ENTERPRISE FOUNDATION LAW
IN A COMPARATIVE PERSPECTIVE

FUNDING ACKNOWLEDGEMENT

Support from the Novo Nordisk Foundation and the Research Project on Long-Term Ownership and Value Creations in Enterprise Foundations as well as Bielefeld University is gratefully acknowledged. The project is funded by Copenhagen Business School, the Augustinus Foundation, the Carlsberg Foundation, the COWI Foundation, the Interogo Foundation, the Lauritzen Fonden, Leo Holding, the Lundbeck Foundation, the Ramboll Foundation, the William Demant Foundation and Bielefeld University.

An open access online version of this book is also available.
Visit https://www.stradalex.eu/ for more information.

strada lex
EUROPE

ENTERPRISE FOUNDATION LAW IN A COMPARATIVE PERSPECTIVE

Edited by
Anne SANDERS
Steen THOMSEN

INTERSENTIA
LEFEBVRE GROUP

Intersentia
Lefebvre Belgium SA
Avenue Jean Monnet 4
1348 Louvain-la-Neuve
Belgium
Email: contact@larcier-intersentia.com

Distribution for the UK, Ireland and
Rest of the World (excl. France, Belgium and Luxembourg)
Ingram Publisher Services UK
1 Deltic Avenue, Rooksley
Milton Keynes MK13 8LD
United Kingdom
Tel: +44 1752 202 301 | Fax: +44 1752 202 331
Email: ipsuk.customercare@ingramcontent.com

Distribution for France and Rest of the World (excl. Ireland and the UK)
Interforum Editis
Avenue de France 92
75013 Paris
France

Distribution for Belgium and Luxembourg
Larcier-Intersentia
Avenue Jean Monnet 4
1348 Louvain-la-Neuve
Belgium

Enterprise Foundation Law in a Comparative Perspective

Artwork on cover: Danny Juchtmans

ISBN 978-1-83970-560-1
D/2026/06040/0116
NUR 827

British Library Cataloguing in Publication Data. A catalogue record for this book is available from the British Library.

FOREWORD

The first edition of the comparative law handbook on Enterprise Foundation Law from 2023 was very well received in German and European literature. The publisher and editors are therefore already presenting a second edition. The first edition, with contributions on seven legal systems, was an unprecedented and innovative presentation of Enterprise Foundation Law in various European countries (Germany, Austria, Switzerland, Sweden, Denmark, Italy) and the USA. The second edition almost doubles the number of country reports to 18, plus a broad-based, highly informative introductory chapter (Thomsen, Foundation Ownership around the World 2025) and a detailed concluding chapter (Sanders/Thomsen/Ørberg) that excellently summarizes the results of the comparative law analysis and the entire volume. New additions include country reports on Liechtenstein (Schurr/Butterstein), the Netherlands (Stokkerman/van Uchelen-Schipper), Belgium (de Wulf), Poland (Osajda/Weber), the Czech Republic (Comstocková/Ronovská), Hungary (Sándor), France (Dupouy), Spain (Emparanza Sobejano/Mejiomil), Portugal (Cunha/Oliveira Martins/Leite), Ireland (Breen), and a contribution on 'Enterprise Foundations and European Law' (van Veen). All others have been updated. The second edition not only provides a welcome completion of the comparative law analysis, but also represents a remarkable achievement in terms of content. It is not possible to discuss the numerous interesting country reports in this foreword, and it would not be appropriate to highlight and describe in detail only the newly added ones or even just a few of them. Following the introductory and concluding chapters, a few brief comments on the occurrence of foundation ownership and the regulation of European foundations are appropriate.

As Thomsen explains in the introductory chapter, which is based on an ongoing research project funded by various foundations, and documents with numerous important empirical data, enterprise foundations account for approximately 0.5% of listed companies worldwide (with 2.1% of global market capitalization, in a worldwide mapping of 237 listed foundations) and for 0.002% of private companies (data for 2019). In the US, the UK, and Japan they are practically non-existent. France has traditionally been very skeptical of foundations, with restrictions only being relaxed since 2019. However, as in some European countries, enterprise foundations are of great economic importance. Just think of Rolex, Carlsberg, or the Guardian, but also MØller-Maersk, Bertelsmann, Robert Bosch, and Investor AB, the holding company of the Swedish Wallenberg companies. In Denmark, Sweden, the Netherlands, and other countries, enterprise foundations are economically very important. In Denmark, they account for more than 60% of total market capitalization (many more empirical and other data in the Danish country report). The explanations for these differences in prevalence and economic significance are not only cultural and political peculiarities – a separate study would be most welcome, for example, in connection with the new field of research on corporate governance and culture – but also, according to the book's convincingly presented and substantiated thesis, differences: 1) in foundation law (on only half-hearted foundation reforms, for example, in Germany, see the German country report by Sanders); 2) in tax treatment (which is prohibitively expensive for foundations in the US, as detailed in Elgar's country report); and 3) in governance constraints. As Thomsen aptly notes at the end of the book, 'Excessive regulation can deter founders and impede the efficient operation of enterprise foundations', a criticism that unfortunately applies more generally to the economy and its regulation in many countries today.

The essence of the comparative law reports and the book is summarized and reflected upon in the concluding chapter on the basis of the most important core questions concerning the enterprise foundation. 1) *Definition:* While there is a certain degree of uniformity in the concept of a foundation, albeit with a few exceptions, there is no legal definition of an enterprise foundation, apart from its legal regulation in Denmark. A practical definition, which is also used in the book and appears to be the most useful in comparative law, is: 'an enterprise foundation is a foundation with a controlling influence in a business', whereby control is understood inconsistently for the enterprise foundation. The country reports therefore quite rightly also deal with foundation-like structures and legal transplants. 2) *Admissibility:* This varies greatly from very broad admissibility to extensive practical prohibition. 3) *Purpose:* The purpose of the foundation as determined by the founder is traditionally a charitable goal in many countries, with considerable differences in what that means. However, most countries now allow generally permissible purposes, albeit with significantly different limits on admissibility. 4) *Flexibility and irrevocability:* There are significant differences in this regard, ranging from a reserved right to amend the statutes, either by the founder himself or by the foundation's board, to the revocation of the foundation as a whole, as is the case in Austria in particular. 5) *Governance/Transparency:* Foundation governance is a key issue across Europe. Control over foundations is mainly exercised by the foundation supervisory authority, and in some countries, such as Austria, by the commercial courts. In a number of countries, such as Belgium, the Netherlands, Poland, and others, there are only private governance mechanisms. It is rightly noted that foundation supervision is no substitute for private governance mechanisms and that governance is 'one of the most important topics of the law of enterprise foundations' (final chapter under 6.1). Adequate transparency is of utmost importance for the proper control of a foundation and, in particular, an enterprise foundation. Unfortunately, this is lacking or deficient in many countries, and the foundation reform in Germany also falls short in this regard. This would include public annual accounts, which are not in sight. 6) *Succession planning:* This has been added in the second edition and is generally an important area of application in theory and practice. Finally, 7) *Tax:* This is a key issue in all the countries examined, both for European foundations and for foundations in general. 8) provides data on the economic significance of enterprise foundations and considerations on future challenges and opportunities. Table 9) is particularly useful: Economic significance of enterprise foundations owning listed companies in relation to stock market capitalization. The data has been updated and supplemented for the new country reports. This reveals surprisingly high differences between individual countries compared to the previous edition. New data for the US does not appear to have been available. Finally, there are some interesting comments on the historical background.

The conclusion remains: foundation ownership, and more specifically enterprise foundation ownership, is a remarkable alternative mode of capitalism based on non-profit rather than for-profit ownership (Hansman), with non-profit meaning that foundations do not have owners or other residual claimants, but can, of course, make a profit. The policy considerations at the end of the concluding chapter are well thought out and should be taken up by legislators and regulators. The legal form of the enterprise foundation deserves further attention and good research, as has been done in an exemplary manner in this book.

Prof. Dr. Dr. Dr. h.c. mult. Klaus Hopt

CONTENTS

LIST OF CONTRIBUTORS

Eugenio Barcellona
Professor of Business Law, DIGSPES (Dipartimento di Giurisprudenza e Scienze Politiche, Economiche e Sociali), University of Eastern Piedmont, Italy

Thomas Barth
Habilitation candidate, Institute for Business Law, University of Economics and Business, Vienna, Austria

Oonagh B. Breen
Professor of Law, Sutherland School of Law, University College Dublin, Ireland

Alexandra Butterstein
Professorship of Company, Foundation & Trust Law, Liechtenstein Business Law School; Member of the Rectorate, Dean Liechtenstein Business Law School

Carolina Cunha
Professor of Commercial and Company Law, University of Coimbra, Faculty of Law, Institute for Legal Research (UCILeR), Portugal

Irma Comstocková
PhD student, Masaryk University School of Law and Practicing Lawyer, Czech Republic

Hans De Wulf
Professor of Corporate Law, Ghent University, Financial Law Institute, Belgium

Sabrina Dupouy
Professor of Private Law, University of Clermont Auvergne, France

Ofer Eldar
Professor of Law, University of California Berkely School of Law, United States of America

Alberto Emparanza Sobejano
Professor of Commercial Law, University of the Basque Country (UPV/EHU), Spain

Rasmus Kristian Feldthusen
Professor, Ph.D., University of Copenhagen, Denmark, Faculty of Law, Deputy Chairman of the Danish Committee on Foundation Governance (appointed by the Minister for Industry, Business and Financial Affairs)

Dominique Jakob
Prof. Dr. iur., M.I.L. (Lund), Professor of Private Law and Director of the Center for Foundation Law, University of Zurich, Independent Advisor, Switzerland

Susanne Kalss
Prof. Dr.Dr. h.c., L.L.M (EUI Florence), Professor of Business and Private Law, University of Economics and Business, Vienna, Austria, Member of the Board of Foundations

Andrea Meijomil Gonzalez
Lecturer of Commercial Law, University of the Basque Country (UPV/EHU), Spain

Katarina Olsson

Professor of Private Law, Faculty of Law, Lund University, Sweden, Chairperson of the Kamprad Family Foundation and Board Member of the Association of Swedish Foundations

Maria Inês Oliveira Martins
Professor of Commercial and Company Law, Faculty of Law, University of Coimbra Institute for Legal Research (UCILeR), Portugal

Mark Ørberg
Assistant professor, Copenhagen Business School, Denmark

Konrad Osajda
Full Professor of Law, Head of the Chair of Commercial and Corporate Law, and Director of the Centre for Family Business Law at the University of Warsaw; member of the Polish Academy of Sciences, the Private Law Codification Commission, and the Studies and Analyses Office of the Supreme Court of Poland

Kateřina Ronovská
Professor of Civil Law, Masaryk University School of Law and Judge at the Constitutional Court, Czech Republic

Anne Sanders
Chair for Civil Law, Company Law, the Law of Family Businesses and Judicial Studies, University of Bielefeld, Germany, Professor II at the Faculty of Law of the University of Bergen, Norway and Part-time Judge at the Higher Regional Court of Hamm, Germany

István Sándor
Professor of Law, Faculty of Law of Eötvös Loránd University, Budapest, Hungary

Francesco A. Schurr
Full Professor (Chair of Italian Private Law and Comparative Law) and Director of the Institute for Italian Law, Law School of the University of Innsbruck, Austria

Christiaan Stokkermans
Professor of Corporate Law, Erasmus University, Rotterdam, and Deputy justice in the Amsterdam Court of Appeals, the Netherlands

Steen Thomsen
Novo Nordisk Foundation Professor of Enterprise Foundations at the Center for Corporate Governance, Copenhagen Business School, Denmark

Marleen van Uchelen-Schipper
Associate Professor of Private Law, University of Amsterdam and adviser at Houthoff, Amsterdam the Netherlands

Wino J.M. van Veen
Professor of Company Law and Law on Legal Persons, Vrije University Amsterdam, Director of the Amsterdam Institute for Financial Law and Corporate Law, Zuidas Institute for Financial and Corporate Law and Counsel Corporate Law Baker & McKenzie Amsterdam, the Netherlands

Anne-Marie Weber
Assistant Professor at the Chair of Commercial Law, Faculty of Law and Administration of the University of Warsaw, Poland

INTRODUCTION

Anne SANDERS and Steen THOMSEN

To put it simply, enterprise foundations are foundations that own companies.[1] The term is not widely known, but many will recognise the names of companies like Bosch, Bertelsmann, Carlsberg, Hershey, Rolex, Investor or Tata Sons, which are owned by foundations or equivalent entities – *Stiftungen*, trusts, *Fonde*, *Stichtingen*, etc. – whose names reflect their legal origins.[2]

Although enterprise foundations have been around for more than a century, they have recently attracted attention as embodiments of the purpose-driven company advocated by Colin Mayer (2013, 2018), the British Academy (2019) or the World Economic Forum (2020) and others. Many enterprise foundations are non-profits without a personal profit motive, which sets them aside from other corporations.[3] Instead, they are bound by their purpose, which typically is to secure the longevity and independence of the companies that they own and to contribute to society by philanthropy. As perpetuities which cannot be dissolved, they are long-term owners. However, not all enterprise foundations are equally altruistic. Some have strong ties to the founding family and continue to donate to its descendants. Others have ties to government organisations, cooperatives or associations which helped establish them.

Enterprise foundation law differs greatly around the world. To our knowledge, Denmark is the only country with codified civil and tax law on the topic. Some countries – such as, until recently, the US – have effectively banned them. Others – like Austria or Germany – seek to limit foundation involvement in the underlying businesses. Most accept that foundations can own businesses as a source of revenue or as a way to serve social needs. The tax treatment of foundations also varies considerably. Enterprise foundation law therefore has to be constructed from various sources including, in particular, foundation law

---

1 100% ownership is not requited. It is sufficient that a foundation has ownership control. Moreover, some enterprise foundations conduct business activities directly through the foundation.

2 Previously used terms for enterprise foundations include: industrial foundations, commercial foundations, *Unternehmensträgerstiftungen*, *Unternehmensstiftungen*, *fondations actionnaires*, *erhvervsfonde*, *erhvervsdrivende fonde*, business trusts and more.

3 In family foundations the family members of the founder benefit from the profits of the foundations.

and tax law. Clearly, there is much to be learned by mapping and analysing the diversity across countries.

This second edition of the book explores enterprise foundation law in 17 nations and analyses how the law influences the prevalence and governance of enterprise foundations around the world. Chapters on enterprise foundations around the world and a chapter on comparative law provide overviews.

The first chapter, 'Foundation Ownership Around the World', by Professor Steen Thomsen of Copenhagen Business School introduces readers to the general topic and to what we know from the empirical literature. This sets the stage for the following country chapters by defining the topic and providing some background information. The chapter introduces a functional definition of enterprise foundations as foundations which own companies. Foundations are independent legal entities, non-profits created by irrevocable donations, typically from the former business owners. They are governed by their charter and a foundation board. The formal foundation purpose varies but often combines a business purpose (being a responsible owner of a business) and philanthropic goals. In some cases (family foundations) foundations may also support members of a founding family.

The chapter provides descriptive information about enterprise foundations around the world focusing on listed companies where we have better information. What are the largest enterprise foundations? Where are they most common? What industries? The chapter ends by a discussion of factors limiting or promoting the spread of enterprise foundations, including enterprise foundation governance, i.e. how the foundations are governed and how they exercise their business ownership. Who sits on the foundation boards? How much stock do they own in the company? Who sits on the company board? What is any is the role of the founding family?

After this introduction, *authors from 17 different legal systems* lay out enterprise foundation law in each of the 17 countries with an eye to answering the following questions:

- Does foundation allow enterprise foundations? If yes, with what qualifications?
- Are enterprise foundations commonly used? What are the reasons for their popularity or lack of it?
- What rules are in place regarding the purpose a foundation must have? Does running an enterprise alone suffice as a purpose for a foundation?
- Does the law impose specific rules on foundation governance?
- Are enterprise foundations subject to supervision by a public body?
- To what extent are enterprise foundations favoured by the tax system?
- What challenges do enterprise foundations face?

Professor Anne Sanders of Bielefeld University starts with a discussion of 'Enterprise Foundations in Germany'. Enterprise foundations have a long history in Germany with businesses like Zeiss, Bosch and Mahle either using foundations or functional equivalents.

Professor Susanne Kalss and Dr. Thomas Barth, both of Vienna University of Economics and Business, have contributed a chapter on 'The Austrian Foundation', focusing on the Law on Private Foundations (*Privatstiftungsgesetz*) in Austria. The Law was set in force in 1993. There exist about 2,500 enterprise foundations in Austria.

'Swiss Enterprise Foundations' are then discussed by Professor Doctor Dominique Jakob, LL.M., of University of Zurich. Swiss foundation law follows a classical foundation model; any foundation purpose is permitted that is not contrary to law or morality and no 'special' foundation form is applicable to enterprise foundations. Switzerland has a great tradition of enterprise foundations which it intends to continue into the future.

Professor Katarina Olsson, LL.D, of Lund University shows the reader that 'Enterprise Foundations in Sweden' are quite a remarkable story. The Swedish definition of an enterprise is an entity which conducts activities of an economic nature with independence and duration. This is a very narrow definition, compared to, for example, the wide Danish definition. Despite not having specific regulation, there are important enterprise foundations in Sweden.

'Enterprise Foundations in Denmark' are discussed by Professor Rasmus Kristian Feldthusen of Copenhagen University. This chapter describes the Danish legal regime of enterprise foundations which are governed by a separate act. Foundation owned enterprises, such as Carlsberg and Novo Nordisk, are regulated by this act.

Professor Eugenio Barcellona, of the University of Eastern Piedmont, introduces the reader to the fascinating history and law of Enterprise Foundations in Italy in the paper 'Industrial Foundations Under Italian Law'. The chapter analyses the legal regime of enterprise foundations in Italy from an historical perspective in order to explore the legal reasons behind the scarcity of industrial foundations.

'Enterprise Foundations in Liechtenstein' (a new chapter in this edition) are addressed by Professor Francesco Schurr, of the University of Innsbruck, and Professor Alexandra Butterstein, of the University of Liechtenstein. Enterprise foundations have a significant presence in Liechtenstein. This chapter explores the key elements of Liechtenstein's enterprise foundations, focusing on foundation governance, corporate governance, beneficiaries' rights, the issue of 'self-serving foundations', will substitutes and other related topics.

'Enterprise Foundations in the Netherlands' (a new chapter in this edition) are discussed by Professor Christiaan Stokkermans, of the Erasmus School of Law, and Doctor Marleen van Uchelen-Schipper, of the University of Amsterdam. Dutch law does not regulate enterprise foundations as such, and foundation law is sufficiently flexible to allow their existence; the chapter provides several examples.

'Enterprise Foundations in Belgium' (a new chapter in this edition) are addressed by Professor Hans de Wulf, of the University of Ghent. Private foundations are often used as enterprise foundations in Belgium, holding a controlling stake in a commercial firm. They rarely have a philanthropic purpose but are mainly used to cement family control over a corporate group, and to pass on that control from one generation to another in a tax efficient way.

The chapter 'Enterprise Foundations: A Polish Perspective' (a new chapter in this edition) was written by Professor Konrad Osajda and Professor Anne-Marie Weber both of the University of Warsaw, Poland. Polish law directly recognises and regulates enterprise foundations, whether they are charitable or private foundations. Charitable foundations may engage in any business activity that is legally permissible. The scope of allowed business activity for private enterprise foundations, on the other hand, is a matter of debate. The newly established flexible Polish family foundation is of special interest for the international discussion.

'Enterprise Foundations in the Czech Republic' (a new chapter in this edition) are addressed by Professors Kateřina Ronovská, and Irma Comstocková Masaryk University, the Czech Republic. Czech law recognises three types of foundations. All three Czech foundations may serve as enterprise foundations and the specific choice, in each case, depends on the exact wishes and goals of the founder.

'Enterprise Foundations in Hungary' (a new chapter in this edition) are discussed by Professor István Sándor of the ELTE Faculty of Law, Hungary. In Hungarian law, foundations play a significant role in economic and social life, and various types are known, which can be categorised based on their purpose and activities. Although the enterprise foundation type is not explicitly recognised, the flexible asset management foundation (AMF) could potentially fulfil this function.

'Enterprise Foundations in France' (a new chapter in this edition) are addressed by Professor Sabrina Dupouy of Aix-Marseille Université. In France, the term '*fondation entreprise*' is used for foundations established by companies for corporate social responsibility (CSR) purposes. However, there are three types of legal structure that can be referred to as a shareholders' foundation: an endowment fund, a recognised public-interest foundation and a sustainability fund. All three of these can be majority or minority shareholders. The endowment fund is becoming very popular.

The chapter on 'Spanish Enterprise Foundations' (a new chapter in this edition) is presented by Professors Alberto Emparanza Sobejano, Andrea Meijomil of Universitad de Pais Vasco. They argue that enterprise foundations in Spain play a crucial role in promoting the country's social, cultural and economic development. Enterprise foundations serve as instruments to channel corporate social responsibility and foster sustainable projects that benefit the community. Their impact is evident in key areas such as education, research, social inclusion and environmental conservation. However, the authors note that enterprise foundations face significant challenges including vague regulation, that hinders uniform operations, and administrative registration issues, that impede transparency and oversight.

Professor Carolina Cunha and Maria Inês Oliveira Martins, both of the University of Coimbra, discuss 'Enterprise Foundations in Portugal' (a new chapter in this edition). Although there is an academic debate over their admissibility, a significant number of authors deem enterprise foundations compatible with the current legal framework in Portugal. Moreover, legal practice tolerates enterprise foundations to some extent insofar as the social interest purpose is not overshadowed by business activity.

'Enterprise Foundations in Ireland' (a new chapter in this edition) are addressed by Professor Oonagh B. Breen. of the Sutherland School of Law, University College Dublin. Enterprise foundations are not commonly known in Ireland, but some structures can be distinguished that could be cautiously classified as enterprise foundations. She concludes that the business case and the philanthropic case provide a rationale for the formalisation of the enterprise foundation concept in Ireland so that enterprise foundations could become a common functional tool for future Irish entrepreneurs.

Professor Ofer Eldar, of the Berkeley School of Law, discusses enterprise foundations in the US under the heading 'Are Enterprise Foundations Possible in the United States'. This chapter first explains the hurdles under US tax law for creating enterprise foundations, particularly taxes on excess business holdings and the unrelated business tax, which may explain why enterprise foundations are rare in the US. However, nonprofit ownership of prominent companies like Patagonia or OpenAI indicate a renewed interest.

The status of 'Enterprise Foundations in European Law' (a new chapter in this edition) is addressed by Professor Doctor W.J.M. van Veen of VU University, Amsterdam. The main findings are that enterprise foundations that carry on business activities are regarded as 'profit-making' according to Article 54(2) TFEU and eligible to invoke freedom of establishment. For holding foundations, this has to be determined on a case-by-case basis. Furthermore, it appeared that establishing, funding and joining a foundation fall under the protection of freedom of association, freedom of expression and the right to property. Freedom of association also covers that foundations must be able to pursue their activities and operate without unjustified interference by the state (section 3.4).

A final, concluding chapter on 'Enterprise Foundation Law in a Comparative Perspective' by Anne Sanders, Steen Thomsen and Assistant Professor Mark Øberg of Copenhagen Business School compares foundation law in the 17 nations. Although all countries permit enterprise foundations in some form, there are great differences in the relevant civil and tax laws, which influence their prevalence and governance.

This book extends the literature on business law beyond its normal focus on corporations. We are confident that this book will be a must-read for officers and directors of foundation-owned companies around the world as well as for lawyers and government officials who work with enterprise foundations. We also hope that it will be read with interest by advocates and critics of company purpose as well as by readers with a general interest in corporate governance. It hopefully offers food for thought for the development of effective foundations by lawyers but also for legal reform.

The preparation of this book has provided valuable input for the European Law Institute project on enterprise foundations, in which the editors of this book served as reporters. The project concludes that enterprise foundations contribute significantly to European society and could contribute even more if legal uncertainty and legal barriers were to be removed. It presents a model law which can be used as inspiration for legislation at the national and European level which seeks to promote establishment and governance of enterprise foundations.

We are sincerely grateful to the contributors to this book for the time and insights they have provided as well as many stimulating discussions. Their efforts have greatly enhanced the current knowledge of enterprise foundations.

FOUNDATION OWNERSHIP AROUND THE WORLD

Steen THOMSEN*

ABSTRACT

A number of important companies around the world are owned by foundations known in the literature as enterprise foundations. In this chapter, we provide a tentative first impression of the extent of foundation ownership around the world by tapping into preliminary research results from an ongoing research project. We find that foundation-owned companies are rare at the global level, accounting for an estimated 0.6% of listed companies, 1.1% of global market capitalisation

* Support from the Research Project on Long-Term Ownership and Value Creations in Enterprise Foundations is gratefully acknowledged. The project is funded by Copenhagen Business School and the Augustinus Foundation, the Carlsberg Foundation, the COWI Foundation, the Interogo Foundation, the Lauritzen Fonde, Leo Holding, the Lundbeck Foundation, the Rambøll Foundation and the William Demant Foundation. This chapter is prepared for A. SANDERS and S. THOMSEN (eds), *Enterprise Foundation Law in a Comparative Perspective*, 2nd ed., Cambridge: Intersentia, 2025. Helpful comments and assistance by David Schröder are gratefully acknowledged. I am grateful to Assistant Professor Caglar Kaya for updating Table 2 and Figure 1 and 2 using an extended dataset and 2024 data.

and 0.002% of companies worldwide. However, in some European countries like Denmark, Sweden, the Netherlands and Luxembourg, they are economically very significant, in some cases (notably Denmark) accounting for more than 60% of total market capitalisation. The most obvious explanation for such national variation appears to be differences in regulation – for example, differences in foundation law and taxation.

1. INTRODUCTION

Enterprise foundations – also known as industrial foundations – are foundations that own companies. This ownership structure is not widely known, but some well-known companies around the world turn out to be foundation-owned (see below).

Figure 1. 20 foundation-owned companies around the world

A.P. Møller-Mærsk – Denmark
Anheuser Busch Inbev – Belgium
Bertelsmann – Germany
Robert Bosch – Germany
CaixaBank – Spain
Carl Zeiss – Germany
Carlsberg – Denmark
DNV – Norway
The Guardian – UK
Hershey – USA
Inter IKEA – Switzerland
Investor – Sweden
Kavli – Norway
Kuehne + Nagel – Switzerland
Lloyd's Register – UK
Mahle – Germany
Novo Nordisk – Denmark
Pierre Fabre – France
Rolex – Switzerland
Tata Sons – India

Source: Thomsen and Kavadis (2022).[1]

1 S. Thomsen and N. Kavadis, 'Enterprise Foundations: Law, Taxation, Governance, and Performance' (2022) 6(4) *Annals of Corporate Governance* 227, 227–333, http://dx.doi.org/10.1561/109.00000031.

Many of them are remarkable companies: A.P. Møller-Mærsk is the world's largest container shipping company; Anheuser Busch Inbev is the world's largest brewer; Bertelsmann is one of the largest publishing companies in the world; Robert Bosch is one of the largest German manufacturing companies; Caixa is the largest retail bank in Spain; Investor is the holding company of the Swedish Wallenberg companies, the leading Swedish business group; Tata Sons is the main holding company of the Tata Group, one of the largest and most admired Indian business groups; Inter IKEA is the franchisor of IKEA, while most IKEA stores are owned by the INGKA Foundation. Brand names like Rolex, Carlsberg, Carl Zeiss and *The Guardian* need no further introduction.

Enterprise foundations have ownership control over all these companies. For example, 51.7% of votes in the Danish shipping company A.P. Møller-Mærsk are owned by the A.P. Møller Foundation, which was created in 1953 by the Danish shipping magnate A.P. Møller to 'safeguard the long-term viability of the group and control by the Mærsk family'.[2]

While enterprise foundations have been studied in Denmark[3] and Germany,[4] we know little about their whereabouts in the rest of the world. A tentative first step towards an international overview was taken by Schröder,[5] who found that foundation ownership was particularly common in the Nordic countries (Denmark, Sweden, Norway and Finland), in the German-speaking Dach region (Germany, Austria and Switzerland) and (somewhat surprisingly) in India. As a share of market capitalisation, he found that foundation owned companies account for about 40% in Denmark, 30% in Austria, 20% in Sweden, 10% in Norway, 5% in Germany and Switzerland and 5% in India.

In this chapter, we extend this work using the same data source for a global mapping of foundation-owned companies around the world. We begin by explaining what enterprise foundations are and then provide a tentative sketch of their global reach. We point to differences in foundation law and taxation as hypothetical explanations for the uneven distribution of foundation ownership around the world.

However, before we engage in this mapping exercise, we owe it to the reader to try to motivate the topic. Why bother with enterprise foundations?

2 Ibid.

3 S. Thomsen, *The Danish Industrial Foundations*, DJOEF Publishing, Copenhagen 2017.

4 M. Herrmann and G. Franke, 'Performance and Policy of Foundation-owned Firms in Germany' (2002) 8(3) *European Financial Management* 261, 261–279.

5 D.J. Schröder, 'Publicly Listed Foundation-Owned Firms around the World: An Overview' (2021) unpublished working paper: https://www.enterprisefoundations.dk/wp-content/uploads/2021/11/Publicly-listed-FoFs-Descriptive-Paper-02112021.pdf.

A first, by now rather obvious, answer to this question is that a number of excellent companies around the world are foundation-owned. These companies seem to make a difference to the world, and one wonders whether it is really a coincidence that so many distinct companies are owned by a very particular ownership structure, which few people have heard about before. Could it be that foundation ownership contributes to corporate excellence? If so, how can we have more of it? Certainly, a more comprehensive assessment of the strengths and weaknesses (or costs and benefits) of foundation ownership is warranted before we can jump to policy conclusions, so the objective here is to examine why it may be interesting to study this question a little bit closer.

A second, closely related motivation is that foundation ownership is an alternative mode of capitalism based on non-profit rather than for-profit ownership.[6] Foundations are governed by a purpose rather than private profit incentives, and in most cases the purpose directly or indirectly obliges the foundation to be a responsible long-term owner. This resonates with recent calls for reform of companies by a corporate purpose[7] and more long-term governance,[8] in which foundation ownership is regarded as a prototype example of a purpose-driven company.[9] Thus, it may be worthwhile to consider foundation ownership as an alternative to conventional capitalist enterprises.

Third, there are other attractive features of foundation ownership which are worth thinking about and may catch the eyes of policy makers. Foundation-owned companies cannot be taken over by hostile raiders. They tend to treat their employees better.[10] Enterprise foundations reduce economic inequality by

---

6 Non-profit is defined by Hansmann (H. Hansmann, 'The Role of Nonprofit Enterprise' (1980) 89(5) *Yale Law Review* 835, 835–901) to mean that foundations do not have owners or other residual claimants. It does not mean that foundation cannot make a profit.

7 A. Edmans, *Grow the Pie*, Cambridge University Press, Cambridge 2020; British Academy, 'Reforming Business for the 21st Century: A Framework for the Future of the Corporation' (2018); British Academy, 'Principles for Purposeful Business: How to deliver the framework for the Future of the Corporation' (2019); Business Roundtable, 'Statement on the Purpose of a Corporation' (2020): https://www.businessroundtable.org/business-roundtable-redefines-the-purpose-of-a-corporation-to-promote-an-economy-that-serves-all-americans; R. Henderson, *Reimagining Capitalism in a World on Fire*, PublicAffairs, New York 2020; C. Mayer, 'Ownership, Agency and Trusteeship' (2019) *European Corporate Governance Institute – Law Working Paper No. 488/2020*, available at SSRN: https://ssrn.com/abstract=3522269; C. Mayer, 'The Future of the Corporation and the Economics of Purpose' (2020), subsequently published in (2022) 58(3) *Journal of Management Studies*.

8 European Commission, 'Study on Directors' Duties and Sustainable Corporate Governance: Final Report' (2020) prepared by EY: https://doi.org/10.2838/472901.

9 C. Mayer, above n. 7.

10 C. Winther Børsting and S. Thomsen, 'Foundation ownership, reputation, and labour' (2017) 33(2) *Oxford Review of Economic Policy* 317, 317–338.

transferring concentrated private wealth to foundations which, in most cases, have a charitable purpose. They contribute funding for research and development (R&D), education, social projects and culture. At the same time, the evidence is that foundation-owned firms perform no worse financially than other private firms.

Finally, while foundation ownership is rare at the global level, it is sufficiently important in some countries – notably Denmark – to be of national economic importance, and even where it is not – as in the US, the UK or Japan – the foundation model may attract attention as an example of steward ownership, which may be of interest for other long-terms owners like family businesses.

2. WHAT IS AN ENTERPRISE FOUNDATION?

The definition of enterprise foundations as 'foundations that own companies' calls for clarification. By a foundation, we mean an independent non-profit entity. 'Non-profit' in this context does not mean that enterprise foundations cannot make a profit, but that they have no residual claimants, i.e. owners or members, who are entitled to receive dividends from the foundation.[11] Although the foundation may choose to donate part of its wealth to outside beneficiaries, they do not have a claim on donations. 'Independent' means that the foundation has its own funds and organisation separate from the founders or other stakeholders. In particular, an enterprise foundation cannot be a government organisation. Enterprise foundations are private entities that operate on market terms. Foundation-owned companies in turn are normal business companies that engage in commercial activities on market terms.

By 'foundation ownership', we mean that one or more foundations have controlling influence in a business company. The foundations do not have to own 100%. Many of the largest foundation-owned companies are publicly listed, as we shall see. But in order to qualify as enterprise foundations, the foundations have to have a controlling influence. It should be noted that controlling influence pertains to voting rights rather than capital shares or dividend rights, and that the definition is functional regardless of the purpose stated in the foundation charter, whether it is philanthropic or not. If a foundation has controlling influence in a business company, it is an enterprise foundation; if not, it is referred to as an ordinary (or general) foundation.

What ownership share is regarded as controlling depends on the circumstances – for example, how much other shareholders own or whether the foundation

[11] H. Hansmann, above n. 6.

has a special say because of shareholder agreements. It may be practical for empirical analysis to set a minimum voting share (say 50%), but in most cases the foundation can exercise effective control with less than that (for example, with 20%). However, usually, the foundation would be required to be the largest shareholder before we talk about foundation ownership.

To supplement the functional definition – enterprise foundations are foundations that own companies – we identify the following key characteristics as part of an extended definition of a standard enterprise foundation:[12]

- Creation by donation (i.e. irrevocable separation from the founder). Once created, the founder cannot take back the donations; attempting to do so would be an act of theft.Independence (a separate legal personality for the foundation). Foundations have no owners. Once created, the founder cannot change the charter or instruct the foundation. Moreover, foundations cannot be dissolved except by government decree. In practice, founders or founding families may be able to exert significant informal influence, but the foundation board has the decision-making power and the responsibility.
- A non-selfish purpose (which goes beyond benefitting the founder). In enterprise foundations, the purpose will often, but not always, involve responsible, long-term ownership of a business company (i.e. a business purpose). Usually, but not always, there will also be a philanthropic purpose served by donations or operating activity.
- A foundation endowment, which includes shares in a company as well as sufficient funds to pay for administrative expenses and philanthropic donations.
- A foundation board of directors or trustees. There may also be an executive management function.
- A foundation charter (including foundation purpose and governance rules).
- Ownership (voting) control of a business company.
- Outside supervision, for example, by a foundation authority, a government organisation or a private court.[13]

We acknowledge that some enterprise foundations – like the Stichting Anheuser-Busch Inbev which owns the company of the same name – do not fit into this standard definition, although we have included them both in the book (see the chapter on Austria in this volume) and in the statistical overview below.

---

12 Cf. H. Kronke, *Stiftungstypus und Unternehmensträgerstiftung*, J.C.B. Mohr, Tubingen 1988; S. Thomsen, 'Foundation Ownership and Economic Performance' (1996) 4(4) *Corporate Governance* 212, 212–221; S. Thomsen and N. Kavadis, above n. 1. Ibid.

13 A detailed explanation of these characteristics can be found in S. Thomsen and N. Kavadis, above n. 1.

We defined these entities as 'family foundations' since they can be altered and sometimes dissolved by founding family members and can therefore be considered to be a kind of extended family ownership.

3. DATA SOURCES

One reason why we know so little about enterprise foundations is that it is difficult to find information about them.

This chapter is based on hand-collected data, extrapolation and estimation. Since there is no global register of enterprise foundations or foundation-owned companies, in most cases (except in Denmark) data has to be hand-collected from a range of other sources. We have relatively good information about publicly listed companies which provide a useful, but imperfect starting point for the analysis given below. We also have some (but more limited) information about private companies, since many (but far from all) countries have publicly available company registers. Finally, we have very limited information about the enterprise foundations which are only systematically registered in one country (Denmark), while only a few countries register foundations at all.

We therefore map foundation ownership around the world first by mapping its prevalence among listed companies and second by reporting what we have found so far from studies of private companies in Europe.

4. THEORETICAL RATIONALE FOR FOUNDATION OWNERSHIP

Given the above characteristics, it seems worthwhile to briefly consider the theoretical rationale for foundation ownership compared to other kinds of private ownership.

Economic agency theory stresses the power of individual incentives, which are missing or muted in enterprise foundations and foundation-owned companies. Moreover, foundation-owned firms cannot diversify risk and attract equity capital when the foundation is reluctant to dilute its ownership and give up control. Hence, according to agency theory,[14] we would under normal circumstances expect foundation-owned companies (non-profits) to underperform and be outcompeted by their more efficient for-profit rivals.

---

14 E.F. Fama and M.C. Jensen, 'Agency Problems and Residual Claims' (1983) 26 *Journal of Law and Economics* 327, 327–349.

However, in some cases there may be economic as well as social value to ownership commitment, which foundation ownership can more credibly provide.[15] As long-term owners, enterprise foundations can enable companies to focus on the long term while avoiding financial short-termism and family succession issues.[16] Because they are less profit seeking, foundation-owned companies may find it easier to gain the trust of their stakeholders.[17] For example, consumers may be more likely to buy from them because they are less fearful of exploitation.[18] Idealistic employees – and other stakeholders – may be more motivated to work for a company purpose than to maximise profits.[19]

In theory, there will be a rationale for enterprise foundations when the benefits of commitment exceed the incentive and financing costs of foundation ownership.

5. A GLOBAL PERSPECTIVE

As research on this topic continues, it seems likely that more and more cases of foundation ownership will be uncovered. Nonetheless, the data to which we currently have access seems to allow for some broad generalisations. In Table 1, we provide some tentative figures.

Globally, foundation ownership is rare. So far, we have found 237 listed foundation-owned firms around the world with a combined market capitalisation of $1.459 billion (or about $1.4 trillion). This is about 0.5% of the world's listed companies (which total around 43,000)[20] and a little more than 2% (2.1%) of global market capitalisation of about $93 trillion at the end of 2019.[21]

15 C. Mayer, above n. 7 (2019).

16 S. Thomsen, T. Poulsen, C. Børsting and J. Kuhn, 'Industrial Foundations as Long-Term Owners' (2018) 26(3) *Corporate Governance: An International Review* 180–196.

17 C. Mayer, above n. 7 (2019).

18 H. Hansmann, above n. 6.

19 R. Henderson and E. Van den Steen, 'Why Do Firms Have "Purpose"? The Firm's Role as a Carrier of Identity and Reputation' (2015) 105(5) *American Economic Review* 326, 326–330.

20 The Organisation for Economic Co-operation and Development (OECD) counted 41,000 companies in 2019: OECD, 'Who are the Owners of the World's Listed Companies and Why Should We Care?' (2022): https://www.oecd.org/corporate/who-are-the-owners-of-the-worlds-listed-companies-and-why-should-we-care.

21 World Federation of Exchanges (2021): https://www.marketsmedia.com/global-market-capitalisation-passed-100-trillion/.

Table 1. Foundation-owned companies around the world

	2019	% of total
Listed foundation-owned companies around the world	237	0.6%
Global market capitalisation of listed foundation-owned companies ($ billions)	1,459	1.6%

Source: The Foundation Project (2022).[22]

This observation immediately raises the following question: if foundation ownership is so great, why is there so little of it? The obvious answer[23] is that foundation ownership requires founders to make the ultimate economic sacrifice – to give away all (or most of) their wealth to a foundation, a sacrifice very few people are willing to make except in special circumstances like exceptional altruism, the absence of close relatives or very high tax rates on private wealth. This implies that foundation ownership is likely to be in permanently short supply, which constitutes a market failure in cases where it is the optimal ownership structure.

Another, less favourable explanation is that foundation ownership is not so great after all in a financial sense. The limited literature on the subject indicates that foundation-owned companies perform no differently than companies with other ownership structures – i.e. they neither systematically underperform or overperform financially.[24]

6. COUNTRY DISTRIBUTION

The geographical spread of foundation ownership around the world appears to be very uneven. In Table 2 we provide a country distribution of the 237 listed foundation-owned companies that we have been able to locate up to 2024.

The first observation is that foundation-owned companies and enterprise foundations can be found around the world, but usually in very small numbers, as noted above. Second, foundation-owned companies tend to be cluster in a few, mainly European, countries. About one-third of the 238 companies (35%) are from the Nordic region (Denmark, Sweden, Norway, and Finland) and about three-quarters are from Europe. Nevertheless, it is possible to find a few examples in many if not all countries around the world – in particular, India has quite a few (mainly Tata companies). As mentioned earlier, it seems likely that we will find many more examples as research in the area progresses.

In terms of market value, enterprise foundations appear to be most important in Denmark, Sweden, Austria, Belgium and Luxembourg.

---

22 The Foundation Project (2022): https://www.enterprisefoundations.dk/.

23 S. Thomsen and N. Kavadis, above n. 1.

24 S. Thomsen, above n. 3.

Table 2. Country distribution of listed foundation-owned companies (2024)

Country	Firms	Total MCAP (USD bln)	Stock Market Size (USD bln)	% of Market Cap
Sweden	36	219.6	1,042.3	21.07%
Denmark	35	642.4	823.8	77.98%
India	26	306.5	4,374.8	7.01%
Germany	17	69.5	2,732.3	2.54%
Japan	17	43.1	6,561.4	0.66%
Austria	15	36.2	157.3	23.03%
Belgium	11	159.0	378.4	42.01%
Norway	10	25.3	343.7	7.37%
Finland	7	15.7	290.7	5.41%
Switzerland	7	172.6	2,405.7	7.17%
Netherlands	6	22.6	1,278.6	1.77%
United States	6	35.0	62,543.5	0.06%
Luxembourg	5	40.5	331.7	12.22%
Pakistan	5	1.0	30.7	3.36%
Türkiye	5	25.1	347.6	7.21%
Brazil	4	4.0	2,295.4	0.17%
Poland	4	2.1	192.1	1.11%
South Korea	4	0.5	2,009.5	0.02%
United Kingdom	4	35.0	4,134.2	0.85%
Italy	3	56.3	737.4	7.64%
Spain	3	45.1	750.7	6.01%
Chile	2	0.0	182.7	0.00%
Croatia	2	0.1	16.9	0.65%
Bangladesh	1	1.3	38.0	3.35%
Canada	1	0.0	3,089.1	0.00%
Cyprus	1	0.6	12.0	5.37%
France	1	0.8	3,202.3	0.03%
Iceland	1	1.7	17.9	9.55%
Liechtenstein	1	0.6	3.7	17.22%
Malawi	1	0.5	3.5	15.21%
Nigeria	1	0.1	36.1	0.40%
Peru	1	0.1	96.1	0.09%
Philippines	1	5.2	227.8	2.27%
Qatar	1	0.5	171.7	0.30%
Saudi Arabia	1	0.5	3,002.3	0.02%
Zambia	1	0.4	2.0	21.05%
Total	247	1,970	103,864	1.90%

Source: S&P Capital IQ.[25]

25 S&PCapital IQ; The Foundation Project (2025): https://www.enterprisefoundations.dk/.

7. PRIVATE FOUNDATION-OWNED COMPANIES

There are many more private (unlisted) than listed foundation-owned firms. Data collection for private foundation-owned firms is still ongoing, but Table 3 below gives an overview of the private foundation-owned firms that we have identified so far.

Table 3. Number of private foundation-owned firms identified in seven European countries

Country	Number
Austria	394
Germany	383
Finland	11
The Netherlands	414
Norway	39
Sweden	85
Denmark	721
Total	2,047

Source: The Foundation project.[26]

Comparing this with the number of listed companies in Table 2, these figures indicate that there are 17 times more private than listed foundation-owned companies in these countries (which have about 120 listed foundation-owned companies compared to the 2047 private foundation-owned companies identified in Table 3 (2,074/120=17)).

If the proportions are the same across the world, there should be 4,000+ foundation-owned companies and an estimated about 2,500 enterprise foundations globally (see Table 4).[27] Although country sources seem to indicate relatively higher absolute numbers in some countries like Germany, foundation ownership probably constitutes substantially below 1% of the world total. Enterprise foundations also seem to be rare compared to philanthropic foundations. According to the Global Philanthropy Report (2018),[28] there are about 260,000 philanthropic foundations worldwide, so 2,500 private foundation-owned companies is less than 1% of all foundations worldwide.

---

26 Ibid.

27 Since some foundations own many companies, we estimate there are fewer enterprise foundations than foundation-owned companies. On Danish data the ratio of holding foundations (which own companies) to foundation-owned companies is about 400/720 = 0.57. If this ratio holds universally, we can use it to estimate the number of enterprise foundations for a given number of companies.

28 P. Johnson, 'Global Philanthropy Report' (2018) *Harvard Institute for Civil Society*: https://www.hks.harvard.edu/centers/cpl/publications/global-philanthropy-report-perspectives-global-foundation-sector.

Table 4. Estimated number of foundation-owned companies and enterprise foundations worldwide

	N	% of total	Total
Private foundation-owned companies in Europe	2,958	0.01%	22,400,000
Private foundation-owned companies worldwide	4,046	0.002%	213,609,000
Foundation-owned companies worldwide	4,284	0.002%	213,650,000
Enterprise foundations worldwide	2,448	0.8%	260,000

Sources: Foundation Project, Statista, OECD, Global Philanthropy Report.[29]

It should be noted that the proportion of private foundation-owned companies relative to the population of private companies seems to be lower than the proportion of listed foundation-owned companies compared to the number of listed companies globally. For example, the estimated number of foundation-owned companies in Europe is 2,958, which accounts for about 0.01% of the European Commission's estimated number of private companies in Europe (22.4 million). The share of the global proportion is even smaller (0.002%). Therefore, it would appear that foundation-owned companies tend to be larger and more frequently listed than companies with other ownership structures. An obvious explanation is that succession to foundation ownership tends to be more common for mature companies, but it is also possible that foundation-owned companies particularly benefit from additional stock market monitoring because foundations lack the strong incentives of private ownership.

Obviously, these numbers are very tentative and should be taken with a very large pinch of salt. Nevertheless, there is little doubt that foundation ownership and enterprise foundations are relatively rare phenomena at the global level.

8. REGULATION AS A CAUSE OF NATIONAL VARIATIONS IN FOUNDATION OWNERSHIP

The highly uneven distribution of foundation ownership around the world indicates that national characteristics strongly influence the spread of enterprise foundations.

An obvious hypothesis is that that the international differences are caused by (national) differences in legislation and regulation. Apparently, enterprise foundation law differs from company law, where legal scholars have identified a range of generic legal attributes that are common to most jurisdictions.[30]

---

29 The Foundation Project (2022): https://www.enterprisefoundations.dk/; Statista, 'Estimated Number of Companies Worldwide from 2000 to 2020 (in Millions)' (2022): https://www.statista.com/statistics/1260686/global-companies/; OECD, above n. 20; P. Johnson, above n. 28.

30 K. J. Hopt and T. von Hippel, *Comparative Corporate Governance of Non-Profit Organizations*, Cambridge University Press, Cambridge 2010.

Legality. Some countries have liberal foundation laws. For example, the Danish Law on Enterprise Foundations allows 'free access to establish enterprise foundations with any kind of purpose', provided that the purpose is sufficiently well defined, legal and not contrary to common decency. In particular, running a particular kind of business or 'owning and ensuring the survival' of a company are legitimate purposes.[31]

Other nations have actively set up enterprise foundations though 'privatization to foundations'.[32] The Italian government transferred more than 80 savings banks and credit institutions to newly established charitable foundations by the so-called Amato Law.[33] A third group of countries – like Lithuania, Slovenia and (until recently) France – appear not to permit enterprise foundations at all.[34]

Taxation. It is perhaps no accident that foundation ownership is particularly prevalent in the Nordic countries, which have the highest wealth taxes in the world. Germany and Austria also have relatively high tax rates. This may have incentivised entrepreneurs to establish enterprise foundations to evade estate and capital gains taxes. In contrast, some countries, like the US, have effectively banned foundation ownership through the use of severe tax penalties.

Governance constraints. Foundation governance rules may also influence the formation and growth of enterprise foundations. Some countries, like Germany, require foundations to have purely charitable goals unless they want to be taxed as companies. Accordingly, German or French foundations are barred from active ownership of business companies, which could make them less efficient owners. Governance rules can also make foundation ownership more or less flexible. In some countries, like Denmark, charters can be changed (by so-called permutation) but in other countries, this is virtually impossible. In some countries, foundations are mainly regulated by the tax authorities (the US), while in others, they are regulated by a government agency (as in Denmark) or by the courts or public prosecutors (as in the Netherlands). Finally, governance rules may make foundation ownership more or less attractive from a family business perspective. For example, in some countries, like Sweden, it is acceptable that the founding family occupies a majority of the board, while in others, like Denmark, it is not.

---

31 S. Thomsen and N. Kavadis, above n. 1.

32 See L.M. Salamon, *Philanthropication thru Privatization: Building Permanent Assets for the Common Good*, Il Mulino, Bologna 2014,. See also W.L. Megginson and L.M. Salamon, 'PtP How-To Booklet no. 2: How to Apply PtP to State-owned Enterprises' (2018) *East-West Management Institute*.

33 C. Leardini, G. Rossi and S. Moggi, *Board Governance in Bank Foundations*, Springer, Berlin 2014.

34 K.J. Hopt, T. von Hippel, H. Anheier, V. Then, W. Ebke, E. Reimer and T. Vahlpahl, 'Feasibility study on a European foundation statute: final report' (2008): http://www.ub.uni-heidelberg.de/archiv/18688, pp. 90–91.

These differences are explored in this book through 17 country chapters and a concluding comparative chapter.

9. SOFT VARIABLES

It is also possible that cultural and political variables play a role in fostering enterprise foundations. For example, the Nordic countries are characterised by high levels of trust and low levels of corruption, which may have facilitated the preponderance of enterprise foundations in this part of the world.

As a preliminary test of this hypothesis, we plot the proportion of foundation ownership (the share of market capitalisation) against levels of trust and levels of corruption in Figures 2 and 3 below respectively. We observe a positive correlation which is also statistically significant in each case. In other words, countries with high levels of social trust and corruption control tend to have higher levels of foundation ownership. Social trust and corruption control tend to be mutually correlated and correlated with other factors, like the rule of law, some of which are reported in the World Bank Governance Indicators. Therefore, it seems premature to explain foundation ownership with any particular indicator; instead, it may be preferable to regard them as expressions of 'good governance', 'social capital' or 'institutional quality'.

Figure 2. Corruption control and foundation ownership

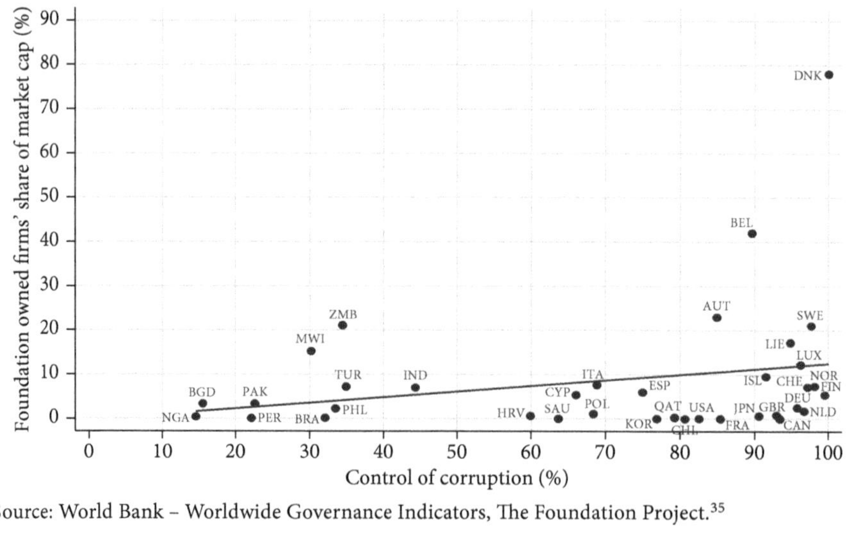

Source: World Bank – Worldwide Governance Indicators, The Foundation Project.[35]

[35] World Bank Corporate Governance Indicators (2021): https://databank.worldbank.org/source/worldwide-governance-indicators; The Foundation Project (2022): https://www.enterprisefoundations.dk/.

Figure 3. Trust in public institutions and foundation ownership

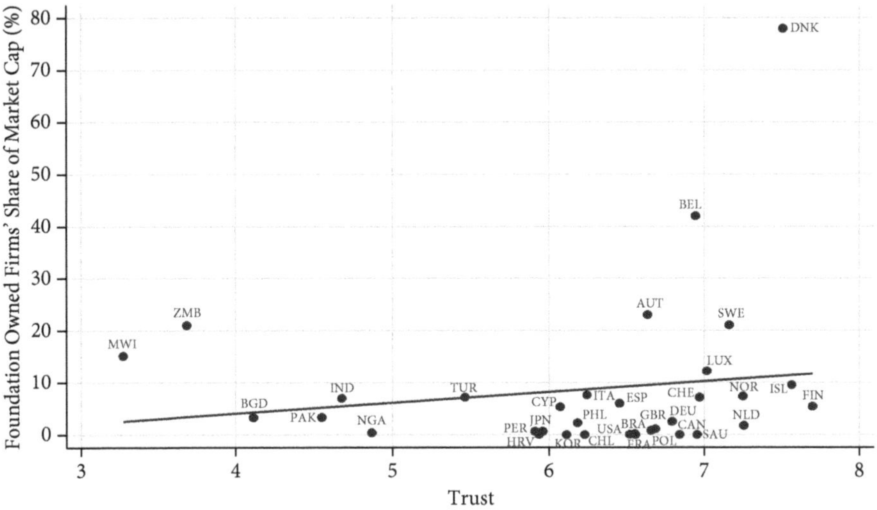

Sources: World Happiness Report, The Foundation Project.[36]

10. CONCLUSION

A number of important companies around the world are owned by foundations known as 'enterprise foundations'. In this chapter, we have provided a tentative first impression of their global reach. We found that foundation ownership is a rarity, accounting for only about 0.5% of listed company assets globally, although in some European countries like Denmark, Sweden and Belgium, they are economically very significant. The most obvious explanation of such national variations appears to be differences in regulation – for example, differences in foundation law and taxation.

We can particularly single out the following factors as hypothetical determinants of the legality of enterprise foundations around the world:

- Legality: in some countries (like, historically, France) it is illegal to establish enterprise foundations. In others (like the US) regulations exist that are specifically intended to limit foundation ownership.
- Relative taxation of private wealth and foundation ownership: high taxation of private wealth which can be avoided by donating to foundations provides a powerful motive to establish them.

36 World Happiness Report (2020): https://worldhappiness.report/; The Foundation Project (2022): https://www.enterprisefoundations.dk/.

- Regulatory constraints: excessive regulation can deter founders and impede the efficient operation of enterprise foundations – for example, by preventing foundations from exercising active ownership or from adapting to new circumstances by charter changes.

ENTERPRISE FOUNDATIONS IN GERMANY

Anne SANDERS*

* I would like to express my gratitude to my former research assistant Dr. iur. Shkelqim Berisha for the inspiration and help he provided for this chapter. I also thank my research assistant Tim Bühring for his help in the updating for the second edition.

ABSTRACT

This chapter discusses the history, terminology and legal framework of enterprise foundations in Germany. Despite its long tradition with enterprise foundations like Zeiss and Bosch, the legal framework is surprisingly complicated. While a major reform legitimised all kinds of purposes for foundations in 2002, administrating and developing a business alone was not accepted as the purpose of a German foundation. Moreover, foundation law was still mainly regulated by the *Länder*, Germany's federal states. However, this has changed. A major reform of foundation law was passed into law on 16 July 2021[1] and came into force on 1 July 2023. While the reform will make foundation law more transparent with the introduction of a centralised register (which comes into effect on 1 January 2026) and has already been improved by its regulation in the German Civil Code, it is doubtful whether the new law is a big step forward for German enterprise foundations or – in part – a lost opportunity.

1. INTRODUCTION AND HISTORICAL CONSIDERATIONS

Enterprise foundations have a long history in Germany, with businesses like Zeiss, Bosch and Mahle either using foundations or their functional equivalents. This chapter discusses the legal framework of enterprise foundations.

---

1 BGBl. 2021 I 2947. For an overview, see R. Hüttemann and P. Rawert, 'Das neue Bundesstiftungsrecht – Darstellung und Analyse sowie Vorschläge für notwendige Reformen der Landesstiftungsgesetze' (2021) 42(33) *Zeitschrift für Wirtschaftsrecht* 3; B. Weitemeyer, 'Das Gesetz zur Vereinheitlichung des Stiftungsrechts – Zur Reform des Stiftungsrechts in Deutschland' (2021) *Zeitschrift für Erbrecht und Vermögensnachfolge* 54; K. Lorenz and J. Mehren, 'Das neue Stiftungsrecht ist da – Kernpunkte der gesetzlichen Neuregelungen und deren Bedeutung für bestehende und noch zu errichtende Stiftungen' (2021) *Deutsches Steuerrecht* 1774; M. Pruns, 'Ein Überblick über das neue Stiftungsrecht' (2021) *Zeitschrift für Steuer- und Erbrechtspraxis* 301; R. Werner, 'Der Regierungsentwurf eines Gesetzes zur Vereinheitlichung des Stiftungsrechts' (2021) *Zeitschrift für die gesamte erbrechtliche Praxis* 482; S. Schauhoff and J. Mehren, 'Die Reform des Stiftungsrechts' (2021) *Neue Juristische Wochenschrift* 2993. For the first commentary of the new law, see M. Orth and M. Uhl, *Stiftungsrechtsreform 2021*, Dr. Otto Schmidt, Cologne 2021; K.J. Schiffer, M. Pruns and C.J. Schürrmann, *Die Reform des Stiftungsrechts*, Zerb Verlag, Bonn 2022.

This introduction will explain basic concepts and terms, the historical developments and importance of enterprise foundations, and the different structures used to organise them. Section 2 focuses on the legal framework after the 2021 reform, discussing the founding of enterprise foundations, their purpose, property, foundation governance and the future German foundation register. Section 3 provides a very brief overview of tax treatment. Section 4 summarises regulatory challenges such as the need to further develop foundation governance and the new movement of steward ownership.

1.1. INTRODUCTION: THE FOUNDATION UNDER GERMAN LAW

Foundations are formed to dedicate property to the pursuit of a long-term goal. Under German law, a number of different legal forms such as trusts and companies are used for such purposes, which will be discussed in detail in section 1.3 below. However, at the centre of this discussion is the legal foundation (*rechtsfähige Stiftung des bürgerlichen Rechts*) regulated in §§80 et seq. of the German Civil Code (*Bürgerliches Gesetzbuch* (BGB)). As of 31 December 2024, there were a total of 26,349 legal foundations in Germany, 89% of which pursued charitable purposes.[2]

Foundations are legal persons that may hold rights, conclude contracts and be liable in tort and contract. Such foundations do not have shareholders or members with the right to decide its fate but only directors with the power to act for the foundation in order to pursue its purpose. A foundation's legal objective or purpose must be prescribed by its founder, which – at least in principle – cannot be changed later on.[3] The foundation authority (*Stiftungsaufsicht*) oversees the realisation of this purpose. Foundations are founded by a unilateral declaration of the founder (*Stiftungsgeschäft*) and the formal recognition (*Anerkennung*) of the respective foundation authority.

Foundations controlling businesses, so-called enterprise foundations, have a long tradition in Germany.[4] Today, they usually do not run enterprises directly, but hold the shares of companies.

2 See Bundesverband Deutscher Stiftungen: Stiftungen Jahresbericht 2024: Der Bundesverband in Zahlen.

3 See B. Weitemeyer in F.J. Säcker, R. Rixecker, H. Oetker and B. Limperg (eds), *Münchener Kommentar zum BGB*, 10th ed., C.H. Beck, Munich 2025; BGB §80, para. 5.

4 S. Thomsen, *The Danish Industrial Foundations*, DJOEF Publishing, Copenhagen 2017, pp. 85–90; on the development of corporate foundations in Germany since the 19th century, see H. Berndt, *Stiftung und Unternehmen*, 5th ed., Nwb Verlag, Berlin 1995, pp. 285–317.

1.2. HISTORICAL DEVELOPMENT

There is a long history of charitable foundations in Germany, which often provided services to fulfil their mission, for example a hospital. However, the history of foundations holding and running enterprises started later. In 1889 the Carl-Zeiss Foundation was founded, which ran the Schott and Zeiss enterprises and is still regarded as the archetype of the German enterprise foundation.[5]

From the start, the federal structure of the German state had a significant influence on the regulation of foundations.[6] Even after the unification of German civil law under the BGB in 1900, the foundation largely depended on the foundation laws of the federal states (*Landesstiftungsgesetze*).[7] While the declaration to found a foundation, its representation by its directors, the change of its purpose and the legal effect of its dissolution were regulated in the BGB from the start, the prerequisites of the formal recognition by the respective authorities were regulated by the laws of the federal states. The BGB did not make any demands in relation to the purposes being pursued, but left that crucial function to the federal states. However, the drafters of the BGB agreed that the long-term pursuit of a special purpose required public permission of some kind.[8]

At the beginning of the 20th century, foundations could only be founded for charitable purposes. Thus, a manual for laypeople in 1902 summarised the prerequisites of founding a foundation as follows:

> Sie setzt voraus: Erlaubten Stiftungszweck (Wohlthätigkeit, Förderung gemeinnütziger Bestrebungen, z.B. Wissenschaft, Kunst-Gewerbe); 2. Stiftungsakt (einseitige schriftliche Erklärung unter Lebenden oder Testament; 3. Vermögen, das für den Stiftungszweck dienen soll; 4. Genehmigung der Landesregierung. [It requires: permissible foundation purpose (charity, support of a public beneficial purpose such as science or decorative art); 2. the declaration to found a foundation in writing or in a will; 3. foundation property to serve the foundation's purpose; 4. authorisation by the government of the federal state].[9]

---

5 D. Jakob, *Schutz der Stiftung*, Mohr Siebeck, Tubingen 2006, p. 17; see also H. Fleisch, 'Unternehmensverbundene Stiftungen' (2018) 4 *Stiftung&Sponsoring* Rote Seiten 2.

6 For a historical overview, see R. Hüttemann and P. Rawert in J. von Staudingers, *Kommentar zum Bürgerlichen Gesetzbuch*, Sellier/de Gruyter, Berlin 2017; BGB preamble to §§80 et seq., paras. 61 et seq.

7 For more details, see R. Hüttemann, A. Richter and B. Weitemeyer, *Landesstiftungsrecht*, Dr. Otto Schmidt, Cologne 2011.

8 B. Mugdan, *Die gesammten Materialien zum Bürgerlichen Gesetzbuch für das Deutsche Reich*, vol. I, 1899, p. 961; R. Hüttemann and P. Rawert, above n. 6; BGB preamble to §§80 et seq., para. 71.

9 *Neuestes Gesetzbuch für den praktischen Gebrauch*, commented by A. Korn, F. Ebstein, A. Kurnicki, P. Plinzner, P. Schwarz and R. Haenschke, Verlag E Globig, Berlin, 1902, pp. 13–14.

While the drafters of the BGB believed in the need to control foundations and their purposes through the requirement of public acknowledgement, foundations and their private money for beneficial purposes were increasingly seen as an opportunity in the second half of the 20th century. In this context, other foundations that did not pursue a public benefit were also increasingly accepted.[10] At this time, the purpose of every permissible foundation was to be approved by the foundation authorities and the foundation law of the states. This could cause considerable differences and discussions as to the permissibility of different foundation purposes. For example, in the federal state of Baden-Württemberg, a foundation with the sole purpose of administrating a business was permissible in the 1980s. Moreover, the purpose of supporting members of a certain family was considered problematic as well. The federal state of North Rhine-Westphalia, for example, did not accept such foundations, so founders chose other federal states for their foundations.[11] In this context, enterprise foundations were also under discussion.[12] In this situation, the call for reform became louder and louder.[13]

A first unification was achieved in 2002[14] by the first federal foundation reform since 1900. In this reform, in §80(2) BGB, federal law regulated foundation purposes for the first time.

> §80 (2) Die Stiftung ist als rechtsfähig anzuerkennen, wenn … die dauernde und nachhaltige Erfüllung des Stiftungszwecks gesichert erscheint und der Stiftungszweck das Gemeinwohl nicht gefährdet. [§80 (2) A foundation is to be recognised as having legal personality if … the long-term and sustained achievement of the object of the foundation appears guaranteed and if the object of the foundation does not endanger the common good.][15]

With this reform, the BGB established a right to have a foundation acknowledged as long as its purpose did not violate the common good. The 'all-purpose

10 See D. Jakob, above n. 5, pp. 13, 19; U. Burgard, 'Das neue Stiftungsprivatrecht' (2002) *Neue Zeitschrift für Gesellschaftsrecht* 697, 699–700.

11 R. Hüttemann, 'Unternehmensnachfolge mit Stiftungen' (2017) *Der Betrieb* 591, 594; on the old practice, see B.-H. Hennerkes, K.J. Schiffer and M. Fuchs, 'Die unterschiedliche Behandlung der unternehmensverbundenen Familienstiftung in der Praxis der Stiftungsbehörden' (1995) *Betriebs-Berater* 209.

12 H. Gummert in V. Beuthien, H. Gummert and M. Schöpflin (eds), *Münchener Handbuch des Gesellschaftsrechts: Band 5: Verein, Stiftung bürgerlichen Rechts*, 5th ed., C.H. Beck, Munich 2021, §81, paras. 33–37; G. Schwarz, 'Die Stiftung als Instrument der mittelständischen Unternehmensnachfolge' (2001) *Betriebs-Berater* 2381; K.J. Schiffer, 'Die unternehmensverbundene Stiftung ist im Gerede' (1999) *Zeitschrift für Erbrecht und Vermögensnachfolge* 424; P. Rawert, 'Der Einsatz der Stiftung zu stiftungsfremden Zwecken' (1999) *Zeitschrift für Erbrecht und Vermögensnachfolge* 294.

13 See with further references D. Jakob, above n. 5, pp. 16–20.

14 BGBl. 2002 I 2634, in force since 1 September 2002.

15 Translation by a team of translators of Langenscheidt's translation service: https://www.gesetze-im-internet.de/englisch_bgb/englisch_bgb.html#p0236.

foundation' ('*gemeinwohlkonforme Allzweckstiftung*') was now explicitly accepted by law.[16] It only requires that a foundation pursues a benefit that is not *harmful* to public benefit rather than beneficial. With this reform, the unclear legal situation in relation to a number of enterprise foundations was settled. The law sparked a 'boom' of new foundations, which became increasingly interesting for legal advisors as tools to organise succession within family businesses.

However, at least since 2014, a new reform of federal foundation law was debated.[17] For this purpose, a working group of federal and *Länder* representatives organised by the federal Ministry of Justice and Consumer Protection was established.[18] In late November 2016, it presented far-reaching proposals.[19] After a hearing with scholars and practitioners, the working group presented a discussion draft on 27 February 2018.[20] The draft recommended a complete regulation of foundation law, but refrained from proposing the establishment of a national foundation register.

The draft was fiercely discussed and a group of the most eminent German foundation scholars even presented an alternative draft.[21] The following draft of the federal Ministry of Justice highlighted important aspects, particularly the demand for a foundation registry,[22] but also considered some less convincing suggestions, especially some that would seriously limit the founder's freedom to design the foundation charter. Fortunately, the next governmental draft amended some important points.[23]

---

16 BT-Drs. 14/8765, p. 9.

17 For an overview of the reform, see R. Hüttemann and P. Rawert, above n. 1, 3–4.

18 Established by the 85th *Konferenz der Justizministerinnen und Justizminister* (Conference of Justice Ministers) on 25 and 26 June 2014 and by the 198th *Sitzung der Ständigen Konferenz der Innenminister und -senatoren der Länder* (Meeting of the Standing Conference of Interior Ministers and Senators of States) on 11–13 June 2014.

19 See '205. Sitzung der Innenministerkonferenz' (2016) *Innenminister Konferenz*: www.innenministerkonferenz.de/IMK/DE/termine/to-beschluesse/20161129-30.

20 'Diskussionsentwurf der Bund-Länder-Arbeitsgruppe "Stiftungsrecht" für ein Gesetz zur Vereinheitlichung des Stiftungsrechts' (2018) available at: https://www.innenministerkonferenz.de/IMK/DE/termine/to-beschluesse/2018-06-08_06/anlage-zu-top-46.pdf.

21 A. Arnold, U. Burgard, M. Droege, R. Hüttemann, D. Jakob, L. Leuschner, P. Rawert, G. Roth, S. Schauhoff, U. Segna and B. Weitemeyer, 'Professorenentwurf zur Stiftungsreform' (2020) 41(10) *Zeitschrift für Wirtschaftsrecht* 3. There were also numerous comments on the draft, including, first and foremost, a statement of the Bundesverband Deutscher Stiftungen of 16 September 2020.

22 German Federal Ministry of Justice, 'Referentenentwurf des Bundesministeriums der Justiz und für Verbraucherschutz, RefE: Entwurf eines Gesetzes zur Vereinheitlichung des Stiftungsrechts' (28 September 2020): https://www.bmjv.de/SharedDocs/Downloads/DE/Gesetzgebung/RefE/RefE_Stiftungsrecht.pdf?__blob=publicationFile&v=3.

23 German Federal Ministry of Justice, 'Gesetzesentwurf der Bundesregierung, RegE: Entwurf eines Gesetzes zur Vereinheitlichung des Stiftungsrechts' (3 February 2021): https://www.bmjv.de/SharedDocs/Downloads/DE/Gesetzgebung/RegE/RegE_Stiftungsrecht.pdf?__blob=publicationFile&v=3.

The federal reform was approved by the Federal Parliament (*Bundestag*) on 16 July 2021 and came into force predominantly on 1 July 2023. It unifies foundation law and aligns federal law in the BGB with the law as commonly accepted by scholars and practitioners. However, it was not meant to change the law in a fundamental way. The opportunity for a more thorough reform was not taken. However, the new law brings improvements, especially a federal foundation register in 2028. While the reform did not address enterprise foundations directly, the reform is also of crucial importance for them and will be taken into account in the general discussion of the legal framework in section 2 below.

1.3. DIFFERENT KINDS OF 'FOUNDATIONS'

When discussing German foundations and especially enterprise foundations, the coverage should not be limited to the foundation that is a legal person, the *rechtsfähige Stiftung*. Other legal forms are also used to achieve the goal of dedicating property to a purpose, especially in the context of enterprise foundations.

1.3.1. The Foundation which is a Legal Person – Rechtsfähige Stiftung

The *rechtsfähige Stiftung*, the legal foundation regulated in §§80 et seq. BGB, has already been introduced. This chapter focuses on this form of foundation, but it should be kept in mind that the practice uses functional equivalents as well.

1.3.2. The Nichtrechtsfähige Stiftung/*Fiduciary Foundation*

Besides the *rechtsfähige Stiftung*, which is a legal person and is regulated in §§80 et seq. BGB, there is also the *nichtrechtsfähige Stiftung*, the fiduciary foundation. It is set up like a trust in a common law system by transferring property to a trustee who promises to administrate it for a certain purpose.[24] It is more flexible and can be set up much more quickly, but has no legal personality and thus lacks the durability many founders desire.

---

24 A. Westebbe, *Die Stiftungstreuhand*, Nomos, Baden-Baden 1993; S. Seyfarth, *Der Schutz der unselbstständigen Stiftung*, Nomos, Baden-Baden 2009, p. 22; K.-H. Muscheler, 'Die unselbstständige Stiftung von Todes wegen und unter Lebenden' (2016) *Zeitschrift für die gesamte erbrechtliche Praxis* 358; V. Kuhn, 'Überblick über zivilrechtliche Grundlagen und ausgewählte Aspekte der Beratungspraxis' (2020) *Zeitschrift für Erbrecht und Vermögensnachfolge* 535.

1.3.3. *The Limited Liability Company (GmbH)*

The German limited liability company, the *Gesellschaft mit beschränkter Haftung* (GmbH), is also used as a more flexible alternative to the foundation.[25] It is a company with legal personality and was introduced in Germany in 1892 as a cheaper, more flexible alternative to the *Aktiengesellschaft* (AG, stock company or stock corporation).[26] The GmbH allowed the owners of smaller businesses to exclude their personal liability by founding a company.[27] Today, the GmbH is much more popular than the AG, with 1,376,420 registered GmbHs and only 13,883 AGs as of 1 January 2021.[28] The reasons for this popularity are the GmbH's flexibility, which makes it useful for small businesses as well as a corporate subsidiary under a holding.[29]

The GmbH, just like the AG, is usually founded to pursue entrepreneurial purposes, but is open for other objectives as well. GmbHs pursuing charitable purposes are quite common and enjoy the same tax benefits as foundations.[30] In the event that a charitable purpose is pursued, tax benefits require that profits are not distributed to shareholders. This goal can be achieved by amendments to the articles of association. However, even the best legal design does not change the most important difference between a foundation and a company that must be taken into account: while a foundation is property with legal personality dedicated to a purpose, a company has shareholders who decide what it does. The articles of association can be changed at any time[31] and shareholders may liquidate the company and keep the proceeds for themselves, even if this means that tax benefits have to be repaid.

Nevertheless, GmbHs are often found in the context of enterprise foundations, whether as an alternative to a foundation, as in the case of Bosch, or to run a business with a foundation as its shareholder.

---

25 H. Fleisch, above n. 5, 3.

26 For major characteristics in English, see M. Schulz and O. Wasmeier, *The Law of Business Organizations*, Springer, Berlin 2012, pp. 38–40.

27 M. Schulz and O. Wasmeier, above n. 26, pp. 4–5.

28 U. Kornblum, 'Bundesweite Rechtstatsachen zum Unternehmens- und Gesellschaftsrecht' (2021) *GmbH-Rundschau* 681.

29 J. Rosengarten, F. Burmeister and M. Klein, *The German Limited Liability Company*, 9th ed., C.H. Beck, Munich 2020, pp. 13–15.

30 See with further references A. Gilberg, 'Die gemeinnützige GmbH in der notariellen Praxis' (2020) *Rheinische Notar-Zeitschrift* 193; B. Weitemeyer, 'Fallstricke der gGmbH' (2021) *GmbH-Rundschau* 57.

31 See with further references A. Schlüter, *Stiftungsrecht zwischen Privatautonomie und Gemeinwohlbindung*, C.H. Beck, Munich 2004, pp. 266 et seq.

1.4. THE CONCEPT AND IMPORTANCE OF ENTERPRISE FOUNDATIONS

Before the introduction of a national, centralised foundation register in 2026, it is still difficult to assess the exact number of German enterprise foundations. However, it is assumed that about 700–2,000 out of the estimated 26,349 foundations in Germany may be described as enterprise foundations holding shares to enterprises worth more than €100 billion.[32]

In Germany, founding an enterprise foundation is a well-known but rarely used option for organising business succession of family businesses.[33] The reasons for this may be that founding a foundation is not that easy – practitioners usually recommend it only for larger enterprises. Moreover, entrepreneurs fear a lack of flexibility. However, the experiences of those businesses making the transfer seem to be positive.[34]

The reasons to choose a foundation as a tool to organise business succession include the wish to keep an enterprise independent, by supporting family members without actually making them holders of shares. A foundation as the main shareholder can also prevent shares from becoming smaller and smaller with the growth of the family. Moreover, the goal of supporting good causes can also be important.[35]

---

32 H. Fleisch, above n. 5, 4; J. Bothello, A. Gautier and A.-C. Pache, 'Families, Firms and Philanthrophy: Shareholder Foundation Responses to Competing Goals' in L. Roza, S. Bethmann, L. Meijs and G. von Schnurbein (eds), *Handbook on Corporate Foundations: Corporate and Civil Society Perspectives*, Springer, Berlin 2019, p. 73, give the number as 500–1,000. For examples, see G. Brandmüller and T. Klinger, *Unternehmensverbundene Stiftungen*, 4th ed., Erich Schmidt Verlag, Berlin 2014, pp. 26–30; H. Gummert in V. Beuthien, H. Gummert and M. Schöpflin (eds), above n. 12, §81, para. 38; on the international significance of corporate foundations today, see L. Roza, S. Bethmann, L. Meijs and G. von Schnurbein (eds), *Handbook on Corporate Foundations: Corporate and Civil Society Perspectives*, Springer, Berlin 2019, pp. 85 et seq.

33 See M. Habersack in Stiftung Familienunternehmen (ed), *Stiftungsunternehmen in Deutschland*, IPRI, Munich 2021; see also H. Fleisch, M. Eulerich, H. Krimmer, A. Schlüter and S. Stolte, *Modell unternehmensverbundene Stiftung*, Erich Schmidt Verlag, Berlin 2018; T. Dahlmanns, 'Errichtung einer rechtsfähigen Stiftung – zugleich Modell der Unternehmensnachfolge' (2020) *Rheinische Notar-Zeitschrift* 417; R. Hüttemann, above n. 11, 591; J. Ihle, 'Stiftungen als Instrument der Unternehmens- und Vermögensnachfolge' (2009) *Rheinische Notar-Zeitschrift* 557 (part 1) and (2009) *Rheinische Notar-Zeitschrift* 621 (part 2); see also P.S. Weinmann, *Die unternehmensverbundene Stiftung*, Tectum Wissenschaftsverlag, Baden-Baden 2024, pp. 125 et seq.; S. Berisha, *Familienunternehmen und unternehmensverbundene Familienstiftung*, Peter Lang, Berlin 2025.

34 H. Fleisch, above n. 5, 6.

35 See G. Brandmüller and T. Klinger, above n. 32, pp. 10–18; see also T. Dahlmanns, above n. 33, 417, 418–419.

A number of different terms are used in the context of enterprise foundations,[36] which, although given in German, will be mentioned here. Though the terminology is not universal, the following terms are most commonly used:

Unternehmensverbundene Stiftung, which may be translated as 'a foundation which is connected to an enterprise', is the most common term used for different kinds of foundations relevant for this chapter and may be roughly translated as enterprise foundation.

Unternehmensträgerstiftung means a foundation which directly administrates a business.[37] The Carl Zeiss Stiftung was the most famous example of this kind of enterprise foundation. However, today, direct enterprise foundations have (almost) vanished. The reason for this is that the foundation regulated in the BGB is simply not designed to run a business.[38] Among other reasons, its charter may only be changed with the approval of the foundation authority and it has no rules designed to secure the interests of creditors.

The *Beteiligungsträgerstiftung*,[39] which may be translated as 'holding foundation', is a foundation which holds shares of a company, usually a flexible GmbH, which runs a business. Today, this is the usual form of German enterprise foundations.[40] The company has its own management, and its articles of association may be changed easily to adjust the company to new challenges.

Sometimes, the term *Unternehmensstiftung* is also used in the discussion.[41] This term, which may be translated simply as 'enterprise foundation' or 'corporate foundation', is mostly used for a foundation founded by a company primarily as an instrument of corporate social responsibility, but that is not running a business or holding shares of a company.[42]

---

36 See H. Gummert in V. Beuthien, H. Gummert and M. Schöpflin (eds), above n. 12, §81, para. 4.

37 G. Brandmüller and T. Klinger, above n. 32, p. 93; A. Godron and P. Thress in M. Feick (ed), *Stiftung als Nachfolgeinstrument*, 2nd ed., C.H. Beck, Munich 2024, §32, para. 1.

38 H. Fleisch, above n. 5, 3.

39 G. Brandmüller and T. Klinger, above n. 32, pp. 117–120; G. Ponath and S. Raddatz in M. Feick (ed), above n. 37, §28, para. 10.

40 D. Jakob and M. Uhl in B. Gsell, W. Krüger, S. Lorenz and C. Reymann (eds), *Beck-online Großkommentar BGB*, C.H. Beck, Munich 2020; BGB §80, para. 476.

41 For example, S. Geibel uses the term for all kinds of enterprise foundations: S. Geibel, 'Unternehmenstiftungen und Governance' in B.P. Paal, D. Poelzig and O. Fehrenbacher (eds), *Deutsches, Europäisches und Vergleichendes Wirtschaftsrecht – Festschrift für Werner F. Ebke zum 70. Geburtstag*, C.H. Beck, Munich 2021, pp. 251, 254.

42 M. Hoffmann-Becking, 'Unternehmensverbundene Stiftung zur Sicherung des Unternehmens' (2014) 178(5) *Zeitschrift für das gesamte Handels- und Wirtschaftsrecht* 491, 492.

1.5. DIFFERENT ENTERPRISE FOUNDATIONS

Federal foundation law does not provide special rules on enterprise foundations. However, different motives and wishes of founders have motivated legal practitioners to develop a number of different types of enterprise foundations. Often, a founder chooses a foundation strategy if no family member or other potential successor is considered trustworthy or qualified enough to take over the business. However, the founding of an immortal legal person as the businesses owner is not enough to guarantee the survival of a business – motivated and competent people are irreplaceable.[43]

1.5.1. Charitable Enterprise Foundations

Founders without a family may wish to keep their businesses independent and commit them to a long-term strategy. However, as will be discussed more fully below, according to the predominant view in the academic literature and foundation authorities, a foundation must have a purpose beyond the administration of a business. This – and possibly tax benefits – can be achieved by choosing a charitable purpose.[44] Founders may also wish to support their families through the foundation. Even a charitable foundation does not make this impossible. However, this kind of support does not go beyond a founder's grandchildren and is therefore not enough to guarantee long-term family security.[45]

1.5.2. Family Enterprise Foundations

Founders with the main goal of supporting their families may found a family foundation,[46] the purpose of which is to support a specific family or families.[47] Such a purpose is a valid foundation purpose under §82 (1) BGB.

---

[43] R. Hüttemann, above n. 11, 591, 596–597.

[44] T. Dahlmanns, above n. 33, 417, 425–427.

[45] A. Schlüter and S. Stolte, *Stiftungsrecht*, 3rd ed., C.H. Beck, Munich 2016, Chapter 7, para. 53.

[46] See C. von Löwe, *Familienstiftung und Nachfolgegestaltung*, 2nd ed., C.H. Beck, Munich 2016; H. Gummert in V. Beuthien, H. Gummert and M. Schöpflin (eds), above n. 12, §80; R. Pauli, 'Die Familienstiftung' (2012) *Zeitschrift für das gesamte Familienrecht* 344; W. Blumers, 'Die Familienstiftung als Instrument der Nachfolgeregelung'(2012) *Deutsches Steuerrecht* 1.

[47] G. Brandmüller and T. Klinger, above n. 32, part 6; T. Dahlmanns, above n. 33, 417, 424–425; C. Stumpf, J. Suerbaum, M. Schulte and R. Pauli (eds), *Stiftungsrecht*, 4th ed., C.H. Beck, Munich 2025; A. Einleitung, para. 17.

There are different ways to structure such a foundation. A foundation's beneficiaries do not have any rights against the foundation and no influence over either the foundation or the business, unless the founder explicitly provides so. This may be exactly what a founder who does not believe that the family could have a beneficial influence on the business wants. In this case, scholars assume that the true motivation for the founder may have been ensuring the long-term wellbeing of the enterprise rather than of the family.[48] However, it is also possible to assign considerable influence to family members.[49]

1.5.3. Double Foundations

With a double foundation, a founder may combine the advantages of a charitable foundation and a family foundation.[50] The enterprise is administrated by a company, usually a GmbH because of its flexibility. The shares of this company are split between a charitable foundation and a family foundation. The family foundation receives shares with voting rights, while the charitable foundation receives shares with capital. In this way, family foundations pay less tax but retain influence over the business. Nevertheless, both foundations may receive an equal amount of dividends, or the family foundation may receive even higher dividends than the charitable foundation.

Usually, tax law is the reason for such constructions. However, other reasons might also be found, for example, the internationally known Robert Bosch enterprise, a producer of household appliances.[51] The enterprise is run by the Robert Bosch GmbH. Shares holding dividend rights are held by the Robert Bosch Stiftungs gGmbH, a charitable company, while the voting rights are held in a partnership whose shareholders change every seven years and include former managers and respected members of the community. This construction uses a GmbH and partnership instead of foundations and combines actual partners with voting rights and the long-term orientation of a foundation.[52]

---

48 R. Hüttemann, above n. 11, 591, 595; S. Berisha, above n. 33, pp. 150–152.

49 K.W. Lange, 'Sicherung des Familieneinflusses durch Stiftungen' in K.W. Lange and K. Windthorst (eds), *Sicherung des Familieneinflusses in Familienunternehmen*, Baden-Baden, Nomos 2017, pp. 95–115; C. von Oertzen and M. Reich, 'Family Business Governance – Sicherstellung der DNA als Familienunternehmen bei von Familienstiftungen gehaltenen Unternehmen' (2017) *Deutsches Steuerrecht* 1118; S. Berisha, above n. 33, pp. 150–607 et seq.

50 T. Dahlmanns, above n. 33, 427; J. Ihle, above n. 33, 621, 634 et seq.; B. Theuffel-Werhahn, 'Fallstricke bei der Gestaltung einer Doppelstiftung' (2015) *Zeitschrift für Stiftungs- und Vereinswesen* 201; V. Auwera, *Die Doppelstiftung*, Centaurus Verlag, Munich 2008, p. 51; M. Feick in M. Feick (ed), above n. 37, §3.

51 For the structure of the Bosch group, the so-called 'Bosch-Modell', see R. Kögel and D. Berg, 'Die Unternehmerverfassung des Hauses Bosch als Grundmodell der Doppelstiftung' (2011) *Zeitschrift für Familienunternehmen und Strategie* 13.

52 See R. Kögel and D. Berg, above n. 51, 13.

1.5.4. *Foundations as a Liable Partner in a Limited Partnership*

The limited partnership (*Kommanditgesellschaft* (KG)) is very popular among family businesses. While the tax advantages that made this form attractive have gone, it still offers other benefits, such as a higher degree of confidentiality and great flexibility.[53]

A KG has at least one partner who is personally liable and at least one limited partner. While traditionally the liable partner was the senior partner running the business and other family members received limited positions, today, the liable partner is usually a limited company, a GmbH (GmbH & Co. KG). The shares of the GmbH are then held by the limited partners and every change among the partners needs to be replicated among the shareholders of the GmbH. In order to avoid such difficulties from arising, there are now constructions where the KG is the shareholder of the GmbH (Einheits-GmbH & Co. KG), a construction that is described as odd, but that is now accepted by jurisprudence.[54]

Another way to structure a business is to use a foundation as personally liable partner (Stiftung & Co. KG).[55] The KG then has an eternal liable partner whose members do not need to be kept aligned with that of the KG because a foundation has no members. While forbidden in Austria and Liechtenstein,[56] this construction (which is used, for example, by Lidl, a supermarket chain)[57] is possible in Germany. It provides stability to a business while still involving the founder's family.[58] However, given current foundation

---

53 A. Sanders and S. Berisha, 'Der persönlich haftende Gesellschafter' (2020) *Neue Zeitschrift für Gesellschaftsrecht* 1290, 1298; regarding the advantages and disadvantages, in addition J. Lieder in C. Bochmann, J. Scheller and J. Prütting (eds), *Münchener Handbuch des Gesellschaftsrechts: Band 9. Recht der Familienunternehmen*, 6th ed., C.H. Beck, Munich 2021, §3, paras. 33–37.

54 See B. Grunewald in I. Drescher, H. Fleischer and K. Schmidt, *Münchener Kommentar zum HGB*, 5th ed., C.H. Beck, Munich 2022, HGB §161, paras. 99 et seq.; R. Werner, 'Die GmbH & Co. KG in der Form der Einheitsgesellschaft' (2006) *Deutsches Steuerrecht* 706; A. von Bonin, 'Die Einheits-GmbH & Co. KG in der notariellen Praxis' (2017) *Rheinische Notar-Zeitschrift* 1.

55 See U. Delp, *Die Stiftung & Co. KG*, R. v. Decker, Heidelberg 1991; P. Höfner-Byok, *Die Stiftung & Co. KG*, Peter Lang, Frankfurt am Main 1996; T. Dahlmanns, above n. 33, 417, 428–429; G. Brandmüller and T. Klinger, above n. 32, pp. 102–116; S. Berisha, above n. 33, pp. 349 et seq.

56 See for the Austrian private foundation (*Privatstiftung*), section 1(2)(1) of the Austrian law of the private foundation (PSG) and for the foundation in Liechtenstein, Article 552, §1, para. 2, s. 1 PGR, in detail: C. von Löwe, above n. 46, §8, paras. 24 et seq. (for Austria) and §10, paras. 19 et seq. (for Liechtenstein); B. Weitemeyer, above n. 1, 54, 56 argues in favour of a ban in Germany, which has not happened yet. However, see the legislative draft of the Green and Liberal Parties: BT-Drs. 13/9320, p. 3 and BT-Drs. 14/336, p. 2.

57 S. Spiegelberger, *Unternehmensnachfolge*, 3rd ed., C.H. Beck, Munich 2022, § 24, para. 197.

58 M. Pawlytta and P.A. Pfeiffer in M. Feick (ed), above n. 37, §31, paras. 17–18; T. Dahlmanns, above n. 33, 417, 429.

law, which will be discussed in more detail below, such foundations must have a purpose going beyond acting merely as a liable partner.

2. THE LEGAL FRAMEWORK

Basic principles of German foundation law have already been explained in section 1 above. In this section, the legal framework will be discussed in more detail in light of the 2021 reform and its effects on enterprise foundations.

2.1. THE FOUNDATION AND ITS PURPOSE

Since the BGB of 1900, the prerequisites for founding a foundation have not changed: there needs to be a declaration of a founder in writing to set up a foundation with a property to pursue a certain purpose. Then as now, the acknowledgement of a public body – the foundation authority – is necessary to bring the foundation into being. This has not changed as a result of the 2021 reform. However, for the first time, federal law now includes a definition in of the foundation in §80 (1) 1 BGB:

> Die Stiftung ist eine mit einem Vermögen zur dauernden und nachhaltigen Erfüllung eines vom Stifter vorgegebenen Zwecks ausgestattete, mitgliederlose juristische Person. [A foundation is a legal person without members which has been provided with property for the perpetual and sustainable pursuit of a purpose set by the founder.]

The 2021 reform has not changed the commitment to the 'all-purpose foundation' in §82 (1) BGB. The administration of the foundation's property was and still is not considered an appropriate purpose for a foundation. A purpose must not be self-serving, but must achieve a benefit for third parties (*Verbot der Selbstzweckstiftung*); a foundation must not be set up to support (only) the founder (*Verbot der Stiftung für den Stifter*).[59]

This principle is understood by the majority of scholars and practitioners to mean that a foundation may not be set up only to run and develop a business, because this purpose would be limited to the administration of the foundation's property (*Verbot der Unternehmensselbstzweckstiftung*).[60]

---

59 With further references, see B. Weitemeyer, above n. 3; BGB §80, paras. 27–28.

60 P. Rawert, 'Die Selbstzweckstiftung oder: Vom Zwecklosen' in M. Fischer, R. Geck and W. Haarmann (eds), *Zivilrechtliches Ordnungsgefüge und Steuerrecht – Festschrift für Georg Crezelius zum 70. Geburtstag*, Dr. Otto Schmidt, Cologne 2018, pp. 87 et seq.; R. Hüttemann and P. Rawert, above n. 6, BGB §80, para. 9; B. Weitemeyer, above n. 3, BGB §80, para. 29; W. Backert in W. Hau and R. Poseck, *Beck'scher Online-Kommentar zum BGB*,

Therefore, under German law, foundations must be founded for another purpose, whether charitable or, for example, for the long-term support of a family.

This understanding has not always been accepted everywhere in Germany. Before the first federal foundation reform in 2002, the federal states were free to regulate foundations and their purposes. Therefore, in the 1980s, founding a foundation with the sole purpose of holding the shares of a business was acceptable in the federal state of Baden-Württemberg. In 1986, for example, the Wala Foundation was founded.[61] It holds the shares to two GmbHs: the Wala Heilmittel GmbH, which produces and distributes organic medicine, and Dr Hauschka, a well-known pioneer of organic cosmetics since 1935. The foundation's purpose reads as follows:[62]

> §2 (1) Es ist Aufgabe der Stiftung, der 'WALA HEILMITTEL GMBH' und der 'WALA Agrikultur GmbH' eine gedeihliche Entwicklung zu sichern. [Article 2 (1) The object of the Foundation is to safeguard the successful development of the company 'WALA HEILMITTEL GMBH' and 'WALA Agrikultur GmbH'.]

Today, it is unlikely that a foundation with this clear purpose of corporate preservation would be accepted.

While the prohibition of foundations with the sole purpose of managing businesses is discussed by academics, practitioners do not see it as a major obstacle, but simply combine other purposes, such as preserving the graves of the founders and supporting a family, with the purpose of managing the business in question.[63] Foundation authorities usually accept such constructions.[64] The founder may name preserving and developing the business as one of a number of purposes and may provide rules, including under which circumstances the business may be sold to and how much in dividends should be paid out to support other purposes (e.g. a charitable purpose).

73rd ed., C.H. Beck, Munich 2022, BGB §80, para. 19; S. Geibel, above n. 41, pp. 251, 254–255; D. Markworth, 'Der Entwurf eines Gesetzes zur Vereinheitlichung des Stiftungsrechts aus unternehmensrechtlicher Perspektive' (2021) *Neue Zeitschrift für Gesellschaftsrecht* 100, 107; A. Sanders, 'Vermögensbindung und "Verantwortungseigentum" im Entwurf einer GmbH mit gebundenem Vermögen' (2021) *Neue Zeitschrift für Gesellschaftsrecht* 1573, 1577 with further references.

61 See https://wala-stiftung.de/en.

62 See the articles of association: https://wala-stiftung.de/files/wala-stiftung/downloads/Satzung_Stiftung_EN.PDF.

63 According to A. Richter in A. Richter (ed), *Stiftungsrecht*, 2nd ed., C.H. Beck, Munich 2023, §10, para. 134, it is a mere problem of finding the right phrasing to escape the prohibition of a (*Unternehmens-)selbstzweckstiftung*; with further references S. Berisha, above n. 33, p. 398.

64 D. Jakob and M. Uhl, above n. 40, BGB §80, para. 483 point out that nowadays the regulatory practice is basically open-minded towards enterprise foundations.

However, there are different opinions in relation to how free the founder is in this respect. Some academics demand that the charitable purpose must always be first, otherwise the foundation may be classified as a '*verdeckte Selbstzweckstiftung*' – a foundation which in reality pursues a forbidden purpose.[65] While foundation authorities have been rather lenient in relation to these, this could change any time.[66]

It might well be argued that the whole doctrine is not convincing.[67] There are considerable differences between foundations simply administering property without any interaction with the outside world and an enterprise providing goods or services to consumers. Such an enterprise necessarily interacts with the world not only because it provides employment to its employees, but also because every business that survives in the market pursuing a lawful objective offers something of value to society. Managing a business is not mere administration because it is always changing and developing, interacting with the market and society.

However, in the official governmental materials of the new law, the doctrine seems to have been reaffirmed, even if it was not included in the text of the law. In the material, the following explanation of the new legal definition of the foundation in §80 (1) 1 BGB, the following sentence can be found:

> Aus dieser für die Stiftung typischen Verknüpfung von Zweck und Vermögen folgt, dass als Stiftungszweck nur ein solcher Zweck in Betracht kommt, der sich durch Nutzung eines Vermögens erfüllen lässt. Der Zweck einer Stiftung kann sich nicht in der Erhaltung des eigenen Vermögens erschöpfen. Auch wenn für die Erfüllung eines Zwecks die Nutzung eines Vermögens nicht erforderlich ist, wie etwa für die Übernahme der Komplementärstellung in einer Personenhandelsgesellschaft ('Stiftung und Co. KG'), kann dieser Zweck nicht in der Rechtsform der Stiftung verfolgt werden. [This typical link between the foundation and its purpose means that only a purpose is acceptable that can be achieved by using property. Preserving the foundation's property is no sufficient purpose. Even if the property is not necessary to pursue the purpose as when a foundation takes on the position as a liable partner in a partnership, this purpose cannot be pursued with a foundation.][68]

[65] For more details, see B. Weitemeyer, above n. 3, BGB §80, para. 163; R. Hüttemann and P. Rawert, above n. 6; BGB preamble to §§80, paras. 225 et seq. Among the indications for this, see P. Rawert, above n. 59, pp. 87, 95–97.

[66] R. Hüttemann, above n. 11, 591, 593; H. Fleisch, above n. 5, 5 argues in favour of long-term orientation of enterprise foundations in the interest of the German economy.

[67] K.J. Schiffer and M. Pruns, 'Zum Lehrsatz vom Verbot der Selbstzweckstiftung' (2012) *Zeitschrift für Stiftungs- und Vereinswesen* 1; K.J. Schiffer and M. Pruns in T. Heidel, R. Hüsstege, H.-P. Mansel and U. Noack (eds), *Bürgerliches Gesetzbuch: BGB, Band 1: Allgemeiner Teil – EGBGB*, 4th ed., Nomos, Baden-Baden 2021, §80, para. 54; D. Markworth, above n. 60, 100, 107–108.

[68] BT-Drs. 19/28173, p. 46.

This statement is discussed as possibly meaning that foundations acting as liable partners in a limited partnership (KG – see section 1.5.4 above) might not be accepted in the future either.[69] However, it is more convincing to assume that the legislator wanted to affirm that foundations may not be founded (only) to perform a certain function or administrate property.[70] However, such foundation constructions probably do not occur in practice in any case.[71] If the legislator had wished to ban foundations acting as liable partners, it would have been necessary to say so explicitly,[72] as is the case in Austria and Liechtenstein, for example.

2.2. DECLARATION TO FOUND A FOUNDATION: *STIFTUNGSGESCHÄFT*

Setting up a foundation requires the declaration of a founder in a special document (*Stiftungsgeschäft unter Lebenden*) or as part of a will (*Stiftungsgeschäft von Todes wegen*).[73] Part of this declaration is the first charter of the foundation. Practitioners and academics agree that the declaration requires careful drafting,[74] but there are relatively few minimum requirements: the founder needs to state at least the foundation's purpose and the property the foundation shall receive to pursue its purpose. Moreover, the founder needs to make provision for the appointment of the first director of the foundation and where the foundation should have its seat.[75]

According to the old and new laws, the declaration needs to be in writing. However, there was a dispute before the reform over whether the declaration

69 See M. Pruns, above n. 1, 301, 302; R. Werner, above n. 1, 482–483; U. Burgard, 'Anerkennungsvoraussetzungen und Grundlagenänderungen' (2021) *Zeitschrift für das Recht der Non Profit Organisationen* 78, 79.

70 D. Markworth, above n. 60, 100, 107; K. Lorenz and J. Mehren, above n. 1, 1774, 1775; M. Feick and J. Schwalm, 'Korrektur bei der Stiftungsreform – Gibt es noch ein happy End?' (2021) *Neue Zeitschrift für Gesellschaftsrecht* 525, 532; see also B. Weitemeyer, above n. 3, BGB §81, para. 31, §80, para. 158.

71 F. Schuck and J. Medinger, 'Stiftungsreform in der entscheidenden Phase: Die geplanten Neuregelungen im Überblick für die Praxis' (2021) *Zeitschrift für Erbrecht und Vermögensnachfolge* 298, 299; K. Lorenz and J. Mehren, above n. 1, 1774, 1775.

72 So also U. Burgard, 'Die Kritik an dem Referentenentwurf eines Gesetzes zur Vereinheitlichung des Stiftungsrechts im Überblick mit Fallstudien' (2021) *Zeitschrift für das Recht der Non Profit Organisationen* 1; G. Ponath and G. Tolksdorf, 'Was lange währt, wird nicht immer gut: Diskussionsfelder des neuen Stiftungsrechts' (2021) *Zeitschrift für Erbrecht und Vermögensnachfolge* 605, 606.

73 In detail, see C. Stumpf in A. Richter (ed), above n. 63, §4; T. Dahlmanns, above n. 33, 417, 421.

74 J. Ihle, above n. 33, 557, 568; S. Schauhoff and J. Mehren, above n. 1, 2993, 2995.

75 With examples: G. Brandmüller and T. Klinger, above n. 32, pp. 34–41.

required another form (for example, notarisation) in certain cases.[76] A number of different assets (e.g. land and shares of a GmbHs) require notarisation both for their transfer and to create enforceable legal claims for their transfer (§311b BGB and §15(4) Act on the private limited company, GmbHG). Therefore, before the 2021 reform, there was a discussion as to whether the declaration of the founder required notarisation if the founder wanted the foundation to receive assets such as land or shares of a GmbH. For an enterprise foundation, which usually holds share to a GmbHs in Germany, this question was of crucial importance. A 2020 decision of the Higher Regional Court of Cologne (OLG Köln)[77] held that notarisation was indeed also necessary for the declaration of the founder and not only for the transfer of the property to the foundation (on this, see §82a BGB.[78] Now, this question is resolved.[79] According to the official explanation of §81 (3) BGB, writing is enough.[80]

2.3. FOUNDATION PROPERTY

Unlike many other legal systems, German company law still requires minimum capital for the founding of companies such as the GmbH[81] and the AG. However, there are no special capital requirements for founding a foundation, let alone an enterprise foundation.[82] §82 (1) BGB requires only that the long-term and sustained pursuit of the foundation's purpose must appear guaranteed.

The 2021 reform introduced in §§83b and 83c BGB for the first time unified federal rules on foundation property and its administration. The new rules

---

76 For a detailed discussion, see K.W. Lange in B. Gsell, W. Krüger, S. Lorenz and C. Reymann (eds), *Beck-online Großkommentar*, C.H. Beck, Munich 2025, BGB §81, paras. 209 et seq.; R. Hüttemann and P. Rawert above n. 6, BGB §81, para. 16.

77 Higher Regional Court of Cologne, 5 August 2019, (2019) *Zeitschrift für Erbrecht und Vermögensnachfolge* 729. For an account that agrees with this, see J. Schwake in V. Beuthien, H. Gummert and M. Schöpflin (eds), above n. 12, §79, para. 146; T. Wachter, 'Stiftungsgründung mit Einbringung eines Grundstücks bedarf der notariellen Beurkundung' (2019) *Betriebs-Berater* 2705, 2706. For a critical view of this decision, see J. Schwalm and M. Thiele, 'Die Form des Stiftungsgeschäfts unter Lebenden: Ausnahmsloser "Vorrang" des §81 Abs. 1 S. 1 BGB' (2020) *Zeitschrift für Erbrecht und Vermögensnachfolge* 523, 525 et seq.; R. Werner, 'Formbedürftigkeit der Übertragung von Immobilien und GmbH-Geschäftsanteilen im Rahmen der Stiftungseinrichtung?' (2021) *Zeitschrift für Steuer- und Erbrechtspraxis* 131; M. Pruns, 'Notarielle Form des Stiftungsgeschäfts bei Zusicherung von Immobilienvermögen?' (2020) *Zeitschrift für die gesamte erbrechtliche Praxis* 163.

78 See R. Hüttemann and P. Rawert above n. 6, BGB §81, para. 17.

79 R. Werner, above n. 1, 482, 483; R. Hüttemann and P. Rawert, above n. 1, 3, 9.

80 BT-Drs. 19/28173, p. 50.

81 In 2008, however, the legislator introduced a sub-form of the GmbH which can be founded with a minimum capital of €1 (see §5a GmbHG).

82 B. Weitemeyer, above n. 3, BGB §81, para. 33; A. Schlüter and S. Stolte, above n. 45, Chapter 1, para. 50; J. Schwake, 'Zum Mindestkapital bei rechtsfähigen Stiftungen bürgerlichen Rechts' (2008) *Neue Zeitschrift für Gesellschaftsrecht* 248.

replace the legislation of the *Länder* on the federal level, defining different kinds of foundation property and its administration. The law now distinguishes clearly between basic property of the foundation (*Grundstockvermögen*), which must be preserved for the future, and 'other' property (*sonstiges Vermögen*) that may be spent pursuing the foundation's purpose. While most foundations have both kinds of property, there are foundations which only have 'other property'. These are foundations for consumption (*Verbrauchsstiftung*),[83] which are meant to spend all their assets.[84] For example, a foundation may be set up to renovate a church and given money to be spent completely until the church is renovated.

While a number of open questions remain,[85] the new law helps to clarify a number of problems. This means that the founder has to provide fewer rules on the foundation property in the foundation's charter.[86]

It is now officially allowed to redeploy the foundation's property and use the proceeds to pursue its purpose. While this position has been widely held by scholars and practitioners before, the new law offers more legal certainty. While the foundation's basic property (*Grundstockvermögen*) has to be retained in full, the legislator also allows more flexibility in the administration of foundation property in §83c (2) BGB. A foundation may now tap into its basic property if it is planned that it will be replenished soon.[87]

2.4. FOUNDATION GOVERNANCE

Foundation governance is a topic of special importance for enterprise foundations.[88] A foundation has no members directing its path, but must pursue a theoretically unchanging purpose set by its founder. Thus, the foundation's

---

83 In detail, see B. Weitemeyer, above n. 3, BGB §80, paras. 41 et seq.; J. Tielmann, 'Die Familienverbrauchsstiftung' (2013) *Neue Juristische Wochenschrift* 2934, 2935 et seq.; R. Hüttemann and P. Rawert, above n. 1, 8, 12–15; with an overview U. Burgard, 'Die Verwaltung und Erhaltung des Stiftungsvermögens nach neuem Recht' (2023) 5 *Zeitschrift für Stiftungs- und Vereinswesen* 159.

84 BT-Drs. 19/28173, p. 46.

85 See, for instance, U. Burgard, 'Nach der Reform ist vor der Reform' (2021) *GmbH-Rundschau* R244, R245.

86 BT-Drs. 19/28173, p. 47.

87 BT-Drs. 19/28173, p. 58.

88 In detail, see B. Schmidt-Schmiedebach, *Stiftung und Governance Kodex*, Springer, Wiesbaden 2015; D. Jakob, above n. 5, pp. 528 et seq.; U. Burgard, 'Foundation Governance' (2015) *Zeitschrift für Stiftungs- und Vereinswesen* 1. For details specifically concerning enterprise foundations, see H. Fleisch and S. Stolte in H. Fleisch, M. Eulerich, H. Krimmer, A. Schlüter and S. Stolte (eds), above n. 33, pp. 154–161; S. Geibel, above n. 41, p. 251.

purpose may be described as the most important guiding principle in foundation governance.[89]

The larger the foundation's property, the greater the risk that others – its directors, the founder's family and potential beneficiaries – will use it for their own goals rather than for the purpose of the foundation. Just like in company law, the necessity of proper governance mechanisms may be explained with the classical principal-agent theory, which sees economic actors as self-interested and possibly opportunistic.[90] Without members looking out for their interests and that of their legal entity, the foundation may be said to be 'helpless'[91] and in need of protection[92] from different parties wishing to use the foundation's means for their own interests. It is the goal of foundation governance to supply this necessary protection.

2.4.1. Board

German law only requires that a foundation has a board with at least one director (*Vorstand*) who can act for the foundation (§§81 (1) 1 lit. d and 84 (1) 1 BGB).[93] In the 2021 reform, there was no change to the required foundation governance or the number of required directors (§§81 (1) Nr. 1 lit. d) and 84 (1)–(2) BGB). However, at least §84 (4) BGB now clearly states that the founder may regulate additional bodies (for example, a supervisory board) in the charter.

However, there is now a small debate as to whether additional by-laws regulating the work of such bodies outside the charter are permissible because §84 (4) BGB prescribes that the composition, duties and rights of such bodies must be set out in the charter.[94] Such by-laws are especially important for the work of enterprise foundations. Nevertheless, it may well be argued that such

89 S. Geibel, above n. 41, p. 251, pp. 253–254; H. Hof in A. Freiherr, V. Campenhausen and A. Richter, *Stiftungsrechts-Handbuch*, 4th ed., C.H. Beck, Munich 2014, §7, para. 1; D. Jakob and M. Uhl, above n. 40, BGB §80, para. 112.

90 In the context of (enterprise) foundations in detail, see B. Schmidt-Schmiedebach, above n. 88, pp. 57 et seq.; S.J. Mühlbauer, *Stiftungsverbundene Unternehmen und Agency-Theorie*, Mohr Siebeck, Tubingen 2018, pp. 59 et seq.; K.W. Lange, 'Die Bedeutung institutionenökonomischer Erkenntnisse für das Verständnis von Herrschaft und Kontrolle in der Stiftung' (2014) 214 *Archiv für die civilistische Praxis* 511.

91 H. Liermann, *Handbuch des Stiftungsrechts*, J.C.B. Mohr (Paul Siebeck), Tubingen 1963, p. 281.

92 See the name of D. Jakob's book (*Schutz der Stiftung*,above n. 5) which may be translated as 'protection of the foundation'; see also N. Thymm, *Das Kontrollproblem der Stiftung und die Rechtsstellung der Destinatäre*, Carl Heymanns, Cologne 2007, pp. 37 et seq., 79 et seq.

93 B. Weitemeyer, above n. 3, BGB §84, para. 3.

94 Critical about this point: U. Burgard, above n. 85, R244, R245; A. Arnold, 'Teil 3: Die Rechtsstellung der Organe und das Stiftungsregister' (2021) *Zeitschrift für das Recht der Non Profit Organisationen* 84, 86.

by-laws are permissible if the charter allows them. This was the practice until now[95] and should not be changed in the future.

The rules with respect to the foundation's directors used to refer to the law of associations (§86 BGB old law). Since 2023, federal foundation law provides its own rules in §§84–84c BGB on the foundation's board and the basic rights and duties of its members. Some scholars have criticised this separation of foundation law from the law of associations with good reason.[96] Germany hosts an impressive number of associations (more than 600,000), but relatively few foundations. The greater number of associations results in more legal procedures and thus more case law clarifying open questions. With the separation of the law of associations and foundations, scholars and practitioners working on foundations may have to wait a long time before the courts have a chance to decide difficult questions.

According to the law, directors and other members of a foundation's governmental bodies work pro bono, unless the charter provides otherwise (§84a (1) 3 BGB). Moreover, the new law includes important rules as to the liability of foundation directors, clearly stating that their liability may be limited. According to §31a BGB, which is applicable to directors of an association as well as of a foundation, the liability of directors working pro bono is limited.[97] However, this rule may be excluded (§84a (3) BGB).

For directors of enterprise foundations, the new §84a (2) 2 BGB is of special importance.[98] It establishes a business judgement rule similar to the one used in German company law (§93 (2) 1 *Aktiengesetz*). It states that directors do not violate their duties if they make a decision on the basis of appropriate information reasonably expecting to act for the benefit of the foundation.[99]

---

95 With further references, see R. Hüttemann and P. Rawert, above n. 6, BGB §86, para. 66; J. Schwake in V. Beuthien, H. Gummert and M. Schöpflin (eds), above n. 12, §79, para. 369.

96 A. Arnold, U. Burgard, M. Droege, R. Hüttemann, D. Jakob, L. Leuschner, P. Rawert, G. Roth, S. Schauhoff, U. Segna and B. Weitemeyer, above n. 21, 3, 4; B. Weitemeyer, 'Professorenentwurf zur Stiftungsrechtsreform 2020' (2020) *Neue Zeitschrift für Gesellschaftsrecht* 569, 571; U. Burgard, 'Der Stand der Stiftungsrechtsreform nach dem Regierungsentwurf' (2021) *Zeitschrift für Stiftungs- und Vereinswesen* 45, 45–46; K. Gollan and A. Richter, 'Der Referentenentwurf zur Stiftungsrechtsreform – So nicht, bitte!' (2021) *Zeitschrift für das Recht der Non Profit Organisationen* 29. For a different opinion, see D. Markworth, above n. 60, 100, 104.

97 A. Sanders and S. Berisha, 'Die Haftung des fehlerhaft bestellten Stiftungsvorstands' (2021) *Zeitschrift für Stiftungs- und Vereinswesen* 50, 58–59 with further references; L. Leuschner, 'Das Haftungsprivileg der §§31 a, 31 b BGB' (2014) *Neue Zeitschrift für Gesellschaftsrecht* 281.

98 See A. Sanders and S. Berisha, above n. 97, 50, 56 et seq.; on the reform in detail, see K.U. Willy, 'Die Stiftungsreform 2021 – Überblick und haftungsrechtliche Fragestellungen' (2022) *Versicherungsrecht* 79, 80 et seq.; K. Uffmann, 'Haftung des Stiftungsvorstands – auch nach der geplanten Stiftungsreform herausfordernd' (2021) *Zeitschrift für Wirtschaftsrecht* 1251; P. Scholz, 'Vorstandshaftung in der Stiftung und Gesellschaftsrechtsdogmatik: Rezeption und Reflexion' (2021) *Zeitschrift für Wirtschaftsrecht* 1937.

99 BT-Drs. 19/28173, p. 61.

Without such a rule, directors incur considerable risks, especially when making financial decisions for foundations with considerable wealth, especially enterprise foundations.

German law does not require that foundation boards be independent of their founders and their family members.[100] Founders or members of their families may even become directors of their own foundations.[101] Unless so provided in the charter, the founder has no position in the foundation, but remains an external force.[102]

2.4.2. *The Foundation Authority (*Stiftungsaufsicht*)*

German foundations are subject to the supervision of the supervisory authority of the respective federal state where the foundation has its seat. The work of the foundation authority is limited to legal supervision (*Rechtsaufsicht*),[103] which especially includes checking and approving changes to foundations' charters, rather than supervision with respect to the expedience of the board's actions. Therefore, the administration of a foundation's property, including a company of which a foundation may hold shares, is usually not reviewed by the foundation authority. However, this may be different, even though it is usually not the case in practice, if a company does not distribute enough profits to support a charitable foundation's purpose. After all, as explained above, according to German law, the foundation's purpose rather than the wellbeing of the enterprise must be its focus. While most foundation authorities do not enforce these principles in the same way, Rainer Hüttemann stresses that founders should not rely on this restraint.[104]

In many foundation laws of the *Länder*, legal supervision of foundations with a private rather than a charitable purpose, especially family foundations, is limited, as in North Rhine-Westphalia (§7 (4) *Stiftungsgesetz NRW*) or was completely abolished, as in Bavaria (Article 10 (1) *Stiftungsgesetz*

---

100 D. Jakob in V. Beuthien, H. Gummert and M. Schöpflin (eds), above n. 12, §119, para. 110.

101 U. Burgard, *Gestaltungsfreiheit im Stiftungsrecht*, Dr. Otto Schmidt, Cologne 2006, pp. 447 et seq.; T. Wernicke, 'Vorstandskontrolle in der Stiftung' (2003) *Zeitschrift für Erbrecht und Vermögensnachfolge* 301, 303; I. Saenger, 'Die Rolle des Stifters in der Binnenverfassungsstruktur von Stiftungen' (2021) *Zeitschrift für Stiftungs- und Vereinswesen* 94, 96.

102 H. Hof in A. Freiherr, V. Campenhausen and A. Richter, above n. 89, §8, para. 99. On the role of the founder in the foundation in detail, see D. Jakob, above n. 5, pp. 103–166; I. Saenger, above n. 101, 94 with further references.

103 BVerwG 22.09.1972, BVerwGE 40, 347, 350; BGH 22 January 1987, BGHZ 99, 344, 348; on the preventive and repressive means of foundation supervision, see B. Weitemeyer, above n. 3, BGB §80, paras. 90 et seq.

104 R. Hüttemann, above n. 11, 591, 594.

Bayern).[105] The foundation authority may limit its supervision if the founder has installed an internal governance mechanism such as a supervisory board.[106]

There have been no studies on the foundation authority's effectiveness. However, anecdotal evidence suggests that practitioners have to wait several months for the approval of changes of foundation charters by some foundation authorities. This suggests a lack of human resources.[107]

While most practitioners do not see public supervision – where it exists – as a great obstacle,[108] there is agreement that public supervision is no substitute for bespoke governance within the foundation, especially in the case of family foundations.[109]

So far, a foundation's beneficiaries have no right to bring a claim against the foundation unless the charter explicitly provides for this. By law, there is also no third party who could enforce the foundation's claims effectively in the event that the board has no interest in doing so – for example, if the liability of board members is in question. In company law, shareholders have a right to bring such claims. In a foundation, which has no members or shareholders, other genuinely interested parties could be found who can bring such claims or can force the foundation authority to act. However, the 2021 reform denied the introduction of a '*actio pro fundatione*' or legal rights for beneficiaries, as demanded, for example, by the 2020 scholarly draft.[110]

2.4.3. *Additional Governance Bodies*

As mentioned above, despite its practical importance, German federal foundation law only requires that the foundation has at least one director to act for it. Given the size and importance of many foundations, especially enterprise foundations, these requirements are highly limited and the supervisory authority is not enough to compensate for such limited foundation governance. This is especially true in the case of family foundations due to the very limited supervision exercised over them.

---

105 For critical accounts of this special treatment, see B. Weitemeyer, above n. 3, BGB §80, para. 104; R. Hüttemann and P. Rawert, above n. 6, BGB preamble to §§80 et seq., paras. 136–137 with further references.

106 J. Ihle, above n. 33, 557, 566; F. Rösner, *Die Konzernierung der Stiftung und ihr Einfluss auf die Pflichten des Stiftungsvorstands*, Nomos, Baden-Baden 2012, pp. 90 et seq.; see also U. Burgard, above n. 101, p. 214.

107 B. Schmidt-Schmiedebach, above n. 88, pp. 76–77; T. Dahlmanns, above n. 33, 417, 421.

108 S. Schauhoff, 'Stiftungen als Unternehmensträgerin' in Gesellschaftsrechtliche Vereinigung (ed), *Gesellschaftsrecht in der Diskussion 2018*, Dr. Otto Schmidt, Cologne 2019, pp. 83, 90.

109 U. Burgard, above n. 88, 1, 3; J. P. Esser, *Stiftungskontrolle und Stiftungsautonomie*, Nomos, Baden-Baden 2024, p. 83.

110 See §85 (3) of the scholarly draft; see also U. Burgard, above n. 96, 45, 47; B. Weitemeyer, above n. 3, BGB §84, paras. 28 et seq. with further references.

Therefore, both scholars and practitioners recommend bespoke governance concepts. It is possible to include directors with supervisory duties on the board so that they can check the actions of their colleagues.[111] Moreover, it is also possible to introduce additional bodies (for example, a supervisory board) to supervise a foundation's directors.[112] Such an additional body may have a strong position, like the supervisory board required by law in a stock corporation (AG), but it can also have merely advisory competences.[113] However, especially for large foundations, including enterprise foundations, a strong supervisory body is advisable.[114]

Besides advising and controlling directors, competences of the additional board may also include the selection, appointment, removal and evaluation of directors, and representing the foundation in interactions with the directors. It is also possible that a supervisory body has veto powers for certain transactions and a duty to organise the annual financial statement with the help of an accountant.[115] An additional board can also be invaluable in terms of helping to prevent and solve conflicts.[116] While the foundation authority is limited to legal supervision, a supervisory board should be qualified to and ready to provide competent advice on questions of expedience.[117]

In family foundations, family members often serve as members on an additional board.[118] However, such family influence should be balanced out with competent persons from outside the family. Since there are no rules concerning a foundation's governance, neither the family nor the foundation is necessarily well protected. In this context, it is important to bear in mind that supervisory authorities have almost completely withdrawn from the supervision of private-benefit foundations.[119] Therefore, such a board[120] should include beneficiaries, like family members, who have a vital interest in a foundation's

---

111 U. Burgard, above n. 101, pp. 427–428; A. Godron and K. Gollan in A. Richter (ed), above n. 63, §6, para. 105; I. Saenger, above n. 101, 94, 96.

112 R. Hüttemann, 'Gemeinnützige Stiftungen in der Nachfolgeplanung' in C. von Bar, H. Hellwege, J. M. Mössner and N. Winkeljohann (eds), *Recht und Wirtschaft: Gedächtnisschrift für Malte Schindhelm*, Carl Heymanns, Cologne 2009, pp. 377, 384; J. Ihle, above n. 33, 557, 571; U. Burgard, above n. 101, pp. 267 et seq.

113 On the possibilities in detail, see U. Burgard, above n. 101, pp. 267–272; D. Jakob, above n. 5, pp. 232–239.

114 R. Hüttemann, above n. 112, p. 377, 384; A. Godron and K. Gollan in A. Richter (ed), above n. 63, §6, paras. 103–107 with further references.

115 See H. Hof in A. Freiherr, V. Campenhausen and A. Richter, above n. 89, §8, paras. 51 et seq. on a possible combination of a board of directors and supervisory bodies – for different competences, see paras. 80 et seq.; see also U. Burgard, above n. 101, pp. 267–268.

116 For instance: D. Jakob, above n. 5, p. 476 recommends a second body to avoid conflict; see also A. Godron and K. Gollan in A. Richter (ed), above n. 63, §6, para. 105.

117 A. Godron and K. Gollan in A. Richter (ed), above n. 63, §6, para. 106.

118 H. Gummert, above n. 12, §80, para. 38; C. von Oertzen and M. Reich, above n. 49, 1118, 1120–1123.

119 R. Hüttemann, above n. 11, 591, 595.

120 T. Wernicke, above n. 101, 301, 302.

administration, but also qualified experts with sufficient independence from the foundation's directors.[121] It is also possible to set up a family council exclusively composed of family members to complement a supervisory board of experts.[122]

2.5. CHANGING THE FOUNDATION'S CHARTER

A major reason not to found a foundation to organise business succession is the perceived inflexibility of foundations. According to the Allensbach/ BDO AG study[123] of 2015, 23% of family businesses could imagine using a foundation to organise succession, but only 1% actually chose it, due to a fear of inflexibility and bureaucracy.[124] While changes to the articles of association of a partnership or limited company require little or no formality, every change to a foundation's charter in principle needs to be approved by the foundation authority.[125] Such authorities have limited resources and are not always quick in responding. This is one of the reasons why a foundation itself is not an appropriate entity to hold a business, but better acts as a shareholder. Nevertheless, a change of a foundation's charter can be important.

Changes to a foundation's charter were an important point of discussion before the 2021 reform. Some scholars argued that founders should be able to change the charter during their lifetime.[126] However, the discussion draft of 2018 did not pursue this goal any further. The 2021 draft explained that such

---

121 See H. Kronke, *Stiftungstypus und Unternehmerträgerstiftung*, Mohr Siebeck, Tübingen 1988, pp. 113 et seq., who sees the respective independence as the most important problem.

122 H. Gummert in V. Beuthien, H. Gummert and M. Schöpflin (eds), above n. 12, §80, para. 37; C. von Oertzen and M. Reich, above n. 49, 1118, 1121.

123 O. Bruttel, K. Schweinsberg and if D Allensbach in BDO AG Wirtschaftsprüfungsgesellschaft (ed), *Nachfolgeregelung in großen Familienunternehmen: Option Stiftungslösung?*, Hamburg 2015, pp. 25, 30: https://epub.sub.uni-hamburg.de/epub/volltexte/2015/37546/pdf/Allensbach_Studie.pdf.

124 According to H. Fleisch, above n. 5, 6, in practice, experiences with enterprise foundations are positive.

125 B. Weitemeyer, above n. 3, BGB §85a, paras. 1 et seq.; T. Dahlmanns, above n. 33, 417, 433; C. Stumpf, J. Suerbaum, M. Schulte and R. Pauli (eds), above n. 47, BGB §85a, para. 3.

126 See, for instance, with further references P. Rawert, 'Öffnung der Stiftung für körperschaftliche Strukturen? – Der noch lebende Stifter und die Verfassung "seiner" Stiftung' in R. Hüttemann, P. Rawert, K. Schmidt and B. Weitemeyer (eds), *Non-profit Law Yearbook 2012/2013*, Bucerius Law School Press, Hamburg 2013, pp. 51–61; D. Jakob, 'Freiheit durch Governance. Die Zukunft des Stiftungsrechts aus rechtsvergleichender Perspektive' in C. Bumke and A. Röthel (eds), *Autonomie im Recht*, Mohr Siebeck, Tubingen 2017, pp. 225–246; B. Weitemeyer, 'Von der Stifterfreiheit zur Stiftungsautonomie. Weiterentwicklung oder Sackgasse?' in C. Bumke and A. Röthel (eds), *Autonomie im Recht*, Mohr Siebeck, Tubingen 2017, pp. 201–224. For a right of founders to change the foundation during their lifetime, see U. Burgard, above n. 101, pp. 370 et seq.

a right would violate the 'nature of the foundation',[127] which has no members constantly changing and adapting its course, but merely a purpose as its lodestar.

The new §§85 and 85a BGB establish a three-step approach with increasing prerequisites for changes of increasing importance.[128] The purpose of the foundation can only be changed in a fundamental way in the event that the purpose becomes impossible to pursue or threatens the common good (§85 (1) BGB). An adaption of the foundation's purpose and major changes to its organisation are possible to align the foundation with new challenges and circumstances (§85 (2) BGB). Other changes can be made as long as they facilitate the pursuit of the foundation's purpose (§85 (3) BGB). Changes can be made by the board of directors or another body. The approval of the foundation authority is always necessary (§85a BGB).

The founder can establish different rules for changes in the original charter and even preclude all changes (§85 (4) BGB). If the founder wants to make changes easier, this is also possible. However, the founder must still give guidance in the original charter in relation to the content and extent of the changes. The more important such changes are, the more detailed the original charter should be.[129] No founder may give carte blanche to the board and its directors or other body of the foundation. Moreover, founders may not retain any right to change the charter themselves after the founding.[130] The charter is to be interpreted in light of the historical or hypothetical will (see also §83 (2) BGB) rather than the actual will of the founder.

Therefore, a careful drafting of the foundation's original charter remains of crucial importance, especially for enterprise foundations.

2.6. THE FOUNDATION REGISTER

The 2021 reform finally included the introduction of a national foundation register in §§82b et seq. BGB and a separate Foundation Register Act (*Stiftungsregistergesetz* (StiftRG)). The register requires much preparation and will start work on 1 January 2028. The introduction of the register was first

---

[127] BT-Drs. 19/28173, pp. 30 et seq.

[128] See in detail T. Schienke-Ohletz and R. Junius-Morawe, 'Möglichkeiten zur Satzungsänderung bei rechtsfähigen Stiftungen nach der Stiftungsrechtsreform' (2021) *Betriebs-Berater* 1886; R. Hüttemann and P. Rawert, above n. 1, 3, 23 et seq.; K.W. Lange, 'Möglichkeiten und Grenzen von Satzungsänderungen nach Inkrafttreten der Stiftungsrechtsreform' (2022) *Zeitschrift für Stiftungs- und Vereinswesen* 207; U. Burgard, 'Die Änderung prägender und sonstiger Satzungsbestimmungen gemäß § 85 Abs. 2 und 3 BGB' (2024) *Zeitschrift für Stiftungs- und Vereinswesen* 39.

[129] BT-Drs. 19/28173, p. 68.

[130] BT-Drs. 19/28173, pp. 30 et seq.

planned for 2026 but was postponed for two years due to technical reasons. It will be administrated by the *Bundesamt für Justiz*[131] in Bonn.[132] All legal foundations need to register there. Foundations founded before 2028 can do so until 31 December 2028. The new law shall increase transparency and facilitate the work of foundation boards, liquidators and foundation authorities.[133] At the moment, persons acting for a foundation need to prove their power of representation with certificates issued by the respective foundation authority. After the introduction of the national registry, foundation authorities can stop issuing such certificates.[134]

Registration in the national register does not convey legal personhood to a foundation;[135] this still requires the approval of the respective foundation authority. However, the register legally protects parties relying on it (§82d BGB that comes into force on 1 January 2028 with the register). Thus, the national register can help to increase the attractiveness of the foundation, and society's trust and acceptance of foundations.[136] It is a pity, that two more years have to pass before this register comes is available.

However, there is a point of discussion which is of special importance for enterprise foundations. According to §15 s. 1 StiftRG, everybody has the right to access the foundation register; there is no need to prove a special interest. This right of access also includes access to the documents on which the registration is based – among others, the original foundation and changed charters. Even a printed version may be requested (§15 s. 3 StiftRG). §15 s. 2 StiftRG provides that if there is a legitimate interest of the foundation or a third party (e.g. a founder or beneficiary), the possibility of inspection is limited (probably by making the relevant offices unidentifiable) or completely excluded.[137]

Scholars and practitioners have criticised this broad right of access during the legislative process and continue to do so now,[138] especially with respect to

---

131 For a critical view on the constitutionality of the register, see J.A. Kämmerer and P. Rawert, 'Fallstricke des Stiftungsföderalismus' (2020) *Zeitschrift für das Recht der Non Profit Organisationen* 273, 275 et seq.; A. Arnold, above n. 94, 84, 88–89; D. Markworth, above n. 60, 100, 108; R. Hüttemann and P. Rawert, above n. 1, 3, 37.

132 For the reasons, see BT-Drs. 19/28173, pp. 32 et seq., 81 et seq., 87 et seq.

133 BT-Drs. 19/28173, p. 81.

134 S. Stolte, 'Reform des Stiftungsrechts – Neuregelung zur Vermögensbewirtschaftung und Einführung eines öffentlichen Stiftungsregisters' (2021) *Betriebs-Berater* 1026, 1028.

135 BT-Drs. 19/28173, p. 81.

136 See D. Markworth, above n. 60, 100, 108; M. Habersack, above n. 33, p. 95.

137 BT-Drs. 19/28173, p. 101.

138 See J. Schwalm, 'Stiftungsrechtsreform ante portas? – Kernbotschaften für die Stiftungspraxis' (2021) *Zeitschrift für Erbrecht und Vermögensnachfolge* 68, 73–74; M. Feick and J. Schwalm, above n. 70, 525, 529; D. Markworth, above n. 60, 100, 109; K. Lorenz and J. Mehren, above n. 1, 1774, 1779–1780; K. Lorenz and J. Mehren, 'Der Referentenentwurf zur Vereinheitlichung des Stiftungsrechts' (2020) *Deutsches Steuerrecht* 2547, 2557; K. Lorenz, 'Publizitätspflichten bei Familienunternehmen und Familienstiftungen – Neues von Gesetzgeber, Verwaltung und Rechtsprechung' (2021) *Die Unternehmensbesteuerung* 386, 392; S. Stolte, above n. 134, 1026, 1029; M. Habersack, above n. 33, p. 95. For even greater transparency, see A. Arnold,

family enterprise foundations.[139] In this respect, it must be taken into account that family enterprise foundations in particular often contain information about the beneficiaries and also about the company in the foundation statutes. It is true that §15 s. 2 StiftRG provides for possibilities of restriction. However, the concrete prerequisites are reserved for a separate regulation (see §19 Nr. 4 StiftRG). However, due to the broad right to inspect the foundation statutes and thus gain access to such information, the business foundation could lose some of its attractiveness as a succession model, especially for family businesses.[140] Of course, it will also depend on how high the requirements for the possibility of restriction will be. In any case, future founders will have to give more thought to what information should be apparent from the foundation statutes in future.[141]

The transparency of foundations is a sensitive topic indeed. In Germany, transparency has already been increased since 2017 by the transparency register (*Transparenzregister*) based on two European money laundering directives.[142] However, with the new right of access to the foundation register, the situation might now change again. It remains to be seen whether the legislator will change the law before the register comes into force or whether practitioners will find other ways to deal with this issue.

3. TAX TREATMENT

Tax treatment is a major aspect for anyone choosing a legal regime to organise a business, including a founder setting up an enterprise foundation. This is a vast topic which will only be briefly discussed here.[143]

It is important to note that a foundation does not enjoy any tax benefits simply because of its legal form. If a founder transfers property to a foundation, whether while alive or after their death, the foundation is usually liable to

above n. 94, 84, 88–89; U. Burgard, above n. 96, 45, 49; K. Lorenz and A. Fassin, 'Das neue Stiftungsregister – Transparenzpflichten und Handlungsmöglichkeiten für (Familien-) Stiftungen (2025) *Neue Juristische Wochenschrift* 1526, paras. 14–17.

139 I am thankful to my former research assistant, Shkelqim Berisha, for pointing out this problem to me. S. Berisha, above n. 33, pp. 214–229; K. Lorenz and A. Fassin, above n. 138, 1526, para. 17.

140 D. Markworth, above n. 60, 100, 109.

141 K. Lorenz, above n. 138, 386, 392.

142 See M. Jurawitz, *Das Transparenzregister*, Berliner Wissenschaft-Verlag, Berlin 2021; specifically concerning foundations, see J. Schwalm, 'Das Transparenzregister im stiftungsrechtlichen Kontext – Alte und neue Herausforderungen (auch) nach der GwG-Novelle' (2020) *Zeitschrift für Stiftungs- und Vereinswesen* 52; J. Kotzenberg and K. Lorenz, 'Bedeutung des Transparenzregisters für Stiftungen – Ein Zwischenbericht' (2020) *Zeitschrift für Stiftungs- und Vereinswesen* 29.

143 For more details, see A. Richter in A. Richter (ed), above n. 63, §10, paras. 196–216; G. Brandmüller and T. Klinger, above n. 32, part 4; T. Dahlmanns, above n. 33, 417, 438–440.

gift and inheritance tax. However, founding a charitable foundation (see section 1.5.1 above) can be privileged.[144] Charitable foundations receive the same tax benefits regarding the income they receive as charitable companies.

The family foundation (see section 1.5.2 above) is set up with the purpose of supporting the founder's family.[145] The legislator reasoned that such a foundation should not be used to dodge inheritance taxes for property still used to provide benefits to the founder's family. Therefore, a foundation set up for the benefit of a certain family needs to pay a special tax every 30 years (*Erbersatzsteuer*) according to §1 (1) Nr. 4 Inheritance and gift tax Act (*Erbschaft- und Schenkungsteuergesetz*, ErbStG).

Double foundations (see section 1.5.3 above) are an example of how foundations are designed to avoid exceeding tax liability. Since the shares holding the capital of the respective company are transferred to the charitable foundation, the transfer is tax-privileged. Nevertheless, the founder's family may be supported by the dividends of the company paid to the family foundation.[146]

4. REFORM AND OUTLOOK

In this final section, current regulatory challenges shall be addressed. Section 4.1 addresses questions still left open after the 2021 reform. Section 4.2 provides brief coverage of the movement of steward ownership.

4.1. AFTER THE 2021 REFORM: GOVERNANCE

The 2021 law did not aim at fundamental reform. Therefore, it is necessary to identify regulatory challenges of the future. David Markworth's ideas are especially interesting in this respect.[147] He argues that the foundation's 'entrepreneurial role' should receive greater attention of the legislator. Weinmann discussed possible reform to improve the legal framework for enterprise foundations in Germany. He proposed a number of interesting suggestions, especially an increased supervisory board to replace the supervision

---

144 See, for instance, §13 (1) Nr. 16 lit. a) ErbStG, §5 (1) Nr. 9 KStG, §10b (1a) EstG, §3 Nr. 6 GewStG and §3 (1) Nr. 3 b) GrStG. In all these norms, the foundation or a donation to the foundation is completely or predominantly privileged under tax law.

145 On the tax law treatment of the family foundation, see in particular A. Richter in A. Richter (ed), above n. 63, §11, paras. 50–146b; an overview is given in T. Schienke-Ohletz and J. Mehren, 'Die inländische Familienstiftung – ein Steuersparmodell?' (2022) *Zeitschrift für Stiftungs- und Vereinswesen* 1.

146 M. Feick in M. Feick (ed), above n. 37, §3, para. 2.

147 D. Markworth, above n. 60, 100.

of the supervisory authority and increased flexibility for founders of enterprise foundations, including the right to revoke the foundation.[148]

In this context, foundation governance should be the focus of new legislative reform. The foundation authority is not qualified, nor does it have the necessary legal competence and resources to monitor enterprise foundations adequately. It is indeed possible that the future may bring special rules for enterprise foundations in this respect. At the moment, foundations do not fall under the same rules of co-determination as companies. It was a goal of the previous government to change this. However, this goal was not realised and it is unlikely that it will be brought back to the table under the current coalition of CDU, CSU and SPD.

In a study on the importance and future of enterprise foundations as a means to organise business succession, Mathias Habersack demanded a mandatory supervisory board to improve the governance of enterprise foundations.[149] This suggestion to improve internal governance mechanisms deserves support.[150] The foundation authority is not equipped to provide competent and timely supervision. Therefore, additional tools of foundation governance are absolutely crucial. While the development of bespoke governance is now left exclusively to founders and their lawyers, the law should demand some basic provisions to secure a minimum level of effective and independent governance.

Another point deserving detailed discussion is the introduction of an '*actio pro fundatione*', the right of certain third parties (in particular, beneficiaries) to bring claims for the foundation[151] and the suggestion to introduce a right to sue the foundation authority in the event of inaction.

4.2. STEWARD OWNERSHIP

Another future challenge may be the movement of so-called steward ownership – '*treuhänderisches Unternehmertum*', '*Verantwortungseigentum*' or '*Gesellschaft mit gebundenem Vermögen*' in German. This is linked to the international purpose debate, criticism of shareholder value primacy and new legal forms such as the US benefit corporation and French *société à mission*. Steward ownership has developed a unique approach focusing on corporate structure

[148] P.S Weinmann, above n. 33, pp. 217 et seq. See also M. Roth, 'Plädoyer für ein Unternehmensstiftungsgesetz' (2025) *Neue Zeitschrift für Gesellschaftsrecht* 1011.

[149] M. Habersack, above n. 33, passim.

[150] See S. Geibel, above n. 41, p. 251; see also D. Jakob and M. Uhl, above n. 40, BGB §80, paras. 165 et seq.; U. Burgard, above n. 88, 1.

[151] See also §85 (3) of the scholarly draft; U. Burgard, above n. 96, 45, 47; D. Markworth, above n. 60, 100, 104; B. Weitemeyer, above n. 3, BGB §84, paras. 28 et seq. with further references.

and business ownership. Rather than combining the pursuit of a prescribed beneficial purpose with profits for shareholders as dual-purpose companies like the benefit corporation, steward owners lead and develop a business without having a right to its profits (the so-called asset or capital lock).[152] In this way, entrepreneurs wish to legally secure a long-term orientation of businesses and show their fundamental commitment to pursue purpose rather than shareholder value.

The so-called 'capital lock' is similar to a foundation. Therefore, under current German law, foundation structures are used to establish steward-owned businesses. Like directors of a foundation, steward owners are paid for their work, but do not receive dividends from the business. A distribution of profits is possible, but such investors may not gain control over the business. Profits shall be reinvested or kept for hard times. The major difference between steward-owned businesses and foundations is that steward owners have voting rights as members and thus constantly develop the business rather than focusing on a founder's foundation purpose that is different from that of the business.

There is fierce discussion on the question if a new legal form should be introduced for steward-owned businesses. A draft prepared by a group of scholars – among them the author of this chapter – was already prepared in 2020 and revised in 2021.[153] This draft proposed a legal basis for steward ownership as a new sub-form of the GmbH, the German limited company.[154] Some eminent foundation scholars in particular have criticised the concept and the idea of creating a hybrid between a foundation and a company.[155]

---

152 In detail, see A. Sanders, 'Binding Capital to Free Purpose: Steward Ownership in Germany' (2023) 19(4) *European Company and Financial Law Review* 623.

153 A. Sanders, B. Dauner-Lieb, A. von Freeden, S. Kempny, F. Möslein and R. Veil, 'Entwurf eines Gesetzes für die Gesellschaft mit beschränkter Haftung mit gebundenem Vermögen' (2021). The draft with explanations in German can be downloaded from: https://www.gesellschaft-mit-gebundenem-vermoegen.de/der-gesetzesentwurf; see also A. Sanders, B. Dauner-Lieb, S. Kempny, F. Möslein and R. Veil, 'Gesetzesentwurf GmbH mit gebundenem Vermögen – Verantwortungseigentum 2.0' (2021) *GmbH-Rundschau* 285; A. Sanders, above n. 60, 1573; S. Kempny and A. Sanders, 'Zum Entwurf einer GmbH mit gebundenem Vermögen' (2021) *NWB Steuer- und Wirtschaftsrecht* 3117; G.R. Rolfes and S. Berisha, 'Der Schutz der Gläubiger des Gesellschafters einer GmbH mit gebundenem Vermögen' (2022) *GmbH-Rundschau* 23; H. Fleischer, 'Ein Schönheitswettbewerb für eine neue Gesellschaftsform mit Nachhaltigkeitsbezug: Zur rechtspolitischen Diskussion um eine GmbH mit gebundenem Vermögen' (2022) *Zeitschrift für Wirtschaftsrecht* 345.

154 See for a discussion in English: A. Sanders, above n. 152, 623, 640 et seq.

155 See, for instance, A. Arnold, U. Burgard, G. Roth and B. Weitemeyer, 'Die GmbH im Verantwortungseigentum – eine Kritik' (2020) *Neue Zeitschrift für Gesellschaftsrecht* 1321; R. Hüttemann, P. Rawert and B. Weitemeyer, 'Zauberwort "Verantwortungseigentum"' (2020) *Zeitschrift für das Recht der Non Profit Organisationen* 296; U. Burgard, 'Verantwortungseigentum in Stiftungsform de lege lata und de lege ferenda' (2021) *Zeitschrift für Stiftungs- und Vereinswesen* 1. See also B. Grunewald and J. Hennrichs, 'Die GmbH in Verantwortungseigentum, wäre das ein Fortschritt?' (2020) *Neue Zeitschrift für Gesellschaftsrecht* 1201; M. Habersack, '"Gesellschaft mit beschränkter Haftung in

However, some practitioners and scholars see the new legal form as an opportunity to found a more flexible alternative to a traditional foundation.[156] While there will always be high demand for the traditional foundation, a new legal form for steward ownership may indeed offer interesting new options for a diverse economy for smaller businesses.

The coalition agreement[157] of the politicial parties that formed the German government elected in 2021 already contained the promise to provide a new legal framework for steward-owned businesses. In 2024, parliamentarians from the parties of SPD, Grüne and FDP that supported the then ruling government, asked the authour of this chapter and the group of scholars who had already worked on drafts in 2020 and 2021, to prepare a new draft for a special corporate form for steward ownership.[158] When the coalition of SPD, Grüne and FDP broke apart in late 2024, it seemed doubtful if the reform process might continue. However, the new coalition of the political parties

Verantwortungseigentum" – ein Fremdkörper im Recht der Körperschaften' (2020) *GmbH-Rundschau* 992; B. Weitemeyer, B.E. Weissenberger and G.T. Wiese, 'Eine GmbH mit ewigem Gewinnausschüttungsverbot – Bahnbrechende Innovation oder volkswirtschaftlich bedenkliche Perpetuierung?' (2021) *GmbH-Rundschau* 1069; K.-G. Loritz and P.S. Weinmann, 'Die GmbH mit gebundenem Vermögen – Kreative Idee oder Legitimation zum Betreiben eines Unternehmens ohne typische Unternehmerpflichten?' (2021) *Deutsches Steuerrecht* 2205; R. Hüttemann, 'Die GmbH mit gebundenem Vermögen – ein Steuersparmodell?!' (2021) *Der Betrieb* 1356; A. Engel and D. Haubner, 'Die GmbH mit gebundenem Vermögen und das Europarecht' (2022) *Deutsches Steuerrecht* 844; V. Obernosterer, 'Die GmbH mit gebundenem Vermögen – eine GmbH mit beschränkter Niederlassungsfreiheit?' (2023) *GmbH-Rundschau* 434; recently B.E. Weissenberger, 'Verantwortungseigentum und GmgV im Realitätscheck' (2025) *Der Betrieb* M6.

156 See, for instance, H.-J. Fischer and K. Fischer, 'Die GmbH in Verantwortungseigentum (VE-GmbH) im Rahmen der Umsetzung globaler Nachhaltigkeitsziele – eine mögliche neue Rechtsform für den Mittelstand' (2020) *Betriebs-Berater* 2122; H.-J. Fischer, 'Die GmbH mit gebundenem Vermögen als eine mögliche neue Rechtsform für den Mittelstand' (2021) *Betriebs-Berater* 2114; W. Servatius, 'Verantwortungseigentum – in dubio Gesellschaftsrecht!' (2021) *Neue Zeitschrift für Gesellschaftsrecht* 569; M. Reiff, 'Entwurf eines Gesetzes für die GmbH in Verantwortungseigentum (VE-GmbH) vorgelegt' (2020) *Zeitschrift für Wirtschaftsrecht* 1750; A. Sanders, above n. 60, 1573; S. Kempny and A. Sanders, above n. 153, 3117; A. Sanders, 'Eine Gesellschaft in Verantwortungseigentum im GmbHG' (2020) *Zeitschrift für Rechtspolitik* 140.

157 'Mehr Fortschritt wagen: Bündnis für Freiheit, Gerechtigkeit und Nachhaltigkeit, Koalitionsvertrag 2021–2025 zwischen der Sozialdemokratischen Partei Deutschlands (SPD), Bündnis 90/Die Grünen und den Freien Demokraten (FDP)' (2021), p. 30: https://www.spd.de/fileadmin/Dokumente/Koalitionsvertrag/Koalitionsvertrag_2021-2025.pdf; see also T. Wachter, 'Zukunft des deutschen Erbschaftsteuerrechts: Der Koalitionsvertrag 2021–2025' (2022) *Der Betrieb* 284, 286.

158 A. Sanders, B. Dauner-Lieb, S. Kempny, F. Möslein, N. Neitzel and C. Teichmann, *Gesetz zur Einführung einer Gesellschaft mit gebundenem Vermögen*, Mohr Siebeck, Tubingen 2024, open access: https://www.mohrsiebeck.com/buch/gesetz-zur-einfuehrung-einer-gesellschaft-mit-gebundenem-vermoegen-9783161640773/; for an English introduction see A. Sanders and N. Neitzel, 'Steward Ownership – Concept, Potential and Implementation in Germany and the Netherlands' (15 March 2025): https://papers.ssrn.com/sol3/papers.cfm?abstract_id=5178366.

currently forming the German government (CDU, SPD) has also taken up the proposal and has embraced the goal to provide a new legal basis for steward-owned businesses with an irrevocable capital lock.[159]

5. CONCLUSION

In Germany, enterprise foundations hark back to a long tradition supported by scholars and practitioners. With the new foundation register, their numbers and economic importance will become even clearer. The 2021 law has clarified much, and the new foundation register will increase transparency. This might increase trust in the foundation but could also make it less attractive to founders who are anxious to protect their privacy. However, the 2021 law was not a real reform, but chiefly an update to the status quo. In particular, questions concerning foundation governance remain the responsibility of founders alone. Therefore, it is unlikely that the discussion will stop now. It also remains to be seen to what extent the discussion about a new legal form for steward ownership will have an impact on foundation law, especially with regard to enterprise foundations.

[159] 'Verantwortung für Deutschland: Koalitionsvertrag zwischen CDU, CSU und SPD: 21. Legislaturperiode des Deutschen Bundestages' (2025), p. 64: https://www.spd.de/fileadmin/Dokumente/Koalitionsvertrag2025_bf.pdf.

ENTERPRISE FOUNDATIONS IN SWITZERLAND

Overview and Current Challenges

Dominique JAKOB*

* The author wishes to thank his assistant Laura Studhalter for her valuable assistance in drafting this chapter.

Dominique Jakob

ABSTRACT

This chapter aims to give an overview of the law and practice of Swiss enterprise foundations and the current challenges in Switzerland. It will try to embed the special form of enterprise foundations into the framework of Swiss foundation law, and will then focus on the specific topics and challenges Swiss enterprise foundations face, such as: the admissibility of self-maintaining foundations; the scope of state supervision; how to deal with reduced flexibility; how to deal with the unfriendly tax environment for charitable (tax-exempt) foundations holding companies; and the unclear situation for mission-based investments, impact investments and entrepreneurial grant-making schemes (by investments in companies). Subsequently, the general need for good 'foundation governance' and, in a family business context, for 'family governance', is discussed as a crucial success factor for enterprise foundations. As a final point, the chapter will provide an outlook into the future.

1. INTRODUCTION

The Swiss foundation law was introduced in the Swiss Civil Code (CC)[1] in 1912 and follows a 'classical' foundation model. According to this notion, a foundation is a legal person that is established by dedicating assets for a specific purpose. After coming into force, the foundation is characterised by the principle of separation and solidification: the founder and the foundation are two separate and independent legal persons, and the original will of the founder is perpetuated and shall guide the foundation for its entire existence. The Swiss foundation is not a corporation (with members like associations or shareholders like stock companies) but is an establishment with an ownerless purpose fund for the benefit of the beneficiaries.[2]

Of course, the foundation as a legal person needs organs to act. However, it is crucial to understand that these organs are, in principle, not allowed to create their own actual will, but must execute the (original) will of the founder. But how can one ensure that only the will of the founder is fulfilled, and that

---

1 Civil Code of the Swiss Confederation of 10 December 1907, as amended, AS 24 233.

2 For a general overview of Swiss foundation law, see D. Jakob and G. von Schnurbein, 'Charitable Foundations, A Practical Guide: Build and Lead Charitable Foundations in Switzerland' (2021) Credit Suisse Group AG (ed); D. Jakob and G. Studen, 'Foundation Law in Switzerland: Overview and Current Developments in Civil and Tax Law' in C. Prele (ed), *Developments in Foundation Law in Europe*, Springer, Berlin 2014, pp. 283–310; D. Jakob, commenting on Articles 80–89a CC in A. Büchler and D. Jakob (eds), *Kurzkommentar ZGB, Schweizerisches Zivilgesetzbuch*, 2nd ed., Helbing Lichtenhahn Verlag, Basel 2017; for a comparative overview, see D. Jakob, '§30 Internationale Stiftungen' in A. Richter (ed), *Stiftungsrecht Handbuch*, 5th ed., C.H. Beck, Munich 2019, pp. 911–983 with special regard to Switzerland, Austria, the Principality of Liechtenstein and Germany.

the organs do not replace the will of the founder with their own actual will? Upon a closer look, the foundation is running into a so-called 'principal-agent problem' because the persons who act are not the persons who own the assets, and the problem is even multiplied as there are no shareholders or members that could control the agent. This is the reason why the historic legislator already decided in 1912 that the foundation (as the only private law entity in Swiss law) needs to be under the supervision of a state authority, the supervisory authority, which has to protect the foundation and has to see that the foundation's organs always fulfil the will of the founder and do not harm the foundation's assets.[3] The competent authority in Switzerland depends on whether the foundation is active at a municipal, cantonal or federal level.[4]

On the other hand, Swiss foundation law is characterised by a great freedom of the founder. Under Swiss foundation law, a foundation can be established for any purpose that is not contrary to law or morality, among which are also business and enterprise-related purposes.[5] Furthermore, the founder is entitled to create the foundation's organisation more or less freely and can decide on the asset structure of the foundation. From that follows – which is important in this context – that a foundation with a business or enterprise-related purpose is a 'classical' foundation and not a 'special' legal foundation form (which the law provides in the case of family, ecclesiastical or pension fund foundations, for which special provisions are applicable). There is, at least in principle, no special law for enterprise foundations, but the normal legal rules for foundations do apply.[6] Hence, enterprise foundations are normal or classical private purpose foundations under Swiss law without any specific provisions.[7]

In this sense, tax-related questions regarding enterprise foundations are also assessed based on the Swiss tax law generally applicable to all legal entities.

---

3 D. Jakob, 'Ein Stiftungsbegriff für die Schweiz' (2013) II *ZSR* 185, 209 et seq. and 315–317; D. Jakob, commenting on Article 84 CC, in A. Büchler and D. Jakob (eds), above n. 2.

4 See Article 84 CC.

5 See decision of the Federal Supreme Court of Switzerland, BGE 127 III 337.

6 Attention must be paid to the accounting rules in Articles 957 et seq. of the Federal Act on the Amendment of the Swiss Civil Code, Part Five, The Code of Obligations (CO) of 30 March 1911, as amended, SR 220, which are effective for all legal forms and for foundations in particular according to the reference in Article 83a CC. Depending on the size of the foundation, different regulatory accounting requirements have to be met.

7 On 1 January 2024 a reform of Swiss foundation law came into force (see the text of final vote, BBl 2021 2992). However, this reform is not aimed at enterprise foundations specifically. In its final form, the revision contains (only) three provisions: a regulation of the supervisory complaint in Article 84, para. 3 CC; a flexibilisation of minor statute amendments in Article 86b CC; and an extension of the founder's right in Article 86a CC from (only) the amendment of the purpose to (also) the amendment of the organisation of the foundation. See the critique on the reform by D. Jakob, 'Die Reform des Stiftungsrechts ist beschlossen – was ist gewonnen, was ist verloren, was bleibt?' in L. von Orelli, J. Jakob, D. Jakob and G. von Schnurbein (eds), 'Der Schweizer Stiftungsreport 2022' (2022), pp. 20 et seq.

Tax law aspects are critically important for prudent and effective asset planning. Therefore, a brief overview of the basic principles of Swiss tax exemption shall be given in the following discussion: enterprise foundations with a purely economic purpose are considered equal to other legal entities with regard to tax law aspects and therefore do not benefit from special tax privileges. On the other hand, enterprise foundations with an exclusively charitable purpose can be exempt from taxation on a federal level for profits that are exclusively and irrevocably committed to these charitable purposes.[8] The same applies to cantonal taxes on profit and capital.[9] Pursuant to Article 56 lit. g of the Federal Act on Direct Federal Tax (FDTA), the acquisition and holding of significant capital stakes in companies are considered to be charitable where the interest in maintaining the company is subordinate to the charitable purpose and no management activities are carried out. Considering limited tax law regulations on charitable status, the practices of the cantonal tax authorities – which are generally guided by the Circular No. 12 issued by the Federal Tax Authority from 1994[10] – are critically important.[11]

2. TYPES OF ENTERPRISE FOUNDATIONS

2.1. BUSINESS OPERATING AND HOLDING FOUNDATIONS

According to this wide-meshed framework of Swiss foundation law, in business reality various forms of business-linked or enterprise foundations have developed. The first distinction can be made between (direct) business operating and (indirect) holding foundations. A business operating foundation operates an economic business itself to fulfil its purpose, which is, for example, the case when a foundation with the purpose of taking care of the elderly runs its own foster home. One other common example would be a hospital run by a foundation.

However, the majority of business-linked foundations are holding foundations, which hold the shares of an operational business. The reasons for this setup can be numerous: if, for example, the shares in the business are held by the foundation as an ownerless entity, these shares do not fall into

---

8 Article 56 lit. g Federal Act on Direct Federal Tax (FDTA) of 14 December 1990, as amended, AS 1991 1184.

9 Article 23 para. 1 lit. f Federal Act on the Harmonisation of Direct Cantonal Taxation and Direct Community Taxation (FTHA) of 14 December 1990, as amended, AS 1991 1256.

10 Circular No. 12 of 8 July 1994, available at: http://www.estv.admin.ch.

11 The tax-exemption criteria in general and for holding foundations specifically will be discussed further in section 3.3.1 below.

someone's estate in the case of death. From a business point of view, such a construct can perpetuate the business independently from individuals, can channel succession matters and can protect the business against hostile takeovers. In a family context, it can support the family while keeping it away from actually running the business. Of course, a structure like this ought to be backed up by means of an effective form of 'family governance'.[12]

2.2. DISTINCTION ACCORDING TO THE PURPOSE OF THE FOUNDATION

It is not quite clear in the Swiss doctrine what will constitute an enterprise foundation,[13] the pure fact that a (somehow substantial part of a) business is held, the possibility of exerting influence on the business, or a purpose that is related to the business. In any case, in business reality we can distinguish different types of enterprise or business foundations according to the foundation's purpose.

2.2.1. Pure Business Foundations

A foundation with the sole purpose of holding a business could be described as a 'pure business foundation'.[14] In this context, two remarks seem to be of crucial importance.

First, for quite a while it was disputed among Swiss scholars if a foundation with an economic purpose was permissible.[15] In 2001 the Federal Supreme Court of Switzerland decided this dispute and held that foundations with a

---

12 See D. Jakob, 'The Role of Foundations in Family Governance' (2020) 26(1) *Trusts and Trustees* 6.

13 For an overview of the controversy, see H. Grüninger, preliminary remarks on Articles 80–89a CC in T. Geiser and C. Fountoulakis (eds), *Basler Kommentar: Zivilgesetzbuch I, Art. 1–456 ZGB*, 67th ed., Helbing Lichtenhahn, Basel 2022, marginal nos. 15 et seq.

14 D. Jakob, 'Ein Stiftungsbegriff für die Schweiz', above n. 3, 188, 273–276; D. Bottge, 'Shareholder Foundations (Holding Foundations) in Switzerland' (2019) 3 *Expert Focus* 180.

15 Against admissibility, see H.M. Riemer, 'Systematischer Teil' in H.M. Riemer, *Berner Kommentar, Die Stiftungen*, Stämpfli Verlag, Bern 1975, marginal nos. 82, 392 et seq.; R. Bär, 'Aktuelle Fragen des Aktienrechts' (1966) 85 *ZSR* 532; M. Pedrazzini and N. Oberholzer, *Grundriss des Personenrechts*, 4th ed., Stämpfli Verlag, Bern 1993, p. 255. In favour of admissibility, see H. Grüninger, *Die Unternehmensstiftung in der Schweiz: Zulässigkeit, Eignung, Besteuerung*, Helbing Lichtenhahn Verlag, Basel 1984, pp. 39 et seq.; P. Liver, 'Rezension zu Riemers Kommentar zum Stiftungsrecht' (1976) 112 *ZBJV* 317; P. Nobel, *Anstalt und Unternehmen*, Diessenhofen 1978, p. 582; R. Portmann, *Wege zur Perpetuierung der Aktiengesellschaft*, Stämpfli Verlag, Bern 1983, pp. 57 et seq.; J.N. Druey, 'Die Rechtsgültigkeit von Unternehmensstiftungen' (1992) *SZW* 174.

(partial) economic purpose are admissible.[16] The Court correctly argued according to the general principles of Swiss foundation law and upheld the neutrality of the legal concept towards all purposes and the freedom of the founder. For foundations in particular which do not strive for tax exemption – where economic purposes, of course, would harm the charitable tax-exempt status of the foundation[17] – this was a welcome decision.

Second, pure business foundations face the potential issue of so-called self-maintaining purposes. According to the general principles of foundation law, a foundation with the only purpose of holding its own assets would not be permissible because it lacks an outward-directed purpose and, thus, constitutes a *perpetuum mobile*.[18] Against this background, one could argue that a pure business foundation is a self-maintaining foundation because the business could be seen as the only self-perpetuated asset (thus leaving aside all the additional outbound effects such a foundation purpose may have). And in fact, some scholars require that a foundation (at least additionally) pursues other outward purposes.[19] However, the discussion has never been conducted as intensively in Switzerland[20] as it has been in Germany.[21] A reason for this might be that Switzerland always had pure business holding foundations, such as the Victorinox Foundation.[22] In practice, it could nevertheless be advisable for founders to install an independent secondary purpose alongside the pure business holding purpose, even if it is solely to avoid discussions and recognition problems with courts or authorities abroad.[23]

---

16 Decision of the Federal Supreme Court of Switzerland, BGE 127 III 337.

17 Circular No. 12, pp. 2 et seq.

18 Cf. D. Jakob, preliminary remarks on Articles 80–89a CC, in A. Büchler and D. Jakob (eds), above n. 2; D. Jakob, 'Ein Stiftungsbegriff für die Schweiz', above n. 3, 272 et seq.

19 Cf. L. Brugger, *Die gemischte Stiftung: Die Stiftung zur Verfolgung unterschiedlicher Zwecke im Lichte des schweizerischen ZGB und des österreichischen PSG*, Helbing Lichtenhahn Verlag, Zürich 2019, pp. 28 et seq. for more details.

20 In the above-mentioned BGE 127 III 337 decision, the Federal Supreme Court of Switzerland left the question of the admissibility of self-maintaining foundations open.

21 D. Jakob, *Schutz der Stiftung, Die Stiftung und ihre Rechtsverhältnisse im Widerstreit der Interessen*, Mohr Siebeck, Tubingen 2006, pp. 51–53 with further references to D. Reuter, preliminary remarks on §80 BGB in *Münchener Kommentar, Bürgerliches Gesetzbuch, Band 1, Allgemeiner Teil*, 4th ed., C.H. Beck, Munich 2005, marginal nos. 42, 50; P. Rawert, 'Der Stiftungsbegriff und seine Merkmale – Stiftungszweck, Stiftungsvermögen, Stiftungsorganisation' in K. Hopt and D. Reuter (eds), *Stiftungsrecht in Europa*, Carl Heymanns Verlag, Cologne 2001, pp. 117 et seq.; P. Rawert, 'Stiftung und Unternehmen' in H. Kötz, P. Rawert, K. Schmidt and W.R. Walz, *Non Profit Law Yearbook 2003*, Carl Heymanns Verlag, Cologne 2004, p. 15.

22 See for further examples of Swiss enterprise foundations H. Grüninger, 'Unternehmensstiftung' in P.V. Kunz, F.S. Jörg and O. Arter (eds), *Entwicklungen im Gesellschaftsrecht V*, Stämpfli Verlag, Bern 2010, pp. 21 et seq.

23 D. Jakob, 'Ein Stiftungsbegriff für die Schweiz', above n. 3, 274 et seq.

2.2.2. *Pure Charitable Foundations (Holding a Business)*

The next possible type would be a pure charitable foundation, i.e. a foundation with the sole purpose to pursue a charitable goal. Accordingly, the business is (or the shares of the business are) only an asset or the only asset of the foundation which is used to fulfil the charitable purpose.[24] In fact, many of the largest Swiss foundations are such pure charitable (business) foundations such as the Jacobs Foundation or the Kühne Foundation holding the Kühne and Nagel Group. Transferring the business to a pure charitable foundation has an important side effect and advantage: the transfer of the business does not levy any gift or inheritance tax if the recipient of the asset itself is tax-free for charitable purposes.[25] Furthermore, a philanthropic vehicle can play a rather important role in a family context as a shared philanthropic activity. It can, for example, serve as a platform where family members of all generations can work together, learn from each other, and share values and experiences.[26] Moreover, it can create a separate management level where family members can learn to take responsibility before taking a leadership role at the business level.[27]

2.2.3. *Family Foundations (Holding a Business)*

Further, Enterprise Foundations can be and often are a tool for the succession planning of family businesses. If their purpose is to provide for the favouring of descendants or other family members of the founder for specific pension purposes, this constitutes a family foundation.[28] The permissible family purposes are narrowly defined in Article 335 CC and, at the same time, the provision prohibits so-called '*Familienfideikommisse*' and, according to the strict jurisdiction, also family maintenance foundations in general.[29] This decisively restricts the possible uses of family foundations in a business context in Switzerland because the provisions may not be circumvented with an enterprise foundation and no benefits may be granted to the beneficiaries without special requirements linked to a specific need.[30] The strict judicial practice

---

24 T. Wüstemann, 'Familienpartizipation und gemeinnützige Stiftungen – rechtliche Herausforderungen und Chancen im nationalen und internationalen Kontext' in D. Jakob (ed), *Stiftung und Familie*, Helbing Lichtenhahn Verlag, Basel 2015, p. 25.

25 See details in section 3.3.1 below.

26 See details in section 3.4 below.

27 D. Jakob, above n. 12.

28 See Article 87 and Article 335 para. 1 CC.

29 D. Jakob, 'Was darf eine Familienstiftung (noch) tun?' in T. Sprecher and L. von Orelli (eds), *Familienstiftungen – neue Perspektiven*, EIZ Publishing, Zürich 2024, pp. 113 et seq., 115 et seq.

30 See decision of the Federal Supreme Court of Switzerland, BGE 127 III 337.

has been heavily criticised by academics in the past.[31] Due to these legal difficulties, in 2022, a political motion was launched to liberalise Swiss family foundations. The aim is to amend Article 335 CC and lift the ban on family maintenance foundations.[32] This is intended to close the gap in Swiss estate planning options, especially after the introduction of a Swiss trust has been rejected. After the Swiss parliament has adopted the motion in 2024, the matter now lies with the Federal Council.[33]

2.2.4. *The Double Foundation Model*

If the founder wishes to profit from a tax-free transfer of assets while at the same time retaining control over the enterprise, it could be considered to create a so-called double foundation model.[34] In this scenario, there are two shareholders – a family foundation or family holding and a charitable foundation – whereby the latter holds the majority of the share capital in the enterprise (which it has normally received as a tax-free donation). The 'trick' is that the share capital and the voting rights are distributed disproportionately between the two shareholders: immensely simplified, one shareholder – the tax-exempt charitable foundation[35] – holds perhaps 90% of the share capital; however, these shares carry only 10% of the voting rights in order to accumulate the actual control in the non-tax-exempt family entity that holds only 10% of the shares but 90% of the voting rights. The rather smart idea behind a vehicle like this is the tax-free transfer of an enterprise while retaining family control. One downside is that public opinion on such a setup might be negative because the construct appears to contain an abusive element: why should the transfer of the enterprise be tax-free when the family remains in control of the assets going to the charitable foundation? By retaining control of the business through voting rights, family members in charge of the family foundation can control the dividends going up to the two shareholders. In the end, a structure like this might save the family a larger sum of money in the form of taxes than

---

31 See D. Jakob, above n. 29, pp. 116 et seq.; D. Jakob, 'Ein Stiftungsbegriff für die Schweiz', above n. 3, 324 et seq. with further references.

32 Motion 22.4445, 'Die Schweizer Familienstiftung stärken. Verbot der Unterhaltsstiftung aufheben' of 15 December 2022.

33 The status of the motion is available at: https://www.parlament.ch/de/ratsbetrieb/suche-curia-vista/geschaeft?AffairId=20224445; see for the whole discussion on Swiss family foundations in the past, present and future D. Jakob, above n. 29, pp. 113 et seq.

34 D. Jakob, 'Ein Stiftungsbegriff für die Schweiz', above n. 3, 185, 276–281; R. Hüttemann, 'Die gemischte Stiftung' in D. Jakob (ed), *Universum Stiftung*, Helbing Lichtenhahn Verlag, Basel 2017, pp. 29, 45; D. Jakob, above n. 21, pp. 78 et seq.

35 Whether this construction is still possible regarding the recent judgement of the Federal Supreme Court, BGE 147 II 287 (see section 3.3.1 below) remains to be seen. However, it seems clear that the Court did not waste any thought on the consequences of its (rather surprising) judgement to special situations such as the present one.

the charitable foundation ends up investing in the charitable purpose over the years. For this reason, the admissibility of this model under foundation and tax law has caused controversy.[36] This model has been intensively discussed in Germany, where there are quite a few well-known family businesses held in such a structure (with the Bertelsmann Foundation being the most prominent example), but should in principle also be possible in Switzerland.[37]

2.2.5. *Mixed Foundations*

The next model would be a mixed foundation – a foundation that pursues more than one purpose, such as a holding, a charitable and a family purpose all in one vehicle.[38] In fact, this structure is quite well known in Switzerland and includes some important family businesses such as the Ernst Göhner Foundation. It can be an efficient structure to use in order to hold the enterprise and to pursue other interests at the same time. This is especially common in Switzerland, where partial tax exemption is, at least in principle, also admissible.[39] However, from a governance point of view, the problem with this structure is that if purposes are mixed in one entity, there is quite a high risk that the interests of the involved persons start drifting apart, especially over the generations.

Typically, in a family context, the authority of the founder remains present within the first generation of family members and is universally respected, whereas in the second or third generation, this authority might dwindle, and the interests start falling apart. Some members of the governing bodies might want to place greater emphasis on the business aspect, while others might wish to focus on the charity; family members, on the other hand, might want to put the emphasis on the wellbeing of the family. In a case like this, conflict resolution can be difficult as it is not easy to restructure a foundation and to provide for the exit of one part. This begs the following question: is the only proper solution from a family governance perspective to build two independent structures instead of a mixed foundation? While this might be an alternative, of course, one could also pay special attention to a prudent drafting of the foundation statutes. Unlike the 1950s, when some famous examples of mixed foundations in Switzerland were established, nowadays we have a more modern understanding of foundations, and it is possible to create a vehicle that is more flexible and thus more suitable in this respect. For instance, one could provide

36 See D. Jakob, 'Ein Stiftungsbegriff für die Schweiz', above n. 3, 276 with further references.

37 D. Jakob, above n. 12. Whether this is still the case after the BGE 147 II 287 decision (discussed in section 3.3.1.2 below) remains to be seen.

38 R. Hüttemann, 'Die gemischte Stiftung' in D. Jakob (ed), *Universum Stiftung*, above n. 34, pp. 29, 30–31, 47; F. Zihler, 'Zulässigkeit von Holdingstiftungen aus der Sicht der Handelsregisterbehörden' (2018) 2 *Reprax* 69, 74–75.

39 Cf. Circular No. 12, p. 6.

for fair exit measures for one of the interested parties or for family members who wish to follow their own path; also, one could establish a robust conflict resolution mechanism in advance.[40]

2.2.6. *No Enterprise Foundation: Corporate Foundations*

Finally, if a *company* establishes a foundation – for example, to fulfil its corporate social responsibility (or, in a family context, a charitable foundation is set up by and next to a family business holding) – Swiss practice speaks of a 'corporate foundation', which is a different structure from an enterprise foundation.[41] Such a charitable foundation would have no holding function whatsoever and therefore does not constitute an enterprise foundation in the given sense.

2.2.7. *Interim Result*

These example structures show that there is not 'the' enterprise foundation under Swiss law and that businesses can be connected to foundations on various levels and for various motives and purposes. The examples also demonstrate the importance of drafting the statutes and setting up these structures in a way that leaves room for adaptability in a world that evolves quickly, and that keeps in mind that there is an intrinsic conflict between the rigid perpetuation on the one hand and the need for certain flexibility on the other hand. Against this background, the emphasis should now be put on specific challenges that enterprise foundations can typically face.

3. CURRENT CHALLENGES

3.1. STATE SUPERVISION AND ASSET MANAGEMENT

As can be seen above, Swiss enterprise foundations are no special legal structures and are regulated by the general provisions of Swiss foundation law. Therefore, the rules of state supervision apply and follow the normal regime of supervision regarding classical foundations.[42]

---

40 D. Jakob, above n. 12.

41 Cf. T. Sprecher, *Stiftungsrecht in a nutshell*, 2nd ed., Dike, Zürich 2023, p. 169; T. Sprecher, P. Egger and G. von Schnurbein, 'Der Swiss Foundation Code' in P. Egger and G. von Schnurbein (eds), *Foundation Governance*, Vol. 11, Helbing Lichtenhahn, Basel 2015, p. 140; T. Gehringer, 'Corporate Foundations as Hybrid Organizations: A Systematic Review of Literature' (2021) 32 *VOLUNTAS* 257, 257–275.

42 See Article 84 para. 2 CC.

While state supervision is sometimes seen as a problem for enterprise foundations, it can be regarded as an advantage or a disadvantage depending on the perspective of the founder who favours more or less external control over his or her foundation. However, in contrast to what is sometimes thought, the supervisory authority will, in principle, not interfere with the business activities or business decisions of the board – especially when it comes to holding foundations.

Of course, the assets of the foundation must be used according to the purpose of the foundation. This can lead to a stricter controlling mechanism for business *operating* foundations regarding business decisions, which are in this structure made at the foundation level.[43] In this regard, *holding* foundations are less problematic as the business decisions are made at the level of the held corporation, and thus usually beyond state supervision.[44]

The bigger problem in fact is that the supervisory authority will have a quite strict control regarding the asset management of the foundation. Also in general, the topic of asset management of foundations can be a difficult subject in practice. The Swiss Civil Code does not contain any provisions on asset management. Solutions must therefore be derived from the general principles of foundation law. As a starting point, the founder's intention takes priority in asset management as well.[45] When setting up a foundation, each founder is free, in the foundation articles, to both define individual regulations on the investment of assets and to stipulate how the foundation assets must be used to achieve the relevant purpose.[46] If the foundation articles do not contain any specifications regarding the investment of assets or leave room for discretion, the foundation board must generally act in accordance with the principles of diligent asset management. According to a quite elderly jurisprudence, these principles include the elements of asset maintenance, security, risk diversification, profitability and liquidity.[47] Based on these principles, while the foundation board should avoid speculative investments, assigning 'gilt-edged status' to investments is not advisable. In addition, according to the Federal Supreme Court, the investment principles laid down in the Ordinance on Occupational Retirement, Survivors' and Disability Pension Plans[48] for staff pension funds

---

43 See A. Meier-Hayoz and P. Forstmoser (eds), *Schweizerisches Gesellschaftsrecht*, 13th ed., Stämpfli Verlag, Bern 2023, §23 marginal no. 21.

44 Ibid.

45 See A. Meier-Hayoz and P. Forstmoser (eds), above n. 43, p. 824; F. Zihler, 'Zulässigkeit von Holdingstiftungen aus der Sicht der Handelsregisterbehörden' (2018) 2 *Reprax* 69 et seq.

46 See Article 84 para. 2 CC.

47 Decisions of the Federal Supreme Court of Switzerland, BGE 124 III 99; 108 II 352, E. 5.a.; for a foundation under federal state supervision, see also VEB 30 (1961) no. 45 p. 78; H. Grüninger, commenting on Article 84 CC in T. Geiser and C. Fountoulakis (eds), above n. 13, marginal no. 14.

48 Articles 49 et seq. in the regulation on occupational retirement, survivors' and disability pension plans (BVV 2), SR 831.441.1.

can be used by boards of trustees of classical foundations as a 'guide'.[49] Since the suitability of these principles of jurisprudence for many, particularly enterprise foundations, is limited, the statutes ideally define a concrete strategic position for the foundation with regard to its assets. However, the day-to-day balancing of investment security against generating returns generally remains at the individual discretion of the foundation board, and these decisions must be made according to the board's best judgement in its proper exercise of discretion. The supervisory authority can only check this exercise of discretion for any error of law and cannot interfere with the result of a lawful exercise of discretion, whether the authority entirely agrees with the decision or not.[50] For instance, if a board decides in its proper exercise of discretion that the special purpose relation of an investment (a so-called mission-based investment) should prevail over the classic criteria (such as diversification), the supervisory authority should respect this decision. However, supervisory authorities sometimes have to be reminded of this rule. It becomes evident that regarding the asset management, every individual foundation is different; what is possible for one foundation may not be permitted for another. However, one must be aware that in this field lurk potential discussions with the supervisory authority.

Another problem in the context of foundation assets can be faced when the foundation wants to separate from or restructure its assets. The question of if a foundation is allowed, for example, to sell the shares it holds, must in principle also be answered in accordance with the asset management criteria described above.[51] This leads to the next topic, which is whether and to what extent a foundation is a suitable structure in a business environment.

3.2. ENTREPRENEURIAL SUITABILITY OF THE FOUNDATION STRUCTURE

3.2.1. *Inflexibility*

The legal framework of foundations is sometimes seen as too inflexible to adapt to the dynamic business developments in an entrepreneurial environment.[52] This fundamental critique could be evaluated in two aspects: first, this reservation is mainly made with regard to Articles 85 et seq. CC, which

---

49 See decisions of the Federal Supreme Court of Switzerland, BGE 108 II 352 and 124 III 97.

50 D. Jakob, commenting on Article 83 CC, marginal nos. 12 et seq. and commenting on Article 84 CC, marginal no. 5, in A. Büchler and D. Jakob (eds), above n. 2; D. Jakob, above n. 12, 316 et seq.

51 See above n. 48.

52 A. Meier-Hayoz and P. Forstmoser (eds), above n. 43, §23 marginal no. 26; H. Grüninger, 'Unternehmensstiftung' in P.V. Kunz, F.S. Jörg and O. Arter (eds), above n. 22, pp. 34 et seq.

constitute difficult conditions for changes in the purpose or the organisation of the foundation. However, this argument ignores a number of practical planning elements. It is possible to formulate a wide foundation purpose that is accompanied by examples or even another (secondary) purpose. Moreover, Swiss foundation law allows the reservation of a statutory founder's right to modify the *purpose* of the foundation.[53] Since 1 January 2024, the right of the founder has been extended: a founder may also reserve a statutory right to amend the foundation's *organisation*.[54] Besides, it is always advisable to outsource the organisational details to separate regulations because they can be modified more easily.[55] Finally, it needs to be noted that the requirements for minor amendments to the foundation deed have been relaxed with the last revision of Swiss foundation law.[56] This shows that Swiss foundation law in fact provides instruments to deal with the need of flexibility in a changing (business) environment,[57] provided that the foundation statutes and regulations are drafted appropriately. Competent legal advice may also consider possible combinations with other legal or hybrid structures to achieve the desired flexibility to maintain the entrepreneurial freedom.[58]

On the other hand, the robust structure of a foundation can be seen as an advantage. In fact, most of the time, the foundation is especially chosen because of its durability and independence, protection against hostile takeovers and ability to facilitate succession planning. Of course, the inevitable degree of rigidity can lead to difficulties, especially if drastic business decisions need to be taken or if restructuring of the business needs to take place by selling the assets or the shares of the foundation. Here, the solution depends on the type of foundation (see section 2.2 above) and the asset purpose relation: is the purpose of the foundation to hold the shares or are the shares only an asset to fulfil a separate purpose? In any case, it usually requires some creativity and legal advice in order to restructure a (held) business in line with the rules of the (holding) foundation. That is the important message: simply the fact that a restructuring

53 See Article 86a CC.

54 See Article 86a CC in force since 1 January 2024; AS 2022 452.

55 H. Hausheer and R. Aebi-Müller, *Das Personenrecht des Schweizerischen Zivilgesetzbuches*, 5th ed., Stämpfli Verlag, Bern 2020, marginal nos. 1297, 1324; H. Grüninger, 'Unternehmensstiftung' in P.V. Kunz, F.S. Jörg and O. Arter (eds), above n. 22, p. 35; decision of the Federal Supreme Court of Switzerland, BGE 76 I 77.

56 See Article 86b CC in force since 1 January 2024; AS 2022 452.

57 H. Grüninger, Unternehmensstiftung' in P.V. Kunz, F.S. Jörg and O. Arter (eds), above n. 22, p. 34; A. Meier-Hayoz and P. Forstmoser (eds), above n. 43, §23 marginal no. 26.

58 A. Meier-Hayoz and P. Forstmoser (eds), above n. 43, §23 marginal no. 27; M. Uhl, *Kooperation im Stiftungsrecht*, Helbing Lichtenhahn Verlag, Basel 2016, pp. 16 et seq.; H. Peter, 'Profit and non-profit purposes: can legal entities serve two masters at once?' (2019) 3 *Expert Focus* 163; V. Pfammatter, 'Hybrid entities in Switzerland: can Swiss entities pursue for- and non-profit purposes at the same time?' (2019) 3 *Expert Focus* 175.

would make sense from a business point of view does not mean that it is automatically admissible and allowed under foundation law.

3.2.2. *Absence of Shareholders*

As is well known, foundations do not have shareholders or any kind of members, because the foundation consists of self-contained assets dedicated to a specific purpose. Therefore, another objection to foundation structures in a business context is the absence of directly interested shareholders to exert pressure on the profitability of the business, which is a decisive aspect of corporations.[59] However, this argument is countered by a number of studies that argue that foundations are the better owners of businesses than profit-driven shareholders.[60] This discussion cannot be conducted here, but it shall be emphasised that there is a multitude of – also in an economic sense – very successful enterprise foundations in Switzerland and other German-speaking countries.[61]

3.3. UNFRIENDLY TAX ENVIRONMENT

3.3.1. *Holding Foundations*

The next challenge is that in Switzerland there is a more and more unfriendly tax environment for charitable tax-exempt foundations that are holding a business. One must recall that the pure charitable foundation is a major foundation model with a large number of important examples.[62] In order to understand why and to what extent holding significant shares of a company is

59 See A. Meier-Hayoz and P. Forstmoser (eds), above n. 43, §23 marginal no. 28; H. Grüninger, 'Unternehmensstiftung' in P. Kunz, F. Jörg and O. Arter (eds), above n. 22, p. 41.

60 Cf. S. Thomsen, *The Danish Industrial Foundations*, DJOEF Publishing, Copenhagen 2017, pp. 25 et seq., 38; H. Hansmann and S. Thomsen, *The Governance of Foundation-Owned Firms*, Copenhagen 2018, pp. 2 et seq.; S. Thomsen, T. Poulsen, C. Borsting and J. Kuhn, 'Industrial foundations as long-term owners' (2018) 26(3) *Corporate Governance: An International Review* 180; M. Habersack, P. Horvath et al., *Stiftungsunternehmen in Deutschland: Gesetzliche Grundlagen, unternehmerische Motive, Reformvorschläge*, Stiftung Familienunternehmen, München 2021, pp. 19 et seq.

61 See A. Meier-Hayoz and P. Forstmoser (eds), above n. 43, §23 marginal no. 47; H. Grüninger, above n. 13, preliminary remarks on Articles 80–89a marginal nos. 17 et seq.; H. Grüninger, 'Unternehmensstiftung' in P. Kunz, F. Jörg and O. Arter (eds), above n. 22, pp. 21 et seq., p. 41; H. Grüninger, above n. 15, pp. 28 et seq.; T. Sprecher and U. von Salis-Lütolf, *Die schweizerische Stiftung*, Schulthess Verlag, Zürich 1999, no. 265; M. Feick, *Stiftung als Nachfolgeinstrument*, C.H. Beck, Munich 2015, pp. 362 et seq.; S. Scherer, *Münchener Anwaltshandbuch Erbrecht*, 5th ed., C.H. Beck, Muünich 2018, §38 marginal no. 24.

62 See section 2.2.2 above.

compatible with or detrimental to tax exemption, a brief look shall be taken at the requirements of tax exemption in general.

3.3.1.1. General Requirements of Tax Exemption

In the first place, a tax exemption requires a 'tax-exemption-worthy' purpose of the foundation. Legal entities are tax-exempt if they pursue specific, charitable purposes. The criteria require two aspects: an activity of a general interest and an altruistic action.[63] To be subsumed under a general interest, which is evaluated from a Swiss perspective, the activity has to take place in the charitable, humanitarian, health, ecological, cultural, educational or scientific sectors.[64] However, not every effort to support individual sections of the population in an economic or social way counts as an effort in the service of the general public; in fact, the pursued purpose has to be seen as worthy of support from a general Swiss social perspective.[65] In addition, the group of possibly eligible beneficiaries has to be open.[66]

The requirement of altruism means that the foundation must pursue neither the interests of the legal entity itself nor those of persons behind it.[67] Altruistic action means sacrifices,[68] not self-helping purposes or commercial interests – business or profit purposes are not charitable purposes.[69] However, not every gainful activity of a foundation is incompatible with tax exemption; it can

---

63 See Circular No. 12, pp. 2 et seq.; decisions of the Federal Supreme Court of Switzerland, BGer 2C_385/2020 25 June 2020, E. 4.2.1; BGer 2C_147/2019 20 August 2019, E. 4.4; BGer 2C_484/2015 10 August 2015, E. 5.3; BGer 2C_251/2012 17 August 2012, E. 2.1.

64 See Circular No. 12, p. 3; and for the criteria in more depth, see M. Greter and A. Greter, commenting on Article 56 FDTA in M. Zweifel and M. Beusch (eds), *Kommentar zum Schweizerischen Steuerrecht: Bundesgesetz über die direkte Bundessteuer*, 3rd ed., Helbing Lichtenhahn Verlag, Basel 2017, marginal no. 29; M. Greter and A. Greter, commenting on Article 23 FTHA in M. Zweifel and M. Beusch (eds), *Kommentar zum schweizerischen Steuerrecht, Bundesgesetz über die Harmonisierung der direkten Steuern der Kantone und Gemeinden*, 3rd ed., Helbing Lichtenhahn, Basel 2017, marginal no. 27a; T. Koller, 'Stiftungen und Steuern' in H.M. Riemer (ed), *Die Stiftung in der juristischen und wirtschaftlichen Praxis*, Schulthess Verlag, Zürich 2001, pp. 66 et seq.

65 Decision of the Federal Supreme Court of Switzerland, BGE 114 Ib 277, E. 2b.

66 Circular No. 12, p. 3; see further M. Greter and A. Greter, commenting on Article 56 FDTA, above n. 64, marginal nos. 30; M. Greter and A. Greter, commenting on Article 23 FTHA, above n. 64, marginal no. 27b.

67 Circular No. 12, p. 3; see further M. Greter and A. Greter, commenting on Article 56 FDTA, above n. 64, marginal nos. 31 et seq.; M. Greter and A. Greter, commenting on Article 23 FTHA, above n. 64, marginal nos. 27c et seq.; see also decisions of the Federal Supreme Court of Switzerland, BGer 2C_166/2020 10 May 2021, E. 6.1; BGer 2C_251/2012 and 2C_252/2012 17 August 2012, E. 2.1.

68 For more details, see M. Reich, 'Gemeinnützigkeit als Steuerbefreiungsgrund' (1989) 58 *ASA* 471.

69 Article 56 lit. g FDTA; Article 23 para. 1 lit. f FTHA; Circular No. 12, p. 3.

be regarded as charitable if it is a meant to fulfil a charitable purpose and is subordinate under that purpose.[70]

3.3.1.2. Specific Tax Exemption Criteria for Holding Foundations

Against this background, it can be seen that foundations pursuing business purposes do not qualify for tax exemption in Switzerland. However, the crucial question is what happens if foundations with charitable purposes hold for profit business-making companies.[71] Here, Circular No. 12 and practice have developed specific criteria.[72]

In order to be compatible with these criteria, it is necessary that the interest in the business is subordinate to the purpose of the foundation. Therefore, the foundation must not have a dominant influence on the business, and a clear separation of the management of the foundation and the company is required (while one connecting person is allowed). As a consequence, the possibility of interference with the business management should be avoided, which would possibly also be the case if another legal entity was holding the majority of the voting rights.[73] As evidence of the fact that the interest in the held business is subordinate to the (charitable) foundation purpose, the authorities have formulated the further requirement of a regular and substantial funding of the foundation by the business[74] and that the foundation must actually be using this funding for its charitable purposes.

However, against this (already quite difficult) background, the Federal Supreme Court of Switzerland dealt with the requirement of subordination in its latest decision of 2021.[75] Here, a non-tax-exempt foundation had transferred its commercial catering business to a 100% held subsidiary company and then applied for tax exemption because of its charitable purpose. In its conclusion, the Court interpreted the requirement of subordination in a new way and no longer referred to the requirement of a regular and substantial alimentation of the foundation by the business. Rather, it surprisingly held that an adequate asset investment diversification was decisive. Having transferred the business of the foundation to *one* underlaying company, which is the *only* asset, this would make the foundation dependent on that company and the interest in the latter would not be subordinate to the charitable foundation purpose.[76] As a result, the Court seems to require investments in various companies or

---

70 Circular No. 12, pp. 3 et seq.
71 See Article 56 lit. g FDTA; Article. 23 para. 1 lit. g FTHA.
72 See Circular No. 12 of 8 July 1994, available at: http://www.estv.admin.ch.
73 Circular No. 12, p. 4.
74 Ibid.
75 Decision of the Federal Supreme Court of Switzerland, BGE 147 II 287.
76 Ibid., E. 8.6.

assets – and not only in one – which might be in line with the general *civil law* principles of asset management (especially the principle of risk diversification), but not with the established *tax* practice and the structure of many charitable Swiss holding foundations.

The described tax criteria for holding foundations are not only vague and difficult to handle in practice; there are also several critical aspects to be pointed out: the tax authorities seem to deny that the investment in one prosperous business can be more reasonable and profitable for a charitable foundation than a more diversified investment in a normal portfolio – however, if such an asset management is deemed admissible from a foundation law perspective (according to the above-mentioned principles),[77] the tax authority should exercise restraint when evaluating the tax exemption and accept the structure. The tax authority and the Court also disregarded the fact that the subsidiary company must pay taxes in an orderly fashion – hence, the assets are already taxed and therefore the foundation does not take any advantage of the tax-free business activity when using the profits for the charitable purpose. Finally, they neglect a clear distinction between the asset management and the purpose of a foundation. That being said, with the new jurisprudence of the Swiss Federal Court, if it is not an outlier decision, there might be a new risk of losing tax exemption or never even getting the exemption if a charitable foundation holds significant shares in only one company.[78]

3.3.2. *Impact Investments and Entrepreneurial Grant-Making*

The next problem is the unclear situation in the Swiss tax environment for mission-based investments, impact investments and entrepreneurial grant-making schemes by investments in companies. If a foundation invests in companies (mostly start-ups or social businesses) and receives shares in return, the situation also results in a special kind of enterprise foundation (mostly with the intention of taking an active ownership role to bring the company forward). The conventional understanding regarding philanthropic foundations used to be that the activities of a foundation are largely limited to the management of the foundation's assets and the distribution of the *income* to the benefit of its purpose. However, the calls for a more impact-oriented approach have been growing louder. The question of whether and when purpose- or impact-related investments are 'permitted' for a certain foundation has therefore been a common issue. From a tax perspective, the criteria for tax exemption must be met so that a tax-exempt foundation does not lose its tax exemption. The challenge is

77 See section 3.3.1.1 above.

78 Covering the whole topic in detail, see A. Opel, 'Steuerbefreiung von Holdingstiftungen' (2021) 4 IFF Forum für Steuerrecht 341.

that the permissibility under foundation and tax law is assessed by authorities on a case-by-case basis. Furthermore, because the Swiss authorities have only recently started to engage more closely with the concept of impact investments, the process of categorising and developing legal admissibility requirements is still ongoing. However, in February 2024 the canton of Zurich announced a change in practice and now also allows entrepreneurial grant-making under a set of reasonable rules (see below).[79] Because foundations traditionally distribute funds *à fonds perdu* and are not meant to act as entrepreneurs (at least from the conventional perspective of the tax authorities), profits from such activities (such as the successful disposal of shares in a start-up)[80] could be regarded as profit-making, which would go against the criteria for charitable status (see section 3.4 below). It is therefore important to demonstrate that such models do not aim to generate profit but rather must be assessed based on their effectiveness at fulfilling the foundation purpose; furthermore, any income from the entrepreneurial approach is only the by-product of the exceptionally effective fulfilment of the purpose.

The crucial question is actually the following: under what conditions can charitable foundations use entrepreneurial funding models without losing their tax exemption, and how can the fiscal authority prevent foundations from abusing their charitable status? Therefore, criteria must be defined that can help to differentiate between genuine entrepreneurial funding models and disguised profit-making activities that would (legitimately) be excluded from tax exemption.[81] In that sense, the Zurich tax authorities clarified that entrepreneurial funding models do not preclude tax exemption, even if a return flow of funds to the foundation is possible, if the following criteria are met: it must be proven that the funds are used in areas where no market (yet) exists and therefore investments are made that profit-orientated third parties would not make; the investments are only permitted within the scope of the actual funding activity; and the returned funds must in turn be used for the charitable purpose.[82]

---

79 Zurich tax book no. 61.1, Tax exemption due to non-profit status (practical note), 1 February 2024, pp. 1 et seq.

80 Cf. T. Sprecher, above n. 41, p. 122.

81 For the suggestions of such criteria by the present author, see D. Jakob and G. von Schnurbein, above n. 2, p. 50; see T. Sprecher, 'Zur steuerlichen Behandlung von neuen Förder- und Finanzierungsmodellen' in B. Eckhart, D. Jakob and G. von Schnurbein (eds), *Der Schweizer Stiftungsreport 2013*, CEPS, Zürich 2013, pp. 19 et seq.

82 Zurich tax book no. 61.1, pp. 1 et seq., above n. 79; cf. T. Sprecher, 'Steuerbefreiung für gemeinnützige Stiftungen (sowie Vereine und andere Organisationen), Praxisänderung des Steueramts des Kantons Zürich' (15 April 2024) *Jusletter*, pp. 9 et seq.; A. Opel, 'Rechtsgutachten zu den steuerlichen Rahmenbedingungen für ein wirkungsvolles Stiftungswesen im Kanton Zürich' (2023) *Universität Luzern*, pp. 48 et seq.

3.4. GOVERNANCE

As a final remark, it should be noted that in order to make an enterprise foundation work, there is a strong need for a good foundation governance (and in a family or family business context, also for family governance).

As foundations are increasingly expected to operate as effectively as possible and should improve in terms of accountability and transparency, effective governance practices are crucial for a foundation that wants to achieve impact and creditability at the same time. Nowadays, founders and foundations should strive for a system to protect the foundation and its purpose fulfilment, as well as for checks and balances and precise standards of actions that lead to an effective foundation governance as a legal and actual regulatory framework.[83]

This is especially true for enterprise foundations as the interaction with the business might lead to conflicts of interest that should be avoided and require measures to ensure that diverging interests can be harmonised.

Since Swiss enterprise foundations often result from a generation transition in a family context, a sensitive look at family governance is also crucial if the foundation should not only work successfully but should also play a part in the wellbeing of a family. The main questions to ask are as follows: how can we take advantage of the additional management level? And how do we integrate family values into legal tools? Here, the role of a shared philanthropic activity is a significant one as it can build a bridge between family values and the business activities.[84] At the same time, it shows that the secret of successful enterprise foundations is a truly interdisciplinary matter.

4. CONCLUSION

As a conclusion, it can be observed that Swiss foundation law provides a liberal environment for different kinds of enterprise foundations. Combined with the freedom of the founder, many structures and solutions are possible. It is therefore not surprising that enterprise or business foundations have a long tradition and many famous examples in Switzerland. On the other hand, there is a general trend towards regulation and stricter authorities, especially regarding the tax exemption for charitable foundations holding or interacting with businesses. Also, a sensitive foundation and family governance is crucial if an enterprise foundation should work successfully over the generations.

---

83 D. Jakob, above n. 12, 314 et seq.; see also T. Sprecher, P. Egger and G. von Schnurbein, *Swiss Foundation Code 2021, Principles and Recommendations for the Establishment and Management of Grant-making Foundations*, Stämpfli Verlag, Bern 2021.

84 Cf. D. Jakob, above n. 12.

If one wants to make a prediction, it seems unlikely that the Swiss legislator will specifically address enterprise foundations in the near future. However, it should be noted that the revision of the Swiss inheritance law has reduced the forced shares of heirs as of 2023 and has thus (among other provisions) facilitated the transfer of businesses in a forced heirship context.[85] Additionally, the political motion to liberalise Swiss family foundations and the potential lift of the ban on family maintenance foundations may – depending on the result – further promote an increase of enterprise foundations in Switzerland in the future.

85 Cf. BBl 2020 9923.

THE AUSTRIAN FOUNDATION

Susanne KALSS and Thomas BARTH

ABSTRACT

In Austria two different types of foundations exist, mainly the Federal foundation and the Austrian foundation. The Austrian Foundation Act was set in force slightly more than 30 years ago and allows foundations to hold shares, manage and to be the head of a group of companies. This type of foundation plays a vital role in the Austrian economy. The law is quite liberal and this requires a careful drafting of the legal framework.

1. LEGAL BASIS AND SIGNIFICANCE

1.1. THE FEDERAL FOUNDATION AND FUND ACT

Austrian foundation law is split into two parts and has two completely different legal bases.

On the one hand, there is the Federal foundation under the Federal Foundation Act (*Bundes-Stiftungs- und Fondsgesetz* (BStFG) 2015).[1] The Federal Foundation Act applies exclusively to non-profit foundations. In addition, there are also nine provincial foundation acts, which also apply only to non-profit foundations. The provincial foundation acts apply to foundations that operate exclusively within the sphere of influence of a state (*Bundesland*). Non-profit foundations must have a non-profit purpose. The foundation is promoted to the public if it benefits the common good. The regulation is based on section 35(2) of the Federal Fiscal Code (BAO).[2]

This type of foundation plays a minor role in Austria. About 700 foundations are organised exclusively as non-profit foundations under the Federal Foundation Act or one of the provincial foundation acts. They are subject to public supervision.[3] The supervisory system is similar to that of an association. At the same time, when a Federal foundation is set up, the founder must submit a founding declaration and confirmation to the Vienna Tax Office, and there

---

1 BGBl. I 2015/106; B. Paus and F. Haslwanter, *Bundes-Stiftungs- und Fondsgesetz 2015*, Linde Verlag, Vienna 2016; M. Melzer and M. Petritz, *Die gemeinnützige Stiftung und der gemeinnützige Fonds nach dem Gemeinnützigkeitsgesetz 2015*, LexisNexis, Vienna 2016.

2 S. Kalss in S. Kalss, C. Nowotny and M. Schauer, *Österreichisches Gesellschaftsrecht*, 2nd ed., Manz, Vienna 2017, Rz 7/8.

3 See for this S. Kalss in S. Kalss, C. Nowotny and M. Schauer, above n. 2, Rz 7/11.

has to be a notice that the founding declaration meets the requirements for non-profit status.

1.2. THE AUSTRIAN FOUNDATION ACT

The second main legal basis for foundation law is the Austrian Foundation Act of 1993 (PSG),[4] which has thus been in force for slightly more than 30 years. This Act forms the legal basis for Austrian foundations. The purpose of the foundation is not limited to non-profit purposes; rather, all permissible purposes can be pursued by the Austrian foundation, so not only non-profit purposes but also self-interested purposes. Since it came into force, the Austrian Foundation Act has only been slightly amended in terms of its organisational framework.

From a tax law perspective, numerous changes were made and tax relief originally granted was withdrawn and brought into line with the general regulations of corporations. After 30 years, the opportunity should be taken to evaluate the performance of the law and to make some adjustments (see section 10 below).

1.3. TAX MOTIVES WHEN THE ACT CAME INTO FORCE

Originally, the popularity and use of the foundation for organising participations was primarily tax motivated. It was a clear concern of the PSG and its accompanying tax laws to make the tax situation particularly attractive for entrepreneurs. Owners of enterprises should be offered an attractive tax framework. The legislator even aimed to attract entrepreneurs and owners to come to Austria from the neighbouring countries and establish a foundation which acts like a holding. Undertakings should be held in Austria and brought to Austria from neighbouring countries, such as Germany and Liechtenstein.[5]

In the past foundations had[6] noticeable tax advantages compared to corporations. The essential ones were as follows:

- At the time that the PSG came into force, inheritance and gift tax was active in Austria. The amount of inheritance and gift tax was based on the value

4 BGBl. 1993/694.

5 G. Cerha, 'Die Vertreibung des Vermögens österreichischer Privatstiftungen ins Ausland' in S. Kalss, *Aktuelle Fragen des Stiftungsrechts: Acht wesentliche Kernthemen*, Linde Verlag, Vienna 2014, pp. 1 et seq., 3 et seq.

6 Most of them have been abolished in the meantime.

of the assets and the 'degree' of the relationship between the transferor and transferee. The tax rate was different if the assets were transferred from mother to daughter in comparison to a transfer between a great-aunt and great-nephew. Therefore, in the case of a transfer of a business or assets, the tax burden could be up to 58% of the value of the taxable base. The transfer of assets to a private foundation, on the other hand, was only subject to a foundation transfer tax (*Stiftungseingangssteuer*) of 2%, i.e. a small fraction compared to the very high inheritance tax.

- Moreover, contributed companies and participations could be sold practically tax free. The hidden reserves then disclosed were not subject to subsequent taxation. The increase in value did not have to be taxed; instead, only the low acquisition value was taken as the basis for taxation.[7]
- For beneficiaries, contributions have always been taxed only at the capital gains tax (*Kapitalertragsteuer*) rate of originally 25% (now 27.5%). Grants from the private foundation are treated as dividend income and are not subject to income tax (*Einkommensteuer*), which, measured with different progression steps, can rise up to 50% and even higher for managers. The above-mentioned tax advantages have been massively reduced during the last two decades.

1.4. ECONOMIC DATA

According to the '*Stiftungsverband*',[8] there are just under 3,000 private foundations in 2025. Currently, the number of foundations is slightly decreasing. Ten years ago, there were more than 3,300 foundations in Austria. The reason for the decreasing number of foundations is, first of all, the lack of new tax incentives. However, it is also due to the fact that the original founders of many foundations have died or are no longer compos mentis. In many cases, the successors of the founders, unless they themselves assume the role of founder, have a limited legal position that restricts their options. Therefore, foundations are dissolved and the foundation assets are distributed to the beneficiaries. The 'price' for this is the tax burden on the donated – currently valued – assets through the imposition of capital gains tax. The competence to decide about the dissolution depends on the statute. In most cases the founder has reserved the right to revoke the foundation. The right to revoke according to section 34 PSG is a highly personal right that cannot be transferred and ends with the death of the founder. Besides this personal right of the founder, the management

7 S. Kalss, 'Die Leistungskraft der österreichischen Privatstiftung für Familienunternehmen' (2018) 117(2) *Zeitschrift für vergleichende Rechtswissenschaft* 221.

8 The '*Stiftungsverband*' is an association that represents in particular the interests of private foundations.

board has the right to dissolve the foundation unanimously if the purpose of the foundation has been accomplished or has become unattainable. In a family business the beneficiaries have to decide after 100 years whether they want the foundation to be continued. The foundations deed may state other reasons. The qualification of the entity as a foundation is not contested in these cases (see also section 2.2.1 below).

When new private foundations are established, their main purpose is to reorganise the family assets and to allocate them to the individual family lines (*Familienstämme*) by establishing individual foundations, so-called sub-foundations (*Substiftungen*), from the main foundation of a family for the various branches of the family. The establishment of a sub-foundation is functionally to be understood as the splitting-off of a foundation. This form of organisation aims to settle internal family disputes or to reorganise assets without disputes and to replicate the division under inheritance law. Thus, both influence and economic participation rights are reorganised.[9] This technique is also used to shift assets from one foundation to another, either in Austria or abroad, and apply specific tax clauses. Foundations have, in total, assets in the triple-digit billion range. In 2016, assets were still around €70 billion.[10] Of these assets, 64% are participations, with an increasing number of around 25% in real estate and securities. Significantly less is invested in private equity and art. Other assets play no role.[11]

Around one-fifth of the Austrian stock corporations (*Aktiengesellschaften*) listed on the Regulated Market of the Vienna Stock Exchange are held by private foundations/enterprise foundations. These foundations hold shares of between 10% and over 96% in these companies.[12] The majority of the 100 largest family businesses in Austria and more than half of the companies listed on the Austrian Traded Index (ATX) are (partially) owned by enterprise foundations. Around 1,830 private foundations hold stakes in around 11,100 companies in January 2025. These companies provide work for more than 350,000 people. In 2023, companies (partially) owned by enterprise foundations paid more than €13 billion in taxes and social security contributions.[13]

---

9 S. Kalss, 'Die Gestaltung von Substiftungen' in *Festschrift für Bernhard Eccher*, Verlag Österreich, Vienna 2017, pp. 425 et seq.; C. Nowotny, 'Substiftungen und ihre Probleme' in *Privatstiftung und Umgründungen: Gedenkschrift für Franz Helbich*, LexisNexis, Vienna 2014, p. 111.

10 S. Kalss above n. 7, with reference to a study presented by economist Helmenstein on 4 December 2015, at the Plattform Familienunternehmen der Industriellenvereinigung.

11 Stiftungsmonitor 2024, a joint empirical study of the Verein Stiftung Next Gen, the Johannes Kepler University and financial services companies specialising in asset management; see also: www.wko.at.

12 See: www.stiftungsverband.at.

13 Position paper of the Austrian *Stiftungsverband* from 22 January 2025 for the 28th legislative period.

In general, these companies are quite successful in economic terms. They have seen enormous growth during the last ten years, in particular the last three years[14] before the invasion of Ukraine.

1.5. NO DIRECT BUSINESS ACTIVITY

Pursuant to section 1 PSG, the private foundation itself may not engage in entrepreneurial activities. It may therefore only hold participations and exercise ownership rights. As such, it may be at the head of a company, a group of companies or manage a group of companies. However, the enterprise foundation may not intervene too intensively in the subsidiaries. The Supreme Court (*Oberste Gerichtshof*) prohibits a so-called tight group management (*straffe Konzernführung*).[15] The enterprise foundation may therefore exercise group management that is not too far-reaching and encompasses all essential management powers. The limit is maintained if the enterprise foundation, as the principal (*Hauptgesellschafter*) or sole shareholder (*Alleingesellschafter*), exercises its statutory shareholder rights.[16] It may also exercise veto rights or typical approval rights in the limited liability company (*Gesellschaft mit beschränkter Haftung* (GmbH)). The strategic decisions close to the owner may be made by the enterprise foundation and a procedure may also be established to implement them in the associated companies.[17] Since the private foundation is not allowed to manage a company itself, Austrian law prohibits the direct enterprise foundation (*unmittelbare Unternehmensträgerstiftung*). It is only permitted within a very narrow framework as a secondary activity, such as the operation of a museum store at a museum foundation (e.g. the Leopold Museum Private Foundation) or the operation of a small canteen in addition to other foundation activities, such as the exhibition of paintings or other works of art. The reason for this is that the interests of the beneficiaries should be protected from claims by creditors against the foundation running the business. A simple entrepreneur (*Einzelunternehmen*) or a personal partner of the partnerships is directly liable to the creditors of the enterprise or the partnership. Therefore, the assets of the foundation should be protected to the benefit of the beneficiaries.

---

14 Ibid.

15 OGH 6 Ob 217/05b, (2006) *GesRZ* 82.

16 S. Kalss and K. Müller, 'Die Stiftung als Instrument der Vermögensweitergabe' in M. Gruber, S. Kalss, K. Müller and M. Schauer, *Erbrecht und Vermögensnachfolge*, 2nd ed., Verlag Österreich, Vienna 2018, §26, Rz 41, 902.

17 S. Kalss and K. Müller in M. Gruber, S. Kalss, K. Müller and M. Schauer, above n. 16, §26, Rz 41; C. Zwick, 'Die Privatstiftung als Konzernspitze' (2009) *GesRZ* 278, 284.

The creditors of a subsidiary of the foundation (*Tochter-GmbH*) cannot hold the foundation directly liable as a shareholder of the company.

However, since the private foundation may hold shares and – as already explained above – may also manage a group of companies, an indirect enterprise foundation is possible. This is also the typical case of an enterprise foundation. In this case, shares or participations are held directly or indirectly. Often, a holding company is placed directly under the enterprise foundation, which in turn holds and directly manages the other participations. According to the different assets, there are different types of enterprise foundations, namely those that actively manage a group of companies and in which the decisive management decisions are made in the enterprise foundation. Other foundations only hold investments as a portfolio and act only as defensive or passive investors without active involvement (portfolio management). Finally, it is also possible to operate a relatively reduced shareholding management, while the operational group management is organised in a subordinate holding company.[18]

1.6. THE PRIVATE FOUNDATION: A LEGAL ENTITY WITHOUT SHARES

The private foundation is a legal entity which exists on a continuing basis and in which no shares can be held. Therefore, there are also no membership rights. As a result, shares and memberships in a private foundation cannot be transferred.

This is because the relevant performance of the private foundation lies in the secure space for the assets – in particular the shares – which have been contributed to it. Neither *inter vivos* nor upon death is a transfer required. On the occasion of the death of a founder or a beneficiary, a share in the private foundation therefore does not have to be transferred. As such, the enterprise foundation is even more stable than a share transfer restriction in a company, more stable than a syndicate agreement (voting agreement) and also more stable than a holding company in which shares or participations are held.

It is precisely this stability and avoidance of division by the shareholder that is a decisive achievement of the private foundation institution. A majority can always be secured without fear of an immediate danger of division if the shares are transferred by a child of an heir.[19]

---

18 S. Kalss, above n. 7, 233 et seq.

19 S. Kalss and S. Probst, *Familienunternehmen*, 2nd ed., Manz, Vienna 2025, Rz 7.1 et seq.

2. THE CONCEPT OF THE PRIVATE FOUNDATION

2.1. THE CONTRACTUAL FREEDOM FOR THE FOUNDATION: NECESSARY CONTROL

The concept of the Austrian foundation is very simple. It is characterised by a high degree of contractual freedom. On the one hand, the Austrian Foundation Act provides only a few requirements and gives the founder merely a few regulatory mandates to regulate certain questions and topics in the foundation's declaration (*Stiftungserklärung*). This is an advantage for contractual freedom and the adaptability to different needs. On the other hand, many questions remain unregulated and therefore, in the absence of a good regulatory by forward-thinking advisors, must first be clarified in a costly legal proceeding. When the law came into force, consulting competence was often lacking and poorly prepared foundation declarations were entered into the commercial register (*Firmenbuch*), which also explains the high number of court decisions.

The private foundation plays a major role in the economy. It also plays a major role in jurisdiction. Currently, eight to ten decisions of the Supreme Court (*Oberste Gerichtshof*) deal with private foundations. This is significantly more than for stock corporations (*Aktiengesellschaften*) and for partnerships (*Personengesellschaften*). Only for limited liability companies (*Gesellschaften mit beschränkter Haftung*) are more Supreme Court decisions handed down per year. This is not surprising, given that there were around 200,000 limited liability companies in 2025. However, this also shows how highly conflict-prone the private foundation is. This is not surprising, given that it is a young law whose boundaries will be shaped case by case. It is a legal form that is very successful, but one where conflicts usually involve large amounts of money.

2.2. THE ESTABLISHMENT OF THE PRIVATE FOUNDATION AND HOW THE PRIVATE FOUNDATION BECOMES A LEGAL ENTITY

2.2.1. Foundation Deeds

The private foundation is established by a foundation deed, which must be drawn up by one or more founders. Pursuant to section 39 PSG, a notarial act is required – i.e. a notary must be involved in the establishment. This elaborate form serves to protect the founder, who is advised by the notary. The notarial act also protects the beneficiaries, who are also to be the addressees of the foundation's purpose.

The foundation deed must contain the essential elements of a private foundation, namely the founder, the purpose of the foundation and the bodies of the private foundation. A number of other matters may be regulated in the foundation deed, such as the individual beneficiaries or the detailed description of the purpose of the foundation, the activity of the foundation and the appointment of the individual bodies. In any case, the foundation deed, if so desired, must also contain the most important founder rights, namely the right of amendment (*Änderungsrecht*) pursuant to section 33 PSG and the right of revocation (*Widerrufsrecht*) pursuant to section 34 PSG, if the founder wishes to exercise them.[20] In addition to the foundation deed, the founder(s) may also draw up a supplementary foundation deed (*Stiftungszusatzurkunde*).

The foundation deed shall be filed for registration in the commercial register (*Firmenbuch*) by the first board of directors. The foundation deed becomes part of the collection of documents kept by the Commercial Register Court (*Firmenbuchgericht*). The commercial register is the register kept by the Court of First Instance in which all corporations, partnerships and other selected legal entities and companies are also registered. The private foundation is therefore part of the general commercial register and general register for companies. All private foundations and the foundation deeds are public.

In addition to the foundation deed, the founder may also draw up a supplementary foundation deed. This is also a deed in the form of a notarial act. The main difference is that the supplementary foundation deed is not public. Therefore, it does not have to be registered in the commercial register in order to be effective. Each foundation may have only one supplementary foundation deed. However, it is possible that a supplementary foundation deed consists of several parts, which are drawn up at different times.[21] In addition, there are sometimes also memoranda of understanding (*Absichtserklärung*) by the founder, in which the founder explains their motivation for the foundation. A memorandum of understanding does not develop any direct normative force and is not directly enforceable. This document can only be used for the interpretation of the foundation deed.[22] In addition to this memorandum of understanding, which is not directly effective, syndicate agreements are concluded by or in private foundations, which bind the founders to each other or bind the private foundation to other partners. They are to be strictly distinguished from the memorandum of understanding.

---

20 OGH 6 Ob 72/11y.

21 Zentrum für Stiftungsrecht, 'Résumé-Protokoll des Fachgesprächs "Aktuelles zum Stiftungsrecht"' (2021) *GesRZ* 380, 385.

22 S. Kalss in S. Kalss, C. Nowotny and M. Schauer, above n. 2, Rz 7/45; C. Nowotny in W. Gassner, P.E. Göth, B. Gröhs and M. Lang, *Privatstiftungen: Gestaltungsmöglichkeiten in der Praxis*, Manz, Vienna 2000, pp. 125 et seq.

With the registration of the foundation in the commercial register (*Firmenbuch*), the private foundation, which had already been established with the foundation deed, has actually become an independent legal entity. The period between the establishment of the private foundation by the notarial act and the registration of the foundation in the commercial register (*Firmenbuch*) is the period of the pre-foundation (*Vorstiftung*).[23] The Austrian foundation comes into legal existence with the registration in the commercial register. No further official permit is required.[24] The foundation's declaration (*Stiftungserklärung*) is a unilateral legal transaction that does not require acceptance or access. The private foundation can be established by one or more individuals or legal entities. The establishment of the foundation consists of two parts, namely the organisational part, in which the foundation constitution and the organisation of the private foundation are determined, and the circumscription of the obligations of the founders, namely the obligation to dedicate assets to the foundation. Thus, the foundation transaction and the establishment of the foundation have an organisational part and a pecuniary part.[25]

2.2.2. *Commercial Register (*Firmenbuch*): In Control*

The Commercial Register Court (*Firmenbuchgericht*) is the only authority that controls the foundation, namely the compliance with the legal regulations when shaping the deed of foundation and when appointing the members of the boards of the foundation. The law does not require a more intensive ongoing control. Thus, there is no authority (*Stiftungsamt*). However, the Commercial Register Court has a supervisory function in the context of non-contentious commercial register proceedings.[26] For example, the Commercial Register Court must examine the foundation declaration when the foundation is established, including the amendment of the deed by the Board of Directors. The Commercial Register Court also has jurisdiction to appoint and dismiss the members of the Board of Directors in accordance with section 27 PSG. This is an official supervisory duty of the Commercial Register Court.[27] Since there is a public interest in the functioning of this institution, this possibility of clarifying and enforcing the law cannot be dispensed nor can this task be transferred from the state court to another institution.[28]

---

23 N. Arnold, *Privatstiftungsgesetz*, 4th ed., LexisNexis, Vienna 2022, §7, Rz 5 et seq.

24 S. Kalss in S. Kalss, C. Nowotny and M. Schauer, above n. 2, Rz 7/36.

25 J. Zollner, *Die eigennützige Privatstiftung aus dem Blickwinkel der Stiftungsbeteiligten*, Manz, Vienna 2011, pp. 41 et seq; S. Kalss in S. Kalss, C. Nowotny and M. Schauer, above n. 2, Rz 7/37.

26 OGH 6 Ob 28/20s point 1.4., (2021) *GesRZ* 95.

27 OGH 6 Ob 28/20s point 1.3., (2021) *GesRZ* 95; S. Kalss, M. Nueber and N. Vavrovsky, (2021) *GesRZ* 148 et seq.

28 Ibid.

The Commercial Register Court has functions similar to supervision in part, and exercises its supervisory duties[29] within the scope of its duty to monitor – for example, whether the foundation deed complies with the legal requirements or whether there is an important reason for the premature dismissal of a board member pursuant to section 27(2) PSG or approval of transactions between a member of the board of directors and the private foundation pursuant to section 17(5) PSG.

3. THE PURPOSE OF THE AUSTRIAN FOUNDATION

Pursuant to section 1 PSG, any permitted purpose is permissible for a foundation. The Austrian foundation may pursue non-profit purposes (such as the financial support of a university or a research institute), or social purposes (such as Concordia Private Foundation). However, the Austrian foundation may also pursue exclusively self-interested purposes, such as supporting the members of a family or supporting certain selected persons who meet certain qualifications circumscribed in the foundation's deed. A private foundation may also combine self-interested and non-profit purposes. Only a few private foundations exclusively pursue a non-profit purpose. In 2020, for example, there were only 17 private foundations in Upper Austria with an exclusively non-profit purpose. About one-third of all Austrian foundations are resident in Upper Austria. A total of 83% exclusively pursue a self-interested purpose, 5% (17 in absolute terms) pursue a non-profit purpose, and 12% of Austrian foundations pursue both self-interested and mixed purposes. Non-profit purposes include the promotion of the economy, technology, science or the support of humanitarian and non-profit organisations, the promotion of education and schools or the support of sick people. In the case of mixed foundations, the promotion of culture and tradition, ecclesiastical purposes or disaster relief can be found.[30]

Simply preserving and developing the business would not be an adequate purpose. The purpose must go further than this – at least to support the founder or the founder's family or other people, the public or special groups of the public (for example, students of a university, inhabitants of a region or members of an association).

The limit is merely unlawful projects such as the promotion of drug trafficking or the facilitation of arms trafficking or smuggling across the

29 S. Kalss, M. Schauer and M. Winner, *Allgemeines Unternehmensrecht und Wertpapierrecht*, 4th ed., Facultas, Vienna 2022, Rz 6/8.

30 E. Lammer, 'Empirische Datenerhebung für Privatstiftungen in Oberösterreich im Jahr 2021', Master's Thesis at the Vienna Universirty of Economics and Business (Wirtschaftsuniversität Wien) (2022), p. 12.

border. In addition, there is a prohibition of self-purpose foundations (*Selbstzweckstiftung*), i.e. the sole purpose of the foundation must not be to merely exist and maintain its assets.[31] It follows from the purpose definition that the foundation must be externally directed and must have a purpose addressee and thus beneficiaries. The law assumes the existence of beneficiaries.[32] The general public may also be beneficiaries. The beneficiaries may be generally circumscribed or specifically designated. Thus, they do not yet have to be specified in the foundation deed (*Stiftungsurkunde*) or in the supplementary foundation deed (*Stiftungszusatzurkunde*). The foundation can also designate a body in accordance with section 9 PSG, which specifies the beneficiaries by name and also the amount of the respective contribution.

4. THE ACTIVITY OF THE FOUNDATION

4.1. ACTIVITIES IN GENERAL

As already explained, the activity of the private foundation (*Unternehmensgegenstand*) is limited. It may not directly manage a company pursuant to section 1 PSG, nor may it assume the position of a partner in a general partnership (*Offene Gesellschaft*), nor may it become a general partner in a limited partnership (*Kommanditgesellschaft*) as a personally liable party. The reason for this is simple: there would be a risk of unlimited liability in favour of the creditors of the registered partnership. This would be in conflict with the legal position and protection of the beneficiaries. As already explained, the private foundation may hold participations. Thus, it may be an indirect enterprise foundation (*mittelbare Unternehmensträgerstiftung*) and is also entitled to group management (*Konzernleitung*). The private foundation may also manage its own assets. It may also sell assets and carry out other activities. The functions of the enterprise foundation are as follows:[33]

- Holding function: it has a holding function and can hold a stable participation in a company (for example 100% or 60% majority).
- Bridging function: if one generation is unable or lacks suitable persons to manage a company, the enterprise foundation can continue to hold the shares and manage them for the next generation.

---

31 OGH 6 Ob 93/06d; OLG Wien 28R 274/04a; Kalss in P. Doralt, C. Nowotny and S. Kalss, *Kommentar zum Privatstiftungsgesetz*, 1995, Linde Verlag, Vienna 1995, 1, Rz 33 et seq.; N. Arnold, above n. 23, §1, Rz 13.

32 S. Kalss in S. Kalss, C. Nowotny and M. Schauer, above n. 2, Rz 7/28.

33 S. Kalss and S. Probst, above n. 19, Rz 7.1 et seq.

- Moderation and mediation function for the family: this provides a permanent institution for discussion and action, and gives the opportunity to keep in touch with the different family members of a family business.
- Entrepreneurial function: the Austrian foundation typically pursues the function of strategic owner (the core shareholder (*Kernaktionär*) or anchor shareholder (*Ankeraktionär*)) and may also assume the function of group management.
- Non-profit function: finally, the Austrian foundation may pursue non-profit purposes.

The Austrian foundation as a whole can therefore realise the will of the founder and act as a custodian of the will (*Testamentsvollstreckung*). At the same time, it can also act like a syndicate agreement among the family members.

4.2. THE ROLE OF A CORE SHAREHOLDER OR HEAD OF A GROUP

As a private foundation may not operate a company itself, but only hold participations, it is well suited as the head of a family business in the sense of holding participations. It is also authorised to carry out individual group management functions; if an enterprise foundation carries out a more strict group management (exercise of all management powers, in particular financing),[34] a supervisory board must be set up. This form of activity is not prohibited. The enterprise foundation can therefore very well fulfil sub-functions of a responsible owner together with the members of the family. The private foundation typically fulfils the role of a core shareholder. A core shareholder is a strategic shareholder who is not only interested in short-term share price increases, but also in the long-term existence of the company and who therefore also wants to influence the strategy of the company. The core shareholder has no entrepreneurial or operational interests of its own that it pursues beyond its shareholding; rather, its aim is to increase the value of the company in the long term by actively participating in its control and support. This function is linked to the long-term holding of shares.[35]

---

[34] OGH 6 Ob 217/05p; S. Kalss in S. Kalss, C. Nowotny and M. Schauer, above n. 2, Rz 7/30; S. Kalss and K. Müller in M. Gruber, S. Kalss, K. Müller and M. Schauer, above n. 16, §26, Rz 41, 902.

[35] S. Kalss and S. Probst, above n. 19, Rz 7.53 et seq.

5. THE ASSETS OF THE FOUNDATION

The initial minimum assets of the foundation are €70,000. The assets need only be actually present at the time of the establishment and registration of the foundation. It must be dedicated to the foundation before its registration in the commercial register. The asset management and investment of the assets is completely free. The law does not stipulate any requirements in this respect. As already mentioned, about two-thirds of the foundation's assets are invested in participations, 20% in real estate and 10% in other assets. The law does not provide for any permanent minimum assets. There are no basic assets (*Grundstockvermögen*) that may not be touched. There are no obligations that the capital must be maintained. The assets may be sold and may also be distributed among the beneficiaries. Thus, in the Austrian foundation, not only may the income be distributed to the beneficiaries, but so too may the substance assets (*Substanzvermögen*) of the private foundation. Thus, there is not only a foundation for use (*Gebrauchsstiftung*), but also a foundation for consumption (*Verbrauchsstiftung*).[36] In the foundation's declaration, i.e. both in the foundation deed and in the supplementary foundation deed, the founder can lay down guidelines for the management of the assets and therefore make specifications to the board of directors. Frequently, certain parts of the assets are excluded from the disposition of the board of directors. Thus, the founder can stipulate certain parts of the assets, for example real estate, and some participations, so-called core assets (*Kernvermögen*), that must not be distributed or disposed of, while other assets can be distributed. If the foundation does not contain any regulations, the board of directors may also set its own guidelines.[37] The assets are subject to internal control. According to the provisions of the Austrian Commercial Code (UGB), the board of directors is responsible for the foundation's accounting and for preparing a balance sheet. If the private foundation has subsidiaries, consolidated financial statements (*konsolidierter Abschluss*) must also be prepared with the subsidiaries. This has a disciplinary function, even if the additional information content is not very great. These financial statements (the balance sheet) prepared by the board of directors must be audited by an auditor (*Stiftungsprüfer*) appointed by the court. The foundation only has a right to propose the appointment of the foundation auditor, i.e. an accountant. The foundation auditor audits the annual financial statements and prepares a report to the private foundation, i.e. to the board of

---

36 S. Kalss in S. Kalss, C. Nowotny and M. Schauer, above n. 2, Rz 7/28; R. Reiter, 'Die Aufgaben des Stiftungsprüfers im Zusammenhang mit unzulässigen Substanzauszahlungen an Begünstigte' (2014) *ZFS* 152.

37 S. Kalss and K. Müller in M. Gruber, S. Kalss, K. Müller and M. Schauer, above n. 16, §26, Rz 198 et seq.

directors. Neither the annual financial statements nor the audit report are filed to the commercial register; the annual financial statements only have to be filed to the tax authorities. However, it is not published and cannot be inspected. The annual financial statements and other accounting documents are accessible to all other bodies and members of bodies of the private foundation. The beneficiaries also have a right to inspect the annual financial statements and to receive a copy pursuant to section 30 PSG. The founder only has such a right if it is granted by the foundation's declaration. They are not entitled to this by law. An external office, who is neither the Commercial Register Court (*Firmenbuchgericht*) nor any other foundation office, controls the management and status of the assets and their use.

6. THE FOUNDER

Pursuant to section 3(1) PSG, one person may establish a foundation, or several individuals or legal entities may be founders of a private foundation. The founder is the person designated as such in the foundation's declaration (*Stiftungserklärung*). It is not absolutely necessary that all co-founders contribute to the foundation's assets. Thus, not every founder has to make a minimum contribution to the foundation.[38] Often, a foundation has a main founder (*Hauptstifter*) who contributes the substantial assets to the foundation, while other founders only dedicate a symbolic amount to the foundation. Minors may become founders. The founder or founders must be named in the foundation deed (*Stiftungsurkunde*) in accordance with section 9(1) and (5) PSG. The status of founder cannot be acquired subsequently – for example, by a subsequent dedication of assets or by a subsequent amendment of the foundation's declaration.[39] As such, the status of founder cannot be subsequently renounced. The historical fact of having established a foundation and therefore of being a founder can no longer be eliminated. However, a founder can subsequently waive the rights to which they are entitled in the context of an amendment to the foundation's declaration. They must declare this to the foundation and this must be executed by means of a declaration of amendment (*Änderungserklärung*) and a notarial act entered into the commercial register (*Firmenbuch*).[40]

38 Explanations of the materials on the law: 1132 Supplements to the stenographic minutes of the Austrian Parliament (*Nationalrat*) 18th GP 21; S. Kalss and K. Müller in M. Gruber, S. Kalss, K. Müller and M. Schauer, above n. 16, §26, Rz 42.

39 OGH 1 Ob 166/04z; N. Arnold, above n. 23, §3, Rz 13; S. Kalss and K. Müller in M. Gruber, S. Kalss, K. Müller and M. Schauer, above n. 16, §26, Rz 44.

40 OGH 6 Ob 78/06y; N. Arnold, above n. 23, §3, Rz 15.

6.1. RIGHTS OF FOUNDERS

The PSG grants only a few rights to a founder. The founder has only marginal rights when dissolving the private foundation. However, the law offers the founder the possibility of retaining comprehensive rights and influence by means of explicit provisions in the foundation's declaration.[41] The founder's most important rights of influence, which they can stipulate in the foundation deed, are the right to amend the foundation's declaration, to revoke the foundation's declaration, to appoint and dismiss board members and to have information rights. A founder can therefore retain a comprehensive right to participate in and shape the foundation, as well as a far-reaching permanent right to shape the foundation similar to that of an owner.

The founder can completely change the purpose and the complete charter,[42] e.g. first to promote vegetarianism and then to promote meat consumption. There has never been any discussion of whether this entity is a foundation, although the founder can change the foundation totally. The foundation was shaped in this manner by the law and therefore opens up this broad scope of ongoing influence of the founder.

The founder may also be a member of a body. They may also be a member of the board of directors; however, section 15(2) PSG then prohibits them from receiving benefits, thus making them a beneficiary at the same time. Being a founder and being a member of a governing body are not mutually exclusive, but it is not permissible to be a member of the board of directors and a beneficiary of the private foundation at the same time.

If the founder has the right to appoint and dismiss members of the board of directors, they also have a material position as a body based on this competence.[43] Therefore, they also have the control rights associated with membership of a body, in particular the right to inspect the foundation documents and the right to file an application with the court in the event of dismissal proceedings.[44]

A founder can therefore continue to interfere with the foundation by granting the right of amendment and revocation. They actually have an extended right of disposal, which is close to a right of ownership. The founder's right to change the foundation is not limited in content,[45] i.e. they can completely

---

41 S. Kalss and S. Probst, above n. 19, Rz 7.10; S. Kalss and K. Müller in M. Gruber, S. Kalss, K. Müller and M. Schauer, above n. 16, §26, Rz 46; C. Nowotny, 'Stifterrechte – Möglichkeiten und Grenzen' (2003) *JBl* 779.

42 OGH 1 Ob 214/09s point 1.9.1.

43 OGH 6 Ob 141/20h.

44 Zentrum für Stiftungsrecht, above n. 21.

45 OGH 1 Ob 214/09s, (2011) *GesRZ* 53.

change the purpose of the foundation, change the beneficiaries and change the object and the asset structure. A total of 90% of all founders reserve the right of amendment. The founder has no right of instructions in the private foundation, but they may stipulate individual founder missions (*einzelne Stifteraufträge*) in the foundation deed or supplementary deed.[46]

6.2. NO INHERITANCE OF FOUNDERS RIGHTS

The right of amendment (*Änderungsrecht*) and the right of revocation (*Widerrufsrecht*) are highly personal and cannot be transferred to another person. Therefore, the right ends when it is granted to a natural person as founder.

However, flexibility is often desirable to respond to changing circumstances. This does not necessarily mean fundamental changes or the dissolution of the foundation but rather changes to maintain its functionality. Continuation and perpetuation can be provided if the right of amendment is granted to a company or other legal entity.[47] Another structure that is sometimes chosen is to stagger the founder rights.[48] This can work in a way that the first founder is entitled to the rights in a first step and other founders only when the first founder dies or is no longer able to act. However, as explained, the status of founder cannot be acquired retrospectively. Such regulations therefore require that the subsequent generation already exists so that they can acquire the status of founder in the course of the establishment of the foundation.

However, according to a recent survey, the right of amendment is often missing for the members of the second and third generation of the founder's family, because these persons were not yet founders or were not granted thus rights as founders.

7. BENEFICIARIES

Beneficiaries are the addressees of the foundation. Pursuant to section 5 PSG, a beneficiary is anyone who, according to the law or the foundation deed, has a right to a donation or an expectancy thereof and is therefore entitled to

---

46 R. Briem, 'Gestaltungsmöglichkeiten in der Privatstiftung' in S. Kalss, *Aktuelle Fragen des Stiftungsgesetzes*, Linde Verlag, Vienna 2014, pp. 61, 92; S. Kalss in S. Kalss, C. Nowotny and M. Schauer, above n. 2, Rz 7/76.

47 S. Kalss and K. Müller in M. Gruber, S. Kalss, K. Müller and M. Schauer, above n. 16, §26, Rz 51; S. Kalss and S. Probst, above n. 19, Rz 7.72.

48 S. Kalss and S. Probst, above n. 19, Rz 7.13, 7.71.

exercise the beneficiary rights.[49] The beneficiary is to be designated as such in accordance with section 5 PSG. By law, beneficiaries have only very minor rights, and they only have the right to receive information and to inspect the foundation deeds as well as the annual financial statements and the accounting documents. They have no further rights of control. By law, the beneficiaries are therefore only the beneficial owners of the foundation. However, they have no participation rights and no rights to shape the foundation.

Ex lege, a beneficiary may request the private foundation to provide information on the fulfilment of the foundation's purpose and to inspect the annual financial statements, as well as the management report, the audit report, the books of account, the foundation deed and the supplementary foundation deed. The beneficiary rights may also be exercised after the expiry of the beneficiary rights. However, the right then only relates to the period of the beneficiary status.

The founder can grant the beneficiary certain rights in the foundation's declaration over and above the statutory provisions.[50] Thus, the beneficiary can be granted economic rights (rights of donation) and rights of influence. In practice, the beneficiaries are often members of the advisory board and have the right to nominate the members of the management board and the advisory board. Often these rights come into force after the death of the founder or the members of the first generation of founders.

The property right could be structured in such a way that not only is an expectation of a donation and of a certain benefit granted, but so too is an enforceable claim. However, this is rare, and an enforceable claim is mainly used, for example, to secure care and utility services or retirement claims.

Possible rights are, for example, control rights that go beyond the legal requirements, such as the initiation of a special audit or participation in an advisory board, or rights of influence on the board of directors, such as appointment and dismissal rights.[51] It is not permissible for a beneficiary to be a member of the board of directors. Section 15(2) PSG excludes beneficiaries from this office. However, not only the beneficiary himself/herself is excluded, but also all his/her relatives in a straight line up to the third degree of the collateral line. Not excluded is the affinity, e.g. the daughter-in-law or the mother-in-law or also the brother-in-law. Also excluded is the spouse. According to section 23(2) PSG, the beneficiaries may not constitute more than half of the members of the supervisory board.

---

49 S. Kalss in S. Kalss, C. Nowotny and M. Schauer, above n. 2, Rz 7/110; Kalss, 'Die einmalige Zuwendung' (2015) *ZFS* 139.

50 S. Kalss and J. Zollner, 'Mitwirkungs- und Kontrollrechte der Begünstigten – Gestaltungsmöglichkeiten des Stifters' (2008) *GesRZ* 126 et seq.

51 Ibid., 131 et seq.; S. Kalss in S. Kalss, C. Nowotny and M. Schauer, above n. 2, Rz 7/111.

8. GOVERNANCE OF THE FOUNDATION

8.1. OVERVIEW

The foundation must have at least two bodies, namely the board of directors and the foundation auditor. Pursuant to section 14 PSG, it is permissible for the founder to establish further bodies in the foundation deed to control or advise the board of directors. The foundation bodies must in any case be determined in the foundation deed, otherwise they do not qualify as bodies.[52] According to the latest opinion of the Supreme Court, the appointment and dismissal of the board of directors establishes the status of a body.[53] In this context, what matters in the case of an institution is not the formal designation, but the decisive and enforceable influence, the decision-making process, and the management and supervision of the private foundation. If a body does not have the status of an executive body (*Organ*), it forms a committee (*Gremium*), which can also be standardised in the supplementary foundation deed or on the basis of a resolution of the board of directors. Committees also have an advisory and control function and can perform important tasks for the private foundation. However, they do not have a function as a body (*Organ*) and cannot, for example, exercise certain control rights and application rights in court. However, internally the significance and competences of bodies and legal committees are quite the same and play an important role in the foundation governance.

8.2. THE BOARD OF DIRECTORS

Pursuant to section 15 PSG, the board of directors must consist of at least three persons. Only individuals can be members of the board of directors. The number of three directors serves the purpose of mutual control. A chairperson must be elected from the board of directors, who has the right to cast a deciding vote in the event of a split vote. In its case law, the Supreme Court has strongly secured the position of the board of directors and has established it as a strong independent body. Thus, according to the case law, a member of the board of directors must be appointed for at least three years; although there is no legal basis for this. A shorter term of appointment is only permissible if

52 OGH 6 Ob 305/01y; OGH 6 Ob 95/15m; S. Kalss and K. Müller in M. Gruber, S. Kalss, K. Müller and M. Schauer, above n. 16, §26, Rz 176.

53 OGH 6 Ob 141/20h; another view OGH 6 Ob 291/02s.

there is an objective reason for it (an age limit). The Supreme Court started this chain of decisions ten years ago without convincing arguments.[54]

A member of the board of directors may only be dismissed by a qualified majority and for an important reason. The latter can only be derived indirectly from the law. In addition, the Supreme Court prohibits the board of directors from being subjected to an excessively narrow framework of transactions requiring approval vis-à-vis other bodies.[55]

The board of directors must exercise the diligence of a prudent manager. The specific level of diligence must therefore be determined in a way that is appropriate to the sector, size and situation of the foundation.[56] The board of directors is subject to the business judgement rule, i.e. it has entrepreneurial discretion (judgement) in its business decisions.[57] Although this is not expressly regulated in the PSG, the Supreme Court has used general principles of law for justification.

The beneficiaries and the close relatives of the beneficiaries, all relatives in the direct line, as well as up to the third degree of the collateral line are excluded from the office of the board of directors.

8.3. THE AUDITOR OF THE FOUNDATION: THE OBLIGATORY CONTROL BODY

The foundation auditor (*Stiftungsprüfer*) is a permanently appointed controlling body of the private foundation. The law expressly standardises their position as a body. The foundation auditor must be appointed by the court. The foundation has only a right of nomination. The foundation auditor may be appointed for a limited or unlimited period. The one-year appointment period as for corporations does not apply in this case.

The auditor of the foundation has to check the legality of the annual financial statements and the accounting. However, their duties go further – namely, they also have the obligation to verify compliance with the purpose of the private foundation by the board of directors and is obliged to provide information to the beneficiary. They are entitled to inspect the audit report. However, the foundation auditor has no obligation to make public any irregularities or, in any case, to notify the commercial register.

---

54 OGH 6 Ob 211/20b; OGH 6 Ob 195/10k; OGH 6 Ob 140/14b.

55 OGH RIS Justiz RS 0115030; OGH 6 Ob 230/13m.

56 P. Csoklich, 'Haftung des Vorstandes einer Privatstiftung' (1999) *RdW* 254; S. Kalss and K. Müller in M. Gruber, S. Kalss, K. Müller and M. Schauer, above n. 16, §26, Rz 198.

57 OGH 6 Ob 160/15w.

8.4. OTHER BODIES

The founder(s) may establish other supervisory bodies in addition to the foundation auditor. In this respect, the founder is free to decide whether this is an advisory board (*Beirat*), a board of trustees (*Kuratorium*) or the beneficiaries' meeting (*Begünstigtenversammlung*). The other bodies may be granted control rights such as information rights, hearing rights and the right to comment. However, the Supreme Court has largely limited the right to consent and genuine control, and it allows only selected measures and matters to be subject to consent.[58] It is at least permissible that the right to appoint or dismiss members of the board of directors is assigned to a supervisory body. The Supreme Court has significantly weakened the other control bodies pursuant to section 14 PSG as a whole through its case law and thus has also shaken the governance of the private foundation, updating a control deficit resulting from the lack of owners and only making it a problem by generally structuring the board of directors so strongly. In addition, it has extended its far-reaching case law on the incompatibility of the supervisory board to other supervisory bodies, so that beneficiaries on the advisory board may exercise even fewer rights. This is disadvantageous because the beneficiaries are the beneficial owners of the private foundation and it is actually they who have a real interest in the functioning of the foundation. The Supreme Court has therefore massively weakened the enterprise foundation as an institution by its very strict view, which is hardly anchored in the text of the law or in the telos of the regulation. The legislator has already required a mandatory third-party management of three non-family members. The Supreme Court extends this restrictive stance to the advisory board and thus the most important controlling body. This largely pushes the family back from management and control. In any case, this is dysfunctional for the long-term functioning of the foundation's business and thus for active entrepreneurial ownership.[59] This strong position of the board of directors sometimes leads to beneficiaries who are represented less in the foundation and in the foundation's bodies seeking help from the court and very often demanding the dismissal of the foundation's board members. The court then has to conduct non-contentious proceedings (*außerstreitiges Verfahren*). This shifts part of the control to the judicial level. In order to forestall this, it is necessary that a foundation's declaration is carefully prepared from the outset and that there is appropriate influence of the family members in the foundation and the corporate holdings held by the foundation.

58 OGH 6 Ob 95/15m, (2015) *GesRZ* 338.

59 S. Kalss and S. Probst, above n. 19, Rz 7.47 et seq.

9. EXAMPLES OF AUSTRIAN ENTERPRISE FOUNDATIONS

Enterprise foundations have a very successful history in Austria. For the many successful family businesses in particular, enterprise foundations offer an opportunity to secure long-term interests and a long-term ownership structure. Some successful enterprise foundation models are:

9.1. B&C PRIVATSTIFTUNG

B&C Privatstiftung is one of the largest Austrian enterprise foundations. It was established in 2000 by two stock cooperations (*Aktiengesellschaften*), namely Bank Austria and Creditanstalt, from which it acquired significant non-banking participations in return for the granting of profit participation rights.[60] The purpose of B&C Privatstiftung is to promote Austrian entrepreneurship. B&C Privatstiftung fulfils its purpose by holding long-term investments in Austrian industrial companies. As a core shareholder, it aims to provide strategic support and long-term planning security to its portfolio companies. B&C Privatstiftung further nominates supervisory board members in the companies to fulfil this role. In addition, B&C Privatstiftung promotes Austrian entrepreneurship by sponsoring academic work and events in the fields of law and economics.

The B&C Group's main investments include majority holdings in the three listed companies: AMAG Austria Metall AG, Lenzing AG and Semperit AG Holding. It also holds and invests in technology growth companies (scale-ups) with an industrial focus through its subsidiary B&C Innovation Investments. B&C Privatstiftung and its associated companies are among the largest enterprise foundations in Austria and, with around 14,000 employees and an estimated gross value added of €1.6 billion,[61] are a key factor in the Austrian economy.

9.2. BANKHAUS SPÄNGLER

Bankhaus Carl Spängler & Co. AG was founded in 1828 and is the oldest private bank in Austria. Today, around 90% of the bank is owned by four enterprise foundations. These represent different family lines. Thanks to this stable and

[60] See 'B&C Privatstiftung: Geschichte' (2025) *B&C Industrieholding*: https://bcgruppe.at/privatstiftung/geschichte/.

[61] 'B&C-Industriebeteiligungen' (2025) *B&C Industrieholding*: https://bcgruppe.at/industrie/.

long-term orientated structure, the bank is already being managed by the seventh generation. Anchoring the ownership structure in enterprise foundations ensures that there is no fragmentation of the shareholding through succession or other divisions. The enterprise foundations are seen as the foundation of the independence of the bank.[62]

A speciality of the structure is that the beneficiaries of the enterprise foundations themselves also hold a minority stake of around 1% in the bank. This structure is intended to fulfil various purposes. On the one hand, it is intended to ensure longevity and stability, while at the same time ensuring that direct influence is not completely lost. On the other hand, the shareholder families and their private foundations are linked by a syndicate agreement to ensure a standardised proceed.[63]

9.3. SAVINGS BANK FOUNDATIONS (*SPARKASSENSTIFTUNGEN*)

Savings bank foundations are a special form of private foundation that can be established by converting a savings bank that holds shares of a bank. Section 27a of the Savings Banks Act (*Sparkassengesetz*, SpG) allows the conversion of a savings bank that has contributed its business or a part of its banking business to a savings bank stock corporation into a private foundation.[64] The (prior) transfer of the banking business to a separate company is required, as a private foundation itself may not engage in direct business activities (see section 1.5 above). Savings banks are already similar to private foundations due to their internal organisation. The founders of a savings bank are not owners, but act as initiators in its establishment and are excluded from participating in the assets and profits of the savings bank.[65] This promotes the non-profit character of a savings bank.

The governance of savings bank foundations differs in some respects from that of private foundations under the PSG. For example, the assets of savings bank foundations must be permanently preserved (section 27a para. 4 no. 4 SpG). Unlike private foundations, savings bank foundations may therefore not be organised as foundations of consumption (*Verbrauchsstiftung*). For savings bank foundations, the prohibition of self-purpose foundations is thus limited.[66]

---

62 'Das Bankhaus' (2025) *Bankhaus Spängler*: https://www.spaengler.at/bankhaus/.

63 'Ein Bankhaus mit langer Tradition' (2025) *Bankhaus Spängler*: https://www.spaengler.at/bankhaus/geschichte/.

64 S. Kalss in S. Kalss, C. Nowotny and M. Schauer, above n. 2, Rz 7/148.

65 S. Kalss and J. Nicolussi, 'Die erste Group Bank AG – Stärkung des wirtschaftlichen Wohlergehens der Kunden als Unternehmenszweck' in H. Fleischer and S. Mock, *Große Gesellschaftsverträge aus Geschichte und Gegenwart*, De Gruyter, Vienna 2021, pp. 283, 312, 333 et seq.

66 S. Kalss in S. Kalss, C. Nowotny and M. Schauer, above n. 2, Rz 7/152.

In addition, no significant governance rights may be reserved, such as in particular the right to amend the foundation declaration, to establish a supplementary foundation deed or to revoke the private foundation (section 27a para. 4 no. 1 SpG). Savings bank foundations therefore differ significantly from foundations under the PSG in terms of their governance. The main purpose of savings bank foundations is the permanent, indefinite pursuit of charitable, benevolent or ecclesiastical purposes.[67]

Savings bank foundations must be established for an indefinite period. They are not allowed to consume their assets. They are therefore particularly well suited, indeed predestined, as long-term business owners. They often have regional roots and promote regional projects and developments. There are currently around 35[68] savings bank foundations that pursue charitable, benevolent or ecclesiastical purposes based on the aforementioned guidelines. However, the focus of their activities lies in their role as an active and forward-looking core shareholder. Savings bank foundations therefore serve above all to actively organise and secure the ownership position in the long term. With 'DIE ERSTE österreichische Spar-Casse Privatstiftung', Austria's largest listed bank, Erste Group Bank AG, is owned by a savings bank foundation.[69] It has over 200 years of corporate history behind it. The 'Sparkasse Oberösterreich Privatstiftung' in Linz, which can look back on over 170 years of company history, is also of great importance, as is the 'Privatstiftung Sparkasse Krems', whose operations also date back to the first half of the 19th century.

10. OUTLOOK

The Austrian foundation is a story of success. The main characters are the open purpose, the liberal legal framework and the strong continuing influence of the founder. The Supreme Court has limited the legal framework to a certain extent. The founder is well advised to shape a strong and well-functioning governance within the foundation. In this way, the Austrian foundation will play an important role in the Austrian economy.

The Austrian private foundation is an important organisational form for companies, especially family businesses. It can fulfil the role of a core shareholder of the holding company or an anchor shareholder.

Since private foundation law is open, it is necessary to carefully prepare the foundation deeds and the interaction of the governing bodies from the outset, otherwise the adverse case law of the Supreme Court will take effect, which has

67 OGH 6 Ob 95/07z; N. Arnold, above n. 23, §27a SpG Rz 15.

68 'Sparkassenstiftungen in Österreich' (2025) *Sparkasse Verband Österreich*: https://www.sparkassenverband.at/de/stiftungen/sparkassenstiftungen-in-oesterreich.

69 S. Kalss and J. Nicolussi, above n. 65, 283, 333 et seq.

an anti-business and anti-family view of the foundation, especially since it wants to keep beneficiaries and thus the typical successor generation of the founders out of the foundation.

In terms of legal policy, it is therefore absolutely necessary to strengthen the position of the family in the governing bodies, especially in the advisory board, and to improve the position of the supervisory body as a whole, namely to grant rights of approval and far-reaching other possibilities of influence in addition to the rights of appointment and dismissal. It also makes sense to make the right of amendment more flexible. Only in this way can the success story of the Austrian foundation be continued in the coming decades.

ENTERPRISE FOUNDATIONS IN SWEDEN

Katarina Olsson

ABSTRACT

This chapter discusses enterprise foundations in Sweden. Although foundations have a long history and a strong tradition in Sweden, there has been little focus on foundations that either conduct business in their own name or own shares in a company. There is a lack of a common understanding of the notion of 'enterprise foundation' and there is no legal definition of it either. Notably, there is also an almost complete absence of a political, legal or economic discussion which results in a situation where enterprise foundations seem to exist more or less unnoticed as a separate category in the foundation world. Greater transparency and a more conscious discussion are needed in order to shed light on this interesting legal entity.

1. INTRODUCTION AND HISTORICAL CONSIDERATIONS

There are almost 19,000 foundations according to the Swedish official registry on foundations.[1] About 1,800 foundations are registered as enterprise

---

1 The registry at the County Administration Boards is available at: https://stiftelser.lansstyrelsen.se.

foundations. However, the number of enterprise foundations is not necessarily accurate. There are probably more enterprise foundations than the registry information suggests. The concept of 'enterprise foundation' in Sweden is not straightforward. The two words 'enterprise' and 'foundation' are inherently complicated and require special attention in a legal discussion.[2] There is no legal definition of an enterprise foundation in Sweden. It is probably not uncommon that a foundation that is presented and described as a charitable foundation is actually a controlling owner of a business entity. Enterprises in themselves are usually profit-driven, but when it comes to ownership, the foundation can provide a legal form that allows for the charitable distribution of wealth. Many enterprise foundations in Sweden are registered according to their purpose, as charitable foundations, even in cases where the foundation has a strong connection to an enterprise. One problem when discussing foundations is that it is difficult to organise and classify foundations into a unified system. Therefore, it is not easy to discuss enterprise foundations. Each author has to present his or her description or definition of the investigated foundations.

We know fairly little about enterprise foundations in Sweden and there seems to be no political or societal interest in discussing these foundations today. Legal writings[3] on the issue are scarce and case law on private law issues is almost non-existent.[4] Enterprise foundations can live a rather quiet life, without attracting attention from the legislator, the judiciary or the academic environment. Myths, lack of transparency and hidden motives have often been at the forefront in the Swedish discussion on enterprise foundations.[5]

Notably for Sweden, relatively few influential family business groups have used foundations to exercise far-reaching control over Swedish industry.[6]

---

2 *Stiftelse* is the Swedish word used for an entity covered by the Foundation Act (*Stiftelselagen* 1994:1220). It is not obvious that the word *stiftelse* is to be translated into 'foundation' in English; however this is the terminology often chosen in Sweden for a text in English.

3 There are only two doctoral dissertations in Sweden that deal exclusively with foundations: H. Hessler, *Om stiftelser*, Norstedts Juridik, Stockholm 1952 (foundations in general); and K. Olsson, *Näringsdrivande stiftelser*, Nerenius & Santérus Förlag, Stockholm 1996 (enterprise foundations). See also, H. Almlöf and K. Olsson, *Svensk stiftelserätt*, Norstedts Juridik, Stockholm 2025. A number of shorter books of a handbook nature, all of them in Swedish, mainly discuss practical issues on foundations. For example, see P. Aamisepp, K. Fagerberg, J. Lindman and B. Löfgren Lewin, *Stiftelsehandboken*, Norstedts Juridik, 4th ed., Stockholm 2023. There is no comprehensive academic study on Swedish foundations in English. Several of the contributions in H. Almlöf, R.K. Feldthusen and P. Lindskoug, (eds.), *Festskrift till Katarina Olsson*, Juristförlaget i Lund, Lund 2025, discuss foundations.

4 When it comes to tax law there is an extensive case law, see M. Berglund, *Beskattning av stiftelser*, IUSTUS, Uppsala 2021.

5 For a discussion on the motives behind the creation of a foundation, which is not always made clear in its purpose, see K. Olsson, above n. 3, pp. 199–210.

6 D. Johansson, M. Stenkula and N. Wykman, 'The Taxation of Industrial Foundations in Sweden (1862–2018)' (2020) 1 *Nordic Tax Journal* 1, 4–5 give a short presentation on family business groups and connected industrial foundations. M. Henrekson, D. Johansson

The fact that, for example, the Wallenberg family business group is controlled by the fifth generation of family members through foundations and the Ax:son Johnson family business group is controlled by the fourth generation indicates that enterprise foundations may be effective in creating and sustaining control over large family business groups.[7] Since there is not much legal research or political discussion on foundations in Sweden, one might conclude that to some extent the foundations are rather poorly understood as actors in the Swedish business life and society in general. However, lately economists have turned their attention to enterprise foundations.[8]

2. HISTORICAL REMARKS

Foundations often come with an interesting history that will help provide the reasons for setting up the foundation, i.e. the founder's ambitions and wishes, but also information that might help in interpreting and applying the provisions in the charter. Sweden has a long history of foundations. The oldest foundations date back to the 16th century,[9] when people donated to religious purposes and for taking care of the poor. In the 18th century, foundations were set up to support education. Higher education and scientific research became more important purposes in the late 19th century. Enterprise foundations are a phenomenon of the 20th century. Foundations are closely linked to the economic and societal development in any country. In order to fully understand how the

and M. Stenkula, 'The rise and decline of industrial foundations as controlling owners of Swedish listed firms: the role of tax incentives' (2020) 68(2) *Scandinavian Economic History Review* 170, 170–191 discuss potential explanations as to why Sweden has seen a decline in the creation of enterprise foundations. The authors point to the importance of tax incentives for the use of enterprise foundations as control vehicles for listed firms.

7 D. Johansson et al., above n. 6, 5. M. Henrekson et al., above n. 6, 174 mention other foundations that are used as controlling vehicles: Dunkerstiftelserna: https://dunkerstiftelserna.se; Söderbergstiftelserna: https://ragnar.soderbergs.org and https://www.torstensoderbergsstiftelse.se; and Kjell och Märtha Beijers stiftelse: https://www.beijerstiftelsen.se. See also D. Johansson, M. Stenkula and N. Wykman, 'The Rise of Private Foundations as Owners of Swedish Industry: The Role of Tax Incentives 1862–2018' (2018) *IFN Working Paper* No. 1245, Research Institute of Industrial Economics, Stockholm.

8 For recent information, see M. Henrekson et al., above n. 6; D. Johansson et al., above n. 6; F. Wijkström and S. Einarsson, 'Comparing Swedish Foundations: A Carefully Negotiated Space of Existence' (2018) 62(13) *American Behavioral Scientist* 1889, 1889–1918.

9 See, for example, Stiftelsen Danviks Hospital, which was created in 1551: https://www.danvikshem.se/historia/grundades-ar-1551. For a comprehensive historical background, see F. Wijkström and S. Einarsson, 'Foundations in Sweden: Their Scope, Roles and Visions' (2005) *Economic Research Institute at the Stockholm School of Economics*, available at: https://www.researchgate.net/publication/273775439_Foundations_in_Sweden_Their_Scope_Roles_and_Visions.

foundations function and are regulated in Sweden, it is vital to understand not only the legal situation but also the societal implications and political aims.[10]

The emergence of a strong welfare state in Sweden in many ways changed how and why foundations were set up. Due to the Swedish welfare system, foundations led a rather quiet existence way into the 20th century. Through the tax system, the state financed education, research, social benefits and economic support for those in need. The foundations provided supplementary grants. According to Wijkström and Einarsson, 'the foundation world is still deeply embedded in the social contract and strong Social-Democratic regime of the 20th century'. The authors refer to this position as a carefully negotiated space of existence.[11]

Sweden, like many other countries in Europe, was a rather poor agricultural country until the start of the Industrial Revolution in the mid-19th century. As Johansson et al. observe, entrepreneurs at that time started successful family businesses controlling large parts of Swedish industry.[12] This of course attracted attention from policy makers and analysts, but it was not until the 1960s that a systematic examination of their influence was conducted. According to the Government Inquiry on Concentration, a number of families and foundations controlled many of the spheres of ownership in the Swedish industry.[13] Henrekson et al. argue that enterprise foundations became a vehicle for corporate control of large listed firms in Sweden in the period between the two World Wars. Wealthy individuals replaced these foundations in the 1990s either through direct ownership or holding companies.[14]

In the 1960s the discussion arose about the permissibility of both concentration of power and foundation ownership. From a political perspective, foundations are not always regarded as beneficial to society. In different inquiries and reports from the government and parliament, one can observe a hostile and suspicious attitude towards private initiatives through foundations. In the debate, arguments can be found that foundations are used for criminal purposes, money laundering or hiding assets in order to benefit the founder.[15]

---

10 For a short background, see F. Wijkström and S. Einarsson, above n. 9; and S. Einarsson and F. Wijkström, 'The EUFORI Study, European Foundations for Research and Innovation, Country Report Sweden' (2015) *European Commission*, section 1.1: https://www.academia.edu/37652874/Sweden_Country_Report_European_Foundations_for_Research_and_Innovation_EUFORI_Study.

11 F. Wijkström and S. Einarsson, above n. 8, 1889.

12 D. Johansson, M. Stenkula and N. Wykan, above n. 6.

13 Government Inquiry on Concentration, 'Koncentrationsutredningen, Ägande och inflytande i det privata näringslivet' (SOU 1968:7).

14 M. Henrekson et al., above n. 6. In the article the authors examine why enterprise foundations became vehicles for control over large companies at the Stockholm Stock Exchange and why the importance of the legal form of enterprise foundations has declined in recent decades. They focus on tax incentives for establishing enterprise foundations as control vehicles.

15 See Government Bill, Prop. 2004/05:50 *Åtgärder mot missbruk at stiftelser* (Measures against abuse of foundations).

Einarsson and Wijkström attribute this criticism to the character of foundations 'as inflexible pools of capital without easily identified proxies for their owners'.[16] The question of using foundations for criminal purposes is currently on the legislator's agenda and new rules are included in the Foundation Act as of 1 January 2025.[17] According to the preparatory works, there are no indications that foundations are particularly prevalent in criminal contexts, but there are examples of foundations being used for illegitimate purposes. Therefore, the protection against financial crime should not be weaker in foundations than it is in other legal entities. A handful of new rules that are similar to the corresponding rules for limited companies and economic associations have been included in the Foundation Act, such as expanded rules on conflict of interest, a duty for auditors to report to the board and to the prosecutor in the event of suspicion of financial crime and a 'straw man' prohibition. The latter rule is sanctioned by criminal penalty, the first of that kind in the Foundation Act.

3. THE FOUNDATION WORLD IN SWEDEN TODAY

Foundations today represent a significant part of the Swedish non-profit sector. The foundations form a heterogeneous group that cannot be defined or described in a uniform way. There are very small foundations in the sense that they have very limited capital, maybe only €1,000. But there are also large foundations with capital of millions of euros and with complicated structures when it comes to purposes and activities. The vast majority of foundations have a charitable purpose. They are grant making, and many of them lead a rather quiet existence, although they perform important tasks that benefit a lot of people and society as a whole.

The enterprise foundations can be categorised as grant-making foundations, although they conduct business in their own organisation or own shares in a business corporation. Such foundations can be controlling vehicles with great influence and power. Although there are some very large enterprise foundations, it must not be forgotten that many of the enterprise foundations are small and there is no family involved or no controlling motive. Foundations are important in several sectors of Swedish society, especially in funding research and education.[18]

---

16 S. Einarsson and F. Wijkström, above n. 10, section 1.1. See also F. Wijkström and S. Einarsson, above n. 8.

17 Government Inquiry SOU 2023:34 *Bolag och brott – några åtgärder mot oseriösa företag* (with a summary in English pp. 29–37) and the Government Bill, Prop. 2024/25:8 *Bolag och brott.*

18 F. Wijkström and S. Einarsson, above n. 8, 1911, conclude that the Swedish foundation sector is complementary rather than a substitute to public financing. However, there is one exception. Funding of scientific research perhaps has a more important function as a substitute. Many of the foundations funding scientific research are owners of businesses,

In the historical context, it is also important to point out the dissolution of the wage-earner funds (*löntagarfonderna*) and the creation of the so-called wage-earner fund foundations (*löntagarfondsstiftelserna*). These huge foundations are not considered as enterprise foundations, but their grant-making to research is often combined with conditions of cooperation with businesses.[19] It is also important not to forget savings-banks foundations (*sparbanksstiftelser*) that own many Swedish savings banks.

Looking at the foundation sector today, it can be concluded that it is a healthy and prosperous legal entity. As the public welfare sector is struggling to finance, for example, education and research, healthcare and care for the elderly, financing from foundations is becoming more and more important. Criticism against the foundation format is seldom heard, and enterprise foundations as a form for conducting or owning business activities are not discussed in Swedish society or in a political or legal context. However, new developments can be observed. Rich young entrepreneurs sometimes create foundations and want the foundation to be an extension of their entrepreneurial experiences. Such a wish can take the form of, for example, social or impact investment rules for investing the foundation's capital. According to the research of Wijkström and Einarsson, 1,400 foundations were created between 2002 and 2012.[20] Compared to the total number of almost 19,000 foundations, this is a rather high rate of new establishment. Foundations of all categories are growing, in terms of numbers as well as assets. Unfortunately, it is not possible to extract any reliable estimate on how many of the new foundations can be categorised as enterprise foundations. The official registries in Sweden are simply not consistent and accurate when it comes to this rather undefined legal entity.

4. SOME WORDS ABOUT TERMINOLOGY

The term 'enterprise foundation' does not have an unambiguous meaning in Swedish law, nor does it expressly refer to a clearly defined type of foundation. The enterprise foundation (*näringsdrivande stiftelse*) concept does not appear in

and thus enterprise foundations according to the terminology used in this book. See also the Government Inquiry SOU 2023:59 *Ny myndighetsstruktur för finansiering av forskning och innovation* (with a summary in English pp. 33–52).

19 See e.g. KK-stiftelsen: https://www.kks.se/om-oss/in-english. The foundation funds activities conducted in collaboration with academic staff and business sector partners. The aim is to build internationally competitive, integrated research and education environments. Eleven foundations were set up with a total capital of €2 billion, all derived from the wage-earner funds. Over the years, political discussions have suggested the dissolution of these foundations and transfer of the money back to the state. The foundation form has proved to be a guarantee of stability and long-term management.

20 F. Wijkström and S. Einarsson, above n. 8, 1894.

the Foundation Act and, as mentioned above, does not have a legal definition.[21] In the preparatory work for the Foundation Act, the foundations are divided into two groups: grant-making foundations (*avkastningsstiftelser*) and activity-based foundations (*verksamhetsstiftelser*). The notion *verksamhetsstiftelse* refers to foundations which 'as a rule fulfil their purpose by carrying on business activities'.[22] This terminology does not recur in the Foundation Act. The fact that a foundation is described as carrying out a business does not entail any legal effects of a private law nature – except that the foundation is obliged to follow certain rules that apply to all organisations that conduct business – but is more a description of foundations with a specific type of purpose and/or activity. Foundations connected to a business in the sense discussed in this book appear in many forms in Sweden: industrial foundations,[23] operation foundations[24] and more rarely enterprise foundations. As far as it has been possible to ascertain, the terminology and language have not given rise to any major problems, either in legal or other respects.

The Swedish private law definition of an enterprise (*näringsidkare*) is someone who professionally runs activities of an economic nature. No profit motive with the business is required in order to be qualified as an enterprise. The business must be of an economic nature, i.e. refer to the sale of goods or services that have an economic value. Professionally conducted activities place demands on a certain scope, regularity and duration. The fact that the activity intends to promote a non-profit or charitable purpose does not constitute an obstacle to considering it as a business activity in a foundation. The term 'business activity' (*näringsverksamhet*) is often used in everyday speech as a description of the company, the enterprise. The entity that runs the business is organised as a natural or legal person, such as a company, an association or a foundation.

In Sweden there is also sometimes a difference between the private law and the tax law notion of business activity (*näringsverksamhet*), which might complicate the discussion. The difference between the private law and the tax law meaning of the concept of 'business activity' is mainly that in private law there is no requirement for profit. This means that the concept of private law is somewhat broader than the concept of tax law. The private law definition thus also includes typically non-profit activities that take place without interest in an economic exchange. The foundation can, for example, run a café at cost price or provide care to the beneficiaries for a heavily subsidised fee. Sometimes the foundations also receive state or municipal grants, which may be the case for a foundation that runs a nursing home, a theatre, a museum or a daycare centre.

---

21 However, the preparatory works refer to *näringsdrivande stiftelse*, e.g. Government Bill, Prop. 1993/94:9, p. 48.

22 Government Bill, Prop. 1993/94:9, pp. 40 et seq.

23 See e.g. M. Henrekson et al., above n. 6; and D. Johansson et al., above n. 6.

24 S. Einarsson and F. Wijkström, above n. 10, section 1.1.

5. DIRECT AND INDIRECT ENTERPRISE FOUNDATIONS

In the eyes of the public in general, a foundation distributes grants for non-profit or charitable purposes. The foundation's wealth consists of assets that can easily be transformed into cash for distribution to the beneficiaries. Swedish tax rules give a very clear incentive for distributing profits and dividends to the beneficiaries (see section 8 below). Business operations, on the one hand, typically require flexibility and some risk taking. The foundation, on the other hand, is expected to be unchangeable and eternal. Business activity may at first glance seem incompatible with the foundation and its lasting purpose. To some viewers, it might seem somewhat strange that a foundation can own a company or conduct a business in its own name. In many enterprise foundations, it is not possible to see from its charter whether the foundation runs or owns a business. This is a crucial difference compared to the companies and associations where the business activity is evident from the documents in connection with their formation, and in some cases also directly from the legal rules. There is a presumption in the law for business activities in limited companies and economic associations. Such presumptions are not linked to foundations.

The relationship between the foundation and the business can be constructed in different ways depending on a variety of causes and factors. Business activities within a foundation may arise in accordance with the founder's instructions in the charter or by decision of the board of the foundation. The design of the purpose provision determines whether the business activity is an aim for the fulfilment of a purpose, will function as a profit generator or in some other way will be part of the asset management. The difference in the way of looking at it is that the business activity is either a purpose in itself or a means for the fulfilment of the purpose. It must follow from the central function of the purpose provision in the charter of the foundation that the connection with the business is regarded as being in line with the purpose. A business activity that cannot be included under the purpose is not acceptable, but can in some cases be part of the asset management.

It is a striking feature that enterprise foundations often operate at the outer limits of what is normally accepted within the concept of a foundation, in terms of either their purpose or activity. Enterprise foundations often also operate on the outer fringes of the 'business' concept. This may, for example, be the case for a foundation that runs a non-profit-oriented business with no real profit motive, where the foundation only strives to cover its costs. Running a certain business does not have to be the sole purpose of the foundation. The foundation may have ancillary, superior or subordinate purposes of a different nature. The assets may also consist of property other than that attributable to the business. There is then often a close connection between other purposes in the foundation and the business activities.

The question of foundations that own shares and therefore could be identified as enterprise foundations have scarcely been discussed in legal terms in Sweden. Sweden is therefore in a completely different situation compared to, for example, Denmark. The 'enterprise foundation' notion generally refers to a foundation that conducts business activities in its own name or that in its capacity as owner or member has a controlling influence and an interest in a business activity outside the foundation. Based on the business operations' relationship to the foundation, there are two forms of enterprise foundations in Swedish law: direct enterprise foundations and indirect enterprise foundations. It could be discussed whether foundations solely in their capacity as owners are to be classified as enterprise foundations. The role of ownership alone cannot generally lead to the foundation being regarded as an enterprise foundation. But additional factors that bind the foundation to a business can lead to it being justified to talk about indirect enterprise.

For pedagogical reasons, it might be interesting to further discuss the two different types of enterprise foundations: direct enterprise foundations and indirect enterprise foundations.[25] Direct enterprise foundations include foundations that run a business in their own name in accordance with an express order from the founder in the charter. The business is the foundation's purpose or object of activity and follows directly from the founder's appointment. From the foundation's point of view, the business is thus originally an external decision that the board has to comply with. A distinctive feature of several foundations in the group is a close and natural connection between the foundation's purposes and the business activities. In its purest form, the business is the foundation's purpose – the foundation shall, for example, run a vegetarian restaurant or a bookstore for children's books. Foundations without an external purpose (called *Selbstzweckstiftung* according to the German terminology) are allowed in Sweden, and unlike other jurisdictions like Denmark, there has been no discussion on the permissibility of this kind of purpose. In these foundations, there is an identity between wealth and business. Since the purpose directly indicates the business activity, these foundations seldom present any problems from a foundation law point of view with regard to the business activity and its compatibility with the purpose. The business can also be the foundation's object of activity – in the examples above, the charter can prescribe that the foundation must spread knowledge about the lacto-vegetarian diet and for this purpose run a vegetarian restaurant, or that the foundation must contribute to the

[25] Writing my dissertation on enterprise foundations in the early 1990s (K. Olsson, *Näringsdrivande stiftelser*, above n. 3), I decided to use the more extended notion and include both direct and indirect enterprise foundations. This has not been criticised or commented on, but it is important to stress that there are no legal effects connected to the terminology itself.

dissemination of good literature for children and run a bookstore. Sometimes it is not even possible to distinguish between foundation purpose and business objects. This is the case if the foundation's purpose is to 'run a bookstore for children's books' or 'publish a journal in law', without any further information in the charter about the specific focus or purpose of the activity.

Indirect enterprise foundations include foundations where the founder has admittedly not prescribed that the foundation shall conduct business activities, but where the board has made the assessment that the foundation's purpose is best met by the foundation conducting business activities. In the examples above, the operation of the vegetarian restaurant and the bookstore in this group of foundations would not appear in the charter. The business activity shall function as a contribution to or a way of fulfilling the purpose and is then the foundation's object of activity, even if it is not expressed in the charter.[26] The business follows from an internal decision by the board of the foundation. The foundation's purpose does not have to have any connection to the business, and the business does not have to have direct support in the charter. However, the purpose and the founder's additional regulations in the charter must not constitute an obstacle for the foundation to conduct business activities.

Many foundations invest their assets in shares of various companies. Some of them might be characterised as indirect enterprise foundations. The share investment can be a way of managing the foundation's capital in order to meet the foundation's purpose with the return on the shares. The shareholding is then a pure investment issue and a means to achieve the purpose. As far as the purpose is concerned, it usually does not matter what type of business is conducted in the company where the founder or the board has chosen to invest all or part of the foundation's assets. However, the share investment can also be based on the fact that the founder or the board has an interest in the company and the business that the company conducts. Of course, such an interest does not exclude an interest in a return on the shares. On closer inspection, it may turn out that the main reason why the foundation was formed is that the foundation should strive for control and influence over the business. Another example includes foundations where the founder or board has chosen the connection to a business activity, because the business activity as such is of interest. Foundations

---

26 A somewhat odd feature in Swedish foundation law literature is the description of a foundation's purpose as consisting of three parts. The first part, the aim (*syftet*), describes what the founder wants to achieve through the purpose. This part is mandatory in all foundations. The second part is the type of activity that is to be conducted in order to fulfil the aim, the object of activity (*verksamhetsföremålet*). The third part is the designated beneficiaries stating who is going to benefit from the purpose (*destinatärskretsen*). The two latter parts are not mandatory in the purpose regulation of the charter. This way of dividing the purpose is not reflected in any legislation on foundations.

that own shares are therefore not included in the group as a way of obtaining a return on capital. In this connection, one can also discuss so-called impact investment, social investment or purpose-based investment, but that is quite another story.

A very large proportion of the number of foundations in Sweden seldom have any decisive influence over the company or any interest in the business. The return on shares, for distribution to the beneficiaries of the charitable purpose, is the primary interest. It is also characteristic that these foundations often have shareholdings in listed companies. Foundations that indirectly run business activities are sometimes referred to as holding foundations according to the corresponding terminology in company law. Through different voting values of the shares, the foundation can be assured of influence over the company even if it only owns a rather small part of the shares. The circumstances of the individual case may determine the influence of the foundation over the business.[27]

The supervision authority (County Administration Boards) does not seem to have any clear view on whether foundations with a business ownership should be regarded as enterprise foundations. Moreover, the tax authorities have their own definitions for tax purposes. Of course, this inconsistency complicates the picture and the legal discussion.[28]

6. THE ADMISSIBILITY OF ENTERPRISE FOUNDATIONS

One of the issues that has been debated, mainly in connection with the preparatory work for the Foundation Act of 1994, is whether the foundation could be used as an organisational form for all conceivable activities and then especially business activities, regardless of the wording of the purpose provision in the charter.

The story of enterprise foundations in Sweden is quite a remarkable one. In the early 1960s it was revealed that many of the large companies in Sweden were owned and controlled by a small number of families, in many cases including foundation structures. During the 1960s and 1970s, there were strong voices advocating against allowing enterprise foundations. But in

27 The Foundation Act has a definition and regulation of 'a group of business entities' in Chapter 1, section 5 that resembles definitions in company law. It should be noted that there is only one place for a foundation in an organisation chart of a foundation company group and that is at the very top of the organisation. The reason for this is simple. A foundation does not have any owners. Nonetheless, statements sometimes imply that a foundation is 'owned' by a family or a company.

28 This section is mainly based on the results in my dissertation: K. Olsson, above n. 3.

the end, the preparatory works to the current Foundation Act concluded that there should not be a ban against enterprise foundations acting in their own name.[29] However, the indirect enterprise foundations were not mentioned. The reason is probably because they were, and still are, not regarded as enterprise foundations according to the foundation law or the authorities. But in an academic discussion, and for comparative reasons, these foundations of course are of interest.

Why are foundations used for business reasons? There are many motives and explanations. One important motive is to secure the future of the company. All shares are irrevocably transferred to the foundation and through a well-formulated and future-oriented charter, the founder's will is secured. Another reason can be lack of family members or no suitable family members for succession as the owners and managers of the company. Sometimes one can see an ideological reason, such as a political view, cultural values or religious values. The tax favours that follow from a non-profit purpose is another motive. Often the charter combines the interest of running and developing the company, and a charitable purpose of some kind.

Ownership and influence in the business world were addressed in several public inquiries and reports during the period from 1960–1990. Some of these inquiries observed the strong ownership by foundations in many areas of the Swedish private business sector. Most of the identified foundations had small shareholdings, but there were also foundations with very large shareholdings.[30] Although several of these investigations are more than 50 years old, there is reason to believe that the ownership situation is not very different today, although some of the families have been replaced by new families.[31]

Up to the Foundation Act in the mid-1990s, foundations as owners of large companies or groups of companies had long attracted interest, mainly from a political point of view. The interest was strengthened by the possibility of keeping the foundation out of the supervisory system, at least until the introduction of the Foundation Act. In the eyes of the public, foundations are still often surrounded by secrecy and mystery, which has helped to further spin myths about charismatic persons such as Ingvar Kamprad, Alfred Nobel, the Wallenberg family and the Rausing brothers and their life's work.

The arguments put forward in the debate up to the turn of the century against business in the form of a foundation have almost exclusively been of a socio-political or legal policy nature. The debate has been characterised by a

29 Government Bill, Prop. 1993/94:9, p. 60.

30 The Concentration Inquiry's report ('Koncentrationsutredningen', above n. 13) (SOU 1968:7), of certain major ownership groups in Swedish business and industry included, among others, the following families or ownership groups associated with foundations: the Wallenberg family, Industrivärden-Svenska Handelsbanken, the Ax:son Johnson family, the Dunker group, the Ericsson family, the Åhlén family, the Kempe family and the Söderberg family.

31 For a closer analysis of the different inquiries, see K. Olsson, above n. 3, pp. 195 et seq.

reasoning about the suitability and need for the foundation form based on such factors as transparency, control, societal benefit and concentration of power.

The arguments for a ban on business activities in the form of foundations were based, among other things, on the perception that the foundation is abused and that business activities entail a risk that the foundation's purposes are jeopardised. The foundation form can be used as a means of concentrating the ownership of the business community to a few people or interest groups. Critics also point to the risk of tax evasion and avoidance, for example by using the foundation as a party to various financial transactions and corporate structures.

Other arguments that are put forward in the discussion against allowing business activities in the form of a foundation include that there are already different forms of associations that are suitable and intended for business activities. The foundation is strongly fixated on the unchanging purpose, which does not provide sufficient flexibility for changing economic situations or changed market conditions. There is a risk that the resources are not used correctly from the point of view of business operations. The great emphasis on the will of the founders can also have an inhibiting effect on business activities. The foundation is best suited for more passive asset management. Enterprise foundations with non-profit purposes have, through tax privileges, a competitive advantage over other forms of business organisations. The tax privileges give the foundation a better financing opportunity. In cases where the foundation has a purpose other than being a trader, there may be a tension between the purpose of the business and the foundation's 'non-financial' purpose. The risk is that the business is not conducted sufficiently efficiently because the profit is to go to the beneficiaries of the foundation or the interest in the business takes over and too little consideration is given to the foundation's purposes. With regard to the importance of business for society as a whole, it has been argued that a business must not be used for purposes that are too self-centred. The legal system should only support what society as a whole benefits from, i.e. non-profit foundations.

To conclude, Swedish law does not generally reject the idea that a foundation's purpose is to run a business or that a foundation's assets consist of a business or shares in a business. In the preparatory works to the Foundation Act in the 1980s and 1990s, the discussion was settled. Enterprise foundations are allowed in Sweden. There are not any restrictions in foundation law for certain purposes or certain commercial activities. There is no discussion today on the admissibility of enterprise foundations.[32]

[32] For a more detailed discussion of the admissibility of enterprise foundations, see K. Olsson, above n. 3, pp. 234–291.

7. THE LEGAL FRAMEWORK FOR ENTERPRISE FOUNDATIONS

Since the late 19th century, there have been discussions about regulating foundations in Sweden. It took almost 100 years to reach the goal of comprehensive foundation legislation. The reason for this reluctance to regulate was a fear that future donors would object to too many compulsory rules on how to set up and administer foundations and therefore would diminish the will to donate. The main private law regulation of foundations today is the Foundation Act of 1994 (*Stiftelselagen* 1994:1220), which came into force on 1 January 1996. This is the first general private law legislation on foundations in Sweden.[33] Many rules in the Foundation Act are default rules. This indicates that the founder's will is of great importance when creating the foundation and later for the board when interpreting the charter of the foundation. A political reason behind the construction of the act was the wish from the legislator to enhance the will to donate to charitable purposes.[34] The rules on taxation of foundations are also generous to those who want to donate to a charitable purpose in the form of a foundation (see section 8 below). The Foundation Act and the preparatory works[35] mention four types of foundations in Chapter 1, section 1: general foundations (*stiftelser i allmänhet*), fundraising foundations (*insamlingsstiftelser*), collective agreement foundations (*kollektivavtalsstiftelser*) and pension and employee foundations (*pensions- och personalstiftelser*). The latter type is used to guarantee employers' pension obligations and personnel benefits to employees.[36] Most enterprise foundations belong to the general foundations group. This also indicates that enterprise foundations are not considered a separate form of foundation according to the legislation.

According to Chapter 1, section 2 of the Foundation Act, a foundation is established when one or more founders donate certain property for independent administration on a permanent basis in order to serve a specific purpose. The property has to be separated from the founder's property and transferred into the hands of someone who can represent the foundation at the time of creation. This is usually one or several members of the board. The charter of the foundation (*stiftelseförordnandet*) must be in writing and signed by the founder or founders, and it can consist of several documents. Often the charter is in the

---

33 The earlier legislation, the Supervisory Act of 1929 (*lag (1929:116) om tillsyn över stiftelser*) had a primarily supervisory focus and contained few private law rules. The Foundation Act is supplemented by an Introductory Act (*lag (1994:1221) om införande av stiftelselagen*) regulating the relationship between existing foundations as of 1996 and the Foundation Act. None of the acts have an official translation into English.

34 Government Bill, Prop. 1993/94:9, p. 303.

35 Government Bill, Prop. 1993/94:9, p. 104.

36 Pension and employee foundations are regulated by a special act on safeguarding of pension commitments (*lag (1967:531) om tryggande av pensionsutfästelse m.m.*).

form of a will or a gift, supplemented by statutes (*stadgar*). The charter carries the legal consequence that the foundation as a legal person is created. A Swedish foundation can never have owners or members. The foundation is 'owned by its purpose' and it is the strong lock between purpose and property that identifies the foundation.[37]

There is no requirement for state approval to set up a foundation. Registration is required with the County Administration Boards (*länsstyrelsen*) and the registry is public.[38] The registration only has an informative and transparency function. The word *stiftelse* has to be included in the name of the foundation. This means that as of 1996, the legal term *stiftelse* is reserved for foundations only. There are no minimum capital requirements, but it must be possible to achieve the purpose in the foreseeable future. A foundation must be durable in the sense that it must exist for a reasonable period of time.[39] There is no eternal requirement and a spend-down foundation is accepted if it is stipulated in the charter.

In order to fulfil the purpose, the foundation must have some sort of management or administration. As a global unique feature, the Foundation Act regulates two organisational forms for managing the foundation. Either the foundation has a separate board consisting of natural persons as board members, which is called own administration or autonomous administration (*egen förvaltning*), or the foundation is managed by another legal person, which is called attached administration (*anknuten förvaltning*).[40] In the latter form of administration, it is the decision-making body of an existing legal person that carries the legal responsibility for administering the foundation. It can, for example, be a university, a state institution, a company or a church. A majority of the foundations in Sweden have attached administration. This is often a cost-efficient way of administration, since many Swedish foundations are rather small. An enterprise foundation can have attached administration, but it is probably rather unusual.

As a general rule in many foundations, the charter states that only return on assets may be distributed. According to the default rules in the Foundation Act, asset management must be acceptable (*godtagbar*). If the founder has regulated the asset management in the charter, it is considered acceptable and has to be followed by the board or the administering body. If the foundation has an autonomous administration, the governing board must not consist of the founder only. Otherwise, there are no requirements as to the number of board

37 The foundation is sometimes described as a self-owning entity (*självägande enhet*).

38 Information on all registered foundations is available at: https://stiftelser.lansstyrelsen.se.

39 Government Bill, Prop. 1993/94:9, pp. 52 and 108.

40 In Chapter 2 of the Foundation Act, there are certain provisions that are common for both types of administration, but also separate sub-chapters for each of the two types of administration.

members. It is often the case that the founder is a member of the board during his or her lifetime. All foundations are also required to have an external audit. State approval is required for all changes of the foundation's purpose. The founder has the right to regulate changes of provisions other than the purpose in the charter. A Swedish foundation may operate abroad if the charter does not forbid this. Sweden also allows foreign foundations to operate in Sweden. There are no restrictions when it comes to foreign funding, and a Swedish foundation can receive donations from abroad. In the individual case, it is of course a question of what the charter allows.

Enterprise foundations that operate a business must be registered before the business begins operating (Chapter 10, sections 6–10 of the Foundation Act). All Swedish foundations are under the supervision of the County Administration Board according to Chapter 9 of the Foundation Act. However, the founder can exempt the foundation from supervision. The effect of this exemption is that the foundation is under very limited supervision. Foundations that carry out business activities cannot be exempt and are always under full supervision even if the founder has stipulated an exemption in the charter (Chapter 9, section 10 of the Foundation Act). There are separate rules in the Foundation Act that target enterprise foundations in three chapters. As mentioned above, the registration of enterprise foundations is regulated in Chapter 10. Chapter 7 regulates foundations that carry out business activities and end up being liquidated or dissolved. Chapter 8 regulates issues concerning the 'business name' of the foundation. These rules have little effect on the everyday life of an enterprise foundation and are of a public law character to protect third parties.

8. TAX TREATMENT

Tax rules[41] that apply to legal persons in the Income Tax Act (*Inkomstskattelagen* 1999:1229) also apply to foundations.[42] As a rule, foundations pay tax on all income and capital gains. A foundation that does not have a non-profit or charitable purpose is fully taxed. Yet, as will be shown below, many foundations receive tax exemptions due to their charitable purpose and activities. A tax-exempt foundation pays tax only on income derived from real property or business activities, but in most cases no tax on dividends from the share holdings. Many enterprise foundations have charitable purposes that allow tax exemption for dividends and capital gains. There is no inheritance tax, gift tax or wealth tax in Sweden.

---

41 I would like to express my gratitude to Lynda Ondrasek Olofsson at Unum Tax for helping me understand the mysteries of the tax law.

42 For an in-depth analysis of the current rules for taxation of foundations, see M. Berglund, above n. 4, which covers relevant legal sources on tax rules concerning all types of foundations.

The tax rules have great practical significance for the design of the foundation's purposes. Therefore, in practice, these rules impose restrictions on the design of the purpose, especially for non-profit and charitable foundations. Since most foundations invest in financial instruments of some kind, the exemption from capital income tax is of the highest importance for the foundation, because more money can be distributed according to the purpose. Since 1942, the basic structure of the legal framework for the taxation of foundations has been more or less the same, offering tax relief for charitable purposes. The rationale behind the fact that a foundation with a charitable purpose is tax-exempt is probably some sort of gratitude from the state. Tax-exempt foundations contribute to activities that otherwise have to be financed by the state through taxes.[43] Also, the state and the regional and local authorities are tax-exempt, and it would be unreasonable to tax foundations that perform tasks that are considered to be charitable and beneficial to society.

A foundation must satisfy three requirements to qualify as a tax-exempt foundation (according to Chapter 7, sections 3–6 of the Income Tax Act): the purpose requirement (*ändamålskravet*), the activity requirement (*verksamhetskravet*) and the completion requirement (*fullföljdskravet*). Sometimes a fourth requirement is mentioned – the recipient requirement (*destinatärskravet*) – which means that the foundation's purpose must not be limited to certain families or specific persons. All requirements must be fulfilled in order to receive favourable tax treatment.

According to the purpose requirement, the foundation must have a charitable, public benefit (*allmännyttigt*) purpose that in one way or another benefits the public good. The tax-exempt purposes are enumerated in Chapter 7, section 4 of the Income Tax Act. These are sports, culture, religion, child and youth care, social assistance, healthcare, environmental protection, politics, Sweden's defence and emergency preparedness in cooperation with authorities, education and scientific research. An abundance of case law sets the limits for the different tax-exempt purposes. As of 2014, the tax-exempt purposes have been somewhat expanded as the enumeration in Chapter 7, section 4 ends with the words 'another equivalent activity'. This might open the way to a more generous application of the tax-exempt area. However, as yet, there is little case law on the interpretation of what type of activities that could be considered as 'equivalent' to the enumerated purposes.

The activity requirement states that the activities of the foundation must be mainly (*huvudsakligen*) to promote charitable purposes. In practice, this means that 90–95% of the foundation's activities must serve to satisfy the non-profit charitable purpose. This condition may be calculated in the form

[43] For a general understanding of the political rationale behind taxation, see: https://www.government.se/government-policy/taxes-and-tariffs.

of, for example, promotion through resources such as money, time or labour. The requirement for activity means that there is little room to act outside of the charitable purpose and still keep the tax-exempt status. The completion requirement states that a foundation's income must, to a reasonable extent, be used to promote the charitable and tax-exempt purpose. Case law has defined 'reasonable' as 80% of the net return. Taxable income shall not be included, nor shall the costs incurred to procure this income. With this requirement, it is not possible for a foundation to, more than to a limited extent, accumulate tax-exempt income over time. This can have a negative effect for enterprise foundations, since there is no possibility of permanently accumulating wealth in the foundation and keeping a tax-exemption.

A difficulty when interpreting the private law rules and tax rules applicable to foundations is that there are some differences in terminology. This sometimes makes it difficult to classify or define certain types or operations and actions conducted by the foundations. An enterprise foundation, where the foundation itself operates a business, is taxed like any other business entity. The corporate income tax rate is 20.6%, which has been slightly lowered in the last couple of years. A foundation that owns an enterprise as a holding foundation can receive dividends tax-free from the business. Dividends are tax-exempt if they are business-related, according to the so-called rules of participation exemption (*näringsbetingade andelar*).[44] This exemption applies to dividends received from a company and to capital gains derived from the sale of shares, provided that the shares qualify as business-related. Unlisted shares that are fixed business assets are always considered as business-related assets. Listed shares that are fixed business assets are considered to be business-related if the participation comprises at least 10% of the company's voting rights or is considered to be necessary in terms of conducting the company's business.[45]

According to Johansson et al., it has been argued that the Swedish tax system has favoured control over business entities through enterprise foundations. This is said to have inhibited entrepreneurship and economic growth. It is held that the favourable tax rules might be one tool for family business groups using enterprise foundations to employ in order to exercise far-reaching control over Swedish industry.[46] Henrekson et al. point out that tax incentives were important for the use of foundations as a control vehicle of listed firms. But the fact that many of these enterprise foundations have to

44 Auditing firms often have information in English on current rules on their websites. See, for example, Deloitte, 'International Tax, Sweden Highlights 2024': https://www2.deloitte.com/content/dam/Deloitte/global/Documents/Tax/dttl-tax-swedenhighlights-2024.pdf. Information in English is also available on the website of the Swedish Tax Agency (*Skatteverket*).

45 Deloitte, above n. 50, p. 2.

46 D. Johansson et al., above n. 6. The purpose of their study was to describe the evolution of tax rules for industrial foundations in Sweden between 1862 and 2018 and to calculate the marginal effective tax rate (METR) on capital income.

use 80% of their net returns on their charitable purpose also means that the foundation is drained of resources. This can be equivalent to a large tax.[47] If, for example, the foundation-controlled company will need new capital, it might be difficult for the foundation to participate. Henrekson et al. build their study on examinations of the Swedish tax system with the conclusion that since the 1980s, there are no motives for setting up an enterprise foundation that can be found in the tax system or rules on taxation. Entrepreneurs tend to control their companies by direct ownership today. This might also explain why there is no discussion on enterprise foundations in Sweden today.

There is no system of tax credit or tax deduction for donations to enterprise foundations. However, a very limited tax deduction for private persons is permitted for gifts. When it comes to corporate donors, some donations can be deducted as business expenses. An individual who receives a grant from a tax-exempt foundation is also exempt from paying tax on the grant, provided that some specific conditions are met.[48]

9. REFORM AND OUTLOOK

The author fears that the reader's confusion might have increased while reading this chapter of the book instead of giving a clear and comprehensive crash course in rules for Swedish enterprise foundations. The first problem is, of course, that there is no definition of 'enterprise foundations' in Swedish legislation. Therefore, it is difficult to identify the legal entity. Foundations as owners of business are not even discussed as a form of enterprise foundations in Sweden.

According to the preparatory works to the Foundation Act, foundations are allowed to conduct business in their own name. There are very few legal rules targeting enterprise foundations and important case law on the issue is absent. There seems to be no political, legal, economic or social encouragement today for setting up enterprise foundations, although advisors active in the consultancy market try to persuade people to set up foundations and let the foundation be the dominant shareholder.

However, foundations run businesses and foundations own businesses in Sweden, regardless of what we call these foundations. Although the legislation is deficient, the political discussion is absent, and the foundations involved in

---

47 M. Henrekson et al., above n. 6.

48 For a more elaborate nutshell summary including several European countries, see DAFNE (Donors and Foundations Networks in Europe and EFC (European Foundation Centre), 'Comparative Highlights of Foundation Laws: The Operating Environment for Foundations in Europe' (2021) Brussels.

enterprises often 'fly under the radar', there are still questions and problems to address.

As seen in this chapter of the book, there are many motives for setting up an enterprise foundation. It gives an entrepreneur the possibility to keep companies under the control of a family for many generations, with a very low level of taxation due to its charitable purpose. Through the foundation, it is possible to keep assets, capital, voting rights and other control mechanisms in one owner's hand. Through generations, the company will avoid inheritance division. Last, but not least, the social status of the family might benefit from the foundation's funding of charitable activities.

However, there are also disadvantages to setting up an enterprise foundation as a control vehicle. The entrepreneur irrevocably loses ownership of the assets. Capital and dividends must be used for this purpose. An aspect that is often overlooked is the fact that the founder can move himself or herself and his or her assets to another jurisdiction. This is not easily done for a foundation.

When focusing on large enterprise foundations with economic, political and social influence and importance as owners, employers and producers, there is a risk of forgetting the smaller ones. Many smaller enterprise foundations run business-oriented activities, perhaps because the foundation format is a good way of cooperating with others without ownership. Maybe the founder wants to label the foundation with a particular ideological idea. These foundations run, for example, schools, nursing homes, museums, newspapers, bookshops and daycare centres. They are also part of the enterprise foundation family.

The Foundation Act is now 30 years old. There have been some minor changes over the years, but no general revision of the legislation. Instead, changes have been more patchwork without attempting a comprehensive approach. The two authorities in the foundation world, the County Administration Boards and the Legal, Financial and Administrative Services Agency, have called for an investigation into a revision of the Foundation Act, but so far, the Ministry of Justice has not taken any action in this respect.[49]

Looking at the statistics, Sweden has a strong and growing foundation sector.[50] Neither foundations in general nor enterprise foundations seem to present any major problems when it comes to management, financing, purpose activity or any other aspect. Once in a while, arguments that foundations are

---

49 The documents are publicly available: *Länsstyrelserna* 2019-07-23 Dnr 206-22738-2019 and *Kammarkollegiet* 2019-06-14 Dnr 1.1-5600-19.

50 F. Wijkström and S. Einarsson, above n. 8, 1909. The authors discuss enterprises set up and controlled by foundations in the sense that different forms of control and power mechanisms can be used to secure influence and control from a group of organisations, a certain family, a value-based community or a public sector body. Somewhat surprisingly the authors state (at 1900) that foundations 'set up and controlled by corporations, were not as many'. The authors convincingly explain that this is an illustration of control and power mechanisms.

used for criminal activities, like money laundering and fraud, are heard, but the reasoning and empirical evidence for these has always been rather weak. However, it is definitely time for a revision of the Foundation Act. Swedish society has changed and the conditions for philanthropy as well as conducting business have developed in the 30 years that have passed. This is not a Swedish phenomenon; it happens all over the world.

Enterprise foundations have two parts: the business side and the foundation side. The two interests do not always coincide. Regardless of the type of business the foundation conducts or owns, it is the foundation issues that are of relevance in this chapter of the book. Rules and legislation on foundations target the business side of the foundation to a very limited extent.

The first item on a wish list would be a definition of enterprise foundations and clear answers on some regulatory issues. Perhaps Sweden is not yet ready for a separate piece of legislation on enterprise foundations as is the case in Denmark. However, some adequate rules are better than no rules. Second, private law and tax law have to share a common view of legal aspects and definitions of enterprise foundations. The foundations have considerable economic power, but there is no registry on the fortune of the foundations. The County Administration Boards sometimes register asset information from foundations' annual reports, but this is not done on a regular or complete basis. This is of course not acceptable.

Foundations are involved in the redefinition of the role and scope of the welfare state of today.[51] Yet, as noted by Wijkström, there is no critical and informed public debate on foundations and their role in contemporary Sweden. I definitely share this view, even some 20+ years after Wijkström first noted this fact.

It is a striking feature that several foundations in Sweden are controlling owners of large firms and company groups. It is even more striking that there is no debate on this. Somehow, as also observed by Wijkström and Einarsson,[52] philanthropy is underanalysed in Sweden because the issues fall under the radar and simply continue to be unnoticed. These large enterprise foundations are often hidden behind the charitable umbrella. Of course, this does not imply any negative aspects, but living in a very transparent society, it is somewhat surprising that decade after decade, these foundations seem to live in the shadows. Research is needed, but so too is a political discussion on the values of foundations running and/or owning enterprises. For a fruitful discussion, it is necessary to lift the veil from enterprise foundations and look behind the curtains.

---

51 F. Wijkström, 'Foundations in Sweden' in M. Bennet and R. Clay (eds), *Foundations in Europe*, Directory of Social Change, London, 2001, p. 245.

52 F. Wijkström and S. Einarsson, above n. 8.

So, what can be done to increase the establishment of new enterprise foundations? As a lawyer, it would be easiest to call for separate legislation of enterprise foundations, as exists in Denmark. But this is probably fruitless since there seem to be no voices advocating for more or different legislation in Sweden. Also, I do not think that the current legislation is an obstacle for the will to donate or set up new enterprise foundations. As shown above, foundations with a charitable purpose already receive favourable tax treatment and the taxation of business activities is neutral. Information is needed so that foundations can do even more good in society. Knowledge is power and on the wish list is definitely an increased degree of transparency when it comes to the two foundation authorities. Creating a best practice, like the Danish example of Recommendations on Foundation Governance, would probably strengthen the management of and create greater self-confidence in the boards.[53] National and international umbrella organisations can also strengthen the impact of the foundation sector.[54]

Foundations have to talk to each other, learn from each other and talk to the rest of the world. In that respect, international contacts are vital. There is a lot to learn from other countries. A catalytic approach to grant giving and partnerships with other foundations or organisations can increase the efficiency of grant giving.

Looking into the crystal ball, the author sees a prosperous future for foundations in general, simply because of the need for charitable purposes as substitutes or complements to state measures. But the author also sees a future for enterprise foundations as long-term sustainable owners of enterprises. One way to start on the road ahead is to increase communication and transparency and to learn from each other. Another way is to persuade the legislator to take more interest in foundations in general and enterprise foundations specifically.

53 Available at: https://godfondsledelse.dk/english.

54 According to F. Wijkström and S. Einarsson, above n. 8, 1905, the creation of a type of umbrella organisation has probably contributed to a less negative attitude towards foundations.

ENTERPRISE FOUNDATIONS IN DENMARK

Rasmus Kristian FELDTHUSEN

ABSTRACT

Denmark has recognised foundations being owners and having a controlling interest in companies since at least 1876. In 1985, Denmark enacted special legislation on enterprise foundations with the Danish Enterprise Foundation Law. Simultaneously legislation was enacted for all non-enterprise foundations, and Denmark has since had two separate pieces of legislation on foundations to thereby suit the different needs and requirements of these two types of foundations. Today the importance of enterprise foundations and their companies to the Danish economy cannot be understated and Danish legislation serves as an example of how to introduce enterprise foundations into a legal system.

1. HISTORICAL BACKGROUND

Enterprise foundations began their existence in Denmark with lawyers, utilising the freedom of contract, drafting charters and transferring assets to 'funds' or foundations, and in the 18th century, also transferring shares in companies, with Carlsbergfondet in 1876 as probably the first actual enterprise foundation. After Carlsbergfondet, many followed – for example, Novo Nordisk Foundation and Egmont H. Petersens Fond.

It was not until 1985 that Denmark enacted legislation on foundations in the shape of two separate laws on foundations, one on enterprise foundations[1] and one on non-enterprise foundations.[2] The reason Denmark chose to have two laws on foundations was that a number of special considerations apply to enterprise foundations, which were deemed to justify a deviation from a number of the general rules and principles. The Committee noted:

> The starting point for the committee's deliberations has been that for enterprise foundations, a reasonable equality should be sought between the rules that must apply to these foundations and the rules that apply to commercial activities that are conducted in other entities. The considerations which have motivated the implementation or consideration of rules on such other forms of business apply to a considerable extent to the enterprise foundations. This applies thus – especially in the case of foundations that directly carry on business activities – securing creditors, co-contractors and employees. In the Committee's view, the aim should be to ensure that the rules applicable to the pursuit of a commercial activity are independent of the form in which the activity is conducted. The rules of law should thus, as a starting point, be 'neutral' in relation to the various forms of business.[3]

In 1986 a separate law on foundation taxation was enacted entailing that foundations – as a point of departure – are taxed the same way as companies (see below section 10).[4]

---

1 Law on Enterprise Foundations (*Erhvervsfondsloven*) consolidated as of 28 December 2021. It is expected that a proposal to revise the law on enterprise foundations in a number of areas will be presented for the Danish Parliament in the Spring of 2026. A number of these changes have been prompted by a report recommending a fundamental revision of the Danish legislation on non-enterprise foundations. This author was chair of the committee that prepared the aforementioned report.

2 Law on Non-Enterprise Foundations (*Lov om ikke-erhvervsdrivende fonde*) consolidated as of 28 December 2021.

3 'Betænkning om fonde afgivet af det af justitsministeren den 14. juli 1978 nedsatte udvalg' (1982) nr. 970, p. 31. The quotation has been translated by the author.

4 R.K. Feldthusen, 'The Danish Law on Foundations' (2016) 22(1) *Trusts & Trustees* 146; S. Thomsen, *The Danish Industrial Foundations*, DJOEF Publishing, Copenhagen 2017;

2. DATA ON THE PREVALENCE AND IMPORTANCE OF ENTERPRISE FOUNDATIONS IN DENMARK

There are approximately 1,400 enterprise foundations in Denmark. The size distribution of enterprise foundations is large, with only a small number of very big foundations. The largest of the Danish enterprise foundations control, through a majority of voting rights, a very large proportion of the dominant companies in Denmark, such as Carlsberg, Danfoss, Mærsk, Novo, Grundfos, J. Lauritzen, Lundbeck and Rambøll.

In 2023 enterprise foundations paid out DKK 18.6 billion in (mainly) charitable distributions.[5]

Professor Steen Thomsen has calculated that enterprise foundations account for 5–10% of the economic activity in Denmark, more than 70% of stock market capitalisation and roughly 50% of the total Danish research and development.[6]

The data on 'foundation-controlled companies' presented below is produced by Fondenes Videnscenter in cooperation with the Center for Corporate Governance at Copenhagen Business School with Professor Steen Thomsen. In the study 'foundation-controlled companies' are understood as companies where an enterprise foundation or philanthropic association owns A- and/or B-shares corresponding to at least 20% of the voting rights and holds more votes than the second and third largest shareholders combined. This definition includes both enterprise foundations covered by the Law on Enterprise Foundations and associations converted from former financial institutions. The study, thus, does not solely pertain to enterprise foundations.[7]

The study also only includes the activities of Danish foundation-controlled companies within the borders of Denmark, as registered in public Danish records.

S. Thomsen and N. Kavadis, 'Enterprise Foundations: Law, Taxation, Governance, and Performance' (2022) 6(4) *Annals of Corporate Governance* 227; R.K. Feldthusen and S. Thomsen, 'How enterprise foundations can sustain sustainability: The European relevance of a Nordic ownership model' in B.K. Sjåfjell and J. Mähönen, *Nordic Company Law: Broadening the Horizon*, Universitetsforlaget, Oslo 2023, pp. 110–128; R.K. Feldthusen, 'Obstacles and Possible Solutions for the Adaptation of Enterprise Foundations' in M. Bartl, R. Claassen and N. van der Horst (eds), 'Whitepaper: Sustainable By Design Industrial Policy for Long-Term Competitiveness in the EU' (2024) Amsterdam/Utrecht: https://www.researchgate.net/publication/383513256_whitepaper-sustainable-by-design-industrial-policy-for-long-term-competitiveness-in-the-eu; R.K. Feldthusen, S. Kalss and C. Teichmann, 'Unternehmensträger mit Vermögensbindung' (2024) *Zeitschrift für Unternehmens- und Gesellschaftsrecht* 862.

5 Danmarks Statistik and Fondenes Videnscenter, 'Fondenes bevillinger i 2023' (December 2023): https://fondenesvidenscenter.dk/app/uploads/Fondes-bevillinger-2023.-Faktaark-FINAL-2.pdf.

6 S. Thomsen, above n. 4, p. 125.

7 Fondenes Videnscenter, 'Fondes erhvervsaktivitet i Danmark 2022' (November 2024): https://fondenesvidenscenter.dk/app/uploads/FINAL.-Fondes-erhvervsaktivitet-2022-1.pdf.

This means that activities abroad, including employees, sales from foreign companies to Denmark and foreign revenue are not included. Consequently, the analysis does not reflect the total business activity of the foundations, as their international business activities are not part of the analysis. However, foreign research and development (R&D) activities are included as the sole exception. The study is based on data from 2022.

Foundation-controlled companies contributed 24% of Denmark's total value added in 2022, an increase from 18% the year before. The 1,291 foundation-controlled companies employed nearly one in ten private sector employees, accounted for 26% of Denmark's total exports and contributed 14% of the country's total revenue.[8]

In 2022, the 20 largest foundation-controlled companies (measured by number of employees) accounted for 86% of the revenue, 91% of the value added and 95% of the exports among foundation-controlled companies.[9]

The foundation-controlled companies employed 12,200 full-time positions in R&D and invested DKK 19.5 billion in internal R&D, corresponding to 34% of all R&D employment and 39% of the total internal R&D investments in Denmark. Additionally, they purchased R&D services worth DKK 25.9 billion, of which DKK 18.4 billion went to Danish suppliers. Overall, there was an increase of DKK 13.9 billion in the R&D activities of foundation-controlled companies from 2021 to 2022, primarily driven by the purchase of R&D services from Danish group companies, which rose by DKK 8.1 billion compared to 2021.[10]

Among Danish companies with more than 500 employees, foundation-controlled companies accounted for 15.4% of these in 2022. In comparison, they made up only 0.2% of companies with fewer than ten employees.[11]

It should be noted that there are also a number of significant non-enterprise foundations in Denmark having sizeable ownership interests in Danish companies, often in conjunction with family ownership – for example, Rockwool Fonden, Ole Kirks Fond and Villum Fonden og Velux Fonden.

3. KEY FEATURES

An enterprise foundation is an independent and self-governing entity without owners and residual claimants that own and control one or more companies. An enterprise foundation is typically established for an indefinite period and may

8 Ibid.
9 Ibid.
10 Ibid.
11 Ibid.

thus be regarded as a strong 'commitment device'.[12] Without the sometimes more short-term interests of (controlling) shareholders, an enterprise foundation can focus on its task to maintain the survival of the business and balance the interests of all stakeholders.

Traditional ownership structures may create continuity problems in the event of any separation or buyout of family members, since each and every family member is subject to the main forces of life, such as love, conflict and death.[13] This is by no means to say that families are not able to also (through multiple generations) run and develop large and successful companies.

An enterprise foundation model may foster social responsibility and ethical behaviour by the business that is owned by the foundation, since it is lacking an impatient controlling shareholder. It could be argued that the business of an enterprise foundation is therefore ideally suited to qualify as an impact or purpose organisation. This adds to the legitimacy of the business and the alignment of the stakeholders, thereby increasing the reputation and expression of the business.[14]

The key features of an enterprise foundation are thus continuity, stewardship, commitment and purpose, often combined with philanthropic distributions of the surplus of the business.

4. SHARE CLASSES

Danish company law allows for having different share classes, cf. the Danish Company Law section 45:

> In limited liability companies, all shares carry equal rights. However, the articles of association may provide for different share classes. In that case, the articles of association must specify the differences between the different share classes and the size of each share class.

Danish law allows for having shares with multiple voting rights, cf. the Danish Company Law section 46:

---

12 On commitment in business, see C. Mayer, *Firm Commitment: Why the Corporation is Failing Us and How to Restore Trust in it*, Oxford University Press, Oxford 2017; and S. Thomsen, T. Poulsen, C. Børsting and J. Kuhn, 'Industrial Foundations as Long-Term Owners' (2018) *Corporate Governance: An International Review* 180.

13 I. Koele and R.K. Feldthusen, 'Shareholder Foundations of Enterprises: The North European Style of Securing Family Businesses for the Long Term – Rising up to the Global Challenge' (2020) 26(7) *Trusts & Trustees* 654 et seq.

14 Ibid.

(1) All shares carry voting rights. However, the articles of association of a limited liability company may provide that certain shares carry no voting rights, and that the voting power of certain shares differs from that of the other shares.
(2) Non-voting shares carry a right of representation only if so provided in the articles of association.

Enterprise foundations most often start out owning all the shares but over time a need for further capital for the benefit of the company arises. It thus becomes in the interest of both the company and the foundation that the foundation dilutes its ownership. It is, however, paramount pursuant to the charter that the foundation maintains its position as the controlling shareholder. The solution here is to create shares with multiple voting rights, thus allowing the foundation to maintain the majority of votes and simultaneously obtain more capital for the company by means of new shareholders. See also Jesper Lau Hansen:

> First of all, the recognition that the acquisition of control is unrelated to the distribution of votes on the individual shares and that the capital structure is thus irrelevant should lead to the conclusion that protection against abuse of control is important *regardless* of whether a jurisdiction allows multi-class MVR share structures or only a single class OSOV structure. The minority needs to be adequately protected against the abuse of control and at all times, and we can be proud of the high level of minority protection available in our Nordic company law legislation.
>
> Second, the realisation that the acquisition of control may be economically efficient despite its increased risk should inform us that this hinges on the capacity of the shareholder to actually control and govern the company efficiently. In the Nordics, and probably elsewhere, we find that controlling shareholders are often tied to the founders, either as a family or, more often, as foundations established by the founder. We also find that these controlling shareholders are long-term owners and that they are very good at running the company by carefully monitoring and if necessary disciplining management to increase performance.[15]

The Danish company legislation allowing for multiple voting shares is thus crucial for the success and proliferation of enterprise foundations in Denmark.

Danish company law provides protection of minority (voting) shareholders against abuse of control by majority (voting) shareholders. Any shareholder, regardless of the size of a shareholder's capital and/or votes, including voteless shares, is entitled to table a motion for the agenda of the company's General

---

15 J.L. Hansen, 'Multiple Voting Rights in Shares – Old Misconceptions and New Challenges' (2023) *Nordic & European Company Law* Working Paper No. 23-06, available at SSRN: https://ssrn.com/abstract=4590616 or http://dx.doi.org/10.2139/ssrn.4590616.

Meeting. Also, any shareholder is entitled to participate in the company's General Meeting and has the right to speak and ask questions to the company's board of directors on any matter on the agenda. This right applies regardless of whether the shareholder only holds one share and even if that share does not provide the holder with a vote.[16]

5. OWNERSHIP STRUCTURES

As stated above, enterprise foundations may either carry on their business within the foundation or – as is most often the case in large enterprise foundations – through a majority ownership in a subsidiary. The foundation may elect to insert a holding company between itself and its subsidiary. Enterprise foundations generally retain a voting majority even where the operating company is listed on the stock exchange.

Below are the different main structures of enterprise foundations regarding their business activity.

Here the operating business takes place inside the foundation.

Figure 1. Structure #1

Source: Produced by the author.

Here the operating business takes place in a subsidiary, with the foundation in turn receiving dividends which it can use for distributions pursuant to its purpose.

Figure 2. Structure #2

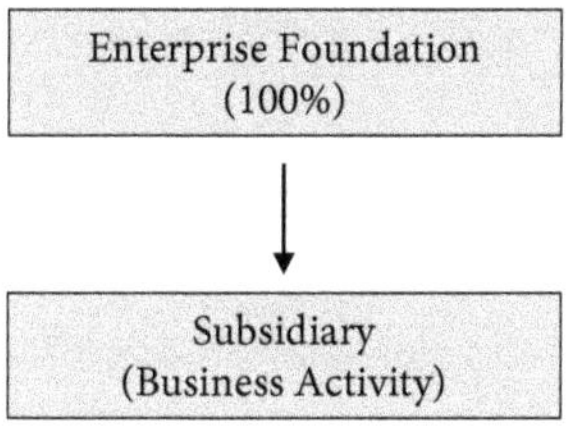

Source: Produced by the author.

[16] R.K. Feldthusen, 'Obstacles and Possible Solutions for the Adaptation of Enterprise Foundations' in M. Bartl, R. Claassen and N. van der Horst (eds), above n. 4.

This is the same as structure #2, with the exception that there are now minority shareholders also having an ownership stake in the operating company. As will be explained below, it might instead be the foundation which has a minority stake in the share capital, but instead has a majority vote in the company.

Figure 3. Structure #3

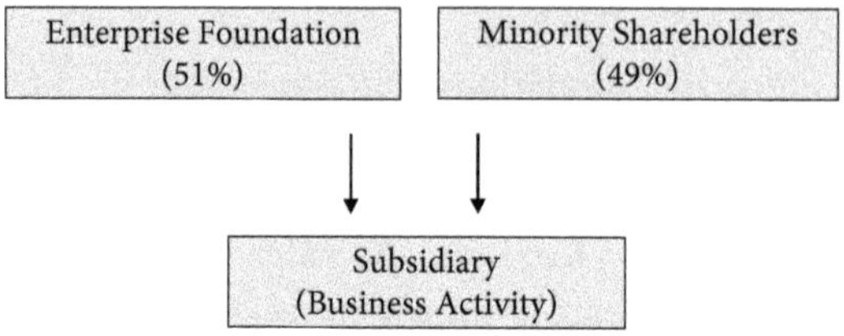

Source: Produced by the author.

Employing holding companies have become more common in large enterprise foundations. There are several reasons for this, but tax is often a factor if the enterprise foundation owns less than 75% of the share capital of the operating company (see section 10 below). Employing a holding company may also serve strategic purposes.

Figure 4 Structure #4

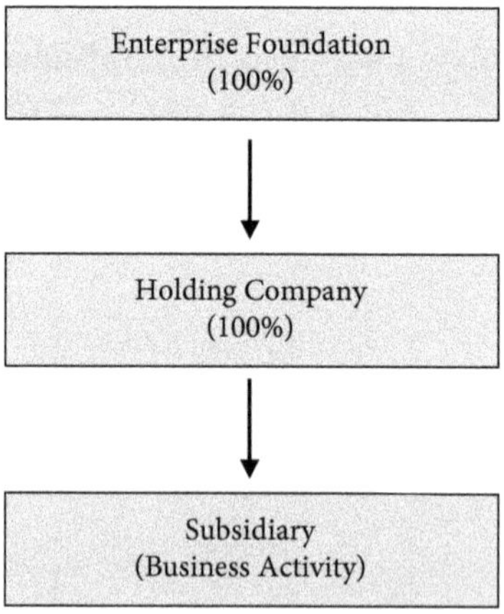

Source: Produced by the author.

The above structures are of course simply generalisations as each foundation group structure is individual and often involves more than one subsidiary, joint venture, etc.

6. SPECIAL DANISH LEGISLATION ON ENTERPRISE FOUNDATIONS

6.1. THE DEFINITION OF 'FOUNDATION'

A foundation is created by a donation (gift or will).

A Danish foundation, whether it is an enterprise or a non-enterprise foundation, is characterised mainly by the following criteria:

a. An irrevocable transfer of property from the founder to the foundation.
b. One or more purposes, being charitable, family and/or commercial.
c. The power to make dispositions of the assets in the foundation rests in a board of directors.
d. The foundation can acquire rights and incur liabilities in its own name (separate legal personality).
e. No natural or legal person outside the foundation has any property rights to the assets in the foundation, which implies that the foundation owns the assets in its own right (self-owned and independent).
f. At least one-third of the members of the board of directors must be independent of the settlor (this does not apply to foundations established before 1985).

Furthermore, the foundation must from the outset be able to exist for at least ten years. The purpose, governance rules, etc. of the foundation are set out in a foundation charter.

6.2. THE DEFINITION OF 'ENTERPRISE FOUNDATION'

The above characteristics apply to foundations in general. In order for a foundation to be an enterprise foundation, it must also fulfil the requirement of carrying out a business activity, either in its own right or through one or more subsidiaries owned or controlled by the foundation (cf. section 2 of the Law on Enterprise Foundations):

> Subsection 1. Pursuant to this Act a foundation is considered being commercial if the foundation:
>
> 1. Trades goods or intellectual property rights, copyright, provides services or the like, for which it normally receives payment,
> 2. Carries out activities involving the sale or lease of real estate, or

3. Has a connection to a limited liability company mentioned in the Companies Act Section 7.[17]

Subsection 2. A foundation is not considered an enterprise foundation if the business activities it conducts, or its connection to the business mentioned in subsection 1, point 3, are of limited scope or only constitute an insignificant part of the foundation's total assets.

Subsection 3. The Danish Business Authority may establish specific rules regarding when a foundation's business activities are considered limited or constitute only an insignificant part of the foundation's assets.

It is a requirement to establish an enterprise foundation that at least DKK 300,000 (approximately €40,000) is donated, either in cash or in kind, to the foundation. When registering a newly established enterprise foundation, the Danish Business Authority conducts a legality check of the charter, and it is a condition that this test is passed in order for there to be a valid enterprise foundation.

The Danish legislator chose a functional approach on how to establish whether a foundation is an enterprise foundation. The reason behind this is that the term 'commercial' or 'enterprise' in the legislation at that time (and also today) encompasses significant variations, making it impossible to formulate a concise, unambiguous and universally applicable concept suitable for use in a proposal for a law on commercial foundations. Consequently, the Law on Enterprise Foundations defines what is to be understood as an enterprise foundation within this legislation.

Enterprise foundations can be linked to business activities either by directly conducting the business themselves or by holding shares or other equity interests in a business, thereby exerting decisive influence over it (holding foundations), cf. section 2, subsection 1, point 3.

The rules in subsection 2, points 1 and 2 address cases where the foundation itself conducts business activities. Subsection 2, point 1, refers to instances where a foundation sells goods or intangible rights (e.g. patents, trademarks or know-how) or provides services or similar offerings (e.g. leasing). To qualify as an enterprise foundation, it is stipulated that the foundation normally receives remuneration in return. It is not decisive whether the business is profitable or whether remuneration is actually paid in a specific situation.

Whether a foundation can be characterised as an enterprise foundation under the Law on Enterprise Foundations is determined not solely by the purpose stated in the foundation's charter but by the activities it actually conducts or the influence it exerts on a business enterprise. Even if the charter specifies the

[17] The quotation has been translated by the author.

purpose as charitable, the foundation may have such a connection to a business enterprise that it is regarded as an enterprise foundation under the law.

Section 1, subsection 2 contains a limitation to the definition of commercial activity, so that a foundation is not considered as an enterprise foundation – and is thus excluded from the scope of the Law on Enterprise Foundations – if the business activities are of limited scope or constitute only an insignificant part of the foundation's total assets. This applies, for example, in cases where the foundation's capital base primarily consists of bonds, mortgage deeds or equity interests such as shares or holdings without associated controlling influence. It also applies in situations where the foundation operates or has the requisite influence over a business that constitutes an insignificant part of the foundation's total asset base. The provision also addresses cases where the foundation's business activities are, in themselves, of limited scope, such as when a foundation owns a small rental property.[18]

The Business Authority has, pursuant to section 1, subsection 3, issued a regulation containing specific rules on when a foundation's business activities are considered limited or constitute only an insignificant part of the foundation's assets:

> Section 1. The business activities of an enterprise foundation are considered limited or constitute only an insignificant part of the foundation's assets if the foundation meets one of the following criteria:
>
> 1) The foundation's gross business revenue is less than DKK 250,000,
> 2) The foundation's gross business revenue accounts for less than 10% of the foundation's total annual income, or
> 3) The foundation's business assets constitute less than 10% of the foundation's total assets.
>
> Section 2. If a commercial foundation fails to meet the criteria in section 1 for three consecutive financial years, the foundation is no longer considered a commercial foundation under the Law on Enterprise Foundations, cf. section 125 of the Law.[19]

If an already existing enterprise foundation no longer fulfils the requirements of being an enterprise foundation it will cease to be subject to the Law on Enterprise Foundations and instead be subject to the Law on Non-enterprise Foundations. This transition is seamless and, importantly, does not incur any taxes. Such a foundation may again in the future become subject to the Law on Enterprise Foundations if the above requirements are fulfilled.

---

[18] 'Betænkning om fonde afgivet af det af justitsministeren den 14. juli 1978 nedsatte udvalg', above n. 3, p. 91.

[19] Bekendtgørelse nr. 1448, 15 of December 2014 on limited commercial activity. The quotation has been translated by the author.

6.3. CAPITAL STRUCTURE

As mentioned above, the capital requirement to establish an enterprise foundation is at least DKK 300,000 (approximately €40,000). Enterprise foundations use the same capital structure as Danish limited liability companies (*anpartsselskaber*) and joint stock companies (*aktieselskaber*) with a division between base capital and free reserves.

The minimum capital requirement relates to the base capital (*grundkapital*) and if the founder wants to establish the foundation with additional funds, the founder has the choice between adding these to the base capital and/or to the free reserves. An enterprise foundation may only make distributions from its free reserves.

Once the enterprise foundation is established, the base capital does not have to be in a special account separate from the foundation's other assets. In the annual report, the base capital is shown as a separate accounting item under equity. The base capital must be stated as an exact DKK amount and cannot be specified as an interval. The base capital also cannot be stated as the assets, e.g. shares in a specific company that the enterprise foundation has received in connection with the establishment of the fund.

The capital structure of a non-enterprise foundation is fundamentally different as its base capital consists of the assets it received when established or which have replaced these, and any capital gains received on these. A non-enterprise foundation does not as such have 'free reserves' but is expected to use the bulk of its net income for distributions.

A founder may specify in the charter that owning the shares of a company is a purpose in itself (see section 6.4 below). In this case, the board of directors is not allowed to divest itself of the shares in the company.

6.4. PURPOSE

Danish law allows a foundation to have any purpose as long as it is not illegal or *contra bono mores*. A foundation may have several purposes – for example, a charitable purpose, a family purpose and a business purpose.

Danish law not only allows an enterprise foundation to either carry out a business or have majority control of a business but also allows the founder to stipulate that the foundation will have a 'business purpose', i.e. that running or owning the business is a purpose of the foundation. This is the case with many of the large Danish enterprise foundations:

Novo Nordisk Foundation:

> [T]o provide a stable basis for the commercial and research activities of the companies in the Novo Group (Novo Nordisk A/S and Novozymes A/S).

Lundbeck Fonden:

> [T]to secure and expand the LUNDBECK GROUP's business.

Bitten og Mads Clausen's Fond:

> The purpose of the foundation is primarily through its holding of shares in DANFOSS A/S – within the provisions of this charter – to strengthen this company for the benefit of all who are connected to the company.

According to the preparatory works of the 1982 report on the first Enterprise Foundation Act, an enterprise foundation may have, as its only purpose, a business purpose. The report states as follows:

> The Committee must emphasise that the purpose of a foundation can be to only pursue business interests, such as to maintain and expand a business enterprise which the foundation either runs itself or in which the foundation owns a significant shareholding. Such foundations exist in practice and the committee's proposal does not change the current law on that point.[20]

The report goes on to state:

> However, the consideration of pursuing the purpose of the foundation and the consolidation of the foundation coincide where the purpose is solely to run the business.[21]

In 2012 a committee charged with drafting a revised act on enterprise foundations reaffirmed the position on an enterprise foundation being allowed to only have a business purpose:

> The Committee emphasises that there is nothing that prevents an enterprise foundation from having only a business purpose and not having an external distribution purpose.[22]

Despite the clear statements in the preparatory works, there is still not a consensus in Danish legal theory on whether an enterprise foundation can have a business

---

20 'Betænkning om fonde afgivet af det af justitsministeren den 14. juli 1978 nedsatte udvalg', above n. 3, p. 98. See also the preparatory remarks to the legislative draft Folketingstidende 1983/84 (2. Saml.), tillæg A, sp. 2846. The quotation has been translated by the author.

21 'Betænkning om fonde afgivet af det af justitsministeren den 14. juli 1978 nedsatte udvalg', above n. 3, p. 115. See also pp. 31 and 115. The quotation has been translated by the author.

22 Erhvervsfondsudvalget, 'Erhvervsfondsudvalgets rapport om fremtidens regulering af erhvervsdrivende fonde' (2012), p. 72. The quotation has been translated by the author.

purpose as its sole purpose. The arguments put forward by the opponents to the above statements are, however, mainly *de lege ferenda* in nature – see, for example, Lennart Lynge Andersen:

> More questionable – with regard to enterprise foundations – is if the purpose is stated as highlighted in the motives (p. 98), e.g. 'The purpose of the foundation is to own and operate N.N.A/S', and the foundation's use of its profits – which must be stated in the articles of association – is concentrated on the limited company in question. Regarding these cases, the motives of the Enterprise Foundation Act are divisive with themselves. The background for the foundation reform and the Enterprise Foundation Act's rules on articles of association and profit use argue that one does not accept a scheme according to which all funds that a foundation receives from a subsidiary can only be used in a continued cycle back to the subsidiary – but opposite here stands the opinion stated in the Foundation Report and the submission of the Minister of Industry. There is no doubt that such foundations existed prior to the fund legislation in 1984 and have existed since 1984.[23]

There is no requirement as to an enterprise foundation making minimum distributions. A minimum requirement for distributions may threaten the interests of the business. This is because foundations by definition do not have owners, and thus only have the revenue stream from the business enterprise and possibly a securities portfolio as a source of financing for the foundation's investments in the business, including for development activities.

Enterprise foundations are, in principle, subject to the same distribution obligations as non-enterprise foundations. However, special considerations apply to enterprise foundations, as these foundations, in addition to fulfilling their charter-based purposes, must also take into account the consolidation and potential further development of the business operations. This includes, for enterprise holding foundations, ensuring the foundation's ability to inject capital into its subsidiary. To the extent that the continuation of the business is an independent purpose of the foundation, these two considerations align.[24]

The Law Committee drafting the report on the proposal for the new law on enterprise foundations stated:

> The importance of the enterprise foundations for the Danish economy via the business activity is far greater than via their distributions. Thus, it is important that the legislation does not impede the business activity of the enterprise foundations.

---

23 L.L. Andersen, *Fonde og Foreninger I – Fondslovene med kommentarer*, 5th ed., Gjellerup, Copenhagen 2003, p. 126. The quotation has been translated by the author. Regarding this discussion, see also E. Werlauff, 'Erhvervsdrivende fonde' (1987) *Juristen* 96; J.H. Mikkelsen, 'En replik vedrørende erhvervsdrivende fonde' (1987) *Juristen* 147.

24 'Betænkning om fonde afgivet af det af justitsministeren den 14. juli 1978 nedsatte udvalg', above n. 3, 35. The quotation has been translated by the author.

> The consideration for the business makes it generally appropriate or even necessary for the foundation to build up reserves which make it possible to participate in later capital increases in the company in connection with mergers or acquisitions, financial crises, major investments and so on. This will be hampered by minimum requirements for distributions.
>
> The business activities of enterprise foundations are quite different and therefore provide widely differing returns depending on industry, competitive position, economic development, tax conditions and so on. It would not make sense to set fixed requirements for distributions across these differences. What is relevant for a foundation's distribution activity is the actual return compared to the company's and the foundation's current situation, while the determination of a return requirement, which must form the basis for a possible minimum distribution, will in any case be based on historical averages. …
>
> In relation to other forms of ownership, foundation ownership is characterised by being long-term, i.e., that the exact requirement for profits in the short term is not exactly the same as in other forms of ownership. This longevity can be challenged by minimum requirements for distributions.[25]

If an enterprise foundation has large free reserves, the state supervisor may enquire about this. If there is no justifiable reason for this, the state supervisor may recommend to the board to consider increasing the foundation's distributions.

Interpretation of the charter and purpose of an enterprise foundation is done solely on the basis of the charter and objectively, cf. the Danish Supreme Court ruling (concerning a non-enterprise foundation, however the same applies to enterprise foundations) in which the Court states:

> It is a fundamental principle of foundation law that the founder irrevocably separates the foundation's assets from their personal estate, as expressly stated in section 1, subsection 2 of the Law on Foundations. As noted in the legislative preparatory works for this provision (Parliamentary Record 2013-14, Appendix A, Bill No. L 114, p. 15), this means, among other things, that the founder's intentions for the foundation must be expressed when drafting the charter (articles of association) or related documents.[26]

It is thus important that all of the founder's wishes and intentions are clearly expressed in the articles of the foundation's charter.

---

25 Erhvervsfondsudvalget, above n. 21, p. 261. The quotation has been translated by the author.

26 The quotation has been translated by the author.

6.5. HARD AND SOFT LAW GOVERNANCE RULES

The Danish Law on Enterprise Foundations includes governance rules (hard law) which are complemented by recommendations on governance (soft law). The soft law governance rules are discussed in section 7 below.

The main governance rules are that a board of directors must comprise of at least three natural persons. The board of directors may employ an executive tasked with the daily management of the foundation, but otherwise this function also belongs to the board of directors. At least one-third of the board of directors must be independent of the founder of the foundation.[27] The board of directors is tasked with only being allowed to pursue the purposes and interests of the foundation.

A majority of the board of directors may not be employed as executives in the foundation, and an executive may not also be chairperson or vice-chairperson of the board. This prohibition is to avoid an unwanted concentration of power in that person. The provision is supplemented by a provision barring a chairperson of the board from performing duties for the foundation that are not part of the position as chairperson, i.e., a 'working chairperson'. However, a chairperson of the board may, where there is a special need for this, perform tasks which the person in question is requested to perform by and for the board.

The management or an equivalent body in the foundation, and members of the management or an equivalent body of the foundation's subsidiaries and of a company which is not a subsidiary, but in which the foundation and its subsidiary exercise a significant influence on the company's operational and financial management, may not appoint members to the board of the foundation. This provision is to avoid bottom-up appointment to the board of the foundation. In other words, is must be the head (the foundation) that wags the tail (of the subsidiary), not the other way round.

The chairperson or vice-chairperson of the board of directors may not be an executive of a subsidiary or of a company that is not a subsidiary, but in which the foundation and its subsidiary exercise a significant influence on the company's operational and financial management, unless the Business Authority (the state supervisor on enterprise foundations) provides permission. This provision is to ensure a degree of separation and independence between the foundation and the management of the subsidiary.

The founder, his or her spouse or permanent cohabitant or persons linked to the said persons by consanguinity or in-laws in the right ascending or descending line or the collateral line as close as siblings, cannot constitute the majority of the board without the consent of the foundation authority.

---

27 Originally the requirement was just one independent person. This requirement was adopted from tax law before there was any legislation on foundations in order to ensure that there was an independent ownership other than that of the founder's economy.

If an enterprise foundation has been established by a company,[28] a person who directly or indirectly owns more than half of the ownership shares or voting shares in the company may not, without the consent of the Business Authority, constitute the majority of the board together with the people so closely linked to a founder, the founder's spouse/permanent cohabitant or family, just as the latter persons cannot, without the consent of the Business Authority, constitute the majority of the board. In the same way, the majority of a founding company's management may not, without the consent of the Business Authority, constitute the majority of the board of directors together with persons who have the above-mentioned specified affiliation with the relevant management members. This provision is to avoid a founder circumventing the prohibition described above by instead establishing the foundation by means of a company.

The members of the board are duty-bound to only pursue the interests and purposes of the foundation.

A member of the board of directors or an executive may not take part in the consideration of questions concerning agreements between the enterprise foundation and the person concerned or actions against the person him- or herself, or about agreements between the foundation and third parties or actions against third parties if the person concerned has a significant interest in them which may be contrary to those of the foundation.

Members of the board of directors or executives may not make such dispositions as to obviously provide the aforementioned or others with an undue advantage at the foundation's expense. Improper board decisions that violate the law or the charter are invalid.

Agreements between the foundation and one or more members of the board of directors or executives are only valid if they are drafted in a way that can be documented later unless they are agreements on usual terms as part of a current account.

The Business Authority has the power to dismiss one or more members of the board of directors if the Business Authority deems it necessary. Nobody else can have a power to dismiss a member of a board of directors.[29] A member may, of course, always resign from the board.

Board members are chosen by means of either co-optation or appointment by third parties, or a combination of both.[30] Third parties can, for example, be an organisation, a public authority, or a private person.

---

28 The general assembly of a company may by vote decide to donate to a charitable purpose, for example, an enterprise foundation with a charitable purpose. Depending on the value of the donation, this can be done by either a simple majority or a supermajority in the company, in some cases with an obligation on the majority shareholders to redeem a minority of the value of their shares should they demand that.

29 The Business Authority may also dismiss the entire board of directors.

30 If the appointment of a board member does not take place according with the foundation's charter, the appointment is done by the Business Authority.

Board members must fulfil certain requirements to be appointed and during their tenure at the board. A member of the board of directors must resign from the board if the person in question is bankrupt, due to long-term illness or other impairment, has proven to be unable to hold the position as a member of the board of directors, commits an act that makes them unworthy to continue to be a member of the board of directors or should generally be considered as being unsuitable to perform the tasks of a board member.

As a non-profit organisation, the enterprise foundation is barred from distributing its net earnings to anyone exercising control over it. Professor Henry Hansmann has described this prohibition on distribution of profits as the 'nondistribution constraint':[31]

> A nonprofit organization is, in essence, an organization that is barred from distributing its net earnings, if any, to individuals who exercise control over it, such as members, officers, directors, or trustees. By 'net earnings' I mean here pure profits – that is, earnings in excess of the amount needed to pay for services rendered to the organization; in general, a nonprofit is free to pay reasonable compensation to any person for labor or capital that he provides, whether or not that person exercises some control over the organization. It should be noted that a nonprofit organization is not barred from earning a profit. Many nonprofits in fact consistently show an annual accounting surplus. It is only the distribution of the profits that is prohibited. Net earnings, if any, must be retained and devoted in their entirety to financing further production of the services that the organization was formed to provide. Since a good deal of the discussion that follows will focus upon this prohibition on the distribution of profits, it will be helpful to have a term for it; I shall call it the 'nondistribution constraint'.
>
> Most non-profits of any significance are incorporated. For these organizations, the nondistribution constraint is imposed, either explicitly or implicitly, as a condition under which the organization receives its corporate charter. Thus, a nonprofit corporation is distinguished from a for-profit (or 'business') corporation primarily by the absence of stock or other indicia of ownership that give their owners a simultaneous share in both profits and control.[32]

In his definition of a non-profit, Professor Hansmann emphasises whether the organisation's net profit can be paid out to people who manage it. The fact that a non-profit creates – and aims to create – profit does (subject to legislation that stipulates otherwise) not matter as to whether an organisation is a non-profit: 'the nondistribution constraint … is the defining characteristic of non-profit organizations'.[33]

---

31 H. Hansmann, 'The Role of Nonprofit Enterprise' (1980) 89(5) *Yale Law Journal* 835.
32 Ibid., 838.
33 Ibid., 842.

According to section 49 of the Law on Enterprise Foundations, remuneration to members of the board of directors and executives may not exceed what is considered customary according to the nature of the position and the scope of work, and what may be considered justifiable in relation to the enterprise foundation and in parents foundations in the group's financial position.

According to section 87 of the Law on Enterprise Foundations, founders, members of the board of directors and executives, auditors or persons holding a senior position in the foundation may not be granted any benefits from the foundation. The aforementioned are only allowed to receive a remuneration which may not exceed what is considered usual according to the nature of the position and the extent of the work involved. The same applies to a person who is connected to one of the persons mentioned by marriage or permanent cohabitation, and the minor children of such persons.

Both of these provisions are expressions of 'the nondistribution constraint' according to which the net profit – regardless of how this may be created – must only be used for the furtherance of the foundation's purpose.

Steen Thomsen comments on this as follows:

> The separation transforms the foundation into a non-profit entity, which, as emphasized by Hansmann …, may make profits but cannot distribute those profits to the organization's members, directors, officers, or other persons who exercise control of the organization.[34]

6.6. CO-DETERMINATION

The Danish Companies Law has rules on co-determination, by granting employees a right to elect company or group representatives to the board of directors of the foundation. These rules apply correspondingly for enterprise foundations and their subsidiaries with some modifications. The rationale behind applying these rules also to enterprise foundations is that electing to conduct business by means of an enterprise foundation should not deprive employees of their right to co-determination. Additionally, applying this requirement also to enterprise foundations ensures a level playing field with companies.

The right to co-determination applies both where the persons are employed in the foundation itself (foundation representation) and where they are employed in the enterprise foundation's subsidiaries (group representation).

The enterprise foundation, respectively the group, must in the last three years have employed an average of at least 35 employees.

The employees may elect a number of members to the enterprise foundation's board of directors corresponding to half of the other board members rounded

34 S. Thomsen, above n. 4, p. 15.

up, but always have a right to elect at least two members, or three members in case of there also being group representation. The board members appointed by the charter of the enterprise foundation must always constitute the majority of the members on the board of the foundation.

There are, of course, situations where an enterprise foundation differs from that of a company and where it is prudent to modify the rules of co-determination. The first modification is where the enterprise foundation has a purpose which provides for distributions to, e.g. charity. Board members, who are elected by the employees, may accordingly only participate in the consideration of questions that do not concern the business enterprise if this is stipulated in the charter of the enterprise foundation. The second modification deals with the election of new board members not being elected by the employees. If the charter states that one or more of the non-employee representative board members are elected by way of co-option, the board members elected by the employees do not participate in this appointment, unless otherwise specified in the charter of the enterprise foundation.

6.7. FAMILY FOUNDATIONS

An enterprise foundation can have a family purpose as either one of its purposes or its sole purpose. This will most often be to benefit the family of the founder. There are no legal restrictions as to how much can be distributed to the family members.

As of 1 January 1985, when the two Danish foundations laws entered into effect, they included a rule against perpetuities. According to this rule, charters which confer on members of a particular family or families a right to preferential distribution shall not have legal effect according to their content to the extent that the preferential right extends beyond those living at the time of incorporation and to one unborn generation.[35] A rule of perpetuities already existed in the Danish Inheritance Act in relation to *fideicommissa*[36] as a consequence of the prohibition in the Danish Constitution against family *fideicommissa*.[37] It was

---

35 To avoid a circumvention of the rule against perpetuities, this applies *mutatis mutandis* to charter which confer on members of a particular family or families preferential rights to hold a particular position or otherwise, including in the form of remuneration, to receive financial benefits from the foundation or from an undertaking over which the foundation has a controlling influence. However, this does not apply to positions as a member of the board of directors.

36 As opposed to a foundation, a *fideicommissum* is not a legal person and is not governed by a board of directors. Instead, a *fideicommissum* relies on the conditions stipulated by the testator on the order of succession. For a comprehensive analysis of *fideicommissa* in Denmark, see R.K. Feldthusen, *Succession*, DJOEF Publishing, Copenhagen 2001.

37 See section 87 of the Danish Inheritance Law: 'Inheritance [which is not subject to forced heirship rules] may be inserted by will in a succession order [*fideicommissum*], so that the

thus natural that this rule would also be made applicable to foundations once legislation was drafted.

The rule against perpetuities similarly applies to provisions in a charter that grant members of a specific family or certain families preferential rights to hold a particular position or otherwise, including in the form of remuneration, receive financial benefits from the foundation or from a company over which the foundation has controlling influence. However, this does not apply to roles as members of the board of directors.

The rule against perpetuities only applies to foundations established on or after 1 January 1985. This was to not infringe upon the legitimate rights of already-established foundations and their beneficiaries. Hence, there are older foundations which today are distributing to later generations of the founder.

For all practical purposes, foundations for the benefit of the founder's family are not established any longer as the tax implications are disincentivising (see further section 10 below).

7. ROLE OF STATE SUPERVISION

Even before Denmark enacted its two foundation laws in 1985, it was possible for foundations to request the receipt of a royal confirmation. By doing so, the foundation would become subject to public supervision by the governmental ministry with the closest connection to the purpose of the foundation, i.e. if the foundation had as its purpose to support culture, then it would be the Ministry of Culture having the supervisory function.

From 1985, the supervision of foundations was assigned to the Danish Business Authority (enterprise foundations) and the National Board of Civil Affairs (non-enterprise foundations).

The Business Authority exercises legal supervision to ensure that the board of directors adheres to the law and the charter of the foundation. The Business Authority does not have the competence to question the board of directors' decisions, which are not in contravention with these legal requirements.

The Business Authority may issue orders on specific matters in relation to the foundation, for example, reduce the board remuneration if it is considered unreasonable, order the board of directors to take the necessary steps to reduce or increase distribution according to the purpose(s) of the foundation, etc.

Several of the provisions in the Danish Enterprise Foundation Act are subject to a fine – for example, for violating the rule against a majority of the members of the board of directors being employed as directors of the foundation and the

---

inheritance goes to an heir or legatee in the first place and then one or more other heirs or legatees in the second or later places. In the case of a will, inheritance or bequest may not be attributed to several unborn persons in succession upon the testator's death'.

rule against a director also being the chairperson or deputy chairperson of the board of directors.

The Business Authority may decide on a special audit (*granskning*) of a foundation, its management or its annual reports. One or more special auditors are appointed at the expense of the foundation and may require all information relevant to the audit.

The Business Authority may remove one or more members of the board of directors. As the removal of board members is a far-reaching intervention, this power is only to be used in situations where a need has clearly manifested itself to dismiss the board member in question and replace this person with a more competent and responsible board member.

The Business Authority is authorised to initiate a lawsuit holding the board of directors, accountants, special auditors, appraisers and/or third parties liable for damages.

If the board is contemplating extraordinary decisions that may entail a risk that the charter may not be complied with or that the foundation will not be able to continue to exist, it must obtain the consent by the Business Authority in advance. It should be noted that this approach cannot be used to achieve a result that is in contravention with the purpose and charter of the foundation. In this case, the board of directors must follow the procedure of amendment of the purpose, which can only be allowed if pursuing the purpose is no longer possible or is clearly unsuitable.

A foundation must apply to the Business Authority if it wants to make amendments to its charter and/or purpose. The criterion for allowing a change of the charter is that the existing provision is not suitable. If the amendment instead concerns the purpose or other material provisions (for example, concerning the dissolution of the foundation), the criterion is that it is otherwise either impossible or unsuitably qualified for the foundation to continue without the requested amendment.

The requirements for allowing a foundation to amend its purpose may, on the face of it, seem rigid with regard to the foundation's business purposes, as changes in the market and competitors, etc. require a flexible and expedited process for amendments. The Business Authority has over the years however proven to understand the needs and wishes of foundations of having their business purposes amended in order for the foundations to stay competitive. Often a need to amend a foundation's business purpose is to raise capital to the company and that means relaxing the foundation's ownership stake, typically from 100% to a lower ownership stake, even below 50%, but then with a requirement to maintain a controlling influence through a majority of votes. Over time, several large Danish enterprise foundations – with the approval of the Business Authority – have amended their business purposes in order to retain a majority of votes (preferential voting shares), but have diluted their ownership:

- Carlsberg Foundation: 75% of the votes and 29% of the share capital in Carlsberg A/S.[38]
- Novo Nordisk Foundation (through Novo Holdings A/S): approximately 77% of the votes and approximately 28% of the share capital in Novo Nordisk A/S, and approximately 74% of the votes and approximately 29% of the share capital in Novonesis A/S.
- A.P. Møller Foundation (through A.P. Møller Holding A/S): 51.45% of the votes and 41.51% of the share capital in A.P. Møller – Mærsk A/S.

The existence of a pragmatic business-oriented state supervisor and the possibility of splitting up shares between share capital and votes have been paramount in ensuring that the foundation-controlled companies have had access to raise more capital.

Any decision made by the Business Authority may be appealed to an administrative complaints board which publishes its decisions, although these are anonymised. Public access is given to decisions made by the Business Authority and documents pertaining to this.

8. RULES ON DISCLOSURE AND TRANSPARENCY

As enterprise foundations are separate legal entities running a business or controlling an operating company, the disclosure requirements have generally been the same as for other Danish limited liability companies, i.e. public annual accounts and registration in a central public business registry.

With the new legislation on enterprise foundations in 2015 came additional requirements as to disclosure and transparency. It is now a requirement that all transactions with related parties, whether at market value or not, are disclosed in the enterprise foundation's annual accounts. The legislation uses the definition of 'related parties' in the International Accounting Standards (IAS 24). If, for example, a member of the board of directors renders services to the foundation at market value, it must be disclosed in the annual accounts.

The foundation must disclose the total remuneration of the board of directors and management in two separate categories in its annual accounts.[39]

---

38 In 2000, the Carlsberg Foundation's board of directors was granted permission to in the future – in connection with a share issue and/or merger – change the purpose of the foundation from having a controlling interest in the Carlsberg Brewery to instead having a 'significant influence', in order to ensure the preservation of 'Carlsberg' as a widespread and recognised beer brand and continue beer production in Denmark.

39 If the information about remuneration will lead to the display of amounts for a single member of a management category, the amounts may instead be stated together for the two categories or omitted if only one category receives remuneration, a pension or a special incentive programme.

The foundation must establish and publish its distribution policy. The requirement is intended to improve public insight into enterprise foundations grant giving. As part of the policy, the foundation must state which main categories to which the board of directors have made distributions during the financial year. The distribution policy must contain any strategy prepared, as well as guidelines and goals that the board of directors follows when making distributions. The distribution policy cannot just be a copy of the foundation's charter but must be an elaboration of how the foundation specifically realises its purpose though its distributions.

In 2014 a Committee on Foundation Governance was established. Its purpose was to issue a set of recommendations on which the enterprise foundations were obligated by law to report, but on a comply-or-explain principle. It is thus voluntary for an enterprise foundation to follow the recommendations, but it must report whether it does or not, and in the latter case the explanation on why it does not follow and how the foundation has instead designed its governance.

Failure to comply with a recommendation is not considered a breach of rules but merely implies that the board of directors has specifically, and for the reasons it has explained, chosen a different approach.

The state supervisor can order the board of directors to account for its response to the recommendations when the foundation:

- fails to address one or more recommendations,
- fails to explain a deviation, provides an explanation for a deviation that is apparently unjustified or without meaning or
- explains a deviation but does not explain what it decided to do instead.

The reporting on the recommendations is made public either through the foundation's annual report and/or its website. The requirement to report applies to all approximately 1,400 enterprise foundations.

As of 2025 there are 19 recommendations divided into the following categories:[40]

1. Transparency and communication.
2. Tasks and responsibilities of the board of directors.
    a. Overall tasks and responsibilities.
    b. Chairperson and the other members of the board.
    c. Composition and organisation of the board of directors.
    d. Independence.

[40] The recommendations can be found at: https://godfondsledelse.dk/english. The author is deputy chair of the Committee on Foundation Governance.

  e. Appointment period.
  f. Evaluation of the performance of the board of directors and executive board.
3. Remuneration of the board of directors and management.

The recommendations are meant to reflect best practice and thus go above and beyond the hard law requirements in the Danish Law on Enterprise Foundations, which can be illustrated with the two recommendations on independence and remuneration mentioned below (sections 2.4.1 and 3.1.1):

> Independence
>
> 2.4.1 It is recommended that at least one third of the members of the board of directors (excluding employee representatives) are independent.
>
> ...
>
> If the board of directors (excluding any employee representatives) is composed of
>
> - three members, at least one member should be independent,
> - four to six members, at least two members should be independent,
> - seven to nine members, at least three members should be independent, or
> - ten to twelve members, at least four members should be independent, and so on.
>
> A board member is not considered independent in this context if, for example, the individual:
>
> - is or has been, within the past three years, a member of the executive board or a senior employee of the foundation, a significant subsidiary, or an important associated company of the foundation;
> - has received, within the past five years, substantial remuneration, including distributions or other benefits, from the foundation, a subsidiary, or an associated company of the foundation, other than as a member of the foundation's board;
> - has had, within the past year, a significant business relationship (e.g. personally or indirectly as a partner, employee, shareholder, customer, supplier or management member in companies with similar connections) with the foundation, a subsidiary or an associated company of the foundation;
> - is or has been, within the past three years, employed by or a partner of the foundation's or its subsidiaries' external auditor;
> - has been a member of the foundation's board or executive management for more than 12 years;
> - is a close relative or otherwise closely connected to persons who are not considered independent;
> - is a founder or a significant donor or contributor;
> - is a board member of the foundation, where the foundation's purpose is to provide support to the board member's family or others closely connected to the board member;

> – is a management member of an organisation, another foundation, or similar entity that has received or repeatedly received substantial donations from the foundation within the past five years; or
> – is a management member of an organisation, another foundation, or similar entity that has granted or repeatedly granted substantial donations to the foundation within the past five years.
>
> In addition to the above, there is also a recommendation on providing information on each member of the board of directors on the following:
>
> – the individual's name and position;
> – the individual's age and gender;
> – the date of joining the board, whether reappointment has occurred, and the end of the current appointment period;
> – the member's specific competencies, if any;
> – the individual's other management positions, including roles in executive boards, boards of directors, and supervisory boards, as well as management committees in Danish and foreign foundations, companies, institutions, and demanding organisational tasks;
> – whether the individual owns shares, options, warrants, or similar instruments in the foundation's subsidiaries and/or associated companies;
> – which members are appointed by authorities, grant providers, etc; and
> – whether the member is considered independent.
>
> Pursuant to the recommendations, the board of the foundation should periodically assess whether its composition and the competencies of its members, both individually and collectively, reflect the requirements of the foundation's purpose, including both its business and charitable objectives, strategy, financial position and other relevant circumstances. The assessment should also consider the board members' ability and willingness to independently and impartially fulfil the foundation's purpose.
>
> Remuneration of management
>
> 3.1.1 It is recommended that any remuneration to the foundation's board members is fixed and not variable. Members of a potential executive board should also be compensated with a fixed remuneration, possibly combined with a bonus which should not be dependent upon accounting results.

The role of a board member in a foundation entails a special obligation to ensure that the board's decisions on remuneration are made solely to fulfil the foundation's purpose and interests, and that the remuneration corresponds exclusively to the responsibility and effort associated with the board position.

The Business Authority is tasked with enforcing the obligation to comply or explain, but whether a foundation complies or instead explains is equally as good.

9. CORPORATE SUSTAINABILITY REPORTING

Enterprise foundations and certain limited liability entities, including cooperative societies, are subject to the Danish Law on Financial Statements but are not regulated under the Accounting Directive[41] because these types of entities are not governed by EU law. In Denmark, enterprise foundations, cooperative societies, and similar entities are therefore generally subject to the same reporting requirements, including – as point of departure – sustainability reporting, as public and private limited companies.

The position of the Danish Government is that certain unique large Danish business forms and group structures, including certain enterprise foundations and cooperative societies, should be included, even though they are not covered by the EU Corporate Sustainability Directive (CSRD).[42] The position of the Danish government is due to the great importance enterprise foundations (and cooperatives) have in Danish society, including the fact that many of Denmark's largest companies are either run in these forms of business or are controlled by them. This position also aligns with the current Danish rules on corporate social responsibility reporting, ensuring that these unique Danish business forms and group structures are not excluded from the regulations simply because they are not governed by EU law.

It should be noted that since distributions from enterprise foundations are treated as a disposition of profit under the Law on Financial Statements, similar to dividend payouts by regular companies. The Danish Government has assessed that this approach should be maintained, so that distributions and their recipients are not subject to sustainability reporting requirements.

10. TAXATION

10.1. INCOME TAXATION

On 1 January 1987 a separate law on taxation of foundations entered into force. As a point of departure, foundations, whether enterprise foundations or

41 Directive 2013/34/EU of 26 June 2013 on the annual financial statements, consolidated financial statements and related reports of certain types of undertakings [2013] OJ L182/19. Enterprise foundations, cooperative societies etc. are however not regulated in this Directive because their types of entities are not governed by EU law.

42 Directive (EU) 2022/2464 of the European Parliament and of the Council of 14 December 2022 amending Regulation (EU) No 537/2014, Directive 2004/109/EC, Directive 2006/43/EC and Directive 2013/34/EU, as regards corporate sustainability reporting [2022] OJ L322/15. It should here be noted that EU on the 14 April 2025 adopted Directive (EU) 2025/794, also known as the 'Stop-the-Clock Directive' which contained key amendments to the Corporate Sustainability Reporting Directive (CSRD), including excluding certain entities from having to report altogether or postponing reporting obligations for certain other entities.

non-enterprise foundations, are taxed in the same way as corporations. This means that foundations are taxed at the same tax rate as companies (currently 22%), and on the same types of income, capital gains, etc. as companies.

However, foundations enjoy greater access to deducting costs and may furthermore deduct charitable distributions from their income. A foundation may also set aside income for later charitable distributions with a deduction if the aforementioned is used for actual distribution within a maximum of five years.

The rationale behind the tax legislation is thus that foundations, which make charitable distributions, should be able to reduce their taxes by the amount of the distributions. Tax deductibility of charitable distributions is important both to encourage foundations to make distributions and to avoid double taxation (as the recipient might be liable to tax of the distribution).[43]

Foundations are not able to be jointly taxed with their subsidiaries. If the foundation owns at least 10% of the share capital, it receives dividends from its subsidiary tax free. However, before any charitable distributions can be deducted in the foundation, the distributions must first be offset against tax-free dividends from its subsidiary.

It is, however, recognised that a foundation may transfer the income of a subsidiary to the foundation, before the income is taxed in the subsidiary, if the foundation uses this income for charitable distributions. Thereby the foundation can achieve a full deduction of the income in the subsidiary in its charitable distributions, effectively avoiding paying any tax. However, this only applies to subsidiaries in which the foundation owns at least 75% of the share capital and only if the subsidiary is owned directly by the foundation, and thus not through other companies, such as a holding company.

10.2. TAX ON THE ESTABLISHMENT OF AN ENTERPRISE FOUNDATION

Establishing a foundation with a charitable purpose does not incur any taxes, whether it is by way of a gift or will. If a business purpose is added, it is still tax free if it is by way of gift, but if it is instead in a will, there is a risk the tax authorities will not grant tax exemption and the foundation will then incur an inheritance tax of 36.25%.[44] Foundations with a family purpose (including as one of their purposes) incur a tax of 20% if the transfer is by way of a gift and 36.25% in inheritance tax if the transfer is by way of a will.

A transfer of tax-relevant assets to a foundation will trigger capital gains which have to be paid by the donor or the estate of the deceased donor. However, it is

43 Non-charitable distributions cannot be deducted by the foundation. Instead, the recipient is only taxed on 80% of the value.

44 This is not logical and is a consequence of Danish tax rules not having been harmonised.

under certain conditions possible to either a) transfer the tax burden onto the foundation or b) altogether avoid paying capital gains on transferring shares in a company to a foundation pursuant to special tax rules implemented to encourage the establishment of more enterprise foundations in Denmark.

Model b) is a favourable way of transferring the shares of a company without either the founder or the foundation incurring any taxes whatsoever. It is, however, a prerequisite, that the shares to be transferred are owned – in practice 100% – by another company (a holding company).

11. FINAL REMARKS

The Danish model in relation to enterprise foundations has proven to be successful and has supported large Danish companies to grow even larger over the years. In a way, the story of enterprise foundations is like the story of the bee. According to traditional laws of aviation, there is no way that a bee should be able to fly, as its wings are too small to get its body off the ground. However, on further inspection, the secret of bee flight, researchers say, is the unconventional combination of short, choppy wing strokes, a rapid rotation of the wing as it flops over and reverses direction and a very fast wing-beat frequency.[45] Correspondingly, according to traditional economic theory, enterprise foundations should be inefficient and outcompeted by their for-profit competitors, as companies are motivated by profit maximisation of their owners, and because enterprise foundations have no owners and board members no personal profit motive.[46] However, the case of Denmark serves as showcase that enterprise foundations actually can fly and prosper and thus are a viable instrument to combine long-termism, purpose, business and philanthropy.

---

45 D.L. Altshuler, W.B. Dickson, J.T. Vance, S.P. Roberts and M.H. Dickinson, 'Short-Amplitude High-Frequency Wing Strokes Determine the Aerodynamics of Honeybee Flight' (2005) 102(50) *PNAS* 18213; and Caltech, 'Deciphering the Mystery of Bee Flight' (2005): https://www.caltech.edu/about/news/deciphering-mystery-bee-flight-1075.

46 S. Thomsen, above n. 4, pp. 25 et seq.

INDUSTRIAL FOUNDATIONS UNDER ITALIAN LAW

Eugenio Barcellona

ABSTRACT

Enterprise foundations are a legal institute that, in the past, has not found widespread application in Italy. This chapter analyses the reasons for this phenomenon and the subsequent evolution of enterprise foundations in Italy. After addressing the cultural and political reasons for which foundations have largely been neglected (section 1), the original provisions of the Italian Civil Code will be analysed (section 2). Then, section 3 will cover the doctrinal developments of the 1960s that reinstated the legitimacy of foundations. Subsequently, the three most important pieces of legislation on the matter will be examined: the 1990s laws on banking foundations (section 4), the 2000 law on recognition of legal personality and on the requirements of the foundation's 'purpose' (section 5) and the 2017 Code of the Third Sector (section 6). The chapter will conclude with a reflection on the current state of enterprise foundations and the directions towards which their further evolution should aim.

1. INTRODUCTION

In Italy, 'industrial foundations' or 'enterprise foundations' – i.e. profit-driven companies held by private law foundations – are a rather rare phenomenon. The reasons for this minor significance are essentially twofold.

The first reason is cultural: it is mainly rooted in the Catholic and Marxist influence that shaped Italian culture. 'Industrial foundations' thrive in those jurisdictions where, to use Max Weber's words,[1] 'the spirit of capitalism' blossoming out of 'Protestant ethics' is deeply rooted:[2] under the Protestant perspective, not only does the pursuit of profit on earth not violate any religious writ, but on the contrary signifies an ascetic and vocational tendency towards productive work. Profit is not merely an instrument of accumulation of wealth to live an opulent life, but rather clear and objective evidence of the success of the entrepreneur's creative endeavour. It is no coincidence that Walter Rathenau's well-known theory of *Unternehmen an sich*[3] originated in a predominantly Protestant context. More than just a money-making machine, an enterprise is an 'institution' that, through profit, ultimately contributes to the wellbeing of the entire community.

---

1 M. Weber, 'Die Protestantische Ethik und der "Geist" des Kapitalismus' in W. Sombart, M. Weber and E. Jaffé, *Archiv für Sozialwissenschaft und Soziapolitik*, Mohr Siebeck, Tubingen 1904–1905, nn. 20–21 (translated into Italian: P. Burresi (trans), *L'etica protestante e lo spirito del capitalismo*, Sansoni, Florence 1970, passim).

2 P. Rescigno, 'Le "non profit organizations" come formazioni sociali' in G. Ponzanelli (ed), *Gli enti 'non profit' in Italia*, CEDAM, Padua 1994, p. 263.

3 The theory of the *Unternehmen an sich* became known to Italian audiences thanks to the publication of W. Rathenau, 'La realtà della società per azioni. Riflessioni suggerite dall'esperienza degli affari' (1960) *Riv. soc.* 912.

Such an institutional view of enterprises never really took root in Italy. The Catholic ethic, unlike the Protestant one, always looked askance at those who handled the 'devil's excrement' (a Catholic expression to describe money).[4] From a very different perspective, Marxism helped to portray the entrepreneur as the 'evil' exploiter of the proletariat. Last but not least, a highly non-meritocratic structure of crony capitalism made the equation 'profit = deserved success' hardly credible.

The second reason for the limited diffusion of 'enterprise foundations' is directly linked to the specific regulatory framework.[5] Italian foundation law has traditionally been very hostile to 'enterprise foundations'.[6] However, such an aversion has been constantly on the wane over the last few decades so that the latest approach, even though it does not yet qualify as 'welcoming', is no longer as markedly 'hostile' as it was at the outset.[7]

This chapter is structured along a chronological timeline of the evolution of the law of foundations: first, the law of foundations as etched in the

---

4 J. le Goff, *Lo sterco del diavolo. Il denaro nel Medioevo*, 5th ed., Laterza, Bari 2012, passim, illustrates the influence of Catholicism over the antagonism against profit-driven economic activities.

5 On Italian foundation law in general, see, amongst others, C.M. Bianca, *Diritto civile, 1: La norma giuridica e i soggetti*, 2nd ed., Giuffrè, Milan 2002, pp. 343 et seq.; F. Galgano (1), 'Delle persone giuridiche' in A. Scialoja and G. Branca (eds), *Commentario del codice civile*, Zanichelli-Foro Italiano, Bologna-Turin 1969, *sub* art. 16, pp. 185 et seq.; F. Galgano (2), 'Fondazione, 1) Diritto civile' in *Enciclopedia giuridica Treccani*, Ed. Enc. It., Rome 1989; P. Rescigno (1), 'Fondazione (dir. civ.)' in *Enciclopedia del Diritto*, vol. XVII, Giuffrè, Milan 1968, pp. 791–814; P. Rescigno (2), *Le fondazioni: prospettive e linee di riforma*, CEDAM, Padua 1989, pp. 480 et seq.; A. Carrabba, *Scopo di lucro e autonomia privata. La funzione nelle strutture organizzative*, ESI, Napoli 1994, pp. 319 et seq.; V. Iudica, 'Fondazioni, fedecommesserie, trusts e trasmissione della ricchezza familiare. Limiti e prospettive del sistema successorio' (1994) II *Nuova giurisprudenza civile commentata* 47; A. Zoppini, *Le fondazioni. Dalla tipicità alle tipologie*, Jovene, Naples 1995, pp. 54 et seq.

6 On enterprise foundations specifically, under Italian law, see, amongst others, R. Costi, 'Fondazioni e impresa' (1968) I *Rivista di diritto civile* 1; P. Rescigno, 'Fondazione e impresa' (1967) *Rivista di Diritto Societario* 812; A. Zoppini, above n. 5, p. 61; A. Zoppini, 'Considerazioni sulla fondazione di impresa e sulla fondazione fiduciaria regolate da una recente legge francese' (1991) I *Rivista di diritto commerciale* 573; D. Vittoria (1), 'Le fondazioni culturali ed il consiglio di amministrazione. Evoluzione della prassi statutaria e prospettive della tecnica redazionale' (1975) *Rivista di diritto commerciale* 297; D. Vittoria (2), *Le fondazioni culturali e il consiglio di amministrazione*, Jovene, Naples 1976, pp. 56 et seq.; A. Barba, *Associazione, fondazione e titolarità di impresa*, Jovene, Naples 1996, pp. 95 et seq.; G. Ponzanelli, *Gli enti collettivi senza scopo di lucro*, 2nd ed., Giappichelli, Turin 2000, pp. 177 et seq.; A. Cetra, *L'impresa collettiva non societaria*, Giappichelli, Turin 2003, passim; G. Baralis, 'Enti no profit: profili civilistici' (1999) *Rivista del notariato* 1091; G.F. Campobasso, 'Associazioni e attività di impresa' (1994) II *Rivista di diritto civile* 581.

7 A survey of 'corporate foundations' (i.e. foundations that are established by corporations, but that do not necessarily own enterprises) that also includes some information about 'enterprise foundations' is provided by Fondazione Bracco and Fondazione Sodalitas, 'Le fondazioni di impresa in Italia: Rapporto di ricerca 2019': https://www.sodalitas.it/public/allegati/_%E2%80%9CLe-fondazioni-d%E2%80%99impresa-in-Italia%E2%80%9D,-Rapporto-di-ricerca,-2019_2019917184724996.pdf.

(very few) provisions of the Italian Civil Code of 1942 is described (section 2). Then, the scholars' evolution that occurred in Italy during the Republican age, with specific reference to the late 1960s (section 3). Subsequently, the most significant legal enactments are examined: (i) the 1990s laws on banking foundations (section 4); (ii) the 2000 law on recognition of legal personality and on the requirements of the foundation's 'purpose' (section 5); and (iii) the 2017 Code of the Third Sector (section 6). The final section is dedicated to the conclusions drawn from the preceding discussion (section 7).

2. FOUNDATION LAW IN THE ITALIAN CIVIL CODE

2.1. INTRODUCTION: THE PERSISTENCE OF THE CIVIL CODE'S OLD RULES

Nowadays, the Italian regulation of foundations is still governed by few and rather incomplete articles of the Italian Civil Code of 1942. It is true that, from the entry into force of the Civil Code until today, certain important special foundation laws have been enacted that have somehow enriched Italian foundation legal regime. Yet, the provisions of the Civil Code have never been amended. It is worth mentioning that, upon the approval of the 'enabling act' (*legge-delega*) that led to the approval of the Code for the Third Sector, the government was originally delegated by the Parliament not only to organically regulate the so-called third sector, but also to coherently revisit the by then outdated regime provided by the Civil Code.[8] As the government failed to fulfil this task, the provisions of the Civil Code technically remain still in force.[9]

We can anticipate our conclusions: the law of foundations set by the Civil Code, as interpreted by the early commentators, represented an insuperable obstacle to the spreading of 'enterprise foundations' in Italy. Here, in brief, are the reasons for this.

2.2. THE LEGACY OF BOURGEOIS IDEOLOGY IN THE INTERCONNECTED REGULATION OF 'FOUNDATIONS' AND 'PROPERTY'

The regime of the 1942 Italian Civil Code testifies to the influence of two different cultural backgrounds: (i) a 'bourgeois' background that can be traced back to the influence that the French Civil Code of 1804 exerted on the Italian

[8] See Article 1, para. 2, a) of the Enabling Act ('*legge-delega*') no. 196 of 6 June 2016.
[9] See section 6 below.

Civil Code of 1865 and then on the Code of 1942; and (ii) an 'authoritative' background that traces back to the specific cultural climate of the two decades of fascism in which the Civil Code of 1942 was drafted.

The bourgeois-liberal ideology did not look favourably upon foundations, since it aimed at modifying the property regime to overcome the feudal regime in order to free the market once and for all. There is indeed a strong systematic link between the Civil Code's regulation of foundations and that of property.[10]

In simplified terms, the feudal regime of property was based on the distinction between the superior property right of the lords (*dominum emines*), giving the lord the right to claim a perpetual rent from its ownership (the land) and the so-called right to use (*dominium utile*), which gave the vassal the right to manage, and benefit of, the asset in exchange for the payment of the census (the rent). The two rights circulated separately, so that the property was, in fact, a divided property (*dominium divisum*).[11] Clearly, such regulation impedes the productive exploitation of the land. As the rent due to the owner of the *dominum eminens* was set once and for all, and, as such, was exempted from market negotiation, a proper management of the costs and revenues of land use, according to rationally capitalistic criteria, was basically impossible. For example, under market conditions, a deterioration in land productivity would have led to a reduction in rent; on the other hand, the feudal regime of *dominum indivisum* radically prevented such an effect, thereby worsening the position of the land exploiter.

The bourgeois regime of property overcomes the inefficiencies of the feudal regime through a revolutionary unification of property regulation: no more separation between *dominum eminens* and *dominum utile*, but rather a sole 'property right' consolidating the right to benefit from the good in the manner deemed most appropriate and the right to sell it on the market or dispose of the leasehold only.[12] Hence, the 'rent' always and in any case due to the holder of *dominus eminens* is abolished, thus creating the conditions for that legal regime, welcomed by capitalistic bourgeoisie, that linked the value of the good's use to the changing dynamics of the market.

The bourgeois regime of property – systematically regulated in the Napoleonic Code of 1804 for the first time – clearly celebrates the liberal ideology of the 'efficient self-interest' that was described in scientific terms by Adam Smith shortly before (1776): since every 'owner' is naturally oriented to

10 R. Costi, above n. 6, 2, highlighted the connection between the legal regime of property on the one hand and the legal regime of foundations on the other hand.

11 The theory of *dominium divisum* in largely addressed in P. Grossi, *Il dominio e le cose*, Giuffrè, Milan 1992.

12 C.B. Macpherson, *Libertà e proprietà alle origini del pensiero borghese – La teoria dell'individualismo possessivo da Hobbes a Locke*, ISEDI, Milan, 1973; P. Grossi, 'La proprietà e le proprietà nell'officina dello storico' in P. Grossi, above n. 11, pp. 648–665.

the maximisation of personal interests (according to the *homo oeconomicus* paradigm) and since the interaction of self-interested owners is naturally oriented towards achieving the best allocation of resources, the more the law incentivises the 'efficient' bourgeois property regime, the more it will procure that scarce resources are destined to their best use. Clearly, the ideology that presides over such regulation of property rights postulates that the efficient use of property can be achieved only with the consolidation in the same individual of the 'management power' (control) on the one hand, and the 'right to the related economic benefits' (ownership) on the other. Since every individual is naturally driven by self-interest (*homo oeconomicus*), the allocation of the economic benefits to the manager itself secures the utilisation most wanted by the market.

Certainly, this bourgeois ideology of property right inspires important provisions originally drawn up by the French Napoleonic Code and still in force today in Italian law under the Civil Code of 1942:[13] (i) the provision allowing the constitution of the right of usufruct (which, in a certain way, mirrors the division between *dominium eminens*, mere property, and *dominium utile*, usufruct), but, notably, only for the maximum duration of the usufructuary's life or, in event that the usufructuary is a legal entity, for a maximum duration of 30 years; (ii) the provision that, coherently, in the case of the constitution of the usufruct by will, forbids the so-called subsequent usufruct (meaning the transfer of the right of usufruct from a first usufructuary to a second usufructuary); (iii) the provision that allows the constitution by will of a perpetual allowance only to the extent that it serves a 'public utility' purpose and, additionally, that enables the release of the allowance payer (thus ultimately allowing the termination of a potentially perpetual obligation); and (iv) lastly, the provision, once again in the field of successions, that prohibits the so-called *fideicommissum* (meaning the testamentary disposition by virtue of which, following the death of the heir, the assets are transferred to another individual chosen by the testator), with the sole exception of a *fideicommissum* established by the caretaker of an individual unable to act and therefore in need.[14] Indeed, (i) a perpetual separation between mere property and usufruct, or (ii) the constitution of perpetual burdens in the absence of a public utility purpose, if allowed, would have jeopardised the 'efficient self-interest' ideology that, on the contrary, postulated the consolidation of 'management power' (control) and related 'economic benefits' (ownership) in the same hands.

In light of the above, one could easily understand why foundations were doomed to face a strong opposition. The bourgeoisie's hostility to foundations

---

13 M.V. de Giorgi, 'Fondazioni di famiglia e attività d'impresa' (2005) II *Nuova giurisprudenza civile commentata* 80.

14 L. Ghidoni, 'Il legato di usufrutto universale' in G. Bonilini and V. Barba (eds), *Le disposizioni testamentarie*, UTET, Turin 2012, pp. 682 et seq.

can be explained by two correlated reasons. First, the allocation of an asset to a legal entity constituted for its perpetual conservation and use for the benefit of certain individuals was thought to pave the way for a subtle reinstatement of the feudal type of property:[15] once the property of the good is transferred to the foundation, such a good is inevitably withheld from circulation and thus its allocation to the most 'efficient' owner is prevented. Second, there was a fear that the disentanglement between the 'management power' and 'claims on economic benefits' could generate inefficient results, according to the same rationale underpinning the perceived efficiency of the 'bourgeois property': a manager with no interest in the results of the management and with no control by an 'owner' has no incentive to ensure the most profitable management of the assets.[16]

The bourgeois-liberal ideology's hostility to foundations – as evidenced, for example, by the French physiocrat Turgot, who advocated for their total prohibition[17] – is at the root of the eloquent silence on the subject by the French Civil Code, which inspired the first unitary Italian Civil Code of 1865 and, later on, the 1942 Code.[18] The Italian legislature of 1942 did not follow the

15 A. Zoppini, 'Quattro tesi per una rilettura delle norme sulle fondazioni' in G. Ponzanelli, above n. 2, p. 78 ('[T]he preposition of an asset to an end – the Idealtypus of the foundation – seemed to the bourgeois legislator, educated to the physiocratic doctrine, incompatible with a political program aimed at promoting the free circulation of profit and the rational exploitation of capital and had, on the other hand, evocated the memory of the "divided property" and the eminent domain')(*'La destinazione di un patrimonio allo scopo, in questo si risolve l'Idealtypus della fondazione, era sembrato al legislatore borghese educato alla dottrina fisiocratica incompatibile con il programma politico vòlto a favorire la libera circolazione della ricchezza e il razionale sfruttamento della ricchezza ed aveva, semmai, evocato il ricordo della "proprietà divisa" e del dominio eminente'*).

16 P. Rescigno (1), above n. 5, p. 803 ('[T]he revolt against this institution, during the Enlightenment and the French revolution, was also based on the risk that through foundations, multiplied by the human desire to achieve immortal deeds, many resources and particular properties would be, in the end, absorbed, in order to achieve goals storically obsolete or no longer felt as useful in society')(*'La rivolta contro l'istituto, nell'età dell'Illuminismo e della rivoluzione francese, prese a motivo proprio il pericolo che attraverso le fondazioni, moltiplicate dalla vanità umana di dare immortalità ad opera dell'uomo, rimanessero a lungo andare assorbite tutte le risorse e le proprietà particolari, e poste al servizio di scopi storicamente superati o non più avvertiti come utili nell'ambiente sociale'*).

17 R. Turgot, 'Fondation. Article de l'Encyclopédie' (vol. VII, 1757) in G. Schelle (ed), *Oevres de Turgot*, vol. I, Librairie Félix Alcan, Paris 1913, p. 593.

18 A. Zoppini, above n. 15, pp. 69–70 ('[T]he reasons for this adversion – which penetrated indistinctly into all legal systems that had the French one as a model – can be summarised essentially in the convergence between the physiocratic dogma, the fear of intermediate bodies hypertrophy, and the conceptual (before than practical) rejection with the fractioning of an asset owned by a single individual')(*'I motivi di questa avversione – che indistintamente è penetrata negli ordinamenti che hanno avuto a riferimento il modello francese – possono compendiarsi essenzialmente nella convergenza tra il dogma fisiocratico, il timore dell'ipertrofia dei corpi intermedi, il ripudio concettuale, prima ancora che pratico, della possibilità di frazionare il patrimonio imputato ad un solo soggetto'*).

French path of total silence, but addressed foundations with few and inconsistent provisions.

Foundations are permitted, provided they are established by public deed (Article 14 of the Civil Code (CC)); the deed of foundation is qualified as irrevocable even by the founder him or herself (Article 15 CC); recognition of legal personality – following which the contributed assets are part of a 'separate patrimony' – is subject to the issuance of a licence and is therefore left to the discretion of the public administration; the purchase of real estate properties is subject to the authorisation of the public administration (Article 17 CC). Lastly, the public administration has the power to transform, or even dissolve, a foundation in the event of the impossibility or 'poor usefulness' of its purpose (Articles 27–28 CC).

Actually, the provisions of the Civil Code do not specify what the purpose of the foundation might be. However, according to an almost unanimous consensus among interpreters of the Civil Code of 1942, foundations could pursue only purposes of 'public utility'.

Such an interpretation, even in the absence of a clear legislative provision, was inferred (i) from the provisions, which are still effective today, that permit a *fideicommissum* in favour of an entity (such as a foundation) only insofar as it is intended to protect a 'needy' individual (Article 692 CC), as well as (ii) from further provisions that admit perpetual allowances only to the extent that they are intended for 'public utility' purposes.

In summary, foundations represented a danger to the bourgeois-liberal ideology that inspired the 1942 Civil Code: there was a risk of the reinstatement of a property regime dangerously similar to the feudal regime and a further risk of an inefficient property regime. However, foundations were not completely neglected (as they were in the French system); on the contrary, they are explicitly tolerated, but only to the extent that, at least according to the prevailing interpretation, they were justified by the pursuit of 'public utility' – a purpose that, generally, should have been fulfilled by the state, but that, exceptionally, could be entrusted to those 'intermediate bodies'[19] that were looked upon suspiciously by the liberal culture.[20] This distrust rested on the following

---

[19] Organised groups of private citizens, other than profit-driven companies, that pursue collective ends.

[20] P. Rescigno (1), above n. 5, p. 793 ('The refusal of the so-called intermediate bodies, and the function that they had absolved up until that point, was mainly aimed against corporativism and, on the other side, Church institutions and activities')('*La negazione dei corpi sociali cosiddetti intermedi, e della funzione ch'essi avevano assolta in un lungo arco di tempo, era diretta a colpire soprattutto l'organizzazione corporativa e, in altra parte della realtà sociale, le istituzioni e le attività della Chiesa*'); G. Ponzanelli, 'Terzo Settore: la legge delega di riforma' (2017) 5 *Nuova giurisprudenza civile commentata* 726 ('The discipline of the Code was characterised by great hostility against intermediate bodies, and would later reveal its structural limitations against this social phenomenon, that spread more and more') ('*La disciplina codicistica era caratterizzata da una forte ostilità nei confronti degli enti intermedi*

assumption: private citizens naturally pursue the objective of maximising their own interests and, thanks to the interaction of selfish individuals, the market achieves the best allocation of resources; instead, it is the state, and the state alone, that naturally pursues 'common good' as its objective.[21]

2.3. THE HERITAGE OF THE FASCIST CULTURE: THE SUBJECTION OF FOUNDATIONS TO 'POLICE LAW'

The Civil Code's regulation of foundations also drew inspiration from a second ideology which is related to the specific cultural climate of the fascist era in which the 1942 Code was approved – a cultural climate whereby, notoriously, the state took an authoritarian and dirigiste approach in relation to private activities.

In this cultural context, it is no surprise that public interference on private activity was (and still is) particularly strong under the Civil Code – especially with reference to 'entities' that were thought to pose a threat to the productive utilisation of goods.

---

e, in seguito, ha accentuato i suoi limiti strutturali nel confronto con un fenomeno sociale che si faceva sempre più diffuso').

21 This was, for instance, the view of A. Solmi, *L'idea fascista nel nuovo Codice civile*, Soc. editrice del Foro Italiano, Rome 1940, pp. 91 et seq. P. Rescigno (1), above n. 5, p. 797 addresses this original approach with these critical words: ('one would read, on the official comments to the new laws, that the assumption, by the state, of all the duties that had something to do with the general interest, reduced the field in which juridical persons "of private character" could operate (and therefore the system of norms set forth by the Civil Code was aimed at controlling the residual space of action of that activity, rather than promoting its expansion)') ('*accadeva di leggere, nei commenti ufficiali ai nuovi testi legislativi, che l'assunzione, da parte dello Stato, di tutti i compiti che toccassero in qualche misura l'interesse della generalità rendeva assai ristretta l'area in cui potessero muoversi le persone giuridiche "di carattere private" (e perciò il sistema di norme predisposte nel codice civile voleva servire piuttosto a controllare quell'àmbito residuo di libera attività, che a favorirne l'espansione)*'). More recently, a similar comment has been made by D. Preite, 'Lo scopo negli enti del primo libro del codice civile: nuovi sviluppi in dottrina e in giurisprudenza' in G. Ponzanelli, above n. 2, p. 285 ('for the traditional liberal culture that inspired the Civil Code the market operated as an instrument of efficient production and resource allocation, as a place of intersection and coordination of people that aimed at economical and egoistical objectives, in particular the maximisation of their profit. The state, on the other hand, was the instrument for the expression of the sum of each individual will. Consequently, entities that did *not* aim at the aforementioned goal appeared extraneous, and almost an obstacle, to both the efficiency of the market and the regular functioning of the state') ('*per la tradizionale cultura liberale che ha ispirato il codice civile il mercato operava come strumento di efficiente produzione ed allocazione di risorse in quanto luogo di incontro e coordinamento di soggetti miranti a scopi economico-egoistici ed in particolare alla massimizzazione del loro profitto. Lo Stato risultava a sua volta strumento ed espressione della somma di volontà individuali. Gli enti che* non *mirano allo scopo suddetto apparivano conseguentemente estranei e quasi di intralcio sia all'efficiente operare del mercato che al normale funzionamento della politica e dello Stato*').

As mentioned earlier, the subordination of recognition of juridical personality to a licensing procedure was already capable of vesting the governmental authority with discretionary power on the establishment of a foundation. However, the 1942 Civil Code goes well beyond that. Indeed, it vests the governmental authority with: (i) the power to control and supervise the foundation's assets; (ii) the power to appoint and substitute the directors in the event of the impracticability of the provisions of the by-laws; (iii) the power to annul the resolution, *inter alia*, on the grounds that they are contrary to 'public order and decency'; (iv) the power to dissolve the foundation in the event of unlawful management; (v) the power to authorise a liability action against the directors and to appoint an extraordinary commissioner to replace them; (vi) the power to order the coordination of the activity of multiple foundations or the unification of their management; (vii) the power to transform or dissolve the foundation in the event of supervening impossibility of purpose or 'scarce utility' and, lastly, (viii) the power to allocate, in the event of dissolution of the foundation, the remaining assets to entities having 'similar purposes' (Articles 25–32 CC).

The fact that this regulation stemmed not only from the liberal ideological distrust towards 'intermediate bodies', but also from the specific cultural atmosphere of the fascist era is blatant. Foundations are subject to what has been disdainfully called 'police law'.[22]

However, attention should be paid to one important aspect: the governmental authority's control and supervision over the management of foundations was not only the result of the specific political and cultural climate, but also a response to the real need to regulate entities without owners. Indeed, in the presence of a (substantial) 'owner' of reference in collective institutions (as is the case with associations or, typically, commercial companies), the incentive for efficient management is closely linked to the incentives of such naturally selfish owners. In the inherent absence of an 'owner' instead (as in the unique case of foundations) – the risk of a manager (the holder of the power, but devoid of risks) acting unlawfully arises from the relevant utter separation

---

22 P. Rescigno (1), above n. 5, p. 797 ('the political climate that saw the birth of the Civil Code naturally lead to adopting, and to some extent also exaggerating, that idea of foundations ... which can be characterised as "police law" ... so that when, on the one hand, the novelty of the Italian Civil Code (in contrast with the Napoleonic Code and the post-unitary Code) was highlighted, it was only about the new discipline of private legal persons, while on the other hand the aim was to minimise the extent of the innovations') ('*il clima politico che vide nascere il codice civile vigente era naturalmente portato a far propria, ed anzi ad irrigidire, quella concezione delle fondazioni ... che può dirsi di "diritto di polizia" ... [c]osì, mentre veniva sottolineata la novità del codice civile italiano (rispetto al code Napoléon e al codice italiano post-unitario), consistente nella disciplina legislativa delle persone giuridiche private, dall'altro lato si cercava di ridurre al minimo la portata dell'innovazione*').

between ownership and control. Liability rules ensure the alignment between management and the purpose pursued; yet, whereas an 'owner' (i.e. the principal) exists, the manager (i.e. the agent) is 'disciplined' by the risk of paying damages; when the 'owner' does not exist, such a mechanism runs the risk of short-circuiting. Thus, a governmental authority vested with the function of controlling and supervising the foundation's management was meant to fulfil the objective need to preserve the functionality of the management. In other words, the governmental power of control and supervision acted as a 'substitute' to the private owner control that could be deemed to be structurally lacking in private foundations thus conceived.[23]

2.4. THE ORIGINAL SCHOLARSHIP'S OPINION OPPOSING 'ENTERPRISE FOUNDATIONS'

Given that this was the legislative framework set by the Civil Code of 1942, it is no surprise that the scholarship's concern of the time focused on 'whether Italian foundations could carry out economic activities' and, specifically, 'whether they could carry out profit-driven economic activities'. The responses to both these queries were negative.

According to the scholarship of the time,[24] there was a rigid distinction between, on the one hand, those entities governed by the First Book of the Civil Code (namely, together with foundations, 'associations' and 'committees') and, on the other hand, the entities governed by the Fifth Book of

---

23 R. Costi, above n. 6, 47 ('for the protection of their interests, the administrative authority – an external body – intervenes, which operates to prevent that this autonomy in the management would lead to an abuse against those for whom the activity should be carried out. To summarise the contraposition between the two organisational models [i.e. company v. foundation], we argue that, while the corporation is the expression of liberty and autonomy, the institution is the expression of the authority; or, in other words, that while in the corporation there is a tendential coincidence between power and risk, in the foundation there is power without risk, and a risk without power') ('*[a] tutela dei loro interessi interviene un organo esterno al gruppo, l'autorità amministrativa, che vigila per impedire che tale autonomia di gestione si traduca in un abuso ai danni di coloro a vantaggio dei quali tale attività deve svolgersi. Volendo esprimere in estrema sintesi la contrapposizione dei due moduli organizzatori* [i.e. company v. foundation] *diremo che mentre nella corporazione si esprime il momento della libertà e dell'autonomia, nella istituzione si esprime il momento dell'autorità; o anche che, mentre nella corporazione v'è una tendenziale coincidenza fra potere e rischio, nella fondazione … v'è un potere senza rischio e un rischio senza potere*'). For a similar opinion, see D. Vittoria (1), above n. 6, 334–335.

24 A. Falzea, 'Brevi note sui caratteri differenziali fra società e associazione' (1947) III *Giur. compl. Cass. civ.* 987; E. Zanelli, *La nozione di oggetto sociale*, Giuffrè, Milan 1962, pp. 53–95; C.M. Bianca, above n. 5, pp. 334–351.

the Civil Code (namely, individual and collective enterprise – hence, commercial companies).

The argument ran as follows: the former (foundations, associations and committees) are totally precluded from carrying out 'economic activities' (i.e. activities directed at the production and exchange of goods or services, according to the definition of 'entrepreneur' provided by Article 2082 CC), which were the prerogative of the latter entities (in particular, commercial companies), to the extent that the pursuit of profit was prohibited for the former and were set as a mandatory purpose for the latter.

In other words, a *summa divisio* was thought to exist between entities governed by the First Book of the Civil Code ('foundations', 'associations' and 'committees') and those governed by the Fifth Book ('individual enterprises' and 'companies'): liberal organisations pursuing idealistic, altruistic or public utility purposes in the former case, and economic activities for profit-making egoistic purposes in the latter case.[25]

Based on such classifications, the widespread opinion was that foundations could not carry out any activity other than mere acts of charity,[26] thereby legitimising 'dispensing foundations' only. Foundations could never pursue any profit-making purpose (which, instead, was a distinctive trait of companies, as prescribed by Article 2247 CC), but only 'public utility' purposes (inherently idealistic and altruistic).

As a result of such an opinion of the predominant scholarship at the time, the Italian jurisdiction was not only hostile to enterprise foundations, but also quite repressive: in the eyes of the first interpreters of the Civil Code, a foundation owning an enterprise and therefore carrying out a profit-driven economic activity was an oxymoron, a mix of 'sacred' (the pursuit of the altruistic 'public utility' purpose, which was primarily reserved for the state) and 'profane' (the pursuit of the selfish goal of profit, naturally sought by individuals).

In this context, it was simply impossible for enterprise foundations to find shelter in Italy: for one thing, they might run the extremely serious risk of being declared unlawful (with the consequent denial, *ab origine*, of legal personality), and also they would have been subject to pervasive public powers of interference, a strong deterrent for anyone intending to assign the management of an enterprise to a foundation.

---

25 This traditional view is examined in critical terms by G. Ponzanelli, 'Le nuove frontiere del primo e quinto libro del codice civile' in G. Ponzanelli, above n. 2, pp. 3–9.

26 This opinion was drawn directly from Article 16 CC which imposes on the by-laws of the foundations to provide for 'criteria and procedures for the supply of allowances' (unofficial translation), thus making purportedly clear that the foundations that the Italian Civil Code had taken into account were charity foundations only.

3. THE NEW CLIMATE IN REPUBLICAN ITALY: THE OPENING BY SCHOLARSHIP AND THE RESISTANCE OF CASE LAW

3.1. THE OPINION OF SCHOLARS

The strong 'hostility' towards 'enterprise foundations' marked by the regulatory framework and by its scholarly interpretation began to fade, at least from an academic point of view, by the end of the 1960s, mainly thanks to the contributions of two distinguished legal scholars.[27]

Three main factors affected the academic debate on the matter. First, after the diffusion of foundations created in Liechtenstein (*Anstalten*) by Italian citizens, scholars had begun to question whether such foreign foundations were compatible with Italian jurisdiction, with favourable opinions beginning to erode the negative attitude of the recent post-war period.[28]

Second, following the Republican Constitution of 1948 and its acknowledgement of the so-called 'intermediate social entities' (that are now explicitly deemed worthy of legal protection), and along with the gradual diffusion of a less state-centric culture, a more favourable attitude towards such 'intermediate bodies' had started to gain momentum.[29]

Third, certain German scholars' opinions promoting an innovative use of foundations[30] began to spread in Italian legal culture. Notably, in Germany, in the aftermath of World War II, a certain stance developed to promote the use of foundations for the socialisation of 'large companies' intended to benefit the entire community.[31] As testified by the coeval US experience, such large companies were characterised by 'owners' relegated to the irrelevant role of minority shareholders without effective influence on management. This called

27 These scholars are notably P. Rescigno (1), above n. 5, pp. 790–814 (a distinguished professor of private law), and R. Costi, above n. 6, 1–49 (a distinguished professor of business law). An analysis of their respective views underlining both the converging and diverging elements thereof is provided by A. Zoppini, above n. 15, 62–63 and, particularly, above n. 4.

28 See L.M. Baiada, 'L'Anstalt, il suo riconoscimento nel diritto italiano e le conseguenze in caso di intestazioni di comodo' (1985) *Rass. dir. civ.* 513.

29 D. Vittoria (1), above n. 6, 299; P. Rescigno (1), above n. 5, pp. 793–795.

30 R. Gordeler and P. Ulmer, 'Der Stiftungszweck in der Reform des Stiftungsrechts, zugleich Überlegungen zur Behandlung von Unternehmensstiftungen un Familienstiftungen im Künftigen Stiftungsrecht (1963) 8(11) *Die Aktiengesellschaft* 292, 292 and 328 et seq.; J. Plagemann, 'Stiftungsunternehmen' (1962) *Aktiengesellschaft* 199; H. L. Steuck, *Die Stiftung als Rechtsform für witschaftliche Unternehmen*, Duncker & Humblot, Berlin 1967, pp. 59 et seq.

31 A. Weber, *Sozialisisierung zugleich als Friedenssicherung*, Lambert Schneider, Heidelberg 1947, pp. 8 et seq.; A. Mitscherlich and A. Weber, *Freier Sozialismus*, Lambert Schneider, Heidelberg 1946, p. 31.

for the emergence of a new 'owner' – indeed, the foundation – capable of overcoming the agency problem between potentially self-referential managers (agents) and the entire constituency of the shareholders or, better, of the stakeholders in general (employees, consumers, local communities).[32] This pro-foundation German stance was favourably viewed by those Italian scholars who tried to rejuvenate Italian foundations.[33]

---

32 R. Costi, above n. 6, 4 ('The *Stiftungsunternehmen* rose as a general instrument for the general organisation of the enterprise during the socialisation programmes advanced in Germany immediately after the war, as a formula that would prevent the reconstruction of private industrial empires, while also allowing the irrenounceable rationalisation of production through big productive units. The shape of the foundation could bind the management of the enterprise to some general interests, such as those of the consumers, the workers and in general the national economy') ('*Lo Stiftungsunternehmen assurse a strumento generale di organizzazione dell'impresa nell'ambito dei programmi di socializzazione proposti in Germania nell'immediato dopoguerra come formula che avrebbe impedito il riformarsi di imperi industriali privati, pur consentendo l'irrinunciabile razionalizzazione della produzione attraverso la concentrazione in grandi unità produttive. La forma della fondazione avrebbe potuto ... vincolare l'esercizio dell'impresa ad alcuni interessi di carattere generale come l'interesse dei consumatori, dei dipendenti e in generale dell'economia nazionale*').

33 P. Rescigno (1), above n. 5, pp. 811–812 ('the tendency ... to declare the legitimacy of such foundations [i.e. enterprise foundations] tried to justify itself on the grounds of positive law, but most of all it wants to claim the "configuration" of the foundation as the best one for the actual configuration and concrete mode of acting of the enterprise. In short, the foundation is considered the most adequate tool, more than any other, to accommodate the developments of modern capitalism. With regard to this "configuration", it claims both the full legitimacy and the intrinsic ability to bend and adapt to the needs and the hidden "institutional" enterprise ideologies. The idea of the "enterprise as such" reduced too much, or even tried to erase, the interest of the "proprietors", meaning the shareholders, ... to transfer to the production facilities, the workers and managers the interest of the company. The foundation seems to fulfil such needs, since the property is just formally attributed to the foundation but, in practice, it presents itself as a "property without subject"') ('*La tendenza ... a dichiarare la piena legittimità di siffatte fondazioni [i.e. enterprise foundations] cerca di giustificarsi sul terreno del diritto positivo, ma soprattutto vuole rivendicare alla "forma" della fondazione la migliore rispondenza all'attuale modo di configurarsi e di concreto operare dell'impresa capitalistica. In breve, la fondazione viene considerata lo schema idoneo, più di ogni altro, a dar veste legale agli sviluppi del capitalismo contemporaneo. Della "forma" descritta si rivendica, dunque, oltre che la piena legittimità la capacità intrinseca di piegarsi alle esigenze e alle ideologie nascoste nelle dottrine "istituzionali" dell'impresa. L'idea della "impresa in sé" riduceva in un margine troppo esiguo o addirittura mirava ad annullare l'interesse dei "proprietari" e cioè degli azionisti ... per trasferire all'organismo produttivo, ai lavoratori, ai managers l'interesse dell'impresa. La fondazione sembra rispondere all'indicato orientamento, per il fatto che la proprietà è solo formalmente imputata al soggetto fondazione e nella sostanza si presenta come una "proprietà senza soggetto"*'); R. Costi, above n. 6, 2–3 ('Of such relevance [i.e. the relevance of enterprise foundations] it was aware of the German doctrine that, in the years immediately following the Second World War, amply debated the *Stiftungsunternehmen* in both political and juridical forums, adopting it as the typical operative instrument for some economic policies officially adopted by the country. The Italian doctrine did not perceive the importance that the structural model of the foundation could have both with regards to the general enterprise doctrine and to that of property; on the other hand, it believed that it could conclude that positive right would postulate a substantial incompatibility between enterprise and foundation, in the sense that this could not be constituted with the sole purpose of exercising an entrepreneurial activity. This

It was thus precisely at the end of the 1960s that a very innovative scholarship orientation went so far as to propose a revolutionary interpretation of the norms of the Civil Code. Since the Code did not explicitly require the pursuit of a public utility purpose, it was concluded that even a completely 'selfish' foundation would not have been incompatible with Italian law.[34] Thus, a use hitherto totally unknown to the practice was revealed: that of an enterprise foundation constituted by an entrepreneur who, on the one hand, entrusts the management of its enterprise to the foundation, but, on the other hand, does so with the aim of making his or her descendants the beneficiaries of the foundation's allowances (and therefore indirectly of the enterprise's profits). In other words, for the first time, the enterprise foundation was suggested as an efficient estate planning tool: an absolute separation between 'ownership' and 'control' could reconcile the need for economically providing for the heirs with the need for institutionally professional management of the enterprise.

Although this was a minority view at the time, it certainly marks the great schism between the legal culture associated with the Civil Code of 1942 and the legal culture that was emerging in post-war and post-fascist republican Italy.

Although some legal scholars have gone so far as to support the complete acceptance of 'family foundations'[35] and, in particular, 'family foundations that have control over a business' (industrial family foundations), the position that prevailed throughout these years falls somewhere between the two.[36]

---

argument cannot be shared: we believe that even in our legal system a *Stiftungsunternehmen* can be hypothesised.') ('*Di tale rilevanza* [i.e. the relevance of enterprise foundations] *si è resa conto quella dottrina tedesca nella quale, sin dagli anni immediatamente successivi alla seconda guerra mondiale, lo Stiftungsunternehmen è stato al centro di ampi dibattiti giuridici e politici assurgendo spesso a ruolo di strumento operativo tipico di alcuni programmi di politica economica ufficialmente proposti per quel paese; la dottrina italiana generalmente non ha avvertito l'importanza che il modello strutturale della fondazione può assumere sia sul piano della teoria dell'impresa, sia su quello della proprietà, ed ha anzi creduto di poter concludere che il diritto positivo avrebbe sancito una sostanziale incompatibilità tra impresa e fondazione, almeno nel senso che questa non potrebbe essere costituita al solo scopo di esercitare un'impresa. Tale impostazione non può essere condivisa: noi crediamo infatti che anche nel nostro ordinamento sia perfettamente ipotizzabile uno Stiftungsunternehmen*').

34 R. Costi, above n. 6, 13–15 ('the structure of the foundation … can be used, just like that of the corporation, to achieve the most diverse goals, and, in particular, it is not true that the foundation must always pursue an interest that does not involve the founder') ('*la struttura della fondazione … può essere usata, così come quella della corporazione, per raggiungere i più diversi scopi e in particolare non è vero che la fondazione debba sempre perseguire un interesse estraneo al fondatore*').

35 R. Costi, above n. 6, 13–15.

36 P. Rescigno (1), above n. 5, pp. 812–813, paved the path for this direction. See also G. Ponzanelli, above n. 25, pp. 3 et seq.; G. Ponzanelli (2), 'Enti senza scopo di lucro' in *Dig. disc. priv., sez. civ.*, VII, UTET, Turin 1991, p. 468; P. Schlesinger, 'Categorie dogmatiche e normative in tema di non profit organizations' in G. Ponzanelli, above n. 2, pp. 275–290.

True, foundations are entities with an 'altruistic' aim. However, nothing prohibits a foundation from obtaining the resources needed to fulfil these 'altruistic' goals by operating an 'egoistic' business. Nor could one argue that this would have blurred the boundaries between 'foundations' and 'companies'. In the case of 'companies', profit is 'the ultimate end': profit is pursued in order to be distributed to the 'owners'. Conversely, in the case of 'foundations', profit is a mere means to an end: it is pursued only for fundraising purposes, so that the funds can be then used for the ideal purpose.[37]

The opening regarding the admissibility of business activities carried out under private law foundations is also the result of the proper interpretation of the definition of 'business' activity.

Although some scholars[38] held that the 'pursuit of profit' was an unavoidable requirement for the attribution of the status of entrepreneur to a person engaging in economic activity, the majority view is rather that in order to qualify as an 'entrepreneur', the objective goal of producing revenues that are at least adequate to cover costs (so-called 'profit in an objective sense', which substantially corresponds to a 'break-even requirement') is sufficient, with the subjective goal of making extra profits for distribution to the enterprise's owners (so-called 'profit in the subjective sense') being only additional.[39] This conclusion, bolstered by the lack of any 'profit' requirement in the code definition of 'entrepreneur' (Article 2082 CC), led the majority scholarship to hold that:

- an individual who *ex ante* plans a productive activity of goods and/or services at symbolic or below-market prices and is thus by definition unable to cover costs with revenues is not an 'entrepreneur';

---

37 F. Galgano, 'Delle associazioni non riconosciute e dei comitati' in A. Scialoja and G. Branca (eds) *Commentario del codice civile, sub* arts. 36–42, Zanichelli-Il Foro Italiano, Bologna-Rome 1967, p. 84; P. Morandi, 'La fallibilità degli enti non profit' (1998) I *Contratto e impresa* 344 ('[it is possible] to distinguish between the ultimate, or institutional, aims of the entity, and the intermediate ones: the former remains of an ideal nature, otherwise a corporation would be formed, while the latter can be pursued for profit, since they are merely instrumental.') (*'[è possibile] distinguere fra gli scopi ultimi o istituzionali dell'ente e quelli intermedi: i primi rimarrebbero comunque di natura ideale, configurandosi altrimenti una società, mentre i secondi possono avere carattere lucrativo, essendo perseguiti in via puramente strumentale'*); G.F. Campobasso, above n. 6, 584–585.

38 For example, A. Rocco, *Diritto commerciale, Parte generale*, S.A. Fratelli Treves Editori, Milan 1936, pp. 255 and 261; A. Arena, *Introduzione allo studio del diritto commerciale e titoli di credito*, Giuffrè, Milan 1936, pp. 43 et seq.

39 This stance was originally adopted by the following scholars: W. Bigiavi, *La professionalità dell'imprenditore*, CEDAM, Padua 1948, p. 75; A. Pavone La Rosa, *Il registro delle imprese*, Giuffrè, Milan 1954, pp. 103 et seq.; G. Ferri, *Manuale di diritto commerciale*, 2nd ed., UTET, Turin 1965, p. 44; F. Roversi Monaco, *Gli enti di gestione*, Giuffrè, Milan 1967, p. 210. Nowadays, this position appears to be accepted by substantially all Italian scholars: G. F. Campobasso, above n. 6, 585.

- instead, an entity – including 'public bodies' (*enti pubblici*) or, more precisely, foundations – that engages in economic activity with the goal of functioning in compliance with the 'break-even requirement' and is therefore self-sustaining via market activity alone, without the need for subsidies (public or private), is an 'entrepreneur'.

The attribution of the status of 'entrepreneur' to foundations engaging in economic activity in accordance with the 'break-even requirement' (or, even more so, with the 'means goal' of pursuing profits to be allocated to the altruistic 'end goal') was, and still is, legally relevant for the following reasons.

The title of 'entrepreneur' (and, in particular, that of 'commercial entrepreneur') comes with all the ensuing legal regime, comprising, *inter alia*, its exposure to bankruptcy.[40] Therefore, once a foundation is given the title of 'entrepreneur', the ensuing consequence should be that in the event of insolvency, it has to be declared bankrupt and made subject to all bankruptcy proceedings. Yet, as to the legal tests to be met in order for a foundation to be declared bankrupt, opinions of scholars are divided.

In particular, while some scholars[41] have expressed the view that whether a foundation is 'exclusively or predominantly' involved in business activity as opposed to its other activities is not decisive in relation to its bankruptcy regime (and therefore that a foundation could go bankrupt even when its involvement in business activity is merely 'ancillary'), other scholars have instead taken the view that foundations could only go bankrupt if their business activities represent their 'exclusive or prevalent' purpose.[42] This conclusion (probably refutable) is reached on the basis of the application by analogy of a rule governing 'public bodies' ('*enti pubblici*') (Article 2201 CC). Because such a rule makes 'public bodies' subject to the legal regime of (commercial) 'entrepreneurs' only on condition that their business activity represents their 'exclusive or main purpose', then (so runs the argument) the same test should also apply to foundations.

40 This is the opinion of the large majority of Italian scholars (see the two following footnotes). Contra, however, M. Greco, 'L'esonero dal fallimento degli enti non profit' in U. Apice (ed), *Imprenditori anomali e fallimento*, CEDAM, Padua 1997, pp. 215–220, who instead expressed the view that, despite the foundation being qualified as 'commercial entrepreneur', it would nevertheless be exceptionally exempt from bankruptcy.

41 This is, for example, the opinion of G. Ponzanelli, above n. 6, p. 185; L. Degani and R. Mozzanica, 'Fondazioni e attività di impresa: l'applicazione dello statuto dell'imprenditore' (2009) 7 *Enti non profit* 9; P. Morandi, above n. 37, 336 et seq; F. Rivellini, 'L'esercizio di attività economica degli enti no profit' (2017) *Diritto. it* 1–5; S. Cerrato, 'Origami giuridici: il fallimento delle fondazioni' (2016) 1 *Giur. It.* 128; G. F. Campobasso, *Diritto commerciale. Diritto dell'impresa*, UTET, Turin 1993, p. 84.

42 This is instead the opinion, for instance, of F. Galgano, 'L'imprenditore commerciale' in F. Galgano (ed), *Trattato di diritto commerciale e diritto pubblico dell'economia*, CEDAM, Padua 2004, pp. 86; F. Galgano, above n. 37, pp. 84 and 102.

The scholarly opinion of those years also raised another extremely relevant issue: that of the 'governance system' of foundations. Since the meagre regulation of the Civil Code mandated the existence of a board of directors only (without any mention of an assembly-type body or a body to which control over the administration was entrusted), it was debated whether the by-laws could provide for a regime such as to ensure the founder (or other person identified in the by-laws) the power to revoke directors and to appoint new ones. The conclusion was mostly negative.[43] Once the assets had been allocated to the altruistic purpose identified in the by-laws, the founder could have well nominated him or self as a director for life of the entity but could not reserve to him or herself or other persons the power to appoint the members of the foundation bodies. In essence, the only system compatible with Italian law would have been that of co-optation, i.e. a regime in which only the directors have the capacity to appoint their successors (with the understanding that the ineffectiveness of the relevant by-laws would have triggered the power of appointment by the government authority).

3.2. THE OPINION OF CASE LAW

While scholarship had eventually widely accepted 'enterprise foundations' and had consequently inferred the ensuing applicability thereto of the legal regime of (commercial) entrepreneurs, case law proved much less clear cut on the point. Although Italian courts have generally abandoned the original rigid stance against the admissibility of 'enterprise foundations',[44] some courts have nevertheless continually failed to draw consistent conclusions from the premise that enterprise foundations are admissible and compatible with Italian law.

---

43 P. Rescigno (1), above n. 5, p. 807 ('bodies of the foundation are neither the founder, ... nor the beneficiaries. In line with the extraneity in the management of the entity, the founder, while he can reserve the right to nominate members for life of the council, he cannot reserve the power to nominate one or all of the administrators in occasion of each subsequent renovation of the council; neither can he reserve the right to dismiss the board of directors') ('*Non sono organi della fondazione né il fondatore ... né i beneficiari. Per la rilevata estraneità all'amministrazione dell'ente, il fondatore, mentre può riservarsi all'atto della fondazione la nomina a vita di membri del consiglio, non può attribuirsi il potere di nominare uno o più o tutti gli amministratori ad ogni successiva rinnovazione dell'organo; né può riservarsi la facoltà di sciogliere il consiglio di amministrazione*'); R. Costi, above n. 6, 44 et seq. This approach started to be criticised in the mid-1970s: see, for example, D. Vittoria (1), above n. 6, 309 et seq.

44 Exemplary early court decisions denying the admissibility of 'enterprise foundations' include: App. Rome, 5 June 1957, in (1957) I *Foro it.* c.1274; Trib. Rome, 11 June 1954, in (1954) II *Dir. fall.* 455; App. Turin, 23 January 1952, in (1952) I *Giur. it.* 2, c.81. More recently, see Cass. Civ., 8 January 1991, n. 81, in (1991) *Società* p. 767; Cass. Civ., 11 September 1997, n. 8963, in (1998) I *Foro it.* c. 2532.

When facing 'foundations carrying out economic activities', for example, certain courts felt the need to requalify such entities as either 'de facto companies' or 'de facto associations' among the founders and/or directors.[45] The consequences of this approach are quite significant.

If it is assumed that a foundation that carries out (commercial) business activities is legitimate, then, in the event of bankruptcy, the foundation is solely and exclusively responsible for its debts and, thus, the principle of limitation of liability continues to apply.

If, on the other hand, the foundation is requalified as a 'de facto company' or as a de facto 'association', then those who are consequently qualified as 'de facto partners' or as 'de facto associates' (acting in the name of the entity) become *personally* and *fully* responsible for the entity's (the company's or association's) debts.[46]

Such a case law position has clearly represented, and continues to represent, a considerable Sword of Damocles hovering over enterprise foundations. The prospect of the requalification of an enterprise foundation as a 'de facto company' or as a 'de facto association' exposes all individuals with important management functions (be they formalised or not) to the serious risk of *personal* bankruptcy and, hence, of potential *personal* indictment for bankruptcy crimes (fraudulent bankruptcy and simple bankruptcy).

It is not difficult to see how such uncertainty concerning the underlying legal framework has been, and continues to be, a substantial deterrent to the establishment of enterprise foundations.

If, in addition, we also consider the strong limitation in term of governance rules imposed by strict interpretation of the scholarship – i.e. the asserted incompatibility of the provision of assembly bodies given by the Civil Code with foundation legal regime; the impossibility of entrusting the founder or third parties with the power to renew the board of directors (with the consequent risk of government interference)[47] – it is clear why, despite the evolution of the scholarship interpretation of the admissibility of enterprise foundations, the

---

45 Amongst others: Trib. Milan, 17 June 1994, in (1994) I *Foro it.* c. 3544; Trib. Milan 16 July 1998, in (1999) *Giur. it.* 1678; Trib. Alba, 24 March 2009, n. 3, in (2009) I *Nuova Giurisprudenza Civile Commentata* 1099, 1099–1102; Trib. Biella, 22 May 2015, in (2016) *Giur. it* 124; Cass Civ., 16 March 2004, n. 5305, in (2005) II *Dir. Fall.* 843. Contra, however, App. Palermo, 7 April 1989, in (1992) II *Giur. comm.* 61; Cass. Civ., 18 September 1993, n. 9589, in (1994) *Fall.* 151. A thorough analysis of this case law is provided by M. Perrino, 'Esercizio indiretto dell'impresa "scolastica", associazione e fallimento' (1992) II *Giur. comm.* 69 and also by A. Cetra, 'L'associazione non riconosciuta che esercita un'impresa commerciale non è una società di fatto fra gli associati' (1999) II *Giur. comm* 442.

46 Partners of a commercial partnership (*società in nome collettivo*) are always personally liable for the company's debts vis-à-vis third parties pursuant to Articles 2267 and 2291 CC. Persons acting in the name of an association are subject to the same legal regime pursuant to Article 38 CC.

47 See above n. 43.

regulatory regime (as resulting from scholarship and case law) turned Italy into a scarcely fertile land for the diffusion and success of industrial foundations.

4. FOUNDATIONS ORIGINATED FROM BANKING REFORMS

4.1. THE AMATO REFORM AND THE 'INVENTION' OF BANKING FOUNDATIONS

In the changing cultural context that began in the late 1960s and followed thereafter, at the beginning of the 1990s, the so-called Amato reform[48] made use of foundations to carry out the privatisation of Italian banks that had hitherto been owned by public bodies according to a state-centric model intended to ensure political control of the national financial system.[49]

On the contrary, the need to reform the banking system according to a market-centric and competition-oriented model stemmed from the pressure exerted by those bodies of the European Community that were institutionally in charge of favouring the liberalisation of the financial systems of Member States. The Italian legislature followed the lead of the EU institutions, yet it did so in such a way as to shield Italian banks against a potential foreign invasion. The Italian political class of the time feared that too abrupt a transition from a public financial system (controlled and protected by the state) to a private financial system (exposed to international competition) would have made Italian banks easy prey for more solid and better equipped foreign financial institutions. A foreign invasion would have exposed the national industrial sector (which has always been heavily reliant on a highly politicalised banking sector) to worldwide financial turbulence.[50]

The 1990 reform implemented the privatisation of banks through two fundamental steps: (i) the transformation of banking businesses into joint-stock companies governed by private law; and, above all, (ii) the transformation of the public state bodies that owned the public banking companies into

48 On the Amato reform, see, amongst others, P. Schlesinger, 'Le c.d. "fondazioni bancarie"' (1995) I *Banca borsa titoli di credito* 421; P. Rescigno 'La fondazione ed i gruppi bancari' (1992) *Banca, Impresa, Società* 389; G. Barbetta, 'La legge Amato e le Fondazioni bancarie: nuovi soggetti nel mondo delle imprese senza fine di lucro' [1992] *Economia e credito* 247; F. Capriglione, 'Privatizzazione e mercato: le fondazioni bancarie' (1996) I *Banca borsa titoli di credito* 336; D. Lucarini Ortolani 'Privatizzazione e fondazione bancaria' (1995) V *Foro Italiano* 120; G. Pagliari, *Le fondazioni bancarie: Profili giuridici*, Giuffrè, Milan 2004.

49 M.V. de Giorgi, 'Fondazioni bancarie e linee evolutive della disciplina comune' [2004] II *Nuova giurisprudenza civile commentata* 643.

50 R. Costi, 'L'ambiguo ruolo delle fondazioni bancarie' [2012] 4 *Diritto della banca e del mercato finanziario* 49.

foundations pre-ordained to hold the controlling shareholdings in the newly established banking companies.

Therefore, for the first time, Italian law itself made use of foundations as an organisation model institutionally entrusted with the operation and control of what were formerly public banks. The two potentially conflicting needs mentioned above were thus fulfilled. On the one hand, the obligation to privatise and liberalise the banking sector was met; on the other hand, newly privatised Italian banks would not fall into the hands of global players due to the allocation of bank shareholdings in institutions statutorily designated to their long-term detention.[51]

A similar reform was only conceivable thanks to the evolution in the scholarship opinion that began in the 1960s, which, with respect to 'foundations', recognised the compatibility between: (i) the pursuit of ultimate goals of public utility; and (ii) the exercise, as a mere means to an end, of business activities and, more specifically, banking businesses.

This is precisely the scheme adopted by the Amato reform for banking foundations: on the one hand, the essential 'object' of the activity is the management or administration of the controlling stake in the privatised bank (i.e. holding the majority of the voting rights in the banking company), which, in turn, seeks to maximise profit like any enterprise; yet, on the other hand, the ultimate 'purpose' of the entity is the destination of profits for public purposes of general importance, namely in the domains of scientific research, education, art and health.[52]

To justify the political decision to privatise the banking system through the formation of banking foundations (BF), the Amato reform was followed by a declaration of the significance of encouraging private non-profit organisations to take over functions traditionally handled by the state at a time when the public welfare system looked financially unsustainable. However, the fundamental logic underlining such a 'creative' approach was to denationalise

51 The original distinctive goal of the newly created foundations was to maintain their control over the newly privatised Italian banks, which was translated into the slogan 'never below 51%' (on this point, see F. Cavazzuti, *Privatizzazioni, imprenditori e mercati*, Il Mulino, Bologna, 1996). In more general terms, the Amato reform modelled the foundations as a new legal entity that would have ensured the permanence of a public ownership of the share capital of the newly privatised banks: S. Rizzini Bisinelli, 'Fondazioni bancarie: strumenti innovativi per la dismissione di partecipazioni' (2000) 5 *Le Società* 542.

52 F. Merusi, 'Il prologo. Il progetto di trasformazione delle banche pubbliche spiegato ad un viaggiatore persiano' in F. Merusi, *Dalla banca pubblica alla fondazione privata*, Giappichelli, Turin 2000, pp. 23 et seq.; M. Tanzi, 'Sulle c.d. fondazioni bancarie: alcune considerazioni critiche' (2013) III *Banca borsa titoli di credito* 266; M. Clarich and A. Pisaneschi, 'Fondazioni bancarie e regioni – commento' (2002) 2 *Giornale di diritto amministravito* 139; A. Zoppini, 'Verso la definitiva separazione tra enti conferenti e banche' (1999) 4 *Il corriere giuridico* 411.

and liberalise the national banking system while retaining the controlling shareholdings in privatised banks in the hands of Italian nationals.

4.2. THE CIAMPI REFORM AND THE GOVERNANCE OF BANKING FOUNDATIONS

Less than ten years after their creation, in 1999 the Italian legislature intervened again on BF regulation with a major reform known as the Ciampi reform.[53]

The Ciampi reform addressed two objectives. First, it was intended to abandon the merely 'formal' privatisation (as accomplished in the 1990s) in order to embrace a 'substantial' privatisation by imposing on BFs partial divestment of their controlling shareholdings in banking companies. Second, the time was ripe to proceed with a more substantial regulation of the governance of those entities that had become major providers of significant resources.

As for the first objective, the Ciampi reform established that BFs pursue 'social utility purposes and the promotion of economic development exclusively' and imposed the obligation to gradually divest their controlling banking shareholdings.

As for the second objective, it provided, for the first time, an analytical regulation of banking foundation governance which, until then, had remained unchanged from the extremely inadequate Civil Code norms.

The governance of banking foundations as resulting out of the 1999 law can be summarised as follows.

First of all, a 'tripartite model of organisation' divided into three fundamental bodies is to be adopted: (i) a founders' council; (ii) a board of directors and (iii) an audit committee. The founders' council is constituted to ensure adequate representation of local public and private entities (regions, municipalities, universities, religious institutions, etc.). It is entrusted with the task of determining 'programs, priorities, and objectives of the foundation' in line with the statutory purpose and it is granted with the power to appoint, revoke and exercise liability actions against the members of the board of directors. The board of directors is in charge of managing the foundation's assets and implementing the strategic guidelines established by the founders' council. The audit committee, composed of individuals qualified to practise as auditors, is tasked with overseeing the legitimacy of the management activity

53 On the Ciampi reform, see, amongst others, G. Oppo, 'Le fondazioni (ex) bancarie: una strana vicenda legislativa' in S. Amorosino and F. Capriglione (eds), *Le 'fondazioni' bancarie. Dalla legge n. 218/90 al D.Lgs. n. 153/99*, CEDAM, Padua 1999, pp. 1–11; G. Mucciarelli, *Attività e impresa nelle fondazioni bancarie*, Giuffrè, Milan 2005, pp. 7–59; G. Pagliari, above n. 48, pp. 157–241; A. Pavone La Rosa 'Fondazioni bancarie e disciplina dell'impresa commerciale' (2000) I *Banca borsa titoli di credito* 1; E. del Prato 'Fondazioni bancarie e categorie civilistiche' (2002) VI *Banca borsa titoli di credito* 739.

(formal legitimacy control which cannot amount to a control on the merits), as well as the obligation to notify the supervisory authority if any management irregularities are detected.[54]

Banking foundations regulation is relevant for our purposes in two different ways.

First of all, the full compatibility between the status of a 'non-profit organisation' and the exercise of profit-driven business activities is unequivocally confirmed. Just as nothing prevents an individual entrepreneur from allocating, for unquestionable personal preference, the profits they derive from their business to general utility purposes, their status as 'entrepreneur' remaining unaffected as a result, nothing prevents an entity that, by law, must pursue altruistic purposes, from operating profit-driven businesses, its qualification as an 'entrepreneur' remaining unquestioned by the same token.

Second, and even more importantly, the full legitimacy of what the Italian scholarship calls 'participation foundations' – i.e. foundations that mix the 'objective element' of a 'dedicated estate' (allocation of assets to a specific purpose) with the 'personalistic element' of an associative body – is also unequivocally confirmed.[55] This replaces the old scholars' opinion under which there was no room for party autonomy to provide for founders themselves or other bodies that, although not founders, were nonetheless interested in a certain allocation of the benefit provided by the entity, to appoint the members of the board of directors of the foundations.[56] Indeed, in the case of BFs, it is

---

54 On the governance of banking foundations, see A. Zoppini, 'L'autonomia statutaria nelle fondazioni di origine bancaria' (2000) *Banca borsa titoli di credito* 399.

55 Authors who supported the admissibility of so-called '*fondazioni di partecipazione*' (participatory or associative foundations, i.e. foundations with an assembly of founders), and did so also before the enactment of the Third Sector Code (TSC), include E. Bellezza and F. Florian, *Le fondazioni di partecipazione*, La Tribuna, Piacenza 2006, passim; A. Zoppini, 'Profili evolutivi della fondazione di partecipazione nella moderna prassi e nella legislazione speciale' in Fondazione Italiana per il Notariato, *Fondazioni di partecipazione*, Il Sole-24 ore, Milan 2007, p. 21; M. Maltoni, 'La fondazione di partecipazione: natura giuridica e legittimità' (2007) X(2) *Quaderni della fondazione Italiana per il Notariato – 'Fondazioni di partecipazione'* 25; A. Fusaro, 'La fondazione tra modello tradizionale e modello partecipativo quale strumento per la tutela delle categorie svantaggiate' (2011) *Vita notarile* 1089; contra, however, A. Zoppini, above n. 15, pp. 102–103.

56 This original position was, for example, expressed by P. Rescigno (1), above n. 5, p. 802 ('[T]he will of the founder is interpreted as an objectivised statement, given to the board of the foundation and destined to give the criterion used to judge the way in which the activity has been carried out, as well as its conformity. The founder remains extraneous to the entity that has been created on the basis of legal recognition, also because of its act of private autonomy; this justifies the opinion that the founder, if the act is an *inter vivos*, cannot reserve themself rights that affect the life and administration of the entity (in particular, it cannot reserve itself the right to nominate, wholly or partially, members of the bodies of the foundation). Decoupled from him, the "will of the founder" remains to guide the life of the foundation') ('*La volontà del fondatore viene intesa come qualcosa di obiettivato, affidato alle tavole della fondazione e destinato a fornire il criterio di giudizio dell'attività svolta e della conformità allo scopo. Il fondatore rimane estraneo all'ente che è nato in virtù di riconoscimento, sulla base, tra*

legitimate that the power to appoint and dismiss the directors of the foundation is entrusted to certain public and private bodies identified in the by-laws. It must be deemed equally legitimate, then, for an enterprise foundation (other than a banking foundation) to reserve the power to appoint directors to the founders or other bodies that are best equipped to ensure a supply of benefits in line with the ideal purposes of the entity as outlined in the by-laws.

In turn, the legislative acknowledgement of the compatibility of a 'participatory' form of governance with the status of a foundation triggers several consequences:

- First of all, the effects of the absence of an 'owner' acting as 'controller' in the common principal–agent relationship is mitigated and the governmental authority's influence on the governance structure and management choices of the entity becomes redundant and can be gotten rid of for good (although the governmental authority is still left with the control over the legitimacy of the entity's management).
- Second, in the event of insolvency, the 'requalification' of a 'foundation' into an 'association' or 'company' is precluded and the bankruptcy of any person in any capacity involved in the management of the bankrupted entity is avoided, thus superseding the case law examined above.

5. FURTHER REGULATORY EVOLUTION: THE LAW ON LEGAL PERSONALITY RECOGNITION AND THE 'PURPOSE' OF FOUNDATIONS

5.1. BEYOND THE LICENCE REGIME AND THE 'LAWFULNESS' OF THE PURPOSE AS SOLE REQUIREMENT

A significant step forward in the evolution of the Italian law of foundation occurred in 2000 with a law that reformed the procedure for recognising legal personality of, *inter alia*, foundations.[57]

---

l'altro, dell'atto di autonomia privata da lui compiuto; e per questo si giustifica l'opinione che il fondatore, se si tratta di negozio fra vivi, non possa preservarsi poteri che incidano sulla vita e l'amministrazione dell'ente (in particolare, non possa attribuire a sé per il futuro la nomina, in tutto o in parte, degli organi della fondazione). Staccata dal fondatore, rimane a indirizzare costantemente la vita della persona giuridica la "volontà del fondatore"')'. Needless to say, this stance concerning the legal constraints on the governance of a foundation made its adoption quite unfit for the purposes of the establishment of an enterprise foundation.

57 D.P.R. 10 February 2000, n. 361 ('Regulation regarding the simplification of recognition procedures for private legal persons and of the approvation of changes to the articles of association and the statute') ('*Regolamento recante norme per la semplificazione dei procedimenti di riconoscimento di persone giuridiche private e di approvazione delle modifiche*

Two novelties are important for our purposes. The first is that the recognition of legal personality is no longer subject to a governmental authority's licence grant,[58] but to an authorisation subject to a mere legitimacy control. The 'statist philosophy' underlying the Civil Code ('the state is master of legal persons') gives way to a more contemporary 'liberal philosophy' ('private citizens are free to adopt any legal scheme consistent with lawful purposes').

Second, with specific regard to 'foundations', the recognition of legal personality is made subject not to the existence of a 'public utility' purpose – which was often assumed as implicit in the case law and also in many scholars' opinion (despite it not being required in any Civil Code rules),[59] – but of a purpose simply qualified as 'lawful'.[60]

According to the majority of commentators, this change is significant because it confirms the full, and now unquestionable, legitimacy not only of foundations that operate a business and then allocate profits to social utility purposes, but also of those that allocate profits for 'selfish', but in any case 'lawful' purposes (for example, benefiting the employees of a certain company).

This precise regulatory evolution has recently led Italian scholars to conclude that the key principle of foundations, far from being that of a presumed 'altruistic purpose', should rather be reduced to the mere prohibition of disbursement of profits to the founder itself, also known as the non-distribution constraint.[61]

---

dell'atto costitutivo e dello statuto'). Pertinent comments on this law can be found in A. Zoppini, 'Riformato il sistema di riconoscimento delle persone giuridiche' (2001) 18(3) *Corriere giuridico* 291; and G. Ponzanelli, above n. 6, passim.

58 Before the enactment of the law at stake, an author had even expressed the view that the traditional 'licence regime' was to be considered incompatible with the Italian Constitutional Charter: V. Mariconda, 'Libertà di modelli organizzativi e statutari per le fondazioni e funzione notarile' (1997) I *Rivista del notariato* 638.

59 The traditional view had instead hitherto been that the purpose of the foundation could not be anything but 'altruistic': see, for example, P. Rescigno (1), above n. 5, p. 806; G. Sicchiero, 'Le fondazioni di partecipazione' (2020) 1 *Contratto e impresa* 19, 34.

60 A. Zoppini, 'Le fondazioni' in D. Carusi, *Associazioni e fondazioni: Dal Codice civile alle riforme annunciate (Convegno di studi in onore di Pietro Rescigno)*, Giuffrè, Milan 2001, p. 72 ('the identification – from which the legislator moved in 1942 – of legal persons, regulated in the First Book of the Civil Code, and non-profit entities, pursuing public utility, has now declined; a textual indication of this trend can be found in the new discipline for the recognition (D.P.R. 10 Febuary 2000, n. 361), which requires only the "sufficiency" of the assets and the "lawfulness" of the purpose, thereby acknowledging that the requirement of the "public utility" is entirely absorbed by the other provisions that the lawmaker gave as sector-specific rules, outside of the Civil Code') (*'l'identificazione – da cui muoveva il legislatore del '42 – tra le persone giuridiche regolate nel primo libro del codice civile e gli enti non lucrativi che realizzano uno scopo di pubblica utilità è ormai venuta meno; un'indicazione testuale in questa direzione si rinviene anche nella nuova disciplina del riconoscimento (D.P.R. 10 febbraio 2000, n. 361), che ai fini della personificazione si limita a richiedere, oltre alla "sufficienza" dei patrimonio, la "liceità" dello scopo, confermandosi così che la rilevanza della "pubblica utilità" è interamente assorbita dalle fattispecie che il legislatore ha previsto quali discipline di settore collocate fuori dal codice*').

61 See, amongst others, G. Ponzanelli, above n. 25, pp. 4–5 and 7–8; A. Zoppini, above n. 15, pp. 67–68; P. Manes, 'Le nuove prospettive in materia di fondazioni' (2018) 1 *Contratto e impresa* 267.

Without prejudice to this limit, Italian foundations are currently deemed to be legitimised in order to pursue any purpose, whether 'altruistic' or 'selfish'.

The identification of the key trait of foundations, not so much with regard of the aims pursued (altruistic or selfish), but rather regarding the so-called non-distribution constraint makes it possible to distinguish 'foundations' and 'commercial companies' in the following terms.

In commercial companies (entities with an ownership structure), it is the 'ownership' of the capital conferred that assigns both (i) the title to participate in the appointment of directors, and (ii) the participation in the profit distribution. On the contrary, in 'participatory'-based foundations (entities with a non-proprietary structure, but with an assembly of participants/founders who appoint and dismiss the directors), (i) the right to participate in the appointment of directors, on the one hand, and (ii) the right to participate in the profit distribution, on the other hand, are structurally non-coincidental and independent from 'ownership'. The first right (appointment of directors) is attributed under the by-laws to the founders/participants, the former being considered the 'former owner', in some sense, as they make contributions to the foundation free of charge and not in exchange for shareholdings. The second right (profit distribution) is given to those beneficiaries who are chosen by the foundation's board of directors based on the criteria outlined in the by-laws.

In other words, as accurately pointed out by the liberal scholars of the 1960s who were favourable to 'family business foundations', the governance structure of a foundation determines an absolute split between 'ownership' and 'control': 'control' is vested in individuals who are 'no longer owners' and therefore 'no longer legitimised' to participate in the profit of the company. Conversely, 'ownership' (i.e. the right to receive the economic benefits of the company) is vested in individuals completely devoid of any voice over the management of the company. Beyond this fundamental difference, once the traditional discrepancy trait based on 'purpose' disappears, the contrast between 'foundation' and 'commercial company' is enormously reduced.

5.2. ABSENCE IN ITALIAN BUSINESS LAW OF AN IMPERATIVE PRINCIPLE OF CORRELATION BETWEEN 'RISK' AND 'POWER'

The fact that a 'foundation' can determine an absolute split between 'ownership' and 'control' requires a thorough examination of its systematic compatibility with Italian law.

Such an arrangement could raise doubts from the same perspective, which, historically, underlines the bourgeois regime of the right to property. In fact, in an 'enterprise foundation', the lack of coincidence between individuals who appoint directors ('participants' and 'non-owners') and individuals who benefit from the entrepreneurial activity ('beneficiaries') creates exposure to the risk of negligence domino effects: (i) negligence by the 'participants' who, being by definition disinterested in management, may not appoint carefully the 'best' directors; and (ii) negligence by the 'directors' who, as an emanation of uninterested parties, could feel free from any 'control' mechanism (with a consequent exacerbation of the so-called agency problem). The managerial efficiency of a company with a similar atypical 'owner' (or, better, a 'non-owner') structure ends up depending on the ability of the 'participants' to become effective interpreters of the interests of the 'beneficiaries'. In other words, one should assume that the 'altruism' of the uninterested 'participants' (the 'founders' of the entity that originated from their free disbursements) is functionally equivalent to the 'selfishness' of the owners concerned (the 'founders' of a company who incorporated it with contributions in exchange of the shareholdings entitling them to the right of profit). Therefore, one could say that the managerial efficiency of a profit-driven company held by a foundation holds up insofar as the *homo oeconomicus* paradigm is replaced by the *homo reciprocans* paradigm.[62] In particular, *homo reciprocans* is that individual who, on the one hand, acts rationally to ensure that the management of the company pursues the maximum profit – and therefore, in this respect, likewise a *homo oeconomicus* – but does so not for personal benefit, but rather to allocate the business's profit to a category of beneficiaries identified not by their capital holding (i.e. as 'owners'), but by their belonging to that category of individuals that the founders wanted to benefit.

Indeed, if one examines the fundamental principles of Italian company law, the compliance with law of a governance structure of a corporation that determines an absolute split between 'ownership' and 'control' could be questioned at first. For example, under company law, as regulated in 1942, the law of

62 Behavioural economics marked the downfall of the *homo oeconomicus* paradigm in favour of other types of economic agents affected by psychological, cognitive, emotional, cultural and social factors. There is probably no single paradigm capable of effectively describing the behaviour of a social agent in every situation, but there is awareness of the inadequacy in that respect of the *homo oeconomicus* paradigm. For an overview of the new paradigms emerged, see E.J. O'Boyle, 'Requiem for Homo Economicus' (2007) 10(2) *Journal of Markets and Morality* 321.
According to Herbert Gintis et al., *homo reciprocans* is 'neither the selfless altruist of utopian theory, nor the selfish hedonist of neoclassical economics. Rather, he is a conditional cooperator whose penchant for reciprocity can be elicited under the proper circumstances'. See S. Bowles, R. Boyd, E. Fehr and H. Gintis, *Homo reciprocans: A Research Initiative on the Origins, Dimensions, and Policy Implications of Reciprocal Fairness*, Cambridge University, Massachussetts 1997, p. 5; on empirical evidence of *homo reciprocans*, see also E. Fehr and S. Gächter 'Reciprocity and Economics: The Economic Implication of *homo reciprocans*' (1998) 42 *European Economic Review* 845; T. Dohmen, A. Falk, D. Huffman and U. Sunde, '*Homo reciprocans*: Survey Evidence on Behavioural Outcomes' (2009) 119 *Economic Journal* 592.

joint-stock companies was governed by the mandatory 'one share, one vote' principle, which aimed precisely at correlating 'ownership' and 'control' on the assumption that only a management influenced by a self-interested profit-seeking individual can ensure the adequate structure of incentives that guarantee efficiency.[63]

If we focus instead on the evolution of company and business law over the last 20 years, then one will notice that the correlation 'ownership'/'control' initially prescribed by the Civil Code of 1942 has now been substantially overcome.

In a nutshell, over the last two decades, the most significant regulatory evolutions in this sense are as follows. First of all, with respect to joint-stock companies (*società per azioni*), after the organic reform of 2003 and the more modest reform of 2016, it is now possible, thanks to the combination of multiple voting shares (with the limit of three votes per share) and no voting shares (issuable to an extent that does not exceed half of the share capital), that a person holding a relatively small minority of the capital (precisely 12.5%) exercises legal control over the company.[64]

Second, and above all, in a limited liability company (*società a responsabilità limitata*), thanks to the admissibility of 'particular rights' to quota holders (whatever the size of the quota), it is now possible for a holder of a minimal fraction of capital to control the company. Thus, Italian law now seems to admit an almost absolute decoupling between 'ownership' and 'control.[65]

---

63 L. Calvosa, *La partecipazione eccedente*, Giuffrè, Milan 1999, p. 160; G. Ferri, 'Potere e responsabilità nell'evoluzione della società per azioni' (1956) *Rivista di Diritto Societario* 35; G. Frè, 'Della società per azioni' in *Commentario del Codice civile Scialoja-Branca*, Zanichelli-Foro Italiano, Bologna-Turin 1972, *sub* art. 2351, pp. 198 et seq.

64 This rule seems to establish only a residual link between 'ownership' and 'control'. See, amongst others, A. Pisani Massamormile, 'Azioni ed altri strumenti finanziari partecipativi' (2003) *Rivista di Diritto Societario* 2195; A. Angelillis and M.L. Vitali, 'Commento *sub* art. 2351' in P. Marchetti, L.A. Bianchi, F. Ghezzi and M. Notari (eds), *Commentario alla riforma delle società*, Egea, Milan 2008, pp. 371; P. Spada, *Appunto in tema di capitale nominale e conferimenti*, Consiglio Nazionale del Notariato, Commissione Studi d'Impresa, Studio n. 127–2006/I, p. 7; J. Sodi, 'L'assegnazione delle partecipazioni non proporzionale ai conferimenti nelle società di capitali' (2009) *Studi e materiali* 587; R. Guglielmo and M. Silva, *I diritti particolari del socio – Vicende della partecipazione tra regole legali ed autonomia statutaria*, Consiglio Nazionale del Notariato, Commissione Studi d'Impresa, Studio n. 138–2011/I, passim; E. Barcellona, *Rischio e potere nel diritto societario riformato fra golden quota di s.r.l. e strumenti finanziari di s.p.a.*, Giappichelli, Turin 2012, pp. 122 et seq.

65 On the admissibility under Italian law of the so-called 'golden quota', see, amongst others, A. Santus and G. De Marchi, 'Sui "particolari diritti" del socio nella nuova s.r.l.' (2004) 1 *Rivista del notariato* 75; R. Rosapepe, 'Appunti su alcuni aspetti della nuova disciplina della partecipazione sociale nella s.r.l.' (2003) 4 *Giurisprudenza commerciale* 479; R. Guglielmo, 'Diritti particolari dei soci nelle s.r.l. e voto non proporzionale' (2010) 3 *Rivista del notariato* 589; M. Maugeri, 'Quali diritti particolari per il socio di società a responsabilità limitata?' (2004) 6 *Rivista di Diritto Societario* 1483; M. Cavanna, 'Partecipazione e "diritti particolari" dei soci' in M. Sarale (ed), *Le nuove s.r.l.*, Zanichelli, Bologna 2008, p. 125; R. Santagata, 'I diritti particolari dei soci' in A.A. Dolmetta and G. Presti (eds), *S.r.l. Commentario*

Finally, with the introduction in 2017 of the new 'social business' model (which can also be organised in the form of a joint-stock company), Italian law has admitted the existence of a company operating in specific sectors of social utility with the purpose of disbursing profit in favour of categories of beneficiaries identified in the by-laws rather than to the owner of the company (founders, shareholders or directors are prohibited from receiving profit) or the reinvestment in the company itself.[66]

This regulatory evolution is clear evidence that the Italian legal system certainly tolerates a governance structure based on an absolute split between management power and the expectation of profits distribution and that therefore no longer postulates any necessary correlation between 'ownership' and 'control' to safeguard the efficiency of the company. The recognition of the sociological relevance of the individual's orientation both to the selfish pursuit of personal interests (according to the *homo oeconomicus* paradigm) and to altruistic and solidarity interests (according to the *homo reciprocans* paradigm) led Italian law to grant private autonomy significant leeway: individuals are free to adopt a governance structure that fully decouples control rights from economic rights.

Not only does the current regulatory framework not oppose such organisational structures, but it actively encourages them. At a time when the welfare state is proving unsustainable for the public treasury, the legal system can only praise the initiative of those private individuals who combine the desire to start a profitable (or at least economically sustainable) business with the desire to share the company's profits with others (the beneficiaries). As a consequence, the favourable impact is twofold. First, a profitable or economically viable business contributes to collective wellbeing by allowing the better allocation of resources. Second, since any company profit is not intended to enrich 'capital', but to allocate wealth in accordance with a solidarity-based

dedicato a Giuseppe B. Portale, Giuffrè, Milan 2011, p. 291; A. Blandini, 'Categorie di quote, categorie di soci' in G. Rossi (ed), *Collana della Rivista delle Società*, Giuffrè, Milan 2009, pp. 95 et seq., particularly p. 97; M. Maltoni, 'La partecipazione sociale' in C. Caccavale, F. Magliulo, M. Maltoni and F. Tassinari (eds), *La riforma della società a responsabilità limitata*, 2nd ed., IPSOA, Milanofiori-Assago 2007, p. 218: V. de Stasio, 'Commento *sub* art. 2468. Quote di partecipazione' in P. Benazzo and S. Patriarca (eds), *Codice commentato delle s.r.l.*, UTET, Turin 2006, p. 137; R. Genghini, 'Le modifiche statutarie' in *Il nuovo ordinamento delle società. Lezioni sulla riforma e modelli statutari*, IPSOA, Milan 2004, para. 4.5; E. Fazzutti, 'Commento sub art. 2468. Quote di partecipazione' in M. Sandulli and V. Santoro (eds), *La riforma delle società*, Giappichelli, Turin 2003, pp. 57–58; P. Revigliono, 'Commento sub art. 2468. Quote di partecipazione' in G. Cottino, G. Bonfante, O. Cagnasso and P. Montalenti (eds), *Il nuovo diritto societario, Commentario*, Diretto da Zanichelli, Bologna-Rome 2004, p. 1807; L. Salvatore, 'La nuova s.r.l.: la disciplina dei conferimenti e delle partecipazioni sociali' (2003) *Contratto e impresa* 239; R. Rordorf, 'I sistemi di amministrazione e controllo nella nuova s.r.l.' (2003) *Società* 666.

66 N. de Luca, 'Tipi societari e impresa sociale: profili notarili' (2019) II *Rivista del Notariato* 449.

paradigm, the private sector contributes to the task of redistribution of wealth that the contemporary state is struggling to achieve.

5.3. THE LEGITIMACY OF FAMILY BUSINESS FOUNDATIONS AND NON-EXISTENCE OF THE NON-DISTRIBUTION CONSTRAINT

The above considerations pave the way to a reassessment of the admissibility under Italian law of the so-called family business foundations.[67] These foundations operate a business with the purely 'selfish' purpose of benefitting the founder's family members.

Once it is established that (i) foundations are simply required to pursue a 'lawful' purpose (and not necessarily a 'public utility' purpose) and that (ii) the absolute separation between 'ownership' and 'control' does not violate any principle of public order under Italian law, there is one inevitable conclusion: no systematic reason prevents the admission or legitimacy of 'family business foundations' with a purely 'selfish' (lawful) purpose.

Notably, if under Italian law there are no reasons for preserving the efficiency of a business when a person holding a minimal quota of the capital exercises control over an entity organised as a 'limited liability company', and if, always under Italian law, there are no reasons for preserving the efficiency of the 'social business' company, where 'shareholders' have no claim over profit and yet exercise control over a social enterprise organised in a corporate form, then one unquestionable conclusion can be drawn. No need for the preservation of business efficiency exists when the management of a family business is handed over to a foundation whose management body is required, under the by-laws, to allocate the profit to the descendants of the founder.

There are also further reasons to believe that family business foundations pursue interests 'worthy of protection' (under Italian law, freedom of contract is always protected when the interests pursued are deemed worthy of protection: Article 1322 CC).[68]

---

67 On family foundations under Italian law, see, for example, P. Rescigno (1), above n. 5, pp. 810–811; E. Moscati, 'Associazioni e fondazioni: finalità fiduciarie e loro rilevanza' (1995) II *Nuova giurisprudenza civile commentata* 25; A. Zoppini, 'Fondazioni e trust quali strumenti della successione ereditaria' in P. Rescigno (ed), *Trattato breve delle successioni e delle donazioni*, vol. I, CEDAM, Padua 2010, pp. 147–195; G. Iorio, *Le fondazioni*, Giuffrè, Milan 1997, pp. 181 et seq; A. Palazzo, 'Il diritto delle successioni: fondamenti costituzionali, regole codicistiche ed istanze sociali' (2004) *Vita notarile* 116; M.V. de Giorgi, 'Fondazioni di famiglia' (1973) II *Rivista di diritto civile* 295. Italian scholars who expressed the view that family foundations are to be deemed to be compatible with Italian law include P. Manes, above n. 61, 265 and 269; M.V. de Giorgi, above n. 13, 79 (but on the condition that the purpose of the family foundation also serves some public benefit).

68 P. Manes, above n. 61, 267–268.

The separation of 'control' and 'ownership' in a family business foundation aiming at distributing profit to the founder's family members ensures unity and continuity to the company's strategic management by shielding it from the risk of heirs' conflict. Furthermore, while the heirs are effectively 'deprived' of management power (unlike the dangerous scenario where this power is placed directly in their hands via the shares in the company), they are not 'deprived' of the right to receive profit, as the family foundation's by-laws mandate for the disbursement of the foundation business's profit in their favour.

Furthermore, the fact that family (business) foundations are undoubtedly legitimate under Italian law from the specific point of view of the absolute decoupling between 'ownership' and 'control' is evident (and undisputedly so nowadays) following the implementation in Italy of the Hague Convention on 'trusts'.[69] Even in a 'trust', one observes a decoupling between 'ownership' and 'control' entirely analogous to that entailed by a foundation. Therefore, if a foreign trust which assigns: (i) management power to the trustees ('managers', but 'non-owners'); and (ii) the associated economic benefits to the 'beneficiaries' ('quasi-owners', but not 'managers') is deemed fully compliant with Italian law,[70] then no valid reason could exist any longer to question the admissibility of a family (business) foundation which substantially replicates the same governance format.

True, certain limits on the constitution of 'family business foundations' derive from Italian inheritance law, which, like other continental legal systems, assigns a reserved portion of the estate to specified groups of individuals (spouses, children and, in some situations, parents). Since, in most cases, the family business (more often the controlling shareholding in a profit-making company) represents almost the entirety of the founder's assets, the gratuitous assignment of such business to a foundation could be challenged by the reserved heirs for violation of their reserved portion under certain conditions. The problem only arises in cases where the potential founder of the foundation has family members who qualify as 'reserved' heirs.[71]

But these inheritance law-related limitations are not insuperable. One could easily think of certain suitable structures to reconcile (i) the need to achieve the desired decoupling between 'ownership' and 'control' and (ii) the need to protect the foundation from the risk of claims from 'reserved' heirs. In particular, it is possible to turn the company that owns the enterprise into

[69] The Hague Convention of 1 July 1985 on the Law Applicable to Trusts and on their Recognition was enacted in Italy with Law no. 364 of 16 October 1989.

[70] See, amongst others, A. Gambaro, 'Problemi in materia di riconoscimento degli effetti dei *trusts* nei paesi di civil law' (1984) I *Rivista di diritto civile* 93; M. Zaccheo, *Gestione fiduciaria e disposizione del diritto*, Giuffrè, Milan 1991, passim; U. Morello, 'Fiducia e trust: due esperienze a confronto' (1990) *Quadrimestre* 239.

[71] A. Zoppini, above n. 67, p. 153; G. Iorio, above n. 67, pp. 82 et seq.

a corporation structure that entitles the holder of a special share (representing a minimal fraction of capital) to full control. This is possible by using both the 'limited liability company' structure (where full control can be attributed to a shareholder with so-called 'particular rights') and the 'limited partnership limited by shares' structure (where the power to manage the company can be attributed to a shareholder[72] whose office as director is irrevocable without their consent). Basically, both the 'limited liability company' structure and the 'limited partnership limited by shares' structure allow the creation of so-called golden shares. Such shares represent a minimal fraction of the capital and are thus endowed with an irrelevant economic value for succession purposes (under Italian law, the testator may always freely dispose of at least a quarter of the estate) while incorporating the right of full control. Therefore, such a golden share could be transferred to the family foundation to ensure that (i) control is transferred according to the rules set out in the foundation by-laws, regardless of the fate of all other non-golden shares, which, instead (ii) enshrine economic rights that circulate in accordance with ordinary 'proprietary' rules. A family foundation, certainly immune from the hereditary disputes, could therefore ensure the unity of the strategic management of the family business, despite being the owner of a substantially insignificant fraction of its capital.

We have now reached the final turning point in the evolution of Italian foundation law: the admissibility under Italian law of family foundations that are potentially identical to a foreign law trust postulates the inapplicability to Italian foundations (whether enterprise foundations or not) of any 'non-distribution constraint', the last alleged mandatory barrier to a true freedom of choice regarding the incorporation of a foundation. Traces of such legal constraints cannot be found in the foundations regime under the Civil Code or in general principles of Italian private law.

Certainly, as mentioned above, Italian law expressly provides a prohibition on the disbursement of profits to founders, shareholders and directors of 'social enterprises'. However, this circumstance reinforces rather than denies the absence of any non-distribution limitation in the case of foundations. First of all, under the '*ubi lex voluit, dixit*' principle, when the law intended to establish a prohibition on the disbursement of profits to certain categories of individuals, it did so explicitly. Second, under a teleological perspective, the rationale behind the regime of social businesses differs from the rationale behind the regime of foundation. In the former case, the company is not an ordinary company under the law, as its by-laws mandate to pursue general interests. In the latter case, the contrary is true, as the foundation may well be the owner of an 'ordinary' non-social business.

---

72 Because such a shareholder can also be a legal entity, this governance layout can last 'forever'.

In conclusion, (i) the legislative amendment of 2000 which legitimised the foundations to pursue any 'lawful purpose' (and not necessarily 'public utility' purposes), (ii) the existence of numerous indexes suggesting that a total split between 'ownership' and 'control' does not contradict any Italian mandatory rule, (iii) the recognition by Italian law of a legal structure (i.e. the trust) that is very similar, in this respect, to family foundations are all elements that consistently point towards the following conclusion. Not only should it be undisputed that a foundation may have as its activity the exercise of an enterprise (including a profit-driven enterprise), but an enterprise family foundation should also be considered an effective estate planning tool that enables the founder/entrepreneur to reconcile both (i) their wish to ensure the unity and professionalism of the business contributed to the foundation (as their 'alter ego') and (ii) their wish to have their descendants benefit from the enterprise's profit. And this would be fully compatible with Italian law, albeit within the limits of inheritance law.

6. THE 'THIRD SECTOR CODE' AND THE 'NOT-FOR-PROFIT FOUNDATIONS': TOWARDS THE REPEAL OF THE RULES OF THE CIVIL CODE?

The study of Italian foundation law would not be complete without addressing the recent organic reform of the not-for-profit sector that resulted in the approval of the 'Third Sector Code' in 2017.[73]

As mentioned above, the Parliament that entrusted the government with the task of organically regulating the 'Third Sector Code' had also delegated to it the additional task of overhauling the provisions of the First Book of the Civil Code that regulate 'foundations', 'associations' and 'committees'.[74] Unfortunately, this opportunity was not taken, so the regime of 'generic' private law foundations (those that do not qualify as 'not-for-profit sector entities') continues inexorably to be, on the one hand, outdated and in need of repeal and, on the other hand, woefully inadequate and resulting in a lack of 'legal certainty'.[75]

The not-for-profit sector code draws its fundamental source of inspiration from the decline of the welfare state and from the ordoliberalist orientation

---

73 A comprehensive history of the evolution of the law of the third sector in Italy is provided by P. Consorti, L. Gori and E. Rossi, *Diritto del Terzo Settore*, 2nd ed., Il Mulino, Bologna 2021, passim.

74 L. Gori and E. Rossi, 'La legge delega n. 106 del 2016 di riforma del terzo settore' (2016) 2 *Osservatorio sulle Fonti* 6.

75 L. Gori, 'Il sistema delle fonti nel diritto del terzo settore' (2018) 1 *Osservatorio sulle Fonti* 15.

that, again due to pressures from the EU, the same Italian Constitutional Charter has now adopted.[76]

The 2001 reform of Title V of the Italian Constitution (devoted to territorial public bodies known as 'regions', 'provinces' and 'municipalities') provided the opportunity to enhance the so-called principle of subsidiarity to constitutional status. The last paragraph of Article 118 of the Constitution establishes that:

> The state, regions, metropolitan cities, provinces and municipalities shall promote the autonomous initiatives of citizens, both as individuals and as members of associations, relating to activities of general interest, on the basis of the principle of subsidiarity.

This is a complete game-changer with respect to the traditional aversion of the liberal state and, even more so, of the authoritarian fascist state, to the so-called intermediate bodies. When the principle of subsidiarity is interpreted not only in a 'vertical' sense (i.e. the higher-level territorial body can only intervene when the lower-level body is unable to pursue the general interest), but also in a 'horizontal' sense (i.e. the public authority only pursues general interest objectives when private initiative is unable to accomplish, on its own, the aim of ensuring the 'common good'),[77] this sanctions a total inversion of the traditional hierarchical order. Thus, private initiative is considered to be meritorious not only when it ensures the most efficient allocation of resources thanks to the competitive dynamics of 'selfishness' (according to the *homo oeconomicus* paradigm), but also when it efficiently organises objectives of solidarity thanks

---

76 S. Benvenuti and S. Martini, 'La crisi del welfare pubblico e il "nuovo" Terzo Settore: la via tracciata dalla legge-delega n. 106/2016' (2017) 2 *Osservatorio Costituzionale* 1.

77 M. Romano, 'I limiti all'autonomia statutaria nelle fondazioni di partecipazione alla luce della riforma del terzo settore' (2019) 2 *Le nuove leggi civili commentate* 355 and, in particular, 357 ('[F]rom the combined reading of Article 118 with Article 117 Const., the central role of private initiative emerges as a means of granting the civil and social rights given to every citizen by the Constitution; many of these rights coincide with the sectors of activity in which non-profit organisations traditionally operate.') ('*Dal combinato disposto dell'art. 118 con l'art. 117 Cost. emerge questo ruolo centrale dell'iniziativa privata nell'assicurare il soddisfacimento dei diritti civili e sociali riconosciuti a ciascun cittadino in attuazione dei principi costituzionali; numerosi di questi diritti coincidono proprio con i settori di attività in cui tradizionalmente operano gli enti non profit*') and 358 ('[T]he transposition of the principle of horizontal subsidiarity in our legal system surely represented a new challenge for non-profit entities, for which a new horizon opened: their initiative has gained priority over the one of the public hand, to which a mere role of integration and organisation of the private initiative is left') ('*Il recepimento del principio di sussidiarietà orizzontale nel nostro ordinamento ha rappresentato indiscutibilmente una nuova sfida per gli enti non profit per i quali si è aperto un nuovo ampio orizzonte: la loro iniziativa ha assunto una rilevanza prioritaria rispetto a quella della mano pubblica, alla quale resta quindi riservato un ruolo di supplenza e di organizzazione dell'intervento privato*'). See also G.U. Rescigno, 'Principio di sussidiarietà orizzontale e diritti sociali' (2002) *Diritto pubblico* 10.

to the spontaneous dynamic of 'altruism' (according to the *homo reciprocans* paradigm).

In 2012, after the well-known sovereign debt crisis, which jeopardised the single currency's survival, and in response to strong pressures from Member States in Central and Northern Europe,[78] the achievement of a net financial balance was made a constitutional principle, effectively outlawing the deficit spending that had financed Italy's welfare structure (and not always in a virtuous way).[79]

The (horizontal) principle of subsidiarity and the principle of net financial balance have shifted the expectations raised by the traditional welfare state to the so-called not-for-profit sector[80] – hence the need to revisit the entire non-profit regime through an organic reform that has given rise to the 'Third Sector Code' (TSC), the expressed purpose of which is, not surprisingly, that of 'supporting the autonomous initiative of citizens who contribute, even in associated form, to pursuing the common good'[81] (Article 1 TSC).

As far as our purposes are concerned, the TSC defines 'third sector entities' (TSEs) as those entities that 'set up for the pursuit, on a non-profit basis, of civic, solidarity and social utility purposes by carrying out, exclusively or principally, of one or more activities of general interest'[82] (Article 4 TSC). Such TSEs may also carry out business activities, but only on an ancillary basis. In fact, the enabling law specifies that foundations (not from the third sector) that primarily or exclusively carry out business activities will be governed by a law that, as of today, has not yet been approved.[83]

Moving on to the aspects that are relevant for our purposes, the TSC provides that the legal form of the TSE can be, *inter alia*, that of the 'foundation'. It then provides, with specific reference to third sector foundations (TSFs), an articulated regime that is even more detailed than that reserved for BFs in the 1990s.[84]

First of all, it is expressly confirmed that the by-laws of the TSF may envisage a 'participatory body';[85] furthermore, it is also implicitly confirmed

---

[78] I. Ciolli, 'I Paesi dell'Eurozona e i vincoli di bilancio. Quando l'emergenza economica fa saltare gli strumenti normativi ordinari' (2012) 1 *Rivista AIC* 1.

[79] S. Benvenuti and S. Martini, above n. 76, pp. 1–2.

[80] G. Ponzanelli, above n. 6, pp. 726–727 ascribes the growth of the third sector to both a government and a market failure. See also A. Zoppini, above n. 15, pp. 80–81.

[81] Unofficial translation.

[82] Unofficial translation.

[83] Article 3(d) of the Enabling Act ('*legge-delega*') no. 106 of 6 June 2016.

[84] G. Donadio, 'La disciplina generale delle associazioni e delle fondazioni del Terzo Settore' (2017) 3 *Non Profit* 127; E. Rossi, 'Il rompicapo dei controlli sugli enti del Terzo Settore' (2017) 3 *Non Profit* 271.

[85] This further attests to the admissibility under Italian law of the so-called '*fondazioni di partecipazione*' (participatory or associative foundations): see above n. 55. After the enactment of the TSC, the same stance has been generally taken by most Italian scholars, including

that the TSF may even adopt an associative structure 'open' to the entry of new participants. If the foundation's by-laws provide for such a 'participatory body', then, unless otherwise specified, the regime provided for third sector associations' assembly becomes applicable. The assembly is therefore essentially competent on the following matters: (i) the appointment and revocation of the corporate bodies; (ii) the appointment and revocation, where required, of the statutory auditors; (iii) the approval of the financial statements; (iv) the promotion of liability action against members of corporate bodies; (v) amendment of the by-laws and (vi) the resolution of dissolution, transformation, merger or division.

The board of directors remains a necessary body, whether appointed by the assembly (if any) or according to the specific rules of the by-laws. It is composed of directors with general representation powers (hence, limits that are not registered in the Single National Register of the Third Sector (RUNTS) cannot be raised as exceptions) and subject to the same rule on conflicts of interest envisaged for directors of commercial companies.

The audit committee, a compulsory body for the TSF, is subject to a regime substantially similar to that envisaged for those of joint-stock companies: (i) it must be composed of individuals with particular requirements of professionalism and independence; (ii) it oversees compliance with the law and the by-laws, as well as compliance with the principle of 'correct administration'; (iii) it monitors compliance with the civic, solidarity and social utility purposes pursued by the entity; and, finally, (iv) it certifies the correctness of the 'economic-financial' statements, as well as of the 'social' financial statements (the preparation of which is compulsory). Moreover, the financial statements of the TSF are subject to a compulsory audit by an external auditor or by an auditing firm when certain size thresholds are exceeded.

Lastly and, again, by analogy with the provisions regarding joint-stock companies, a certain percentage of participants may report 'reprehensible facts' to the audit committee (which, when the complaint is raised by a qualified minority, must report it to the assembly). Additionally, with authorisation from a certain percentage of the participants, the audit committee, the auditor or the public prosecutor may act before the competent court to report 'serious management irregularities'. This report may also lead to the judicial revocation of the corporate bodies and the appointment by the court of one or more administrators.

G. Sicchiero, 'Le fondazioni di partecipazione' (2020) 1 *Contratto e impresa* 19, 20; P. Manes, above n. 61, 267 and 269; and M. Romano, above n. 77, 368–370 ('[T]he legislator [has] indirectly confirmed that participatory foundations are not atypical foundations, and that the foundation is a model upon which statutory autonomy can be implemented, even though there are precise limits') ('*Il legislatore [ha] indirettamente confermato che la fondazioni di partecipazione non sono fondazioni atipiche, e che la fondazione è un modello sul quale l'autonomia statutaria può innestarsi, seppure con limiti precisi*').

These rules are extremely important as they mark the definitive abandonment, in the case of TSF, of that 'police right' of authoritarian origin, which authorised governmental authority to intervene *ex officio* in the control and supervision of foundations. A much more liberal protection mechanism left essentially to private initiative now takes its place, eliminating that 'threat' of public intervention in the management of foundations that acted as an enormous deterrent on the spreading of such a model.

Fundamental to our purposes and highly debated by the first interpreters of the TSC, is the question arising from the inclusion (Article 3, para. II TSC) of the principle according to which the rules of the Civil Code continue to apply to TSE (and, therefore, also to the TSF) (i) 'insofar as not provided for by this Code [i.e. the TSC]' and (ii) only 'to the extent compatible'.[86]

In reality, since the regime dictated by the TSC is more detailed than that set by the Civil Code, the aforementioned provision should entail, even regardless of the 'compatibility' clause, the substantial total repeal (or rather the inapplicability) of the Civil Code regime to all 'third sector entities', including 'not-for-profit foundations'.[87]

A fundamental question for our purposes is whether the legal regime dictated by the TSC is applicable by analogy to entities that cannot be qualified as belonging to the third sector: this would be the case for a foundation that does not carry out activities of 'general interest' for 'civic, solidarity and social utility' purposes (as required for foundations that are TSEs), but rather exclusively or mainly carries out a business activity with non-altruistic (yet 'lawful') purposes.[88]

The early commentators provided a non-uniform response to this question: both the pro-analogy and anti-analogy[89] opinions have adherents.

Naturally, should the opinion of those supporting the application by analogy of the TSC discipline to foundations outside the third sector prevail and, in turn, the application of the TSC regime renders the one dictated by the

86 Unofficial translation.

87 M. Romano, above n. 77, 366–367.

88 G. Ponzanelli, above n. 20, 728; P. Consorti, 'Profili generali della riforma del 2017' in P. Consorti, L. Gori and E. Rossi, above n. 73, p. 60.

89 M. Romano, above n. 77, 367. Early commentators questioned whether and to what extent the provision contained in the new decree could by analogy also apply to entities carrying out non-altruist purposes (i.e. not qualifying as third sector entities). In this regard, on the one hand, some scholars are of the opinion that those rules of the TSC that protect the general interest can be applied by analogy (in this sense, see G. Posio 'Norme del CTS applicabili a tutte le fondazioni di partecipazioni' in G. Sicchiero (ed), 'Le fondazioni di partecipazioni' (2021) *Ipsoa* 2512; G. Iorio, 'Il codice del terzo settore e le associazioni: i riflessi civilistici della nuova disciplina' (2018) 17 *Ianus* 15, 23 et seq.). On the other hand, other scholars argued instead that, in light of the specific purposes of third sector entities, it is not possible to extend the application of TSC's special provision by analogy (in this sense, see G.D. Mosco, 'L'organizzazione degli enti del Terzo settore tra codice civile, leggi speciali e autonomia privata' (2021) 2 *LUISS Law Review* 72, 81).

Civil Code structurally inapplicable, as the case should be, the consequences would be enormous. It would mark the end of what remains of the outdated 'police law' of the 1942 Civil Code.

Unfortunately, the fact that the legislature of the TSC chose not to intervene on the rules of the Civil Code and, instead, delegated the regime of foundations that wholly or predominantly engage in economic activity to another yet-to-be-approved law makes this conclusion not entirely clear. As long as the relevant areas of regulatory uncertainty exist on such an important front as the relationship between private activity and public control, the terrain of Italian law will remain 'fertile' ground only to a limited extent for purely private company foundations, albeit far less 'sterile' than it originally was.

7. CONCLUSION

Italian foundation law has undergone an extraordinary evolution from the Civil Code of 1942 to date. Due to (i) solicitations from the more vanguard scholarship of the 1960s and (ii) special legislation enacted in recent decades (a) on 'banking foundations' in the 1990s, (b) on the recognition of legal personality and 'purpose' in 2000 and (c) on the regime of the 'third sector' in 2017, the following conclusions can finally be drawn:

- Foundations can legitimately exercise 'business activities' not only on an ancillary or instrumental basis, but also on an 'exclusive or prevalent' basis; in other words, 'enterprise foundations' have today acquired 'citizenship rights' even in Italy.
- Despite the initial resistance to the founder's right to, directly or indirectly (through an ad hoc body), appoint and dismiss directors, foundations can now adopt the so-called associative model, which contemplates the devolution of authority to an assembly body that appoints and removes directors.
- Since the foundation can now pursue any 'legitimate purpose' and since it can no longer be argued that our law mandatorily prescribes a necessary correlation of 'ownership' and 'control' in the management of businesses, there are no longer any obstacles to consider legitimate even purely 'selfish' foundations such as family business foundations – there is no rule that imposes the so-called non-distribution constraint for foundations.
- By way of analogy with the tripartite model of the organisation initially adopted for the BF and now replicated for the TSF, the governance of any foundation (even if not belonging to the 'third sector') should preferably be articulated in three bodies: (i) the 'board of directors', which has always

been required by law, but also (ii) the 'audit committee' (now required) and (iii) the 'founders' council' (not required, but admitted).

- Since the regime of private controls envisaged for the TSF replaces public control prescribed under the Civil Code, if the regime of TSC is generally applied to foundations outside the 'third sector', the threat of *ex officio* interference by governmental authorities provided by those articles of the Code that are still formally in force no longer exists.

In a nutshell, the Italian legal infrastructure is already less hostile towards, if not moderately welcoming towards, enterprise foundations. In order to overcome the doubts that still exist among practitioners, a limited reform of the Civil Code clarifying the private nature of the Italian legal regime by the explicit repeal of all those rules of fascist inspiration is certainly desirable.

The evolution of foundation law that has been examined here appears to be inextricably connected with the concurrent evolution of property rights and, in particular, of the rights of ownership of enterprises, to which the former appears inevitably linked.

The changed attitude towards foundations indeed appears to be strongly interconnected with the changed 'sociological' context. The evolution from (i) the original rules of the Civil Code, strongly influenced by the Napoleonic Civil Code of the early 19th century to (ii) the new law on 'subsidiarity' (including in the horizontal sense) and 'third sector', which, on the contrary, appears to be influenced by the constitutionalism of ordoliberal inspiration, which encourages private entrepreneurial initiative not only for self-interested purposes, but also 'common good' purposes, albeit pursued via profit-driven activities.

The 19th century law, which still casts its long shadow over the Civil Code of 1942, was intended to discourage *ancien régime* forms of ownership – i.e. land ownership protecting the rent of an unproductive class (the old nobility) – and to favour the new revolutionary ownership; ownership of capital oriented to entrepreneurial uses for the benefit of the new bourgeoisie. Therefore, such laws intended to supplant a socio-anthropological model rooted in *homo gaudens* (the noble *rentier*) with a new model of *homo oeconomicus*, incarnated in the new hero of modernity (the bourgeois entrepreneur). In this context, any organisation – such as foundations – capable of jeopardising the market-oriented use of property was seen with suspicion and relegated to the market's periphery.

Contemporary law, in a phase in which the capitalist model has by now found maximum diffusion and is certainly no longer threatened by the 'unproductive' pressures of a class of 'passive' owners, has a completely different need now. Indeed, today the need is that of encouraging private individuals to make up for that function of guarantor of the 'common good' of the welfare state, which the contemporary state, heavily indebted and constitutionally limited by 'ordo-liberal' budget constraints, is no longer able to appropriately fulfil. In brief, the contemporary need is no longer to safeguard the *homo oeconomicus* paradigm, but on the contrary to ensure its 'happy' coexistence with the *homo reciprocans* paradigm – hence the legislative favour not only for 'social businesses', but also for those 'businesses' which, although not 'social' (as they do not pursue aims of 'social utility'), can nonetheless contribute to the 'common good' both indirectly, through the exercise of a profitable economic activity (like any profit-making enterprise with a traditional ownership structure) and directly through the concurrent pursuit (not compulsory, but certainly permitted) of ends that can benefit the whole community, under the peculiar ownership structure of a 'foundation'.

Many scholars, myself included, stand by in the hope that our legislature will run the 'last mile' and finally make Italian law favourable to 'enterprise foundations' to the same extent as the most advanced (at least under this respect) Scandinavian or Northern European laws are.

ENTERPRISE FOUNDATIONS IN LIECHTENSTEIN

Francesco A. Schurr and Alexandra Butterstein

ABSTRACT

In 1926 Liechtenstein introduced legislation that equally encompasses both private interest foundations, such as family foundations, and charitable foundations. The Liechtenstein legal framework does not provide a statutory definition of the enterprise foundation but rather confines its regulatory provisions to establishing the parameters under which foundations may permissibly conduct commercial business operations. Since the latter half of the 20th century, numerous Liechtenstein foundations with specific purposes linked to business enterprises have been established. Thus, there is a significant presence of enterprise foundations in Liechtenstein. The purposes of these enterprise foundations include holding company shares, preserving business integrity, aligning the interests of the founder's family with the development of the business, ensuring the productivity of the underlying company, a link with philanthropic purposes and succession planning as well as balancing interests of the underlying companies' stakeholders. This chapter explores the key elements of Liechtenstein enterprise foundations, focusing on foundation governance, corporate governance, beneficiaries' rights, self-serving foundations, will substitutes and related topics.

1. INTRODUCTION

The competition between the European legal systems which recognise enterprise foundations is not only played out in tax law, but in particular in private law and corporate law. In the recent past, issues regarding corporate governance and foundation governance[1] have been discussed intensively in the business community as well as in the legal community, especially in those scenarios

[1] See D. Jakob, *Die liechtensteinische Stiftung*, Liechtenstein Verlag, Vaduz 2009, paras. 442 et seq.; B. Lorenz in H. Heiss, B. Lorenz and M. Schauer (eds), *Kommentar zum liechtensteinischen Stiftungsrecht*, 2nd ed., Helbing Lichtenhahn, Basel 2022, PGR Article 552 §9, paras. 1 et seq.; J. Gasser, *Liechtensteinisches Stiftungsrecht*, Stämpfli, Bern 2019, PGR Article 552 §9, paras. 1 et seq.

where foundations are linked to businesses.[2] When comparing Liechtenstein foundation law to the corresponding laws in other jurisdictions in Europe, it is striking that there is a broad range of mechanisms available to achieve a tailor-made governance structure for each individual enterprise foundation. It seems that Liechtenstein stands out in this respect among competing jurisdictions in Europe, especially since the 2009 total revision of Liechtenstein foundation law.[3]

Furthermore, Liechtenstein's legal system contains attractive options with particular regard to the formation of mixed-purpose foundations combining both common-benefit purposes and private-benefit purposes. The founder is free to choose the purpose of the foundation. It is a necessary component of the foundation declaration (Article 552, §16, para. 1, clause 4 of the Persons and Companies Act (PGR)).[4] A distinction is made between charitable and private foundations. The predominant form of private-benefit foundation is the family foundation, which is established for the benefit of one or more specific families. If, in addition to the primary purpose of a pure family foundation, such foundations also pursue charitable or other (secondary) private benefit purposes, they are referred to as mixed family foundations.[5]

It is evident that a foundation may also be legally associated with a company. However, it should be noted that these enterprise foundations do not constitute a distinct category of foundation. Instead, they are established as either charitable or private-benefit foundations, contingent upon their designated purpose.[6] In Liechtenstein, such enterprise foundations are generally permitted, although a distinction must be made between two different forms: (i) the enterprise foundation, which itself operates a company, does not play a major role in practice, as this is only permissible for charitable foundations if it directly serves their charitable purpose; and (ii) the holding foundation, which generally holds the primary shares in a company and is therefore capable of exerting influence, is of considerably greater practical importance.[7] In this context, it is possible to organise a holding foundation as a family foundation with charitable purposes.[8]

---

2 See F. Schurr, 'Die Foundation Governance als Schlüsselelement im Wettbewerb der Stiftungsrechtsordnungen' (2010) 2 *Die Privatstiftung* 64; A. Butterstein, 'Die Governance der liechtensteinischen Stiftung als Instrument für die Nachfolgeplanung' (2024) 3 *Die Privatstiftung* 100.

3 Law of 26 June 2008 on the Amendment of the Persons and Companies Act, *Liechtenstein Law Gazette* 2008, No. 220 (*Gesetz vom 26.6.2008 über die Abänderung des Personen- und Gesellschaftsrechts, LGBl.* 2008, Nr. 220); on the 2009 total revision, see Marxer & Partner, *Liechtensteinisches Wirtschaftsrecht*, Manz, Vienna 2021, paras. 9.3 et seq.

4 See M. Schauer in H. Heiss, B. Lorenz and M. Schauer (eds), above n. 1, PGR Article 552 §1, paras. 6 et seq.; D. Jakob, above n. 1, paras. 41 et seq.

5 See A. Butterstein, above n. 2, 100, 101.

6 See D. Jakob, above n. 1, para. 120.

7 See M. Schauer, above n. 4, PGR Article 552 §1, paras. 28 et seq.; D. Jakob, above n. 1, paras. 122 et seq.

8 See A. Butterstein, above n. 2, 100, 102.

Entrepreneurs wishing to choose a jurisdiction to realise and combine their personal common- or private-benefit and entrepreneurial goals by establishing a foundation (*Stiftung*, *Fondazione*, *Stichting*, etc.) will have to take numerous factors into consideration in order to be able to identify the ideal location in which to realise their project. In practice, advisors use a variety of criteria to determine the suitability of a jurisdiction to realise the founder's intentions. In many circumstances, one of the first significant criteria might be the impact that taxation will have on the foundation as well as on its beneficiaries. Besides these tax considerations, increasingly more importance is being attributed to purely civil law factors in deciding upon the choice of the jurisdiction.[9] In this regard, emphasis is often placed on the degree of flexibility associated with determining the foundation's purpose and the associated freedom of the founder:[10] for example, the option of transforming a priori a common-benefit foundation into one with a private-benefit purpose and vice versa.[11] Where the selection of a location for a foundation is concerned, attention is also increasingly being paid to the issue of foundation governance (as well as on the corporate governance of the underlying companies). The Liechtenstein multidimensional foundation governance can help the organisation of the foundation and the company to interlock in a meaningful way.[12] This is a comprehensible standpoint when the roots and the origins of the foundation are taken into consideration.

According to the European understanding of foundations, a foundation is an ownerless entity holding assets. It is ultimately only subject to the will of its founder, as originally expressed by him/her on the formation of the foundation. The compliance with and observance of the foundation's purpose over decades or even centuries requires a careful balance to be struck between its administration and supervision. Typically entrepreneurs look for: jurisdictions with a high degree of legal certainty with regard to pursuing the foundation's purpose over a long period of time; the greatest degree of freedom possible for the founder in establishing the internal organisation of the foundation; confidentiality concerning the formation of the foundation; and a high degree of expertise among the official authorities and courts involved. From these criteria, a link between structure and function – i.e. the inextricable connection between a foundation's governance and its purpose – stands out. The main focus of the

---

9 See F. Schurr, 'The Foundation Governance under Liechtenstein Foundation Law' in C. Prele (ed), *Developments in Foundation Law in Europe*, Springer, Dordrecht 2014, p. 176.

10 See F. Schurr, 'The change of beneficial interest within the Liechtenstein Private Purpose Foundation – can the principles of solidification and flexibility coexist?' (2020) 26(6) *Trusts & Trustees* 556.

11 On the rules that can be enacted in the foundation documents regarding the transformation from a common-benefit to a private-benefit foundation in the future, see, e.g. F. Schurr, 'Die gemeinnützige Stiftung in Liechtenstein – Potential für die Zukunft' in F. Schurr (ed), *Gemeinnützige Stiftung und Stiftungsmanagement*, Schulthess, Zürich 2010, p. 82.

12 A. Butterstein, above n. 2, 100, 106.

2009 total revision of Liechtenstein foundation law was on the creation of an efficient system of foundation governance. The 2009 total revision brought the Principality's foundation law into line with modern standards and requirements. Since their entry into force on 1 April 2009, the provisions contained in Article 552, §§1–41 PGR[13] provide the Principality of Liechtenstein with the legal framework upon which to hold its own in an ever harsher competitive environment for the creation of enterprise foundations.[14]

2. DEFINITION OF ENTERPRISE FOUNDATIONS IN LIECHTENSTEIN

Until now, the concept of enterprise foundation has not been defined clearly in the legislation or case law of the Principality.[15] However, in Liechtenstein practice, three types of enterprise foundations, thus of foundations that closely link a foundation with an enterprise, are recognised.[16] The first, and most common model for such a close interconnection, is the foundation's role as a significant corporate shareholder. Second, there are foundations which hold shares and additionally have contractual links with businesses that allow them to give directions and to determine the strategy etc. In this regard, the foundation can be granted additional rights of influence and control over the entrepreneurial decisions of the family business in the company's articles of association.[17] The third and least relevant type are foundations that operate businesses directly

13 Law of 26 June 2008 on the Amendment of the Persons and Companies Act, *Liechtenstein Law Gazette* 2008, No. 220 (*Gesetz vom 26.6.2008 über die Abänderung des Personen- und Gesellschaftsrechts, LGBl.* 2008, Nr. 220).

14 For an analysis of the Liechtenstein foundation law in the light of recent revisions in neighbouring jurisdictions, see A. Butterstein, 'Die liechtensteinische Stiftung im Umfeld aktueller Reformen in der Schweiz und in Deutschland' (2022) 43(4) *Liechtensteinische Juristenzeitung* 209. Furthermore, Liechtenstein is considered a model state in the implementation of international regulations on anti-money laundering (see the 2023 Activity Report of the newly created Financial Intelligence Unit: Stabsstelle Financial Intelligence Unit (SFIU), 'Jahresbericht 2023. Stabsstelle Financial Intelligence Unit (SFIU) des Fürstentums Liechtenstein' (2024): www.llv.li/serviceportal2/amtsstellen/stabstelle-financial-intelligence-unit/fiu_jahresbericht_2023_de.pdf) and tax data exchange (see M. Amann, 'Automatischer Informationsaustausch in Steuersachen und Datenschutz' (2018) *Liechtensteinische Juristenzeitung* 1; a comparison of the tax laws of a German and a Liechtenstein family foundation disproves the widespread belief that Liechtenstein foundations have a major tax advantage over foreign foundations, see K. Kutac, 'Die Familienstiftung in Deutschland und Liechtenstein' (2021) *Internationales Steuerrecht* 409).

15 See D. Damjanovic, 'Unternehmensstiftung in Liechtenstein – ja, nein, vielleicht?' (2023) 3 *Liechtensteinische Juristen-Zeitung* 142; D. Jakob, above n. 1, para. 119.

16 See J. Gasser, above n. 1, PGR Article 552 §1, paras. 15 et seq.

17 See A. Butterstein, above n. 2, 100, 106.

or that hold personal liability in partnerships that manage enterprises.[18] In Liechtenstein, this is only possible in accordance with Article 552, §1, para. 2, clause 1 PGR if it directly serves the achievement of a common-benefit purpose of the foundation. All three categories fall under the concept of a Liechtenstein enterprise foundation.[19] This chapter will focus primarily on the first model, thus, the model where foundations own companies.[20]

In Liechtenstein, it is quite common that foundations hold large stakes in capital corporations with operating enterprises and/or to be contractually connected with business operators or having such operators as beneficiaries.[21] These two models allow the business foundations to grant financial stability for themselves and the company, to sustainably secure the company's existence and to give the underlying companies running the businesses the flexibility and independence to adjust to various situations in the market. Furthermore, these two types of business foundations can help to realise an asset lock that might be relevant in terms of a steward ownership.[22] Thus, the strategic position of foundations (e.g. regarding stakeholder interests) can be realised in the long run.[23] Whenever foundations operate as corporate shareholders, their influence over the company is granted primarily through the exercise of the membership rights in the underlying company.[24] Moreover, the foundation may be granted additional appropriate rights of influence and control over the entrepreneurial decisions of the family business in the articles of association of the company, taking into account the entrepreneurial freedom of the management.[25]

Thus, it seems to be essential to distinguish foundations that hold stock as a form of neutral investment from those foundations that have been specifically

---

18 See K.J. Hier, 'Der Stiftungszweck der Unternehmensstiftung' in F. Schurr (ed), *Wandel im materiellen Stiftungsrecht und grenzüberschreitende Rechtsdurchsetzung durch Schiedsgerichte*, Schulthess, Zürich 2013, pp. 23–54.

19 See I. Wohlgenannt, *Verbot von Selbstzweckstiftungen in Österreich und Liechtenstein*, Manz, Vienna 2015, pp. 74 et seq.; F. Schurr, J. Gasser and T. Hosp, 'Verantwortlichkeit und Abberufung des Stiftungsrats – Privatrechtliche und steuerrechtliche Fragen im Zusammenhang mit der Unternehmensträgerstiftung' (2012) 4 *Liechtensteinische Juristen-Zeitung* 166; on the various types of links between a foundation and a business from a comparative perspective, see F. Schurr, *Die Stiftung mit unternehmerischer Verantwortung*, Nomos, Baden-Baden 1998, pp. 27 et seq.

20 See A. Sanders and S. Thomsen, 'Enterprise Foundation Law: Introduction' in this volume, pp. 1 et seq.

21 See K.J. Hier, *Die Unternehmensstiftung in Liechtenstein*, Liechtenstein Verlag, Vaduz 1995, pp. 9 et seq.

22 On the concept of *Verantwortungseigentum* in the context of foundations, see e.g. R.K. Feldthusen, S. Kalss and C. Teichmann, 'Unternehmensträger mit Vermögensbindung' (2024) *Zeitschrift für Unternehmens- und Gesellschaftsrecht* 862, 864; A. Sanders, 'Binding Capital to Free Purpose: Steward Ownership in Germany' (2022) *European Company and Financial Law Review* 622.

23 See D. Damjanovic, above n. 15, 142, 145.

24 See I. Wohlgenannt, above n. 19, pp. 76 et seq.

25 A. Butterstein, above n. 2, 100, 106.

established in order to realise precise entrepreneurial goals in respect of one or more defined companies.[26] From a general point of view it needs to be emphasised that probably most of the foundations headquartered in Liechtenstein somehow hold shares in operating companies. However, many of these foundations are likely to regard these company shares as an arbitrary asset, that can be replaced at any time, e.g. by bankable assets, real estate, etc. whenever such a change in the investment strategy seems convenient. It goes without saying that these scenarios do not fall under the category of enterprise foundations.

3. PURPOSES OF ENTERPRISE FOUNDATIONS

3.1. THE BUSINESS RELATED PURPOSES

As was previously mentioned, enterprise foundations do not belong to a separate category of foundation enshrined in law; they are structured as charitable or private-benefit foundations in line with their purpose.[27] In order to be qualified as an enterprise foundation according to the discussion in Liechtenstein, there needs to be *inter alia* a defined intention of the founder[28] regarding the business. This entrepreneurial intention has to be mirrored in the purpose of the foundation, e.g. with the following wording:

> The purpose of the X foundation is to exert influence on the management of the companies held directly or indirectly by the X foundation through appropriate measures, and thereby to promote the continuity and expansion of the assets. Furthermore, the purpose is that the X foundation shall ensure the financial support and promotion of the founder of the companies held directly or indirectly by the foundation and his/her family members, as long as they exist, by making distributions and granting other economic benefits.[29]

Founders of enterprise foundations typically set up the foundation and bring in the shares that they are holding in the business because they want to make sure that their personal ideas about the company's management, its business strategy and its future development are realised in the long run.[30] Thus, it is

---

26 See K.J. Hier, above n. 21, pp. 14 et seq.

27 See A. Butterstein, above n. 2, 100, 106; M. Schauer, 'Grundelemente des neuen liechtensteinischen Stiftungsrechts und die rechtsvergleichende Perspektive' in F. Schurr (ed), *Das neue liechtensteinische Stiftungsrecht*, Schulthess, Zürich 2008.

28 See H. Böckle, 'Die Unternehmensstiftung im Spannungsfeld zum Pflichtteilsrecht' (2013) *Liechtensteinische Juristen-Zeitung* 141.

29 A similar wording has been used by the Liechtenstein Supreme Court, OGH 9.1.2014, 04 CG.2012.438, GE 2014, 206, quoted also in J. Gasser, above n. 1, PGR Article 552 §1, paras. 15c et seq.

30 See I. Wohlgenannt, above n. 19, pp. 72 et seq.

typical for enterprise foundations that the goal of economic sustainability of the business is reflected prominently in the foundation's purpose defined in the foundation documents: rules contained in the foundation deed, the supplementary foundation deed and regulations of the enterprise foundation need to make sure that the foundation governance is adequate.[31] The checks and balances in the internal setup of the enterprise foundation are essential for the successful achievement of the founder's intentions on the level of the underlying company.[32]

3.2. OTHER PRIVATE-BENEFIT PURPOSES

The family members of the founder often find themselves in the position of being beneficiaries of the foundation. However, it happens frequently that these family members consider the establishment of the Liechtenstein enterprise foundation as contrary to their own interests. Thus, there is a constant risk of internal conflicts.[33] This is due to the asset lock produced by the transfer of the company's shares in the foundation. This asset lock creates a main obstacle to future transfers of the same shares to the family members of the founder. Thus, it might be a challenge to balance the company's interests on one hand and the family's interests on the other.[34] Things might get even more complicated whenever an enterprise foundation pursues *inter alia* charitable purposes. Thus, it is essential that the different purposes – e.g. the economic (social and environmental) sustainability of the business, the support and maintenance of family members, the philanthropy, etc. – are reflected equally in the definition of the foundation's purpose in the foundation deed, the supplementary foundation deed and the regulations and that the foundation governance is adequately balanced. The founder's intentions need to be defined clearly in the wording of those articles of the foundation deed, the supplementary foundation deed and the regulations that are dedicated to the purpose. Thus, these articles always need to be interpreted in the light of the (presumed) intentions of the founder at the time of the establishment of the foundation.[35]

---

31 On categories of foundation documents, see D. Jakob, above n. 1, paras. 197 et seq.; B. Lorenz above n. 1, PGR Article 552 §16, paras. 4 et seq.; J. Gasser, above n. 1, PGR Article 552 §16, paras. 7 et seq.

32 See J. Gasser, above n. 1, PGR Article 552 §1, paras. 15 et seq.

33 On the topic of conflicts between beneficiaries and foundation bodies, see F. Schurr and A. Butterstein, 'Rechtslage in Liechtenstein' in M. Nueber and M. Gass (eds), *Konfliktlösung in Privatstiftungen*, Verlag Österreich, Vienna 2019, paras. 34 et seq.

34 See K.J. Hier, above n. 18, p. 28.

35 See D. Jakob, above n. 1, paras. 21 et seq.

3.3. CHARITABLE PURPOSES

Over the last 15 years, Liechtenstein has become one of the most efficient hubs for philanthropy in the European Economic Area (EEA).[36] The above-mentioned 2009 total revision has created a very innovative regime of foundation governance for charitable foundations allowing for the foundation surveillance authority (*Stiftungsaufsichtsbehörde*, STIFA) and the Princely Court (*Fürstliches Landgericht*) to safeguard well-balanced foundation governance.

Charitable enterprise foundations typically rely on the underlying for-profit company whose shares are kept by the foundation to receive regularly the dividends necessary to make the charitable distributions. This model is used, e.g. if a founder without descendants sets up a foundation in order to grant scholarships to young talented musicians, while the funds for these distributions of the foundation originate in the dividends paid by the underlying company to the enterprise foundation. Under these circumstances, the intentions of the founder as defined in the foundation purpose embrace the maintenance of the family business on one hand and the charitable purpose (e.g. distributions to scholarships for young talented musicians) on the other. There might also be charitable purposes that relate to the company, such as, e.g. the distribution to family members of the underlying enterprise's staff that are in need. In all scenarios the foundation's assets and the income must be used in line with the charitable purposes.[37]

3.4. PROTECTION OF ASSETS AND SUCCESSION PLANNING

The enterprise foundation typically serves as a tool for the protection of both the enterprise per se and its relationship with the market.[38] The reason for setting up such a foundation might be to preserve the so-called productive assets in a broader sense and to ensure growth.[39] By transferring the company's assets to the foundation, many founders may also intend to preserve the unique corporate culture of the business, e.g. relating to customer interactions, product quality, affordability and design of the products as well as the relations to the employees. It is quite common that the intention of the founder to preserve her/his life's work

36 The creation of the Association of Liechtenstein Charitable Foundations and Trusts (*Vereinigung lichtensteinischer gemeinnütziger Stiftungen und Trusts*/VLGST) can be regarded as one of the essential milestones in this evolution, see: www.vlgst.li.

37 See K.J. Hier, above n. 18, p. 28.

38 See F. Schurr, 'Wealth preservation by using trusts or private foundations in a civil law environment' (2019) 25(6) *Trusts & Trustees* 587; R.K. Feldthusen, S. Kalss and C. Teichmann, above n. 22, 862, 867.

39 See F. Schurr, 'Wesensmerkmale der Asset Protection anhand ausgewählter Fragen des liechtensteinischen Rechts' in F. Schurr (ed), *Handbuch des Vermögensschutzes für Liechtenstein, Österreich und die Schweiz*, Manz, Vienna 2015, §1, paras. 46 et seq.

or the work of her/his ancestors has priority over the interests of the individuals involved in the wealth planning strategy, such as, e.g. the family members and/ or other persons that are close to the founder. There are various prominent examples of successful succession planning[40] of globally acting businesses (such as Ikea, Interogo Foundation or the Kuno Frick Family Foundation[41] etc.) where a Liechtenstein foundation's role is to protect the assets. There are also some foundations associated with enterprises, although it is not known whether they only hold shares or are involved in the organisation of the management.

3.5. FAMILY GOVERNANCE

It happens quite frequently that the founder has the intention to link the members of the family to the business. Under Liechtenstein law, there are two ways to realise this liaison. The first way is to insert clauses into the foundation deed, the supplementary foundation deed or regulations that allow the family members to take an active role in the management of the underlying companies. Furthermore, the founder can set up rules in these foundation documents that allow for the distribution of profits from the enterprise to the family members. Thus, these family members would have the status of discretionary beneficiaries.

Anyway, it is typical for Liechtenstein enterprise foundations that distributions to family members are restricted in order to allow reinvestments into the business. This approach is chosen primarily by founders whose first goal is to preserve the family business for various generations. For the founder, providing for the family takes precedence over distributing profits, with enterprise preservation being the best way to secure this provision. They seek to ensure long-term family support through the business, involving descendants either directly as managers or indirectly as foundation board members.

4. INTERPLAY BETWEEN VARIOUS OBJECTIVES AND BENEFICIARIES

The foundation is used as a legal tool to grant a balanced interplay between various objectives of the founder, such as entrepreneurial goals, maintenance of the family, charitable intentions, etc. that are often contradictory. Among the choice of the descendants that benefit (indirectly through the distribution of the foundation) of the company's profits, the founder might choose persons that are

---

40 See M. Mathauer, *Unternehmensstiftung zur Nachfolgeplanung*, Recht & Wirtschaft Verlagsanstalt, Vaduz 2016, pp. 54 et seq.

41 For the integration of the Bank Frick in the Kuno Frick Family Foundation, see: 'About Bank Frick' (2025) *Bank Frick*: www.bankfrick.li/en/about-bank-frick.

talented to get a leading role in the enterprise and motivate them (through a discretionary distribution policy) to be focused and successful. On the contrary, the founder might rather choose weak and vulnerable family members that would not be in a position to make a career because of, e.g. health issues. Whenever the founder is concerned about the maintenance of a good personal relationship between the family members, he/she will consider equal treatment that implies a higher level of social harmony. If the setup of an enterprise foundation is intended as a will substitute, the founder often implements the principle of equal treatment between descendants in order to mirror succession law. In fact, many jurisdictions have embraced in their succession law the principle of equal treatment between heirs. Many founders of Liechtenstein enterprise foundations have implemented demands and expectations linked to the distribution to beneficiaries in order to motivate them to develop abilities as potential managers of the underlying company. Furthermore, it is very common that the founder wants to provide entrepreneurial opportunities to his/her descendants through a business that he/she has inherited or that he/she has established. Under these circumstances, the foundation can serve as a suitable tool to ensure that descendants that are interested and qualified seize the opportunity to achieve a role of entrepreneurial responsibility on the level of the underlying company or on the level of the enterprise foundation. The foundation can also contribute when it comes to maintaining the goodwill of the less talented family members towards the family enterprise whose shares are kept by the enterprise foundation. In the long run, this goodwill might be relevant because these family members might in the future again have qualified and interested offspring. As far as the concept of an enterprise foundation as a will substitute is concerned, it is essential to highlight that founders typically intend to create legal certainty regarding the business that they have established or inherited. This means that they use the foundation in order to maintain the productivity of the business beyond their death and to grant economic support to the family members. Finally, it should be noted that the founder should not reserve any founder's rights for him/herself in order to ensure the institutionalisation of the company-related foundation as a will substitute.[42]

5. COMPATIBILITY OF PURE BUSINESS PRESERVING FOUNDATIONS WITH THE LEGAL FRAMEWORK

5.1. INTRODUCTION

What the founder intends with the enterprise foundation must primarily be enshrined in the provisions regarding its purpose. As far as the purpose of

42 See A. Butterstein, above n. 2, 100, 105.

enterprise foundations is concerned, it seems to be wise to distinguish various categories. The first one is the foundation that has the sole purpose to preserve the business.[43] We could label this category as a 'pure business preserving foundation'. Whenever the preservation of the enterprise is just one of various goals of the founder, along with, e.g. the maintenance of family members and/or philanthropy, we could label such a foundation as 'mixed business preserving foundations'.

Since the 2009 total revision of foundation law, a self-serving foundation is considered to be in contrast with the law.[44] According to Article 552, §1, para. 1 PGR a foundation is a legally and economically independent special-purpose fund which is formed as a legal entity (legal person) through the unilateral declaration of will of the founder. According to the quoted provision, the founder allocates the specifically designated foundation assets, stipulates the purpose of the foundation, entirely non-self-serving and specifically designated, and also stipulates the beneficiaries. Thus, Article 552, §1 para. 1 PGR requires the founder to define both the directly outward-facing, clearly specified purpose of the foundation and the beneficiaries.[45] This requirement seems to be particularly relevant for enterprise foundations since it is applicable: 1) to foundations aimed at preserving a business as well as; 2) to those established for the benefit of the founder's descendants; or 3) to those established for charitable purposes. It goes without saying that the requirement for a directly outward-facing purpose defined in Article 552, §1, para. 1 PGR excludes the possibility of a purely self-serving foundation. Unfortunately the legislator did not give a precise explanation of when a purpose is considered outward-facing, but it does define a purely self-serving foundation as one that exclusively manages (its own) assets and permanently accumulates and reinvests profits without ever distributing those profits for a specific (charitable) purpose or to specifically defined beneficiaries (e.g. descendants).[46]

At this stage it is important to emphasise that enterprise foundations whose purpose is to preserve a business definitely do not fall under the concept of an unlawful self-serving foundation. The preservation of a business is a purpose that goes beyond the mere management of assets and the reinvestment of the profits. That is due to the fact that the preservation of a specific enterprise is a complex endeavour that requires the bodies of the foundation to deal with many questions and to interact – indirectly through the underlying company – with many stakeholders, such as employees, customers, suppliers, etc. As further argument in favour of the compatibility of the enterprise foundation with the

---

43 On the various definitions of the term business (*Unternehmen*) under Liechtenstein law, see D. Damjanovic, above n. 15, 142, 144.

44 Thus, a pure self-serving foundation cannot be recognised and thus does not separate the assets from the assets of the founder, see F. Schurr, above n. 39, §1, paras. 60 et seq.

45 See K.J. Hier, above n. 18, p. 30.

46 See D. Damjanovic, above n. 15, 142, 145.

sole purpose to preserve the business, we would like to stress the definition of an outward-facing purpose through the definition of self-serving foundations. The 2009 total revision of Liechtenstein foundation law did not address explicitly the question whether 'pure business preservation foundations' fall under the concept of self-serving foundations. The omission of any explicit restrictions can be interpreted as a deliberate effort to allow Liechtenstein foundations to be used as structures for the maintenance of businesses on a very broad spectrum of goals, including the sole preservation of the business as a legitimate goal. Due to the unclear legal situation and the lack of case law, in practice, an additional outward-focused purpose is chosen in order to avoid an unlawful charitable self-serving foundation.

5.2. NECESSITY TO DEFINE BENEFICIARIES

The above-mentioned provision of Article 552, §1, para. 1 PGR requires the founder not only to define the purpose of the foundation, but also its beneficiaries.[47] This wording is highly confusing and needs to be corrected in the light of Article 552, §16, para. 1 PGR. This provision contains a list of elements that need to be included in the foundation deed. At clause 4 the legislator makes it clear that the foundation deed needs to define the purpose of the foundation, including the designation of tangible beneficiaries, or beneficiaries identifiable on the basis of objective criteria, or of the category of beneficiaries, unless the foundation is a charitable foundation or the beneficiaries are evident from the purpose of the foundation, or unless there is instead express reference to a supplementary foundation deed regulating this. Hence, there are no doubts that it is fully in line with the law if a foundation has the sole purpose to preserve a business.[48]

5.3. OUTWARD-FACING PURPOSE

With the requirement of an outward-facing purpose and the associated description of a self-serving foundation, Liechtenstein has a formal regulation addressing the self-serving nature of foundations.[49] A foundation whose purpose is solely the preservation of a business can be described as a 'corporate self-serving foundation'. As mentioned previously, such a foundation is admissible under Liechtenstein law, because the foundation interacts indirectly with the

47 See P. Panico, *Private Foundations*, Oxford University Press, Oxford 2014, para. 7.07.

48 See K.J. Hier, above n. 18, pp. 33 et seq.

49 See K.J. Hier, above n. 18, pp. 31 et seq; M. Walch, 'Zum Verbot der Selbstzweckstiftung' (2021) *Zeitschrift für Stiftungswesen* 35.

stakeholders of the underlying company and therefore does not operate as an isolated entity, such as a foundation that simply reinvests all the profit generated out of the investment of its assets.

5.4. RESTRICTIONS REGARDING DISTRIBUTIONS

Even since before the 2009 total revision of Liechtenstein foundation law, such a 'corporate self-serving foundation' has never been prohibited. The understanding of self-serving foundations as defined in Article 552, §1, para. 1 PGR does not preclude corporate-related arrangements, provided there is a serious purpose in the preservation of a specific business and not merely a pretext. Anyway, in practice, most of the enterprise foundations are not limited to the goal of preserving a business, but typically have as a second purpose the maintenance of family members or a charitable purpose. Furthermore, it needs to be highlighted that deferred or otherwise restricted distributions to beneficiaries align with the founder's intentions and their practical implementation in enterprise foundations. Founders often wish to ensure that their descendants remain connected to the business across generations, either as business leaders or as beneficiaries of its profits. To achieve this, founders aim to strengthen the financial position of the business sustainably, limiting profit withdrawals from the corporation. Naturally, this requires the foundation, as a shareholder, to exercise its voting rights accordingly. If the foundation is also to retain earnings itself – whether for later reinvestment into the corporation (i.e. the business) or investment into other enterprises – this must also be defined by the founder. It is advisable to secure this flexibility for the foundation. However, this necessitates that the founder defers and restricts the foundation's distributions from retained earnings over time. Special ownership structures involving enterprise foundations are primarily established in practice for large, profitable and high-growth companies. The profits generated – and potentially retained by the enterprise foundation – are therefore substantial, often far exceeding the needs of a single generation of descendants, even with an elevated standard of living. It is therefore logical for the founder to impose restrictions on distributions, typically limiting them annually to a small percentage of the profits received or retained by the foundation.

5.5. NON-EXISTENCE OF SELF-SERVING ENTERPRISE FOUNDATIONS BECAUSE OF A NECESSARY ULTIMATE BENEFICIARY

The question needs to be raised whether a foundation can ever truly serve a purely self-serving purpose. Enterprise foundations anyway do not do so for the reasons stated previously in this chapter, but they could still protect their existence by pointing to the ultimate beneficiary. In fact, every foundation, including every enterprise foundation, has an ultimate beneficiary as per Article 552, §8 PGR. This could either be explicitly designated in the foundation deed, the supplementary foundation deed or regulations or, in the absence of designation, default to the state of Liechtenstein. A distribution, however, occurs at the latest in favour of the ultimate beneficiary when the foundation is terminated.[50]

6. MANAGEMENT OF THE ASSETS OF ENTERPRISE FOUNDATIONS

6.1. GENERAL PROVISIONS

The foundation is required to pursue ownership interests, regardless of whether its purpose is limited to business preservation. The shareholding in the corporation is always part of the foundation's assets, and it is often its most significant component. Under Article 552, §25, para. 1 PGR, the foundation board is required to manage these assets in accordance with the founder's intent and the foundation's purpose, following principles of sound management. This implies a general duty of loyalty to the foundation. The board must act exclusively in the foundation's interests, making this the sole guiding principle of its conduct. Under Article 552, §25, para. 2 PGR, the founder can establish specific and binding management criteria. Regardless of whether the foundation's purpose is limited to business preservation, founders often impose special obligations on the foundation board regarding the management of corporate shareholdings. Even if the shareholding is merely a means to pursue a foundation purpose unrelated to the business, founders often impose additional obligations. Once again, the foundation board is naturally required to pursue the foundation's ownership interests.

6.2. RESTRICTIONS ON THE SALE OF THE BUSINESS FOR BUSINESS PRESERVATION FOUNDATIONS

Whenever there is a business that must be preserved according to the foundation's purpose, a lucrative sale of the business is questionable. It goes without saying that the business preservation as a purpose can only be pursued if the foundation does not sell the business. This means that the purpose cannot be achieved if the

50 See K.J. Hier, above n. 18, p. 37.

foundation sells its shareholding in the business-operating corporation for profit or is outright prohibited from selling it.

If the foundation's purpose is solely business preservation, it would be entirely logical to require the foundation to sell the business if it could no longer ensure its preservation in any other way or if keeping it would jeopardise or prevent its sustainability. This applies regardless of whether the sale is explicitly mandated or not. In such cases, the guiding principle is that the foundation must prioritise the preservation of the business over its own existence. Anything else would contravene the legal pursuit of the purpose and thus be impermissible. Therefore, selling the business is not prohibited; in extreme cases, it is even necessary.

If the foundation has no purpose other than business preservation, it is not required to sell the business as lucratively as possible. Instead, it must sell the business in a timely manner – before its connection to the foundation causes it lasting harm or threatens its existence. The sale proceeds only matter insofar as they are reinvested in the business to pursue the foundation's purpose.

Different rules apply if the foundation's purpose extends beyond business preservation. For instance, the foundation might be required to sell the business if other investments appear more stable and profitable. In this case, the sale must indeed be as lucrative as possible to ensure a smooth transition to other assets. However, if the foundation's purpose is limited to business preservation, the accusation of being unable to sell the business lucratively is unfounded.

7. FOUNDATION GOVERNANCE WITHIN ENTERPRISE FOUNDATIONS

7.1. INTRODUCTION

In European legal tradition, foundations are more or less the only type of legal entity which exists without a so-called corporate element.[51] As a result, the legal concept of shareholders is completely missing in the concept of foundations. In Liechtenstein, not only foundations, but also establishments (*Anstalten*) and business trusts (*Treuunternehmen*) fall under the category of legal persons without members/shareholders.[52] The unique Liechtenstein establishment can

51 See F. Schurr, 'Beneficiaries' rights and foundation governance in Liechtenstein' (2015) 21(6) *Trusts & Trustees* 674.

52 Establishments (*Anstalten*) and business trusts (*Treuunternehmen*) can be established with or without shareholders. Only the foundation-like establishments (*stiftungsähnliche Anstalt*) and the business trust with legal personality without members (*Treuunternehmen mit Rechtspersönlichkeit ohne Mitglieder*) is comparable in its structure and function with the Liechtenstein foundation.

be organised in two different ways: either as a foundation or as a corporation.[53] Despite the absence of an international equivalent, the establishment has already been recognised as a corporate entity by foreign courts.[54] Furthermore, Liechtenstein law is the only legal system in continental Europe that recognises not only the foundation but also the trust, which has been incorporated into the PGR as a legal transplant. In contrast to the foundation, the trust does not possess legal personality. Due to the Hague Trust Convention and the European freedom of establishment, the trust is also recognised by other civil law states.[55]

It needs to be highlighted that the category of so-called participants in the foundation (*Stiftungsbeteiligte*), as defined in Article 552, §3 PGR, shall not be confused with the concept of shareholders of companies or members of associations. On the contrary, the category of participants in the foundation embraces the entitled beneficiaries; the prospective beneficiaries; the discretionary beneficiaries; the ultimate beneficiaries. The provisions of Liechtenstein foundation law define specific rights and duties of these persons.[56] None of these persons has a legal status that resembles the role of a shareholder of a company. This is because a foundation is a special purpose fund which belongs to itself and is subject only to its own purpose. Whenever such a shareholder-like power is granted (e.g. to the founder and/or to a beneficiary in a provision of the foundation deed, the supplementary foundation deed and/or the regulations), the assets of the foundation cannot be considered to be separated from the personal assets of the holder of these powers. Thus, such a construction would be detrimental for the desired effect of a working protection of the assets of the Liechtenstein enterprise foundation.[57]

The autonomous nature of the special purpose fund requires the setup of an organisational structure by means of which the long-term pursuit of the foundation's purpose – e.g. in the field of the maintenance and development of the underlying company running a business – is rendered possible, even after the death of the founder. The logical consequence of this is that tighter control mechanisms are ultimately necessary for foundations than for companies. Having said this, it is imperative that the realisation of the purpose is not hampered by complicated regulatory bureaucracy or insufficient expertise on the part of the

---

53 See M.U. Fischer, 'Die liechtensteinische privatrechtliche Anstalt nach Art 534 ff PGR – Ein Wanderer zwischen den Welten' in H. Schumacher and W. Zimmermann (eds), *90 Jahre Fürstlicher Oberster Gerichtshof: Festschrift für Gert Delle Karth*, Jan Sramek Verlag, Vienna 2013, pp. 169, 176 et seq.

54 See German Federal Court of Justice, BGH 3.12.2014, NJW 2015, 623.

55 See F. Schurr, 'Rechtliche Ausgestaltung und Anwendungsbereiche des Trusts in Liechtenstein' (2017) 1 *Zeitschrift für Stiftungs- und Vereinswesen* 12; A. Butterstein, 'Rechtsvergleichende Betrachtung der Errichtung einer Substiftung und des Trust Decanting' (2020) 41(3) *Liechtensteinische Juristen-Zeitung* 208.

56 See M. Schauer in H. Heiss, B. Lorenz and M. Schauer (eds), above n. 1, PGR Article 552 §3, paras. 1 et seq.

57 See F. Schurr, above n. 39, §1, paras. 60 et seq.

regulators. Therefore, every foundation finds itself on a fine line between the rigidity usually associated with regulation and the flexibility needed to pursue its purpose.[58] The Liechtenstein system of foundation governance represents a combination of the beneficiary-based control model (typical, e.g. for the Austrian private-benefit foundation) and the public-authority control model (typical, e.g. for the Swiss or German charitable foundation). Liechtenstein law therefore enables a foundation governance model that is adapted to the respective purpose of the foundation and distinguishes between the supervision required for common-benefit foundations, which are subject to state supervision, and for private-benefit foundations, which are generally controlled by the beneficiaries or supervised by courts acting in response to petitions. It goes without saying that the relevance of functioning foundation governance is particularly relevant in the field of enterprise foundations.[59]

7.2. STRUCTURES OF GOVERNANCE OF ENTERPRISE FOUNDATIONS

Other than in most of the other European jurisdictions, Liechtenstein foundation law can be categorised as particularly flexible and thus suitable for the creation of a tailor-made enterprise foundation. The legal provisions regarding the foundation governance contained in Article 552, §§1 et seq. PGR are in many cases optional. This means that most of the governance structures that will be discussed in this chapter can be adapted still further in the deed of the Liechtenstein enterprise foundation.[60]

As far as foundation governance is concerned, it is necessary to distinguish between the common-benefit and the private-benefit foundation. Only the first category of foundations, those that have a predominantly common-benefit purpose, is subject to an external supervision by the Foundation Supervisory Authority (*Stiftungsaufsichtsbehörde*, STIFA). On the contrary, private-benefit foundations are not subject to compulsory supervision by this public administrative body. For the latter type of foundations, a considerable emphasis is placed on the beneficiaries as an internal control body.[61] Enterprise foundations under Liechtenstein law may fall under the first or the second model, depending whether the distributions made by the enterprise foundation shall be made according to the foundation deed, the supplementary

---

58 See F. Schurr, above n. 9, p. 178.

59 See e.g. the information about the foundation governance of the Interogo Foundation (IKEA) on the website: www.interogofoundation.com/foundation-governance/foundation-governance.

60 See F. Schurr, above n. 9, p. 179.

61 See D. Jakob, above n. 1, paras. 453 et seq.

foundation deed and/or the regulations, e.g. to charitable organisations or, e.g. to members of the family of the founder. The fact that family foundations, for example, can exist completely independently of state supervision clearly gives Liechtenstein a definite competitive advantage over other jurisdictions. Merely by determining the purpose of the foundation on its formation, it is possible to ascertain whether the future foundation will be subject to supervision by STIFA.[62]

According to Article 552, §29, para. 1 PGR, STIFA is responsible for supervising enterprise foundations that fall under the definition of common-benefit foundations.[63] Common-benefit foundations are understood as foundations that fulfil purposes for the benefit of the general public. This is taken to be the case when a foundation's activity serves the common good in a charitable, religious, humanitarian, scientific, cultural, moral, social, sporting or ecological sense, as defined in Article 107, para. 4a PGR. This provision is applicable to all legal persons such as foundations, companies, associations, establishments, etc. In Liechtenstein, there is also a special feature which should be mentioned: a common good is also deemed to be served even if only a specific category of persons benefits from the foundation's activity.

A unique feature in the Liechtenstein system is that external governance is not reserved exclusively for common-benefit foundations. Private-benefit foundations can choose to place themselves under such supervision by so determining in the foundation deed (i.e. by opting in).[64] This means that public administrative bodies can also become involved in monitoring more than just the philanthropic sector. This model can be attractive for enterprise foundations where the founder intends to avoid that the beneficiaries (e.g. the children or grandchildren) of the founder receive detailed information (e.g. about the assets, the revenues, etc.). If, on forming a private-benefit enterprise foundation, no choice is made to opt in, the foundation's internal governance structure will form the basis of supervision. In such cases, it is left to the foundation participants (Article 522, §3 PGR) to exercise their control functions.[65]

On international comparison, Liechtenstein stands out with its combination of external and internal governance which has been in place since the 2009 total revision of its foundation law. The same applies to the approach of combining supervision by STIFA with that of the mandatory audit authority. This approach has been borrowed from Switzerland, where Article 83c of the Swiss Civil

62 See F. Schurr, above n. 9, p. 180.

63 On the differences between the supervision exercised by an administrative body as compared to a court, see K.J. Hier, above n. 18, pp. 112 et seq.

64 As stated by the head of STIFA during the Foundation Law Day at the University of Liechtenstein on 20 November 2024, as of September 2024, the number of private-benefit foundations under STIFA's supervision was 31, in contrast to 1,390 common-benefit foundations.

65 See D. Jakob, above n. 1, paras. 474 et seq.

Code (ZGB) also provides for cooperation between audit authorities and the supervisory authority.[66] In contrast, supervision of private foundations in Austria is undertaken by the courts – not by any administrative authorities. This approach has the advantage that the judiciary is politically independent. The mandatory provisions concerning state supervision contained in Liechtenstein foundation law are tempered by the fact that STIFA and the courts cooperate with one another where punitive measures are required. This almost completely prevents the work of STIFA from being influenced by political considerations. With regard to the duties and responsibilities of STIFA as set out in the new Liechtenstein foundation law, a distinction must be made between areas requiring preventative and punitive measures.

7.3. RULES ON PREVENTATIVE AND PUNITIVE MEASURES

In Article 552, §29, para. 3 PGR the scope of the preventative measures available have been defined clearly. Under this provision, STIFA is entitled to request information from a foundation and to order an inspection of a foundation's books and documents, which is to be carried out by an audit authority.[67] The same article governs the scope of the punitive measures available. STIFA can ensure that executive bodies are dismissed, special audits are carried out or resolutions passed by the executive bodies are set aside, if these are to the benefit of a foundation. Such measures may, however, not be carried out by STIFA itself. Instead, a petition must be filed in court within the framework of special non-contentious civil proceedings. It can be summarised that there is a combination of two models, which leads to a so-called supervision of the supervisors: ongoing state supervision is combined with supervision by the courts which only act on the basis of petitions. When the 2009 total revision entered into force, there were concerns about the shared competences of the surveillance authority and the court, especially as far as the risk of an increase of bureaucratic work was concerned.[68] The high expenditure required for involving two public institutions (administrative authorities and courts) can be justified using the argument that abuse will be completely eliminated by this sophisticated system of governance and that this in turn will contribute greatly to creating trust and confidence in the system of Liechtenstein foundation law. There is no doubt that in the current competition amongst jurisdictions, the dual system of supervision has become the essential criterion for ensuring that Liechtenstein, rather than another

66 See F. Schurr, above n. 9, pp. 180 et seq.

67 See D. Jakob, above n. 1, para. 460.

68 See F. Schurr, above n. 9, pp. 181 et seq.

jurisdiction, is chosen as the location of preference for the creation of enterprise foundations that operate internationally and thus require a structure that is suitable for cross-border activities.[69]

7.4. INTERNAL AND EXTERNAL GOVERNANCE OF PUBLIC-BENEFIT ENTERPRISE FOUNDATIONS

As far as common-benefit enterprise foundations in Liechtenstein are concerned, internal governance has also been given due consideration. An audit authority within the meaning of Article 552, §27 PGR is of relevance in this context. For each foundation subject to the supervision of STIFA, an audit authority has to be established and responsibilities are delegated to this internal body. For only foundations that manage minor-value assets, STIFA may request the appointment of an audit authority. Courts are also involved in appointing an audit authority: a court makes the appointment of an audit authority on recommendation by the founder concerned, as defined in Article 552, §27, para. 3 PGR. In making such appointments, the potential for any obvious conflicts of interest must be considered. Such conflicts of interest are clearly present where members of another executive body of the foundation, employees of the foundation, people with close family connections with members of executive bodies of the foundation, and beneficiaries of the foundation are involved.[70]

7.5. SUPERVISION OF PRIVATE-BENEFIT ENTERPRISE FOUNDATIONS

As indicated above, it is typical for private-benefit enterprise foundations to exist under Liechtenstein law without being exposed to any type of external governance whatsoever. As mentioned previously, private-benefit foundations may choose to place themselves voluntarily under the supervision of the state as carried out by STIFA. Thus, in the default model, any influence of a public authority is limited to any action taken by the court on the basis of a petition that has been filed by a foundation participant (founder, beneficiaries or executive bodies) or in very rare and clearly defined cases *ex officio*.[71]

---

69 See A. Butterstein, 'Modernes Stiftungsrecht im Lichte grenzüberschreitender Stiftungstätigkeit' in F. Schurr (ed), *Segmentierte Stiftungen – Anerkennung – Vermögensverwaltung – Nachfolgeplanung – Philanthropie*, Schulthess, Zürich 2018.

70 See D. Jakob, above n. 1, para. 390.

71 See F. Schurr, above n. 9, pp. 184 et seq.

As far as foundations not subject to public supervision are concerned, responsibility for supervision lies with the beneficiaries of the foundation. It is therefore ultimately the beneficiaries who are the mainstay of the internal governance structure.[72] The beneficiaries have their own separate interest in ensuring that the foundation's purpose, as outlined in the foundation documents, is in fact pursued.[73] The strong role played by beneficiaries as a body enforcing compliance with the foundation's purpose represents a significant advantage of the legal situation in Liechtenstein with regard to foundation governance. This distinguishes the approach taken in Liechtenstein foundation law from that of some other jurisdictions.

On examination of the structural design of the new Liechtenstein law on foundations with regard to private-benefit foundations on the whole, it becomes clear that the supervisory vacuum left by the lack of official supervision is filled by the active role undertaken by beneficiaries. Anyway, beneficiaries falling within the framework of foundation governance cannot be compared to shareholders of a company. This is due to the fact that beneficiaries cannot assume the same functional role held by shareholders of a company. This is because shareholders represent a corporate element which would be incompatible with the foundation's character as an ownerless fund.[74] Nevertheless, the beneficiaries do, to some extent, hold a legal position similar to that of an owner. Drawing a comparison between foundation beneficiaries and equitable owners of trusts cannot be justified dogmatically; on a functional comparison, however, it becomes clear that they have equivalent legal functions.[75]

A beneficiary's entitlement to supervise is primarily shaped by supervisory rights. Pursuant to Article 552, §9 PGR, beneficiaries are entitled to inspect the foundation deed, the supplementary foundation deed and any regulations. Furthermore, they may request the disclosure of information, reports and accounts. For this purpose, beneficiaries have the right to inspect the business records and documents and to produce copies, and also to examine and investigate all facts and circumstances, in particular accounting, personally or through a representative. At the same time, the supervisory rights delineate the boundaries of beneficiaries' rights. The fundamental purpose of the right of information is to ensure the adequate preparation and protection of the beneficiaries' primary rights. According to Article 552, §33, para. 3, §34, para. 2 and §35, para. 1 PGR, beneficiaries are entitled to the right of application and party status in non-contentious proceedings.

---

72 See F. Schurr and A. Butterstein, above n. 33, paras. 40 et seq.
73 See Liechtenstein Supreme Court, OGH 23.7.2004, LES 2005, 392.
74 See D. Jakob, above n. 1, para. 87.
75 See F. Schurr, above n. 9, p. 185.

7.6. CATEGORIES OF BENEFICIARIES OF ENTERPRISE FOUNDATIONS

Beneficiaries are not all equally entitled to conduct supervision.[76] Beneficiaries are systematically classified into categories in Article 552, §§5 et seq. PGR. First, there is a limitation in place according to which beneficiaries only have a right to information insofar as their legitimate interests are concerned. In this context, beneficiaries with a vested interest have a right to supervision under Liechtenstein law, as specified in Article 552, §5 together with §6, para. 1 PGR. In addition, prospective beneficiaries also qualify for entitlement to supervise if they hold an interest in a future benefit, as pointed out in Article 552, §5 together with §6, para. 2 PGR. Ultimate beneficiaries have a legal claim; the supervisory entitlement arises on the dissolution of the foundation, as specified in Article 552, §5 together with §8 and §9, para. 3 PGR. Holding an expectation of acquiring a benefit, but without any legally enforceable claims to entitlement, leads to being classified as a discretionary beneficiary.[77] By way of this classification, discretionary beneficiaries who also have a current prospect of receiving a benefit at the discretion of the foundation's governing bodies have a legitimate interest in receiving information about the foundation and are therefore entitled to a supervisory role. Clearly, discretionary beneficiaries should be viewed as a particularly effective supervisory body as they ultimately could stand to lose their future interests and therefore are more attentive: any decision made by the foundation council which could have a negative impact on the extent of the discretionary beneficiaries' benefit could become an occasion for preventative supervision.[78] It needs to be highlighted that a person holding a contingent expectation to a discretionary future benefit is excluded from claiming any entitlement to supervise.[79]

7.7. RESTRICTION TO CASES OF PRESENT INTEREST

Beneficiaries' supervisory rights are also restricted by the requirement of a so-called present interest. The use of this element leads, however, to a certain degree of legal uncertainty. In the past, the existence of present interest was put into doubt when a request for information made by a beneficiary pertained to an incident which occurred prior to a person gaining his/her status as a beneficiary.[80] In this context, a beneficiary is only awarded an entitlement to obtain information

---

76 See F. Schurr, above n. 51, 674, 676.
77 See F. Schurr, above n. 9, p. 186.
78 See D. Jakob, above n. 1, para. 479.
79 See F. Schurr, above n. 51, 674, 676.
80 See Liechtenstein Supreme Court, OGH 7.2.2008, LES 2008, 272.

in very specific exceptional cases. This includes in circumstances where incidents have occurred prior to a person gaining his/her status as a beneficiary, which, however, have a direct effect on his/her current beneficial interest.[81] Nevertheless, in 2015, the Liechtenstein Supreme Court ruled that beneficiaries possess rights to information and disclosure, even in circumstances that occurred prior to their becoming beneficiaries.[82]

7.8. THE FOUNDATION'S INTERESTS IN CONFIDENTIALITY v. THE BENEFICIARIES' INTERESTS IN TRANSPARENCY

Under exceptional circumstances, the right of supervision may also be restricted where the need to protect the foundation outweighs the interests of the beneficiaries in obtaining information: abuse, in particular, should be prevented, as pointed out in Article 552, §9, para. 2, clause 2 PGR.[83] In accordance with this provision, rights to information and disclosure must not be exercised with dishonest intent, in an abusive manner or in a manner which conflicts with the interests of the foundation or other beneficiaries.[84] It is not entirely clear when a beneficiary's right of supervision can be denied due to the existence of a foundation's fundamental and conflicting interest. A foundation's interests in maintaining confidentiality alone will be unlikely to suffice. Otherwise every private-benefit foundation not falling under the supervision of STIFA would be able to exist without any supervision whatsoever. It is for this reason that high benchmarks must be set when allowing any conflicting interests to prevail.[85] For the purpose of ensuring effective supervision, a decision in favour of beneficiary rights should be made in cases of doubt when weighing the conflicting interests involved, i.e. the foundation's interests in protecting its privacy and the beneficiaries' interests in receiving information.[86] This is due to the fact that a founder is able to strip down or minimise beneficiaries' information rights by implementing the use of other control mechanisms. On drawing up a foundation, he/she is able to do this, if necessary, to pursue the specific privacy interests involved. If this institutionalised option to minimise the information rights of beneficiaries had not been provided to founders under Liechtenstein law, the foundation would certainly not enjoy the same level of protection as it currently does.[87]

---

81 See D. Jakob, above n. 1, para. 487.
82 See Liechtenstein Supreme Court, OGH 4.9.2015, LES 2015, 210.
83 See F. Schurr, above n. 9, pp. 187 et seq.
84 See F. Schurr, above n. 51, 674, 676.
85 See Liechtenstein Supreme Court, OGH 23.7.2004, LES 2005, 392 et seq.
86 See F. Schurr, above n. 9, p. 188.
87 See Liechtenstein Supreme Court, OGH 7.2.2008, LES 2008, 272.

7.9. EXCLUSION BY VOLUNTARILY INVOLVING STIFA

In accordance with Article 552, §12 PGR, beneficiaries can be denied their information rights if the enterprise foundation is voluntarily placed under the supervision of STIFA. With regard to the mutually exclusive options of supervision being exercised either by STIFA or by beneficiaries, one point should be highlighted. Beneficiaries often feel compelled to check the work done by STIFA. This is true for both common-benefit foundations subjected to compulsory supervision and private-benefit foundations subjected to voluntary supervision. Moreover, a beneficiary's entitlement to receive information cannot be denied where STIFA omits to carry out its information duties, as this would lead to the manifestation of a supervisory vacuum. In this situation, beneficiaries are granted a so-called emergency right of supervision. In practice, however, this situation only arises in extremely exceptional circumstances because STIFA usually fulfils its supervisory duties efficiently.[88]

7.10. PRIVATE CONTROLLING BODY

It needs to be highlighted that the submission to supervision by STIFA is not the only method used to reduce the beneficiaries' rights to information. Under Article 552, §11, para. 1 PGR, an option is provided to reduce the beneficiaries' rights to a bare minimum by appointing a private controlling body. In such cases, beneficiaries are not entitled to information regarding, e.g. the assets of the enterprise foundation or regarding any payments which have been made to other beneficiaries. Instead, the rights of beneficiaries to information are bundled into a private controlling body which acts in lieu of any beneficiaries.[89]

Whenever there is a complex beneficiary structure (e.g. conflicts between children of the founder regarding their management roles in the underlying companies) it makes sense to bundle the efforts of controlling institutions within a foundation and unite these in a private controlling body. The interests of beneficiaries often conflict with those of the foundation. Thus, it is common that the information rights of beneficiaries are exercised in an abusive manner.

It should be noted that a private controlling body can take the shape of an audit authority, a representative with sufficient expertise or a founder personally, as outlined in Article 552, §11, para. 2 PGR. If an audit authority is to act as a private controlling body, it must be appointed by the court. Furthermore, the provisions governing conflicts of interest must be observed. In court proceedings

88 See F. Schurr, above n. 9, p. 188.

89 See F. Schurr, above n. 51, 674, 676 et seq.; A. Butterstein, 'Registerpublizität und Stiftungsaufsicht im Lichte der jüngsten europäischen Rechtsprechung' in T. Husemann et al. (eds), *Strukturwandel und Privatrecht*, Nomos, Baden-Baden 2019.

for the appointment, STIFA clearly has no standing, as is also the case with the appointment of an audit authority for common-benefit foundations. Furthermore, a person that is close to the founder may be appointed as a private controlling body. In such cases, however, an appointment by the court is not required. A founder may personally act as a supervisory body provided that he/she is not also one of the beneficiaries. If a private representative is appointed as a controlling body of the enterprise foundation for the purpose of curtailing beneficiaries' information rights, a situation arises which resembles one on the appointment of a protector under common law trust laws. As regards the enforcement of rights by means of supervision by appointing a private controlling body, the following point may be made: the beneficiaries are at liberty to have the requirements for the private controlling body reviewed by a court of law. This means that a foundation must demonstrate that a private controlling body exists and has been set up properly if it wishes to be able to shield itself against beneficiaries' claims for information.[90] If, in such a case, a foundation demonstrates that a founder has been personally appointed as the supervisory body, proof must be provided that he/she is not also a beneficiary. In case an audit authority is set up, for the appointment of which the court is instrumental, a court order making the appointment is sufficient to deny beneficiaries their entitlement to information or to reduce this to a minimum.

8. ALTERING THE PURPOSE OF ENTERPRISE FOUNDATIONS

Effective, long-term management of enterprise foundations often requires altering a foundation's purpose. In the field of common-benefit foundations, STIFA may apply to the court within the framework of special non-contentious civil proceedings pursuant to Article 552, §33 PGR if one of the following conditions is fulfilled: the purpose has become unachievable, impermissible or irrational or if circumstances have changed to the extent that the purpose has acquired a quite different significance or effect.[91] The idea behind this provision is to prevent a foundation from becoming detached from the intention of its founder. Any amendment of the purpose must be consistent with the presumed intention of the founder concerned. In such cases, the presumed intention of the respective

---

90 See D. Jakob, above n. 1, para. 510.

91 See F. Schurr, 'The change in beneficial interest within the Liechtenstein Private Purpose Foundation – can the principles of solidification and flexibility coexist?' (2020) 26(6) *Trusts & Trustees* 556. In the case of foundations that are not subject to the supervision of the Foundation Supervisory Authority, the judge may make the amendments described at the request of a participant in the foundation (in particular the beneficiaries), see Article 552, §35, para. 1 PGR.

founder must be established by applying the interpretative rules of the allusion theory (*Andeutungstheorie*).[92] This doctrine requires two steps to be taken: the intended purpose must be determined by analysing the facts of the specific case and the statements made by the founder in that case; thereafter, the question of whether a commensurate allusion of the intended purpose has been achieved must be answered.[93] Pursuant to Article 552, §33, para. 3 PGR, foundation participants are also entitled to file a petition in court for the amendment of a foundation's purpose. If no such application for amendment is made by STIFA, foundation participants may petition the court in place of STIFA.[94]

STIFA may also file a petition for the amendment of other contents of a foundation deed or a supplementary foundation deed. Foundation participants are also entitled to petition the court to this effect.[95] This is because an order for supervisory measures may be issued by the court on the basis of a petition filed by either STIFA or the other foundation participants. Both STIFA and other foundation participants can therefore act as applicants in special non-contentious civil proceedings. Under Article 552, §3 PGR, founders, entitled beneficiaries, prospective beneficiaries, discretionary beneficiaries, ultimate beneficiaries, the executive bodies of foundations and members of these executive bodies are deemed to be participants of the enterprise foundation. Typically, subsequent donors are not considered to be foundation participants because of their exclusion from the exhaustive list provided in Article 552, §3 PGR. Thus, subsequent donors are not qualified as petitioners, even though they would hold an interest in filing petitions.[96]

9. PROTECTED CELL COMPANY (PCC)

Since the beginning of 2015, registered holding foundations and exclusively non-profit foundations have had the option of so-called 'segmentation' (*Segmentierte Verbandsperson*, Protected Cell Company, Article 243 to Article 243g PGR).[97] The assets of a segmented foundation consist of the core assets and the separate assets of the individual segments. However, only the foundation itself has its own legal personality, not the individual segments. In contracts with third parties,

92 See Liechtenstein Supreme Court, OGH 3.8.2000, LES 2000, 240; OGH 6.3.2008, LES 2008, 354 et seq.

93 See H. Bösch, *Liechtensteinisches Stiftungsrecht*, Stämpfli, Bern 2005, pp. 493 et seq.

94 See F. Schurr, above n. 9, pp. 183 et seq.

95 See F. Schurr and S. Büchel, 'Überlegungen zur Anpassung und Änderung des Stiftungszwecks' (2009) *Liechtenstein Journal* 110.

96 See D. Jakob, above n. 1, paras. 468 et seq.

97 See F. Schurr and I. Wohlgenannt, 'Einführung der segmentierten Verbandsperson in das liechtensteinische Personen- und Gesellschaftsrecht (PGR)' (2015) 1 *Liechtensteinische Juristen-Zeitung* 23.

it can be agreed that a specific segment is liable, while the core assets are only secondarily liable. In addition to the mandatory contents of the foundation deed pursuant to Article 552, §16, the foundation deed of a segmented foundation must include: a declaration that it is a segmented foundation; provisions regarding the organisation and representation of the segmented foundation; the specific designation of the individual segments; and the areas of activity of the individual segments.[98] Segmentation is also possible retrospectively, provided that a reservation of amendment in favour of the founder or the foundation bodies is anchored in the statutes. Otherwise, a transformation can also be applied for in court.[99] The segmentation of a holding foundation is particularly interesting in order to reduce the risks of cross-liability between various subsidiaries. Whenever an enterprise foundation is used as a will substitute, the segmentation of the holding foundation allows for a more differentiated structure of succession planning and thus for a clear separation between the entrepreneurial assets of the subsidiaries attributed to each individual.

10. SPECIAL NON-CONTENTIOUS CIVIL PROCEEDINGS

Like the participants involved with common-benefit foundations, those involved with private-benefit foundations have a right to petition the court within the framework of so-called special non-contentious civil proceedings, as outlined in Article 552, §35, para. 1 PGR. Involving the courts is, in this regard, the only method of being able to verify the external governance structures existing for private-benefit foundations. The involvement of the courts in response to a petition filed by foundation participants leads to a state supervisory body (the courts) having a direct effect on foundations. Courts may intervene *ex officio* in very rare cases, for example where the Office of the Public Prosecutor or STIFA issues a communication to this end.[100]

11. CONCLUSION

Liechtenstein has established itself as a premier location for enterprise foundations due to its flexible legal framework, which accommodates the needs of founders seeking to preserve businesses and create long-term governance structures. A notable feature of Liechtenstein's legal framework is its allowance

98 The last two pieces of information can also be regulated in a set of regulations pursuant to Article 552, §18 PGR.

99 See Marxer & Partner, above n. 3, para. 9.99.

100 F. Schurr, above n. 9, pp. 189 et seq.

for greater flexibility in defining the purposes of businesses, including those with a primary focus on business preservation.

This flexibility aligns with the evolving understanding of self-serving purposes, as seen in both legal literature and practice. In Liechtenstein, the emphasis is on ensuring that the foundation's structure can meet its intended goals, whether they involve securing the continuity of a business, maintaining employment, or achieving other objectives in a free-market context. Additionally, Liechtenstein's regulatory environment and foundation laws provide tools to address concerns regarding transparency, governance, and the balancing of various stakeholder interests. These measures serve to enhance the stability and reputation of enterprise foundations.

Liechtenstein is too small to host a large number of industrial enterprises. However, such businesses can be controlled from Liechtenstein, particularly through domestic holding structures. The necessary infrastructure for expertise and personnel is well suited to Liechtenstein's scale and generates economic and social value that would be challenging to achieve otherwise.

ENTERPRISE FOUNDATIONS IN THE NETHERLANDS

Christiaan Stokkermans and Marleen van Uchelen-Schipper

ABSTRACT

Dutch rules on foundations *(stichtingen)* are flexible. They facilitate all kinds of foundations but do not contain special rules on enterprise foundations. A structure often used in the Netherlands is where a foundation acquires shares for the account of beneficial owners, whilst issuing depositary receipts for the shares to such beneficial owners. Dutch foundations may (and do) also hold company shares for their own account and even operate businesses themselves. Dutch foundations also feature in protective structures, for instance as call option holders of protective preference shares of listed companies or as holders of golden shares in steward ownership structures.

1. INTRODUCTION

Foundations and their predecessors have a long history in the Netherlands, leading back to medieval 'houses for the poor', hospitals and museums. Nowadays, foundations are used for a wide variety of purposes. Many foundations are charities, but foundations can be used for totally different purposes. For example, investment funds not structured as legal entities can be set up with a foundation as nominee owner of the fund assets. According to information from the Dutch Chamber of Commerce, over 250,000 foundations are currently registered in the Dutch Commercial Register. Ranking behind the private limited liability company (BV) (of which there are more than 400,000), the foundation is the second most popular type of legal entity in the Netherlands. The Dutch foundation can be characterised as a rather flexible, not-for-profit type of legal entity.

Dutch law does not regulate enterprise foundations as such, and foundation law is sufficiently flexible to allow their existence. Therefore, we will first describe the legal framework for and characteristics of Dutch foundations in general (section 2). After that, we will zoom in on Dutch enterprise foundations in practice and discuss a variety of concrete examples (section 3). In this chapter, the term 'enterprise foundation' refers to a foundation that holds a controlling interest in a business corporation. Structures in which a foundation owns and runs a business itself will be briefly discussed as well. We will end with some thoughts about opportunities for Dutch enterprise foundations going forward.

2. DUTCH FOUNDATION LAW

2.1. LEGAL FRAMEWORK FOR DUTCH FOUNDATIONS

Despite the long history of foundations in the Netherlands, the first law on foundations only entered into force in 1956. Currently, the rules on foundations are laid down in Book 2 (Legal Persons) of the Dutch Civil Code (DCC).[1] They offer much flexibility.

Incorporation requires a notarial deed stating the name of the incorporator(s), containing the charter (articles of association) and naming the first board members.[2] Neither governmental approval nor the contribution of any capital is required for such incorporation. After its incorporation, the foundation and its charter must be registered at the Dutch Commercial Register but this is not a requirement for its existence. This registration is a duty of the foundation's board members. As long as this first registration has not taken place, each (management) board member can be held liable for legal actions performed on behalf of the foundation. In addition to name, seat and purpose, the charter must contain rules for appointment and removal of board members, and for the destination of property after dissolution of the foundation. A foundation is incorporated for an indefinite period of time.[3]

An important change to legislation in the Netherlands was enacted per 1 July 2021.[4] It came in response to incidents with semi-public institutions that often use the foundation form (such as government funded social housing, healthcare and educational institutions). In one of these incidents, a managing director of a government funded housing institution had speculated with the foundation's funds; its bankruptcy could only be avoided by similar institutions stepping in. The aim of the 2021 legislative change is to further professionalise management and (where applicable) internal supervision at foundations. The duties of the board are clarified, conflicts of interest rules are introduced and director liability rules are tightened.

Sector legislation and comply-or-explain based sector codes, where applicable, often provide additional regulation, especially rules on governance and external supervision. This includes semi-public sectors such as social housing, healthcare and education. Cultural institutions, such as museums, which are usually set up as foundations, have their own informal sector regulation as well. Local governments and other public or private organisations that grant subsidies generally require these institutions to comply with the special code for cultural institution, the Cultural Governance Code. Pension funds must, by law, use the foundation as a legal form and a pension fund foundation must comply with certain sector rules and apply the Pension Fund Governance Code.

Foundations with a charitable purpose can benefit from certain tax advantages, subject to conditions and registration as a public benefit organisation (PBO);[5]

1 The foundation rules are in Title 2.6 (Articles 2:285 et seq.) DCC; the general provisions for legal persons in Title 2.1 (Articles 2:1 et seq.) DCC apply to foundations as well.
2 Article 2:286 DCC.
3 Article 2:17 DCC.
4 (2020) *Staatsblad* 507 and 508.
5 In Dutch: *algemeen nut beogende instelling* or ANBI.

this will be discussed in section 2.7. Charities with fundraising activities can (also) apply for CBF recognition (reference is made to section 2.5), the Dutch private fundraising label, subject to compliance with certain rules.

Furthermore, Dutch law mandates a few extra rules for any foundation operating a business of its own. Such foundations are often informally referred to as 'commercial foundations' and will be further discussed in section 3.5.

2.2. PURPOSE AND PROPERTY

The charter of a foundation must set out its objects, its purpose. Any purpose is allowed as long as it is not illegal or contrary to public order (such as a threat to national security).[6] For instance, the foundation's purpose can be to administer (family) property or to run a business. The aim of the foundation must be to employ its property in furtherance of the purpose set out in its charter. A foundation's assets can consist of contributions made by the founder, earnings from its activities, contributions from affiliated entities, donations, subsidies and/or other government contributions. However, a foundation is not required to have any property. It might, and sometimes does, exist without property, for instance if it is merely set up as a governance device (e.g. to take decisions in deadlock situations between joint venture partners).

An amendment to the foundation's charter, including a change of its purpose clause, may only be effected if expressly authorised by the charter.[7] If the (management) board – with or without the approval of the supervisory board, if any – is allowed to change the purpose clause, the board's duty implies that, in doing so, the board must consider the interests of the foundation's stakeholders. Whether a change is legitimate depends *inter alia* on the type and nature of the foundation, its stakeholders and the origin of its assets and funds. Should the charter not allow amending the charter, amendment will (still) be possible by court order, on the request of a qualifying interested party.[8]

A foundation can be converted into another type of legal entity, such as a Dutch BV (*besloten vennootschap*). It will require an amendment of the charter and court permission. If a foundation is converted to a BV, the first shareholders must be appointed in the deed of conversion. By law, the conversion of legal form will give rise to an asset or capital lock: the foundation's property at the time of

6 Article 2:20 DCC.

7 Article 2:293 DCC.

8 Article 2:294 DCC provides that the District Court may amend the charter upon request of a founder, the board of directors or the Public Prosecution Office, if an unchanged continuation of the charter would lead to consequences which reasonably could not have been the intention at the incorporation of the foundation.

conversion, and any proceeds thereof, will be earmarked and may only be used in furtherance of the foundation's original purpose.[9]

2.3. NO DISTRIBUTIONS; NO MEMBERS

A foundation may not make distributions to incorporators or members of its bodies, or third parties, except for distributions with a charitable or social character to third parties.[10] The reference to 'distributions with a charitable or social character' must not be interpretated narrowly. For instance, if the incorporator or his family member suffers from a rare disease, a foundation can be set up and funded to make resources available for the treatment of such disease. Contractual payments such as directors' remunerations are not deemed distributions. A contractual payment which cannot reasonably be regarded as a *quid pro quo* may violate the distribution prohibition. This may not be easy to establish; case law on this subject is scarce.[11] The restriction on distributions also applies to the spending of any liquidation surplus after dissolution of the foundation.

A foundation holding mere legal title to assets which are beneficially owned by others (e.g. the incorporators or their family members, or third-party investors) is usually referred to as a trust foundation (a 'STAK'). This particular use of foundations will be further explained in section 3.1.

Another key feature of Dutch foundations law is the prohibition for foundations to have members.[12] A foundation may establish bodies other than a (management) board and supervisory board, for instance a participants' or stakeholders' council, but it may not have a body that can be equated with the general meeting of members of an association in terms of composition and powers. The scope of this membership prohibition is not entirely clear. It is ultimately up to the courts to determine whether the membership prohibition is breached in a specific case; there is very little case law on this matter. The ultimate consequence of violation of the membership prohibition is that the court can dissolve the foundation. However, the foundation would then first be given the opportunity to amend its charter or to convert into another type of legal entity.[13]

---

9 Article 2:18(4), (5) and (6) DCC.

10 Article 2:285(3) DCC.

11 Court of Appeal, The Hague, 19 December 2023, ECLI:NL:GHDHA:2023:2684 and Court of Appeal, Amsterdam, 9 June 2020, ECLI:NL:GHAMS:2020:1499 (*Stichting ANV Fondsen*).

12 Article 2:285(1) DCC.

13 Article 2:21 DCC.

2.4. FOUNDATION GOVERNANCE

A foundation is required to have a (management) board, consisting of one or more (managing) directors. Specific (sector) rules may require a minimum of three directors. Other organs (e.g. supervisory board, advisory board) are optional, except in certain regulated sectors. For instance, sector rules and governance codes for healthcare institutions (hospitals) and social housing institutions prescribe internal supervision in the form of a separate supervisory board. Managing directors can be individuals or legal entities. Supervisory directors may be individuals only. The actions of the boards must be guided by the interests of the foundation, which is defined by its purpose and includes taking due account of the interests of its stakeholders.[14]

Many general governance rules in the DCC applicable to foundations were originally designed for companies. For instance, the conflict of interest rules in the DCC prescribe that a director having a personal interest that conflicts with the interest of the legal entity must leave the decision-making to the other (non-conflicted) directors. If all directors are conflicted, however, the default rule in company law mandates that the decision be left to the general meeting of shareholders. By contrast, if all directors of a foundation are conflicted the board may still decide, with an obligation to explain the decision in writing.

A two-tier structure (management board and supervisory board) is well suited to organise internal supervision. Pursuant to the DCC, the task of a supervisory board is to supervise the policy of the management board and the general course of affairs in the foundation. In addition, a supervisory board is charged with giving advice to the management board, solicited and unsolicited. Having sufficient and up-to-date information is considered essential for proper supervision. Therefore, the management board must, in a timely manner, provide the supervisory board with the information necessary for the latter to perform its duties. Moreover, at least once a year, the management board must inform the supervisory board in writing of the main points of the strategic policy, the general and financial risks and the management and control systems used.[15] If a supervisory board is installed, it will also have the power to suspend managing directors (except if the charter provides otherwise). The foundation's charter may vest additional powers in the supervisory board, such as approval rights in respect of important management board decisions.

Sector regulation, where applicable, often mandates specific governance requirements. Under governance codes for the social housing and healthcare sectors, for instance, foundations operating in the sector must have a two-tier board structure (with separate management and supervisory boards). Sector regulation

14 Article 2:291(3) DCC and Article 2:292a(2) DCC.
15 Article 2:292a(11) DCC.

may also comprise additional rules on supervisory board composition (diversity, independence, etc.), self-evaluation and accountability. For instance, sector rules for healthcare institutions stipulate that the supervisory board is composed in such a way that the supervisory directors can operate independently and critically towards each other, the management board and any particular interest.

Foundations desiring or required to set up internal supervision may alternatively provide for a one-tier structure.[16] A one-tier board consists of two types of directors: executive and non-executive directors. As far as regulated sectors are concerned, the one-tier board is mainly found in the pension sector and sometimes in (primary) education. Additional bodies, such as a participants' or stakeholders' council, can be added voluntarily and granted specific rights in the charter such as prior approval rights for certain board decisions.

The foundation's charter must contain rules on the appointment and removal of directors. In a two-tier structure, the power to appoint and remove managing directors is often granted to the supervisory board. The supervisory board usually provides for its own succession. However, this right can be granted to another corporate body such as a participants' council or even to an outsider, such as local government. Instead of a direct right to appoint directors, the charter can grant a (binding) nomination right to a corporate body or an outsider. For healthcare institutions and social housing institutions, sector rules prescribe that the right to appoint and remove managing directors is granted to the supervisory board and the right to appoint and remove supervisory directors to the supervisory board itself. In addition, in these semi-public sectors, a mandatory clients council (patients or tenants) may nominate one or more supervisory directors. Foundations with a works council (*ondernemingsraad*) or similar employee representation body – this concerns, e.g. large commercial foundations and many semi-public institutions – must seek advice from this body when a director is nominated or proposed to be removed.[17]

Dutch corporate co-determination rules (*structuurregime*) apply to qualifying large NVs (*naamloze vennootschappen*) and BVs, cooperatives (*coöperaties*) and mutuals (*onderlinge waarborgmaatschappijen*),[18] but not to foundations. The enterprise foundation is relevant, however, to application of the co-determination rules to the underlying company (NV or BV). Under the standard co-determination rules: (1) the qualifying company must have a supervisory board; (2) the works council may nominate one-third of the supervisory board members; (3) important management decisions are subject to supervisory board approval; and (4) management board members will be appointed and may be removed by the supervisory board. In international groups, the international

16 However, in the social housing and healthcare sectors, a two-tier board is mandated.

17 Article 30 of the Dutch Works Council Act.

18 Articles 2:63a–2:63j DCC (cooperatives and mutuals), Articles 2:152–2:164a DCC (NVs) and Articles 2:262–2:274a DCC (BVs).

holding company will be fully exempted, in which case a relaxed regime will apply to the Dutch operating company (or sub-holding for the Dutch activities) meeting the qualification criteria. Under the relaxed regime, the management board members are appointed and removed by the shareholders (as in companies without co-determination), allowing the international holding to exercise control. Another instance where this relaxed rule applies is where a foundation holds all shares in a company qualifying for co-determination for its own account.[19] So, if an enterprise foundation owns for its own account all shares in a Dutch company qualifying for (and not exempted from) corporate co-determination, then that company may apply the relaxed version of the co-determination rules.

2.5. EXTERNAL SUPERVISION

Foundations in sectors such as social housing, healthcare and education are supervised by external supervisors (inspections) on the basis of sector regulation. Fundraising charitable foundations will usually seek recognition from the Central Fundraising Agency (*Centraal Bureau Fondsenwerving*, in short: the CBF); they will then be subject to supervision by the CBF. A special team of the Dutch Revenue Service supervises foundations qualifying as a public benefit organisation (PBO) (see section 2.7). In addition, service providers to foundations such as banks and notaries must screen their clients and – in case of legal persons – request information regarding the ultimate beneficial owners. A notary must refuse to incorporate a foundation or amend its charter if that would be contrary to law or public policy or has an unauthorised purpose.

The Public Prosecution Office (*Openbaar Ministerie*) can seek the removal or suspension of foundation directors through the court if the directors neglect their duties, other serious circumstances warrant such a decision or important changes to circumstances so require. The right to start such court proceedings also accrues to qualifying interested parties, which, depending on circumstances, may include former directors, founders, beneficiaries of foundation assets, benefit recipients and subsidy providers.[20] The court has removed directors, for example, where they used donations received by the foundation for private purposes or violated the distribution prohibition.[21] A director removed by the

---

19 Article 2:155a(1)(b) DCC (for NVs) and Article 2:265a(1)(b) DCC (for BVs).

20 Article 2:298 DCC.

21 Court of Appeal, The Hague, 19 December 2023, ECLI:NL:GHDHA:2023:2684 and Court of Appeal, Amsterdam, 9 June 2020, ECLI:NL:GHAMS:2020:1499 (*Stichting ANV Fondsen*). More cases are discussed in M. van Uchelen-Schipper, 'Stichting en extern toezicht' in B.C.M. Waaijer, M. van Uchelen-Schipper, B.J. Kuck, P.H.N. Quist, E. Schmieman, J.D.M. Schoonbrood, K.A. Breuker, G.J.C. Rensen, S.J.C. Hemels and B.F. Assink, *De stichting, een onbegrensde rechtsvorm?*, SDU, The Hague 2024.

court may be excluded from becoming a managing or supervisory director of another foundation for a period of five years after removal.

The Public Prosecution Office holds a number of civil law powers. For example, the Public Prosecutor has tools under company law and bankruptcy law to prevent abuse of legal entities. With regard to foundations, the Public Prosecutor may request information from the foundation's board if good faith compliance with the law and the foundation's charter is in doubt.[22] Going one step further, the Public Prosecution Office may request the court to remove a foundation director on one or more of the grounds stated in the law, as mentioned above.[23] So far, the Public Prosecutor has rarely used these special provisions with respect to foundations.[24]

2.6. DISCLOSURE AND TRANSPARENCY

Each foundation must be registered in the Dutch Commercial Register (which is a public register). This includes registration of its board members. A foundation is not required to publish annual reports, save a few exceptions. An exception applies to foundations operating a business within the meaning of the Commercial Register Act, if that business is medium-sized or large. These are subject to the same annual reporting requirements as NV and BV companies.[25] The meaning of the term 'business' in the Commercial Register Act will be further discussed in section 3.5 which deals with commercial foundations. A business is 'mid-sized or large', if annual turnover in at least two subsequent years exceeds €6 million.[26]

Here we add that one may question whether an enterprise foundation, i.e. a foundation acting as controlling shareholder, will as such be deemed to operate a business. Generally, this will not be the case, as the foundation's involvement with the policies of the underlying company and its subsidiaries will normally be limited. The foundation may impose, and monitor compliance with, a rather generic set of principles, such as a mission statement, but will leave business strategy and group management to the board of the company of which it directly owns the shares. That company will often be a holding company exercising central leadership over the group it forms with its subsidiaries and therefore will be obliged to publish both company and consolidated financial statements.[27] However, as we will see in section 3.5, a foundation with for-profit activities

22 Article 2:297 DCC.
23 Article 2:298 DCC.
24 For a recent case, see Court of Appeal, Amsterdam, 20 June 2023, ECLI:NL:GHAMS:2023:1395.
25 Articles 2:300 and 2:360(3) DCC. See also Article 2:300a DCC for director liability risk in the case of non-compliance.
26 Articles 2:360(3) and 2:396(1)(b) DCC.
27 Articles 2:361 and 2:406 DCC.

involving more than 15 hours of work weekly in the foundation itself[28] will generally be deemed to have a 'business' within the meaning of the Commercial Register Act. Even then, active leadership of the group's business by the shareholder foundation will not easily result in that foundation becoming subject to annual reporting requirements, including consolidated accounts for the group as a whole. This is because the foundation's own business would normally not meet the 'medium-sized or large' threshold.

A requirement similar to NV and BV annual reporting obligations applies to foundations in certain (mainly publicly funded) sectors, such as social housing, healthcare and education.[29] The same applies to fundraising charitable foundation recognised by the CBF. Foundations that qualify as a public benefit organisation (see section 2.7) must publish their financial statements under rules issued by the Dutch Revenue Service.

A draft bill that was recently passed by the Dutch House of Representatives (*Tweede Kamer*) proposes that all foundations be required to file a balance sheet and statement of income and expenditure, annual accounts or similar financial statements with the Commercial Register.[30] Certain governmental supervisory authorities will be given access to this financial information through a non-public part of the Commercial Register. The purpose of this bill is to counter abuse of foundations, especially abuse for bankruptcy fraud, tax fraud, terrorist financing or money laundering. The bill is not yet passed by the Dutch Senate (*Eerste Kamer*) and has been widely criticised.

Another disclosure requirement derives from EU legislation on ultimate beneficial owners (UBOs).[31] The board of a foundation must maintain a register of beneficiaries, meaning persons receiving funds from the foundation.[32] The foundation's board must provide information from this register upon the request of governmental authorities, such as the Dutch Revenue Service. If the amount a beneficiary receives is more than 25% of the total amount the foundation distributes in a year, the person or entity receiving this amount must be registered

---

28 If the foundation is the controlling shareholder in an operating company and this operating company is so closely intertwined with the activities of the foundation that the whole functions as an economic entity, the tax authorities may look at the economic reality.

29 For instance, healthcare institutions must publish annual accounts on the basis of Article 40b *Wet marktordening gezondheidszorg* (Wmg) in combination with *Regeling openbare jaarverantwoording Wmg*.

30 Proposal of Civil Society Organisations Transparency Act (*Wet transparantie en tegengaan ondermijning door maatschappelijke organisaties* (WTMO)) (2024–2025) *Kamerstukken I*, 35 646, A.

31 Since 2020, Dutch entities must register and maintain information on their ultimate beneficial owners (UBOs). A UBO of a foundation is an individual who directly or indirectly has an ownership of more than 25% or can exercise more than 25% of the voting rights in respect of changes of the charter. The managing director of the foundation will qualify as a (quasi) UBO if no individual meets the criteria.

32 Article 2:290 DCC.

as an ultimate beneficial owner in the general UBO-register that is accessible for public authorities.

2.7. TAXATION

Foundations are not subject to Dutch corporate income tax (CIT), unless the foundation is a registered social housing institution or if it operates a business itself.[33] The meaning of 'business' under the Dutch CIT Act will be further discussed in section 3.5, dealing with commercial foundations.

The mere holding of shares in a company does not qualify as operating a business, so enterprise foundations are usually not subject to CIT. Enterprise foundations and companies they hold shares in may benefit from this, e.g. for the purpose of managing excess cash. Say the company intends to save cash for possible future investments or acquisition: when saving it at company level, any accrued interest would constitute company profits subject to CIT. Alternatively, the company could make a distribution to its enterprise foundation, its shareholder,[34] which can make tax-free profits out of it. The enterprise foundation can reinvest savings plus profits in the company as a capital contribution if needed for allowing the company to make investments or acquisitions.

Foundations can seek the status of a public benefit organisation (PBO) (*algemeen nut beogende instelling* or ANBI) to benefit from certain tax advantages.[35] Donations given to a PBO are tax-deductible (subject to limitations), and donations received and given by a PBO will not be subject to inheritance tax and gift tax.

To qualify as a PBO, the foundation must be registered as such with the Dutch Revenue Service. Registration is available on application, provided certain criteria are met. The foundation's activities must almost entirely (at least 90%) be focused on the public benefit (as opposed to serving private interests); the foundation's organisation and the persons directly involved in the organisation must meet integrity requirements; no one director may have majority control over the assets of the foundation (as a result, a PBO must have at least three directors); and the directors' remuneration must be restricted to an expense allowance or a minimum attendance fee.[36] In addition, a PBO may not have more assets than

---

33 Article 2(1)(d) and (e) of the Dutch Corporate Income Tax Act.

34 The distribution will be subject to a dividend withholding tax; except if the foundation is subject to CIT, it can reclaim the dividend tax. See Article 10 of the Dutch Dividend Tax Act 1965.

35 Article 5b of the General Act on State Taxes (*Algemene wet inzake rijksbelastingen*); and Articles 1b to 1e of the Executive Order for the General Act of State Taxes (*Uitvoeringsregeling AWR Algemene wet inzake rijksbelastingen*) 1994.

36 Executive directors employed by the foundation are exempted from this restriction on remuneration.

necessary for delivering on its purpose (anti-hoarding requirement). For this reason, the foundation's assets must remain limited, and the costs must be in reasonable proportion to its expenditure. A PBO must also draw up a policy plan and publish certain information on its own website. Finally, funds remaining after its dissolution must be allocated to a public benefit (general good) objective identical to the foundation's objective.

On the whole, these PBO requirements are not necessarily incompatible with enterprise foundations gaining PBO status. In fact, enterprise foundations with PBO status do exist, in particular where the underlying company is itself pursuing public interests (e.g. a BV operating a private university, such as Nyenrode Business University, or a social enterprise). However, combining PBO status with active shareholdership of a company not pursuing a public interest may be difficult from a tax perspective. In that case, a second foundation may be set up specifically for the public benefit activities; the latter foundation may then act as PBO, depending either on donations from the former foundation or on distributions directly from the company (for which purpose the PBO foundation could, for instance, hold non-voting shares). Two separate foundations (a mission foundation or holding foundation and a separate charitable foundation) are for instance incorporated in the structure of Tony's Chocolonely and TBI mentioned hereafter.

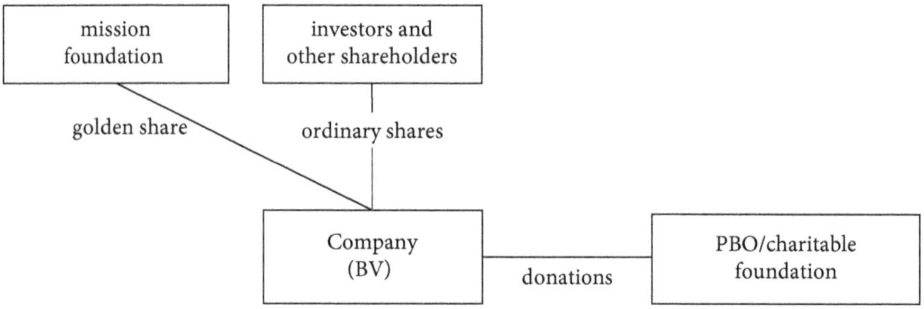

Tony's Chocolonely Mission Foundation is a holder of a golden share in Tony's Factory BV (reference is made to section 3.4). The charitable foundation, the Chocolonely Foundation, is not a holder of shares in the company and has no influence in the company. This foundation was incorporated by Tony's Factory BV but is an independent organisation and its object is to support the company's mission. The company donates 1% of its net revenue yearly to this charitable foundation.[37] As the Chocolonely Foundation is a PBO, the company can deduct its donation from its CIT due.

[37] 'Chocolonely Foundation', *Tony's Chocolonely*:https://nl.tonyschocolonely.com/en/pages/chocolonely-foundation.

3. ENTERPRISE FOUNDATIONS IN PRACTICE

3.1. TRUST FOUNDATIONS

A structure often used in the Netherlands is where a foundation acquires shares for the account of other persons (beneficial owners), whilst issuing depositary receipts for the shares (DRSs) to such beneficial owners. Those beneficial owners are then called DRS-holders. DRSs are contractual instruments. As the transferor of the shares will retain the beneficial ownership (represented by the DRSs), the foundation will not need to pay a purchase price. The transaction is not a donation either. Ownership of the shares is transferred only in order for the shares to be 'managed' by the foundation. The foundation will draw up a set of general terms and conditions applicable to the DRSs it issues, usually called trust conditions. Such trust conditions may or may not limit the transferability of the DRSs. A foundation issuing DRSs is usually called a trust foundation, or in Dutch a 'STAK'.[38]

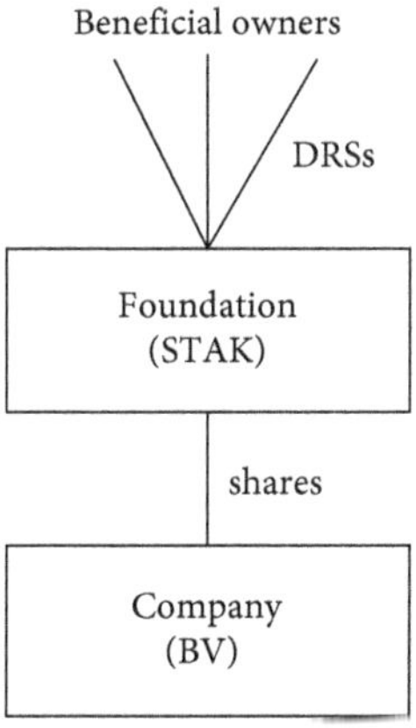

Pursuant to the trust conditions, the financial interest in the underlying shares will accrue to the DRS-holders, the beneficial owners. As a result, any distributions on shares will be passed on to the DRS-holders. This may be distributions of profits of the company, but those are not foundation profits as the beneficial interest in the shares sits with the DRS-holders, not the foundation. The right to attend and speak at the company's shareholder meetings, the voting rights and other membership rights attached to the shares will accrue to the trust foundation as the formal shareholder. DRS-holders will also have the right to attend and speak

[38] STAK is short for *stichting administratiekantoor*. According to information obtained from the Dutch trade register, approximately 42,500 foundations are named '*stichting administratiekantoor*', so can be expected to be trust foundations.

at shareholder meetings if the DRSs are issued 'with the company's cooperation' (for NVs) or those rights are granted by the company to DRS-holders (for BVs).[39]

Trust foundations (STAKs) are frequently used for family businesses. The foundation usually is the sole or majority shareholder of the holding BV of the family business. One reason to incorporate a family trust foundation is to facilitate generational succession of ownership within the family, whilst concentrating control over the company. The board of a family trust foundation will consist of some of the family members and/or outsiders. In a family context, DRS-holders are often divided into family stakes, e.g. ensuring each stake may nominate one board member.

Usually, much time and effort is invested in drafting a policy document for the family's ownership of the business *(familiestatuut)* and aligning all family members behind it. Cultivating such shared vision is considered an important prerequisite for sustainable family ownership and the long-term success of the company.[40] Important as well is to clearly define the precise roles of each of the boards and the trust foundation with respect to the company, to avoid tensions over the distribution of powers (risk of crowded structures).

Trust foundations are used outside the context of family businesses as well, e.g. in the context of equity participations for employees. Rather than the company issuing shares to employees, the latter would receive DRSs issued by a trust foundation. Either the majority shareholder or company management would control the trust foundation. Yet another purpose for which trust foundations can be used is protection of a company's mission.

3.2. TRUST FOUNDATIONS FOR LISTED COMPANIES

Trust foundations have been used frequently, and are still used sometimes, by listed companies, as an anti-takeover device and to shield the company against undue shareholder influence. The percentage of Dutch listed companies using DRSs as an anti-takeover device was 20% in 2001 and 8% in 2023.[41] To achieve said protection, the DRSs are listed, not the shares. A DRS-holder may be allowed to exchange his/her DRSs for underlying shares (and vice versa).[42] However, as

---

39 Article 2:117(2) DCC (for NVs) and Article 2:227(2) DCC (for BVs).

40 I. Matser and J. van Zwol, *Goed eigenaarschap – Voor synergie tussen familie en bedrijf*, BigBusinessPublishers, Utrecht 2023.

41 R. Abma, 'Corporate governance en engagement' in T.M.C. Arons, P.W.J. Coenen and G.F.E. Koster, *100 jaar VEB*, Wolters Kluwer, Deventer 2024, para. 19.5.2, referring to the percentage of Dutch AEX and AMX companies. The AEX index is composed of Dutch companies that trade on Euronext Amsterdam (formerly known as the Amsterdam Stock Exchange) and the AMX is a mid-cap index.

42 Under the former listing rules of the Amsterdam Stock Exchange, this was a requirement.

only DRSs are listed and traded at the stock exchange and investors often wish to be able to sell quickly (if need be), most investors would rather accept the lack of voting rights than suffer the delays of such conversions.

In 2004, in an effort to strengthen checks and balances within listed companies, the effectiveness of such structures was restricted by the introduction of Article 2:118a DCC (applicable to Dutch NVs).[43] Under this statutory provision, holders of listed DRSs must be granted a power of attorney to vote the underlying shares at shareholder meetings. In practice, not all DRS-holders will request a power of attorney, leaving the trust foundation with many shares it may vote itself, unless it has committed that it will not do so. In addition, powers of attorney requested by DRS-holders may be refused or revoked only, if a hostile bid is made for the shares, or if DRS-holders (alone or with other DRS-holders or shareholders) have acquired a 25% stake in the company, or if the trust foundation determines that voting by DRS-holders would seriously go against the company's interests. As conditions to refusing or revoking powers of attorney to DRS-holders in such circumstances, the board of the trust foundation must be independent from the company, and the DRSs must have been issued with the company's cooperation.[44] A few examples are included below.

3.2.1. ABN Amro Bank N.V.

After a fierce takeover battle and a financial crisis (2008), a slimmed-down version of ABN Amro Bank N.V. ended up being wholly owned by a trust foundation set up by the Dutch government (NLF). NLF's sole DRS-holder is the state of the Netherlands. Later, NLF transferred part of its ABN Amro Bank shares to another trust foundation (STAK AAB), which issued DRSs listed on Euronext Amsterdam. STAK AAB's purpose is to protect both the interest of its DRS-holders and the company's independence, continuity and identity. Article 2:118a DCC applies to the DRSs issued by STAK AAB. Hence, when refusing or revoking powers of attorney of the DRS-holders, STAK AAB will vote the shares it holds itself; it will then primarily focus on the interests of the company, which include those of customers, savers and deposit holders, shareholders, DRS-holders, employees and the society in which the company performs its activities.[45]

---

43 This concerns DRSs (for shares in an NV) admitted to trading on a regulated market or a multilateral trading facility as referred to in Article 1:1 of the Financial Supervision Act (*Wet op het financieel toezicht*) or a system comparable to a regulated market or multilateral trading facility from a state that is not a member state of the European Union.

44 Article 2:118a DCC; see also Article 5:71(1)(d) of the Financial Supervision Act (*Wet op het financieel toezicht*), exempting such trust foundations from mandatory bid rules.

45 'Shareholder structure' (2025) *ABN AMRO*: https://www.abnamro.com/en/about-abn-amro/information/shareholder-structure?selectedTabs=STAK%20AAB; 'Stichting Administratiekantoor Continuïteit ABN AMRO Bank' (2025) *ABN AMRO*: https://www.stakaab.org/nl/home.

3.2.2. *Triodos Bank N.V.*

Triodos Bank N.V. is owned by a trust foundation to support its mission that focuses on sustainable banking and investing. Non-tradable DRSs were issued to institutional investors and private citizens alike. To provide them with an exit opportunity, the company promised to repurchase DRSs at a price based on intrinsic value. During the Covid-19 epidemic, it terminated this scheme due to solvency needs, leaving DRS-holders dissatisfied, with no reasonable exit opportunity. Next, in 2023, the DRSs were admitted for trading on a multilateral trading facility, allowing for transactions once a week. This triggered application of Article 2:118a DCC, leaving the trust foundation less powerful than before. In practice, DRS-holders sold at around one-third of the pre-Covid-19 price. To enhance trade (and hopefully stock prices), the DRSs were listed on Euronext Amsterdam in June 2025.[46] Article 2:118a DCC continues to apply.

3.2.3. *FastNed B.V.*

A trust foundation (Fast) owns all shares of FastNed B.V., the Dutch company building and operating charging stations for electric vehicles. DRSs issued by Fast are listed on Euronext Amsterdam. These DRSs are not subject to Article 2:118a DCC, as that statutory provision applies to NVs only, not BVs like FastNed. The purpose of the trust foundation is to support FastNed's mission, which is to accelerate the transition to electric mobility. The board members of the trust foundation are appointed by the meeting of DRS-holders; they must be independent from the company.[47]

3.3. PROTECTIVE PREFERENCE SHARES FOUNDATIONS

A rather common protective device for Dutch listed companies involves preference shares. In 2023, 57% of the Dutch listed companies used preference shares for this purpose.[48] The structure features a foundation usually called a continuity foundation (*stichting continuiteit*). For clarity, we use the term protective preference shares foundation. Most (if not all) structures of this kind were put in place at the time of the company's initial public offering (IPO).

46 'Triodos Bank zoekt op Euronext redding voor vastgelopen certificatenhandel' (14 May 2024) *Het Financieele Dagblad.*

47 'Corporate Governance', *Fastned*: https://www.fastnedcharging.com/en/for-business/investor-relations/corporate-governance.

48 R. Abma, above n. 41, para. 19.5.2.

Typically, the foundation is granted a call option for preference shares in the listed company, exercisable in the event of a serious threat to the company's interests, such as a hostile takeover or undue shareholders activism.[49] Often, the call option is for (at most) as many shares as will represent 50% of the votes exercisable in the general meeting after exercise in the event all issued shares would be represented the meeting. Given absentee experience with listed companies, not all of the other shares will be represented at general meetings to follow. Thus, full exercise of the option hands the foundation an absolute majority. Sometimes, the call option is for a maximum of 30%. The foundation's purpose, as included in its charter, is usually to protect the interests of the company, including (where applicable) its independence, continuity and identity, whilst taking the interests of all stakeholders of the company into account. These structures always provide for a mechanism allowing for cancellation of the preference shares once their existence is no longer warranted for their intended protective purposes.

As a result of exercising its call option, the foundation's voting rights may go from 0% to over 30%, the Dutch threshold for a mandatory public offer for all shares in the company.[50] The mandatory offer regulation was first included in Dutch law in 2007. To avoid the public offer requirement, the foundation will either exercise its call option up to a maximum of 30% or rely on a specific exemption from the mandatory offer rules. The exemption concerned is given in case the foundation is a legal entity independent from the target company, whose purpose is to serve the company's interests, and which will hold the shares for a maximum of two years from the time a hostile bid is made, to protect the target company.[51]

This exemption to the mandatory offer rules is more restrictive than the previous Amsterdam Stock Exchange rules for allowing protective preference share structures. To rely on the current exemption, the foundation must be independent from the company; what independence means here is not entirely clear. We also note that the exemption is not drafted towards protecting the company against threats other than hostile bids, such as activist shareholders demanding changes to the company's strategy.

A structure like this is set up, e.g. for the Dutch listed insurance company NN Group N.V. The name of the foundation concerned is Stichting Continuïteit NN Group. According to its charter, the objects of this foundation are to protect the interests of the listed company NN Group N.V.:

49 Article 2:96(1) and (5) DCC.

50 Articles 5:70 and 1:1 of the Financial Supervision Act (*Wet op het financieel toezicht*).

51 Article 5:71(1)(c) of the Financial Supervision Act (*Wet op het financieel toezicht*).

> the businesses maintained by the company and the entities with which the company forms a group and all persons involved therein, in such way that the interests of the company and those businesses and all persons involved therein are protected to the best of its abilities, and by making every effort to prevent anything which may affect the independence and/or the continuity and/or the identity of the company and of those businesses in violation of the interests referred herein above.[52]

Faced with a protective preference shares structure, parties interested in a takeover may be deterred from even making a hostile bid for the listed company shares. Sometimes, a hostile bid is announced anyway. In some of these occasions, it all ended in a takeover anyway, whether at a higher price or by another party, with or without the foundation exercising its call option. On other occasions, fierce support by the foundation board of the company's strategy, including exercise of the call option, was successful to stave off the hostile attack. This was the case, for instance, when Mexican company América Móvil attempted to takeover Dutch telecoms provider Royal KPN in 2013.[53]

3.4. GOLDEN SHARE FOUNDATIONS

The term 'golden shares' is often used for shares which, under the company's charter, have special powers attached such as binding nomination rights, approval rights for share issues, as well as veto powers concerning profit distribution, investment decisions and amendment of the company's articles of association, etc. Often, they carry little to no financial interest in the company and virtually no votes in the company's general meeting of shareholders. Such shares are traditionally referred to as priority shares *(prioriteitsaandelen)* and are often held by a foundation, generally referred to as a priority foundation *(stichting prioriteit)*. For clarity, we prefer the term 'golden share (foundations)'.[54]

In the past, a considerable number of listed companies had golden shares outstanding with a golden share foundation, mainly as an anti-takeover device.[55] In such structures, the board of the foundation would partly consist of directors of the company. The use of such anti-takeover devices has declined over the past 25 years.

---

52 See: www.nn.nl.

53 'América Móvil drops KPN takeover bid' (17 October 2023) telecoms.com: https://www.telecoms.com/communications-service-provider/am-rica-m-vil-drops-kpn-takeover-bid.

54 The term 'priority' could be misunderstood to refer to some sort of financial preference. Also, golden shares often have no actual 'priority' in a meaningful sense of the word.

55 In 2001, 34% of the Dutch listed companies used priority shares but in 2023 this percentage was down to 11%, R. Abma, above n. 41, para. 19.5.2.

3.4.1. *Stichting Prioriteit Aalberts*

Aalberts, the Dutch technologies group, is headed by Aalberts N.V., a listed company applying a golden share structure. The golden (priority) shares issued are held by *Stichting Prioriteit* 'Aalberts N.V.'.[56] The foundation board consists of managing and supervisory directors of the company plus an independent director. The powers attached to the golden (priority) shares include, *inter alia*, the making of binding nominations for appointments to the company's management and supervisory boards, and vetoes with respect to the issue of ordinary shares and changing the company's articles of association.[57] The object of the foundation is to promote good governance in Aalberts N.V., in particular by ensuring the company's continuity. It endeavours to achieve this objective by acquiring and holding all priority shares in the capital of the NV. The objects of the foundation explicitly exclude transferring or otherwise disposing of the priority shares to parties other than the NV and acquiring ordinary shares in the NV.[58]

Structures involving golden share foundations exist with non-listed companies as well. The golden shares may, for instance, be designed to grant special control rights to founders or their families or serve to protect the company's (social) purpose or mission.

3.4.2. *Tony's Chocolonely Mission Foundation*

Tony's Chocolonely, the Dutch ethical chocolate maker, provides an example in the latter category.[59] Tony's Factory B.V. is a private company owned by one of its founders, two former directors, some current employees and an investment vehicle backed by the founders of Innocent Drinks. An investment vehicle backed by two families behind AB Inbev, the Belgian brewing giant, is also an investor in Tony's. In 2023, the company issued a golden share to Stichting Tony's Chocolonely Mission Foundation, which may not be sold except to the company itself. The foundation's objectives are to protect the company's mission and objects. The golden share carries the right to veto certain changes to the company's articles of association, including the mission statement therein.

56 See: www.aalberts.com.

57 See Aalberts' 'Annual Report 2023', p. 137 (accessible through the company's website: www.aalberts.com).

58 Article 2 of the charter of Stichting Prioriteit 'Aalberts N.V.'

59 'Introducing: Tony's Mission Lock – a future-proof legal structure for impact companies' (31 May 2023) *Tony's Chocolonely*: https://tonyschocolonely.com/nl/en/our-mission/news/introducing-tonys-mission-lock-a-future-proof-legal-structure-for-impact-companies. See also '"Golden shares" to safeguard sustainability at Tony's Chocolonely' (31 May 2023) *Guardian*: https://www.theguardian.com/business/2023/may/31/golden-shares-to-safeguard-sustainability-at-tonys-chocolonely.

Moreover, the foundation has the right to contribute a section to the company's annual report, to receive and request information from the company, and, if need be, to start inquiry proceedings at the Enterprise Chamber of the Amsterdam Court of Appeals. The foundation board members are referred to as 'mission guardians'. According to the foundation's charter, its board consists of a maximum of three members. New members are appointed by the board (co-optation). The charter of the foundation does not include provisions on the composition of the board. This mission foundation is distinct from the Chocolonely Foundation, mentioned in section 2.7, which receives 1% of the company's net revenue yearly for activities such as creating conditions to ban slavery.[60]

3.5. COMMERCIAL FOUNDATIONS

A foundation can operate a business itself. As indicated, such foundations are often informally referred to as 'commercial foundations'. Terminology can be somewhat confusing, as distinct statutory provisions may mean different things when referring to a 'business'.

To determine whether a foundation must register a 'business' with the Dutch Commercial Register, in addition to its registration as a legal entity, 'business' refers to a separate entity in which through contribution of labour or funds services or goods are delivered, or things are produced, on a for-profit basis.[61] The number of hours spent on economic activities may indicate whether activities are structural and of sufficient scope to be considered a business. As a rule of thumb, a foundation with for-profit activities involving more than 15 hours of work weekly in the foundation itself will generally be deemed to have a 'business' under this regulation.[62] As discussed in section 2.6, this definition is also relevant under annual reporting rules.

For certain other purposes, the term 'business' is defined differently. A foundation is subject to Dutch corporate income tax (CIT) if it exercises a business. This is the case where the foundation performs economic transactions for the purpose of making profit with the use of an organisation of capital and labour, or is engaged in a similar activity in competition with the activities of commercial entities.[63] Under legislation requiring the institution of a works

---

60 See above n. 37.

61 Business within the meaning of Article 5(a) of the Dutch Commercial Register Act (*Handelsregisterwet*) 2007 and Article 2 of the Dutch Commercial Register Decree (*Handelsregisterbesluit*) 2008.

62 Policy Rule from the deputy minister for Economic Affairs regarding the notion of 'business' in the Commercial Register Act, 'Het ondernemingsbegrip in het handelsregister' (2008) 123 *Staatscourant* 15, WJZ 8074645.

63 Business within the meaning of Article 2(1)(e) and 4(a) of the Dutch Corporate Income Tax Act (*Wet op de vennootschapsbelasting*) 1969.

council, the term 'business' refers to a separate entity in which paid labour is performed.[64]

It is important to note, therefore, that a foundation may not have a commercial purpose or activity, or seek to generate profits, and still be obliged to register a 'business', set up a works council and/or pay corporate income tax. This is all subject, of course, to other requirements for such obligations being fulfilled, including that the 'business' must be operated at the level of the foundation itself and not at the level of a subsidiary thereof.

Foundations operating a business itself may act as enterprise foundations at the same time, by holding shares in companies, e.g. a social housing foundation may have set up subsidiary companies for construction projects or commercial ventures. Likewise, a pension fund foundation (with activities of its own not qualifying as a business) may be a controlling shareholder of an asset management company.

Social enterprises[65] in the Netherlands are undertakings whose primary objective is to have a social impact rather than generating profit for owners or shareholders. They act from a social mission (impact first). A social enterprise operates by providing goods and services for the market in an entrepreneurial and innovative manner and uses its profits primarily to achieve its social objectives.[66] In the Netherlands, social enterprises do not have a separate legal form. According to the European Social Enterprise Monitor 2024,[67] 23% of social entrepreneurs use the single foundation as their legal form (and 14.9% use a combination of a BV and a foundation).

3.5.1. Social Enterprise Examples

An example of a commercial foundation that operates a social enterprise is Oefenen.nl, an enterprise that developed a portal for lower educated (young) adults, including migrants, who want to improve their language skills. Organisations can buy a licence that gives access to training material, workbooks and tracking systems. Other examples are the 'fair trade shops', such as Stichting Counting Flowers. It trades handmade scarfs, tablecloths and bath

---

64 Business within the meaning of Article 1(1)(d) of the Dutch Works Councils Act (*Wet op de ondernemingsraden*).

65 According to the European Commission leaflet, 'The Social Business Initiative of the European Commission' (18 December 2015) Ref. Ares(2015)5946494, in the EU a social enterprise is an undertaking (business): 'whose primary objective is to achieve social impact rather than generating profit for owners and shareholders, which uses its surpluses mainly to achieve these social goals, which is managed in an accountable, transparent and innovative way, in particular by involving workers, customers and stakeholders affected by its business activity'.

66 Reference is made to the definition used by Social Enterprise NL: www.social-enterprise.nl/english.

67 Social Enterprise Monitor 2024 | Social Enterprise NL.

towels and works with and buys directly from small independent entrepreneurs in emerging countries. Also, there are about 180 fair trade shops in the Netherlands called *wereldwinkel.* Many of these incorporated their own local Stichting Wereldwinkel. These foundations qualify as PBOs (for tax purposes, see section 2.7).

Commercial foundations can also operate a business without being a social enterprise.

3.5.2. The Efteling

The Efteling is the largest theme park in the Netherlands. This fantasy- and fairytale-based amusement park opened in 1952.[68] The founders were driven by a social/cultural spirit rather than a commercial one so they incorporated a foundation to own and operate the business. This made it a commercial foundation within the meaning discussed here. Later, following expansion and diversification of the park and activities (other attractions; hotel accommodations, etc.), a separate BV was set up for each business division, all BV shares being owned by the original foundation. As a result, that foundation now meets the description of a full shareholder foundation as discussed hereafter. The purpose of this foundation is to maintain the park and its recreational activities and to promote tourism, as well as to support social community projects aimed at children.

3.5.3. Jaarbeurs

A similar trajectory of an (initially) not-for-profit business starting in a not-for-profit structure and ending up in a BV owned by a full shareholder foundation, is Jaarbeurs. It concerns trade fairs, meetings and a large events location. It started in 1916, as exports and imports declined due to World War I. Organisations representing commercial businesses, backed by the government, incorporated an association for organising fairs to promote more local trade. Later, the business expanded, the association was converted into an enterprise foundation (Stichting Koninklijke Nederlandse Jaarbeurs) and the business was hived down into a holding company (Jaarbeurs Holding B.V.) and subsidiaries.[69] The foundation and its group companies share the same purpose: to organise trade fairs, conferences and events. In addition, the objects clause in the foundation's charter mentions it may hold shares in companies.

---

[68] 'Efteling' (2025) *Wikipedia*: https://en.wikipedia.org/wiki/Efteling.

[69] 'Jaarbeurs' (2025) *Wikipedia*: https://en.wikipedia.org/wiki/Jaarbeurs; see also:https://www.jaarbeurs.nl/en/over-ons.

3.6. FULL SHAREHOLDER FOUNDATIONS AND STEWARD OWNERSHIP

By 'full shareholder foundation' we refer to a foundation that holds all shares or a controlling shareholding in a company for its own account. The difference with the trust foundation is that the latter holds the shares in the company for the account of others, the DRS-holders. These shareholder foundations can, but need not, be part of a company's steward ownership structure.[70] Steward ownership can also take other forms, e.g. using a trust foundation, see e.g. Triodos.[71]

In some of the foundation charters we studied, the purpose of the foundation is the long-term continuity of the enterprise, but a shareholder foundation can also have a charitable or combined purpose. For tax reasons explained in section 2.7, the charitable foundation being a PBO is usually separate from the shareholder foundation. Besides the objects clause, we looked at governance clauses. Some aim for foundation board independence, at least for the majority of the board members, from the underlying company. By contrast, the boards of other enterprise foundations are composed of one or more managing and supervisory directors of the company and a member of the company's works council, plus sometimes one independent. This latter structure is in line with the steward ownership principle that 'power over the company is held by people directly connected to the company's operation and mission'.[72] Some examples are discussed below.

3.6.1. *Stichting HaskoningDHV*

Stichting HaskoningDHV holds 75% of the shares in Koninklijke HaskoningDHV Groep B.V., a Dutch global consulting engineers' firm. The other shareholder is a trust foundation that holds all class B shares, for which it issued DRSs to

70 According to the Purpose Foundation (https://purpose-economy.org/en/whats-steward-ownership/), steward ownership is 'a corporate ownership structure that presents an alternative to shareholder value primacy. It ensures that companies prioritize their long-term purpose over short term profits – by legally enshrining two principles:
Self-determination: Power over the company cannot be speculated with but is held by people directly connected to the company's operation and mission: stewards ....
Purpose-orientation: Profits are means to a purpose, not a goal in itself. Value created in the company cannot be extracted by the shareholders. Profits are reinvested, used to cover capital costs or donated.'

71 Various examples of steward ownership can be found on the website of We Are Stewards: https://www.wearestewards.nl. In April 2024, the Dutch parliament approved a motion to commence drafting a Dutch steward ownership legal form, the *rentmeestervenootschap*. According to the motion, there is a growing demand for alternative business structures where profit maximisation is not the only defined goal. The motion also considers that establishing such business models is now relatively costly and time-consuming. A draft legislative proposal for such form is not available yet.

72 See: https://www.purpose-economy.org/en/whats-steward-ownership/.

employees. The purpose of Stichting HaskoningDHV is to look after the interests of the group and all those involved in it, with a view to the group's continuity, independence and identity. The board of Stichting HaskoningDHV consists of five members, of which only one is independent. The supervisory board and the management board of the company each appoint one member, the (combined) works council and selected staff each appoint one member. The fifth member is an independent external individual appointed by the four members and acts as chairperson.

3.6.2. *Stichting Aandelen Remeha*

Stichting Aandelen Remeha is the sole shareholder of Remeha Group B.V., which heads a large group of companies that sell and manufacture heating equipment. Remeha was founded in the 1910s, during the well-advanced industrial revolution. The founder started a bicycle shop and later a plumbing company focusing on installing central heating systems. This became a family business that established itself as a frontrunner in the Netherlands on selling central heating boilers. In the 1960s the company became a key player in the transition to gas and started to develop high efficiency boilers. The foundation was incorporated in 1982 by the son of the founder. The main motivation was to ensure the continuity of the company which is still the main objective today. Moreover, the objective was and is to ensure and protect employment within Remeha in the long term. In addition, according to the objects clause in the charter, the foundation's objects are to contribute to training and development of professionals, in particular with a view to promoting sustainability and innovation. Managing and supervisory directors of the company and members of the works council cannot be appointed as a member of the foundation board. The foundation board consists of a minimum of five and a maximum of seven members to be appointed by that board itself. One board member is appointed on a binding nomination by the descendants of the company's founder and one on a binding nomination from the workers' council. Per the charter, the board must prepare a profile for its composition with due observance of expertise, experience, affinity with the foundation's purpose and background.

3.6.3. *Stichting Albron*

Another example is Stichting Albron, a foundation holding all shares of Albron B.V., a large foodservice company. The objective of the foundation is to ensure the continuity of the activities of the company and its subsidiaries. According to the charter, the foundation holds shares in and may finance Albron and may devote funds to social objectives related to the company's activities. The board of Stichting Albron consists of one or two members A and two or three members B. Members A can only be supervisory directors of Albron B.V. who are appointed on the nomination of the foundation. As some of the other companies discussed in this chapter, Albron B.V. is subject to the Dutch co-determination rules (*structuurregeling*) discussed at the end of section 2.4.

3.6.4. *Stichting TBI*

Stichting TBI holds all shares of TBI Holdings B.V., the parent of a large technical equipment, building and infrastructure group. The TBI structure was set up to save healthy business parts of Ogem, the former large industrial conglomerate (and colonial gas and electricity company), which was mismanaged and went bankrupt in 1983. The TBI group comprises more than 20 separate businesses operating under their own names (not TBI) in a rather decentralised group governance structure.[73] The board of Stichting TBI consists of at least three members to be appointed by the board. According to the charter, the majority of the board members consists of persons who were previously managing or supervisory directors of TBI Holdings B.V.

3.6.5. *Former Cooperatives*

Cooperative banks and mutual insurance companies may also end up as companies with an enterprise foundation as a full shareholder or in a comparable structure. Insurance company Aegon provides an example. It resulted from the merger of two insurance companies in 1983, one a mutual and the other a listed NV company. The mutual's business was contributed to the NV in exchange for newly issued shares. At the same time, the mutual was converted into an association with its board members also serving as the sole members of the association. That association's purpose was aligned with the NV's interests. The association was the NV's majority shareholder. Later, after dilution resulting from subsequent acquisitions by the NV, the association's interest was reduced to less than 20%. With a structure similar to multiple voting shares, its voting power was kept at higher levels. The association and this structure still exist. However, since Aegon NV sold its Dutch business to ASR, its main operations are in the US, and the Dutch NV was converted into a Bermuda company.[74]

3.7. LOST STRUCTURES

The famous Royal Packaging Industries Van Leer exists no more. In its heyday it was the world's largest producer of steel oil barrels and a large producer of

73 See: https://www.tbi.nl.
74 'Redomiciliation to Bermuda completed' (30 September 2023) *Aegon*: https://www.aegon.com/newsroom/news/press-releases/2023/redomiciliation-bermuda-completed.

other packaging material. In 1971, the son and heir of founder Bernard Van Leer set up an enterprise foundation (Van Leer Groep Stichting) and transferred all company shares to it. He also set up a charity foundation (Bernard Van Leer Stichting). The enterprise foundation transferred all dividends received to the charity foundation in order to advance education for young children worldwide. The structure survived until 1996, when the company's shares were listed at the Amsterdam Stock Exchange. Three years later, a takeover by Finnish consumer packaging company Huhtamäki took the company private again; in 2001, Huhtamäki sold the industrial packaging part of former Van Leer on to the US-based company Greif Brothers.[75]

Another sad story is about the former PCM Publishers (PCM Uitgevers). This publishing house resulted from a merger between three leading Dutch newspapers. Each was originally owned by 'its own' foundation. These were classic enterprise foundation structures, suited to protect the newspapers' missions. As a result of the merger, these foundations became the three shareholders of a holding, with separate newspaper subsidiaries and a book publishing subsidiary as well. One of the foundations, Stichting Democratie en Media (SDM), was majority shareholder. Then, PCM Publishers came to a strategic crossroads: SDM favored expanding the newspaper business, whereas the company boards championed diversification through acquisitions in the book publishing sector. The infighting resulted in the sale of PCM Publishers to a private equity firm in a leveraged buyout in 2004, which drained the company's financial resources. No substantial investments were made.[76] Three years later, SDM and the other two foundations reacquired PCM Uitgevers to save it from downfall. Fairly soon after that, they sold the majority of the shares in the company to Belgian commercial publisher De Persgroep and PCM was renamed De Persgroep Nederland. However, SDM still holds some shares, including a priority share, in the capital of De Persgroep Nederland. It also holds shares in the Dutch online journalist platform De Correspondent and makes financial contributions to various initiatives in line with its mission. As an independent foundation SDM supports free press and aims to protect the independence and continuity of journalism.[77]

We discussed protective preference shares foundations in section 3.4. Some of these protective devices for listed companies have been dismantled because of fears for what was called the 'Dutch discount'. The Dutch Minister of Finance mentioned around 20 years ago that Dutch listed companies would be worth

---

75 Van Leer's company archives were donated to the Amsterdam municipality archives in 2004; a Dutch summary is available at Koninklijke Van Leer | Stadsarchief Amsterdam.

76 This episode resulted in court proceedings attracting much media attention. In a landmark decision, it was determined mismanagement had occurred. Court of Appeal (Enterprise Chamber), Amsterdam, 27 May 2010, ECLI:NL:GHAMS:2010:BM5928 (*PCM*).

77 Wie we zijn – Stichting Democratie en Media – Stichting Democratie en Media.

10–30% less compared to foreign companies because of protection schemes, although the basis of the information was unclear. It was in this climate, in 2004, that the board of ABN Amro Bank decided to waive the company's anti-takeover defence measures. This was supposed to lead to foreign investors participating in the bank and to a higher share price. The board did not consider a hostile takeover likely because of the necessary interference from the Minister of Finance. It turned out to be a miscalculation. In 2007, a banking consortium formed by the Royal Bank of Scotland, Banco Santander and Fortis Group launched a hostile takeover bid and took over the ABN Amro Bank shares after the Minister of Finance greenlighted the acquisition. After this takeover, the bank was divided into three parts. Belgian/Dutch bank Fortis acquired the Dutch activities of ABN Amro Bank but faced financial difficulties soon after. In 2008, the Dutch government had to step in to acquire the Dutch parts of Fortis, including ABN Amro Bank. Later, in 2015, ABN Amro Bank was reintroduced to the Amsterdam Stock Exchange. This time, a trust foundation was incorporated which issued listed DRSs for the ABN Amro Bank shares (see section 3.1).

4. OPPORTUNITIES GOING FORWARD

Clearly, a wide variety of enterprise foundations exist in the Netherlands. We have discussed trust foundations issuing DRSs for the shares they hold. As a result, the financial interest in the shares sits with the DRS-holders, with the voting rights attaching to the shares accruing to the foundation. We have also discussed protective preference shares foundations for listed companies, golden share foundations, as well as commercial foundations (operating a business themselves), full shareholder foundations and steward ownership structures.

Dutch law offers much flexibility to tailor foundations to specific needs. Advisors have room for creativity. Entrepreneurs and investors have options to choose from. A level of complexity derives from tax and accounting rules and an increasing amount of foundation governance regulation. The latter especially applies to specific business sectors, not to enterprise foundations as such. There is a tendency towards strengthening external supervision, by the Dutch Tax Revenue, the Public Prosecutor's office and others. This concerns foundations generally, including enterprise foundations.

Enterprise foundations provide a structure for the exercise of shareholder ownership rights. A key feature concerns the foundation's purpose as described in its charter. For instance, that purpose may be to support the company's interest, to provide mission protection or anti-takeover protection, etc. Other key elements of the structure relate to the foundation's board composition (rules on appointment and removal; and director qualification requirements), and the type of their shareholding (type of shares and time for which they are held). Depending on the circumstances, the division of powers between foundation board and company board require special attention to avoid infighting. For instance, this concerns their respective roles in respect of the company's mission, strategies and major decisions such as on investments, divestments, dividends and financing.

The company and various other stakeholders will depend on the foundation's policies. This includes capital investors other than the foundation, such as the DRS-holders of a trust foundation, and the outside shareholders of a company which is majority-owned by a full shareholder foundation. This puts the foundation in some sort of agency relationship with stakeholders. As a result, the foundation may need to manage expectations, by being transparent about its basic ownership policies.

We use the term full shareholder foundations in reference to foundations holding shares for their own account. A variety of backgrounds may result in such structures. An enlightened business owner may have donated the shares for sustainability and charitable purposes. Other examples include the not-for-profit venture evolving into an enterprise foundation plus company structure, and professional services firms (with little capital needs, initially) set up as such from the start.

The pool of investors and entrepreneurs willing to create such structures may be limited. In addition, these full shareholder foundations can be less rent seeking than some other capital investors, but their own ability to provide the company with additional equity will be limited. Equity funding may be needed to finance sustainability investments, research, innovation and business expansion. This limited reach of full shareholder foundations may be overcome by allowing outside shareholders in the company (with the foundation potentially retaining multiple voting rights). Dutch-style trust foundations (DRS structures) serve a similar purpose. Other solutions for this dilemma include more restrained protection devices such as protective preference share structures (for listed companies) and golden share foundations. Dutch law allows all of these.

For listed companies, the effectiveness of two types of structures is limited by law. First, a trust foundation must grant voting powers to DRS-holders unless the company interests are 'seriously' jeopardised. The scope of the 'seriousness' requirement is not quite clear, but it clearly implies a limitation for potential protection. Second, the use of protective preference shares structures is limited as a result of the mandatory bid rules. Normally, a shareholder acquiring a 30+% interest must make a public bid for all outstanding shares in the company. The foundation may benefit from an exemption, but the scope of that exemption is very limited (only available after a hostile takeover bid is announced and for a maximum of two years). The proportionality of these restrictions – in comparison to the latitude given to the use of multiple voting rights, for example – can be questioned. Maybe corporate law should be more permissive towards independent trust foundations and protective preference shares foundations aiming to protect the company's interests or purpose. This would require legislative changes in the Netherlands and – as far as the mandatory bid rules are concerned – EU legislation as well.

The Tony's Chocolonely example discussed herein explains how golden share foundations may serve as mission guardians. As noted, golden shares may have certain special powers but will normally have very little or no voting power in the general meeting. Hence, a golden share foundation will have little influence on certain decisions. For instance, Dutch law does not allow that the golden share foundation be given a veto right with respect to the appointment or removal of directors by the general meeting. In support of structures designed to protect the company's interest, the Dutch legislator might consider allowing such veto rights, subject to the foundation being independent and required to act in the company's interest.

Finally, enterprise foundations may serve businesses irrespective of the sector in which they operate. Their potential for use in high societal impact sectors may be particularly interesting. Examples of such sectors are healthcare, childcare, accountancy and legal services, to name a few. These are all sectors that are or may be opened up, more and more, for commercial business models and equity investments. Enterprise foundations may help to ensure that shareholder ownership rights in these sectors are exercised responsibly, which will require a broad stakeholder perspective rather than a narrow view dominated by the financial interests of shareholders. Regulators of these sectors may take that into account as a potential tool for protecting public interests where private equity investments are needed.

ENTERPRISE FOUNDATIONS IN BELGIUM

Hans De Wulf

ABSTRACT

Belgian foundation law is not very developed. Private foundations, which may pursue a wider range of disinterested goals than public interest foundations, were only introduced in 2002. Such private foundations may pursue any type of activity, including holding and administering shares, as long as they do not distribute any of the profits they make with those activities. There is no state supervisory authority for foundations in Belgium. Judges are allowed to intervene in the governance of foundations when no other options are available to solve a problem, and foundations cannot be wound up without court approval. There is little to no control in Belgium on whether foundations actually respect their disinterested purpose, except indirectly by the tax authorities, who will regularly subject foundations to the much higher corporate taxation rates if they find that a foundation runs a business or distributes profits (but holding shares, even a controlling stake, in a company is not regarded as running a business).

Private foundations are often used as enterprise foundations, holding a controlling stake in a commercial firm. But in Belgium, enterprise foundations are almost always part of a so-called certification arrangement, whereby the foundation issues certificates (depository receipts) to the shareholders who contributed their shares to the foundation. On the basis of those certificates, the foundation has a contractual duty to pass on to the holders of the certificates any income it receives from the company. It is therefore universally accepted in Belgium that a private foundation distributes the income it receives from the shares it manages, as long as it also pursues a disinterested goal, which typically will be to maintain the family character of a firm. Certification arrangements are even stimulated by Belgian law, as private foundations that engage in certification are exempt from the wealth tax that is applicable to other private foundations. Thus, enterprise foundations in Belgium almost never have a philanthropic purpose, or at least this is never the main purpose of the enterprise foundation: they are mainly used to cement family control over a corporate group, and to pass on that control from one generation to another, in a tax efficient way.

Public interest foundations could also lawfully manage controlling stakes in firms, as long as they reinvest any income from those shares in their non-profit purpose. However, to date, public interest foundations are very rarely used as enterprise foundations (in Belgium) because they would not be allowed to act as a certification vehicle.

1. INTRODUCTION

As this chapter will explain, enterprise foundations – foundations holding a controlling stake in a commercial firm – are often used to help structure the exercise of shareholder control in large companies in Belgium (for small companies, a foundation control structure is too expensive to set up and maintain). However, it is very rare for enterprise foundations in Belgium to also have philanthropic goals, in spite of the requirement for every Belgian foundation to pursue a so-called disinterested goal.[1] Usually, the main purpose of such a Belgian enterprise foundation is to cement family control over a firm. Frequently an additional goal is to have the foundation bear the cost of certain family expenditures. They are often used for succession planning in families that control a business – succession planning both in the sense of transferring a business to the next generation while paying as little taxes as possible, but also in the sense of making sure only the 'right' family members (children) get access to the levers of power within the business group, whereas others will only share in the cash flows the business generates.

The use of enterprise foundations to organise family control over a business is often accompanied by a so-called certification arrangement[2] through which voting and profit rights attached to the shares owned by the foundation are split up and allocated to two different groups of persons (e.g. two branches of a family or founding family members and external investors). The availability of the certification technique is probably the main reason why the so-called 'double foundation model' that is common in some other European countries like Germany, Switzerland or Denmark, is rarely, if ever, used in Belgium.

Belgian entrepreneurs often set up enterprise foundations under Dutch law rather than under Belgian law, although less so since 2019 than before that date. One of the reasons for that is probably that while public interest foundations have existed in Belgium since 1921 (that is, at least, the year when it became possible for them to acquire legal personality and hence capacity without specific recognition in a specific act of parliament), private foundations, which are more suitable for enterprise foundations and were indeed introduced into Belgian law in order to enable entrepreneurs to use a Belgian memberless control holding, were only introduced in 2002. At the time of writing, Belgium's best-known public interest foundation, the King Baudouin Foundation (KBF), is exploring whether it or satellite foundations it would set up could also act as an enterprise foundation, with a philanthropic purpose. If the KBF goes ahead with its plans and is successful, this could no doubt have a catalysing effect in Belgium on the use of philanthropic foundations as enterprise foundations.

1 For the disinterested goal requirement, see Article 1:3 of the Belgian Code on Companies and Associations (hereafter referred to through its official acronym in Dutch: WVV).

2 Which we explain in section 5 of this chapter. The creation of certificates ('*certificaten*' in Dutch, '*certificats*' in French, sometimes translated as 'depository receipts' in English) is partly governed by Article 7:61 WVV.

2. BELGIAN FOUNDATION LAW GENERALLY[3]

2.1. TWO TYPES OF FOUNDATION: PRIVATE AND PUBLIC INTEREST

Today, two types of foundations exist under Belgian law: the public interest foundation (hereafter: PIF) and the private foundation. They are both memberless legal persons that can only be set up through a notarial deed, at the request of one or more founders who transfer for free some assets to the foundation. They are both non-profit organisations meaning that, though they are allowed to make a profit with their activities, they may not distribute such profits. They must pursue a so-called disinterested goal (see below, section 2.3).[4] There are no minimum asset requirements for either private or public interest foundations (but of course the definition of foundation implies that *some* assets are contributed to the foundation from the start).

It has been possible to create public interest foundations since 1921.[5] They are only allowed to pursue seven types of activities, exhaustively listed in statute:[6] philanthropic, religious, philosophical, scientific, artistic, pedagogical or cultural purposes and activities.[7] Private foundations were only introduced in 2002.[8]

---

3 Foundations are governed by Book 11 of the WVV, which also deals with foundations as the third main type of private law organisational form, and which was adopted in 2019. There is little up-to-date, post-WVV non-tax related literature on foundation law, but since the 2019 Act did not fundamentally change the statutory rules on foundations, much of the pre-2019 but post 2001 literature remains relevant. The leading handbook is D. Van Gerven, *Handboek stichtingen*, Kalmthout/Biblo, Antwerp 2004, p. 442, and R. Van Boven, *De Belgische stichting*, 2nd ed., Intersentia, Antwerp 2020, p. 313 is also much consulted. In French, one may mention V. Simonart, *Associations sans but lucratif, associations internationales sans but lucratif et fondations*, Bruylant, Brussels 2016 and A. Benoit-Moury, O. Caprasse and J. De Leenheer (eds), *ASBL, fondations et associations internationales*, die Keure, Bruges 2004. A leading comment on the impact of the 2019 reform on non-profit law generally (including foundations, with, e.g. a discussion of the meaning of the requirement of a 'disinterested purpose') is M. Coipel, 'L'intégration des ASBL, des AISBL et des fondations dans le nouveau Code' in O. Caprasse, H. Culot and X. Dieux (coords), *Le CSA sous la loupe. Le nouveau droit des sociétés et des associations*, Anthemis, Limal 2019, pp. 489–518.

4 See Article 1:3 WVV, which defines foundations under Belgian law.

5 An Act of 27 June 1921 introduced for the first time the possibility for non-profit associations and public interest foundations to obtain legal personality without being recognised in a separate, specific act of parliament. This 1921 Act, which was thoroughly reformed by an Act of 2 May 2002 that, among other reforms, introduced *private* foundations into Belgian law, was the equivalent for non-profit organisations of the Companies Act until both the Companies Act and the 1921 Act on non-profit organisations were merged into the WVV, effective 1 May 2019.

6 Article 11:1 WVV.

7 The textbook example of a kind of activity or purpose a PIF would not be allowed to pursue are sports-related activities. Thus, a Belgian PIF may not own or support any type of sports club, nor could it lawfully support sporting events.

8 By an Act of 2 May 2002, amending the 1921 Act on associations and foundations. At that time, there were about 320 public interest foundations in Belgium, see E. Wymeersch,

They can pursue any type of activity, as long as they do not distribute profits. The main reason why the Belgian parliament introduced private foundations in 2002 was in order to allow Belgian entrepreneurs to use a Belgian foundation as the vehicle for holding a controlling stake of shares in closed companies and act as a so-called certification vehicle.[9] Before the private foundation was introduced in Belgium, Belgian entrepreneurs wanting to use a foundation as a control vehicle had to go to the Netherlands and use a Dutch foundation.[10] As we will see, even today such shareholding foundations are often set up in the Netherlands, under Dutch law, by Belgian entrepreneurs.

Both types of foundations (public and private) are governed by Book 11 of the 2019 Belgian Code of Companies and Associations (cited here as WVV, the official abbreviation in Dutch), which also contains the statutory rules on foundations even though the latter are not mentioned in the name of the Code. Book 11 is a short 'Book' within the Code, containing only 16 articles (sections), although other parts (Books) of the Code are also relevant, like the rules on annual accounts and auditing in Book 3 or the rules on mergers and transformations in Book 13, in addition to the definition of 'foundation' under Belgian law in Article 1:3 of the Code.

Article 1:3 of the Code defines foundations essentially as legal persons without members, set up by one or more founders, and that pursue a disinterested goal. This implies foundations may not award any financial advantage to the founders, directors or any other person, except when such an award of financial benefits is part of the pursuit of the disinterested goal of the foundation.[11] Article 1:3 of

---

'Stiftungen im belgischen Recht' in K. Hopt and D. Reuter (eds), *Stiftungsrecht in Europa*, Carl Heymanns Verlag, Cologne 2001, p. 276. For discussions of the private foundation from shortly after its introduction, see (in addition to the articles by Lavrysen and De Wulf cited below in footnote 11): P. Nicaise and I. Banmeyer, 'Les fondations' in Centre d'Études Jean Renauld (ed), *Le nouveau droit des ASBL et des fondations*, Bruylant, Brussels 2002, p. 329; H. Briet, 'La nouvelle loi sur les ASBL, fondations et associations internationales' (2002) *R.G.E.N.* nr. 25.281; D. Van Gerven, 'De private stichting en de stichting van openbaar nut' (2003) T.B.B.R. 347; B. Sarteau, 'Les fondations privées' (2003) *Revue du Notariat belge* 6; L. Weyts, 'De private stichting: een nieuwe uitdaging voor het notariaat' (2004) 2 *T. Not.* 78, 80; J. Malherbe and M. de la Serna, 'Fondation belge, trust et fondation etrangère – régime fiscal' in Centre d'Études Jean Renauld (ed), *Le nouveau droit des ASBL et des fondations*, Bruylant, Brussels 2002, p. 349.

9 Certification is explained in section 5 below.

10 For a comparison between Dutch and Belgian enterprise foundations just after the Belgian private foundation had been introduced as a possible certification vehicle, see P. Lavrysen, 'De private stichting: een volwaardig alternatief voor de Nederlandse stichting-administratiekantoor?' (2002) *T.B.H.* 667, 673 et seq.; see also H. De Wulf, 'De private stichting als instrument van familiaal vermogensbeheer' in J. Bael, R. Deblauwe and C. De Wulf, *Familiale vermogensplanning. Cyclus Delva 2003–2004*, vol. 30, Wolters Kluwer, Mechelen 2004, pp. 569–625.

11 E.g. a foundation that has as its goal (according to its articles of incorporation) to financially support excellent Belgian students who want to pursue their studies at top US universities may of course distribute scholarships to such students.

the WVV thus makes clear that foundations may not distribute profits, either directly or indirectly. Indirect (profit) distributions are defined in Article 1:4 of the WVV as any transaction involving a foundation as a result of which its assets decrease or its liabilities increase and for which the foundation either does not receive anything in return, or consideration that is manifestly too low (in view of market prices and practices established at arm's length) compared to whatever the foundation performed in exchange for such consideration. Or, as handbooks and practitioners would put it, an indirect distribution is any transaction between the company and a third party that is manifestly not performed at arm's length, i.e. at market 'prices', to the detriment of the foundation.[12]

'Enterprise foundation'[13] is not a concept used in Belgian statute but more generally is not a legal concept in Belgium, nor do practitioners use the expression. Nevertheless, private foundations are sometimes used as vehicles for running small commercial businesses and, more frequently, for holding controlling stakes in (for-profit) companies. It is just that nobody in Belgium outside academia would call such foundations 'enterprise foundations' and, more importantly, they are not subject to different private law, organisational rules than any other type of foundation. But there are some specific tax rules for foundations whose exclusive or almost exclusive activity is holding shares in companies.[14]

2.2. SOME HISTORY ON PERMITTED ACTIVITIES AND PURPOSE

To this day, Belgian law uses a quite strict and clear-cut distinction between companies, which must pursue profit distributions,[15] and associations and

12 The textbook example is the case of a foundation director who owns a building that the foundation rents, as offices, from the director, but with the rent set at a level that far exceeds market prices for renting such a building. Such transactions can be declared null and void, but very few claims for voidance are brought. Rather, the rule on no profit distributions is mainly, indirectly, enforced by the tax authorities, who will tax such transactions as profit distributions. If tax authorities find that a foundation engages in such transactions on a regular basis, they will tax the income (and the unlawful distributions) of such a foundation using corporate tax rates, whereas normally foundations that stick to the rules are taxed at much lower rates than (for-profit) companies, under the system of so-called 'legal person taxation', where 'legal person' in fact refers to non-profit organisations (whereas companies under Belgian law are always for-profit organisations).

13 In the sense of a foundation that holds a controlling interest in a company, either (and most commonly) by holding shares in the company or by directly owning and operating a business.

14 See section VII.2 and Article 147 of the Belgian (Flanders) Gift Tax Code. The rule was originally introduced by the 15 July 1998 Belgian Certification Act.

15 Article 1:1 WVV. Book 8 of the WVV deals with 'social enterprise' companies: these are cooperative companies (other company forms, like private or public corporations, cannot adopt the label) that pursue a 'social goal' and have to reinvest about 95% of their profits into that goal. They can only use the 'social enterprise' label if they are recognised as such by a government agency, see Article 8:5 WVV. (This requirement was introduced in 2019 because it

foundations, which are organisations that may not pursue profit distributions.[16] Of course, these non-profit organisations may turn a profit, but if they make a profit, they must reinvest it in whatever disinterested goal they are pursuing according to their articles of incorporation. They may not distribute it.

Until 2018, Belgian law distinguished between 'traders' (who professionally engaged in activities earmarked as 'commercial' by section 2 of the then Commercial Code, which was abolished in 2018) and 'non-traders'. Associations and public interest foundations were not allowed to engage in commercial activities (as defined in section 2 of the Commercial Code). This prohibition came on top of the ban on profit distributions for associations and both types of foundations. Private foundations were allowed, from their introduction into Belgian law in 2002, to engage in commercial activities, but were also subject to the ban on profit distributions. This led to tensions and difficulties of interpretation, e.g. when a private foundation owned and ran a chain of 'bio-shops', where supposedly only healthy foods were sold. The foundation also ran workshops and organised talks on healthy living. Commercial food shops had already successfully sued the predecessor organisation of the foundation, namely an association (VZW-ASBL) on the basis of unfair competition, and now successfully sued the successor foundation. The Court of Appeal of Antwerp ruled that the foundation engaged in the same type of activities as commercial firms and that there were indications that profits from the 'bio-shops' indirectly benefitted organisations (including a health insurer) affiliated with one of Belgium's main political parties.[17] The case illustrated how difficult it was for foundations whose activities were exactly the same as those of for-profit commercial companies to convincingly argue that they were operating with the required disinterested goal and not even indirectly awarding financial benefits to outsiders.

---

was felt that previously, when all company types could, from 1995, award themselves the label of 'social company', provided their articles of association contained ten mandatory provisions (like a one share one vote rule and the possibility for employees to become shareholders), the label had been abused by companies that in reality did not really pursue a social goal). But even these 'social profit' companies must sooner or later mandatorily distribute profits to shareholders, either through dividends or upon dissolution, when the net assets are distributed among shareholders. Non-profit companies are simply not allowed under Belgian law.

16 On the distinction between profit and non-profit organisations after the 2019 reform, see e.g. H. De Wulf, 'Het onderscheid vennootschap-vereniging na de invoering van het Wetboek van vennootschappen en verenigingen' in D. Bruloot and H. De Wulf (eds), *Het nieuwe ondernemingsrecht, Cyclus Delva*, vol. XLIV, Wolters Kluwer, Mechelen 2020, pp. 219–249.

17 Court of Appeal, Antwerp, 17 November 2005 (2006) *TBH-RDC* 443, with a case note analysing the possibility for foundations to engage in business activities: H. De Wulf, 'Economische acitiviteiten van private stichting en VZW: woordspelletjes versus de bestrijding van concurrentievervalsing' (2006) 4 *TBH-RDC* 447.

In any case, in 2018, the legal distinction between traders and non-traders was abolished[18] and since then there can be even less doubt that private foundations may engage in business activities (as long as they reinvest any profits they make in a disinterested goal).

In the 19th century, Belgian politics was dominated by the fight between 'liberals' (proponents of free markets, free speech, state education and sometimes vehemently anti-religious) and Catholics. The liberals were distrustful of non-profit organisations – often associated with religious orders and the Catholic Church – which they feared would lead to the unproductive use of assets that would be kept out of market transactions (fear of the 'dead hand') and would accumulate within the Church, thus contributing to the wealth and (hence) influence of the Church. This attitude among liberal politicians is why a generalised possibility for non-commercial non-profit organisations to obtain legal personality (and hence legal capacity) without, as a rule, government control, was only introduced in 1921 through the so-called 'Law on non-profit associations', which also introduced so-called 'public foundations', which this chapter calls public interest foundations (PIFs). PIFs were (and are) still subject to some form of government control, in that their articles of incorporation must be submitted to the Ministry of Justice, where one or two civil servants are tasked with checking whether the PIF can be expected to, in actual practice, pursue a disinterested goal.[19] Only when the ministry approves, and this approval is translated into a Royal Decree,[20] can the PIF obtain legal personality, namely on the day the Royal Decree approving their articles of incorporation is published in the Annexes to Belgium's Official Gazette.[21]

By 2002, when the 1921 Act on associations and public interest foundations underwent a major modernisation, mindsets had, of course, evolved, and the time was ripe for private foundations. These can pursue any type of activity but must have a disinterested goal to pursue. This means that they may certainly not distribute profits, but must also indicate in their articles of incorporation which specific disinterested (in the sense of morally or socially praiseworthy) goal they pursue.[22]

---

18 By an Act of 15 April 2018 ('*houdende hervorming van het ondernemingsrecht*'), *BS* 27 April 2018, 36.878.

19 Article 2:6, §4 WVV.

20 In Belgian law, 'Royal Decree' is the name given to executive orders approved by a cabinet minister or the cabinet (government) as a whole. In the hierarchy of norms, they rank just below parliamentary legislation, and they can indeed only be lawfully adopted on the basis of an act of parliament (legislation) that awards the power to a minister or the government to issue Royal Decrees about the relevant subject matter.

21 Article 2:6, §4, 2nd subparagraph WVV.

22 Article 2:11, §2, 3° WVV.

2.3. THE MEANING OF THE 'DISINTERESTED GOAL' REQUIREMENT

It is not completely clear or undisputed whether, for foundations, the requirement to have a disinterested goal is a separate, additional requirement on top of the rule that they may not distribute profits.[23]

As indicated, a major distinction in Belgian law is between for-profit organisations, which must distribute profits (namely companies), and non-profit-organisations, which may make a profit but may not distribute it (namely associations and foundations (private and public)). The ban on profit distributions has always been and still is a fundamental feature of all non-profit organisations in Belgium. As also previously explained, until 2018, non-profit associations and PIFs were, in addition, not allowed to engage in commercial activities. But for associations, statute did not state, until the 2019 reform, that they had to pursue a disinterested goal. For public interest foundations, of course, statute did from the start determine that they should pursue one of only seven types of goal/activity, but again, did not use the expression 'disinterested goal' (until May 2019). When they were introduced in 2002, private foundations were allowed to engage in any type of activity, including commercial activities, as long as they did not distribute any profits they made, but reinvested such profits (if any) in whatever the goal was they pursued through their activities. But statute from 2002 onwards also defined private foundations as entities that acted for a disinterested goal. It was the first time the concept of 'disinterested goal' was introduced in Belgian legislation on private law legal persons (companies, associations and foundations). Since it was clear from the start that private foundations were allowed to engage in any type of activity, including commercial activities, most scholars and commentators argued that the 'disinterested goal' mentioned as part of the statutory definition of what a private foundation is, was simply a reference to the ban on profit distributions and nothing else.[24] Indeed, in the parliamentary committee that discussed the adoption of the 2002 Act introducing private foundations, it was explicitly stated

---

23 See H. De Wulf, 'Het onderscheid vennootschap-vereniging na de invoering van het Wetboek van vennootschappen en verenigingen' in D. Bruloot and H. De Wulf (eds), above n. 17, pp. 241–243 on the history of the concept of 'disinterested goal' in Belgian statute and why it was introduced into Belgian law, for the first time, in 2019, for non-profit associations as well. Belgium's leading foundation law attorney, Dirk van Gerven, and myself share the opinion that the concept of 'disinterested goal' should be removed from statutory texts, but we cannot of course deny that it is presently there.

24 See D. Van Gerven, above n. 3, pp. 47–48 and his discussion of how the meaning of this concept was not completely clear from the start; P. Lavrysen, above n. 10, 673; H. De Wulf, above n. 10, p. 571; A. van Zantbeek, 'Behoud van controle door familie- de Belgische Private Stichting' in A. Verbeke, *Handboek estate planning Deel 6*, Larcier, Brussels 2008, p. 40; R. Van Boven, above n. 4, p. 28.

that the expression 'disinterested goal' was intended as a replacement of the more traditional 'without a profit-seeking goal'.[25]

When the Code on companies, associations and foundations was rewritten from scratch in 2019 (a year after the distinction between commercial and non-commercial activities had been abolished), a new definition of 'association' was adopted in Article 1:2 WVV which also referred to 'disinterested goal'. For associations the law states that they must pursue a disinterested goal through their activities and in the next sentence that they may not distribute profits, either directly or indirectly. For foundations, the statutory definition (Article 1:3 WVV) states that their assets must be assigned towards a disinterested goal and, again in a separate sentence, that they may not distribute profits directly or indirectly. Within the four-person committee (of which I was a member) that had been tasked by the Minister of Justice to write the 2019 Code, there was a shared aversion to using nebulous concepts like 'purpose' or 'goals' to distinguish separate legal forms like companies and foundations from each other or to determine what types of activities could be pursued through which legal form.[26] For the committee, all that mattered was that non-profits like foundations and associations could not distribute profits. 'Goals' and 'purpose' were concepts that the committee considered were best left to theologians or French post-structuralist philosophers, but were tools with no purpose within the kingdom of law, whose citizens are all pragmatic hard-nosed lawyers. The legal meaning of 'disinterested goal' to the committee was simply that entities that are not allowed to distribute profits would normally not be animated by the pursuit of profit as their main reason for existing.

But the mindset and intentions of the drafters of a statutory text are completely irrelevant to its interpretation. And it cannot be denied that the statutory definition of both 'foundation' and 'association' refers to the pursuit of a disinterested goal in one sentence, and formulates the profit distribution ban in the next sentence. If a single article of a law code uses two different expressions, it is obvious that, unless there are clear indications that the second expression ('non-profit-distributing') is only meant to explain the meaning of the first expression ('disinterested goal'), the two expressions have a different, independent meaning. In addition, Article 2:11, §2, 3° WVV states that the foundation articles of incorporation must 'precisely' state the disinterested goal and the activities that the foundation will pursue. This requirement (which in the 2019 reform was simply copied from the previous legislation on private foundations, as opposed to a new wording of the definition of foundation) makes clear that the law regards having a disinterested goal as something different and separate from acting as a non-profit (not distributing profits).

25 *Parl. St. Senaat*, 2000–2001, nr. 2-283/11, 45–46.
26 I have explained this in the article cited above in n. 23.

All this is more or less in the same spirit as the tax approach to non-profits under Belgian law. Non-profit organisations (foundations and associations) are taxed at much lower rates than companies, who in Belgium are by definition for-profit.[27] Non-profits that actually distribute profits, are taxed as for-profits.[28] But contrary to what one might expect, it is not whether a foundation distributes profits or not which will determine whether it enjoys the lower rates of non-profit taxation: any legal person that runs a 'firm' as understood in tax law (see Article 180 of the Belgian Code on Income Tax) is taxed as a for-profit corporation, even when it never distributes any profits. This means an enterprise foundation exercising control over the shares of a commercial firm better have an explicit disinterested goal which it pursues if it wants to retain its privilege of being subject to non-profit taxation.[29]

3. THE LACK OF PUBLIC OVERSIGHT AND THE ENFORCEMENT OF ASSET LOCK RULES

It seems several countries with a tradition in foundations have quite well-equipped and pro-active supervisory authorities, especially concerning philanthropic/public interest foundations. In Denmark, for instance, supervisors seem to work quite closely with foundations and their boards.[30] Nothing similar exists in Belgium. For private foundations there is no supervision at all, though as will be detailed shortly, courts may intervene when foundations do not respect the no-distribution rule. There are probably two civil servants within the Ministry of Justice who spend part of their time supervising public interest foundations, but this supervision only takes place at the moment the foundation is set up (control of the goal of the foundation and its articles, see Article 2:6, §4 WVV) and in the rare cases where the articles of incorporation are changed.

In addition, there is government control on gifts to foundations. Since 1921 and to this day, all foundations in Belgium, both private and public interest, are subject to the rule that any gift to a foundation with a value larger than €100,000 must be approved by the government through a Royal Decree.[31] The

27 See Articles 220, 180 and 181 of the Belgian Code on Income Tax for non-profit taxation versus Article 179 of the same Code for company taxation. See generally on taxation of non-profits C. Meskens and B. van Vlierden, 'Rechtspersonenbelasting' in Tiberghien (ed), *Handboek voor Fiscaal Recht*, Wolters Kluwer, Mechelen 2024, pp. 909–928.

28 See Articles 180 to 182 of the Belgian Code on Income Tax and, e.g. L. De Meyere and S. De Raedt, 'Fiscale Implicaties van de nieuwe definitie van vereniging' in D. Bruloot and H. De Wulf (eds), above n. 16, p. 313.

29 See section 8.2, on taxation.

30 See BR.K. Feldthusen, 'Enterprise Foundations in Denmark' in this volume.

31 Article 11:5 WVV.

rule does not apply, however, to so-called 'hand gifts'.[32] This traditionally meant that something was physically handed over from the donor to the beneficiary without involvement of a notary, so that according to Belgian law no gift tax had to be withheld. It has long been accepted that the transfer of money between bank accounts can be structured as a 'hand gift' and most lawyers would argue that the same applies to transfers of book-entry securities between securities accounts (but note that under Belgian law, shares registered in a shareholder's name cannot be treated as book-entry, 'dematerialised' securities and therefore cannot be donated through a hand gift, but always require the intervention of a notary (for gifts, not for sales), who will withhold gift tax). As a result of these rules, most large gifts of money and securities to foundations, especially by the founders, are structured as 'hand gifts' or 'bank gifts'.

3.1. ENFORCEMENT OF THE NO DISTRIBUTION RULE

The rules that a foundation must pursue a disinterested goal and that it may neither directly nor indirectly distribute profits are sanctioned through potential nullity of the foundation as such. Article 11:5 WVV contains an exhaustive list of four grounds for nullity of a foundation. One is that the goal for which the foundation was set up, or the activities listed in the objects clause, are incompatible with mandatory statutory rules or public order. Nullity on this ground will occur very rarely; an example would be a foundation the articles of which make explicitly clear that the foundation intends to distribute profits. This example is separately listed as the fourth possible ground for nullity: when a foundation has been set up with a goal to provide its founders, directors or others with direct or indirect financial advantages, it can be declared null and void, except if the distribution of financial advantages happens in accordance with the disinterested purpose as defined in the articles.[33] While there may be a fair number of foundations in Belgium that distribute profits in actual practice, extremely few will list this as one of their goals in the articles, and it is only that which Article 11:5 WVV targets with nullity.

If a foundation distributes (directly or indirectly) profits or assets, such a distribution can be voided (last sentence of Article 1:3 WVV) unless the foundation can show that the distribution was performed in the pursuit of the disinterested goal of the foundation (e.g. if the goal of a foundation is to award

[32] About this exception, with numerous references, see R. Van Boven, above n. 3, pp. 131–132, nr. 344.

[33] Practitioners tell us that some founders chose to use (often Luxembourg-based) professionals to act as founders to foundations, in the hope of avoiding legal trouble when the foundation (to which the 'real' founder will contribute assets after the foundation has been formally set up by the advisor) turns out to arguably distribute money to the benefit of the founder or his/her family members.

scholarships to financially disadvantaged students, then of course the foundation may distribute money to such students). The directors who have signed off on such a distribution will have violated their duties to the foundation, but since foundations have no members, the risk for directors of being sanctioned is very low[34] – unless the foundation is declared bankrupt after an unlawful distribution, in which case the insolvency trustee may sue the directors. Otherwise, tax authorities will usually limit themselves to taxing the distribution, not suing directors (or the foundation) and public prosecutors have other priorities.

Article 2:114, §1, 3° and 4° WVV allows the Enterprise Court to forcibly dissolve a foundation if it violates the non-distribution rules. 3° allows for dissolution if the foundation uses its assets or income for a goal that is incompatible with the purpose for which it was set up. 4° allows for dissolution if the foundation violates the rule that it may not directly or indirectly distribute profits, unless the distribution is in support of the disinterested goal of the foundation. Article 2:114, §1 awards the power to sue for the dissolution of the foundation to the founder, any of his/her heirs or beneficiaries, any director, or any party that can show an interest in the dissolution and the public prosecutor. But as mentioned before, public prosecutors have other priorities.

Indeed, since there is no Belgian government agency in charge of supervising foundations or the non-profit sector, and since checking whether foundations respect the non-distribution rule is understandably not a priority for public prosecutors,[35] the actual supervision of foundations, at least regarding whether they respect the non-distribution rule, is performed by the tax authorities. On the basis of Article 180 of the Belgian Code on Income Tax, these can subject non-profit organisations to the much higher rates of corporate income tax when they establish that the entity either runs a firm or distributes profits. Thousands

34 Article 11:13 WVV states that the Enterprise Court can dismiss (forcibly remove) directors who have been grossly negligent, but it does not indicate who would be competent to seize the court – which means it must be assumed anyone showing an interest (within the meaning of Article 17 of the Code on Civil Procedure) could seize the court. Article 11:13 WVV does not imply that the only way to remove directors against their wishes is through the court: no doubt the articles of incorporation of the foundation may also contain rules on this (e.g. awarding this right to a simple majority of the other directors), as long as the articles do not try to curtail the powers of the courts.

35 I have no knowledge of a foundation ever being wound up at the request of the public prosecutor's office. This does sometimes happen to associations who distribute profits, though. A relatively recent case that reverberated in legal circles was Court of Appeal, Mons, 9 March 2021 (2022) *TBH-RDC* 625, where the Brussels public prosecutor successfully sued for the dissolution of an association which had as its stated purpose to help sick and injured people and also to exercise the profession of ambulance driver. The association was held to be indirectly distributing profits to a company controlled by the directors of the association, through service contracts between the association and the company whereby the company charged disproportionately high prices for its services. The Court of Appeal ruled that the claim for forced dissolution was in principle justified, but granted the association a stay of execution in order to allow it to rewrite the contracts and/or convert its business into a company.

of non-profits are thus systematically subjected to corporate income tax, but I have no figures on foundations specifically, and it may very well be that the vast majority of such cases pertain to associations, not foundations.

3.2. CONTROL ON ASSET LOCKS IN CASE OF DISSOLUTION, MERGER AND TRANSFORMATION

Could founders or their heirs or family members distribute the assets of the foundation to themselves upon the foundation's dissolution, or by merging or transforming the foundation into an entity with less stringent rules on asset locks? Normally this is not permitted[36] and not possible. Foundations cannot be dissolved by their board (and there are of course no members who could decide the dissolution). They can only be dissolved by a court, upon the request of one of the founders, a director, the public prosecutor or a 'third party with an interest'.[37] A court decision is required even when the foundation was set up for a fixed term or when the articles contain an explicit condition that leads to dissolution if it is met (resolutory condition). In addition to those two cases, foundations can be dissolved when their purpose or goal has been fully realised; when they are no longer able to pursue the goal or purpose for which they were set up; when its assets or income are used for a different purpose than the one fixed in the founding act; when it distributes profits, directly or indirectly, or acts contrary to public order or the Code of Companies and Associations (which also deals with foundations) or when it violates its own articles in a serious way; or finally, if it is subject to an obligation to publish annual accounts (because it is a large foundation or active in a specific sector like healthcare) and does not perform that disclosure, not even after having been sued for dissolution.[38]

Since foundations have no members, when they are dissolved their assets cannot be distributed among such members (after all debts have been paid, which in any case of course needs to happen first). The assets (if any) that remain after all debts have been paid (to the extent possible) can only be assigned to another non-profit[39] and in accordance with the articles.[40] The court that dissolved the foundation will check the so-called 'plan for the assignment of assets' to make

36 However, Article 11:2, second paragraph WVV provides that the articles of the foundation may provide that the founder or his/her beneficiaries may take back the assets that the founder contributed, or the equivalent value in money, if the foundation has fully realised the goal for which it was set up. The textbook example is a villa or castle that was contributed to a foundation whose sole purpose was to renovate the building.

37 Article 2:114, §1 WVV.

38 For this closed list of grounds for dissolution of a foundation, see Article 2:114 WVV.

39 Article 2:11, §2, 6° WVV.

40 Article 2:11, §2, 6° WVV, see also Article 2:140 WVV for the rule that after dissolution a judge needs to check whether the assignment is in accordance with the articles of the foundation.

sure it respects those rules. The assets cannot be assigned to anyone without the court's consent.[41]

In the sector of 'social profit companies' (companies that pursue some 'social goal' other than benefitting their shareholders, and who may only distribute a limited amount of their profits, but must reinvest about 95% of profits in whatever their 'social goal' is) Belgium has witnessed some abuses or at least successful attempts to circumvent the asset lock rules applicable to such entities through mergers with or transformation into a for-profit entity.[42] Is anything similar possible for foundations?

Transformations – in the technical sense of a legal person adopting another legal form without any break in legal personality – are not allowed for foundations, except that a private foundation may transform itself into a public benefit foundation (PIF) through a notarial deed, if the transformation and the articles of the PIF are recognised by Royal Decree,[43] in practice by the civil servant of the Ministry of Justice tasked with dealing with the approval of PIFs. Remarkably, statute does not say who can decide such a transformation, so it must be assumed that the board may take the decision, though it could be assumed that the board could only apply to the Ministry of Justice/the Ministry could only approve the transformation if it is not obvious that transferring the assets of the private foundation to a PIF is not compatible with the wishes of the original founder. It would be hard to accept that the board of a private family foundation that manages shares of one or more commercial firms could legitimately transform that private foundation into a public foundation, potentially against the wishes of the current family members. Certainly, this should never be allowed if the private foundation hitherto acted as a so-called STAK, which stands for '*stichting administratiekantoor*', being the kind of private foundation that holds shares (a controlling stake) in an operating company and is used as a vehicle for certification – an arrangement we discuss in detail in section 5 below. STAKs (henceforth we will use this acronym to indicate a foundation that issues certificates in exchange for the shares that it holds) are under a contractual duty to pass on to holders of certificates issued by the STAK any income they receive based on the shares they hold. Public interest foundations may not, however, pass on such income and cannot act as a STAK, and therefore if a STAK were transformed into a PIF, this would radically undermine the intentions of the founder of the STAK. Therefore, such a transformation should not be allowed. If it were performed anyway, such a transformation should therefore be regarded as a breach of duty by the foundation towards the certificate holders, so that the certificates would be automatically converted into shares again and the foundation would lose those

41 See Article 2:140 WVV.

42 See S. Cools, 'Asset lock bij verlies erkenning als sociale onderneming' (2021) *TRV-RPS* 970.

43 Article 14:67 WVV.

shares as an asset.[44] But in any case, in view of the need to obtain consent from the Ministry of Justice for the transformation of a (even private) foundation, there is no danger of 'asset leakage'.

Mergers and divisions of private foundations are also possible, but they can only merge with legal entities that continue their disinterested purpose.[45] Such a merger is only possible if the board of the foundation unanimously decides to perform such a merger. The way statute is formulated gives the impression that the board can always decide to engage the foundation in a merger or division, but it could be argued that the founder can lawfully exclude this possibility in the articles. On the other hand, there can be little doubt that the board derives a competence to merge the foundation into another foundation or public law entity from Article 13:1 WVV even when the articles are silent on the matter. The statutory provisions have been drafted in a suboptimal way, but it still seems pretty clear that foundations can only merge with other foundations or similar entities:[46] a private foundation may be absorbed through a merger by another private foundation or a public foundation, university or other public law legal person. The assets of the absorbed foundation must form a separate accounting fund (without legal personality) within the absorbing entity and may only be used for the pursuit of the same disinterested goal the original (absorbed) foundation had.[47]

4. THE USE OF FOUNDATIONS IN BELGIUM, INCLUDING AS ENTERPRISE FOUNDATIONS

There can be no doubt that private foundations may engage in any activity that a for-profit company could also engage in. In other words, private foundations may engage in business activities. This includes running a business or holding shares in a company, either a controlling stake or not.

Belgian private foundations can be used to run a business directly, but this rarely happens. At least several hundred small businesses like 'social clubs', 'cultural centres' (event centres) and even ordinary bars, cafés and teahouses are organised as non-profit associations but is it is rare for such businesses to organise as foundations.[48]

I am not aware of any large business in Belgium being directly run by an enterprise foundation and am confident there are no such enterprise foundations.

44 See Article 7:61, §1, last subparagraph WVV.
45 Article 13:1, §1 WVV.
46 See Article 13:2, §2 WVV.
47 See Article 13:2, §2, 2nd section WVV.
48 One example was the chain of bio-shops that gave rise to the court case (Court of Appeal, Antwerp,17 November 2005) discussed in above n. 17.

But there certainly are hundreds of private foundations that hold a controlling stake in large, sometimes even listed firms. Such a foundation could act as a mere holding entity, but very often, when a controlling stake is contributed to a foundation, such an enterprise foundation is part of a 'certification agreement', which we will discuss in section 5 below. Such a certification structure entails that while the foundation is the controlling shareholder of a company in which it holds shares and exercises the voting rights attached to such shares, the foundation is contractually obliged to pass on any income it receives from the underlying operating company to holders of certificates that the foundation has issued. As mentioned previously, foundations that are part of a certification setup are called '*stichting administratiekantoor*' (very literally translated: 'foundation-management office') or STAK.

4.1. GENERAL USE OF FOUNDATIONS IN BELGIUM

Let us first look at some figures on the use of foundations in Belgium in general. Research by journalists and the business data provider Graydon showed that in early 2024 there were 2,105 private foundations registered in Belgium.[49] (Only) 349 of those had an exclusively philanthropic, non-family-related, more or less society-oriented purpose. In addition, 88 were to support religious organisations and 104 had as their main goal to preserve or promote the work of an artist. About 110 foundations were intended to financially support a handicapped person. The journalists also identified at least 517 so-called 'family foundations' – about a quarter of all private foundations – defined as foundations that will financially support families, usually the generations that will come after that of the founder(s). In most of those cases, such a family foundation also pursues goals other than supporting the children and grandchildren of the founder. The articles will first list three or four other goals, such as collecting art or keeping an existing collection together, awarding prizes to top performers in a certain artistic or scientific sector or scholarships for promising students. Only then will they mention things like 'in a spirit of care, carrying the burden of certain family expenditures' or 'in order to maintain family solidarity' fund certain amenities. In practice, it is very hard to ascertain which types of expenditure get priority – the family-related expenditures or those that are directed towards outsiders. What is striking is that the articles of many of these family foundations are quite

49 L. Bové, P. Depuydt and S. Souris, 'Private stichting dient om belangeloos doel te steunen, niet om je familie te verwennen' (23 March 2024) *De Tijd*. Unless otherwise indicated, all figures concerning foundations in this paragraph are from this article in Belgian daily newspaper '*De Tijd*'. I contacted the journalists but they were not prepared to share the database they had assembled with the help of Graydon, a leading provider of company data in Belgium.

explicit and detailed in what costs exactly can be covered by such foundations, e.g. the cost of a gardener or a cook, certain costs for the upkeep of villas, yachts, airplanes, etc. Sometimes specific monthly allowances are mentioned, like in one probably extreme case, 'a maximum monthly allowance of 600,000 euros, according to reasonable estimates of what is required for a normal life'. I agree with critics who argue that this type of allowance for all family members, or for the upkeep of the family castle or estate if it is not open to the public as a museum, are pure and simple distributions which cannot be justified by other activities of the foundation that do benefit non-family outsiders. One cannot convincingly argue that since the allowance is paid or the cost is borne in order to maintain family solidarity, equality among family members or in order to maintain a family estate in the family where it has been for decades or centuries, these distributions serve a disinterested goal and are therefore[50] allowed. The new Belgian government that was formed in early 2025 announced that it would look into the regulation of the non-profit sector, and apparently one of the government's main goals would be to uproot this type of abuse of private foundations.[51]

4.2. ENTERPRISE FOUNDATIONS IN BELGIUM

Turning to enterprise foundations, in early 2024 there were about 380 private foundations in Belgium that operated as STAKs, that is held a controlling or at least major stake in an operating company, as part of a certification arrangement.[52] These data are necessarily incomplete, as it is well-known that Belgian controlling shareholders in the past often preferred to set up a foreign, usually Dutch, foundation to administer the controlling stake in 'their' company. Fully a third of those 380 STAKs had been set up in 2023 according to the same journalistic research. It had been public knowledge for a long time that in several listed Belgian companies the controlling shareholder (or group of shareholders, like a family) had structured its control through a foundation.

---

50 Article 1:3 WVV (the definition of foundation) makes clear that foundations may distribute money if this is part of the realisation of their disinterested goal.

51 See *Federaal regeerakkoord 2025–2029* (February 2025), p. 47.

52 P. Depuydt, L. Bové and S. Souris, 'Van Donald Muylle tot Kinepolis: families geven bedrijf door, maar niet de stuurknuppel' (1 April 2024) *De Tijd*. According to the same journalistic research, there were, at the end of 2023, 258 Belgian private foundations controlled by non-Belgians. Only 40 of those had purely philanthropic purposes; all the others were family, enterprise or family enterprise foundations. The best-known example, often referred to, is a foundation controlled by the important French entrepreneur Bernard Arnault. According to the journalists, that foundation holds the shares in two holding companies that together hold shares with a value of €3 billion in companies of the LVMH group, see L. Bové, P. Depuydt and S. Souris, 'Honderden families steken fortuin in stichting, maar daar is amper controle op' (27 March 2024) *De Tijd*.

To the best of our knowledge this is still the case in, for instance, AB InBev (the world's largest brewer), Colruyt (a supermarket chain), Lotus Bakeries (a very successful producer of gingerbread cookies to go with coffee), Ter Beke (prepared foods), Bekaert (mainly producing different kinds of steel wire), etc. But as the journalists documented, most STAKs are in control of private, unlisted, but sizeable firms.[53] Many of those private firms have existed for several decades, but the newspaper article also mentioned several tech startups.[54] I suspect that in case of a startup already having a foundation to administer the shares of a controlling shareholder, the foundation is more intended as an anti-takeover device than as a vehicle for family tax and succession planning, but must stress this is speculation.

Would a *public interest* foundation be allowed to act as an enterprise foundation? As far as I know there are, as yet, no public interest foundations in Belgium that act as enterprise foundations. As mentioned before, public interest foundations may only pursue seven kinds of activities[55] or goals listed in Article 11:1 WVV. But current legislation contains no limitations on the kinds of *assets* a public interest foundation is allowed to own.[56] There can therefore be no doubt that public interest foundations may own shares that constitute a controlling stake in a commercial company. But at the same time, it seems equally clear that a PIF could not lawfully have as its only objective or activity to act as a holding and exercising control. It must pursue at least one of the seven objectives listed in Article 11:1 WVV and therefore would have to use the income it receives from the shares it owns to pursue those philanthropic, scientific, artistic, etc. goals. This also implies that the fiduciary duties of the foundation's directors instruct them to exercise the voting rights (if any) attached to the shares that the foundation owns in such a way that the foundation derives at least some income from the shares it owns. This means the foundation board would have to at least sometimes vote in favour of dividend distributions (by the operating company, to the extent that the general meeting of the operating company has a say on that, as is the case in Belgium, where the general meeting of shareholders of a company votes on profit distributions, but based on a proposal drafted by the board).

[53] One example is DPG Media (one of Belgium and the Netherlands' leading media companies). But also much smaller (but still sizeable) firms like clothing retailer JBC or kitchen builder Dovy.

[54] E.g. Showpad or TechWolf or Droia (the latter is more of an investment fund/holding company).

[55] The literal, 1921 text of the statutory provision says that a public interest foundation can be recognised (by the relevant government service) 'if it is aimed at the realization of a work ("*oeuvre*" in French) of a philanthropic ... nature'. I take the reference to 'work' to be a reference to activities.

[56] Until the Act of 2 May 2002 abolished that rule, the legal capacity of PIFs was deemed to be limited by the fact that they could not own rights to real estate unless that real estate was necessary to fulfil the purpose of the foundation, see Article 35 of the Act of 27 June 1921, D. Van Gerven, above n. 3, p. 399, nr. 374.

Sometimes this could lead to clashes with management or, less likely, minority shareholders of the operating company, who sometimes may prefer retention of profits within the company, for instance to fund research and development in the near future.

Whereas a PIF could, consequently, act as an enterprise foundation, it could not lawfully act as a STAK,[57] since STAKS have a contractual duty to forward any dividends and related income they receive from the operating company to holders of certificates. In other words, STAKs have to distribute any income they receive from the shares they hold, which would be completely incompatible with the requirement to pursue one of the seven goals permitted by statute. Neither could a PIF act with the mixed purpose of acting as a STAK for the certificated shares it holds and pursuing philanthropic, public interest goals with the other assets it holds. The income distributions it would have to make as part of the certification would simply be incompatible with the public interest purpose of any PIF. To be clear, a STAK organised as a *private* foundation could have a mixed purpose, namely acting as a STAK for the shares it holds and at the same time pursuing a philanthropic goal with its other assets and income that is not related to the certificated shares. (But users of such a mixed purpose private foundation should be aware that in that case, the wealth tax discussed below in section 8.2 will be levied on those other, non-share, assets, whereas single purpose STAKs are exempt from that wealth tax).

5. ENTERPRISE FOUNDATIONS AND CERTIFICATION AGREEMENTS

5.1. THE CERTIFICATION TECHNIQUE

Certification[58] is a technique that Belgian lawyers copied from their Dutch colleagues, who seem to have invented it.[59] It is by now so well-established

---

57 Correctly stating that a public interest foundation cannot act as a STAK: D. Van Gerven, above n. 4, nr. 257.

58 For general overviews of the legal rules and practices concerning certification in Belgium, see e.g. (from a vast literature) D. Van Gerven, above n. 3, pp. 276–395; M. Tison, 'Certificering van aandelen naar Belgisch recht (Wet van 15 juli 1998)' in A. Verbeke (ed), *Handboek Estate Planning*, Larcier, Brussels 2009, pp. 240 et seq.; F. Hellemans and R. Tas, 'De certificering van effecten (W. 15 juli 1998)' in A. Benoit-Moury, M. Denef and K. Geens, *Nieuw vennootschaps-en financieel recht 1999*, Jan Ronse Instituut (ed), Kalmthout/Biblo, Antwerp 2000, pp. 13–58; A. Verbeke, 'Certificering van effecten. Nuttig instrument voor successieplanning?' (1999) 3 *Not. Fisc. M.* 43; F. De Bauw and E. Pottier, 'La certification de titres émis par une société anonyme' (1999) *TBH-RDC* 523.

59 On certification ('depository receipts') and the use of private foundations for that purpose in the Netherlands, see the chapter in this book on the Netherlands by Christiaan Stokkermans and Marleen van Uchelen-Schipper.

that, since 1998, the Belgian Code on Companies and Associations (WVV) has regulated it, introducing a limited number of mandatory rules on certification.[60]

Certification is an essentially contractual arrangement whereby shareholders in a commercial, for-profit company contribute their shares to a holding entity which always is a legal person, usually a non-profit, and in most cases a private foundation.[61] As just mentioned, it is usually assumed – correctly, in my opinion – that *public interest* foundations cannot be used as certification vehicles,[62] as they are only allowed to pursue seven goals listed in statute, and certification or cementing control over a family firm is not one of those permitted goals. Of course, one could argue that as long as the income generated by the shares that the foundation owns is used for the philanthropic, artistic, scientific, etc. purposes allowed by law, there is no legal issue. But that argument would be unconvincing, because a STAK will have to forward all income it receives to the certificate holders, leaving no income to pursue philanthropic goals.

The foundation acting as a vehicle for certification is set up by the shareholders in the company (all or some of them) who contribute their shares to it, as part of the certification arrangement. The foundation becomes the new shareholder in the company, usually the controlling shareholder, and frequently the sole shareholder, for instance when a husband and wife who set up a successful company 20 years earlier contribute all their shares to a foundation (STAK). Simultaneously with the contribution of the shares to the foundation, the founders enter into a contractual arrangement with the foundation: the certification agreement. In exchange for the contribution of their shares, the former shareholders receive certificates, issued by the foundation.[63] These certificates represent a contractual claim against the STAK, obliging the STAK to immediately distribute to the certificate holders any income the STAK receives from the operating company. This income could result from dividend distributions, but unless otherwise specified, any income (originating from the company) will be covered by the agreement, for instance also the liquidation surplus that is distributed among shareholders when the company has been dissolved. If the STAK 'immediately' distributes the income it receives, the STAK will be tax transparent: there will be no taxation (withholding tax or other) at the level of the STAK on the occasion of

60 See Article 7:61 WVV.

61 If it is not a foundation, it usually is a VZW-ASBL, that is, an association.

62 See D. Van Gerven, above n. 3, p. 282, nr. 275.

63 This type of certificate has nothing to do with the share certificates (in Dutch, the exact same word is used as for the certification certificates) that a company that has issued registered shares must, according to Belgian law, issue to the shareholders registered in the company's share register, as proof of their registration as shareholders through what in effect is an excerpt from the share register, just like people can print bank statements showing how much money there is in their bank account.

the payment from the company to the STAK.[64] The certificate holders receiving the income will be taxed, though. Private foundations are in principle subject to an annual wealth tax of (at the time of writing) 0.45% on the value of their assets. However, this wealth tax does not apply when the assets of the foundation mainly consist of company shares that have been certificated in accordance with the certification rules of the 1998 Certification Act (among other things this implies a 'one on one' certification: for every share that is certificated, only one certificate is issued. Certification arrangements may deviate from this 'one on one' rule, but the issuing foundation will then not be tax transparent).[65]

Certification allows the parties involved to split voting and other governance rights from rights to profits and other cash flows. The STAK will be a controlling or sole, at the very least, substantial shareholder in the operating company. It exercises al the rights attached to the shares it owns. But the STAK is under a contractual duty to pay onwards any income it receives from the shares to the certificate holders. The latter have no rights *in rem* on the shares, only a contractual claim against the foundation – of which they are not members, since a foundation by definition has no members.

At the moment when the STAK first issues certificates, these are often awarded to the contributors of the shares, who usually are also the founders of the STAK foundation. These initial certificate holders will then often donate their certificates, within a brief period, to their children or other beneficiaries. But it is not uncommon for the certificates to be awarded directly to the children or other beneficiaries of the former shareholders who contributed their shares to the STAK (in such a case, parents contribute their shares to the STAK and the STAK issues certificates to the children; the transaction thus constitutes an indirect gift by the parents to the children). Sometimes the parents will first donate their shares to their children, with the understanding – which can be contractually imposed as part of the gift agreement – that the children themselves will contribute the shares to a STAK, perhaps with the parents as initial board members of the STAK.

How the rights attached to the shares that the STAK owns are exercised is determined by the foundation board. In entrepreneurial families where those in power (e.g. the founders of the company, who also set up the STAK) do not want all family members to have an equal share in governance powers in the company (mainly voting power), the founders of the STAK will make sure to exclude from the STAK board those family members they want to exclude from power. The textbook example is that of a wealthy family with a paterfamilias who founded a successful business empire and who has three children or three family branches in the second generation. The parents want their children (all family branches)

---

64 Rule introduced by Article 13 of the Act of 15 July 1998 (Certification Act). See also e.g. Ruling (of the competent Belgian tax authorities) nr. 2018.0644, 18 September 2018 on the principle and the conditions for this tax transparency.

65 See Article 150, 2nd paragraph, 5° Code on Gift Taxes.

to share equally in the wealth created through the company, but they do not trust the two sons near the levers of power in the company, only their daughter (or, e.g. not the Kardashian and Jenner family branches, only the Wests). So, each child/family branch receives the same number of certificates, but only one child/family branch is appointed to the foundation board.

According to Belgian law, the default rule[66] is that a certificate holder may return his/her certificates to the STAK in exchange for the shares against which the certificates were issued.[67] The certificate holder can thus reverse the certification arrangement. However, this would allow certificate holders to undermine the whole set up, which was intended to cement control over the company at the level of the STAK and thus (only) with those family members who are members of the STAK board. That is why it is allowed, and standard practice, to provide in the certification agreement (issuing conditions of the certificates) that the certificate holder does not have the right to exchange his/her certificates for the shares.[68] The WVV does contain the mandatory rule, however, that certificates will be changed back into shares in two cases. First, when the foundation is declared bankrupt, dissolved or enters another situation of '*samenloop*', i.e. *concursus creditorum*.[69] Second, when the foundation disregards its duties towards the certificate holder(s) or when it grossly neglects the interests of those holders.[70] The most obvious example of a violation of foundation duties would be if the foundation fails to forward to the certificate holder any income it received from the company. What constitutes gross negligence concerning the interests of certificate holders is less clear and can be more controversial. An example could be that the STAK board uses its voting power in the company to 'manifestly unreasonably' block any dividend payments by the company, so that holders of certificates do not enjoy any income from the company. 'Manifest unreasonableness' is the standard under Belgian law used to judge whether voting behaviour of a shareholder constitutes an abuse of its voting power.[71] Needless to say this is a vague standard, but it should be clear that Belgian courts are reluctant to rule that the exercise of voting rights was manifestly unreasonable; they will rightly only condemn extreme cases where it is clear that the voting shareholder (in this case the foundation) more or

---

66 See Article 7:61, §1, last subparagraph, 1st sentence WVV.

67 This swap is called '*royering*' with the Dutch technical legal term invented by Dutch lawyers, derived from the French verb '*royer*', to scrap, delete, strike off (the register).

68 Article 7:61, §1, last subparagraph, 2nd sentence WVV. In legal Dutch, the certificates are then called '*niet-royeerbaar*', i.e. not eligible for exchange (against shares).

69 Article 7:61, §2 WVV.

70 Article 7:61, §1, 6th subparagraph, 2nd sentence.

71 See Article 2:42, 2° WVV about nullity of company decisions because of 'abuse of right' or 'abuse of powers'. The 'manifest unreasonableness' criterion was developed by courts (see especially, Court of Cassation, 10 September 1971 (1972) *Arr. Cass.* 31), but was recently codified in Article 1.10 (new) Belgian Civil Code.

less intentionally voted in such a way as to harm the interests of the certificate holders without any (or a negligible) advantage to the company or its other stakeholders/shareholders.[72]

Is the foundation board allowed to sell or more generally alienate the shares for which it issued certificates? The default rule is that it cannot but the certification agreement may provide otherwise. If the shares were issued by a listed company, however, the rule that the foundation that issued certificates in exchange for those shares may not alienate those shares is mandatory.[73]

Certification arrangements can serve several purposes simultaneously. Contributing the shares to a foundation – from an economic perspective: gifting them – could be done to provide the foundation with income to serve a philanthropic purpose. But in the vast majority of cases, in Belgium the purpose is to cement the control of a family or coalition of shareholders over the underlying company and keep the family/coalition together, since individual family/coalition members will no longer be able to sell the shares (and the foundation board will also be subject to limits on its power to alienate the shares, often through provisions in the articles of the foundation, sometimes as a result of a shareholder agreement to which the foundation is a party). But this is not a certification, simply the creation of a holding in order to keep a controlling block of shares together. If the creation of the holding foundation is followed by a certification, the purpose of the latter will be to split up voting and profit rights. The intention is to simulate the effects of an English trust, which is a legal phenomenon that is not possible under Belgian law (beneficial 'owners' are never 'owners' – who have rights *in rem* – under Belgian law).

5.2. CERTIFICATION AND DISTRIBUTIONS BY THE STAK

It is always difficult to explain to people who first learn about Belgian foundation law and certification arrangements that it is unobjectionable that foundations that function as STAKs simply pass on the income they receive from the operational company to certificate holders, who often are either former shareholders in that company or the children or grandchildren of such former shareholders. Are these not simply distributions and therefore outlawed? Well, yes; the payouts are doubtless distributions. Nevertheless, there can be no doubt that is perfectly legitimate to use a private foundation under

72 For a discussion of court cases and literature about this topic, see generally F. Pollefeyt and B. Tilleman, *Handboek nietigheid van besluiten van rechtspersonen*, Intersentia, Brussels 2024, pp. 331–363.

73 See (both rules, listed and unlisted company) Article 7:61, §1, 5th paragraph WVV.

Belgian law as a holding company/STAK: the main, decisive reason why Belgian parliament created the private foundation in 2002 was to offer a Belgian vehicle to Belgian entrepreneurs who wanted to set up a certification arrangement, and to avoid the need for such entrepreneurs to set up a Dutch foundation.[74] Indeed, during parliamentary proceedings that led to the adoption of 2002 Act it was explicitly stated that private foundations could act as a STAK as part of a certification arrangement and that their disinterested goal would then usually be keeping family control over the underlying company.[75] The Belgian legislator simultaneously, and of course very deliberately, created a wealth tax exemption for those private foundations that mainly administer shares, in other words STAKS.[76] One sometimes hears the argument, in defence of STAK foundations, that they do not distribute profits: they simply pass on the income they receive from the operating company. And indeed Belgian tax law will treat the STAK as a tax transparent entity if it immediately (within 14 days) forwards the company income to the certificate holders. But even though the income the STAK receives is simply passed on, and this income is not generated by production or service activities of the STAK itself, there is no denying these pass-on payments are distributions. Would one deny that when an ordinary holding company receives dividends from, say, three subsidiaries and then distributes a dividend of its own exclusively consisting of the money it received from the subsidiaries, that this would also from a legal perspective be a profit distribution? The pass-on argument cannot save the STAK because it is wrong. The only way to justify foundations being used as STAKs is that such a STAK foundation will have a disinterested goal, and foundations may distribute money if this is part of the pursuit of their disinterested goal (Article 1:3 *in fine* WVV). For STAKs the disinterested goal will usually be something like maintaining the family character of the underlying business, making sure it is run in the interest of all stakeholders, with a long-term view, contributing to the local economy, keeping a certain industry Belgian, etc. One can of course try to argue that such goals/purposes are only a thin veil over the real purpose: maintaining family control in order to enrich that same family. But then again, it bears repeating that the main reason why Belgium introduced private foundations into Belgian law in 2002 was to enable this STAK practice. If the law were changed or courts decided that pass-on payments by STAKS would henceforth be illegal, the only effect would be that Belgian entrepreneurs would again have to systematically resort to a Dutch STAK instead of a Belgian one.

---

74 E.g. H. De Wulf, 'De private stichting als instrument van familiaal vermogensbeheer' in J. Bael, R. Deblauwe and C. De Wulf, above n. 10, p. 611.

75 See the parliamentary proceedings at *Parl. St. Senaat*, 2000–2001, nr. 2/283-13, 46.

76 See Section 8. Article. 150, 2nd paragraph, 5° Code on Gift Taxes.

5.3. USE OF DUTCH FOUNDATIONS BY BELGIAN ENTREPRENEURS[77]

The private foundation used to administer the shares of a Belgian company and that issues certificates pertaining to these shares need not be Belgian.[78] As mentioned, the practice of certification developed in the Netherlands and was then copied in Belgium. Initially Belgian entrepreneurs used Dutch foundations (registered in the Netherlands, set up through a Dutch notary) for their certification arrangements because in Belgium private foundations did not exist. Precisely in order to offer a Belgian vehicle to entrepreneurs, the private foundation was introduced into Belgian law in 2002.[79] For various reasons, Belgian entrepreneurs until at least 2020 still preferred to use Dutch foundations as vehicles for certification (less so when the foundation is a mere holding and certainly not if the main purpose is philanthropy or to bear expenses that a family has to bear like the upkeep of its castle or private jet). Statistics about this do not exist, but it is what every specialist law firm or notary's office will tell you. Specialist notaries in (the southern part of) the Netherlands would often be able to service French-speaking Belgian entrepreneurs in the latter's native language.

Why did Belgian entrepreneurs go to the Netherlands for so long – and still sometimes do – for STAKs? As far as I know, there is no systematic research on this question but company advisors will often mention three reasons. First – but this is no longer true now that the Belgian law has been in force for more than 20 years – Dutch notaries and other advisors had more expertise in drafting the required contracts. Second, the tax treatment of various transactions in which foundations may be involved was more certain in the Netherlands than in Belgium and more generally there were more precedents (case law) concerning foundations and certification in the Netherlands than in Belgium. Third, until a 2019 reform of Belgian law, the Dutch governance arrangements were perceived to be more flexible. In particular, the previous Belgian rule that every private foundation needed a collegiate board consisting of at least three people was

---

77 For an article (by three tax lawyers) comparing the use of a Dutch versus a Belgian foundation as an enterprise foundation controlling a Belgian company, see P. Souffriau, E. De Nolf and E. Kustermans, 'Controlebehoud bij aandelen: de Belgische PSAK of de Nederlandse STAK?' (2021) 3 *Vermogensplanning in de Praktijk* 4.

78 This has never been disputed under Belgian law, see e.g. M. Tison, above n. 58, p. 175; F. Hellemans and R. Tas, above n. 58, p. 52.

79 That this was the main goal of the government when it proposed the bill to introduce private foundations into Belgian law is clear from the report of parliamentary proceedings in Verslag van de Commissie Justitie, *Parl. St. Senaat*, Z, 2000–2001, nr. 293/16, 146. That same document, at 69, stressed that other legal persons than foundations could also be used as STAKS.

regarded as bothersome by some, e.g. when the two founders of a company wanted to be the only directors of the enterprise foundation to which they had contributed their shares. The Belgian board rule was abolished starting 1 May 2019 so Belgian private foundations can now function with only one or two directors if they so wish.[80]

In recent years, Belgian entrepreneurs have in great numbers begun to prefer Belgian foundations to Dutch ones. Advisors give several reasons for that.[81] First is the 2019 reform, meaning that the board of a Belgian foundation may now also consist of just one director. But for most enterprise foundations, it would be puzzling to have just one director. Second is the developments in Dutch tax law, meaning it is now easier to have a fully tax transparent STAK in Belgium than in the Netherlands. Third, the rules on the UBO (disclosure of who is the ultimate beneficial owner) in the Netherlands allow almost anybody to consult much of the data in the UBO,[82] whereas access to UBO register details is restricted in Belgium (to certain professionals who show a legitimate interest, excluding, e.g. journalists or the general public).[83] But fully one third of the 380 or so Belgian STAKs in existence at the end of 2023 had been set up after 2022.[84] This makes it likely that many of those were conversions of Dutch STAKs into Belgian ones because of the introduction into Belgian law of a new tax rule by the so-called '*Programmawet*' (a budget Act) of 22 November 2022, implying that if a taxpayer sets up a Dutch foundation over a Belgian company, he/she is engaging in a 'legal construction' ('*juridische constructie*'), that is, using a foreign vehicle that is regarded with suspicion by Belgian tax authorities and which persons subject to Belgian income tax must notify to the tax authorities, with one consequence being that the tax authorities receive the possibility to perform checks on tax returns for longer (ten years) than usual. Practitioners have reported that this has led to an exodus from the Netherlands of Belgian-controlled foundations because taxpayers want to avoid being branded as users of 'legal constructions'.[85]

---

80 See Article 11:6 WVV.

81 See the legal advisors cited in P. Depuydt, L. Bové and S. Souris, 'Van Donald Muylle tot Kinepolis: families geven bedrijf door, maar niet de stuurknuppel', above n. 52 and see P. Souffriau, E. De Nolf and E. Kustermans, above n. 78.

82 M. Zwankhuizen and M. den Dubbelden, 'Het Nederlandse UBO-register: een overzicht van de belangrijkste kenmerken' (2020) 3 *Vermogensplanning in de Praktijk* 42, 44.

83 See Article 7, 3° of the Royal Decree of 30 July 2018 ('*betreffende de werkingsmodaliteiten van het UBO-register*'), *BS* 14 August 2018.

84 See P. Depuydt, L. Bové and S. Souris, 'Van Donald Muylle tot Kinepolis: families geven bedrijf door, maar niet de stuurknuppel', above n. 52.

85 See P. van Maldegem, 'Vrees voor Kaaimantaks doet Belgen uit Nederlandse stichtingen stappen' (12 December 2023) *De Tijd*; D.-E. Philippe, 'De Nederlandse stichting worstelt met de Kaaimantaks' (6 June 2024), available at: www.lexgo.be.

5.4. SOME CONFLICTS OF LAWS ISSUES WHEN SHAREHOLDERS OF A BELGIAN COMPANY USE A DUTCH CERTIFICATION ARRANGEMENT[86]

As mentioned, many Belgian entrepreneurs who set up a certification use a Dutch STAK. This was common practice before Belgium legislated on certification in 1998 and introduced private foundations in 2002, but it still is common practice today (2025). The parliamentary proceedings concerning the 1998 Certification Act confirmed that not only pre-1998 Dutch certifications of Belgian shares remained valid after the Belgian Act had become effective, but also that it remained possible after the Act had become effective to enter into new certification arrangements concerning the shares of a Belgian company in accordance with Dutch law and/or use a Dutch certification vehicle.[87] The question arises which, if any, Belgian rules on certification and STAKs would apply if a Belgian operating company uses a Dutch STAK and a certification under Dutch law. For a detailed treatment of these sometimes controversial questions, we have to refer to specialist literature.[88] Here we limit ourselves to some remarks about the general approach to these issues.

If the STAK is a Dutch foundation, that is with a registered office in the Netherlands (and therefore normally founded through the services of a Dutch notary), it will be governed by Dutch law on foundations, not by Belgian law, since both Belgium and the Netherlands apply the incorporation theory to all legal persons,[89] meaning that it is irrelevant that, for instance, the foundation was set up by a Belgian citizen or that the board of such a Dutch STAK consists of Belgians who live in Belgium and always meet in Belgium. Under the 'real seat doctrine' these would have been relevant elements to conclude that the Dutch foundation would in fact be governed by Belgian law, but the real seat doctrine has been abolished by the new 2019 Belgian Companies Act, as of 1 May that year (and the Netherlands have applied the incorporation theory since the

86 For discussions of these issues, the best treatment is probably M. Tison, 'Gevolgen van de Belgische certificeringswet 1998 op bestaande certificeringen naar Nederlands recht', Boek 3 topic 47 in A. Verbeke, *Handboek estate planning, algemeen deel 3: Vermogensplanning met effect bij leven: rechtspersoon*, Larcier, Brussels 2009, pp. 253–260. See also F. Hellemans and R. Tas, above n. 59, pp. 52–55; W. Goossens, 'Certificatie naar Nederlands recht van effecten van Belgische vennootschappen; nog enig belang na de invoering van de Belgische wet betreffende de certificatie van effecten?' (1999) *Stichting & Vereniging* 60 and from before the 1998 Belgian certification law: P. Hamer, 'Administratiekantoor de droit néerlandais et actions de sociétés de droit belge: convention de vote et de blocage?' (1993) *R.P.S.* 285, 289; F. Bouckaert, 'Nederlandse administratiekantoren en Belgisch internationaal privaatrecht' (1989) *T.R.V.* 183.

87 Explanatory memorandum, *Gedr. St. Kamer*, 1997–1998, nr. 1430/1, 3. See on the matter, M. Tison, above n. 87, p. 254.

88 See especially M. Tison, above n. 87, pp. 253–260.

89 See Article 110 Belgian Code on for Belgian law.

1970s). If the STAK is governed by Dutch law, Dutch law will of course govern any mandatory rules on board composition or other aspects of foundation governance. Likewise, it will determine what types of clauses can be lawfully included in the articles of incorporation of the STAK.

The certification of shares itself is a contractual operation. The subsequent relationship between the certificate holders and the STAK is also governed by contract, and not by the articles of the STAK. First, a contract is concluded between the initial shareholders and the foundation (that was usually founded by those same shareholders) whereby the shareholders contribute their shares to the foundation in exchange for certificates that give their holder (the former shareholders or their beneficiaries) certain contractual rights (claims) against the foundation (STAK).

When certification was first regulated in the Belgian Companies Act in 1998, the explanatory memorandum to the Act proclaimed that even when the issuer of certificates (the STAK) was not Belgian, Belgian certification rules would be applicable as soon as the shares (or other financial instruments) issued by a Belgian company were 'certificated'.[90] This statement cannot be accepted without some reservations or nuances. It certainly seems right that the question whether shares can be certificated would be governed by the law governing the company that issued those shares and not necessarily by the country whose laws govern the content of the certification contract. But since the relationship between the STAK and the certificate holders is a contractual one, private international law rules on contracts will prevail, and in case of a Dutch STAK, this will mean Dutch law applies unless parties to the certification agreement have explicitly chosen to apply Belgian law to it, using the choice of law possibility offered to them in contractual matters by Article 4.1 of the Rome I Regulation.[91] At least within the EU, the Rome I Regulation would be applicable to determine the *lex contractus*.[92] According to Article 4.2 of Rome I, the law of the country where the contracting party that effects the 'characteristic performance' has its habitual residence would apply. Since one may assume that issuing the certificates (and distributing the funds that these give a claim to) is the characteristic performance in a certification, Dutch law would apply.[93]

The relationship between a shareholder and the company that has issued the shares and more specifically the question which rights against the company the shareholder has, is governed by the *lex societatis*,[94] the law of the company, at

---

90 Explanatory memorandum, *Gedr. St. Kamer*, 1997–1998, nr. 1430/1, 3.

91 See e.g. M. Tison, above n. 87, p. 257, nr. 370.

92 Regulation (EC) 593/2008 of 17 June 2008 on the law applicable to contractual obligations (Rome I) [2008] OJ L177/6.

93 See in that sense e.g. F. Hellemans and R. Tas, above n. 59, p. 54, nr. 67.

94 This has traditionally been accepted in western European countries, sometimes on the authority of the French '*Royal Dutch Shell*' court decision (Cass. Fr. Civ., 17 October 1972, *RCDIP* 1973, 520, case note H. Battifol). The decision ruled that when a Dutch company had

least for registered ('nominative') shares.[95] This means the relationship between a Dutch STAK and the Belgian operational company (OC), whereby the STAK is a shareholder in the Belgian company, will essentially be governed by Belgian company law. It is therefore usually – but not universally – assumed that the rules on whether certificates can be exchanged back into shares is governed by the *lex societatis*, as this is regarded as a question concerning the conditions under which one can become shareholder and therefore pertains to the company-shareholder relationship.[96] It would be good for legal certainty if everyone could be convinced of this view, but it needs to be said that it seems equally convincing to argue that the question of '*royeerbaarheid*', i.e. exchangeability of certificates against shares, is one that pertains to the relationship between the STAK and the certificate holders.

6. GOVERNANCE: BOARDS AND CHANGES TO THE FOUNDATION ARTICLES

6.1. BOARDS AND COURT INTERVENTIONS

Every foundation is run by one or more directors.[97] Until 1 May 2019, a board consisting of at least three people was required and since then only one director is sufficient. The first directors are appointed by the founders and they will often appoint themselves as one of the directors or as the sole director.

If the founder appoints more than one director, the directors will function in a collegiate way (decisions require a simple majority among those present at a meeting, half of the directors being required to be present for valid decision-making).[98] It is not completely clear whether this is a mandatory or merely default rule but in the absence of wording in statute like 'unless the articles provide otherwise', the best interpretation is that this is a mandatory rule.

Since foundations have no members, the articles will have to deal with director succession. The most common solution is that the current board may

issued shares and these paper shares were held in France by French shareholders, the validity of those shares and hence the rights shareholders had against the company was governed by Dutch law, and not by the law of the country where the shares were held (France)), and for Belgium the rule is confirmed in Article 111, §1, 6° and 7° of the Belgian Code on Private International Law.

95 For dematerialised shares, the law applicable to the intermediary where the shareholder/ultimate beneficial owner holds a securities account may also be relevant.

96 M. Tison, above n. 86, p. 255; F. Hellemans and R. Tas, above n. 58, p. 55, both with further references to the majority of Belgian doctrine on the 1998 Certification Act.

97 Article 11:6 WVV. This article also confirms that legal persons may be appointed as directors. Thus, a private company could be appointed as a/the director of a private foundation.

98 Article 11:6, 2nd paragraph WVV.

co-opt new members, i.e. select its own successors. The articles could contain eligibility requirements. It is also not unheard of – and perfectly legal – for the founder to provide in the articles who the first generation of successors will be. For example, a founder could provide that she and her husband would be on the original board and that upon their death or when certain conditions are met, their children (or some, specifically indicated children) would succeed them as foundation directors.

Belgian law contains no rules on foundation board composition. More specifically, there is no requirement for foundation boards to be independent of the founders or family members. Indeed, in family foundations the board often consists of the founders and/or family members.

When setting up the foundation, the founder could provide in the articles for other governance bodies than the board. Nothing in the law prevents the creation of a dual board model, with a supervisory board and an executive board. But since foundations are, by definition, memberless, one should take care not to create the equivalent of a general meeting of members under the guise of creating an advisory council. As is the case for so much in Belgian foundation law, the (implications of the) statement in the previous sentence remains untested before courts. In any case, what is, in a foundation, the practical difference between a general meeting and a supervisory board which in the articles receives the power to appoint executive board members? Well, one difference is that I think it would not be allowed to create a body which could appoint the supervisory board members that can, in turn, appoint the executive board members.

In family foundations, the need may be felt to create a family council that tries to look after the family interests. A family council is a common feature of family firms. Such a council could not be given powers to represent the foundation towards outsiders in addition to the directors. I think it should be allowed to provide in the articles that the actual directors may not take certain decisions without first *consulting* the family council. But if one wants to provide a *veto right* to family council members, they should be appointed as directors. In any case, supposing a provision in the articles would require the consent of non-directors such as a family council for certain acts through which the directors represent the foundation vis-à-vis third parties, the validity of such directorial acts would not be affected by the lack of family council consent, since Article 11:7, §2 WVV applies the *Prokura* doctrine to foundation directors.[99]

Is there any possibility for courts to intervene in foundation governance? Yes, but this will have to be based on the general competence of courts to adopt so-called provisional measures or measures as part of summary proceedings.[100]

99 The *Prokura* doctrine entails that a legal person (e.g. foundation) cannot rely against third parties on limitations in the articles of association or other documents of the legal powers of representation vested by statute in directors or other 'organs' of the legal person.

100 See primarily Articles 19 and 584 of the Belgian Code on Civil Procedure.

Book 11 WVV (dealing with foundations) contains no rules on court interventions in governance matters, except the general possibility to changes to the articles as meant in Article 11:4 WVV. Belgian courts have, since the 1970s, awarded themselves the possibility to appoint 'provisional administrators' ('*voorlopig bewindvoerder*', '*administrateur provisoire*') in all private legal persons.[101] These are court-appointed persons who will exceptionally and temporarily replace the whole board (very rare) or a specific board member, or whose permission the actual directors need for certain decisions as listed by the court in its order. Neither the Companies Act nor any other legislation awards courts the power to appoint such 'provisional administrators'. But courts have ruled that their general power to issue orders to provisionally deal with any issue brought before them[102] also allows them to temporarily replace directors or limit the powers of the remaining directors. Courts rightly make sparse use of this self-created power, and if they do, it is because the plaintiff has been able to convince the court that the governance structures of a company or foundation are seriously malfunctioning in a way that cannot be remedied by mechanisms internal to the company or foundation. I have no knowledge of this possibility ever being used towards a foundation, but it would be possible.

6.2. CHANGES TO THE ARTICLES OF INCORPORATION AFTER THE FOUNDING ACT

Is it possible to change the articles of incorporation of a foundation that govern the way the foundation functions? Belgian legislation contains no general rules on the matter, except Article 2:11, §2, 5° WVV which says that the articles of incorporation of the foundation must mandatorily contain rules on how the articles can be changed. If the articles do not explicitly indicate anyone, like the board, who is allowed to change the articles, nobody can[103] except the Enterprise Court of the district where the foundation has its registered office, and then only in the cases meant in Article 11:4 WVV (which will be discussed shortly). There is of course no general meeting that could change the articles. The founder who founded the foundation has irrevocably parted with the assets he/she attributed to the foundation. He/she may not change the articles,[104] but of course it is not uncommon for founders to sit on the initial board of the foundation – indeed

101 E. Pottier and M. De Roeck, 'L'administration provisioire: bilan et perspectives' (1997) *TBH-RDC* 203 is the classic text describing the evolution of case law about this topic.

102 See Article 19, para. 2 and Article 584 of the Code on Civil Procedure.

103 See D. Van Gerven, above n. 3, p. 103.

104 Unless, I would argue, if he/she has reserved this power in the initial articles. But there is no authority on this question in Belgium. In any case, the founder (or anyone else) can never be allowed to change the articles in such a way that the founder would have a claim to assets of the foundation.

sometimes the founders are the only initial board members – and if anyone is given the power (in the articles) to change the articles, it will usually be the board. But it should be clear that board is not entitled to change the articles if it has not been given that power in the articles. The articles could provide that only certain provisions in the articles can ever be changed or could also, conversely, explicitly list provisions which should never be changed.

Article 11:4 WVV provides that if maintaining the articles unchanged would have consequences which the founder reasonably could not have wanted, and the persons entitled to change the articles do not act, the Enterprise Court can change the articles. Statute adds that the court should keep as close as possible to the existing articles. The reference to consequences the founder clearly could not have wanted implies that the court cannot change the purpose or goal for which the foundation was set up (nor can anyone else for that matter).[105] The court can be seized by any board member or the public prosecutor's office – it may not act on its own initiative.

7. STRUCTURING THE CONTROL OF THE FOUNDATION OVER THE ENTERPRISE GROUP

In Belgium as in other countries, the control of an enterprise foundation over a business can be structured in essentially four ways.

The first possibility is that a foundation directly owns the assets (and liabilities) that form a business. This is extremely rare to non-existent in Belgium, unless in the case of very small businesses. Small businesses like 'cultural centres' that operate a pub or snack bar, or 'biofood shops' that also organise events on healthy food or sustainable living, sometimes organise as non-profits, including as private foundations. They usually do so in the hope of benefitting from lower tax rates applicable to non-profit organisations and sometimes also hoping for other benefits, like government subsidies for certain activities organised through non-profit organisations.[106] Very often this is done to evade rules applicable to regular commercial business that the founders and people in control of the non-profit find too cumbersome. This of course only makes sense when statute attaches the benefits to having a specific legal form, belonging to the non-profit categories, such as associations and foundations.

105 See e.g. D. Van Gerven, above n. 4, p. 104.

106 Until 1 May 2018, non-profits could not be declared bankrupt in Belgium, provided they did indeed in actual practice refrain from distributing profits and did not engage in what was then considered by law to be commercial activity. Since a 2018 reform, all legal persons can be declared bankrupt (also some organisations that lack legal personality), irrespective of their activities, purpose, legal form or whether they are for-profit or non-profit.

In a second model, the holding foundation holds shares directly in a commercial company. It can be the sole, majority or minority shareholder.

The third approach consists of the holding foundation, which could be philanthropic, holding a controlling stake in an intermediate holding, usually a (private) company but potentially another, private, foundation, which in its turn holds a controlling stake in the operating company. In this case, the top holding foundation does of course not hold shares in the intermediate foundation but dominates the latter's board. The subsidiary foundation would then often pass the income it itself received from the operating company to the philanthropic holding foundation.

In a fourth case – rare in Belgium – there are two holding foundations but neither is a subsidiary of the other one ('double foundation model'). Sometimes, one of two holdings will be a partnership or a private company. In this structure, the operational company (OC) is controlled by a foundation holding the voting rights in the OC, whereas a second holding is a foundation, closed company or partnership that receives the profits and other cash flows distributed by the OC. If the whole group is dominated by a family, the family will normally be primarily in charge of the foundation holding voting rights whereas other investors will (often) control the entity to which profit rights are awarded. Sometimes the foundation receiving the dividends from the OC will have purely or mainly philanthropic goals. Or the structure could be complicated by adding a philanthropic entity that has a contractual claim to the dividends which are directly received from the OC by another entity. The split between voting rights and profit rights will be achieved by awarding one holding entity shares with profit rights but no voting rights, and the other shares with voting rights and very limited profit rights (or no profit rights at all, but many jurisdictions seem to have outlawed shares without any profit rights attached). This approach seems mainly useful in jurisdictions which are unfamiliar with the Dutch-Belgian technique of certification, which is an alternative way of separating voting and profit rights.

All these models are possible in Belgium, but the first is rare anywhere in the world, and the fourth (double foundation) is rare in Belgium even though it seems to be used quite frequently in, for instance, Denmark, Germany and Switzerland.[107] That the double foundation structure is rare in Belgium is probably explained by the fact that a certification arrangement is regarded as a more convenient and cheaper way of splitting up voting rights from cash flow rights. Another reason is that, as mentioned before, few enterprise foundations in Belgium are used for philanthropic purposes; rather, they are used to cement

---

107 See the chapters on those countries in this book and also (mainly about Swiss law) G. Neri-Castracane and D. Bottge, 'The double holding foundation model' (2024) 3 *SZW/RSDA* 283.

a family or shareholder coalition's control over a company. For such a family control purpose, it is often not necessary to split voting rights from cash flow rights whereas if the ultimate beneficiary of the cash flow rights is a philanthropic organisation (usually a foundation), the controlling family shareholder will want to retain control over voting rights.

If the enterprise foundation is a private foundation acting as a family foundation that is simply pursuing control over the OC on behalf of the family or a controlling group of former shareholders, there is nothing problematic about the foundation holding the shares directly without the intermediation of a holding company.

If the enterprise foundation has philanthropic goals, it seems advisable to always use a holding company (or private foundation acting as a STAK in a certification arrangement) to actually hold and administer the shares, even though such an extra level (the holding as intermediary) may create some immediate costs. This is especially true if the OC still has minority shareholders. First, an intermediate holding allows the board of the foundation to concentrate on philanthropy and the board or director of the holding company to concentrate on managing the shares and thinking about the governance of the OC. Precisely because the holding company and its board will intervene, as controlling shareholders, in the governance of the OC, it seems quite useful to have a 'waterproof compartment' between the philanthropic enterprise foundation and the OC. This is also why it is probably unwise to have joint directors on both boards, that is to have directors who are both on the foundation and on the holding board. This would lead to piercing of the compartment (but not to legal veil piercing). If there is a conflict between the holding as controlling shareholder and the other shareholders in the OC – potentially leading to litigation, perhaps even to litigation against the directors of the holding – it may be helpful that the enterprise foundation itself, and its directors, are somewhat removed from this tussle. Of course, if such litigation leads to successful claims that are enforceable against the assets of the holding, the foundation will directly feel the financial impacts (e.g. if some of the shares owned by the holding are seized). Likewise, often –most of the time – investors or contractual partners (suppliers, banks, etc.) of the OC will know that the foundation lurks behind the holding. Still, being once removed from the actual OC is useful, particularly when the OC or its board gets into reputational difficulties, e.g. because the OC committed tax fraud.

Directors of the philanthropic organisation will also need different qualities than those of the vehicle that exercises control over the commercial company. The latter will need to be more attuned to the needs of business and investor expectations.

If a philanthropic foundation is part of the control structure and does indeed act as the controlling shareholder of the operating company, but the latter also has minority shareholders, the two major governance problems are probably the following.[108] First, like every controlling shareholder, the foundation will be tempted to pursue private benefits of control. But that is not an issue specific to enterprise foundation-controlled groups. The problem is exacerbated, however, if the foundation has a philanthropic purpose. Most investors do not have philanthropic goals at all but pursue a high return on their investment. The opposition or difference in interests between regular return-oriented investors and philanthropic investors is probably greater than between regular controlling and minority shareholders. The foundation may want the OC to concentrate on projects that are less risky but generate a dependable cash flow that can be used to fund the philanthropy, whereas regular investors may prefer the company to take more risks, e.g. in creating or conquering new markets. Potentially, the foundation could act short-termist, in that it prefers dividend distributions rather than massive investments in research and development (R&D) which could be beneficial for the company in the long run but loss-making in the short term.

The second potentially major problem is more or less the opposite of the first; namely that even if a philanthropic foundation is the controlling shareholder, if the company needs large investments, the commercial minority shareholders who could provide (part of) that funding could overrule the hitherto controlling shareholder (foundation) and force the OC to move away from serving the needs of that philanthropic shareholder.[109] This issue is beautifully illustrated by events at OpenAI.[110] For a long time, OpenAI was structured as a non-profit. Microsoft then became a minority shareholder and initially injected about $10 billion into the company. Microsoft was a minority shareholder and the board of OpenAI was still under fiduciary duties to serve the non-profit purpose of OpenAI, which centred around the creation of safe general artificial intelligence (AI) systems. But the same type of consideration that moved OpenAI to seek out Microsoft as an investor with the massive financial firepower needed to fund the acquisition of the large numbers of high-end chips that were, at the time, deemed necessary to develop advanced large language models (LLMs) led to the board having its

108 The (already) classic analysis of governance issues around enterprise foundations is of course H. Hansmann and S. Thomsen, 'The Governance of Foundation-owned Firms' (2021) 13 *Journal of Legal Analysis* 172.

109 This governance issue is also highlighted, together with an insightful discussion of other issues concerning enterprise foundations and governance, in O. Eldar and M. Ørberg, 'The Anatomy of Nonprofit Control of Business Enterprise' (31 January 2025) *European Corporate Governance Institute* Law Working Paper No. 820/2025, available at http://dx.doi.org/10.2139/ssrn.5119965, especially p. 27.

110 The story is told in P. Olson, *Supremacy: AI, ChatGPT and the race that will change the world*, Macmillan, London 2024. One of the general topics covered in this book is how, though founders like Demis Hassabis and Sam Altman had different views on how to best attempt to develop general AI, both DeepMind and OpenAI initially attached considerable importance to keeping AI safe for humanity, but how both organisations had to cope with the pressure that came from the need to attract a large outside investor in order to fund their extremely expensive research (far too expensive for even the richest universities in the world such as Stanford).

hand forced when they fired CEO Sam Altman for not pursuing the non-profit goals of Open AI, and to OpenAI eventually pursuing a for-profit status.

8. TAX TREATMENT[111]

As always, when someone who is not a tax lawyer writes a general text about a legal phenomenon with some added tax remarks, what follows is not meant as an in-depth discussion of tax rules applicable to foundations, but is only meant to provide some information on tax matters that could be helpful in understanding why private or public interest foundations are used or not as enterprise foundations.

8.1. NON-PROFIT VERSUS FOR-PROFIT TAXATION

In Belgium, companies with legal personality are subject to corporate income tax.[112] Foundations and associations, which may not distribute profits, are subject to non-profit taxation[113] (confusingly called 'legal person taxation'[114] even though for-profit corporations are of course also legal persons). The rates of non-profit taxation are lower than those in company tax.[115] But the non-profit taxation status is not only lost when a non-profit legal form (association or foundation) distributes profits, but also as soon as the tax authorities establish that the non-profit runs a 'firm' as defined in Belgian tax law, even when it never distributes profits, and unless the firm is active in one of the 'preferred' non-profit activities listed in Articles 181 and 182 of the Belgian Code on Income Tax (WIB), such as education or care for the elderly.[116] Oddly, even today

---

111 On taxation of foundations, see extensively R. Van Boven, above n. 3, pp. 241–313; on non-profit taxation in general, see C. Meskens and B. van Vlierden, above n. 27, pp. 909–928 (updated every year). On some tax issues concerning foundations that were litigated in the recent past, see V. De Brauwere and L. Wautelet, 'Fondations privées belges et fondations étrangères: quelle fiscalité depuis l'apport par le fondateur jusqu'aux distributions aux bénéficiaires?' (2022) 8 *Rec.gén.enr.not.* 318. On the wealth tax that applies to private foundations, see D. Deschrijver, *De patrimoniumtaks: Een dode hand-heffing op overschot?*, Wolters Kluwer, Mechelen 2024. See also the annual review of developments in non-profit taxation in the *TRV-RPS* law review, e.g. D. Deschrijver, O. Hermand and P. Malherbe, 'Kroniek fiscaal recht voor vennootschappen en verenigingen 2022' (2023) 4 *TRV-RPS* 221.

112 Article 179 of the Income Tax Code.

113 See Article 220, 3° WIB (Belgian Income Tax Code).

114 '*Rechtspersonenbelasting*' in Dutch, see Article 220 of the Income Tax Code (WIB 92).

115 See Articles 220 to 223 of the Income Tax Code, which also make clear that for foundations, not all income or profits are taxed, but only certain types of income.

116 See L. De Meyere and S. De Raedt, above n. 28, pp. 313–350, who discuss this issue mainly with respect to associations, but their analysis is equally applicable to foundations; see also L. Debroe and M. Peeters, 'De fiscaalrechtelijke gevolgen van de invoering van het nieuwe

(2025) 'firm' or 'business' (Dutch '*onderneming*', French '*entreprise*') is defined for tax purposes with reference to the commercial law concept of 'commercial activity'[117] that was abolished in the rest of Belgian law in 2018, provided such activities are performed through a durable organisation that produces goods or offers services on a market with a view of being a going concern. In order to subject a foundation to corporate tax rates, the tax authorities do not need to prove that a foundation (unlawfully) distributes profits, but it can use such profit distributions as an indication that the non-profit is running a business.

The main reason for this tax law approach is the conviction that organisations that exercise the same type of activities, should be subject to the same legal rules, including on taxation. When in 2018–19 the rules on the type of activity that a non-profit association could lawfully perform were relaxed (scrapping of the ban on commercial activities), small and medium-sized enterprise (SME) interest groups expressed worries that unfair competition from non-profits to for-profit companies would get even worse[118] – even though the 2018–19 reform also had the effect of subjecting all entities running a firm to largely the same economic law rules – including extending the possibility for non-profits to be declared bankrupt,[119] even introducing an irrebuttable presumption that every private legal person runs a firm in the sense of the Code of Economic Law[120] that codifies most economic regulation applicable to 'firms'.

There are several reasons why this approach to taxation is misguided and undesirable, and incompatible with the private law approach to the for-profit company versus non-profit association or foundation distinction, but we need not and cannot go into that matter here. As a matter of positive law (the law as it stands), it is clear that under current Belgian tax law, a private organisation will be subject to corporate income taxation when it runs a business, even if it is not allowed by law to distribute profits (and thus is not a company) and does not in actual fact even indirectly distribute profits. It would be better policy to tax as

---

Wetboek van vennootschappen en verenigingen' in H. De Wulf and M. Wyckaert (eds), *Het WVV doorgelicht*, Intersentia, Antwerp 2021, p. 762.

117 Article 2, §1, 5° a of the Income Tax Code defines which companies are subject to Belgian corporate income tax, and refers to either pursuing profits or running a firm/business, and for the latter refers to 'commercial, industry or agricultural activities' ('*handels-, nijverheids- of landbouwverrichtingen*'); see also ComIB 1992 nr. 179/10 (the official commentary on the Code of Income tax by the tax authorities, indicating how they interpret its provisions) and for instance L. De Meyere and S. De Raedt, above n. 29, p. 317.

118 See H. De Wulf, 'De totstandkoming van het Wetboek van vennootschappen en verenigingen: enkele impressies over het maken van wetgevingsworsten' in I. Claeys (ed), *Recente wetgevende hervormingen: nieuw en beter?, XLVe Cyclus Delva*, Kluwer, Mechelen 2021, pp. 130–132 about the fears of the corporate sector of unfair competition by no-profits and how this influenced the legislation leading to the new 2019 Companies Act (WVV).

119 This possibility did not exist until 2018, when Book XX of the Belgian Code on Economic Law (WER) was amended, see the definition of firm and debtor for purposes of Book XX WER in Article I.23, 7° and 8° WER, as introduced by Act of 11 August 2017, effective 1 May 2018.

120 See Article I.1, 1° of the WER (above n. 120).

non-profits all associations and foundations that run a business but reinvest all profits in their activities because by law they may not distribute those profits, but that is, again, not how Belgian tax law is currently applied.

However, holding a controlling stake in a company and managing those shares is as such *not* a commercial activity within the meaning of tax law, so foundations who act as holding entities will as a rule remain subject to non-profit taxation. Only when a foundation would itself directly run an enterprise would it become subject to corporate taxation. Article 181, 8° of the Belgian Code on Income Tax explicitly mentions foundations that are exclusively used as certification vehicles (STAKs, in other words) as being exempt from corporate income taxation, and hence subject to the favourable non-profit-taxation regime.

8.2. TAXATION OF STAKs AND CERTIFICATION ARRANGEMENTS

As mentioned before, if a STAK immediately, i.e. within 15 days after receiving them, passes on any dividends it receives from the operating company to the holders of certificates, the foundation will be tax transparent: the income from the operating company will only be taxed at the level of the certificate holders. In addition, when assets such as shares are contributed to a foundation, any hitherto unrealised added value that is expressed upon the contribution is as a rule not taxed. Both rules were introduced by Article 13 of the so-called Certification Act of 15 July 1998. They also apply when a Dutch STAK is used by a Belgian founder contributing the shares of a Belgian company to the foundation.[121]

Effective from 1 January 2018, the Belgian tax rules on the use of foreign entities to save taxes[122] were amended and subjected to a so-called 'Cayman tax' which applies to entities that, in the jurisdiction where they are registered, are either not subject to income tax at all or to less than 1% of the tax they would have to pay if they were subject to Belgian income tax. Since Dutch foundations are not subject to income tax at all provided they do not run a business, and STAKs are not deemed to run a business, Dutch STAKs that hold shares in Belgian companies will as a rule be subject to this Cayman tax.[123] As explained before, an amendment of 22 November 2022 to tax law implies that Dutch STAKs (with shares in Belgian companies) will also be regarded as suspect 'legal constructions' that the STAK founder has to specifically mention in his/her tax returns – making it likely the tax authorities will pay closer attention to all

121 For all this, see, e.g. P. Souffriau, E. De Nolf and E. Kustermans, above n. 77, 16.

122 See Article 2, 13 b) of the Income Tax Code.

123 See e.g. G.D. Goyvaerts and C. Coudron, 'De kaaimantaks als de yin en yang van de Belgische fiscaliteit. Een kritische commentaar bij de invoering van het nieuwe EER-KB en niet-EER-KB' (2019) *TFR* 849, 891–895.

his/her tax affairs – and giving rise to an extended ten-year period during which tax authorities may check and correct the tax returns by the founders. As mentioned, these developments have made many Belgian entrepreneurs decide to convert their Dutch STAKs into Belgian ones, or at least not set up new STAKs in the Netherlands. Belgian enterprise foundations are not subject to this 'Cayman tax' as they are in principle subject to income tax.[124]

Private foundations are in principle subject to a wealth tax,[125] introduced because Belgian policy makers feared that once the private foundation became available from 2002 onwards, it would be used by estate planners to save money on taxes, and especially gift and inheritance tax, so that parliament wanted these revenue losses compensated with a wealth tax. This is a progressive tax on the value of the assets of a private foundation above a certain threshold, and with certain exclusions that need not detain us here. For a long time, the top rate was 0.17% but this top rate was increased to 0.45% from 2024 onwards on the part of the assets whose value exceeds half a million euros.[126] But from the start, private foundations whose assets exclusively consist of shares that are subject to a certification agreement (that corresponds to the definition in the 1998 Certification Act) were exempt from this wealth tax, and this remains the case today.[127] This can only be explained by a desire on the part of Belgian legislators to stimulate the use of Belgian foundations for certification purposes, and to do a tax favour to entrepreneurs. Many other people find it odd that a philanthropic private foundation is subject to a wealth tax but a foundation managing the shares of a wealthy family, to the financial benefit of that family, is not. Public interest foundations are always exempt from this wealth tax, and this is probably the only remaining reason to set up a PIF instead of a private foundation. But as explained, PIFs are not allowed to act as STAKs.

9. CONCLUSION

Enterprise foundations are common in Belgium, but they are usually pure 'family foundations', used only to cement and organise the control of a family over a commercial company. Contrary to what is observed in several Scandinavian or German-speaking countries, these foundations rarely have a philanthropic

124 Article 181, 8° of the Income Tax Code.

125 See Article 147 of the Flemish Code on Gift Taxes (W. Succ.). A similar rule applies in Brussels and Wallonia (the other two regions in Belgium where gift tax rates are a regional, not a federal matter). This wealth tax is officially called 'tax for the compensation of gift taxes' (meaning: to compensate the loss that the Belgian state suffers in gift tax revenue as a result of the use of private foundations).

126 Assets below €50,000 are not taxed, between €50,000 and €250,000 the rate is 0.15%, and between €250,000 and €500,000 it is 0.30%.

127 See Article 150, 5° of the Code on Gift Taxes.

purpose. Very often, the holding foundation that exercises control over an operating company will issue certificates (depository receipts) that give their holders a contractual claim against the holding foundation to all the income the foundation receives from the operating company. Probably the availability of the certification technique explains why 'double foundations' are not commonly used in Belgium (in a double foundation model, one foundation, with a philanthropic purpose, receives the cash flows from the operating company, another foundation exercises the voting rights in the underlying company). Tax rules are in favour of private foundations that act as certification vehicles, for instance by exempting foundations that act as certification vehicles from the wealth tax that other private foundations are subject to. Neither public interest nor private foundations are subject to meaningful government checks. There is no foundation authority in Belgium. Tax authorities will often subject foundations that run a business or indirectly distribute profits to corporate income tax (instead of the more favourable non-profit tax regime), but again certification vehicles are exempt from this. Whereas in the past Belgian entrepreneurs usually used Dutch foundations as certification vehicles, since 2019 and especially since 2023, they have developed a preference for Belgian foundations.

ENTERPRISE FOUNDATIONS

A Polish Perspective

Konrad OSAJDA* and Anne-Marie WEBER

* This chapter is a result of research financed by the Polish National Science Centre, project number: 2021/41/B/HS5/00857. The authors would like to thank Krzysztof Grzegorczyk for his assistance in editing the manuscript.

ABSTRACT

This chapter examines the legal framework governing enterprise foundations in Polish law, focusing on their operation under the two distinct statutory frameworks regulating charitable foundations and family foundations. It provides an analysis of how these frameworks enable and shape the activities of enterprise foundations within the Polish legal system. The discussion begins with an overview of the historical development of foundation law in Poland, followed by an outline of the current regulatory environment for enterprise foundations. The chapter then highlights the key similarities and differences between charitable enterprise foundations and (private) family enterprise foundations, particularly in terms of their capacity to conduct business.

1. INTRODUCTION

This chapter explores the concept of enterprise foundations within the framework of Polish law. It examines the legal provisions governing the engagement of foundations in business activities, with particular attention to the regulatory conditions under which they may hold ownership of companies.[1] This introduction provides a succinct overview of the historical evolution of foundation law in Poland, establishes a typology of foundations, and outlines the contemporary legal framework applicable to them. Section 2 focuses on the legal regime applicable to charitable foundations, analysing the prerequisites for their establishment and their capacity to engage in business activities. Section 3 discusses the recently enacted legislation on the so-called family foundation (*fundacja rodzinna*), emphasising its role as a mechanism for implementing the private enterprise foundation model. Finally, section 4 concludes the chapter by synthesising the key findings.

---

1 In reference to the functional definition of an enterprise foundation as provided by the first chapter of this volume ('Foundation Ownership Around the World').

1.1. A SHORT HISTORY OF POLISH FOUNDATION LAW

1.1.1. Before 1918

The history of foundations in Poland[2] dates to the 12th and 13th centuries, when the first foundations were set up – mostly to run hospitals. A new wave of foundations originated in the 16th century, their primary aim being the support of students of the Jagiellonian University in Cracow. Later, new foundations took care of orphans and conducted cultural activities, for instance, running public libraries.[3] When Poland lost its independence in 1795 and its territory was partitioned among Austria, Prussia and Russia, the legal systems of the respective powers were imposed on the Polish lands. Foundations were regulated in the Austrian[4] and Prussian partitions.[5] In the central region, where the French *Code Civil* was introduced during the era of Napoleon I, foundations were not regulated; however, they were not dissolved and continued to function in practice. In the territory governed by Russian law, the establishment of foundations was permitted only in exceptional cases, each requiring formal administrative approval.[6]

Alongside the development of charitable foundations, Polish nobles established so-called *ordynacje*, which can be regarded as the precursors of modern private foundations. They were modelled on the Spanish *mayorazgos*[7] and introduced in Poland in the 16th century. Some of these estates endured

---

2 See more: M. Wawrzyński, *Fundacje w Polsce: Zarys historii i stan w latach dziewięćdziesiąty ch. Bariery i możliwości działania*, Ulica Lipowa, Warsaw 1997.

3 P. Suski, *Stowarzyszenia i fundacje*, Wolters Kluwer, Warsaw 2018, p. 359.

4 Particularly §646 ABGB (*Allgemeines bürgerliches Gesetzbuch*, version from 31 December 2016: https://www.ris.bka.gv.at/NormDokument.wxe?Abfrage=Bundesnormen&Gesetzesnummer=10001622&FassungVom=2016-12-31&Artikel=&Paragraf=646&Anlage=&Uebergangsrecht= (accessed 20 January 2025)).

5 Chiefly §§80–88 BGB (*Bürgerliches Gesetzbuch*, version from 18 August 1896, RGBl. p. 195) and other laws.

6 H. Konic, *Prawo osobowe: Wykład porównawczy na tle prawodawstw obowiązujących w Polsce w zestawieniu z kodeksem szwajcarskim. Część pierwsza*, Księgarnia F. Hoesicka, Warsaw 1924, p. 227.

7 *Mayorazgos* were introduced in Spain by the *Leyes de Toro*, enacted by King Ferdinand II of Aragon in 1505 (the text is available here: https://faculty.georgetown.edu/sallesrv/courses/SPAN-459/span459/pdfs/leyes_toro/leyes_96.pdf). These laws formally sanctioned and standardised the rules of inheritance for entailed estates, reinforcing the power and prestige of major noble families. *Mayorazgos* ensured that estates could only be inherited by the eldest son (under the right of primogeniture), thereby preventing their division among descendants. The institution of *mayorazgo* played a crucial role in Spain's social and economic structure until the 19th century, when it was abolished as part of liberal reforms. For further information, see I.M. Melero Muñoz, 'El mayorazgo' (2022) *Encrucijada de mundos*: https://grupo.us.es/encrucijada/el-mayorazgo.

for remarkable periods, with perhaps the most renowned example being the *Ordynacja Zamojska*, which existed from 1589 to 1944.[8]

1.1.2. 1918–1945 (1947)

Poland regained independence in 1918, and shortly thereafter, a decree on foundations was promulgated[9] – the Decree on Foundations and Confirmation of Donations and Legacies from 8 February 1919.[10] This decree only applied in the central and former Russian-ruled territories of Poland. The former German and Austrian regions continued to be governed by the respective German and Austrian laws on foundations. Subsequently, the Decree of 22 October 1947 extended the 1919 decree to encompass the entire Polish territory. Moreover, before World War II, certain foundations were established directly through statutes enacted by Parliament, such as the foundation *Zakłady Kórnickie.*[11]

1.1.3. After 1945 (1947)

The concept of a foundation was perceived as incompatible with the principles of the socialist state. As a result, the Decree of 24 April 1952[12] dissolved all foundations. The decree functioned similarly to a nationalisation law, as it transferred the assets of the dissolved foundations directly to the state. However, the Decree did not apply to foundations with their seat located abroad, or those possessing at least part of their assets outside the country.

The new act on foundations (hereinafter: Foundation Act or FA) was passed in 1984 and remains in force, albeit with some amendments.[13] It should be stressed that, for the first time, the law directly addressed enterprise foundations, though in a limited capacity, by including provisions governing the engagement of foundations in business activities.[14]

From 1989 onwards, Poland underwent a significant shift in its economic system, transitioning to a market economy. As a result of the introduction of the principle of freedom of economic activities, numerous new businesses were established. After approximately three decades, many of those founders began

---

8 G. Jędrejek, *Regulacje prawne dotyczące ordynacji zamojskiej*, (2012) t. XXII, nr 3, *Roczniki Nauk Prawnych*, 7.

9 See more about the history of the legislative work concerning the decree: A. Strzebińczyk, *Droga do uchwalenia dekretu o fundacjach i o zatwierdzaniu darowizn i zapisów z 1919 roku*, (2023) 5(79) *Forum Prawnicze* 99.

10 Dz.U. Nr 15, poz. 215. The decree is available only in Polish: https://eli.gov.pl/eli/DU/1919/215/ogl (accessed 20 January 2025).

11 Ustawa z 30.7.1925 r. o Zakładach Kórnickich, Dz.U. Nr 86, poz. 592.

12 Dekret o zniesieniu fundacji z 24.04.1952 r., Dz.U. z 1952 r., Nr 25, poz. 172.

13 Ustawa z 06.04.1984 r. o fundacjach, Dz.U. z 2023 r., poz. 166.

14 This issue is dealt with in section 2.

contemplating the transfer of their businesses to the next generation. This prompted an increasing discourse on what became known as the 'succession law of entrepreneurs'.[15] Specifically, a coalition of entrepreneurs and legal experts advocated for the introduction of a concept primarily known in German-speaking countries – the private foundation. As a result, such a type of foundation was regulated in Polish law in 2023 by introducing the so-called 'family foundation' (hereinafter: Family Foundation Act or FFA).[16]

1.2. TYPOLOGY OF FOUNDATIONS IN POLISH LAW

Due to the absence of a unified foundation law, the typology of foundations in Poland is complex. Two criteria can be applied to produce a classification of foundations under Polish law: the regulatory framework governing them – whether public or private law – and their specific purposes.[17]

In terms of the regulatory framework, foundations can be categorised into those governed by general laws on foundations, which belong to the realm of private law,[18] and those regulated by individual statutes pertaining to specific foundations, rendering them subject to public law.[19]

The latter can be referred to as 'public law foundations'[20] or 'statutory foundations'. The relevant statutes define their purposes, organisational structure and the extent to which they may engage in business activities,[21] with each regulation being unique. Such foundations may be funded by public resources (state or local communities),[22] or funded privately.[23]

The majority of foundations, however, are established by individuals – whether natural persons or legal entities – under the general laws governing foundations. These 'private law foundations' are governed by private law, hence

15 See K. Osajda (ed), *Prawo spadkowe przedsiębiorców*, C.H. Beck, Warsaw 2022.

16 Ustawa z 26.1.2023 r. o fundacji rodzinnej, Dz.U. poz. 326.

17 Foundations could be put into different categories according to more detailed criteria that results in more detailed classifications – see for example: G. Gura, *Ustawa o fundacjach: Komentarz*, C.H. Beck, Warsaw 2021, pp. 3–5 (the author distinguishes eight categories of foundations); L. Stecki, *Fundacja. Część druga i trzecia*, TNOiK, Toruń 1996, pp. 156–167 (the author proposes several different criteria that could be used to differentiate foundations).

18 It is briefly described in section 1.3.

19 See as an example, Ustawa z 20.2.1997 r. o fundacji – Centrum Badania Opinii Społecznej, Dz.U. Nr 30, poz. 163.

20 P. Suski, above n. 3, p. 389.

21 See as an example, Article 11 of the statute above in n. 19, which states that CBOS (this is the name of the foundation set up by the statute) may conduct business activities to accomplish its goals according to the provisions of its charter.

22 For example, Wieś Kościuszkowska Foundation – see Ustawa z 23.3.1929 r. o utworzeniu państwowej fundacji pod nazwą 'Wieś Kościuszkowska', Dz.U. 1929, Nr 24, poz. 248.

23 For example, Zakłady Kórnickie Foundation – see Ustawa z 30.7.1925 r. o Zakładach Kórnickich, Dz.U. 1925, Nr 86, poz. 592.

their labelling. They are established upon registration in a designated registry, a process akin to the incorporation of companies. They may be further classified based on their purposes.

With regard to the second criterion, namely the purpose pursued by a foundation, three categories can be distinguished. The first encompasses foundations with highly specific purposes, which are established by individual statutes. This category comprises the aforementioned public law foundations. The second category consists of charitable foundations, which are established to pursue socially beneficial purposes.[24] Finally, the third category consists of family foundations, which may be created to serve entirely private purposes and interests. Nonetheless, Polish law does not preclude such foundations from also pursuing public or charitable purposes.

Traditionally, another criterion used to differentiate foundations is their independent legal status, based on whether or not they possess legal personality. This distinction divides them into independent and non-independent foundations.[25] Under Polish law, however, all foundations are endowed with legal personality, so that only independent foundations are legally recognised.[26]

Although Polish law does not provide a formal definition of a 'foundation',[27] the term is generally understood to denote a legal person whose assets are dedicated to the pursuit of specific purposes. The foundation administers its assets, which it owns in a formal legal sense, but it does not enjoy them as a beneficiary. In this sense, the legal title is distinct from the beneficial title. This structure bears some resemblance to trusts in the common law system; however, as indicated above, unlike trusts, under Polish law, foundations constitute independent legal entities.

1.3. ARCHITECTURE OF THE REGULATORY FRAMEWORK

There is no unified body of law governing foundations in Poland. On the contrary, the legal framework is highly fragmented, and there is no legal definition of a

24 A subtype of this category forms foundations set up by churches because regulations concern the state – church relations apply to them. See more on this subtype of foundations under Polish law: G. Radecki, *Fundacje zakładane przez osoby prawne Kościoła katolickiego w Polsce*, Wydawnictwo Uniwersytetu Śląskiego, Katowice 2009; G. Radecki, *Fundacje zakładane przez kościelne osoby prawne (zagadnienia wybrane)* (2004) 11 *Rejent* 122.

25 P. Suski, above n. 3, p. 391.

26 L. Stecki, above n. 17, pp. 362–366. However, some authors claim that it is possible to set up a non-independent foundation by a donation or a last will. It is also claimed that rules on foundations should be applied to non-independent foundations *per analogiam*. See more about non-independent foundations in Polish law: H. Cioch, 'Fundacje niesamodzielne' in S. Wójcik (ed) *Prace cywilistyczne. Księga pamiątkowa dla uczczenia 40-lecia pracy naukowej profesora Jana J. Winiarza*, Wydawnictwo Prawnicze, Warsaw 1990, pp. 17–24.

27 G. Gura, above n. 17, p. 1. It is not unique from comparative perspective – see more on notions of 'foundation' in different jurisdictions: H. Cioch, above n. 26, pp. 23–28.

'foundation' under Polish law.[28] Instead, the applicable rules must be derived from various sources. These sources of Polish foundation law can be categorised into three main groups. The first comprises statutes establishing individual foundations through specific legislative acts. The second group includes laws governing charitable foundations (FA). The third group pertains to the recently enacted legislation on family foundations (FFA). These sources originate from different historical periods and follow distinct structures. For this reason, and particularly from the perspective of enterprise foundations, they must be analysed separately. Such an analysis is undertaken in sections 2 and 3, with the first group excluded, as it does not allow for the deduction of general principles relevant to the functioning of enterprise foundations in Poland.

It is worth noting that the question of whether the current 'parallel' regulatory technique to foundations should be maintained remains unresolved in Polish law. This fragmented approach is atypical when compared to other areas of regulation; for instance, all companies – whether partnerships or corporations – are regulated within a single legal framework under the Code of Commercial Companies.[29] A unified regulation of foundations would offer significant advantages, allowing general issues to be addressed in a common section while still allowing for specific provisions for particular types of foundations.

1.4. ENTERPRISE FOUNDATIONS

Enterprise foundations represent one of the most recent developments in the evolution of foundation types, with the German Carl-Zeiss-Stiftung often cited as an early example of this type. However, enterprise foundations face significant challenges, particularly in the area of taxation. Compared to corporations, enterprise foundations are typically granted preferential tax treatment by law, which has raised concerns about potential inequities since one of the motivations for their establishment is the avoidance of high inheritance taxes.[30]

There are divergent approaches across jurisdictions concerning the admissibility and regulation of enterprise foundations. In some legal systems, foundations are permitted to engage in business activities, while in others, such activities are strictly prohibited. Furthermore, the regulatory frameworks differ: in very few jurisdictions, enterprise foundations are governed by dedicated statutes, whereas in others, their regulation is fragmented across various legal provisions.

---

28 See more about theoretical approaches to defining 'foundation', including comparative and historical remarks: H. Cioch, *Fundacje w ujęciu prawa polskiego*, AWH, Lublin 2000, pp. 14–25.

29 Kodeks spółek handlowych z 15.9.2000 r., the amended text: Dz.U. 2024, poz. 18.

30 H. Cioch, *Prawo fundacyjne*, Wolters Kluwer, Warsaw 2011, pp. 42–43.

As indicated above, in Poland, the regulatory framework adressing foundations has undergone significant changes over time. The Polish foundation law, passed in 1919, did not permit foundations to engage in any business activities. This restriction was lifted with the enactment of the law of 1984, which introduced a more permissive framework.[31]

Despite these developments, Polish law neither defines nor explicitly recognises enterprise foundations as a distinct legal category. Rather, it regulates the business activities of foundations indirectly, by specifying the scope and methods through which such activities may be undertaken. Owing to the absence of a unified foundation law, however, the regulation of economic activities differs depending on the type of foundation in question: statutory (public law) foundations, charitable foundations and family (private) foundations.

As noted above, the first group of foundations is too specific and unique to be included in this chapter, as the regulations governing the business activities of statutory foundations are intricately linked to the provisions of their respective individual statutes. Consequently, this chapter will focus on the remaining two categories of enterprise foundations – charitable foundations and family foundations – which will be examined in detail in the following sections.

The detailed analysis of charitable enterprise foundations and family (private) enterprise foundations must be preceded by certain general remarks. The Polish Constitution (Article 20)[32] guarantees the freedom of economic activity for all individuals. With some limitations concerning specific types of business activities (e.g., banking services), it is sufficient to register such an activity – no licence or permission is required. However, the law may impose restrictions on the scope of business activities, particularly concerning certain categories of legal entities. Foundations are among those subject to such statutory limitations, which will be examined in greater detail in the subsequent sections of this chapter.

These statutory limitations are exclusive in nature, as Polish law on legal persons does not recognise the doctrine of *ultra vires*. Consequently, it is not legally possible to restrict the scope of economic activity of a legal entity through its charter or bylaws in a manner enforceable against third parties. Such restrictions, if included, would only serve as internal guidelines and could form the basis for holding board members accountable for non-compliance. However, they would not have any legal effect in limiting the foundation's activities vis-à-vis external parties.

2. CHARITABLE FOUNDATIONS

Currently, more than 30,000 charitable foundations are registered in Poland, with over 18,500 of them considered entrepreneurs. This section analyses

[31] Ibid., p. 43.

[32] Konstytucja Rzeczypospolitej Polskiej z 2.4.1997, Dz.U. Nr 78, poz. 483.

the establishment, purpose and governance of charitable foundations, with particular attention to those features that make them suitable for use as enterprise foundations.

2.1. DEFINITION AND PURPOSE

The FA defines a charitable foundation by reference to its purposes. According to Article 1 FA, a foundation may be established to pursue socially or economically beneficial objectives that align with the fundamental interests of the Republic of Poland.

The purpose of a foundation is determined by the founder in the founding act (Article 3, section 2 FA) and constitutes a mandatory element of the foundation's charter (Article 5, section 1 FA). Although the fact that the foundation's objective is defined by the founder and not by the state, Article 1 FA underscores the 'public nature' of charitable foundations.[33] Accordingly, a foundation's objective must: (i) align with the fundamental interests of the Republic of Poland; and (ii) be socially or economically useful (Article 1 FA). Additionally, the objective must be tied to the pursuit of a public interest goal, a requirement not expressly codified in the statute but widely affirmed in legal scholarship and jurisprudence.[34]

Consequently, a foundation established under the FA may not be directed solely towards particular or individual interests that lack a broader dimension of public utility.[35] For this reason, foundations created on the basis of the FA are classified as charitable foundations.

The terms 'interests of the Republic of Poland' and 'socially or economically useful' as employed in Article 1 FA are general clauses, the meaning of which may vary depending on the current geopolitical and social context,[36] and which must be interpreted in light of the Polish Constitution.[37] To guide interpretation, the legislator has provided an illustrative, non-exhaustive catalogue of a charitable foundation's objectives, including the protection of health, the development of the economy and science, education and upbringing, culture and the arts, social welfare and assistance, environmental protection and the care of historical monuments. A charitable foundation may pursue several objectives simultaneously.[38]

---

33 M. Dumkiewicz in A. Kidyba (ed), *Ustawa o fundacjach. Komentarz*, Wolters Kluwer, Warsaw 2023, LEX/el., Art. 1, para. 2.

34 Ibid., para. 2; A. Rzetecka-Gil, *Ustawa o fundachach. Komentarz*, Wolters Kluwer, Warsaw 2018, LEX/el., Art. 1, paras. 3, 6; B. Niemirka, *Statut fundacji*, C.H. Beck, Warsaw 1998, p. 46; P. Bielski, 'Commentary on the Supreme Court Resolution of 1 February 2000, III CZP 36/99' (2000) 11 *Rejent* 121.

35 M. Dumkiewicz, above n. 34, Art. 1, para. 2.

36 G. Gura, above n. 17, p. 3.

37 P. Suski, above n. 3, p. 347.

38 A. Kidyba in A. Kidyba (ed), above n. 34, Art. 5, para. 4.

Socially useful objectives are pursued in the interest of society. The notion of 'society', however, should not be understood merely as the aggregate of its individual members.[39] If society were equated with the totality of its constituents, objectives directed at particular societal group – such as students of a particular university, individuals suffering from a specific illness or the unemployed – would fall outside the scope of 'socially useful objectives'. Such a restrictive interpretation would clearly contradict the purpose of the FA.[40] Accordingly, a socially useful objective need not extend to all members of society but may legitimately be directed toward a defined social group.

Economically useful objectives should primarily be understood in connection with the foundation's business activities, particularly the generation of income from such activities, which is subsequently reinvested to advance the realisation of the foundation's charitable goals.

The objectives of a charitable foundation not only define the scope of its activities but also determine its pool of beneficiaries.[41] This circle may be relatively narrow (e.g. people with a particular disability), provided that its composition is not definitively predetermined or restricted to specifically designated individuals (e.g. individuals A, B, C).[42] The eligibility criteria must therefore be framed in abstract and general terms, ensuring that the group of beneficiaries, even if small, remains open to change over time.[43] Consequently, a foundation may still be regarded as pursuing a socially useful objective even if, in practice, its beneficiary is a single individual, so long as that individual qualifies under such general criteria.[44] The permissible objectives of a foundation, as outlined in Article 1 FA, are generally understood to preclude the establishment of private foundations aimed at serving private interests, in particular private family foundations.[45]

The objective of a charitable foundation can be defined in a finite manner. In such cases, it is possible to determine the exact moment when the goal has been achieved, such as the construction of a support centre for the elderly. Alternatively, the objective may be formulated in an open-ended manner.[46] In this case, the goal does not have a fixed point of completion. An example would be the promotion of a healthy lifestyle among the elderly.

---

39 G. Gura, above n. 17, p. 3.

40 R. Trzaskowski, *Działalność statutowa a działalność gospodarcza fundacji – prawo i praktyka*, Oficyna Naukowa, Instytut Wymiaru Sprawiedliwości, Warsaw 2003, pp. 19–21.

41 P. Suski, above n. 3, p. 415.

42 J. Dominowska, *Prowadzenie działalności gospodarczej przez fundacje. Studium prawne*, Wolters Kluwer, Warsaw 2016, p. 97.

43 M. Dumkiewicz in A. Kidyba (ed), above n. 34, Art. 1, para. 1.

44 A. Rzetecka-Gil, above n. 35, Art. 1, para. 6.

45 H. Cioch, 'Pojęcie i rodzaje fundacji. (Wybrane zagadnienia na tle prawnoporównawczym)', (1987) 2 *Państwo i Prawo* 70; P. Suski, above n. 3, p. 421; A. Rzetecka-Gil, above n. 35, Art. 1, para. 10.

46 J. Dominowska, above n. 43, p. 91.

Pursuant to Article 5, section 1 FA, the foundation's charter may contain provisions that regulate the modification of the foundation's objective or changes to its charter. It is undisputed that the objective and the charter of a foundation can be modified if the latter contains provisions explicitly permitting such changes. However, considerable debate surrounds the question of whether the objective of a foundation can be altered in the absence of any provisions in the charter authorising such modifications.

One strand of legal doctrine and case law maintains that if the foundation's charter does not include provisions permitting changes to its objective or charter, such changes are prohibited. On this view, the objective and charter are to be regarded as immutable.[47]

More liberal interpretations have also been advanced, suggesting that modifying the foundation's objective may be permissible even in the absence of explicit provisions in its charter[48] or even contrary to an explicit prohibition.[49] The adoption of this view would, however, have the troubling effect of disregarding the founder's intent as expressed in the founding act and charter.[50]

Consequently, it should rather be assumed that the founder may choose to preserve the foundation's objective rigidly, either by refraining from including provisions for its modification or by explicitly precluding changes, or, conversely, may decide to allow flexibility by permitting potential adjustments.[51] The latter scenario may manifest as a detailed charter provision outlining the prerequisites, procedures and scope of permissible changes to the foundation's objective. Alternatively, the charter may contain a general clause allowing for the alteration of the foundation's objective without further specification, thereby omitting details on the procedure and conditions for such changes and potentially rendering its application more demanding.

Another issue arises when the foundation's charter includes provisions permitting amendments to the charter in general, yet fails to specifically address changes to the foundation's objective. While the objective of the foundation is an obligatory element of the charter under Article 5, section 1 FA, this alone does not suffice to justify the assumption that a general provision permitting amendments to the charter also

47 A. Goldiszewicz, 'Znaczenie celu fundacji i dopuszczalność jego zmiany' in P. Litwiniuk, A. Milewska and M. Wasilewski (eds), *Prawne i ekonomiczne uwarunkowania funkcjonowania fundacji*, Wydawnictwo SGGW, Warsaw 2019, p. 70; see also resolution of the Supreme Court dated 7 July 1993, III CZP 88/93, OSNC 1994/1, poz. 14 which holds that altering the purpose of a foundation, as determined by the founder and set out in the statute, may only occur if expressly permitted by the statute and in compliance with the specified conditions therein.

48 H. Cioch, 'O potrzebie dokonania zmian w polskim prawie fundacyjnym' in A. Kubicka (ed), *Księga pamiątkowa dla uczczenia pracy naukowej Profesora Kazimierza Kruczalaka*, Wydawnictwo Uniwersytetu Gdańskiego, Gdańsk 1999, p. 70 [(1999) 5 *Gdańskie Studia Prawnicze* 70].

49 L. Stecki, *Fundacja. Część pierwsza*, TNOiK, Toruń 1996, pp. 213–214.

50 A. Goldiszewicz, above n. 48, p. 70.

51 M. Dumkiewicz, above n. 34, Art. 1, para. 3.

permits unrestricted changes to the foundation's objective.[52] Unlike other mandatory elements of the foundation's charter, the provision defining the foundation's objective merely reiterates and potentially clarifies the founder's intent expressed in the founding act. It should be assumed that in the absence of a specific clause that either permits or forbids the change of a foundation's objective, a general change-of-charter clause only allows for amendments that do not create inconsistencies with the founder's original intent.[53]

In most cases, amendments to the foundation's objective and charter are executed by the board. However, if the charter establishes a governance structure involving additional bodies, changes proposed by the board may, for instance, require their approval or consultation. Additionally, the authority to amend the foundation's objective or the charter may be conferred entirely on a particular body or individual. For example, the founder may reserve for themselves the authority to modify the foundation's objective or charter, thereby retaining an instrument of influence over the foundation after its establishment.[54]

Any amendment to the charter must be reported to the National Court Register by the board. The jurisdiction of the registry court includes assessing the admissibility of the amendment and verifying the documents forming the basis of the application. Amendments to the foundation's objective and modifications to its charter remain subject to ordinary internal and external oversight mechanisms.[55] An *ex ante* approval of such changes by the public oversight authorities is not required.

2.2. ESTABLISHMENT

Under the regime of the FA, foundations are legal entities without members. They may be established either by individuals (natural persons), irrespective of nationality or place of residence, or by legal entities with their registered offices in Poland or abroad (Article 2, section 1 FA). The registered office of a charitable foundation, however, must be located within the territory of Poland (Article 2, section 1 FA) and must be specified in its charter (Article 5, section 1 FA). Where a foundation intends to operate within a single voivodeship,[56] its registered office must be located in that voivodeship (Article 5, section 3 FA).

---

52 Ibid., Art. 1, para. 3.

53 B. Niemirka, above n. 35, p. 93; M. Dumkiewicz, above n. 34, Art. 1, para. 3.

54 A. Kidyba, above n. 34, Art. 5, para. 14.

55 See in detail below section 2.3.3.

56 A voivodeship (*województwo*) is the highest-level administrative division in Poland, equivalent to a province. Poland is divided into 16 voivodeships, each with its own government and administrative structures, including a voivode (governor) appointed by the central government and a regional assembly (*sejmik wojewódzki*). Voivodeships function as key units of territorial self-governance and state administration.

A charitable foundation is established through a unilateral juridicial act of the founder,[57] which must be made in the form of a notarial deed, referred to as the founding act (in Polish: *akt fundacyjny*) (Article 3, section 1 FA). An exception applies where the foundation is created in the founder's last will *mortis causa*, in which case notarisation is not required.

In the founding act, the founder must specify the foundation's objective and the assets allocated for its achievement (Article 2, section 2 FA). These assets may consist of money and securities, as well as movable and immovable property transferred to the foundation (Article 2, section 3 FA). Despite the narrow wording of the provision, it is generally accepted that any property or right of determinable value that is owned by the founder and is transferable, or capable of being established, may be designated for the realisation of the foundation's objective.[58]

The FA regime does not prescribe a minimum value of the foundation's initial (founding) assets. Some commentators argue that the assets designated in the founding act must be sufficient to achieve the objective for which the foundation is established.[59] This view, however, overlooks the fact that the foundation's objective may also be realised through the growth of its initial assets, either through donations or by conducting business activities.[60] A similar view was expressed by the Supreme Court in its judgment of 12 February 2002.[61] In this ruling, the court reaffirmed that the legislator did not specify a minimum threshold for the foundation's initial assets and that these assets hese assets may increase or decrease over time.

There are no legal obstacles to the establishment of a foundation by more than one founder, whether this involves several natural persons, several legal persons or any combination of natural and legal persons acting jointly.[62] The establishment of a foundation by other foundations is also to be regarded as permissible, provided that it is consistent with the founding act and charter of the establishing foundation.[63] A categorical rejection of such a possibility finds no support in the applicable legal provisions and would unduly restrict the foundation's legal capacity. Where, in a given case, the creation of a foundation by another foundation were to conflict with its objective or charter, the appropriate supervisory mechanisms would apply.[64] However, the legal act of establishing a foundation by another foundation would not be subject to the sanction of absolute nullity.[65]

57 P. Suski, above n. 3, p. 408.
58 M. Dumkiewicz, above n. 34, Art. 3, para. 4.
59 H. Cioch in A. Kidyba and H. Cioch (eds), *Ustawa o fundacjach. Komentarz*, 2nd ed., Wolters Kluwer, Warsaw 2010, p. 37; A. Rzetecka-Gil, above n. 35, Art. 3, nb. 5.
60 M. Dumkiewicz, above n. 34, Art. 3, para. 4.
61 Supreme Court judgement of 12.02.2002 r. (I CKN 1388/99), LEX nr 53162.
62 P. Suski, above n. 3, p. 329.
63 M. Dumkiewicz, above n. 34, Art. 2, para. 2.
64 See in detail section 2.3.3.
65 M. Dumkiewicz, above n. 34, Art. 2, para. 2.

The founding act is made subject to a suspensive condition, namely the successful registration of the foundation with the National Court Register (in Polish: *Krajowy Rejestr Sądowy*) which maintains the 'register of associations, other social and professional organisations, foundations, and independent public healthcare institutions' (in Polish: '*rejestr stowarzyszeń, innych organizacji społecznych i zawodowych, fundacji oraz samodzielnych publicznych zakładów opieki zdrowotnej*') (Article 7, section 1 FA; Article 1, section 2, para. 2 of the Act on the National Court Register/NCRA).[66] Upon registration, the foundation acquires legal personality (Article 7, section 2 FA). The court registers the foundation after confirming that the legal actions underlying the registration have been undertaken by an authorised person or body and are valid. The court also verifies that the foundation's objective and charter comply with legal regulations (Article 9, section 1 FA).

The founder establishes the foundation's charter, which defines its name, registered office, assets, objectives, principles, forms and scope of activities as well as the composition and organisation of the board, the method of its appointment and the duties and rights of the board and its members (Article 5, section 1 FA). The charter may also include other provisions, particularly those concerning the foundation's business activities, the conditions under which it may merge with another foundation, changes to its objective or charter, and the possibility of establishing other governing bodies alongside the board (Article 5, section 1 FA). Importantly, the foundation's charter must align with the founding act.[67] The founder may forgo the personal establishment of the charter and authorise another natural or legal person to determine its content (Article 6, section 1 FA).[68]

The court notifies the two public supervision authorities – the minister responsible for the scope of the foundation's activities and objectives, as well as the district governor (in Polish: *starosta*) responsible for the location of the foundation's registered office – about the foundation's registration and sends the foundation's charter (Article 9, section 2 FA). If the foundation's objectives fall within the scope of two or more ministers' responsibilities, the court notifies the relevant minister, whose area of activity is most closely related to the foundation's primary objectives (Article 9, section 3 FA). The founder may designate the minister responsible for the foundation's objectives (Article 5, section 2 FA). Their declaration in this regard must be attached to the charter and submitted to the court handling the foundation's registration (Article 5, section 2 FA). If the foundation's objectives are broad and fall within the jurisdiction of several ministers, there is no impediment to designating multiple ministers. The court will then assess which minister is responsible for the

---

66 Act on the National Court Register (hereinafter: NCRA) – ustawa z dnia 20.08.1997 (Dz.U. Nr 121, poz. 769); H. Cioch, above n. 31, pp. 51–54; P. Suski, above n. 3, p. 401.

67 A. Kidyba in A. Kidyba (ed), above n. 34, Art. 5, para. 1.

68 If the founder established the foundation in a will but did not set its charter or authorise another person to do so, the provisions of Book IV of the Civil Code (Ustawa z dnia 23 kwietnia 1964 r. – Kodeks cywilny, Dz.U. 1964 nr 16 poz. 93, amended) regarding instructions (*polecenie*) apply accordingly (Article 6, section 3 FA).

largest number of the foundation's objectives. If the founder were to designate a minister who is not competent based on the foundation's objectives, the court is not bound by the founder's designation.

Upon registration, a foundation acquires legal personality, thereby attaining independence and autonomy. This results in a separation between the founder and the foundation. From that moment, the founder no longer derives the right to independently make decisions regarding the foundation or to directly influence its operations by virtue of their status.[69] While the severance of ties between the founder and the foundation does not have to be absolute, from the moment of registration, any powers the founder may hold over the foundation derive not from their status as founder, but rather from statutory provisions granting them specific rights or from their membership in the foundation's governing bodies.[70] Once a foundation is entered into the register, it is no longer possible to acquire the status of a founder. Individuals making contributions to a registered foundation are instead referred to as donors.[71]

2.3. GOVERNANCE

2.3.1. Regulatory Sources

Charitable foundations operate based accordance with the provisions of the FA and their charters (Article 4 FA). Since the FA is a relatively general legal framework,[72] the proper drafting of the foundation's charter is of paramount importance.[73] In practice, the charter will largely determine the foundation's ability to function effectively to pursue its objective.

As indicated above, the foundation's charter, established by the founder prior to the foundation's registration, contains crucial information on the foundation's governance. As a minimum requirement in that regard, the charter should indicate the composition and organisation of the management board, the method of its appointment and the duties and rights of both the management board *in corpore* and its members (Article 5, section 1 FA). The charter may also enrich the governing structure of the charitable foundation by establishing other bodies alongside the mandatory management board (Article 5, section 1 FA).

Besides the charter, the necessity of additional internal regulations (by-laws) may arise from the specificities of a given foundation. In particular, these

69 L. Stecki, above n. 50, p. 371.

70 A. Kidyba, 'Kilka uwag na temat statusu fundatora po wpisie fundacji do rejestru' in P. Litwiniuk, A. Milewska and M. Wasilewski (eds), above n. 48, p. 108.

71 M. Dumkiewicz, above n. 34, Art. 2, para. 1.

72 C. Wiśniewski, 'Tworzenie i funkcjonowanie organizacji pozarządowych – wybrane problemy cywilnoprawne' (1999) 4 *Glosa* 1.

73 A. Kidyba in A. Kidyba (ed), above n. 34, Art. 4, para. 3.

regulations may be employed to establish the rules of operation for governing bodies, such as the management board or other bodies foreseen by the charter. It should be assumed that the foundation's governing bodies may issue such regulations, though it is also possible that the founder or another authorised person establishes them.[74] The latter, however, is deemed admissible only prior to the foundation's registration.[75] Similar to the charter, the internal regulations should provide for procedures for their amendment.

2.3.2. Management

A charitable foundation operates through its bodies in a manner prescribed by law and its charter (Article 38 of the Civil Code).[76] The management board (in Polish: *zarząd*) is the only obligatory body of the foundation.[77] It is tasked with administering and overseeing the foundation's operations and represents the foundation in external matters (Art 10 FA). The establishment of the management board is a prerequisite of the foundation's registration.[78]

Only natural persons can be members of the management board.[79] The charter must specify the number of members on the board (Article 5, section 1 FA). This can take the form of a definite number or a range (e.g. three to five). A single-member board should be deemed permissible. The charter must also delineate the management board's internal structure. This entails defining the organisational layout, the division of tasks and the designation of specific functions, such as the president, vice-president, etc. It also involves determining the rules for convening the management board. Additionally, it is crucial to establish the appropriate majority required for adopting resolutions, as well as the quorum and other related procedural aspects.[80]

The method of appointing of the management board's members must be detailed in the charter (Article 5, section 1 FA). An act of appointment encompasses any form of action that establishes an organisational relationship between the foundation and the management board member, resulting in the authorisation of an individual to perform the relevant duties. This can include appointments by other bodies of the foundation, designations by third parties, or drawing lots. The granting of appointment powers to the founder is permissible.[81]

---

74 Ibid., para. 3.

75 Ibid., para. 4.

76 If a foundation is unable to be represented or to conduct its affairs due to the absence of a duly appointed body the court is obligated to appoint a legal guardian.

77 P. Suski, above n. 3, p. 373.

78 A. Kidyba in A. Kidyba (ed), above n. 34, Art. 10, para. 2.

79 B. Niemirka, above n. 35, p. 157; A. Rzetecka-Gil, above n. 35, Art. 5, para. 7.

80 A. Kidyba in A. Kidyba (ed), above n. 34, Art. 5, para. 6.

81 See resolution of the Supreme Court of 1 February 2000 (III CZP 36/99), OSNC 2000/7–8, poz. 124.

Exercising their right, a founder may also appoint themselves to the management board.[82] It is conceivable to implement a concept of absolute competence of the founder if the founder appoints themselves as the sole member of the board and the board is constituted as a single-person structure. An appointment can also follow a mixed approach, where each member of the board, or some of them, is appointed *via* a different procedure.

It is important to note that if the founder or any specifically named person is to be the appointing authority, the procedure for appointing the management board in the event of their death (or the liquidation of the legal entity) must be specified in the charter. Personally conferred rights related to the appointment of the foundation's management board do not transfer to the legal successor of the individual or legal entity who was granted such rights.[83] The term of office for members of the management board may be determined in a calendrical manner or by other means. In addition to the rules governing appointments, a foundation's charter typically outlines personal requirements for management board members, including criteria for independence.

The charter must stipulate the rights and duties of the management board and its members (Article 5, section 1 FA). A precise delineation of these competences is particularly important where the foundation's governance structure includes additional bodies. In that scenario, it seems meaningful to define the rights and duties of the management board in relation to other bodies and their respective competences. The description of the rights and duties of individual members of the management board may be linked to the division of tasks within the board's structure. However, these rights and duties are always to be interpreted in light of the collective rights and duties of the entire board.

The foundation's charter may grant equal status for all management board members. It is also possible for the president of the board to be granted preferential rights, such as voting privileges, the authority to convene meetings or the role of chairing proceedings. Such privileges may also extend to the chairing of meetings, which could, for instance, apply to the vice president if the president of the foundation's management board is absent. The charter also frequently regulates the remuneration of board members.

2.3.3. Supervision

The public interest, which underpins the objectives of a charitable foundation within the framework of the FA, is precisely why oversight mechanisms are essential for these foundations.[84] The supervisory system is designed to ensure

---

82 A. Kidyba in A. Kidyba (ed), above n. 34, Art. 5, para. 7; A. Rzetecka-Gil, above n. 35, Art. 5, para. 8. This view has also been rejected in the literature: P. Suski, above n. 3, p. 440.

83 A. Rzetecka-Gil, above n. 35, Art. 2, para. 4.

84 J. Dominowska, 'Skuteczność i efektywność nadzoru nad fundacjami w Polsce' in P. Litwiniuk, A. Milewska, M. Wasilewski (eds), above n. 48, p. 32.

that foundations operate within the confines of the law, uphold public order, and faithfully pursue the objectives outlined by the founder, all while managing the entrusted assets in a responsible manner. The instruments of external and internal supervision, therefore, serve not only the interests of the charitable foundations themselves but also the public interest and the interests of the founder.

In the FA, supervision over foundations is geared towards external 'public' oversight. The system is, however, neither centralised nor uniform. Oversight is carried out through a dual scheme, involving both the courts and public authorities and is thereby substantially governed by the respective public law framework.[85] The supervisory bodies are the court (Article 12 FA) and the competent minister or district governor (Articles 13 and 14 FA).

According to the first supervisory mechanism, at the request of the competent minister or district governor, the court may assess whether the foundation's activities comply with the law, its charter, and the objective for which it was established (Article 12, section 1 FA). It is generally accepted that in the event of an inconsistency, the competent authority is under a duty to submit such a request to the court.[86] A significant flaw in this mechanism is that its application can only result in a judicial declaration that the foundation's actions are inconsistent with the law, its charter, or its objective, without any accompanying sanction.[87] The court is not empowered, within the framework of this procedure, to impose obligations on the foundation, to suspend its management board, or to order its dissolution and liquidation.[88]

To provide the competent minister with relevant information enabling an assessment of the proper achievement of its objectives, the foundation is required to submit an annual report on its activities, setting out the key aspects of its operations during the reporting period (Article 12, section 2 FA). The report must be prepared in electronic form, using a template provided in the Public Information Bulletin on the official website of the office servicing the Minister of Justice (Article 12, section 2b FA) and it must also be made publicly available by the foundation (Article 12, section 3 FA).

Another supervisory mechanism available to the competent minister and district governor enables them to apply to the court for the annulment of a resolution of the foundation's management board that is in serious contradiction with the foundation's objective, the provisions of its charter, or the law (Article 13 FA). Each of the grounds listed constitutes an independent basis for annulment:

---

85 M. Swora, 'Nadzór nad stowarzyszeniami, fundacjami oraz prowadzeniem działalności pożytku publicznego' (2003) 12 *Państwo i Prawo* 68; S. Kidyba, *Wybrane zagadnienia związane z nadzorem nad fundacjami – uwagi de lege lata i de lege ferenda* (2007) 9 *Przegląd Prawa Handlowego* 32.

86 H. Cioch, above n. 60, p. 269.

87 J. Dominowska, above n. 86, p. 38.

88 M. Dumkiewicz, above n. 34, Art. 12, para. 2.

the occurrence of any one of them is sufficient to justify the application.[89] The competent authorities may also request the court to suspend the execution of the resolution until the case is decided (Article 13 FA). This supervisory measure applies exclusively to resolutions adopted by the management board of the foundation. It does not extend to the annulment of resolutions made by other bodies that may be established within the foundation pursuant to its charter.

Furthermore, the FA establishes a framework for the compulsory management of charitable foundations. Where the actions of the management board materially violate legal provisions, the foundation's charter, or its stated objectives, the competent minister or district governor may impose a deadline for rectifying the deficiencies (Article 14, section 1 FA). Alternatively, they may require the replacement of the foundation's management board within a specified timeframe (Article 14, section 1 FA). If the deadline for rectification expires without result, or if the foundation's management board persists in acting in a manner inconsistent with the law, the charter or the foundation's objectives, the competent minister or district governor may petition the court to suspend the management board and appoint a compulsory administrator (Article 14, section 2 FA). The compulsory administrator assumes representation of the foundation in all management matters, including legal proceedings, and is tasked with taking the necessary measures to restore the foundation's proper functioning (Article 14, section 3 FA). The court may revoke its decision to suspend the foundation's management board and appoint a compulsory administrator upon the request of the foundation's management board, provided that the circumstances demonstrate that the actions in violation of the foundation's objectives, its charter or the law will be discontinued (Article 14, section 4 FA).

Beyond external oversight, the FA also permits internal supervisory mechanisms. Specifically, supervision powers may be vested in a supervisory board. The procedures for the establishment and operation of such an additional body must be outlined in the foundation's charter (Article 5, section 1 FA). The supervisory board's competences typically include evaluating the performance of the management board, which encompasses granting discharge, appointing and dismissing its members, and establishing remuneration policies. Additionally, the supervisory board is often responsible for representing the foundation in matters concerning its relations with individual members of the management board. However, the supervisory board's competences must not encroach upon the management board's autonomy in the administration of the foundation's affairs. At most, the supervisory board may have a role in influencing these processes.[90]

89 M. Dumkiewicz, above n. 34, Art. 13, para. 1.
90 A. Kidyba in A. Kidyba (ed), above n. 34, Art. 5, para. 2.

2.3.4. *Advisory Powers*

The charitable foundation's charter may establish various mechanisms aimed at providing advice and guidance to the management board. In particular, advisory powers may be conferred upon a separate advisory body of the foundation. The rules governing the establishment and functioning of such a body should be defined in the foundation's charter (Article 5, section 1 FA). In most cases, such a body takes the form of an advisory council (in Polish: *rada fundacji*). The charter may also establish a founders' council (in Polish: *rada fundatorów*).

In cases where such additional bodies are established within a charitable foundation, the principle of presumption of competence in favour of the management board applies. This principle must be respected in delineating the respective competences of the management board and the advisory or founders' council.

2.4. BUSINESS ACTIVITY

2.4.1. *Statutory Scope of Business Activity*

Under the legal framework of the FA, a charitable foundation may engage in business activity to further its objectives. However, a fundamental question regarding the business activities of a charitable foundation is whether it can be established solely to pursue economic objectives. Specifically, can it centre its operations around conducting business activities? A purely linguistic interpretation of Article 1 of the FA would suggest that this is possible.

Some have argued that such an interpretation cannot be accepted due to the wording of Article 5, section 5 FA, which states that 'a foundation may conduct business activity to the extent necessary for achieving its objectives'.[91] This was understood to imply that the foundation's primary objectives must be socially useful, and business activities may be undertaken to fulfil these goals, meaning the foundation can *also* pursue economically useful objectives.[92] Other authors, however, strictly differentiate between the pursuit of economic objectives and the conduct of business activity. Consequently, they claim that foundations *may* pursue solely economic objectives and that the limitations that follow from Article 5, section 5 FA only impact the scope of their business activity.[93]

91 H. Cioch, *Prawo fundacyjne*, Zakamycze, Kraków 2005, p. 59.

92 K. Kruczalak, 'Niektóre zagadnienia polskiego prawa fundacyjnego' in M. Bączyk (ed), *Księga pamiątkowa ku czci profesora Leopolda Steckiego*, Dom Organizatora, Toruń 1997, pp. 154–155; L. Drożdżewicz, *Powstanie fundacji* (2004) 2 *Nowy Przegląd Notarialny* 24, 31; G. Gura, above n. 17, p. 3.

93 M. Dumkiewicz, above n. 34, Art. 1, para. 2; A. Kidyba, *Prowadzenie działalności gospodarczej przez fundacje* (1999) 10 *Przegląd Prawa Handlowego* 1, 2; A. Rzetecka-Gil, above n. 35, Art. 1, paras. 7, 8.

As indicated above, irrespective of these varying interpretations it is generally agreed that a foundation's objective – even if solely economic – may not only serve the interests of the founder or individuals connected to them but must bear a public nature.[94] Therefore, it should be assumed that Article 5, section 5 FA precludes business activity from being considered the foundation's sole or primary objective. The provision stipulates that any business activity cannot be pursued solely for its own sake.[95] Engaging in profitable business activity is thereby essentially a means of obtaining funds for the pursuit of the foundation's objectives, thus serving a supportive role.

As previously noted, one of the requirements for a foundation to engage in business activity is that such activity must be conducted within a scope that directly supports the achievement of its objectives (Article 5, section 5 FA). Notably, however, the scale of a foundation's business activity is not explicitly restricted by law. In principle, the broader the foundation's objectives, the greater the permissible scale of its business activity. However, determining with certainty whether these inherently ambiguous boundaries are respected poses a significant challenge at the outset, particularly during the drafting of the foundation's operational framework.

2.4.2. Formal Requirements for Conducting Business Activity

If a charitable foundation pursues business activities, the value of the foundation's assets allocated for this purpose must not be less than PLN 1000 (Article 5, section 5 FA). Without a doubt, this minimum does not offer substantial guarantees for either the foundation's creditors or the foundation itself. The risk that funds allocated for achieving the foundation's objectives may be diverted to subsidise its business activity is, of course, inherent.

Another formal requirement stipulates that a foundation that conducts business activity must be registered with the entrepreneurs' register (in Polish: *rejestr przedsiębiorców*) (Article 36, para. 13 NCRA). While this register is also maintained by the National Court Register, it is distinct from the aforementioned register of associations, other social and professional organisations, foundations and independent public healthcare institutions. Currently, almost 18,500 charitable foundations are registered in the entrepreneurs' register.[96]

In order for a foundation to conduct business activities, its charter must explicitly specify the type of activity to be undertaken (Article 11, section 1 FA). A critical element in clarifying this issue is defining the concept of business activity itself. According to the applicable legal definition, business activity is understood as organised income-generating activity carried out in its own name and on a

---

94 M. Dumkiewicz, above n. 34, Art. 1, para. 2; A. Rzetecka-Gil, above n. 35, Art. 1, paras. 3, 6; B. Niemirka, above n. 35, p. 46; P. Bielski, above n. 35, 121.

95 R. Trzaskowski, above n. 41, p. 157.

96 Data obtained through the public search engine of the National Court Register: https://wyszukiwarka-krs.ms.gov.pl/ (accessed 20 January 2025).

continuous basis.[97] Charitable foundations that conduct business activity are commonly classified as 'not-for-profit organisations'. They differ from 'non-profit organisations' in that business activities can be conducted with the aim of generating profits. The essential distinction, however, lies in the allocation of profits: rather than being distributed among members or participants, profits must be devoted to the foundation's statutory objectives and used exclusively to further those goals.[98]

The FA does not specify the organisational and legal forms for conducting business activities by charitable foundations. A previously applicable regulation of the Council of Ministers from 2 December 1985 outlined the forms in which foundations could engage in business. It stated that business activity may be conducted by a separate organisational unit (facility) established by the foundation's board, or by the foundation itself; the foundation may also engage in business activity through participation in a company.[99]

Even in the absence of a comparable regulatory basis that would currently be applicable, it should be assumed that a charitable foundation's business activity can be carried out either through a separate unit or without organisational separation directly by the foundation. In the first case, this is most commonly done in the form of a financially and organisationally distinct enterprise, either a 'facility' (in Polish: *zakład*) or an entity separate in the legal sense, which is owned by the foundation. Specifically, it is generally accepted that foundations may hold ownership rights in partnerships or companies.[100] External approval is not required for allocating the foundation's capital in such ownership rights.[101] Since, under the FA regime, a charitable foundation can own a company, this mode of operation aligns with the fundamental premise of the definition of an enterprise foundation.

There are some controversies, however, as to whether the foundation's ownership of a company can be qualified as the conduct of business activity. It is being raised that not every form of participation in a company confers upon the foundation the status of an entrepreneur. According to one view, this status arises only where the foundation, directly or indirectly, exercises or is capable of exercising a dominant influence over the company's operations.[102] Other authors, by contrast, question whether the mere ownership of shares in a company can be considered a business activity at all.[103]

This debate becomes relevant primarily in the context where such classification influences the foundation's legal rights and obligations, including the requirement

---

97 Act of 6 March 2018 – the Entrepreneurs' Act (Ustawa z dnia 6 marca 2018 r. – Prawo przedsiębiorców, Dz.U. z 2018 r. poz. 646, as amended), hereinafter: EA.

98 M. Szydło, *Pojęcie przedsiębiorcy w prawie polskim* (2002) 7–8 *Przegląd Sądowy* 72, 92–93.

99 See Rozporządzenie Rady Ministrów z 02.12.1985 r. w sprawie prowadzenia przez fundacje działalności gospodarczej, amended text: Dz.U. 1985, Nr 57, poz.293.

100 J. Dominowska, above n. 43, pp. 281–331.

101 H. Cioch, above n. 93, p. 45.

102 Ibid., p. 45.

103 A. Kidyba in A. Kidyba (ed), above n. 34, Art. 5, para. 25; B. Niemirka, above n. 35, p. 218.

to specify all types of business activity in its charter (Article 11, section 1 FA), the duty to apply for entry into the entrepreneurs' register within the National Court Register (Article 36, para. 13 NCRA), the allocation of a minimum founding capital (PLN 1000) (Article 5, section 5 FA), the authorisation to grant a commercial power of attorney (in Polish: *prokura*) (Article 109^1 Civil Code) and adherence to the proportionality principle, which ensures that the scope of economic activities aligns with the foundation's objective (Article 5, section 5 FA). Regardless, however, of whether company ownership qualifies as business activity, the establishment and operation of an enterprise foundation remains a permissible and viable modality within the framework of the FA regime.

The operation of charitable enterprise foundations under the FA may also involve participation in larger group structures. Within such frameworks, a foundation may occupy various roles, in particular as the controlling entity or as a controlled entity.[104] Some argue that the groups' activities should align closely with the nature of the endeavours pursued by the charitable foundation to ensure that the foundation's involvement in the holding serves as a means to bolster its objective rather than divert its focus.[105] In any case, a foundation's integration into a holding structure should enhance its ability to achieve the objectives outlined in its charter.[106]

2.5. TAXES

Since foundations established under the FA operate in the public interest and thereby assume functions that would otherwise fall within the responsibilities of public authorities, it is considered consistent with the public interest to support their activities through appropriate tax privileges.[107] Such privileges encompass both exemptions from tax liabilities for the foundation itself and tax incentives for individuals and entities supporting its activities. Such measures not only strengthen the foundation's capacity to fulfil its statutory objectives but also foster broader societal participation in philanthropic initiatives.

Regarding the privileges granted to the foundation itself, any acquisition by a foundation – whether through inheritance, bequest, or donation – of money, other movable property, or property rights is exempt from inheritance and donation tax (Article 16 FA). Foundations may also benefit from tax exemptions provided by other laws. However, unlike the exemption outlined in Article 16 FA, these exemptions are not automatically granted to foundations solely based on their legal-organisational status. Instead, they depend on the presence of other

104 L. Stecki, above n. 17, pp. 302 et seq.

105 Ibid.

106 L. Stecki, above n. 17, p. 302; A. Kidyba in A. Kidyba (ed), above n. 34, Art. 5, para. 25.

107 A. Kidyba in A. Kidyba (ed), above n. 34, Art. 5, para. 26.

characteristics, particularly those related to the foundation's specific objectives.[108] An example of this is the exemption from the civil transaction tax, provided that the organisation conducts civil law transactions solely in connection with its unpaid public benefit activities, as defined by the provisions on public benefit activity and volunteering (Article 8, point 2a of the Civil Transactions Tax Act).[109]

2.6. EXAMPLES OF CHARITABLE FOUNDATIONS

Among the largest and most well-known Polish charitable foundations that are entered into the entrepreneurs' register are *Fundacja Dzieciom 'Zdążyć z Pomocą'*,[110] which provides financial and rehabilitative support to children with disabilities, and *Fundacja Siepomaga*,[111] a crowdfunding platform dedicated to raising funds for medical treatments. While these foundations engage in some business activities, their primary focus remains on accumulating charitable donations.

A more typical example of a charitable enterprise foundation that pursues its statutory objectives primarily through business activities *Fundacja Leżę i Pracuję*,[112] which operates a marketing agency that employs individuals with quadriplegia, integrating them into the workforce. Another example is *Fundacja na Zielonym*[113], which promotes ecological education and sustainable agriculture through a business focused on local farming, particularly running a market for organic produce. The *Fundacja Poland Business Run*[114] organises a corporate relay race, with revenue from registration fees, sponsorships, and virtual participation used to fund prostheses, wheelchairs, and rehabilitation for individuals with disabilities.

3. PRIVATE ENTERPRISE FOUNDATIONS

For many years, Polish law did not recognise private foundations.[115] This changed recently with the enactment of the law on family foundations, a relatively comprehensive regulation consisting of 145 articles.[116] Family foundations have

---

108 J. Dominowska, above n. 43, pp. 124 et seq.

109 Civil Transactions Tax Act – Ustawa z dnia 09.09.2000 r. o podatku od czynności cywilnoprawnych (Dz.U. Nr 86, poz. 959).

110 The official website of the foundation: https://dzieciom.pl/.

111 The official website of the foundation: https://www.siepomaga.pl/.

112 The official website of the foundation: https://lezeipracuje.pl/.

113 The official website of the foundation: https://nazielonym.pl/fundacja-na-zielonym/.

114 The official website of the foundation: https://polandbusinessrun.pl/en.

115 As a result, wealthy Polish businessmen tended to establish private foundations abroad, chiefly in Liechtenstein.

116 Although this is a new regulation, the literature is growing rapidly. It is mostly in Polish; however the following papers are available in English: A. Moszyńska, 'New regulation of family foundations in Poland and their usefulness in intergenerational estate planning' (2024)

become much more popular in practice than initially anticipated. Within 18 months of the statute's enactment, nearly 4,000 applications for registration were filed at the court registry, resulting in the registration of almost 2,000 foundations.

Family foundations were introduced in Poland with the explicit aim of facilitating the succession of family businesses.[117] This purpose is crucial in determining the intended 'proper' use of this legal instrument. While the legislator sought to incentivise the establishment of family foundations by granting significant tax privileges, the use of such a foundation solely for tax avoidance purposes may constitute an abuse of the legal framework. This could result in serious consequences, including the obligation to repay all due taxes along with substantial interest penalties for delayed payment.

3.1. DEFINITION AND PURPOSE

The FFA defines a family foundation in its Article 2 as a legal person established to gather assets, manage them in the interest of the beneficiaries and serve the beneficiaries. The founder specifies the detailed purpose of the family foundation in its charter.

Although the foundations established under the FFA are referred to as 'family foundations',[118] typologically, they are private foundations because they may be established to provide services to anyone, not just family members of the founder.[119] Moreover, the aim of a family foundation may be mixed[120] as it may also be tasked with serving charitable objectives.

3.2. ESTABLISHMENT

A family foundation is established by a founder. The FFA allows the establishment of such foundations by more than one person, except where it is created by way of a last will (Article 12 FFA). The founders do not have to be members of the same

30(3) *Trusts & Trustees* 118; A. Sikorska-Lewandowska, 'Foundations in Poland and the Possibility of Running a Business by Them' (2024) 21(3) *European Company Law Journal* 64; T. Krzywański and K. Gajdziński, 'Polish family foundation – a grand finale of a long saga' (2023) 29(6) *Trusts & Trustees* 594.

117 See official justification of the new law available here: https://orka.sejm.gov.pl/Druki9ka.nsf/0/17118C9A9F6DE247C125890500329D3E/%24File/2798.pdf (pp. 5–6).

118 See more about the genesis and history of family foundations: L. Stecki, above n. 17, pp. 169–170.

119 It is commonly accepted that the correct criteria to differentiate family foundations are their aims and the beneficiaries who are family members (*fundatio iure sanguinis*).

120 Contrary, incorrectly, T. Krzywański and K. Gajdziński, above n. 117, 595. L. Stecki argues that the mixed aim should be typical for every foundation because it is not pragmatic to strongly differentiate charitable and private goals, L. Stecki, above n. 17, p. 171.

family; they may be unrelated persons. Legal entities may not act as founders, as this role is reserved exclusively for natural persons. Founders must possess full legal capacity (Article 11 FFA).

There are two ways to set up a family foundation: through a unilateral juridical act, the 'founding act', or by way of a last will (Article 21, point 1 FFA). In both cases, the documents must be executed in the form of a notarial deed (Article 22 FFA).

The FFA specifies the documents required to establish a family foundation, including the founding act, the foundation's charter, an inventory of assets, and the appointment of the governing bodies. Moreover, contributions to the foundation's fund must be made, with a minimum of PLN 100,000 (roughly €24,000). Finally, the foundation must be entered into the register in order to acquire legal personality (Article 21 FFA).

A so-called 'family foundation in organisation' comes into being upon the execution of the founding act or the disclosure of a last will (Article 23, section 1 FFA). In this interim form, the foundation acts in its own name, manages and safeguards its assets, and may acquire rights, assume obligations, and initiate or defend against legal proceedings (Article 23, section 3 FFA). Representation of the family foundation in organisation may be exercised by the founder, an authorised representative, or, in specific cases, the management board (Article 23, section 4 FFA). Legal personality is granted to the family foundation at the moment of its registration (Article 4, section 1 and Article 24 FFA). At that point, the foundation in organisation becomes a fully established family foundation. The court maintains the register of family foundations (Article 4, section 2 FFA), and everyone has the right to obtain certified copies, extracts, certificates and other information from this register (Article 111 FFA), however it is possible only in the courthouse (the registry is not available online).

3.3. GOVERNANCE

The governance structure of a family foundation is modelled on the corporate governance of limited liability companies. Given its complexity, a detailed presentation is not feasible within the context of this chapter. Instead, the focus will be on the most essential elements and regulations.

The governing bodies (boards) of a family foundation comprise the management board, a generally optional supervisory board and the beneficiaries' assembly (Article 43 FFA).

The management board may consist of one or more members (Article 56 FFA). Board members are appointed for a three-year term, unless otherwise specified in the foundation's charter (Article 61, section 1 FFA).[121] As a rule, appointments and dismissals are made, by the founder. Following the founder's

[121] Members may serve multiple terms.

death, this competence passes to the supervisory board, or, if no supervisory board exists, to the beneficiaries' assembly (Article 61, section 3 FFA).

The management board is with managing the affairs of the family foundation[122] and representing it externally[123] (Article 54, section 1, point 1 FFA). Its statutory duties include pursuing the objectives outlined in the charter (Article 54, section 1, point 2 FFA), safeguarding the foundation's financial liquidity and solvency (Article 54, section 1, point 3 FFA) and ensuring the fulfilment of the foundation's obligations towards its beneficiaries (Article 54, section 1, point 6 FFA). Management board members are required to perform their functions with due diligence and with loyalty to the foundation (Article 55, section 1 FFA).

Members of the management board are liable for damages resulting from unlawful actions, unless they can demonstrate the absence of fault. A board member is not deemed to have breached the duty of due diligence where, acting loyally towards the family foundation, they operate within the limits of reasonable business risk. This includes situations in which decisions are based on information, analyses, and opinions that, under the circumstances, should reasonably be taken into account when making a careful assessment.[124]

A supervisory board is mandatory only where the number of beneficiaries exceeds 25 (Article 64, sections 1 and 2 FFA). It may consist of one or more members (Article 66 FFA), who are appointed for a five-year term, unless the charter provides otherwise (Article 68, section 1 FFA).[125] The founder appoints and dismisses the members of the supervisory board. After the founder's death, this responsibility passes to the beneficiaries' assembly unless the charter provides otherwise (Article 68, section 3 FFA).

The supervisory board is tasked with overseeing the management board's compliance with legal requirements and the foundation's charter (Article 65, section 1 FFA). The foundation's charter may also expand the supervisory board's competences, for example by requiring the management board to obtain its prior approval for specific actions (Article 65, section 2 FFA).

The beneficiaries' assembly is composed of those beneficiaries designated in the foundation's charter as members of the assembly (Article 70, sections 1 and 2 FFA). This may encompass all beneficiaries or only a select group, with the founder enjoying full discretion in determining membership criteria. Beneficiaries may also be designated based on specific characteristics, allowing

---

122 In multi-member boards, all members are responsible for the managing the foundation's affairs, unless otherwise specified in the foundation's charter (Article 58, section 1 FFA).

123 In multi-member boards, at least two members must act jointly to represent the foundation, unless the foundation's charter provides otherwise (Article 59, section 1 FFA). Declarations made to the foundation can be directed to any board member (Article 59, section 2 FFA).

124 The same rules regarding liability apply to the members of the supervisory board (Article 67 FFA).

125 Members may serve multiple terms (Article 68, section 2 FFA).

for flexibility in the composition of the assembly over time. For instance, the founder may stipulate that all descendants will become members upon reaching the age of 18. As a result, even children or grandchildren who were not yet born at the time of the foundation's establishment will eventually become members of the assembly as they come of age.

The management board convenes the beneficiaries' assembly,[126] unless the charter provides otherwise (Article 71, section 1 FFA).[127] The beneficiaries' assembly must adopt resolutions on approval of the foundation's annual financial statements (Article 72, point 1 FFA), granting discharge to members of the governing bodies (Article 72, point 2 FFA), the allocation or covering of net financial results (Article 72, point 3 FFA) and the appointment of an auditing firm for an audit of the financial statements is required (Article 72, point 4 FFA).[128]

The founders hold a special position within the structure of a family foundation, allowing them to exert influence not only at the stage of its establishment but also throughout its operation.[129] Only a natural person may become a founder (Article 11 FFA). They have the right to appoint and dismiss members of the management board and supervisory board unless the charter specifies other rules (Article 61, section 3 and Article 68, section 3 FFA). The founders may challenge the resolutions of the foundation's governing bodies by filing lawsuits to annul decisions that contradict the foundation's charter or its purpose, or to invalidate those that violate the law (Article 82, section 1 FFA). Additionally, the founders hold the right to make changes regarding the beneficiaries of the foundations or their entitlements, as outlined in the foundations' charter (Article 14, section 2 FFA). While their comments, opinions or recommendations regarding the foundation's activities are not legally binding, the founders may submit them to the governing bodies for consideration (Article 15 FFA). In certain circumstances specified in the charter, the founders may also decide on the dissolution of the foundation.[130]

---

126 Unless the foundation's charter states otherwise, the assembly is valid regardless of the number of votes represented (Article 73, section 1 FFA).

127 The foundation's charter may list the situations when a beneficiary is entitled to call the management board to convene the assembly (Article 71, section 4 FFA). If the management board fails to convene an assembly within two weeks of receiving a request, the registration court may authorise the requesting beneficiary to convene it (Article 71, section 6 FFA).

128 And on other matters specified in the foundation's charter or law (Article 72, point 5 FFA).

129 A. Moszyńska correctly observes that the strong legal position of the founder under Polish law may lead to the use of family foundations for purposes unrelated to intergenerational estate planning. For instance, they may be utilised to safeguard the founder's personal assets or even to conceal them. This concern is particularly relevant for individuals who are legally required to publicly disclose their assets due to their high-ranking positions, such as politicians (A. Moszyńska, above n. 117, 125–126).

130 Depending on the reason for the dissolution of a family foundation, the decision may be made by the board, the beneficiaries' assembly, or the court. The court may act either on its own initiative or in response to a petition submitted by a beneficiary.

Furthermore, they are responsible for drafting the foundation's charter (Article 26, section 1 FFA) and may, in this process, confer upon themselves additional rights.

3.4. BUSINESS ACTIVITY

3.4.1. *Scope of Business Activity*

A family foundation may operate as either non-profit or not-for-profit organisation. A non-profit foundation refrains entirely from conducting business activities. By contrast, a not-for-profit foundation is permitted to engage in business activities;[131] however, all income generated must be reinvested into fulfilling the foundation's stated purpose.

The FFA explicitly authorises family foundation to conduct business activities, but it also places limits on their permissible scope. Article 5 FFA provides a closed list of activities that may be undertaken by a family foundation. According to this provision, a foundation may:

1) dispose of property, provided that the property has not been acquired solely for the purpose of subsequent disposal;
2) lease, rent or make property available for use on another basis;
3) join or participate in commercial companies, investment funds, cooperatives and entities of a similar nature, established either in the country or abroad;
4) acquire and dispose of securities, derivative instruments and rights of a similar nature;
5) grant loans to companies in which the family foundation holds shares or stocks, partnerships in which the family foundation participates as a partner or beneficiaries;
6) trade in foreign currencies owned by the family foundation to make payments related to the foundation's activities;
7) produce plant and animal products processed in a manner other than industrially, with the exception of processed plant and animal products obtained within the framework of the conducted special departments of agricultural production and products subject to excise tax, provided that the amount of plant or animal products originating from own cultivation,

[131] It is worth noting that according to the first draft of the Polish law on family foundation they were forbidden to conduct any business activities; this rule was subsequently reversed (A. Pardej in A. Mariański (ed), *Fundacje rodzinne. Aspekty prawne i podatkowe*, Wolters Kluwer, Warsaw 2023, pp. 129–130). See more about the history of legislative procedure regarding this issue: W. Kotowski and A. Turska-Tomczykowska in P. Tomczykowski (ed), *Fundacja rodzinna. Aspekty prawne i podatkowe. Komentarz*, C.H. Beck, Warsaw 2023, pp. 18–22.

breeding or rearing, used for the production of a given product constitutes at least 50% of this product; and
8) engage in forestry management.

The catalogue of activities is broad,[132] and many enumerated categories require further interpretation, which will be examined in greater detail below. Given that the legislation only entered into force in 2023, no established practice or case law has yet developed in this area. Nevertheless, two key issues have already emerged as points of discussion. First, the catalogue lacks internal consistency, as not all the listed activities are classified as business activities under Polish law. Second, the legal consequences of engaging in activities not included in the catalogue remain unclear and are a subject of significant debate.

Polish law defines business activity as organised profit-oriented activity carried on in one's own name and on a continuous basis (Article 3 of the Entrepreneurs' Law).[133] Anyone engaged in business activity is classified as an entrepreneur and is registered in a designated register, with separate registries for legal persons and natural persons. This definition of business activity is broad and flexible, while ensuring adaptability, also creates uncertainty: in practice, it is often difficult to determine whether a given activity falls within the scope of business activity and therefore triggers the obligation to comply with the relevant regulatory framework.

As a general principle, business activity presupposes active involvement in the conduct of economic operations. Mere profit derived from the use of assets does not automatically qualify as business activity. For example, renting out an apartment does not in itself constitute business activity. Likewise, the mere holding of shares in a company is not regarded as business activity under Polish law.

Against this background, the FFA introduces a conceptual inconsistency when it identifies holding shares in companies as a form of business activity. While this is largely a theoretical issue with limited practical consequences, the same cannot be said of the controversy surrounding the permissible scope of business activity for family foundations, which raises far more significant practical concerns.

The wording of Article 5 appears clear and definitive: a family foundation is permitted to engage in business activity solely within the categories explicitly enumerated in this provision. This raises a critical question regarding the consequences of a foundation conducting business activities outside the prescribed scope. This issue remains unresolved in case law, making it a subject of considerable debate. Two competing interpretations emerge.

---

132 Comparatively, the scope of permitted business activities is broader than in many jurisdictions (T. Krzywański and K. Gajdziński, above n. 117, 595).

133 Prawo przedsiębiorców (the Entrepreneurs' Act, EA, above n. 99) as amended on 6 March 2018, the amended text: Dz.U. 2024, poz. 236.

The first interpretation posits that conducting business activity beyond the scope outlined in Article 5 is unlawful.[134] Under this view, any contracts entered into by the foundation in connection with such unauthorised activities would be deemed null and void as they contravene the law.[135] As a result, the family foundation could be exposed to liability for losses or damages arising from the termination of these activities. Moreover, the foundation could potentially seek recourse against its management board members, claiming reimbursement for damages incurred on the grounds that the management board members violated the law by involving the foundation in unlawful business activities.

The second interpretation suggests that a family foundation may, in principle, engage in any type of business activity permitted by law; however, only with regard to the types of business activities listed in Article 5, a family foundation enjoys tax privileges.[136] According to Article 6, §1, point 25 of the Legal Persons' Income Tax Act (hereinafter: LPITA),[137] a family foundation does not pay income tax as every other legal person. However, Article 6, §7 of the same act stipulates that the exemption referred to in para. 1, subpara. 25 does not apply to the economic activities of a family foundation that exceed the scope defined in Article 5 FFA. This provision implies that the legislature indirectly acknowledges the possibility of a family foundation conducting business activities outside the catalogue of Article 5 FFA. This interpretation currently prevails in legal scholarship.[138] It is primarily justified by the need to ensure stability and predictability in business activities. Nevertheless, the current wording of Article 5 leaves room for ambiguity and requires amendment and clarification to reconcile its provisions with the broader regulatory framework.

Having explained the importance of the regulation limiting the scope of business activities that family foundations can conduct, the specific types of permissible activities will now be detailed further.

First, a family foundation may dispose of its property. This is essential because family foundations are established for the long term and changing circumstances may require restructuring of the foundation's assets. The ability to dispose of property thus ensures flexibility in asset management. However, commercial

134 D. Leszczyk points out that the application of Article 58 of the Polish Civil is not excluded by Article 5 so potentially it could be applied; however she does not favour such interpretation (see: D. Leszczyk, in P. Grabowski and D. Leszczyk (eds), *Ustawa o fundacji rodzinnej. Komentarz*, C.H. Beck, Warsaw 2023, p. 19.

135 According to Article 58 of the Polish Civil Code every juridical (legal) act contrary to law is null and void.

136 See for example: R. Adamus in R. Adamus and P. Stec (eds), *Fundacje rodzinne. Komentarz: Linia orzecznicza*, C.H. Beck, Warsaw 2024, p. 69; A. Krysik, *Ustawa o fundacji rodzinnej. Komentarz*, C.H. Beck, Warsaw 2024, p. 23.

137 Ustawa z 15.2.1992 o podatku dochodowym od osób prawnych, amended text: Dz.U. 2023, poz. 2805.

138 See for example: R. Adamus above n. 137, p. 69; A. Krysik, above n. 137, p. 23; D. Leszczyk, above n. 135, p. 19).

transactions involving the purchase of property with the explicit intention of resale are prohibited. This restriction is justified by the risk inherent in such speculative activities, which would be inconsistent with the primary purpose of family foundations, namely, the preservation and safeguarding of assets, rather than engaging in high-risk investment strategies.

Second, a family foundation may rent, lease or allow others to use its property on any legal basis. Crucially, such activity must generate income for the foundation and therefore cannot be carried out gratuitously.

Third, a family foundation may participate in entrepreneurial ventures as a member, partner or shareholder of various business entities. The law provides a broad, non-exhaustive list of permissible entities, commercial partnerships,[139] corporations,[140] investment funds, cooperatives and mentions 'other entities of a similar nature'. Foundations can hold either minority or majority shares, potentially enabling them to indirectly run enterprises. Additionally, the law does not preclude a family foundation from owning a single-member company, allowing it to establish an entity explicitly for operating a business on its behalf.

Fourth, a family foundation may engage in securities trading, which includes buying and selling all types of securities and derivatives, even highly speculative instruments. In contrast to property transactions, there are no restrictions on trading securities, allowing a family foundation to buy assets solely for the purpose of resale. While this competence offers considerable flexibility and can serve as a useful tool for asset management, the absence of statutory safeguards exposes the foundation to significant financial risks. Such an approach appears difficult to reconcile with the core objective of family foundations, namely the long-term preservation and protection of assets.

Fifth, a family foundation may extend loans, though this competence is subject to statutory limitations. Loans may only be granted to a specific group of recipients, including corporations in which the foundation holds shares, partnerships where the foundation is a partner, and beneficiaries. Among these, granting loans to beneficiaries aligns most closely with the primary purpose of family foundations. The inclusion of corporations and partnerships as potential borrowers raises concerns. Notably, even a minority shareholding is sufficient to qualify a company as an eligible recipient. This seems overly broad and could expose the family foundation to excessive financial risk. A more prudent approach would be to restrict lian activities to entities in which the foundation holds a controlling stake.

---

139 Polish law recognises the following types of commercial partnerships: commercial partnership (*spółka jawna*), professional partnership (*spółka partnerska*), limited partnership (*spółka komandytowa*) and partnership limited by shares (*spółka komandytowo-akcyjna*).

140 Polish law recognises the following types of corporations: limited liability company (*spółka z ograniczoną odpowiedzialnością*), simple joint-stock company (*prosta spółka akcyjna*) and joint-stock company (*spółka akcyjna*).

Moreover, the consequences of breaching these statutory limitations remain unclear. If the only penalty is the loss of tax privileges, the regulatory purpose of restricting loans is undermined.

Sixth, a family foundation may engage in foreign currency trading, but only to the extent necessary for making payments connected with its activities. This restriction aims to mitigate risks typically associated with currency trading. Yet, as with the loan-related provisions, if violations only lead to tax penalties, the effectiveness of this safeguard becomes questionable, potentially jeopardising the foundation's financial stability.

Seventh and eighth, where a family foundation operates as an agricultural producer (e.g. runs a farm), it may produce plant and animal products that are processed in a non-industrial manner. However, at least 50% of the raw materials used in the production must come from the foundation's own cultivation, breeding or rearing. Additionally, if the foundation owns a forest, it is permitted to engage in forestry management activities. These provisions, while specific, align with the broader goal of allowing family foundations to manage and sustain their assets effectively.

Although the range of business activities expressly permitted for family foundations is diverse, it shares a common underlying feature: the foundation is conceived as a vehicle for generating income primarily through the passive use of its assets, rather than through active entrepreneurial engagement.[141]

An analysis of the statutory framework reveals two main points. First, the range of activities permitted is broad, providing flexibility for the foundation to manage and sustain its wealth. Second, the regulation of these activities is not without controversy and will require interpretation through practice and judicial decisions as case law develops.

The statutory catalogue also raises two further questions of principle. The first concerns whether a family foundation itself can qualify as an entrepreneur, directly operating an enterprise rather than merely participating in one passively. The second concerns the extent to which the scope of permitted business activities may be contractually restricted through the foundation's charter, thereby enabling the founder or those vested with amendment powers to calibrate the foundation's business involvement in line with their own preferences and objectives.

3.4.2. Status as an Entrepreneur

The most fundamental and straightforward type of business activity involves directly operating an enterprise and holding ownership of it. According to Polish law (Article 55[1] of the Civil Code), an enterprise is an organised complex of

---

141 M. Paszczela in M. Guzek, M. Lejman, M. Paszczela and M. Stefaniak (eds), *Fundacja rodzinna. Komentarz do przepisów podatkowych*, C.H. Beck, Warsaw 2024, p. 53.

material and non-material components created to conduct economic activity. While it is composed of various elements – such as individual properties or real estate – Polish law uniquely recognises a unified and singular right to the enterprise as a whole. This right is akin to ownership, allowing the enterprise to be treated as a singular entity that can be the subject of legal transactions, such as sales or donations.

Typically, the owner of an enterprise is considered to be conducting business activity through the operation of the enterprise. This raises an important question in the context of family foundations: can such a foundation own an enterprise and thereby engage in business activity directly? This issue is particularly significant because ownership of an enterprise implies active involvement in managing and profiting from it, which contrasts with the predominantly passive income-generating model that family foundations are generally expected to follow.

Article 5 of the FFA does not explicitly permit a family foundation to operate an enterprise, as this activity is not included in the catalogue of permitted business activities. The regulation is inconsistent with the provision that allows family foundations to operate a specific type of enterprise – namely, an agricultural farm. According to Polish law (Article 55^3 of the Civil Code), an agricultural farm is agricultural land together with forest land, buildings or their parts, equipment and livestock if they form or can form an organised economic whole, and with the rights connected with the running of an agricultural farm. This definition bears a strong resemblance to a definition of an enterprise. Furthermore, both an agricultural farm and an enterprise can be treated as a unified object of legal transactions, such as sale or donation. Despite these parallels, the FFA treats them differently, permitting family foundations to run agricultural farms while excluding the direct operation of enterprises. This distinction appears arbitrary and raises interpretative challenges. Allowing the operation of an agricultural business suggests that family foundations are capable of managing complex economic ventures. However, the explicit prohibition on running other enterprises seems to contradict this, creating a lack of coherence in the regulatory framework.

Although, as indicated in the above analysis, a family foundation is not permitted to operate an enterprise directly, this does not preclude it from owning an active enterprise. Article 5, §1, point 2 FFA permits family foundations to lease various assets. An enterprise, as a whole, can not only be sold but also leased to an 'operator' under various legal arrangements. The owner of the enterprise is entitled to receive rent in return. This type of business activity is fully permissible for family foundations. Consequently, it can be concluded that a foundation may be endowed with an enterprise and legally acquire ownership of it.

Alternatively, a family foundation can operate an enterprise indirectly. According to Article 5, §1, point 3 FFA, a foundation may become a shareholder of a company. There are no restrictions on the types of business activities that such a company may undertake. Consequently, there are no barriers to owning or managing an enterprise through this arrangement. Where the company is controlled by the foundation, the foundation would be able to exercise decisive influence over the enterprise's strategic direction and key decisions.

The analysis demonstrates that the legislator intentionally established a barrier (or veil) between the active operation of an enterprise and a family foundation. This approach considers the inherent functions of family foundations. While such foundations are not entirely excluded from owning or indirectly operating an enterprise, this structure ensures that the foundation is shielded from the risks and liabilities associated with the enterprise's operations. Although the foundation may lose the asset itself (i.e. the value of the enterprise), it is difficult, if not impossible, to hold the foundation liable for the enterprise's debts.[142]

In conclusion, a family foundation can be regarded as an appropriate mechanism for ensuring the succession of an enterprise. However, the foundation itself cannot operate the enterprise directly. Instead, it has two options: it can lease the enterprise to an operator who will manage it independently while paying the agreed rent to the foundation, or it can establish a company and transfer the enterprise to that company. In the latter case, the company will operate the enterprise, but the foundation will retain control over the company and, in turn, indirectly over the enterprise.

3.4.3. *Internal Limitations of the Scope of Business Activity*

The final issue to be considered in the context of family enterprise foundations concerns the possibility and effectiveness of restricting the scope of permissible business activities in the foundation's charter. This matter is explicitly regulated for charitable foundations: Article 11, section 1 FA allows charitable foundations to conduct only those types of business activities specified in their charter. By contrast, no equivalent provision exists in the statute governing family foundations.

This legislative silence leads to the conclusion that any restrictions on business activities included in a family foundation's charter will not be enforceable against third parties (*erga omnes*). This results from the general rejection of the *ultra vires* doctrine in Polish law governing legal persons. Nonetheless, this does not prevent a founder from incorporating such restrictions into the foundation's charter. These provisions will remain effective exclusively within its internal governance framework (*inter partes*).

Consequently, an activity prohibited by the family foundation's charter would still be legally valid but would violate the charter. In such cases, members of the

142 It cannot be totally excluded because in specific situations potentially the doctrine of piercing the corporate veil could be applied.

board who authorise or engage in such activities may be held liable vis-à-vis the foundation for any losses incurred by the foundation as a result.[143]

3.5. TAXES

According to Article 30 FFA, the beneficiaries of a family foundation may include natural persons, such as the founder, as well as non-governmental organisations conducting public benefit activities. Income earned by natural persons as the foundation's beneficiaries – both during the existence of the foundation and upon its dissolution – falls under 'other sources of income' as outlined in Article 20, section 1g) of the Personal Income Tax Act (hereinafter: PITA). Founders and their closest family members, i.e. spouses, descendants, ascendants, stepchildren, siblings, stepfathers, and stepmothers are, under Article 21, section 1, point 157 PITA, exempt from income taxation. A broader family group including sons-in-law, daughters-in-law and in-laws enjoy a 10% tax rate (Article 30, section 1, point 17 a) PITA). A 15% tax rate applies to other individuals who benefit from the assets of the family foundation (Article 30, section 1, point 17 b) PITA).

As signalled above, family foundations are subject to the LPITA. Under Article 6, §1, point 25, they are generally exempt from income taxation. Therefore, if a family foundation generates income within the scope of business activities indicated in Article 5, section 1 FFA, it remains tax neutral. Exceeding the specified scope of business activities may result in the imposition of a 25% penalty tax rate.

With respect to income derived from leasing, rental, or similar agreements concerning assets made available to the foundation's beneficiaries or related entities, the family foundation is subject to the standard income tax rate of 19%. The scenarios in which the family foundation is obligated to pay a 15% tax on its income are limited to the following triggering events:

1) the transfer of a monetary benefit to the beneficiary, in accordance with the provisions of the foundation's charter;
2) the transfer, in line with the charter's provisions, of a non-monetary benefit to the beneficiary, especially benefits that involve granting the beneficiary the use of the foundation's assets;
3) the transfer of a benefit related to so-called hidden benefits; or
4) the transfer of assets in connection with the dissolution of the family foundation.

---

[143] A. Pardej, above n. 132, p. 145.

In conclusion, the family foundation presents a potentially attractive option within the Polish tax landscape, particularly for those seeking to manage wealth across generations while benefitting from certain tax advantages. The preferential income tax rates for founders and their family members, along with the general tax exemptions for the foundation itself, make it a compelling structure.[144] At the same time, careful attention must be paid to the statutory limitations on the scope of permissible activities and to the risk of tax penalties should the foundation exceed these boundaries.

3.6. EXAMPLES OF FAMILY FOUNDATIONS

The law on family foundations has been in force for only about two years, which limits the availability of extensive examples of family enterprise foundations. Moreover, founders and beneficiaries typically place a high value on privacy, resulting in limited public access to information about their operations. Nevertheless, a number of notable examples can be identified, most of which involve family foundations established by the founders or executives of major publicly listed companies.

Members of the management board of STS Holding S.A. have established several family foundations, including MJ Foundation Fundacja Rodzinna, Fundacja Zbigniewa Jaroszka Fundacja Rodzinna, Fundacja Marcina Walczysko Fundacja Rodzinna and Fundacja Zdzisława Kostrubały Fundacja Rodzinna.[145]

The two families that founded Oponeo S.A.[146] also decided to establish family foundations, one of which is Fundacja Rodzinna Topolewscy Corvus Albus Fundacja Rodzinna. They transferred shares in the company to the foundation, ensuring that the foundation will exercise the rights embedded in those shares.[147]

The founders of Cyber_Folks S.A.[148] transferred their shares in the company to a family foundation they established. As relatively young entrepreneurs, they chose to use the family foundation as a long-term corporate governance instrument.[149]

---

144 T. Krzywański and K. Gajdziński interestingly notice that the foreign foundations of Polish clients will be granted the same privileges because entities from various Member States of the EU cannot be treated differently solely on the basis of their different residence (T. Krzywański and K. Gajdziński, above n. 117, 600).

145 'Fundacje rodzinne wśród firm rodzinnych notowanych na GPW' (2025) *Portal Kancelarii Prawnej PragmatIQ o sukcesji*: https://pragmatiq.pl/zmianawarty/fundacje-rodzinne-wsrod-firm-rodzinnych-notowanych-na-gpw/#Fundacje_rodzinne_zakladane_przez_polskie_firmy_rodzinne_notowane_na_gieldzie.

146 The official website of the company: https://www.ir.oponeo.pl/en.

147 See above n. 147.

148 The official website of the company: https://investors.cyberfolks.pl/company-pages/o-nas.

149 See above n. 147.

The president of the IMMOBILE S.A. group of companies,[150] along with a member of the supervisory board, transferred their shares to a family foundation they created, named Fundacja Rodziny Jerzych Fundacja Rodzinna. As a result, the foundation became a shareholder, ensuring that its beneficiaries – both current and future family members of the founders – will benefit from the company's profits.[151]

4. CONCLUSIONS AND OUTLOOK

Polish law does not recognise enterprise foundations as a separate category of business entities. Instead, it provides distinct regulations on entrepreneurship (business activity) and various types of foundations. The two key statutes – the Foundations Act (FA) and the Family Foundation Act (FFA) – each address the conditions under which foundations may conduct business activities. While the underlying principles of these regimes display significant similarities, their detailed provisions differ in important respects.

A primary similarity between the statutes on charitable foundations and family foundations lies in the recognition of enterprise foundations as a permissible form. Both statutes allow founders to choose whether to establish a non-profit foundation refraining entirely from business activity, or as a not-for-profit entity, authorised to engage in business activity, provided that profits are reinvested in pursuit of the foundation's objectives. In this sense, Polish law directly acknowledges and regulates the possibility of enterprise foundations, whether charitable or private.

The crucial distinction between charitable and private enterprise foundations concerns the scope of permissible business activities. It is undisputed that charitable foundations may engage in any business activity that is legally permissible. However, a founder may impose limitations on the scope of such activities, as each type of business activity must be explicitly stated in the foundation's charter.

The scope of allowed business activity for private enterprise foundations, on the other hand, is a matter of debate. One interpretation is that it is strictly limited by law, and any activities beyond those permitted are illegal. An opposing view holds that a family foundation may engage in any type of business activity, but it enjoys tax privileges only for activities specifically enumerated by the legislator. Significantly, the FFA does not require family foundations to enumerate business activities in their charters, meaning that, in practice, the management board may involve the foundation in any activity it considers conducive to advancing the foundation's objectives.

---

150 The official website of the group of companies: https://immobile.com.pl.

151 See above n. 147.

The historical trajectories of the two models also diverge. Charitable foundations have existed in Poland since 1984, with approximately 30,000 foundations currently registered, many of which are engaged in business activities. In contrast, practical experience with private foundations remains limited, as they were only introduced into Polish law in 2023. Nonetheless, within 18 months of the statute's enactment, nearly 2,000 family foundations were successfully established. This rapid uptake has been accompanied by controversy, as concerns have been raised that the new regime may be exploited primarily for tax optimisation rather than for succession planning. It is therefore likely that the debate on amendments to the FFA, particularly those aimed at curbing certain tax privileges and reinforcing the role of family foundations as instruments of intergenerational wealth transfer, will shape the core discussion in the coming years.

ENTERPRISE FOUNDATIONS IN THE CZECH REPUBLIC

Irma COMSTOCKOVÁ and Kateřina RONOVSKÁ*

* Irma Comstocková is PhD student at the Masaryk University School of Law, and a practicing lawyer; Kateřina Ronovská is a professor of Civil Law at the Masaryk University School of Law, and a Vice-president at the Constitutional Court of the Czech Republic.

ABSTRACT

This chapter summarises the historical development and the current state of foundation law in the Czech Republic. It provides an explanation as to why enterprise foundations are not firmly embedded in the Czech legal culture, unlike in the jurisdictions of some of the country's direct neighbours. It follows with a presentation of the important milestones which enabled the concept to take root in the Czech Republic and a discussion of the legal forms currently available for use as enterprise foundations. It considers the advantages and shortcomings of the individual legal structures and provides examples of practical use. It concludes with a brief comparison of these legal forms and an outlook for the future.

1. INTRODUCTION AND HISTORICAL CONSIDERATIONS

1.1. FROM MONARCHY TO POST-REVOLUTIONARY YEARS

Shared history, geographic proximity as well as cultural similarities constitute factors contributing to the shaping of a country's legal system and its individual fields. In the case of the Czech Republic and the foundation sector, this is true on multiple levels.

The nearly 400 years of the country's existence within the Austro-Hungarian Monarchy impacted the development of the Czech legal system. It meant, along with other things, that the private foundation sector was inadequately regulated. The Austrian Civil Code (ABGB), which was also applicable within the territory of the Czech Kingdom, contained only a single brief provision relating to foundations and the foundation field[1] was thus regulated predominantly by public law. In the mid-19th century, state supervision over the foundation sector was eventually institutionalised via a king's decree.[2]

The new Czechoslovak Republic, as it came into existence after World War I, adopted the Austrian regulation of legal persons, which was underdeveloped at that time. 'Pre-Republic' foundations, which were originally established for the benefit of those who became Czech citizens, were handed over under the special provisions of the Treaty of Saint-Germain. However, the subsequent economic crisis and the advance of fascism prevented the newly established foundation field from further developing.

---

1 Section 646 ABGB recognised the existence of foundations as entities distinct from specific concepts of inheritance law. Foundations represented entities distributing income in favour of public benefit institutes such as churches, schools, hospitals and orphanages or in support of specific private individuals.

2 K. Ronovská, 'K historickému vývoji nadací ve střední Evropě' (2011) 19(2) *Časopis pro právní vědu a praxi* 124.

The situation after the Communist coup d'état in 1948 contributed to a further decline, resulting in a complete ban of all foundation legislation in 1953 and the liquidation of nearly all existing foundations. Only one foundation in the Czech Republic survived this regime, albeit in a much-restricted form, and the survival of this institution can be mostly attributed to the personal bravery and abilities of the scientists sitting on its governing and supervisory boards.[3]

The overall decline of the foundation sector during the Communist era is a heritage shared with other countries of Central and Eastern Europe. This shared legacy of communism reflects equally on the common evolution after the fall of the Iron Curtain when these countries, including the Czech Republic, slowly rediscovered the potential of foundations and recodified their foundation legislation.

However, in the Czech Republic in the 1990s, the revival of the foundation sector was not a political priority of the Czech governments. A delay in the development of the foundation legislation can thus be observed in comparison with many western European countries. The first two post-revolutionary decades were marked by a very narrow conceptual approach to the foundation legislation. This attitude stemmed primarily from a fear of a potential abuse of the foundation legal form. Therefore, foundations could only be set up for public benefit purposes and there were strict legislative limitations implemented as to the management of the foundation assets. This tightly constructed regulation contained in a separate legal act[4] remained in effect until the second decade of the 21st century. This led to a rather slow development of the entire sector and to a limited practical use of the foundation as a legal form.

The historical considerations discussed in the previous paragraphs contributed to the fact that, unlike in countries of similar legal cultures such as Germany or Switzerland, there is no long-term tradition of placing an entire or a significant portion of a business enterprise into a foundation as either a tool of transgenerational wealth transfer or in favour of society at large. Thus, despite a more recent development described in the following section, the concept of an enterprise foundation has no historical roots in this territory.

1.2. CURRENT LANDSCAPE

A significant change to the pattern of strict regulation was brought by a recodification of the Czech Civil Code in 2014[5] which was marked by an overall increase in respect for the autonomy of the owner's will. For the foundation

[3] The concerned foundation, the Hlavka Foundation ('*Nadání Josefa, Marie a Zdenky Hlávkových*') was established in 1904 by architect Josef Hlávka and is still in existence.

[4] Act No. 227/1997 Coll., on Foundations and Endowment Funds.

[5] Act No. 89/2012 Coll., Civil Code.

legislation, this meant a notable liberalisation of the foundation's designated purpose and an increase in the autonomy of the founder's will to create a foundation in line with his/her true intentions and needs.[6] Most importantly to the main topic of this chapter, this liberalisation also meant that foundations could get involved in business activities, whether directly or indirectly, including via holding of significant shares in business corporations.

Apart from the positive elements of liberalisation of the foundation purpose and the increased autonomy of the founder's will, the recodification also brought about a degree of confusion as it provided for an array of legal forms with overlapping purposes: foundations (*nadace*) and foundation funds[7] (*nadační fond*), civil law trust-like structures (trust funds[8] – *svěřenský fond*), public benefit institutions (*ústav*) and ancillary funds (*přidružený fond*).

The forms with the characteristics most closely related to the needs of an enterprise foundation in terms of asset designation, purpose definition and corporate governance are the first three types of entities. Of these, foundations and foundation funds possess a legal personality while the trust fund (Czech trust-like structure) represents an entity without a legal personality derived from a Québécois style of civilian trust with asset ownership belonging neither to the trustee nor the beneficiaries.[9] The main body of the remaining text will thus be devoted to these three entities.[10]

6 For futher see: K. Ronovská and P. Lavicky, 'New Czech Foundation and Trust (like) Law: initial experience and reactions' (2016) 22(6) *Trust & Trustees* 641: https://dx.doi.org/10.1093/tandt/ttw062.

7 Foundation funds were already regulated by Act No. 227/1997 Coll., on Foundations and Endowment Funds, along with classical foundations. They were considered 'younger siblings' of foundations, somewhat easier to establish and run. There is no standard terminology used for the translation of this Czech instrument. The most direct translation can be represented by the term '*foundation fund*', which, however, carries a different meaning in other jurisdictions, e.g. a separate fund set up by a foundation for a specific purpose. Alternatively, the term '*endowment fund*' could be used; however, this term may imply the existence of a permanent or a minimal income producing endowment and this is not a necessary condition for the entity's existence. The term 'foundation fund' is thus used throughout the chapter as the slightly more convenient of both options, even though imprecise, but consistent with past use of these terms in other publications of the authors in English.

8 The term 'trust fund' is at times used throughout the chapter to avoid the repetition of the longer descriptions such as 'civilian trust-like structure' or the original terminology in Czech and, at the same time, to distinguish it from the term 'trust' as understood in common law countries.

9 For characteristics of possible legal forms see also: K. Ronovská and V. Pihera, 'Estate planning on the edges of time: The Czech Perspective' (2017) 23(6) *Trusts & Trustees* 648: https://dx.doi.org/10.1093/tandt/ttx067.

10 The legal form of an ancillary fund is typically used for the management of assets which are supposed to be held separately from other assets of the foundation while the creation of a new foundation is not considered necessary or efficient. The assets in the fund are thus managed by the main foundation while the ownership of the assets is supposed to remain with the donor. However, there appears to be a discrepancy between the intention of the legislator as declared in the introductory notes to the new Civil Code and the actual wording

It could be argued, however, that the introduction of all three structures was not necessary, and that the Czech legislature could have simply used the legal form of a foundation to cover all the designated purposes. A proper explanation of the journey leading to the current state would be rather lengthy. In brief, the legal form of a foundation fund was introduced by the Act on Foundations and Endowment Funds of 1997.[11] This form was originally envisaged as a less strictly regulated foundation-type structure which could also be used for private benefit purposes, including asset management or corporate holdings, while foundations would continue to be dedicated to public benefit activities only. However, this intention was abandoned in the legislative process and ultimately both foundations and foundation funds were introduced as entities exclusively for public benefit purposes by the Act.

Therefore, the idea of an entity which could be used also for private benefit purposes re-emerged about 20 years later during the recodification of the Civil Code via the civilian trust-like structure trust fund (*svěřenský fond*). Nevertheless, the legal forms of a foundation and foundation fund were liberalised in 2014, when the new Civil Code and all recodification laws entered into effect. Thus, all three forms have coexisted since 2014 in the same Civil Code for purposes ranging from public to private benefit, including the possibility of holding of corporate entities.[12]

1.3. ECONOMIC DATA

As discussed in the previous section, the Czech Republic belongs to the group of civil law countries that implemented both a liberal concept of foundation legislation as well as a civil law style trust-like structure. Even though the purpose of their establishment overlaps to some degree, the economic data suggest specific trends in the popularity of their use.

According to the information provided by the non-profit organisation Donors' Forum (*Fórum dárců*),[13] there were over 3,100 foundations and foundation funds registered as of 2023 of which the simpler foundation funds represented a little

of the regulation. Charitable associations, on the other hand, are historically used in the direct provision of public or private services available to all on an equal basis under the fulfilment of specified conditions. It combines the features of a corporation (personal basis) and those of a foundation (asset basis) and represent what could be labelled as a 'universal legal entity.' Although it can perform business activities under conditions similar to foundations, its main purpose and focus remains in the direct provision of services – a feature which renders it less suitable for the use as an enterprise foundation.

11 Act No. 227/1997 Coll., on Foundations and Endowment Funds.

12 See further K. Ronovská and V. Pihera, 'Private foundations in the Czech Republic: 10 years on the road' (2022) 28(6) *Trust & Trustees* 528.

13 See: www.donorsforum.cz. In 2023 there were 574 foundations and 2,612 foundation funds.

over 80%. The total number was further split approximately 85% to 15% in favour of entities set up by non-corporate founders, whether for public or private purposes. In both categories, foundation funds represented roughly 80% of all entities. Nearly CZK 2.3 billion was devoted to public purpose causes via these entities in 2022. In comparison to previous years, there is a clear upward trend in the total number of existing entities – an increase of nearly 40% between 2018 and 2023.

The upward trend for trust-like structures is even steeper; their number has nearly quadrupled between 2019 and 2024 to approximately 6,000 trust funds. Asset managers estimate this number will continue to grow steeply in at least the next ten years.

In terms of purpose of establishment, foundations are still perceived as entities devoted primarily to public benefit or charitable causes, while foundation funds are more commonly used for both private and public benefit purposes and trust funds predominantly for private causes.

2. LEGAL FORMS FOR ENTERPRISE FOUNDATIONS

The following sections introduce the basic characteristics of foundations, foundation funds and trust funds, and compare the advantages and drawbacks of each for use as 'enterprise foundations'. In doing so, consideration is given namely to the following features: long-term orientation and irrevocability in principle; focus on public benefit purpose; flexibility in purpose design and its change; governance structure; ability to assume an active role in the management of a larger business; and tax treatment advantages, if any exist. Wherever possible, a reference is provided to examples of practical use.

2.1. FOUNDATION

Czech foundations represent entities endowed with legal personality and features typical for continental foundations: non-membership base, identifiable assets and irrevocable dedication of assets to a particular purpose. They are set up to provide 'a permanent service in favour of a societal or economically beneficial purpose'. Their intended duration in perpetuity and the irrevocable character of asset contribution distinguishes them from other entities discussed in this chapter. The concept of 'sunsetting' – planning an end date for the foundation – is not specifically built into the Czech legislation, although such a construct is not excluded by some scholars. According to the law, a foundation can be dissolved once it reaches its designated purpose; at this moment, however, a planned purpose consumption is a rather theoretical concept within the Czech legal environment.

2.1.1. *Foundation Purpose*

Foundations can be set up for 'public benefit or charitable purposes'.[14] Despite the definition not being entirely clear and a bit narrow, it can be considered that a foundation may be established for any lawful purpose, of public and private benefit. In addition, since the tax legislation makes a clear reference to family foundations, legal practice relies on a broader interpretation of 'charitable purpose' in favour of pure private benefit purpose, including family foundations.

Public benefit foundations can apply for and receive the status of a 'public benefit taxpayer'[15] which is related to certain tax benefits (e.g. no tax on gains at the foundation level if gains are expended in line with the foundation's public benefit purpose). Foundations with a private benefit purpose (e.g. family foundations) cannot become public benefit taxpayers. The existence of mixed-purpose foundations is not excluded by the Civil Code; however, from a tax perspective, they would be treated entirely as private purpose foundations irrespective of their partial public benefit purpose and lose any tax benefits tied to their partial activities towards the public good. Therefore, splitting their activities into two separate entities seems like a more viable approach.

It is prohibited to set up foundations fulfilling illegal purposes as well as foundations supporting activities of political parties. Foundations serving exclusively business purposes are also forbidden. Business activities are possible, but only as a means by which a non-business purpose is achieved. Direct enterprise foundations are thus banned except for business activities ancillary to the main non-business purpose. Indirect performance of business activities via holding of shares in for-profit corporations is permitted; however, even in these cases such holdings must serve the main declared purpose of the foundation, public benefit or charitable. Both types of business activities may be prohibited by the founder in the foundation deed. There is also another limit – foundations can never become partners with unlimited liability. Foundations set up for the sole purpose of preservation and development of a business or self-preservation and maintenance of its assets are not allowed.

2.1.2. *Foundation Registration and Changes to its Deed*

Foundations are set up by the declaration of a founder or multiple founders in a special document called the foundation deed or as part of the founder's will. More detailed regulation of the organisational structure and decision-making processes is embodied in the foundation statute issued at the latest within a month from its incorporation. All foundations are registered with a public

---

14 Section 306 of Act No. 89/2012 Coll., Civil Code.

15 Article 17a, section 2 of Act No. 586/1992 Coll., on Income Tax.

registrar (Register of Foundations). Information about foundations and founding documents are publicly accessible and available online without the need to prove any legitimate interest.[16]

The foundation deed, including the foundation purpose, may be changed during the lifetime of the founder or after his/her death by a decision of the founder or another foundation body designated by the foundation deed, and in a manner stipulated in the foundation deed, unless such change is excluded in the founding documents. Special attention should thus be paid to the drafting of the deed in this respect. The founder cannot reserve the right to revoke the foundation, and such right cannot be vested in any other foundation body. Sunset foundations, as mentioned above, are currently more or less a hypothetical concept.

In case of a substantial change in circumstance, the foundation deed can be changed even without such mechanism envisaged by the deed, unless such change is specifically excluded by the deed. In specific cases, a decision on the change can also be passed by the courts. A change from a public benefit to a charitable purpose always requires the involvement of a court. Third-party rights and the rights of the current beneficiaries are specifically protected by law in case of the adoption of a later change to the deed or foundation purpose.

2.1.3. Minimal Capital and Asset Management

Foundations have dedicated minimal capital, the use and disposition of which is restricted by law.[17] This part of the foundation assets represents a foundation endowment which shall be preserved and is meant to produce a permanent income in support of the foundation's activities. However, the amount is not restrictively high, approximately €20,000.

The asset management of a foundation is governed by the general provisions of the Civil Code which require a standard of due professional care with respect to the managers. It is generally agreed that the provisions regarding full asset management apply, which means that management towards asset growth and multiplication rather than mere preservation is desired. This approach is fully compatible with enterprise holding. Further guidelines or restrictions may be contained in the foundation documents.

There are no nationwide industry standards such as rules applicable to pension funds further refining the style of asset management within non-profit organisations, including foundations. The newly adopted Czech Foundation Codex,[18] built on the Swiss model, contains some basic provisions regarding the establishment of the foundation's investment strategy, its approval and supervision.

---

16 Access to selected information defined by law may be restricted based on application.

17 The endowment cannot, for example, be pledged or used as collateral.

18 Available in the Czech language only at: nadacnikodex.cz.

All foundations whose basic assets or annual turnover reach approximately €200,000 must have their end-of-year financial statements audited by an independent auditor. Annual reports, including the audited results, must be filed with the Register of Foundations and are publicly available online. The transparency of all foundations is thus high. However, similar rules apply to corporations; keeping an enterprise within a domestic corporate holding structure or directly does not provide any benefits in respect of transparency.

2.1.4. Governance, Beneficiaries and External Supervision

Foundations are managed by a board of directors and are internally supervised by a supervisory board (or a single comptroller if a supervisory board is not established). Both the board of directors and the supervisory board must have at least three members; a full supervisory board instead of a comptroller must be established if the foundation's basic assets (endowment) reach ten times the minimal required capital (circa €200,000).

Czech law does not require that foundation boards be independent of their founders and their family members; however, members of foundation bodies, employees and the members of their families cannot become beneficiaries of the foundation. The same applies to the founder, except for specific cases envisaged by law, and the members of the founder's family, unless the foundation was set up for their support. These rules are criticised by legal doctrine and practice and are often teleologically reduced or replaced by the will of the founder as these limitations do not make sense for private benefit foundations when family members are involved in the foundation management. These should not be of concern for enterprise foundations set up as vehicles for achieving common good. In either case, family members could be involved in the work of additionally set up corporate bodies such as family councils or advisory committees which are not regulated by the Civil Code. Protectors, unlike in other jurisdictions, are neither provided for by law nor regularly used. The Czech Foundation Codex mentioned in section 2.1.3 provides for a non-binding set of recommendations for foundation governance and good practice that is being adopted by foundations in practice in addition to legal regulation and rules set forth by the founder in the foundation charter.

The position of beneficiaries is not comprehensively regulated by a separate provision and references to their rights are scattered across various sections – whether related to cases of adoption of changes to the foundation deed or to conflict of interest between the rights of beneficiaries and the prohibition of their position on the statutory bodies.

External supervision over foundations consists of several levels: (i) the foundation deed must be drafted by a notary which represents basic guarantee of compliance with laws; (ii) a foundation's existence is conditioned by its entry into the Register of Foundations maintained by the reginal courts; compliance of the founding documents with law and the appointment of their statutory bodies is thus reviewed by a state's authority. Any change to the statutory bodies and the founding documents is subject to further review by courts. Citizens proving legitimate interest or the foundation itself may turn to courts also in other specific events such as when changes to the founding documents touch upon their rights or in case the members of the foundation's statutory bodies violate the foundation's internal documents or law and have not been removed from their position; (iii) external control is further carried out by an external auditor which is obligatory for all foundations with an entry capital over CZK 5 million as well as via the duty to publish annual reports in the Register of Foundations maintained by the courts (this obligation is similar to the legal requirements placed on business corporations, cooperatives and other selected entities and physical persons carrying out business activities); and (iv) external control is also exercised by the financial authorities, in particular in the case of public benefit foundations enjoying public payer status. There is no special external authority supervising the foundation sector such as the supervisory authorities in Switzerland, Lichtenstein or Denmark with their specific powers to intervene in the life of foundations or offering aid upon request.

2.1.5. Tax Regime

Regarding tax treatment, an approach of general 'tax neutrality' among foundations, foundation funds, trust funds and corporations has been adopted by the Czech legislator, except for entities with public benefit taxpayer status. Entities established for the sole purpose of doing business (e.g. trust funds with such purpose) and family foundations and foundation funds established for the purpose of supporting selected groups of individuals such as the founder's family members, including entities with mixed purpose, cannot, under any circumstances, be granted such status.

An entity granted a public benefit taxpayer status is not subject to an income tax on gains on the condition that these gains are further distributed in compliance with its statutory public benefit purpose (no time limit is set; however, long-term retention of gains without distribution would likely be questioned by the financial authorities). Furthermore, contributions to foundations and foundation funds with a public benefit taxpayer status represent a tax deduction on the side of the donor; contributions to trust funds are never tax deductible even in the case of public benefit trust funds.

Otherwise, there is no tax duty attached to the initial or later contribution of assets to all these entities and there is no tax attached to the transfer of dividends from the operating for-profit corporation to the holding entity. Regarding gains at the level of a holding entity, a standard corporate tax applies, unless the entity is granted the status of a public benefit taxpayer as described above. Contributions to beneficiaries are taxed as income at their individual tax bracket in the case of foundations and foundation funds and as capital gains by withholding tax in the case of trust funds, except for beneficiaries of entities with public benefit taxpayer status, where no tax applies at distribution. In the case of distributions from the contributed assets, tax may not apply depending on the relationship of the beneficiary to the founder.

2.1.6. *Inheritance Law and Rights of Forced Heirs*

Czech law recognises rights of forced heirs. Forced heirs are children of the testator and their descendants. Minor children are entitled to at least three-quarters of their statutory share, adult children to at least a quarter thereof. However, there are features specific to Czech law which are uncommon in other jurisdictions[19] – there is, for instance, no 'clawback mechanism' which is present in some related jurisdictions like Austria, Germany or Switzerland, which means there are no time limitations before the death of the testator for donations *inter vivos* which would cause such gifts or the value thereof to be included in the total estate for the calculation of the forced shares. There is only a three-year time limitation (possibly extendable by the testator) for the inclusion of all gifts to a forced heir among his or her compulsory share. In contrast to certain other jurisdictions, it is thus possible to donate all or part of the assets of the testator, including an enterprise, to a foundation (foundation fund or a trust funds) to avoid forced heirs and their compulsory share. Under the prevailing opinion of legal scholars, it would work similarly for gifts *mortis causa*.

2.1.7. *Conclusion*

It follows from the above that the Czech foundation represents a suitable vehicle for holding business corporations or controlling parts thereof, in particular if the goal of the founder is to contribute to common good via such enterprise holding (public benefit foundation). In case of private benefit foundations holding enterprises, the rules on conflicts of interest between statutory body membership and the position of beneficiaries may be an obstacle, depending on the desire of the family members to be involved in the governance bodies of the foundation. In addition, public benefit foundations may achieve more favourable tax treatment. In both cases, the restricted disposition rights with respect to the foundation endowment may represent an issue in the performance of business activities at the enterprise level.

---

19 K. Ronovská and V. Pihera, 'The unbearable lightness of forced heirship: the Czech perspective' (2018) 24(6) *Trust & Trustees* 547.

However, both types offer relative flexibility in their purpose definition and the subsequent change thereof; their legislative framework provides for a robust governance structure and mechanism of internal supervision and for reasonable asset requirements and asset management rules.

2.1.8. Examples of Practical Use

Having concluded that a Czech foundation may, depending on the goals of the founder, represent a suitable vehicle for use as enterprise foundation, the question then arises as to whether it is used in practice given the missing tradition and despite its historical perception as an entity set up for public benefit causes. Some founders still rely on foreign jurisdictions due to their long tradition in the industry, developed legal environment, additional privacy and a possibly more beneficial tax treatment. For instance, the family of traditional Czech beverage company Kofola[20] has recently decided to contribute their business to a Lichtenstein-based foundation and, according to the company's official statements,[21] the stability of the local legal environment was one of the primary reasons to look abroad.

On the other hand, there are areas in which alternative enterprise ownership forms, such as public benefit foundations, are finding use. One such area is independent quality journalism. According to a study conducted by the Reuters Institute for the Study of Journalism at the University of Oxford in 2011:

> problems afflicting news organisations in many parts of the West [arising from economic pressure of the changing landscape of media and news] are leading to a resurgence of interest in alternative forms of ownership and control of [media companies].[22]

The study found that the primary goals of these alternative ownership forms were the reduction of influences of commercial aspects on content, improvement of sustainability and preservation of core journalistic values.

In the Czech context, there are several publishers operating news organisations which are (or were)[23] either controlled by a public benefit foundation or in which

---

20 The valuation of Kofola was estimated between CZK 5 and 8 billion in 2022.

21 'Majitelé Kofoly zakládají rodinnou nadaci, která má pomoci se zajištěním nástupnictví a správou firmy pro další generace' (21 August 2024) *Kofola*: https://www.kofola.cz/aktuality/majitele-kofoly-zakladaji-rodinnou-nadaci-ktera-ma-pomoci-se-zajistenim-nastupnictvi-a-spravou-firmy-pro-dalsi-generace.

22 D.A.L. Levy, '1. Why look at Charitable and Trust Ownership of News Organisations?' in D.A.L. Levy and R.G. Picard (eds), *Is There a Better Structure for News Providers? The Potential in Charitable and Trust Ownership*, Reuters Institute for the Study of Journalism (University of Oxford), Oxford 2011, pp. 3–18.

23 One of the companies where such an attempt failed was Echo Media a.s., a publishing company established in 2014 which publishes a conservative weekly '*Echo*', a magazine similar

a public benefit foundation holds a relevant, although not controlling, stake. The most prominent of these is the joint stock company N Media a.s. (a publisher of the liberal daily *Deník N* which was contributed by its founders to a public benefit foundation (Nadace Independent Press – Independent Press Foundation)). The purpose of the foundation is to promote 'long-term accessibility of independent quality news, to contribute to the control mechanism of liberal democracy and to cultivate and educate society'.[24] The foundation controls the publisher with 66.7% of voting shares and control is exercised via independent directors at the supervisory board of the publisher in addition to the exercising of shareholders' rights. The foundation holds stakes in other media houses, including the liberal weekly *Respekt*, in which it holds a share of 25%, with the remaining shares owned by similarly minded investors and journalists working for the weekly. Control at *Respekt* is exercised in conjunction with other investors.[25]

The establishment of *Deník N* was inspired by its Slovak predecessor *Denník N*, which was established in 2014 by the core journalists of the daily *SME* in response to a presumed threat of a takeover by the financial group Penta.[26] The protection of independent quality journalism lays also at the heart of the foundation ownership of its Czech counterpart, whereas media companies have become a valuable asset for groups or individuals who may be interested in purchasing them for reasons incompatible with the preservation of their independent news coverage.

Another example of practical use can be found in asset management by the Catholic Church. In 2012, the Czech government passed an act on the restitution of church property confiscated during the Communist regime. The single largest beneficiary of the restitution was the Catholic Church, which then relinquished some of the assets in favour of other minority churches. The total amount of real assets returned was valued at approximately CZK 75 billion; another circa CZK 59 billion is gradually paid in annual instalments. When the total amount is paid off by 2030, state subsidies to the Church cease and Church operations will have to rely primarily on income from investments and for-profit activities. These will

to the British *Spectator* in its political orientation. The majority (of 51%) was owned by the 'Foundation on Freedom of Speech and Expression' whose purpose was 'to protect freedom of speech and democratic principles of the society'. The remaining 49% was owned by an independent investor. The magazine was continuously loss-making since its foundation, and it was entirely acquired in 2021 by an independent investor whose aim is to build a larger conservative media house in the Czech Republic.

24 Article 2.1 of the foundation charter of the Independent Press Foundation available online at Veřejný rejstřík a Sbírka listin – Ministerstvo spravedlnosti České republiky: https://or.justice.cz/ias/ui/vypis-sl-firma?subjektId=1103009.

25 There are three classes of shares with various voting rights. Standard majority for all decisions requires always either all corporate owners to agree, or, if they cannot all agree, all journalist owners must be in favour along with at least two of the three corporate owners for the decision to pass.

26 'V Česku vzniká nový deník inspirovaný Denníkem N' (26 June 2018) *MediaGuru*: https://www.mediaguru.cz/clanky/2018/06/v-cesku-vznika-novy-denik-inspirovany-dennikem-n/.

have to cover not only the personal and maintenance costs of the organisation, but also the costs of its public benefit activities in the fields of healthcare, education and others.

The Church must thus learn to be an 'entrepreneur'. However, given its primary purpose of existence, all gains of such endeavour must serve higher societal goals. Holding assets in enterprise foundations might thus seem ideal from the perspective of long-term duration and public benefit purpose. It may also seem more acceptable to society, which does not traditionally associate churches with for-profit activities.

The business activities of the Catholic Church currently focus on some traditional areas such as wood processing, wineries and breweries. However, it is also venturing into areas such as construction, the running of photovoltaic power plants and real estate development. The Prague Archdiocese, which has recently started implementing the discussed holding structures into its business organisation, has adopted the use of both public benefit foundations and trust funds. So far, it has established public benefit foundations for the holding of assets and businesses which are considered core assets of the Church or activities with a clear public benefit mission (e.g. forestry and church schools).[27] On the other hand, assets and businesses considered potentially disposable (non-core to church activities) are held in trust funds which provide for more operational flexibility.

2.2. FOUNDATION FUNDS

Foundation funds are entities with a legal personality, which were originally meant to serve the purpose of less strictly regulated foundations not necessarily established for an indefinite period of time, whose purpose could possibly be also private. However, as described in section 1.2, this intention of the legislator failed and up until the recodification of the Civil Code in 2014, they were allowed to be set up exclusively for public benefit purposes. Since the 2014 Civil Code reform, they can also be used for private benefit purposes.

2.2.1. Purpose and Duration

Currently, they represent entities belonging to the same corporate group as foundations (*fundace*) but with a higher degree of flexibility in purpose definition, governance and asset management. Their purpose is defined in a broader manner than in the case of foundations as 'any public benefit or economic purpose'[28]

27 There are no special church trusts or foundations within Czech law; general legislation applies also to the for-profit activities of religious organisations.

28 Section 394 of Act No. 89/2012 Coll., Civil Code.

which, unlike in the case of foundations, clearly includes also pure private benefit purposes. However, since they are regulated in the same section of the Civil Code along with foundations, it is derived from higher principles of law that they cannot be set up for business purposes only, nor is it allowed to set them up for self-fulfilling purposes.

Foundation funds are not necessarily set up for long-term duration – long-term duration is not part of their statutory definition. It depends on the will of the founder whether they will be set up for perpetuity or in support of shorter-termed ad hoc projects. For this reason, their establishment does not require the existence of an untouchable income-producing endowment of a minimal required value. Funds supporting their activities can thus be secured on an ad hoc basis. Certain statutory limitations to asset disposal still apply, but all assets can be consumed if it is permitted by the foundation fund's statute.

2.2.2. *Governance*

The internal organisation of a foundation fund is similar to a foundation, but the regulation is less strict. For instance, there are no rules regarding conflicts of interest between the positions on the governing bodies and the ones of beneficiaries, which may be more practical for family foundations holding businesses where family members as beneficiaries desire to participate in the life of the foundation fund also via membership in its statutory bodies.

The governing bodies are identical to the governing bodies of a foundation – a board of directors and a supervisory board (or a single comptroller). Additional bodies can be set up. There are no mandatory rules regarding annual reports or their audits, thus there is a lower degree of forced transparency. This higher degree of privacy may, again, be welcomed by private purpose entities including those holding for-profit corporations. However, their existence is entered into a public registrar just like foundations, along with founding documents and end-of-year financial results. The Register of Foundations plays a similar role of an external supervisory authority as in the case of foundations.

In general, the less precise regulation of foundation funds is interpreted as a feature providing the founder with a greater decision-making power in the design of its functioning rather than as an indication of an indirect application of the rules governing foundations (analogous application can apply where necessary). On the other hand, the lack of precise regulations may lead to issues regarding interpretation.

2.2.3. *Conclusion and Practical Use*

In summary, foundation funds have the advantage of legal personality and a standard corporate governance structure like foundations, which may be appealing to those looking for structures more native to the local legal environment, coupled with more flexibility in design and fewer restrictions. They represent a suitable vehicle for holdings for-profit businesses with the mission being for public or private benefit. Just like foundations, private benefit or mixed-purpose foundation funds cannot become entities with public benefit taxpayer status.

Foundation funds are thus functionally closer to the trust-like structure of trust funds in their flexibility, but unlike trust funds, they are still more commonly set up for public benefit purposes given their historical roots. However, more families are currently considering them as a vehicle for transgenerational wealth transfer, including for holding of family businesses. One recent example is the Matera family from northern Moravia who set up foundation fund PROMET Family Foundation as a vehicle for transgenerational transfer of a family engineering enterprise. According to its founding deed, the foundation fund was established for private benefit purposes, including supporting the needs of the Matera family members.

2.3. TRUST FUNDS[29]

The Czech trust funds represent a specific continental trust-like structure without a legal personality.[30] The Czech version is based on the Québécois *fiducie*/trust, with the ownership of the assets belonging to neither the trust nor the trustee or the beneficiaries, and represents a so-called 'patrimony by appropriation'.[31] The role of a founder in the life of the trust fund is also stronger than the role of a settlor in a typical Anglo-Saxon trust (the founder has, for instance, strong supervisory powers over the trustees), while the position of beneficiaries is somewhat weaker than in a typical trust (the will of a founder prevails over the position of beneficiaries who are not perceived as economic owners of the assets to the same degree as in Anglo-Saxon trusts).[32]

---

29 For more information on Czech trust funds, refer to K. Ronovská, E. Dobrovolná, B. Havel and V. Pihera, *Property and Trust Law in the Czech Republic*, 1st ed., Wolters Kluwer, Alphen aan den Rijn 2020.

30 Some legal scholars argued that legal personality could be derived from legal principles (interpretation of registration of the founding documents as quasi-incorporation). However, the question has been resolved by the Czech Supreme Court in 2020 which confirmed the absence of legal personality.

31 The *fiducie*/trust, introduced in 1991 in the Civil Code of Quebec, is not equivalent to the trust of common law, it rather corresponds to trust-like structures under civil law. It represents a concept of 'patrimony by appropriation' which becomes an autonomous entity – the owner of the property dedicated to the specific purpose intended by the settlor. Its patrimony forms a juridical universality which the law sees as independent of the persons involved with the trust.

32 V. Pihera and K. Ronovská, 'Svěřenské fondy a fundace v desátém výročí nového občanského zákoníku' (2024) Contribution to Conference on the 10th Anniversary of the New Civil Code, Olomouc.

The establishment of a trust fund requires setting aside assets in favour of the trust, the existence of a contract between a founder and a trustee, a statute in the form of a notarial deed and registration in a special registrar of trust funds. The requirement to register trust funds with a registrar was adopted in 2016, two years after the new Civil Code came into force. In contrast to the Register of Foundations, which is freely available online, access to the registrar of trust funds is restricted to those proving legitimate interest.

2.3.1. Purpose and Duration

The purpose of the trust can be 'in the sphere of public benefit or purely private, including in the benefit of a specific person or in their memory'.[33] Public benefit trust funds cannot have business activities as their main purpose. Trust funds can also be set up as investment vehicles. Of the entities discussed in this chapter, the purpose of a trust fund is the broadest of all.

Trust funds are typically set up for a definite period at the end of which the beneficiaries may take possession of the entrusted assets. They may, however, be set up also for an indefinite period. A limit of maximum 100 years of duration applies to private trust funds. It is further possible under Czech law to set up a revocable trust fund. Its usability as a vehicle for an enterprise foundation thus depends on the exact design of the trust fund's structure. The settlor can freely design the trust fund's purpose to include business activities or put herself in the position of a beneficiary as well as one of the trustees.[34] She can also open the trust fund to revocability. Turning it into a suitable holding vehicle for a business corporation would thus require a careful design of the trust fund's structure to best fit the interests of an enterprise foundation. The time limit imposed by law on private trust funds may be of concern.

2.3.2. Governance

The internal organisation of a Czech trust fund consists of a trustee (or a board of trustees), beneficiaries and an elective supervisory or advisory board. Protectors may also be appointed. From the perspective of governance, foundations and foundation funds may represent a more suitable vehicle for holding businesses as they create standard corporate bodies. Their governance structure may also be more suitable for family businesses in which family members are not interested in running the for-profit corporation but would like to remain otherwise engaged in its indirect management, i.e. on the corporate bodies of the holding entity. While trust-like structures may create bodies such as family councils or advisory committees, these may be perceived as less prestigious.

---

33 Section 1449 of Act No. 89/2012 Coll., Civil Code.

34 In such a case, another trustee must be appointed, and they must act in concert.

As mentioned above, trust funds do not possess legal personality. This could possibly be a disadvantage when dealing with more conservative third parties such as banks, which may perceive the possession of a legal personality as a sign of stability and lower risk.[35] However, Czech trust funds share some corporate features with foundations and foundation funds due to their existence being conditioned upon the registration in a registry of trusts, which reduces this difference (foundation and foundation funds come into existence upon their registration as legal entities into the foundation register).

One of the most important differences lies in the rights of beneficiaries. Although the rights of beneficiaries in a Czech trust fund are weaker than in their Anglo-Saxon counterparts, they have firmer rights to the assets of the trust than do the beneficiaries of a foundation or a foundation fund. Depending on the circumstances, these vested rights in assets may compete with the best interest of other stakeholders in an enterprise foundation or the corporation it controls.

2.3.3. *Statutory Changes*

As mentioned earlier, a foundation's statute can be changed in several ways after its founding, including with respect to its purpose. The primary mechanism of such change relies on the rights reserved by the founder or vested into another statutory body by the founder in the statute. The brief regulation of a foundation fund by the Civil Code is interpreted as providing the founder with the autonomy to set up the mechanisms for a change which he/she desires. The only limitation is compliance with good morals and the basic principles of foundation laws.

The regulation of trust funds, on the other hand, does not provide for many opportunities to a later change in the statute. The only possible change envisaged by the Civil Code is a change via a court decision in the case that it were possible to achieve the purpose intended by the founder in a better way. This leads some scholars to the conclusion that no other ways of statutory changes are available. Others argue that the omission of another expressed method should not be interpreted as though there were no other methods left up to the founder. As the interpretation remains unclear, any such change should be approached with caution, in particular should trust funds be used as enterprise foundations.

2.3.4. *Practical Use*

As documented in section 2.3 generally, Czech trust funds have become quite a popular tool in asset management, including in transgenerational wealth transfer involving holding for-profit corporations. They are appreciated for their flexibility, including in relation to asset disposition, and lower visibility to the

35 Assets in trust funds generally represent additional risk factor with banks.

public eye. The initial caution people had in using this form diminished when the tool was used by the then Prime Minister Andrej Babiš for the management of his large business conglomerate, Agrofert a.s., due to new legislation on conflicts of interest between a governmental position and the conduct of business.

3. SUMMARY

It follows from the above comparison that all three entities could serve as enterprise foundations and the specific choice would, in each case, depend on the exact wishes and goals of the founder.

The design of the Czech public benefit foundation most closely resembles the definition of an enterprise foundation as proposed by the European Network of Enterprise Foundations,[36] which has, however, not been adopted by this project. This definition, among other features, requires that there be no individual beneficiaries of the foundation (including no family members with rights to the foundation assets) and that income from the business be used in support of philanthropic activities – features distinguishing such entity from a typical family or other private benefit foundation. In addition, public benefit foundations have long-termism built into their statutory definition as well as permanent income producing foundation endowment such as for-profit enterprise. Their legal standing as entities with obligatory statutory and supervisory bodies, reasonable external supervision, relative flexibility in the adaptation of the statute, including changes to the foundation purpose, financial and ownership transparency vis-à-vis a public register and an advantageous tax regime may all play role in favour of this choice. Certain restrictions, such as rules on conflicts of interest between the position of beneficiaries and the membership in statutory bodies, including limitations in the definition of the foundation purpose (public benefit must prevail over indirect entrepreneurial activities), may not constitute an obstacle to this choice in case public benefit is the raison d'être of such foundation.

If more flexibility is desired, for example, in the design of the entity's purpose or in the composition of the membership on the statutory bodies, and more privacy is required or needed while a standard legal entity with traditional statutory bodies is preferred, a foundation fund with a carefully drafted statute matching the needs of an enterprise foundation mentioned above, in particular a long-term duration, at least a partial public benefit purpose and a permanent income-producing endowment, may be the preferred option. Flexibility may, however, come at the price of losing certain tax benefits.

36 'European Network of Enterprise Foundations to be hosted by Philea' (7 August 2023) *Philea*: https://philea.eu/european-network-of-enterprise-foundations-to-be-hosted-by-philea-from-autumn-2023/.

Finally, trust funds may seem like the best of all possible worlds to some – flexible in their design, with the one potential exception of a later change to the trust fund's purpose, more private to the public eye than the previously mentioned entities and benefitting from a developed legal environment due to their popularity. However, more firmly vested rights of beneficiaries to the assets of the trust make this option inherently less compatible with a pure public benefit purpose. In addition, their governance structure may be perceived as more suitable for entities holding assets in favour of third parties for a defined period rather than for perpetuity.

4. OUTLOOK

The underdevelopment of the foundation sector throughout the 19th and much of the 20th century, as well as a ban on private ownership and entrepreneurial activities during the Communist era, caused a gap in the development of the sphere of family planning via structures such as foundations and trusts. However, with the recent legislative reforms and the first post-revolutionary generation of entrepreneurs entering the phase of transgenerational wealth transfer, one can observe a steady increase in the interest in options available to those contemplating such steps.

Even with the legal infrastructure now in place, it is not guaranteed the market will follow suit. As some practitioners observe, many founders still find it difficult to give up ownership or control in favour of third-party entities and the requirements to reserve as much power as possible are not rare. Nevertheless, the sentiment is gradually changing, with the founders of some the larger enterprises setting the example. At the same time, the attitude towards philanthropy as an integral part of private wealth is changing – it is becoming the norm, in particular among younger business leaders.

Nevertheless, the idea that a company built for generations may end up in a foundation or a similar entity out of the complete control of the founder or his/her family and, in addition, serving primarily public benefit purposes rather than supporting the members of the given family, is far from mainstream thinking. Legislative changes towards the creation of at least partial tax advantages for mixed-purpose foundations or trust funds might help encourage the establishment of such an environment. Such an approach was considered during the initial legislative process by the financial authorities, however, it has not been mentioned since. A growing interest and awareness of entrepreneurs of the entire pool of options may, hopefully, initiate debates regarding useful legislative changes.

ENTERPRISE FOUNDATIONS IN HUNGARY

István SÁNDOR

ABSTRACT

In Hungarian law, foundations play a significant role in economic and social life, and various types are known, which can be categorised based on their purpose and activities. Although the enterprise foundation type is not explicitly recognised, the asset management foundation type could potentially fulfil this function, particularly given the flexibility of the regulations governing foundations in Hungary.

1. A BRIEF HISTORICAL OVERVIEW

1.1. THE PRE-WORLD WAR II PERIOD

In Hungary, foundations played a significant role in society, particularly in the non-profit sector, where they gained prominence by providing an appropriate private law framework for civil cooperation aimed at achieving various public interest goals. Their emergence and historical role are closely linked to this function, which, beyond religiously motivated purposes, gradually expanded to include secular objectives and the management of family wealth relationships.[1] Moreover, the 21st century marked a significant breakthrough in the use of foundations explicitly for private purposes, effectively transforming their historically established role in legal history.

Foundations have been an integral part of Hungarian social and legal life; however, their regulatory framework was developed in the 19th century primarily with a focus on state supervision.[2] The private law rules governing foundations were shaped by judicial practice, much of which was incorporated into the 1928 Private Law Bill. Although the bill never came into force, its provisions were applied in practice on a customary law basis. At the beginning of the 20th century, foundations were primarily distinguished by whether they were established for religious or secular purposes and whether they were public or private foundations. Among the private foundations, one of the most characteristic types was the family foundation. This was primarily distinguished from the entail (*fideicommissum*) in that the assets of a family foundation were not owned by individual family members. Instead, the family members had only obligational rights against the foundation, which was an independent legal entity. In contrast, in the case of a family entail, family members were both possessors and owners of the assets, but an alienation restriction was imposed to protect the interests of family members designated as heirs.

1.2. THE SOCIALIST ERA

The political shift in Hungary after 1948, driven by the rise of socialist ideology, led to the banning of social organisations and the obstruction of their operations.

---

1 See for this I. Sándor, 'Remarks about the History of Foundations' (2021) 12(1) *Journal on European History of Law* 105.

2 See for this I. Sándor, 'The transformation of foundation law in Hungary, with particular regard to private foundations' (2023) 29(6) *Trust & Trustees* 553.

According to the 1949 Constitution, only the party, trade unions, youth organisations and the Patriotic People's Front were allowed to operate as social organisations. As a result, private individuals were not permitted to establish associations (thousands of associations had already been dissolved by a decree of the Minister of the Interior in 1946), and the creation of foundations was also prohibited for the private sphere in 1949.[3] Understandably, the regulation of foundations was omitted from the Civil Code of 1959.[4]

1.3. THE POST-TRANSITION PERIOD

In 1987, the first legislation was enacted that established the private law rules for foundations and placed them within the chapter on legal entities of the old Civil Code.[5] It declared the legal personality of foundations and stipulated that they could only be established for a lasting public interest purpose. Although the regulation covered only the main rules and left many issues to judicial practice, it laid down the framework for modern Hungarian foundation law.[6] The new Civil Code, which came into effect in 2014,[7] placed the private law provisions for foundations in Book III (Legal Entities). It aimed to broaden the framework of private autonomy in this area, particularly with the general rule on the dispositive nature of legal entities.[8] A significant innovation was that it allowed for the establishment of family foundations. One of its main novelties was that it only required a lasting purpose from the foundation, no longer mandating a public interest goal, thereby enabling the creation of foundations for private purposes as well.[9]

In 2019, regulation of asset management foundations (AMFs) was introduced,[10] allowing both existing and newly established foundations to carry out asset management activities for the purpose of fulfilling tasks specified in the founding document or providing financial benefits to beneficiaries. The specific provisions concerning AMFs are contained in a separate piece of legislation,[11]

3 Decree-Law No. 2 of 1949; for a detailed analysis, see Z. Csehi, *A magánjogi alapítvány. Történeti és dogmatikai alapok* [*The Private Law Foundation: Historical and Dogmatic Foundations*], Gondolat, Budapest 2006, p. 87.

4 Act IV of 1959 on the Civil Code of the Hungarian People's Republic; hereinafter referred to as the Old Civil Code.

5 Decree-Law No. 11 of 1987 on the amendment of certain civil law provisions.

6 Z. Csehi, above n. 3, p. 89.

7 Section 3:378-3:404 of Act V of 2013 on the Civil Code; hereinafter referred to as the Civil Code.

8 Z. Csehi, 'Az Alapítvány' ['The Foundation'] in L. Vékás and P. Gárdos (eds), *Kommentár a Polgári Törvénykönyvhöz* [*Commentary to the Civil Code*], vol. I, Wolters Kluwer, Budapest 2014, p. 593.

9 For its international trend see P. Panico, *Private Foundations: Law and Practice*, Oxford University Press, Oxford 2014, pp. 5–8.

10 Hereinafter referred to as AMFs.

11 Act XIII of 2019 on Trust Foundations; hereinafter referred to as the AMF Act.

while the rules of the Civil Code serve as background regulation. AMFs have two subtypes: those established for private purposes and those established for public interest purposes.[12] In the latter case, further special regulation applies to AMFs performing public duties.[13]

According to the database of the Central Statistical Office, the number of foundations in Hungary has consistently been around 20,000 over the past 20 years, although it shows a slight decreasing trend. In 2005, there were 22,255 foundations registered, while in 2023, the number was 19,193.[14] According to the current court registry, in 2025, there were 829 public foundations and 130 asset management foundations.[15]

2. THE CONCEPT AND TYPES OF FOUNDATIONS

2.1. THE CONCEPT OF THE FOUNDATION

In defining the concept of a foundation in Hungary, it is important to highlight that it is an independent legal entity created to achieve a specific lasting purpose.[16] A foundation is a legal entity without owners, an independent legal subject, with assets separate from its founder, manager (representative) and beneficiaries. A foundation can be established for the legal achievement of a lasting purpose, which does not necessarily have to be of public interest. The foundation is independent from its founder (at least in part)[17] and has its own governing body and potentially other organs. Its operation is carried out within the framework defined by the founding document and the applicable laws.

2.2. TYPES OF FOUNDATIONS IN HUNGARIAN LAW

Under the current effective Hungarian law, the following types of foundations are recognised based on their establishment and purpose:

---

12 See for this I. Sándor, 'Key Features of Private Foundations in a Comparative Law Approach: With Special Emphasize on Asset Management' (2021) 29(6) *European Review of Private Law* 885.

13 Act IX of 2021 on public interest asset management foundations performing public duties.

14 See: https://www.ksh.hu/stadat_files/gsz/hu/gsz0012.html.

15 See: https://birosag.hu/ugyfeleknek/civil-szervezetek/civil-szervezetek-nevjegyzeke. It should be noted that the significant number of public foundations includes those established before 2006, when any municipal government could also create a public foundation.

16 This most recent handbook provides detailed information about foundations in Hungarian literature: B. Gábor Szabó, A. Menyhei and I. Sándor, *Az alapítvány: Történeti, tipológiai, működési, adózási és vagyonkezelési omnibus* [*The Foundation: Historical, Typological, Operational, Taxation, and Asset Management Omnibus*], HVG-ORAC, Budapest 2021.

17 See the founder's rights in section 3.5 ('The Founder').

- public foundations;
- political party foundations;
- private foundations, which include family foundations; and
- AMFs, which can be either for private purposes or for public interest, with the latter including those performing public duties.

Starting from 2006, the establishment of a public foundation is only authorised by the government based on specific statutory authorisation.[18] The regulation of public foundations, in this form, has been removed from the scope of the Civil Code, and currently, the framework for their operation is provided by government decrees and other legal regulations established based on specific statutory authorisation. Therefore, the distinction between a public foundation and a private foundation is made based on the founder, not the purpose.

Private foundations can further be categorised based on their specific characteristics.[19] They can be established for public interest purposes or private purposes, and they have additional subtypes. A political party foundation can be established and operated with transparency guarantee rules to support political training, research, scientific and educational activities aimed at promoting citizen awareness, assisting in the formation and expression of the will of the people and developing political culture.[20]

In everyday life, the term 'family foundation' is used to refer to private foundations where the founder, the supporters (associates, joiners) and their relatives can be beneficiaries. The founder and the associate can be beneficiaries if the purpose of the foundation is the care of the founder's scientific, literary or artistic works. Furthermore, the founder's and the associate's relatives can be beneficiaries if the purpose of the foundation is the care of the relative's scientific, literary or artistic works, the care and maintenance of the relative, covering their healthcare costs or supporting their education through scholarships or other means.[21]

An AMF can be established to manage the assets designated by the founder and to use the income derived from these assets to fulfil the tasks specified in the founding document and provide financial benefits to the person or persons appointed as beneficiaries. The AMF can be established for both public interest

18 See, for example, Government Decree No. 1099/2017 (III. 6.) on the establishment of the Otto von Habsburg Foundation and the provision of the conditions and resources necessary for its operation; and Government Decree No. 1859/2017 (XI. 23.) on the establishment of the Wacław Felczak Foundation and the provision of the conditions and resources necessary for its operation.

19 Section 3:378(1) of the Civil Code no longer requires that the foundation's lasting purpose be of public interest.

20 Act XLVII of 2003 on foundations engaged in scientific, educational, research, and informational activities supporting the operation of political parties.

21 Section 3:386(1)–(2) of the Civil Code.

and private purposes. In the case of a public interest AMF, the beneficiaries are not predetermined individuals; instead, the foundation's activities are aimed at achieving specific goals. An AMF is considered to be of public interest if three conjunctive conditions are met: it is established for one of the public interest purposes listed in the AMF Act, the circle of its beneficiaries is open regarding the individuals concerned and the founder has requested its classification as a public interest foundation.[22]

In addition to the previous distinctions, a different type of categorisation for foundations is based on the public benefit status.[23] Public benefit activity is any activity that directly or indirectly serves the fulfilment of a public task specified in the founding document, thereby contributing to the satisfaction of the common needs of society and the individual.[24] The public benefit status grants various tax benefits to foundations, and obtaining and maintaining this status requires meeting a complex set of conditions. It is worth noting that the status of a public interest AMF also entitles the foundation to acquire public benefit status if the foundation requests it.

2.3. THE ENTERPRISE FOUNDATION IN HUNGARIAN LAW

Hungarian statutory law does not regulate enterprise foundations, so we will now examine the legal framework available for the creation and operation of foundations with such a function.

As a general rule, a foundation can carry out any activity not prohibited or restricted by law. A foundation – excluding an AMF – can engage in activities according to its primary purpose and may only engage in economic activities secondarily.[25] Therefore, a foundation – excluding an AMF – cannot be established for the purpose of conducting business activities, and its primary activity cannot be directed toward this.[26] An organisation is considered primarily engaged in economic or entrepreneurial activities if the annual total revenue from its economic or entrepreneurial activities reaches or exceeds 60%

22 Section 4(2) of the AMF Act.

23 The detailed conditions for this are outlined in Act CLXXV of 2011 on the right of association, public benefit status, and the operation and support of civil organisations.

24 Regarding the applicability of social enterprises in Hungary see I. Sándor, 'Social Enterprises in Hungary' in D. Brakman Reiser, S.A. Dean and G. Lideikyte Huber (eds), *Social Enterprise Law. Droit des entreprises sociales: A Multijurisdictional Comparative Review. Une étude comparative multi-juridictionnelle*, Intersentia, Cambridge/Antwerp/Chicago 2023, pp. 275–324.

25 Section 18(1) of Act CLXXV of 2011 on the right of association, public benefit status, and the operation and support of civil organisations.

26 Section 3:379(1) of the Civil Code and section 17(1) of Act CLXXV of 2011 on the right of association, public benefit status, and the operation and support of civil organisations.

of its total annual revenue.[27] If it is determined for a given year that the civil organisation is primarily engaged in economic or entrepreneurial activities, the tax authority may initiate a legality audit procedure against the organisation. A further restriction is that a foundation cannot be an unlimited liability member of another legal entity (e.g. a partner in a general partnership, etc.). Based on the rules outlined above, a foundation can engage in economic activities and hold shares or ownership interests in business entities, but this cannot be its primary activity. Accordingly, the closest equivalent to an enterprise foundation in Hungarian law is the AMF. On the other hand, the primary goal and activity of an AMF is asset management, although it cannot engage in other activities (such as manufacturing, trading, etc.).[28]

In line with the above, we will now specifically examine AMFs in relation to legal regulations governing foundations, with an emphasis on the differences between public interest and private interest AMFs.

3. THE AMF

3.1. ESTABLISHMENT

The establishment of a foundation takes place in two phases. The first step is the preparation of the foundation's deed of establishment and its signing by the founders. The foundation can be created not only through a legal transaction between living individuals but also by a written will or inheritance agreement in the event of death. However, an AMF can only be established with a private document certified by an attorney-at-law or with a public deed.[29] The foundation can be established for a fixed or indefinite period.

In Book III, on legal entities, of the Civil Code, the principle of disposability primarily applies. This means that the founders can deviate from the provisions of the Code in the foundation's deed regarding their relationship with each other and with the legal entity, as well as the rules governing the organisation and operation of the legal entity. However, deviations are not permitted in these areas if they are explicitly prohibited by the Civil Code, or if they would clearly violate the rights of the foundation's creditors, employees or the minority of the founders, or if they would obstruct the proper supervision of the legal entity's lawful operation.[30]

27 Section 2, point 7 of Act CLXXV of 2011 on the right of association, public benefit status, and the operation and support of civil organisations.

28 Section 2(2)–(3) of the AMF Act.

29 Section 9(1) of the AMF Act.

30 Section 3:4(1)–(3) of the Civil Code.

The court makes a decision on the application in a non-litigation procedure, and the foundation obtains its legal personality upon the final registration in the registry. The registry court exercises legality supervision over foundations during their operation as well. The procedure may be initiated by the court *ex officio* or upon request. A request may be submitted by an authority or administrative body authorised to oversee the foundation's activities in the performance of its statutory duties; by a person with a legal interest in the procedure who provides reasonable evidence of such interest; or by a person obligated by law to initiate the procedure.

3.2. PURPOSE

As a general rule, the founding deed must include the foundation's purpose, which must be long-lasting. The goal of the foundation shall be described in a declarative form and, according to judicial practice, the activities the foundation intends to carry out must be defined in a manner consistent with the foundation's purpose, with sufficient precision. The exact definition of the foundation's goal is significant for several reasons. During the registration process, it must be verified whether the foundation's purpose is durable and, if not, its registration may be refused. Furthermore, it impacts the foundation's later operation, as the foundation can only carry out activities in accordance with the purposes specified in the founding deed. It is also crucial that the foundation's assets must be sufficient to achieve its goals. Another important consideration is that the foundation's purposes can only be modified in exceptional cases.[31]

In the case of a public interest AMF, the law exhaustively defines the possible purposes, which include financing or supporting educational, higher education, research, healthcare, charitable, social, family, child and youth protection, cultural, or sports activities, or maintaining and operating institutions that carry out such activities.[32] In contrast, a private purpose AMF may be established for

---

31 'The expansion of the foundation's objectives, in the context of applying section 3:393(1) of the Civil Code, represents a modification of the foundation's purpose. Modifications can only be made if the foundation's original purpose has been realised or if its realisation has become impossible. Nevertheless, the expansion of the objectives may be acceptable in certain cases, provided that it does not jeopardise the achievement of the original foundation's goals (especially if it is accompanied by appropriate financial contributions), but it must not be abusive'. This is the position taken in the 37th resolution of the National Conference of Courts' Civil Law College Heads, held on 18–19 May 2015 ('Conditions for Modifying Foundation's Objectives').

32 Section 4(1) of the AMF Act. Several former state-maintained higher education institutions have been transformed into institutions operated by AMFs. The first of these was the Maecenas Universitatis Corvini Foundation (Corvinus University of Budapest; Government Resolution 1810/2019 (27 December 2019)).

the purpose of providing financial benefits to the person or persons designated as beneficiaries.

A public interest AMF cannot be established for the benefit of the founder, the joiner, the foundation's officers, the members of the foundation's organs or their relatives. This provision is not violated by the compensation paid to the foundation's officers under contract. In contrast, a private purpose AMF may be established explicitly for the benefit of the founder, the joiner and their relatives.

The author of this chapter would like to emphasise the close relationship between the foundation's purpose and its activities. Fundamentally, the foundation can only carry out its activities to achieve its purpose, meaning that any deviation from this may raise issues regarding the civil law liability of the board of trustees and could potentially have tax implications.[33]

3.3. THE ASSETS OF THE FOUNDATION AND THEIR USAGE

It is mandatory to define the amount, timing and method of the financial contribution to be provided to the foundation. While foundations generally do not have specific, quantified asset requirements, for AMFs, a minimum starting capital of HUF 600 million is required,[34] which must be provided to the foundation at the time of its establishment.

During the operation of the AMF, the legal minimum capital must be maintained. The AMF will be dissolved if its assets do not reach the minimum capital amount for three consecutive years; this will be regarded as the impossibility of achieving the foundation's purpose.

3.4. THE ACTIVITY OF THE FOUNDATION

In the case of AMFs, there is a special provision that they can only engage in asset management activities. However, this asset management activity is two way, as the foundation is not only allowed to manage the assets provided by the founder as its own capital, but it is also entitled to establish a separate trust relationship with the founder or third parties. This type of asset management relationship

---

33 It is important to highlight the following case decision: 'Exemption from local (land) property tax for real estate owned by the foundation may only be granted if the foundation uses and utilises the property to carry out the core activities outlined in its founding document'. In the specific case, the circumstances did not justify the determination that the core activities of the foundation were being carried out on the properties in question. Therefore, the claimant foundation was not entitled to property tax exemption for the properties in question under section 3(3) of Act C of 1990 on local taxes. The decision was made in the Supreme Court's ruling No. Kfv. 35.721/2016/9 in an administrative case review.

34 Approximately €1.5 million.

largely corresponds to the concept of a trust under common law and the Hague Convention.[35]

Under Hungarian law, it is also a mandatory rule that the managed assets form separate pools distinct from the assets of the settlor, the trustee and the beneficiary. Furthermore, the trustee is considered an office-holder, the settlor and beneficiary do not have the right to give instructions, and both of them have independent *locus standi* against third parties who acquire assets from the trust assets in bad faith or without consideration (tracing).[36] In the case of the AMF, a so-called hybrid trust structure can be established, the essence of which is that the AMF both manages its own assets and can enter into agreements with the founder or third parties for asset management (trust) in which it acts as a trustee. This trustee function is not the same as the foundation's managing body (board of trustees), as the AMF itself will be the asset manager. In such a trust relationship, the managed assets constitute a separate estate from the AMF's own assets and have an independent legal existence. From the perspective of creditors, full asset segregation takes place, meaning there is no overlap between the AMF's own assets and the trust assets derived from a third party under the trust agreement. For example, the AMF's creditors cannot claim the assets managed by the AMF on the basis of the trust agreement with a third party. The AMF can be a trustee in multiple such trust relationships, and these managed assets form separate, independent estates, which are distinct from each other and from the AMF's

---

35 Convention of 1 July 1985 on the Law Applicable to Trusts and on their Recognition, prepared by the Hague Conference on Private International Law, entered into force 1 January 1992.

36 For detailed information regarding the Hungarian trust in the English-language literature see especially I. Sándor, *Fiduciary Property Management and the Trust: Historical and Comparative Law Analysis*, HVG-ORAC, Budapest 2015, pp. 378–392; I. Sándor, *Property and Trust Law in Hungary*, 3rd ed., Wolters Kluwer, Alphen aan den Rijn 2024, pp. 209–224; Á. Menyhei, and I. Sándor, 'Trust in the Hungarian Law' in I. Sándor (ed), *Business Law in Hungary*, Patrocinium, Budapest 2016, pp. 406–421; I. Sándor, 'The appearance of trust laws in the Eastern part of Continental Europe' in F. Barrière (ed), *La fiducie: assise théorique et applications pratiques. Trusts in civil law jurisdictions: operational and theoretical perspectives. Actes du colloque tenu le 29 septembre 2017 à l'Université Lyon 2*, LexisNexis, Paris 2018, pp. 57–82; I. Sándor, 'The Introduction and Concept of Trust-like Legal Devices in Some Central and Eastern European Countries' in I. Szabó (ed), *Central European Legal Studies: Selected Essays on Current Legal Issues from a Comparative Legal Approach*, vol. 1, Partium, Oradea-Nagyvárad 2023, pp. 95–108; I. Sándor, 'The Phenomenon of Asset Protection Trusts and Their Emergence in Hungary' in T. Nochta (ed), *Central European Civil Law Studies 2024*, Partium, Oradea-Nagyvárad 2024, pp. 31–44; I. Sándor, 'Different Types of Trust-Like Regulations in Eastern Europe – A Comparison' (2016) 66 *Studi Urbinati, A – Scienze giuridiche, politiche ed economiche: Fiducia, trusts, affidamenti. Un percorso storico comparatistico* 437; I. Sándor, 'Different Types of Trust from an Ownership Aspect' (2016) 24(6) *European Review of Private Law* 1189; I. Sándor, 'An Overview of Trust Law in Hungary' (2023) 4 *Zeitschrift für Stiftungswesen* 116; Z. Borbély, 'Thoughts on Understanding the Increased Requirements Regarding the Hungarian Trustee' in T. Nochta (ed), *Central European Civil Law Studies 2024*, Partium, Oradea-Nagyvárad 2024, pp. 173–174; Á. Menyhei, 'Development of the estate planning industry through the introduction of the trust in Hungary' (2016) 22(6) *Trust & Trustees* 660.

assets. This legal structure provides a unique opportunity for the creation of segregated, limited liability sub-assets without legal personality, which can be applied in numerous practical situations (e.g. projects, etc.) and is therefore quite popular.

At the same time, the Hungarian regulation is unique in that it distinguishes between occasional trustees and professional trustee enterprises.[37] Under the Trustee Act, almost anyone can be a trustee, but only in a single trust relationship (so-called 'ad hoc trustee'). If a trustee is involved in multiple trust management relationships, their activity is considered professional, and such activity can only be conducted with the authorisation of the Hungarian National Bank. To obtain this licence, the trustee must meet strict capital, material and personal requirements. Furthermore, if someone is an ad hoc trustee, the trust management relationship must be registered with the Hungarian National Bank.

Trust management relationships established by an AMF are not subject to the Trustee Act,[38] and therefore benefit from various exemptions. It is not considered an ad hoc trustee, so it is not required to register the trust management relationship with the Hungarian National Bank. On the other hand, trust management activity carried out by an AMF is not regarded as professional trust management and thus cannot be classified as a professional trustee undertaking.

If the founder of the AMF has made a unilateral declaration in the founding deed regarding the trust management of the assets, they can validly reserve the right to issue instructions. The trust management relationship does not terminate with the termination of the AMF without a legal successor; it is possible to appoint a new trustee. However, an important limitation is that the AMF must be considered the exclusive beneficiary of the managed assets, and as the beneficiary, it is obliged to manage these assets in accordance with the objectives set out in the foundation's founding deed. However, with a few exceptions, the provisions of the Civil Code regarding trust agreements also apply to AMFs.

In terms of legal structure, the first public interest AMF case is illustrative. In the case of the Maecenas Universitatis Corvini Foundation which took over the operation of Corvinus University, the law and government decree adopted in 2019 provided for the donation of founding assets to the foundation.[39] As its initial assets, the foundation received money, real estate and the university's maintenance rights (as a property right) from the Hungarian state. In addition, the state, as the settlor, transferred shares in two Hungarian blue-chip companies, MOL and Richter Gedeon, along with the dividends attached to those shares,

---

37 A trustee engages in professional trust management activity if they operate under at least two trust management relationships. Section 3(1) of Act XV of 2014 on trustees and their activities; hereinafter referred to as: Trustee Act.

38 Section 2(3)b) of the AMF Act.

39 Act XXX of 2019 on the donation of assets to the Maecenas Universitatis Corvini Foundation and the Budapest Corvinus University. Government Decision No. 1810 of 2019 (XII. 27.) on the Maecenas Universitatis Corvini Foundation.

into the trust of the Corvini Foundation as trustee. The segregation is important because the foundation is free to dispose of its own assets within the framework of the founding document, while the assets received under the trust (shares) are separate. In the case of the foundation's insolvency (liquidation), these trust assets are not considered part of the foundation's liquidatable assets. In the event of the foundation's dissolution or termination without a legal successor, the ownership of these assets reverts to the state. Moreover, the foundation is obligated to perform the trust asset management free of charge for the state, meaning that the costs arising under the trust arrangement can only be accounted for against the received dividends. This structure provides the opportunity for the AMF to have its own assets while also financing its operations from income derived from separated assets (managed assets) without the managed assets serving as collateral for the AMF's creditors in case of insolvency.

3.5. THE FOUNDER

The founder can be either a natural person or a legal entity; however, an important restriction is that a foundation cannot establish another foundation. It is possible for the foundation to be established by multiple individuals together, and in such cases, the founders exercise the founder's rights jointly.[40] In this case, it is not mandatory, but there is the possibility to regulate the founders meeting.

The practice regarding foundations previously regarded the founder's rights as tied to the individual founder, and the transfer of these rights was not considered valid. Moreover, designating another person to exercise these rights was only gradually allowed by the judicial practice. The current Civil Code allows and regulates the possibility for the founder to appoint another person to exercise their rights, or even to transfer the founder's rights to someone else, in the event of the founder's death, dissolution without a legal successor, or if, for any other reason, the founder is permanently unable to exercise their rights.[41] The Civil Code itself creates the transferability of the founder's rights by expressly allowing their transfer. However, it is important to note that such a transfer is only effective if it is registered in the court registry.[42]

The founder can designate another person or even one of the foundation's bodies to exercise the founder's rights. To avoid conflicts of interest, if a body of the foundation is authorised to exercise the founder's rights, the authorised body cannot exercise these rights in relation to its own members, leaders or those in charge of oversight.[43]

---

40 Section 3:395(1) of the Civil Code.

41 Section 3:394(1) of the Civil Code.

42 The reasoning of the judgement No. P. 20.255/2017/45 of the Eger Court.

43 Section 3:394(3) of the Civil Code.

In the case of any AMFs, the founder may designate the board of trustees to exercise the founder's rights, while in the case of a non-public AMF, the founder may also designate the asset supervisor instead of the board of trustees, or if the founder has reserved these rights in the founding document or has not provided any provision regarding this, they may transfer these rights to the foundation itself. The founder may also stipulate in the founding document that their rights will pass to the foundation upon their death, dissolution without a legal successor, or when a specific condition stated in the founding document occurs.

The foundation and its goals may be supported by other individuals beyond the founder, if permitted by the founding document. The legislator grants broad freedom to the founder regarding whether to allow such support and, if so, under what conditions, and whether the supporters acquire any rights with respect to the foundation.[44] A prerequisite is that support can only be provided to a foundation that has already been registered, and the rights and obligations of the supporters are defined by the founding document. It is also possible for the joiner to be authorised to exercise the founder's rights, in which case the joiner may exercise the founder's rights jointly with others authorised to do so.

The founder has the right to withdraw their founder's declaration until the foundation's registration is final.[45] This rule is mandatory, and the founder cannot deviate from it and after the final registration, the founder no longer has this right. After the foundation's establishment, the founder may exert influence over the foundation's operations in two cases: one is the modification of the founding document, which must not harm the foundation's goals. The other important right is the dismissal of persons holding positions in the foundation's bodies, the appointment of new individuals and the determination of their remuneration. However, the founder has no managerial or directive authority over the foundation's operations. There is no obstacle for the founder to be a member of the board of trustees, but in this case, their exercised rights are no longer founder's rights, but executive rights.

For public AMFs, the rules regarding incompatibility between the beneficiaries, the founder and the supporters are applicable, while for private interest AMFs, these rules do not apply.

3.6. THE BOARD OF TRUSTEES

The board of trustees ('curatorium') is the executive body of the foundation, and its members are the foundation's operative officers. The individuals acting on

44 Section 3:383(1) of the Civil Code.
45 Section 3:381 of the Civil Code.

behalf of the foundation are authorised to represent the foundation and manage its internal organisation.

The founder has the right to appoint the members of the board of trustees ('curators') and establish the rules for its operation. The founder has considerable discretion in this regard and may decide whether to appoint an individual or a body for this purpose. The founder is also entitled to determine the rules governing the representative's actions and the board's operations.

For public benefit AMFs, the board must consist of at least five natural persons. In the case of private benefit AMFs, the board must include at least three natural persons, at least two of whom must have a permanent domestic residence.[46] The Civil Code's provision that only natural persons may be members of the board is considered a mandatory rule according to judicial practice. The founder may also appoint a curator for the sole management of a private benefit AMF, and the same rules for the board will apply accordingly.[47]

The board is authorised to make decisions regarding the foundation's management that are not within the founder's scope of authority. Curators are obligated to carry out their executive duties in accordance with the foundation's interests. Board members are, in principle, entitled to challenge certain decisions of the foundation in court if those decisions are unlawful or contrary to the provisions of the founding deed.

The expectations regarding the internal care required from the senior officers and their related responsibilities should be assessed according to the rules of their mandate. Based on their mandate, board members are bound by a duty of care, which may vary depending on whether their work is compensated or voluntary. If they are compensated, their scope for exoneration is narrower, and only circumstances outside their oversight or unforeseen events that make it impossible to mitigate the damage will be considered.[48] If they work on a voluntary basis, the level of care expected is lower, and liability arises only in cases of intent, failure to provide information or fault.[49]

Board members are required to perform their duties with the care typically expected from persons holding such office, and if they cause damage to the foundation, they are liable according to the general rules of civil law. Judicial practice provides several case decisions that can serve as guidance for assessing the level of care expected from board members. This reflects the adoption of the 'business judgement rule' in domestic judicial practice.[50] For instance, a senior officer cannot be held liable solely for making a poor business decision, even if

---

46 Section 3:397(2) of the Civil Code.

47 Section 3:397(5) of the Civil Code.

48 Section 6:142 of the Civil Code.

49 Sections 6:147(1)–(2) of the Civil Code.

50 Á. Fuglinszky, *Kártérítési jog* [*Law of Damages*], HVG-ORAC, Budapest 2015, pp. 136–140.

it causes harm to the legal entity.[51] The senior officer is also not liable for losses incurred by the legal entity during its operations unless the loss was caused by their fault.[52]

3.7. THE SUPERVISORY BOARD

The founders are required to establish a supervisory board consisting of at least three natural persons in the founding deed, with the task of overseeing the management to protect the public benefit AMF's interests. In the case of a private interest AMF, the founding deed may stipulate that the foundation will not have a supervisory board, and in such cases, the duties and powers of the supervisory board are exercised by the foundation's asset supervisor. On the other hand, if the founder of a non-public AMF has designated the asset supervisor to exercise the founder's rights instead of the board of trustees, the appointment of a supervisory board is mandatory. The founding deed may set qualifications, educational requirements, and other professional criteria for the president and members of the board of trustees and supervisory board.

3.8. THE FOUNDATION'S ASSET SUPERVISOR

The foundation's asset supervisor has the right and obligation to monitor the asset management of the foundation in accordance with its objectives, independently of the foundation's supervisory board. In case of an AMF, the designation of an asset supervisor is mandatory in two cases. Both types of AMFs are subject to the rule that if the founder designates the board of trustees to exercise the founder's rights, or transfers those rights to the foundation, an asset supervisor must be appointed. In the case of a private interest AMF, the founder may stipulate that no supervisory board be established; in such cases, the appointment of an asset supervisor is required to exercise the functions of the supervisory board.

The founder may empower the AMF to appoint the foundation's asset supervisor in the founding deed. In this case, the appointment of the asset supervisor is decided jointly by the board of trustees and the supervisory board, but the designation and appointment must be approved by the registering court.[53]

Only an audit firm, auditor, law firm, lawyer or another person with a clean criminal record and a higher education degree in the relevant field specified in

51 Court Decisions, Journal of the Curia of Hungary No. 2004/372.
52 Repository of Court Decisions No. 2008/1767.
53 Section 7(3) of the AMF Act.

the founding deed can be designated or entrusted as the asset supervisor. The founder, members of the board of trustees and supervisory board, the president, other officers, employees, auditors, or beneficiaries of the AMF or their relatives cannot serve as the foundation's asset supervisor. The founding deed may establish additional conflict of interest rules for holding this office.

If the operations or actions of the board of trustees or supervisory board exercising the founder's rights do not comply with the law or the founding deed, the asset supervisor is entitled to call the concerned foundation body to comply with the regulations. If the body does not comply, the asset supervisor may initiate a legality supervision procedure with the registering court.

The asset supervisor has the right to provide an opinion on issues falling within the scope of the founder's rights exercised by the board of trustees. The asset auditor has the same rights as the supervisory board to inspect foundation documents and to access information.

3.9. THE AUDITOR

The AMF is required to engage a permanent auditor. To perform its duties, the permanent auditor may inspect the legal entity's documents, accounting records and books. The auditor may request information from the executive officers, members of the supervisory board and employees of the legal entity and may examine the legal entity's payment accounts, cash registers, securities and inventory, as well as contracts.

If the permanent auditor notices any changes in the foundation's assets that threaten the satisfaction of claims against the foundation, or if the auditor detects circumstances that may lead to the liability of the members of the board of trustees or supervisory board for their activities in those roles, the auditor is required to promptly initiate actions at the board of trustees to make necessary decisions by the exerciser of the founder's rights. If the initiative does not lead to results, the auditor must inform the registering court responsible for overseeing the legality of the foundation about the discovered circumstances.[54]

3.10. OTHER BODIES

The largely dispositive regulation of foundation law allows for the establishment of other bodies as well. The only limitation is that the scope of these bodies'

[54] See Act LXXV of 2007 on the Hungarian Chamber of Auditors, audit activities, and public oversight of auditors.

powers cannot diminish the rights of the board of trustees, the supervisory board or the auditor.[55] In the case of AMFs, this could practically include, for example, an investment advisory committee or another body composed of individuals competent in professional matters.

3.11. THE BENEFICIARIES AND THEIR RIGHTS

Distribution may be granted from the foundation's assets to the person who is designated as the beneficiary in the founding deed, or – if the founding deed does not provide for it – by the competent foundation body. The beneficiary cannot claim any rights against the foundation, except if the founding deed specifies the beneficiary, the distribution they are entitled to and the timing of the performance in the necessary manner, or if the board of trustees has decided on a benefit for the beneficiary, communicated the decision to them and the beneficiary has accepted the conditions of the benefit.

Therefore, the legislator has not provided the beneficiary with a legal title against the foundation's assets that would allow them to assert property rights. If the beneficiary and their entitlement are clearly defined, they can only assert an *in personam* claim against the foundation. However, if there is any uncertainty regarding the beneficiary's claim, it should be considered as an uncertain future claim.[56]

3.12. THE TRANSFORMATION OF A FOUNDATION

It is a mandatory general provision that the foundation cannot change its form, meaning that it cannot transform into another type of legal entity. The foundation can only merge with another foundation and can only split into other foundations, and the general rules for legal entities in the Civil Code must be applied to such procedures.[57] The founder can decide on the merger of the foundation with another foundation or the splitting of the foundation only after fulfilling the provision of assets specified in the founding deed. A further safeguard is that the merger or split cannot result in the depletion of the foundation's assets or endanger the foundation's objectives.

---

55 Section 3:401 of the Civil Code.

56 See for this Z. Steixner, 'Can We Cross the Bridge before We Come to It? Conflict Prevention and Arbitration-based Dispute Resolution in Asset Management Models in Hungary' in T. Nochta (ed), *Central European Civil Law Studies 2024*, Partium, Oradea-Nagyvárad 2024, pp. 185–190.

57 Section 3:402(1) of the Civil Code.

3.13. THE DISSOLUTION OF A FOUNDATION

Under the general rules of the Civil Code, a foundation terminates if:

a) the foundation has achieved its purpose, and the founder has not defined a new goal;
b) the realisation of the foundation's purpose has become impossible, and there is no possibility of modifying the purpose or merging with another foundation; or
c) the foundation has not engaged in activities for the realisation of its purpose for three consecutive years.

In the case of AMFs, these situations are supplemented by a provision stating that if the foundation's assets fail to reach the minimum capital amount for three consecutive years, it must be considered that the realisation of the foundation's purpose has become impossible.[58] According to the general rule of the Civil Code, the founder cannot terminate the foundation.[59] However, a private interest AMF may be dissolved upon the request of the founder.[60] If any of the termination causes occur, the board of trustees must inform the person or body exercising the founder's rights to take the necessary measures, and it must notify the supervisory board and the auditor of the termination cause. If the person or body exercising the founder's rights does not take any action within 30 days, the board of trustees must notify the registering court of the termination cause. The board members are jointly liable for damages arising from the delayed or omitted notification to the foundation and third parties.

In the case of a foundation's dissolution without a legal successor, the remaining assets, after satisfying creditors' claims, will be disposed of by the decision ordering the deletion. In the case of a foundation's dissolution without a legal successor, after the creditors' claims are satisfied, the remaining assets will belong to the person designated in the founding document. However, the assets owed to the founder, joiners, other donors and their relatives cannot exceed the value of the assets donated to the foundation by the founder, joiners or other donors. The founder may allocate the donated assets to a foundation or association with the same or similar purpose as the foundation in the event of its dissolution if the founding document does not dispose of the assets in such a case or the fulfilment of the disposal is impossible. If the founding document or the founder does not allocate the assets upon the foundation's dissolution, or if the designated person or the designated foundation or association refuses to

58 Section 10(1) of the AMF Act.
59 Section 3:403(1) of the Civil Code.
60 Section 11(1) of the AMF Act.

accept or cannot acquire the assets, the registering court will allocate the assets to an organisation defined by law.

In all of the above-mentioned cases, the registering court will determine the occurrence of the event that leads to the foundation's termination in a non-litigation civil procedure.

4. TAXATION ISSUES

The foundation form generally does not result in any differences in taxation compared to other business organisations. If the foundation acquires public benefit status, it may qualify for various tax, stamp duty and customs payment benefits. Among AMFs, those with public interest purposes are automatically considered public benefit organisations upon request. Regarding asset donations to AMFs and the expenditure of such assets, the rules applicable to trusts should be applied, which are particularly favourable.

The establishment of an asset management arrangement is essentially free of charge, as the AMF as trustee does not provide consideration to the settlor or founder for transferring the managed assets. For an individual settlor, the trust agreement leads to a decrease in assets, meaning it does not generate income and therefore does not create a personal income tax obligation.[61] If the settlor is a foreign individual, a tax liability may arise based on the tax laws of their state of tax residence. For a domestic business entity as the settlor, no corporate tax obligation arises if the trust arrangement is recorded in the settlor's books at the book value of the transferred assets.[62] In the case of a foreign legal entity as the settlor, no corporate tax liability arises in Hungary. As a general rule, trust arrangements are not subject to value added tax[63] or stamp duties.[64]

The AMF's identity and own assets must be separated from the managed assets. In relation to the management of the assets, the AMF acts as the legal owner and representative of the managed assets. From an accounting perspective the managed assets are considered as a business entity,[65] and from a tax perspective they are regarded as a taxpayer with their own tax identification number, and they are considered a domestic taxpayer for corporate tax purposes.[66] In this regard, it is important to take into account the statutory exemption from tax

61 The second sentence of section 9(3) of Act CXVII of 1995 on personal income tax. If the settlor is an individual acting as a sole proprietor under the scope of the Act, then it is considered income according to section 49/B(4a) of the Act.

62 Section 40/A of Act C of 2000 on accounting.

63 Section 17(5) of Act CXXVII of 2007 on value added tax.

64 Section 17/D(1) of Act XCIII of 1990 on duties.

65 Section 3(1), point 2 of Act C of 2000 on accounting.

66 Section 6(1), point e) and section 11(2) of Act CLI of 2017 on tax administration; and section 2(6) of Act LXXXI of 1996 on corporate tax and dividend tax.

payments applicable to the managed assets.[67] Since the managed assets are not a legal person or entity, they are not considered a taxpayer for value added tax purposes.[68] In terms of local taxes, the managed assets are also regarded as a business entity, and therefore, they are subject to local tax obligations.[69]

The distribution of assets from the managed wealth to the beneficiary may trigger corporate tax obligations on the side of the managed assets. In assessing this, it is important to distinguish between the initial capital, which is the value of the assets transferred by the settlor to the AMF at the inception of the trust relationship, and the income, which is the profit generated during the asset management.

The distribution of assets from the managed wealth to a beneficiary, whether a foreign or domestic private individual, from the initial capital is exempt from personal income tax in Hungary. However, any distribution from the income of the managed wealth is subject to tax, as it is a transfer of value charged against the reserve, thus qualifying as a dividend.[70] For a foreign resident private individual, the distribution of income from the managed wealth is also considered a dividend which is subject to withholding tax. In this case, the double taxation agreement between the state of the beneficiary's tax residence and Hungary, if applicable, must also be taken into account.

A distribution from the income of the managed wealth to a domestic business entity beneficiary is also considered a dividend, while a distribution of the capital part of the managed wealth to the beneficiary will be treated as other income for the beneficiary.[71] If the beneficiary is the same person as the settlor, there is no tax base; otherwise, tax obligations arise.

From the perspective of duty payments, the legal framework 'looks through' the AMF. The acquisition of the managed wealth and its profits by the beneficiary is treated as if the beneficiary obtained the managed wealth and its benefits directly from the settlor or founder. If, under the trust agreement, the beneficiary paid consideration for the beneficiary's entitlement, the transaction is considered in return for payment and the rules for the duty on onerous transfers of property apply. However, if the distribution to the beneficiary is a gratuitous transaction, which is predominantly the case in practice, it triggers a gift duty obligation, except if the beneficiary is the settlor or the founder of the AMF.[72]

---

67 Section 20(1)(b) of Act LXXXI of 1996 on corporate tax and dividend tax.
68 Section 5(1) of Act CXXVII of 2007 on value added tax.
69 Section 52(26) of Act C of 1990 on local taxes.
70 According to section 66, para. (1), point a), subpoint ae) of Act LXXXI of 1996 on corporate tax and dividend tax; see also section 1, para. (5) of Act LIII of 2018 on social contribution tax.
71 Section 4(28/b) of Act LXXXI of 1996 on corporate tax and dividend tax.
72 Section 17/D(2)–(3) of Act XCIII of 1990 on duties.

5. CONCLUSIONS

The concept of the 'enterprise foundation' is not explicitly recognised as a separate legal category under Hungarian law. However, the regulations governing foundations are generally flexible, and the specific provisions related to AMFs offer a particularly good opportunity for fulfilling the function of an enterprise foundation. Of particular note is the possibility of establishing a hybrid trust in the case of AMFs, which allows for both holding functions and other wealth management activities to be implemented.

In terms of taxation, the public benefit status can provide certain advantages. AMFs enjoy particularly favourable tax and duty payment rules, which further contribute to the interest in this area. Overall, Hungarian foundation law offers a broad range of possibilities for establishing foundations with various purposes and activities. In the case of AMFs, which are closest to the concept of an enterprise foundation, there is significant potential for the development of structures similar to foreign models in this area.

ENTERPRISE FOUNDATIONS IN FRANCE

Sabrina Dupouy

ABSTRACT

Enterprise foundations in France are structures that hold company shares to ensure business continuity while funding public-interest initiatives. There are three forms: '*la fondation reconnue d'utilité publique*' – the public benefit foundation (heavily regulated with high capital); '*le fonds de dotation*' – the endowment fund (flexible and accessible);and '*le fonds de pérennité*' – the sustainability fund (focused on economic stability). They protect against hostile takeovers, preserve corporate identity and support social and environmental commitments. However, French law remains restrictive, often opposing public interest and economic goals. The European Enterprise Foundation model law is a source of inspiration and suggests for example more freedom and sustainability for these models.

1. INTRODUCTION

1.1. ORIGINS OF THE FOUNDATION

The concept of the foundation first appeared in Greek and Roman antiquity: a foundation is independent of its founder and requires, in principle, an irrevocable transfer of property.[1]

But it is traditionally from the opinion of the French Council of State of 24 December 1805 and Article 910 of the Civil Code of 1804,[2] which required public interest establishments to obtain administrative authorisation in order to accept donations and legacies, that the system of recognition of public interest, characteristic of foundations,[3] was really built.

This was followed by Law no. 87-571 of 23 July 1987 on the development of philanthropy, which defined the concept of a foundation in Article 18, para. 1 where it states the following, in general terms:

> A foundation is an act by which one or more natural persons or legal entities decide to irrevocably allocate property, rights or resources to the realisation of a work of general interest and not for profit.

This law created the legal status of the foundation. In 1987, this was the only type of foundation in existence.

Until the passing of this law, the foundation had no legal existence in the French legal landscape. This was due to the historic hostility of the republican state to this institution, which was too contrary to the individualism of 1789.

---

1 H. Souleau, *L'acte de fondation en droit français*, Th. dact., Paris 1968.

2 P.-H. Dutheil, *Juris Corpus Droit des associations et fondations*, Dalloz, Paris 2016, n° 63.01; M. Pomey, *Traité des fondations d'utilité publique*, PUF, Paris 1980.

3 At least the largest and most famous of them.

Whereas foundations had flourished under the *Ancien Régime*, and probably because of this, they were held from 1804 in suspicion by the Civil Code.[4]

Since then, French legislation has been active for several reasons. First and foremost, it was felt necessary to create a new category of legal entity, one that would be able to carry out its activities over the long term, thanks to the autonomy of resources provided by a separate asset base.[5] This patrimonial autonomy makes it possible to choose which philanthropic fields to invest in, while managing the sums invested as closely as possible. Foundation philanthropy is also a means of strengthening family cohesion and unity. Family members can be invited to reflect on the foundation's main principles and methods of action, and to define its areas of intervention. In this way, a foundation can act as a link between different generations.[6] For a variety of reasons, a foundation can also be a means of protecting or even passing on a family business. More generally, the emergence and success of foundations is evidence of a simultaneous retreat of the state and an increase in corporate intervention in the public interest.

However, as we will study below, the notion of shareholder foundation is not defined in French law. Indeed, the legislator has not given a general definition of the notion of foundation, as he has done for example for a '*société*' (a company) in Article 1832 of the Civil Code.[7] However, it is accepted that several conditions must be cumulatively met, and this applies to all types of foundation: the creation by a single founder, whether an individual or a legal entity; an irrevocable allocation of assets, rights or resources (gifts) at inception (initial endowment) or during its lifetime (additional endowment or resources); non-profit-making; realisation and/or support of actions of general interest; and simple governance based on a governing board or equivalent. Thus the advantages of a shareholder foundation are various. First, the shareholder foundation protects the company's capital through the irrevocable nature of the transfer of shares to the shareholder foundation (which can be reinforced by inalienability clauses). Second, the holding of capital provides the foundation with regular income. The third advantage lies in the tax benefits.

Nevertheless, the economic role of foundations is not as far-reaching as it could be. There are several reasons for this, perhaps the lack of a legal basis, the fear of deviating from the very nature of the foundation, or the need for a

4 A.-S. Mescheriakoff, 'Notion de fondation en droit français' (2025) *Lamy Associations*, n° 805-2.

5 D. Roskis, 'Fondation d'entreprise' (2017) 1 *Revue d'économie politique*, p. 285.

6 J. Mestre and S. Dupouy, 'Par-delà les générations: la structure juridique de la foundation' in A.-L. Fabas-Serlooten, S. Lacroix-de Sousa and J. Mestre (eds), *Les Juristes au soutien du transgénérationnel*, Mare&Martin, Le Kremlin-Bicêtre 2023, p. 285, especially p. 287.

7 Article 1832: 'A company is formed by two or more persons who agree by contract to allocate assets or their industry to a business enterprise in common, with a view to sharing the profits or benefitting from any savings that may result. In the cases provided for by law, it may be set up by an act of will by a single person. Partners undertake to contribute to losses' (translated).

reference point. As French positive law is not a complete set of rules, there is a degree of legal uncertainty and lack of clarity on some issues. If necessary, the judge will have to decide a question by relying on other branches of law, such as contract law, company law or the law governing associations.

There are three types of legal structure[8] that fulfil the functions of a shareholder foundation: *le fonds de dotation* (the endowment fund), *la fondation reconnue d'utilité publique* (the public benefit foundation) and *le fonds de pérennité* (the sustainability fund). All three of them can be majority or minority shareholders.

The first is *la fondation reconnue d'utilité publique* (the public benefit foundation), which has been authorised to hold shares since 2005. In 2008, *le fonds de dotation* (the endowment fund) was created, offering more or less the same advantages as the public benefit foundation, but with much greater flexibility. The formalities involved in setting it up and the rules governing its operation are far less demanding, and in this respect, it is enjoying great success today. There were 2,665 'active' endowment funds in 2023.[9]

One of the major differences between the public benefit foundation and the endowment fund is the size of the initial endowment. The average initial endowment for the public benefit foundation is €1.5 million, while that for the endowment fund is just €15,000.

Then, more than ten years later, in 2019,[10] two new legal regimes were created to encourage the development of responsible capitalism: *les sociétés à mission* and *le fonds de pérennité* (the sustainability fund). This fund is constituted by the free and irrevocable contribution of capital securities – shares or corporate units – of one or more companies carrying on an industrial, commercial, craft or agricultural activity, with philanthropic activity optional.

According to Bruno Le Maire (Minister of the Economy, Finance, Industrial and Digital Sovereignty from 2017 to 2024) during the debates before the special commission of the National Assembly, 'the objective is to ensure the transmission and sustainability of our businesses, particularly family businesses'.[11] According to Le Maire:

> this new structure must be clearly distinguished from foundations recognised as being in the public interest or endowment funds, which have a philanthropic purpose: it will primarily have an economic vocation, which is to guarantee the long-term stability of companies.[12]

---

8 We will explore these legal regimes further below.

9 C. Amblard (updated by S. Couchoux), 'Les fondations d'entreprise en chiffres' (2024) *Lamy Associations*, n° 815-1.

10 Law no. 2019-486 of 22 May 2019 on the growth and transformation of businesses (PACTE).

11 Sénat (J.-F. Rapin), 'Rapport n° 207, fait au nom de la commission des affaires européennes sur le projet de loi relatif à la croissance et à la transformation des entreprises' (2018–2019).

12 Ibid.

The *fonds de pérennité* is a kind of antechamber to the shareholder foundation. It is a laboratory, a status that enables us to try our hand at the shareholder foundation. The pursuit of a general interest is optional, and dissolution is possible. With this fund, founders can try the adventure of a shareholder foundation and, if they do not like the idea, they can walk away. In fact, if the founders find that the commitments required are too great or do not correspond to their real aspirations, they can use this fund as a simple economic management tool, like a holding company.

1.2. DEFINING THE SCOPE OF THE STUDY

In the chapter 'Introduction' (earlier in this volume), written by Anne Sanders and Steen Thomsen,[13] it is explained that the definition includes not only foundations in a classical sense, but also other legal structures employed to construct long-term oriented action. According to Anne Sanders and Steen Thomsen,[14] the most important point is that the enterprise foundation controls a business either as a shareholder or administrates a foundation directly.

In accordance with this definition of 'enterprise foundation', we do not include *la fondation d'entreprise* (the French corporate foundation) in this chapter. *La fondation d'entreprise* has existed since a law was passed in 1990:[15]

> Any civil or commercial company, as well as public establishments of an industrial or commercial nature, cooperatives, provident institutions and mutual societies, may set up a non-profit legal entity, known as a company foundation, with a view to carrying out a work of general interest.

This type of foundation has proved highly successful in practice, and there are now more than 400 of them. Among the largest are the foundations set up by EDF, GDF, Louis Vuitton, Alstom, Vivendi, L'Oréal, Danone, Orange (formerly France Télécom), Cartier and others. The Louis Vuitton Foundation,[16] for example, has been committed to art, culture and heritage for almost 25 years. The Hermès Foundation, for its part, is committed to the public interest in four areas: passing on know-how, creating works of art, protecting the environment and encouraging

---

13 A. Sanders and S. Thomsen, 'Introduction' S. Thomsen and A. Sanders (eds.), in *Enterprise Foundation Law in a Comparative Perspective*, Intersentia, Cambridge 2023 p. 1, esp. p. 2.

14 Ibid., p. 2.

15 Law no. 90-559 of 4 July 1990 creating company foundations and Decree no. 91-1005 of 30 September 1991.

16 See 'Un lieu dédié à la création', *Fondation Louis Vuitton*: https://www.fondationlouisvuitton.fr/fr/fondation.

acts of solidarity.[17] The KPMG Foundation, which supports initiatives that contribute to the social and professional integration of disadvantaged groups.[18]

According to Article 19-2 of Law no. 87-571, a foundation is established for a fixed term of more than five years, and may be renewed for a period of at least three years, possibly with the support of new founders. At the end of this period, the founders or some of them may decide to extend the foundation for a further period of at least three years. Founding companies must commit to a multi-year program of action, with a value of at least €150,000 euros. This sum may be paid in instalments over a maximum period of five years. However, a corporate foundation may not make public appeals for donations, nor receive gifts or bequests (except in the case of donations from employees of the founding company or group). Under the terms of Article 19-9 of the same law, corporate foundations are required to draw up an annual balance sheet, income statement and notes to the accounts, which must be submitted to a statutory auditor. Article 19-10 of the same law entrusts the administrative authority with the task of ensuring that the corporate foundation is operating properly and stipulates that every corporate foundation must send the administrative authority an annual report, together with the auditor's report and the annual financial statements.[19]

With regard to shareholdings per se, it is interesting to note that Article 19-3 of Law no. 87-571 stipulates in para. 6 that if the corporate foundation holds shares in founding companies or companies controlled by them, it may not exercise the voting rights attached to these shares.[20] Despite this ability to hold equity interests, the corporate foundation cannot be qualified as a shareholder foundation for several reasons. First of all, because it is created by the company, there is a risk of confusion between the corporate purpose of the corporate foundation and the interests of its founders, who, it should be remembered, are first and foremost companies. This point is all the more important as the corporate foundation is increasingly becoming the social arm of a company's corporate social responsibility (CSR) approach, with the attendant risk of 'gender confusion'. Then, at the time of extension, the founders commit to a new multi-year action programme, as defined in Article 19-7, and, if necessary, supplement the endowment defined in Article 19-6. This is the main difference between this type of foundation and the shareholder foundation, whose activities are necessarily

17 See 'La Fondation' (2021) *Fondation d'Entreprise Hermès*: https://www.fondationdentreprise hermes.org/fr/la-fondation.

18 J.-L. Chaussende, 'Témoignage. La démarche de la fondation d'entreprise KPMG France' (2012) 461 *JA* 33.

19 C. Debbasch, 'Le nouveau statut des fondations: Fondations d'entreprise et fondations classiques' (1990) *D.* 269.

20 This *de jure* exclusion of any possibility of active management of the company held by the foundation clearly demonstrates that the legislator had, in the case of the corporate foundation, identified active management as incompatible with the exercise of the foundation's general interest mission, implying disinterested management and non-profit-making.

more long term. Lastly, unlike the charitable foundation, whose creation is always disinterested, the corporate foundation stems, on the contrary, from the desire to institutionalise the patronage actions of an industrial or commercial company. More precisely, in today's competitive, media-driven society, 'companies are faced with a new imperative: to improve their communication'.[21] The corporate foundation creates value for the company by enhancing its image. Corporate philanthropy through the corporate foundation is thus recognised as a corporate communications strategy.[22]

Since the term enterprise foundation tends to cause misunderstandings in the French discussion, we use the term shareholder foundation (*fondation actionnaire*).

2. THE CONCEPT OF FRENCH SHAREHOLDER FOUNDATION

No article of law defines what a shareholder foundation is. There is a general agreement that a foundation is an irrevocable allocation of assets to realise a work of general interest. Upstream, the company owner dispossesses him/herself by donating all or part of his/her shares to a foundation created for this purpose. Downstream, the foundation supports public interest causes, notably through the dividends it receives from the company. The shareholder foundation is special in this respect, because in addition to the philanthropic action usually entrusted to a foundation, it is also entrusted with the mission of protecting the company that has been donated to the foundation, in line with a certain strategy and values: 'The aim is to safeguard the values of a company and give it an extra soul'.[23] They include large companies such as Pierre Fabre, as well as small and medium-sized companies. A review of relevant literature indicates a commonality amongst the subjects of interest in the presence of a visionary entrepreneur who exhibits a marked humanist tendency.[24] There are different types of companies that are likely to turn to a foundation as a shareholder: the family business handed down from generation to generation, the fast-growing startup (which wants to preserve

---

21 Sénat (P. Laffitte), 'Rapport n° 213, fait au nom de la commission des Affaires culturelles sur le projet de loi relatif aux fondations et modifiant la loi n° 87-571 du 23 juillet 1987 sur le développement du mécénat' (1990), p. 22. 'Une bonne communication est nécessaire pour que les personnels de l'entreprise, les clients, les pouvoirs publics, les médias aient le sentiment de mieux la connaître. Il est devenu difficile sinon impossible à une grande entreprise de rester silencieuse' (p. 7).

22 Ibid., p. 9.

23 A. Jevakhoff and D. Cavaillolés, 'Le rôle économique des fondations' (April 2017) *IGF Rapport* N° 2017-M-008, p. 27.

24 V. Seghers, G. Ferone Creuzet and E. Nordstrom, 'La fondation actionnaire, un levier de transmission et de contribution des entreprises au bien commun' (October 2023) *RLDA* 7813.

certain values without worrying about future fundraising), or any company that wants to ensure that social and environmental issues are considered in its business activities in a more sustainable way.

Some basic rules to be observed when setting up a foundation are the same for shareholder and non-shareholder foundations. All foundations in France must comply with certain formalities when they are set up. For a foundation to get legal capacity, a specific procedure must be followed. It is an approval by decree of the Council of State, or an administrative authorisation.

Shareholder foundations are non-profit organisations, but they can manage a business directly – around 20% to 30% of the organisation's total funding. However, to avoid the risk of losing its non-profit status, the company may be forced to turn its activities into a subsidiary. The purpose of this profit-making activity is the funding of the foundation's activities which are of general interest.

That is why there is a controversy about what a shareholder foundation is. Some representatives of public benefit foundations[25] (which can be shareholder foundations when it holds shares in a company) assume that only this type of foundation is a shareholder foundation, because it is subject to administrative control through the presence of state representatives on its governing board. The non-profit nature of the public benefit foundation is reinforced by its tax status. The public benefit foundation is exempt from business taxes. Donations made by taxpayers benefit from tax reductions equal to 66% of their amount, up to a limit of 20% of taxable income for those made by individuals, and 60% of their amount, up to a limit of €20,000 or 0.5% of sales when they are made by companies subject to income tax or corporation tax. Donations and bequests made by individuals are also exempt from transfer duties and are eligible for a reduction in the property wealth tax (IFI) up to 75% of their amount, up to a limit of €50,000. According to certain schools of thought, this disinterested management justifies tax exemption and is proof of foundation character. In our view, this is an outdated conception of the notion of general interest. We believe that shareholder foundations have a hard time fitting into the French legal landscape because of this requirement that non-profit activities be predominant. However, the most important thing is that profits from profit-making activities should be allocated to general interest projects carried out by the shareholder foundation. The French vision of the public interest therefore needs to evolve, especially at a time when public interest causes are increasingly supported by structures with hybrid financing methods such as shareholder foundations.

Furthermore, the shareholder foundation's function is not limited to the realisation of a work of general interest. To achieve this goal, it also plays a more original role, that of a shareholder that enables it, among other advantages, to

---

[25] See below for a definition.

secure a permanent source of funding. And it is precisely this role of shareholder that is difficult to establish in the French tradition.

In France, it is difficult to fully accept the concurrence of interests between the general interest and the economic interest. In other words, the notion of the shareholder foundation, as it exists in Denmark, has difficulty taking root.[26]

It is generally accepted that the sole mission of a foundation, even a shareholder foundation, is philanthropic. For the tax authorities, for example, the fact that a shareholder foundation holds shares in a company is a means to an end, and nothing more. In short, in French thinking, a shareholder foundation serves the general interest, not the particular interest of the company in which it is a shareholder. Of course, it benefits from advantages and facilities, in terms of taxation or legacy, but that is where it ends.

The way the Pierre Fabre Foundation, a major public benefit foundation, is run reflects this idea. The Pierre Fabre Foundation holds its stake in Pierre Fabre through a 'passive' holding company, Pierre Fabre Participations, which is not involved in the operational management of the Pierre Fabre Group.[27] The governing board of Pierre Fabre Participations is made up of members appointed for life and any co-option of a new director is subject to the approval of the Pierre Fabre Foundation. The Pierre Fabre Foundation and the company Pierre Fabre Participations have the same chairperson.

And yet, after discussions with the heads of other shareholder foundations, it is *possible* and *even necessary* to be both philanthropically oriented and at the service of the company's performance. In fact, there is a gap between the image of the French-style shareholder foundation, which focuses exclusively on the general interest, and the expectations of certain business leaders. Perhaps this is why the shareholder foundation is not yet very popular with French companies, because such an image can be discouraging to economic actors.

Indeed, to be very attractive in the context of ecological crisis and competitive pressures, a legal vehicle cannot be just philanthropic. Some major companies, such as Pierre Fabre Laboratories, have set up shareholder foundations, and, even if the economic interest of society is not clearly expressed, it does exist. And yet the two are intimately linked: the general interest of the foundation is intimately linked to the private interest of the foundation. For example, each year, the foundation, as a shareholder, decides how much of its profits are to be reinvested in the company and how much is to be raised for its public interest initiatives. The amount that can be allocated to community projects thus depends on the company's performance.

However, French law has never declared that sponsorship and shareholder status are incompatible for a foundation. In other words, the fact that a

26 Prophil, 'Voyage au pays des fondations actionnaires' (March 2015).

27 See 'Notre actionnariat' (2025) *Laboratoires Pierre Fabre*: https://www.pierre-fabre.com/fr-be/notre-groupe/notre-actionnariat.

foundation is a shareholder in a company does not deprive it of the tax benefits associated with general interest. More precisely, the application of the 'common law' sponsorship tax scheme set out in Articles 200-1-b and 238 bis-1-a of the French General Tax Code requires six conditions to be cumulatively met by a foundation in order for it to benefit from the advantageous general interest tax scheme. The first condition is laid down by law, while the others are set out in tax administration doctrine. First of all, the foundation must be involved in one of the fields covered by the General Tax Code: art, culture, heritage, social, environmental, education, higher education, research, amateur sport, etc. Finally, it must act or support actions in France or in the European area (with exceptions for humanitarian or environmental projects, or those contributing to the promotion of French culture, language or scientific knowledge abroad).

Lastly, one shareholder foundation can be transformed into another. This is the case for the sustainability fund, whose net assets are transferred on dissolution to a beneficiary designated in the foundation's by-laws, another sustainability fund, the public benefit foundation or an endowment fund.

3. THE THREE TYPES OF FRENCH SHAREHOLDER FOUNDATION

Funds and foundations held €40 billion in assets in 2021, an increase of 37% over the 2017–2021 period.[28]

3.1. THE PUBLIC BENEFIT FOUNDATION

Defined by Article 18 of Law no. 87-571, a foundation is recognised as being in the public interest by decree of the Council of State. This is a demanding condition. It may receive donations and bequests from individuals or legal entities other than the original founders. In principle, it is created 'for eternity'. It must carry on the personality of the deceased founder, who wished to 'defy death'.[29]

Like all foundations, the public benefit foundation must have a real public interest objective. And, in application of the principle of speciality of the foundation provided for in Article 18-3[30] and its restrictive interpretation by the French Council of State, the corporate object of the company must be similar to that of the foundation.[31] To guarantee its independence and longevity, it must

---

28 Observatoire de le Philanthropie, *Les fondations et fonds de dotation en France, Enquête nationale 2001–2022*, 6th ed., Fondation de France, Paris 2023, p. 27.

29 M. Pomey, above n. 2, p. 83.

30 Law no. 87-571 of 23 July 1987 on the development of philanthropy.

31 CE, avis, 24 mai 1977, Rec. CE 1977, p. 418.

also have a very substantial endowment, with a minimum capital of €1.5 million, paid out over a maximum period of ten years from the date of its creation[32] and which is legally irrevocable.[33] Although the French Council of State has never ruled on the amount, a minimum endowment of around €1.5 million is required.[34]

The Council of State's standard foundation by-laws of 22 April 2020 state that:

> the income from the endowment must be sufficient to finance the foundation's corporate purpose. This financing can be presumed to be sufficient when the endowment reaches at least one and a half million euros and in view of the resources forecast over the last three years of operation. Beyond this amount, it is recommended that other financial and real estate assets held by the foundation be allocated to a reserve fund.[35]

If the endowment is the result of payments spread over ten years, as authorised by the amended 1987 law, these payments must be effective, failing which recognition as a public utility may be withdrawn by the administrative authority. The founder may decide to pay out the endowment in instalments, according to a schedule laid down in the by-laws. In this case, the by-laws must specify the number of instalments, their amount, the founder required to make them and the payment schedule.[36] Failure to comply with the payment schedule laid down in the by-laws may result in withdrawal of recognition as a public benefit foundation and dissolution of the foundation (standard by-laws, Article 13). The endowment cannot be taken over, even if the foundation is dissolved. But this principle does not mean that the endowment is inalienable. In other words, if it is appropriate to sell certain elements of the endowment, the by-laws can provide for this and ensure that the assets disposed of are replaced by those obtained or acquired in return. In addition, practice has seen the development of temporary donations of usufruct, which enable a foundation to obtain regular income. In such cases, the irrevocability of the endowment does not prevent the return of the usufruct to the settlor at the agreed term. In order to undertake the activities for which it was established, the foundation may, over time, utilise the assets received at the time of its inception. This is known as a consumable endowment. It is also possible to retain the assets received and use the income from these assets.

There are several principles governing the formation and life of the foundation. First of all, as mentioned above, there is the principle of speciality.

---

32 Law no. 2003-709 of 1 August 2003 on sponsorship, associations and foundations.

33 S. Couchoux and A. Vinas, 'Les fondations reconnues d'utilité publique' (2025) *Lamy Associations*, n° 809-14.

34 C. Nouel, 'Les "fondations actionnaires"' (2020) 2 *BJS* 49.

35 Article 11, note no. 29.

36 Article 11, no. 32.

Recognition as a public utility requires compliance with the principle of speciality, which stipulates that the activities of any public non-profit establishment must be strictly in line with its purpose, otherwise it will lose its nature.[37]

The 1987 law does not specify how public interest foundations are to operate. As a result, governance is governed by the foundation's by-laws and internal regulations. The foundation's governance can be organised around the usual governing board or a supervisory board and a management board.[38] However, another characteristic principle of the foundation, the principle of independence of the foundation from its directors, requires a certain degree of organisation. The composition of the foundation's governance must respect this principle of independence in order to obtain and maintain recognition as a charitable organisation. The practical consequences of this principle of independence are far-reaching. In application of this principle, a foundation recognised as being in the public interest is independent, founded and endowed by its founders, is not dependent on anyone, serves no particular interest and is not, directly or indirectly, managed exclusively or principally by its founders.

The independence of a public benefit foundation from its founders is based on the principles of the Civil Code relating to gifts, in particular Article 893, which states that 'a gift is an act by which a person disposes of all or part of his property or rights free of charge for the benefit of another person …', and Article 894, which states that 'a gift inter vivos is an act by which the donor disposes of the thing given …', which can only be derogated from by law. In consequence, the Conseil d'État, in its doctrine and in the standard by-laws of public benefit foundations, prohibits founders or their representatives from holding more than a third of the positions on the foundation's governing board or supervisory board (depending on the chosen mode of governance), and therefore from holding a majority in the decision-making body, but it now even seeks to oust their heirs or successors as much as possible, or even to make them disappear altogether.

La Fondation des Treilles (the Foundation des Treilles) case illustrates the legitimate fear that this legal organisation arouses in its founders. The Fondation des Treilles was created by Anne Gruner-Schlumberger and recognised as a charitable organisation in 1986 to manage a centre for study and research in the fields of science, literature and the arts. On the death of its founder and

---

37 H. Ripert, *Le principe de la spécialité chez les personnes morales de droit administratif: son application en matière de dons et legs* (thesis) 1906.

38 A. Verjat, 'Fondations d'utilité publique. Gouvernance de la fondation' in P.-H. Dutheil, above n. 2, n° 63.124: 'The Governing board is a sovereign body which appoints the officers, decides on delegations of powers, adopts all decisions and oversees their implementation. Public interest foundations operating with a governing board under the control of a supervisory board have what is known as "two-headed governance", as the functions of management and control are clearly separated and entrusted to two distinct bodies. It is therefore a case of two-headed executive power, a principle inspired by corporate law'.

in accordance with her wishes, her granddaughter was appointed president. However, following differences of opinion between the board members and another foundation set up by the same founder, the Fondation des Treilles statutes were amended for the first time in 2004, at the request of the Conseil d'État, to reduce the number of family representatives – the founders' college now comprising just three members, in accordance with the 'three-thirds' rule, with four *ex officio* members and five qualified personalities. Most surprising of all, however, is the appointment of a Councillor of State as president of the Foundation.

The Minister of the Interior's decree approving these changes to the by-laws was first challenged before the administrative courts on the grounds of *ultra vires* non-compliance with the founder's wishes and misuse of procedure. However, the Conseil d'État rejected this request in a ruling dated 16 April 2010,[39] stating that:

> the arguments based on the fact that the amendments made to the foundation's by-laws disregard the founder's wishes cannot be usefully invoked in support of an appeal for excess of power.

According to lawyer Xavier Delsol,[40] the conclusions of the public rapporteur in this case are likely to discourage people wishing to set up a public benefit foundation and invest themselves personally:

> The French concept of foundations recognised as being of public utility is dominated by the principle of non-patrimoniality: in other words, once the foundation has been set up, it must escape the exclusive control of the founder … We believe that by submitting to the administrative authorities for approval a project that conforms to these standard statutes, the founder should be deemed to have accepted in advance that, through successive modifications, the public utility of the foundation may evolve in a direction that he or she had not necessarily wished.[41]

In 2005, a parliamentary amendment was introduced into a law relating to companies, known as the *loi Dutreil*[42] with the aim of securing the transfer of the majority of shares in Laboratoires Pierre Fabre to a public interest foundation. It was done especially for Pierre Fabre. Before that amendment, it was illegal for a public interest foundation to hold shares. In the past, a public benefit foundation was not allowed to hold all or part of the capital of a company with an economic purpose because of its public interest nature.

---

39 CE, 16 avril 2010, n° 305649.

40 X. Delsol, 'Quelle gouvernance pour les Fondations RUP? Un plaidoyer pour les fondateurs' (2011) 448 *Juris associations* 34.

41 CE, 16 avril 2010, n° 305649, conclusions of the public rapporteur.

42 Law no. 2005-882 of 2 August 2005 in favour of small and medium-sized enterprises.

Consequently, Article 18-3 was incorporated into the French legislation on corporate philanthropy,[43] which stipulates that:

> in the context of the sale or transfer of a company, a foundation recognised as being in the public interest may receive shares in a company with an industrial or commercial activity, with no limitation on the threshold or voting rights, provided that the foundation's principle of speciality is respected.

After that, the Law of 22 May 2019, (*Loi PACTE*)[44] gave a new, broader wording, since it was no longer necessarily linked to a transfer transaction. The first paragraph of Article 18-3 of Law no. 87-571 now stipulates that:

> A foundation recognised as being in the public interest may receive and hold shares in a company carrying on an industrial or commercial activity, with no limit on capital or voting rights.

In more detail, the second paragraph of Article 18-3 states that:

> A foundation recognised as being in the public interest may receive and hold shares in a company with an industrial or commercial activity, without limitation as to capital threshold or voting rights. When these shares give the foundation control of the company within the meaning of Article L. 233-3 of the French Commercial Code, the foundation's by-laws must specify how, in application of the principle of speciality, the foundation will manage these shares without interfering in the management of the company, and the conditions under which the foundation will decide, in particular, on the approval of the company's accounts, the distribution of its dividends, the increase or reduction of its capital, as well as on decisions likely to lead to a modification of its by-laws.[45]

When these shares give the foundation control of the company according to Article L233-3 of the French Commercial Code, the foundation's by-laws must specify how, in application of the principle of specialty,[46] the foundation manages these shares without interfering in the management of the company. They must also specify the conditions under which the foundation is to vote on the approval of the company's financial statements, the distribution of dividends, the increase or reduction of its capital, and on decisions likely to entail a modification of its by-laws.

La section de l'Intérieur deduced from these terms that the principle of speciality governing a public interest foundation does not prohibit it from

43 Law no. 87-571 of 23 July 1987 on the development of philanthropy.
44 Law no. 2019-486 of 22 May 2019 on the growth and transformation of businesses.
45 Law no. 87-571 of 23 July 1987 on the development of philanthropy.
46 The principle of speciality is set out in Article 18-3 of Law no. 87-571 of 23 July 1987 on the development of philanthropy.

exercising control over a company with an industrial or commercial activity in a field unrelated to the general interest mission which justified its recognition as a public interest establishment, but it does oblige it to exercise its rights as a shareholder or unitholder under conditions specified in its by-laws and designed to ensure that the foundation does not interfere in the management of the controlled company, that it operates in a disinterested manner and that it devotes itself exclusively to fulfilling its mission, while taking care to preserve the value and yield of the assets that enable it to finance its activity.[47]

In order to comply with this legal provision and for tax reasons, it could be necessary to interpose a holding company between the two entities in the event of a foundation holding a majority stake in a commercial company. The Varenne Foundation,[48] for example, was recognised as a public benefit foundation a long time ago, by decree on 7 October 1988. Today, it is the majority shareholder in the La Montagne press group. Its aim is to promote the press and communication in all its forms, to encourage young people to enter the professions and trades of the press, and to provide moral or material assistance to all professionals in the sector, active or retired, and their families. It helps to promote democracy, tolerance and good press and communication practices, through its many local initiatives.

Another example, the Christophe et Rodolphe Mérieux Foundation[49] holds a 32% stake in Institut Mérieux. The Mérieux Foundation bases its action on historical expertise in clinical biology and a global approach to public health issues, with one objective: to fight in the field against infectious diseases affecting developing countries.

Also, the Avril Foundation[50] was recognised as a public benefit foundation by decree on 11 December 2014. The Avril Foundation supports the transition of agriculture towards models that create sustainable economic, social and environmental value, and works in the regions to promote healthy, sustainable food for all. In Africa, the Foundation aims to contribute to the country's protein self-sufficiency, through active support for the structuring of supply chains and for agro-ecological initiatives that promote crop biodiversity and soil preservation. It controls the limited partnership with shares Avril SCA, in which it holds (the majority) 50.7% of the voting rights (but only 34.7% of the dividend rights). The aim of this arrangement is to ensure that the foundation does not interfere in the management of the company, while at the same time enabling it to make structuring decisions (choice of directors).

---

47 Section de l'Intérieur, 'Fondation Avril' (23 July 2019), n° 397.890.

48 See: https://www.fondationvarenne.fr.

49 See: https://www.fondation-merieux.org.

50 See: https://www.fondationavril.org.

It should be noted, however, that a report by the French Inspectorate of Finance, published in April 2017,[51] states that, while possible in public benefit foundations, majority shareholding in a company's capital has remained fairly rare. The authors of the report therefore advocate the use of other forms of foundation in the broadest sense, principally endowment funds, to fulfil this function.

As a conclusion, the principle of independence devised and imposed by the Conseil d'État is one of the main obstacles to the development of charitable foundations in France. While the founders must 'contribute' an initial endowment of a very high amount, which is also open to criticism,[52] they will not be able to directly control 'their' foundation. How can we justify today a principle of independence based essentially on the legal regime governing gifts when, for example, endowment funds, which have a philanthropic capacity equivalent to that of public interest foundations, are not bound by the same principle?[53] Alongside the principle of independent governance, the principle of financial independence, which translates into the requirement for a high, intangible initial endowment, is the second major obstacle to the development of public benefit foundations in France. In 2008, these two very strict principles led to the emergence of a new form of 'competing' foundation, the endowment fund, which gives the project owner complete freedom to define the rules of governance within a legal and philanthropic framework (donations) similar to that of the public utility foundation.

3.2. ENDOWMENT FUND

This new form of foundation in the French landscape is directly inspired by the American endowment fund.[54] The endowment fund's unrestrictive legal status and attractive tax treatment have won the favour of new philanthropists, even if it is regrettable that the creation of a new foundation status has been favoured over the simplification of the public utility foundation status requested by practitioners.[55]

The endowment fund was created in 2008.[56] In 2024, there were over 2,455 active endowment funds[57] out of a total of 7,392 funds and foundations in

---

51 Inspection Générale des Finances (IGF), 'Rapport d'activité' (September 2018), p. 54.

52 S. Couchoux, 'Le fonds de dotation'(2025) *Lamy Associations*, n° 809-52.

53 The governing board of an endowment fund can be totally controlled by the founders.

54 S. Couchoux and A. Vinas, above n. 34, n° 810-1.

55 Fidal avocats, 'Étude Fidal "Évolution des Fondations 2009–2018: les fonds de dotation en vedette"' (7 November 2018) *Fidal*: https://www.fidal.com/fr/actualites/etude-fidal-evolution-des-fondations-2009-2018-les-fonds-de-dotation-en-vedette.

56 Law no. 2008-776 of 4 August 2008 on the modernisation of the economy.

57 I. Scolan and P. Gaboriau, 'Fonds de dotation en pratique' (June 2024), p. 1, available online: https://www.centre-francais-fondations.org/wp-content/uploads/2024/10/Guide-Fonds-de-dotation-en-pratique-2024-10-1.pdf.

2024.[58] In accordance with Article 140 of the French law of 4 August 2008 on the modernisation of the economy (*Loi de modernisation de l'économie*):[59]

> I. – An endowment fund is a non-profit legal entity governed by private law, which receives and manages, by capitalisation, assets and rights of any kind donated to it free of charge and irrevocably, and uses the income from the capitalisation to carry out a work or mission in the general interest, or redistributes it to assist a non-profit legal entity in carrying out its works and missions in the general interest.
>
> An endowment fund is created by one or more individuals or legal entities for a fixed or indefinite period.

When the endowment fund was established in 2008, no initial endowment was mandatory, the reference text merely stating that 'the founder(s) may provide an initial endowment to the fund'. Since the entry into force of Decree no. 2015-49 of 22 January 2015 the founder must contribute an initial endowment in cash, which may not be less than €15,000. An endowment fund can be set up simply by registering with the prefecture with an initial capital of €15,000. It has almost all the same tax benefits as a public interest foundation provided that its management is disinterested.[60]

The report by the French Inspectorate of Finance[61] noted in particular that the endowment fund was undoubtedly the most suitable instrument for majority ownership of a company. However, and this is a major difference, unlike associations or public benefit foundations, endowment funds may not receive public funding of any kind. The very few derogations granted will be subject to a joint decree by the ministers responsible for the economy and the budget. Public establishments and local authorities setting up an endowment fund must take care not to grant any gratuitous benefits, such as the provision of premises or staff, as this would be considered a disguised subsidy.[62]

---

58 Centre français des Fonds et Fondations (CFF), Les entreprises pour la Cité and Ernst & Young Société d'Avocats (EY), '2024: Panorama des fondations et fonds de dotation créés par des entreprises mécènes' (2024), p. 9, available online: https://www.centre-francais-fondations.org/wp-content/uploads/2024/10/ey-panorama-des-fondations-2024.pdf.

59 Law no. 2008-776 of 4 August 2008 on the modernisation of the economy.

60 BOI-IS-CHAMP-10-50-10-20, 7 June 2017, §60: 'The disinterested nature of an organisation's management is proven if the following conditions are met: the organisation is managed and administered on a voluntary basis by persons who have no direct or indirect interest, either themselves or through an intermediary, in the results of its operations; the organisation makes no direct or indirect distribution of profits in any form whatsoever; the organisation's members and their successors cannot be declared beneficiaries of any part of the assets, subject to the right to take back contributions'.

61 IGF, above n. 52, p. 55.

62 I. Scolan and P. Gaboriau, above n. 58, p. 57.

At the time of its creation, by-laws must be drawn up for all endowment funds. The drafting of the by-laws is unrestricted, and the French government does not impose any standard statutes, unlike for foundations recognised as being in the public interest. As with all foundations, the governing board is the sovereign governing body of the endowment fund, and as such has very broad powers. It takes all decisions in the interests of the fund. It is not possible to set up a 'dual' form of governance with a supervisory board and a management board in an endowment fund.

The fund is 'administered by a governing board comprising at least three members appointed, for the first time, by the founder(s)'.[63] In addition to this legal obligation, the fund's by-laws are free to set the composition and operating rules of the governing board, including the number of directors and their number, terms of office, right of veto, powers of representation, rules governing appointment, dismissal, quorum and majority, number of board meetings and procedures, presence of guests, etc. On this point, the by-laws expressly state that the governing board is composed of a minimum of three members. On this point, the by-laws fully express the application of the principle of contractual freedom that characterises the governance of an endowment fund, unlike other foundations.[64]

Furthermore, directors' duties are generally performed free of charge, but this principle is not enshrined in law, unlike in the case of other types of foundation (like corporate foundations). As a result, members of the governing board of an endowment fund may benefit from the administrative tolerance whereby the granting of an indemnity to directors does not call into question the disinterested nature of the management, provided that it does not exceed three-quarters of the minimum wage (*salaire minimum interprofessionnel de croissance*/Smic).[65] In addition, and most importantly, under the provisions of Article 261, section 7, para. 1°(d) of the French General Tax Code, it is possible to remunerate officers (board members) of an endowment fund up to an annual ceiling equal to three times the social security ceiling. The number of directors remunerated varies according to the fund's own resources: one director may be remunerated if the fund's resources are between €200,000 and €500,000; two directors if the fund's resources are between €500,000 and €1 million; three directors if the fund's resources exceed €1 milion. The income threshold is assessed 'on average over the three financial years preceding that in which the remuneration is paid'. Consequently, it is not possible to remunerate one or more of the fund's

63 Law no. 2008-776 of 4 August 2008 on the modernisation of the economy, Article 140, para. V.

64 S. Couchoux, 'Le fonds de dotation publique' (2025) *Lamy Associations*, n° 810-18.

65 BOI-IS-CHAMP-10-50-10-20, 7 June 2017, §100.

directors before the expiry of the three-year period required to verify that the own resources conditions have been validated over this period.[66]

It is important to note that the non-profit nature of an organisation may be called into question:

> if there are economic links between the two entities, or if the directors of the subsidiary are also directors of the association, or if there are family ties between the director of the association and the director of the subsidiary.[67]

In order to avoid this type of situation, it is common to set up a holding company between the foundation and the company. For example, the endowment fund called Pour une Presse Libre holds all the shares in Mediapart through another company called Pour la Protection de l'Indépendance de Mediapart, which is a passive holding company.

About governance, unlike public benefit foundation, the governance of endowment funds is freely organised, which distinguishes them from public benefit foundations which are subject to administrative supervision. Consequently, the organisation of the endowment fund is more flexible. It is administered by a governing board comprising at least three members, appointed for the first time by the founder. The fund's by-laws must specify its composition as well as the conditions of appointment and renewal. In particular, the governing board is responsible for producing the endowment fund's annual report and financial statements, and in this capacity responds to any requests for explanations from the statutory auditor.

In addition, above an endowment of €1 million, the fund must set up an investment advisory committee. This committee will be responsible for considering the investment policy, the policy for investing and monitoring the fund's endowments. In principle, unless otherwise stipulated in the by-laws, the directors are free to make their own choices and may therefore decide not to accept the proposals put forward by the investment committee. The appointment of committee members is governed by Article 2 of the Decree of 11 February 2009,[68] which stipulates that the persons chosen must not be members of the governing board, and must be qualified to carry out expert appraisals and investment studies. The renewal of members and the duration of their mandates must be stipulated in the by-laws. A duration of three to four years and an initial partial renewal of members is recommended to enable the gradual renewal of the body while preserving a certain continuity.[69] Four other committees can also be created but there is no obligation to do so. These are: the Honorary Committee,

---

66 S. Couchoux, 'Le fonds de dotation publique' (2025) *Lamy Associations*, n° 810-18.

67 BOI-IS-CHAMP-10-50-20-10, 3 October 2018, §610.

68 Decree no. 2009-158 of 11 February 2009 on endowment funds.

69 I. Scolan and P. Gaboriau, above n. 58, p. 18.

made up of donors/patrons, to whom a role must be assigned and a role defined in order to include them concretely in the life of the fund; the Scientific Committee (or Committee of Experts), which can advise the governing board and pre-select projects for funding; the Ethics Committee, which can ensure that by-laws and procedures in force concerning the probity and ethics of people, actions and decisions are implemented and respected; and the Strategic Committee, made up of qualified individuals from a variety of backgrounds, to consider longer-term strategy.[70]

And there are two types of funds. On one hand, there are operational funds, which carry out their own public interest activities and manage their assets with this objective in mind.

An example of a clause for an operator fund is:

> The purpose of the endowment fund is to carry out any initiative in the field of contemporary and living artistic and cultural creation, by the following means:- the production and organisation of shows, concerts, events and demonstrations;- the payment of grants to artists;- the constitution and animation of networks of spectators and the provision of information to the public on the fund's activities and cultural and artistic news;- the organisation of workshops, courses, training courses and any activity promoting the dissemination of arts and culture.[71]

On the other hand, there are funds that help other not-for-profit legal entities achieve their objectives by providing them with financial resources. These are known as redistributing endowment funds.

An example of a clause for a redistribution fund is:

> The purpose of the endowment fund is to contribute to the protection of the natural environment, to participate in the preservation of animal, plant and mineral biodiversity, and to promote public education on all issues relating to the preservation of the planet's heritage. Within the strict framework of its purpose, the endowment fund may select and finance any project for the protection of the natural environment or for raising awareness of the challenges of biodiversity and the conservation of natural heritage, presented by a public interest organisation.[72]

In 2022, the breakdown of endowment funds by type of operation was 77% redistributing funds and 23% operating funds.[73]

---

70 Ibid., p. 19.

71 Legal Affairs Department of the Ministry of the Economy, Finance and Industrial and Economic Sovereignty, 'Clausier pour la rédaction des statuts d'un fonds de dotation' (December 2023), p. 6.

72 Ibid.

73 I. Scolan and P. Gaboriau, above n. 58, p. 22.

There are also funds that both operate and redistribute, known as mixed funds. An example of a clause for a mixed fund is:

> The purpose of the endowment fund is to facilitate the development of children and to protect all children, whatever their nationality, in France or throughout the world, to ensure their future. The fund will give priority to supporting projects presented by humanitarian organisations. In order to achieve its objectives, the fund will use all means it deems appropriate, and in particular:- information and education initiatives in the health field, whether these involve working with the populations concerned, training those involved at local level, or organising conferences or colloquia, in particular to publicise innovative practices that can serve as a reference,- direct support in the health field for vulnerable children, with the financing of scientific studies in the pharmaceutical field,- finally, cooperation initiatives with humanitarian organisations and support for all child protection projects.[74]

In most cases, endowment funds use only the income from their assets to carry out their activities. These are capital endowment funds. The fund may also invest in a range of movable and immovable assets, including shares, as indicated in Article 1 of the Decree of 11 February 2009.[75] In the case of the Jean-Noël Foundation,[76] the endowment fund holds 85% of the assets and therefore the capital of NAOS, while a company called B612 holds 51% of the voting rights and therefore has the decision-making power. The originality of the model is based on the separation of capital and decision-making powers with a view to creating value and ensuring the sustainable development of all NAOS activities in a spirit of loyalty, fairness and independence. This system of governance sacralises the company, its cause and its '*raison d'être*'.

Another example, Yann Rolland, CETIH's main shareholder, has contributed 40% of his shares to a philanthropic endowment fund called Superbloom.[77] As part of a capital reorganisation, Yann Rolland, who held 50.5% of CETIH's shares, has irrevocably transferred 40% of his holding to this philanthropic endowment fund, which in effect becomes a 35% shareholder in the group. He and his family manage this fund, the dividends of which are used exclusively for philanthropy and charitable associations, particularly those focusing on the theme of fragility.

As far as controls are concerned, they are very light when the company is set up. On creation, when the by-laws are filed and the application for declaration is submitted, the relevant departments of the prefecture check that the by-laws contain the minimum legal requirements. During the life of the endowment fund, the prefect ensures that it is operating properly and may request any documents

74 Legal Affairs Department of the Ministry of the Economy, Finance and Industrial and Economic Sovereignty, above n. 72, p. 7.

75 Decree no. 2009-158 of 11 February 2009 on endowment funds.

76 See: https://www.jeannoelthorel-foundation.org/.

77 See: https://superbloom.fr/.

and investigations he/she deems necessary. To this end, within six months of the end of the financial year, the endowment fund must send the prefecture to which it reports, by registered letter with acknowledgement of receipt, the activity report, the annual financial statements and the auditor's report.

Firstly, the activity report: each year, the endowment fund must draw up an activity report which, like the financial report, must be submitted to the governing board for approval.[78] If the activity report has not been submitted within the timeframe mentioned in the first paragraph, or if the report is incomplete, the administrative authority may give the endowment fund formal notice to comply with its obligations within one month.

Secondly, the annual financial statements (including balance sheet, income statement and notes) must be sent to the prefecture within six months of the year-end and published on the Direction des Journaux Officiels website. Thirdly, *le rapport du commissaire aux comptes* (the statutory auditor's report) must also be sent to the prefect within six months of the year-end. A statutory auditor is appointed when the endowment fund's resources exceed the threshold of €10,000 during management. The auditor certifies the accounts for the year in which this threshold was exceeded.

The statutory auditor has a specific duty to alert endowment funds when,[79] in the course of his or her work, he or she becomes aware of facts likely to jeopardise the continuity of the fund's activities. He/she first requests explanations from the chairperson of the governing board and the chairperson of the fund is required to reply within 15 days. The statutory auditor informs the administrative authority and if these provisions are not complied with, or if the statutory auditor finds that, despite the decisions taken, the continuity of the business remains compromised, he/she draws up a special report and, in writing, a copy of which is sent to the administrative authority, invites the chairperson to have the governing board, convened in accordance with the conditions and deadlines laid down by decree, to deliberate on the facts raised. If, following the meeting of the fund's governing board, the auditor finds that the decisions taken do not ensure the continuity of the business, he/she informs the administrative authority of his/her actions and communicates the results.

In addition, the statutory auditor contributes to the transparency of any transactions between the fund and its directors that fall within the scope of Article L612-5 of the French Commercial Code. Each year, he/she is required to

---

78 It must contain a certain amount of information, such as a report on the endowment fund's activities, a list of public interest actions financed by the endowment fund and their amounts; a list of legal entities benefitting from redistributions and their amounts; whether the endowment fund makes a public appeal for generosity and whether the legal thresholds have been exceeded; the statement of use of resources collected from the public; a list of gifts received.

79 Law no. 2008-776 of 4 August 2008 on the modernisation of the economy, Article 140, VI, para. 4 and Decree no. 2009-158 of 11 February 2009 on endowment funds, Article 5, para. 2.

draw up a special report on the existence or otherwise of such transactions, which will be sent to the prefecture after being presented to the fund's governing board. Given the specific nature of this mission, it is advisable to choose an auditor familiar with the legal, tax and accounting particularities of endowment funds. Finally, there is a procedure for dealing with serious malfunctions. Under this procedure, the prefect may decide to suspend the fund's activity for a maximum of six months if serious malfunctions are observed. Serious malfunctions are those which affect the achievement of the endowment fund's purpose,[80] for example, when the endowment fund uses up all or part of the capital endowment it has received or if the by-laws do not authorise the use of this endowment.[81]

In addition to *ex post* administrative control, financial control may also be implemented. As soon as the endowment fund has recourse to public generosity, it will be subject to the control of the Cour des Comptes, which will verify the conformity of expenditure with the objectives pursued by the appeal to public generosity.[82] If necessary, the Cour des Comptes will attach to its report a declaration of non-compliance between the objectives pursued by the endowment fund and the expenses incurred, which will be forwarded to the minister responsible for the Budget. It is therefore necessary to pay particular attention to potential conflicts of interest. As a legal entity under private law, an endowment fund may employ staff for its own activities. However, these employees are subject to private law and the provisions of the French Labour Code. French law strictly regulates conflicts of interest. In corporate law, for example, salary increases for directors bound to the company by an employment contract are strictly regulated.[83]

3.3. THE SUSTAINABILITY FUND

Article 177-I of the 2019 Law[84] lays down the principle of setting up a sustainability fund through the unavoidable free and irrevocable contribution of capital securities or shares in one or more operating companies or group holding companies in order to manage these securities or shares, exercise the rights attached to them and use its resources with the aim of contributing to the economic sustainability of this or these companies[85] and, if it so wishes, to carry

80 Decree no. 2009-158 of 11 February 2009 on endowment funds, Article 9.

81 Law no. 2008-776 of 4 August 2008 on the modernisation of the economy.

82 Law no. 91-772 of 7 August 1991 on representation leave for associations and mutual societies and to the control of the accounts of organisations appealing to public generosity, Articles 5 and 7.

83 I. Balensi, (1977) *Revue des société* 251.

84 Law no. 2019-486 of 22 May 2019 on the growth and transformation of businesses. Application Decree no. 2020-537 of 7 May 2020 on sustainability funds.

85 P.-H. Conac, 'Le fonds de pérennité: the French Privatstiftung?' (2019) 3 *RTDF* 29, 30.

out or finance works or missions in the public interest.[86] The main idea here is to create an irremovable shareholder;[87] on the other hand, general interest activities are optional, unlike the endowment fund and the public benefit foundation.

The sustainability fund, for its part, can be considered a shareholder foundation when it has chosen in the foundation's by-laws to pursue an activity of general interest (this is an optional purpose).[88] Moreover, in accordance with the nature of the fund, Article 900-4 of the French Civil Code provides that the sustainability fund may be judicially authorised to dispose of the securities or shares subject to inalienability if the economic survival of the company or companies so requires.

It should be noted that as of 31 December 2023 there are only six. It is not yet very popular mainly due to its unattractive tax regime[89] because it carries on a business comparable to that of a holding company, which is lucrative by nature. It is therefore subject to commercial taxes under ordinary law. Gifts, whether made by individuals or corporations, are not tax deductible. Gifts made by individuals are subject to a 60% transfer tax. On the other hand, under Article 38, section 7 quater of the French General Tax Code, companies subject to corporate income tax that transfer a holding to a Sustainability Fund are entitled to a tax deferral. According to this article:

> the capital gain or loss resulting from the irrevocable transfer, free of charge, of equity securities or shares to a sustainability fund when it is set up is included in the income for the financial year during which these securities or shares are subsequently sold.

The endowment of the *fonds de pérennité* is made up of the securities or shares contributed by the founder(s) at the time of its creation, as well as assets and rights of any kind that may be contributed to it free of charge and irrevocably. Article 910 of the French Civil Code, which provides, in particular and under certain conditions, for a right of opposition by the representative of the state, does not apply to such gifts.

The legislature found it was good idea to establish an irremovable shareholder because putting a company's assets in perpetuity funds means making them safe and, above all, separating them from the interests of individual shareholders,

---

86 J.-J. Lubin, 'Le fonds de pérennité: la fondation actionnaire à la française' (2019) 9 *RFP*, étude 22.

87 N. Dupouy and A.-F. Zattara Gros, 'Les fonds de pérennité: aspects juridiques et fiscaux' (2019) 47 *JCP N* 1321.

88 J. Mestre, 'Fonds de pérennité' in J. Mestre and B. Lemercier, *Le Lamy Sociétés commerciales*, Lamy, online 2024, n° 1661.

89 Ministère de l'Économie, des Finances et de la Relance (B. Rocher), 'Rapport Rocher: Repenser la place des entreprises dans la société: bilan et perspectives deux ans après la loi Pacte' (2021), p. 54. R. Mortier, 'Pourquoi il faut corriger la fiscalité du fonds de pérennité' (2019) 42 *JCP N* 808: according to this author, the legislator should simply exempt the creation of the sustainability fund from transfer duties.

now known as beneficial owners. By its very nature, a *fonds de pérennité* can devote its resources to contributing to the economic sustainability of the company whose shares it holds. What is more, the economic sustainability of the company is intended to benefit the fund in return, so that it can carry out or finance works or missions in the public interest. The shares of the company or companies concerned are indeed inalienable. However, where the *fonds de pérennité* controls one or more of these companies, within the meaning of Article L233-3 of the French Commercial Code, as a result of the bequest or acquisition or of the situation prior to the latter, the contributor or testator, at the time of the bequest, or the governing board, at the time of an acquisition, may decide that this inalienability does not apply to all or part of the securities or shares within the limit of the fraction of the share capital which is not necessary for the exercise of this control.

In addition, the management of equity securities by the sustainability fund is of major importance in stabilising a company's shareholder base. Indeed, at first glance, it is clear from the legal rules that the fund is a veritable manager of company shares. It collects the shares of one or more companies it manages with a view to ensuring their long-term survival. This is the meaning of Article 177 of the 2019 Law,[90] which created the fund as an entity that manages the shares or corporate units transferred to it by its founders. It manages the company's shares to make an obligatory contribution to the company's economic survival or, on an optional basis, to carry out works of general interest. As such, it can exercise control over the company's managers, dismissing them if necessary. In exercising this control, the fund has the power to put a stop to any managerial, social or patrimonial policy that may have a negative impact on the company's perennity. In brief it may act as an active shareholder.[91] In order to achieve the objective of longevity and apply the principles chosen by the founder, the new structure should be able to exercise voting rights in the investee company as the law states. Indeed, in addition, the Decree of 2020[92] specifies:

> An account of the way in which the sustainability fund has managed the securities or shares making up its endowment, exercised the voting rights and other rights attached there to, and used its resources.

Regarding the formal requirements to be observed when creating it, the by-laws must be drawn up in writing. In particular, they determine the name, object, registered office and operating procedures of the *fonds de pérennité*, as well as the composition, conditions of appointment and renewal of the governing board and management committee. The object of the by-laws must include an indication

---

90 Law no. 2019-486 of 22 May 2019 on the growth and transformation of businesses.
91 S. Couchoux, 'Le fonds de pérennité: quel avenir ?' (2022) 187 *RLDA* 38.
92 Decree no. 2020-537 of 7 May 2020 on sustainability funds.

of the principles and objectives applied to the management of the securities or shares of the company or companies in which the fund is a partner, to the exercise of the rights attached thereto and to the use of the fund's resources, as well as an indication of the actions envisaged in this context. It also includes, where applicable, an indication of the works or missions of general interest that the fund intends to carry out or finance. The sustainability fund is registered with the prefecture of the department in which its head office is located.

The governance of the *fonds de pérennité* is simple. It is administered by a governing board comprising at least three members appointed, for the first time, by the founder(s) or, in the case of a bequest made to the *fonds* before it is set up, by the persons designated by the testator to set it up. The governing board is vested with the broadest powers to act in all circumstances on behalf of the *fonds de pérennité*, within the limits of its corporate purpose. Clauses in the by-laws limiting the legal powers of the governing board may not be invoked against third parties. Furthermore, in dealings with third parties, the governing board binds the *fonds de pérennité* by acts falling within its purpose. Acts performed outside this scope are null and void, without this nullity being enforceable against third parties acting in good faith.

The by-laws must also provide for the creation of a management committee reporting to the governing board, comprising at least one member of the governing board and two members who are not members of the board. This committee is responsible for the ongoing monitoring of the company or companies referred to in point I of Article 197 of the 2019 Law[93] and makes recommendations to the governing board on the financial management of the endowment on the exercise of the rights attached to the securities or shares held, and on the actions, and associated financial requirements, making it possible to contribute to the economic sustainability of these companies. The committee may also propose studies and expert appraisals. Each year, the *fonds de pérennité* draws up accounts that include at least a balance sheet and an income statement. These accounts are published within six months of the end of the financial year. The *fonds de pérennité* appoints at least one statutory auditor, chosen from the list mentioned in point I of Article L822-1 of the French Commercial Code, whenever the total amount of its resources exceeds €10,000 at the close of the last financial year. In this case, the annual financial statements are made available to the statutory auditor at least 45 days before the date of the governing board meeting scheduled to approve them. When, in the course of his/her work, the statutory auditor identifies facts likely to jeopardise the continuity of the fund's operations, he/she informs the governing board and seeks its explanations. The governing board is required to respond within a time limit set by decree. In the absence of a response, or if the measures taken appear insufficient, he/she draws

93 Law no. 2019-486 of 22 May 2019 on the growth and transformation of businesses.

up a special report which he submits to the governing board, a copy of which is sent to the Management Committee and the administrative authority, and invites the board to deliberate on the facts raised, under the conditions and within the timeframe specified in Article 9 of the Decree of 7 May 2020.[94]

Finally, it should be noted that the administrative authority ensures that the perpetuity fund is operating properly. To this end, it may request any documents and carry out any useful investigations. Each year, the perpetuity fund must send the administrative authority an activity report, together with the auditor's report and the annual financial statements. And if the administrative authority observes serious malfunctions affecting the achievement of the fund's purpose, it may, after a formal notice which has not been followed up within six months, decide, by a reasoned decision published in the *Journal Officiel*, to refer the matter to the judicial authority for dissolution.[95]

4. THE LITTLE-KNOWN BENEFITS OF SHAREHOLDER FOUNDATION

The term *shareholder* in connection with *foundation* is not meaningless. We are witnessing a mutation in the foundation landscape, a mutation whose existence we must accept, to identify its risks and benefits.

The term 'shareholder foundation' includes not only foundations, a general-interest concept, but also the notion of corporation. And the deeper nature of what a corporation is and why it exists in the legal landscape cannot be overlooked, at the risk of undermining its very groundwork. So, there are many reasons why the shareholder foundation is becoming more and more popular and why it will continue to do so in the future. It seems that the future success of foundations lies in this balance between the private and the public interest, between the economic and the human.

4.1. A PROTECTIVE SHAREHOLDER

First and foremost, the foundation is a protective shareholder, helping to affirm the company's identity.

94 Application Decree no. 2020-537 of 7 May 2020 on sustainability funds.

95 In particular, Article 5 (Decree no. 2020-537 of 7 May 2020 on sustainability funds) clarifies what is meant by serious malfunctions. These include, in particular, where they affect the achievement of the fund's purpose, the fact that the fund disposes of or consumes all or part of its endowment in breach of legal or statutory provisions, or disposes of its resources in breach of its statutory purpose, or has failed to send activity reports to the prefecture for two consecutive financial years despite having been given formal notice to do so.

As a shareholder, a foundation can make it easier for the values of a company to shine through, as the Pierre Fabre company has done. The Pierre Fabre company, founded in 1962 by Mr. Pierre Fabre, is an international French pharmaceutical and dermo-cosmetics group with revenues of almost €3 billion by 2023 (€2.83 billion precisely), and its foundation works in the field of healthcare. Another example is Mobil Wood, a small business based in the north of France, which specialises in ecological store fixtures and fittings. Today, it employs 180 people and generates sales of €20 million. In 2018, it sold part of its capital to an Ulterïa endowment fund, passing on 10% of its shares. It pursues two public interest missions: education and societal and ecological transition in the territories where Ulterïa is based. It is even in the DNA of certain shareholder foundations, since in application of the principle of specialty, introduced by the Council of State and imposed on the *public benefit foundation*, the foundation must own shares in a company related to its corporate purpose.

The identity of the company is also preserved by a shareholder foundation.[96] It can be a way of raising funds for a startup, while protecting the company against subsequent fundraising (such as hostile takeover bids when the company is listed) that could distort its DNA. For example, Yann Rolland was the main shareholder in CETIH. He created the Superbloom endowment fund to guarantee CETIH's independence. Here are the words of Yann Roland:

> I would have been extremely saddened and deeply affected if the company had fallen into the hands of financiers or even a competing industrial family. We had to ensure the company's independence.[97]

However, care must be taken because, although the contribution made to the shareholders' foundation is irrevocable, the shares held by the shareholders' foundation are only relatively unsellable. In the case of a usufruct[98] gift, for example, the irrevocability of the endowment does not prevent the restitution of the usufruct to the grantor at the agreed term. Indeed, this cannot be permanent for fear of violating the foundation's fundamental rights and freedoms, such as freedom of contract, property rights, etc.

The shareholder foundation also makes it possible to ensure that non-financial interests are effectively considered. A shareholder foundation enables a company to acquire a long-term, non-profit shareholder dedicated to the public interest. From this point of view, the shareholder foundation can be the guarantor of

---

96 C. Dagbedji, 'L'apport du fonds de pérennité à la longévité des entreprises' (2024) 5 *Revue des sociétés* 281.

97 Interview of 8 March 2024.

98 J. Mestre and S. Dupouy, above n. 6, especially p. 287.

compliance with various legal obligations relating to the consideration of social and environmental issues. More generally, it is also a shareholder guaranteeing compliance with the performance of the *contrat de société* (partnership agreement) 'taking into account social and environmental issues', as now stipulated in Article 1833 of the French Civil Code introduced with the 2019 *Loi PACTE*.[99]

The creation of a shareholders' foundation is therefore a way to anticipate the risk of litigation. For example, created in the summer of 2021 by the Rolland family, Superbloom is the first French family endowment fund to become a shareholder in a *société à mission* (mission company). The 'mission company'[100] label requires companies choosing to adopt it to make strong social and environmental commitments. And a strong sign of respect for these obligations is the creation of a shareholder foundation whose purpose is precisely to meet these requirements.[101]

Beyond this example, it is true that step by step, companies are becoming obliged to take environmental and social interests into account. Legislation is evolving in this direction. For example, *la directive relative au devoir de vigilance* (the Directive on corporate sustainability due diligence)[102] imposes many transparency obligations on companies. In the same way, and more generally, the law imposes *un devoir de bon comportement en matière de durabilité* (a duty to behave in a sustainable way).

4.2. AN AMBITIOUS SHAREHOLDER

The shareholder foundation is also ambitious. First and foremost, it attracts investors. According to the investment fund Alter Equity,[103] the presence of an endowment in a company's capital suggests that its shareholders are committed to strong values – and that is attractive! Such a shareholder is very important for a company because this is in line with current trends.[104] Expectations of companies today are high; they have a role to play in addressing contemporary

99 Law no. 2019-486 of 22 May 2019 on the growth and transformation of businesses.

100 Article 1835 of the Civil Code, 'The by-laws may specify a raison d'être, consisting of the principles which the company adopts and for which it intends to allocate resources in order to carry out its activity'.

101 S. Couchoux, 'Mécénat et fondation comme supports de l'entreprise "à impact"' (2020) 165 *RLDA* 47.

102 Directive (EU) 2024/1760 of 13 June 2024 on corporate sustainability due diligence [2024] OJ L1760/1.

103 See: https://www.alter-equity.com/mission.

104 B. Oppetit, 'Éthique et vie des affaires' in *Mélanges offerts à André Colomer*, Litec, Paris 1993, p. 327.

societal challenges such as environmental protection and the defence of human rights.

It is also a way of ensuring the company's long-term future.[105] It is firstly a shareholder who is willing to stay with the company for a long, even very long time. Unlike companies, the legislator has not specified the period, which suggests that these foundations can be set up for a fixed or indefinite period. And second, it is a shareholder willing to financially support the company for years to come. They can do this by exercising their right to participate in collective decisions. A voting right will clearly be in the best interests of the company. However, particular care should be taken in the selection of directors to ensure that they have the necessary skills to take on the role of shareholder.

5. FOUNDATION STRATEGY

The values of the founder or owner, as well as the values of the business being transferred, are often at the heart of the strategy. Strategy can be difficult to organise and requires considerable thought and consultation. First and foremost, the strategy must be coherent between the company's business and the foundation's public benefit activities. Second, governance must be fair. Care must be taken to ensure that the foundation does not fall into the trap of *green and social washing*.

In practice, shareholder foundations often draw up *une charte* (commitments), which is appended to the by-laws to give it a certain normative force. It is possible, for example, to stipulate that the foundation will have stronger political rights with regard to certain strategic decisions. For example, the foundation may be called upon to approve any change in the company's capital structure, such as the entry or exit of a shareholder, a capital increase, the allocation of voting and dividend rights, or the appointment of senior management. For example, it could reject a hostile takeover bid or dismiss a CEO (which would be difficult to imagine in the context of a shareholder foundation, which is often chaired by the company's CEO). The foundation can also give its opinion on the evolution of the social and environmental commitments of the company in which it is a shareholder, and, for example, advocate obtaining certification (such as ISO 14001 on environmental management systems).

In these by-laws, it is important to specify the foundation's means of action in order to prevent potential conflicts between the company and the foundation over the points listed above. A clause may first provide for a privileged right to information and warning, or a mechanism for the amicable resolution of conflicts

[105] A. Jevakhoff and D. Cavaillolès, above n. 24, p. 25.

through a mediation committee, for example. And if need be, the foundation can use its prerogatives as a shareholder, such as the right of veto.

6. PERSPECTIVES

Looking to the future, and in the light of the 'Draft contribution to a European Enterprise Foundation model law',[106] let us now consider what might be in store for French law in the future.

6.1. A COMMON DEFINITION FOR ALL SHAREHOLDER FOUNDATIONS

The European enterprise foundation model law notably offers as a source of inspiration an Article 1 dedicated to this definition. This definition is firmly rooted in reality, as it is based on the notion of control. In this project, the notion of control is broadly apprehended in Article 1 (Définitions):

> A controlling interest can be assumed if the enterprise foundation holds a majority of votes in the company (holding enterprise foundation) or if the foundation conducts a business itself (operating enterprise foundation). If a foundation does not hold a majority of votes in a business, a shareholder agreement or an otherwise dispersed shareholder structure may still suffice for the foundation to exercise effective control and classification as an enterprise foundation.

In France, as mentioned above, there is no common definition of shareholder foundations in legislation or case law. It is through a combination of practice and legal doctrine that the three types of shareholder foundation – public interest foundation, endowment fund and perpetuity fund – are described as shareholder foundations. In order to establish greater legal certainty and in the interests of education, it might also be interesting to enshrine such a legal concept in French law, based as it is in this draft on the concept of control. In France, it is not so much a legal and social barrier as a lack of awareness of the advantages of a shareholder foundation.

There is, however, one major obstacle to such a definition. Under French law, the term 'foundation' is reserved exclusively for foundations recognised as being in the public interest. Only the the public benefit foundation may use the single

106 A. Sanders, S. Thomsen and M. Ørberg, 'Draft contribution to a European Enterprise Foundation model law Including guidelines (best practice recommendations) and tax principles' (January 2025), prepared for the European Law Institute project on enterprise foundations.

term 'foundation' in their title, by-laws, contracts, documents or advertising.[107] For an endowment fund, the term 'foundation' may not be used in the name. Conversely, the use of the term 'endowment fund' is not compulsory. In practice, however, it is possible to use the English term 'foundation' in the name of endowment funds, particularly when they have international ambitions.

6.2. TO ADOPT SUSTAINABLE BEHAVIOUR

As mentioned above, the foundation's corporate purpose is naturally sustainable. The examples described above illustrate the fact that it is either human values that are chosen, or environmental protection. Sustainability values are therefore only partially taken into account.

Given this observation, the question arises as to whether it would be appropriate to create the equivalent of Article 1833 of the Civil Code for shareholder foundations. Pursuant to the second paragraph of Article 1833 of the French Civil Code: 'A company shall be managed in its corporate interest, taking into consideration the social and environmental challenges of its activity'. For the sake of consistency of legislation, it might be worth extending such a rule to shareholder foundations. Indeed, in addition to companies, under French law, other private not-for-profit legal entities – such as mutual societies[108] and provident institutions[109] – must also take sustainability issues into account when carrying out their activities.

In the same vein, the 'Draft contribution to a European Enterprise Foundation model law'[110] refers to the requirement for foundations to adopt 'Responsible Business Ownership'. In Article 2, para. 2, the model law establishes the obligation for shareholder foundations to act as responsible owners, bearing in mind the long-term interest of the company and its stakeholders:

> Regardless of its purpose, an enterprise foundation must exercise its ownership of business companies in a responsible way bearing in mind the long-term interest of the company and its stakeholders.

It should be noted that this notion of stakeholders is understood in a broad sense in this draft European law:

---

107 Law no. 87-571 of 23 July 1987 on the development of philanthropy, Article 20.

108 Code de la mutualité, Article L.111-1: 'Elles sont gérées en prenant en considération les enjeux sociaux et environnementaux de leur activité'.

109 Code de la sécurité sociale, Article L.931-1: 'Les institutions de prévoyance sont des personnes morales de droit privé ayant un but non lucratif, administrées paritairement par des membres adhérents et des membres participants définis à l'article L. 931-3'.

110 A. Sanders, S. Thomsen and M. Ørberg, above n. 107.

> Stakeholders include not only the foundation's beneficiaries, its employees and the employees and minority shareholders of a company it controls. Moreover, it includes the interests of communities benefitting from the foundation and or the business. The interest of the environment may also be included. If a national legislator wishes to so, concepts such as planetary boundaries and doing business without doing harm may be explicitly mentioned.

This vision of stakeholders, encompassing not only stakeholders but also non-financial interests, is in line with the spirit of Article 1833 of the French Civil Code, which focuses on the sustainable operation of a business.

6.3. FREEDOM TO MANAGE THE FOUNDATION GOVERNED BY THE BY-LAWS

A principle of freedom runs very strongly through these European guidelines, which France could learn from. In an original way, the project enshrines the freedom to choose an object dedicated solely to responsible business ownership.

6.3.1. Freedom to Choose the Purpose

Article 2 of the draft model law,[111] entitled 'Purpose', makes it possible for a shareholder foundation to choose as its purpose a 'responsible corporate ownership' within the meaning of Article 4. Could this be possible in France? At present, in France, this is not possible because the three types of shareholder foundation studied above require the foundation's purpose to be philanthropic. However, allowing a shareholder foundation to have such a purpose would be beneficial in France. Generally speaking, in fact, companies are now being asked to demonstrate responsible governance and to take account of sustainability issues in their strategic decisions. The responsibilities of companies in terms of sustainability are constantly increasing. Against this backdrop, it would be highly beneficial for the company to have a shareholder specifically dedicated to these issues. Not only would the shareholder foundation protect the company from the risk of litigation if sustainability issues were not taken into account, but it would also be committed to making the best decisions for the company over the long term. The focus would no longer be on short-term returns, but on protecting the long-term future of the company and the environment in which it operates.

---

111 Ibid.

6.3.2. *Freedom to Manage the Assets*

Article 7 of the draft model law, entitled 'Distribution and foundation property', makes it possible for a shareholder foundation, unless the by-laws provide otherwise, to administrate, sell, reinvest and restructure its assets irrespective of whether they have been donated by its founders or received later through donations or profits. Here again, this freedom to manage assets is not found in all French shareholder foundation statutes, and French law could draw inspiration from this freedom. This would certainly increase their attractiveness.

6.3.3. *Freedom to Remunerate the Governing Board*

Article 18 of the draft model law, entitled 'Remuneration', states that:

> Members of the enterprise foundation governing board shall be remunerated by a fixed fee proportionate to the workload and responsibility involved. Alternatively, the governing board may decide not to renumerate its members.

It is a real job, and it requires real work, to take on the role of shareholder and manager – and the tasks that go with it – and it is important to ensure that they are fairly remunerated, not least in terms of motivation. Despite this, French law provides a very strict framework for remuneration. However, it is interpreted rather flexibly by the courts. For example, in a ruling handed down by the Versailles Administrative Court of Appeal on 22 September 2016,[112] the judge did not hesitate to interpret the spirit of the law in a way that was favourable to the remuneration set up:

> The fact that the remuneration of the ten directors exceeds the limit of three times the social security ceiling is not such as to call into question the disinterested nature of the management of a foreign foundation seeking to be treated for tax purposes as a foundation recognised as being in the public interest under French law. The amount of remuneration and benefits in kind must be assessed in the light of the duties imposed and taking into account the specific rules of the state in which the foundation is resident. The task of managing and investing the foundation's resources requires the full-time services of four directors, with total assets of €2.5 billion and an annual operating budget of €100 million. The directors are personally responsible for the financial consequences of their decisions, which are subject to ongoing control by independent chartered accountants and an internal control committee.

It would therefore be beneficial if legislation regarding this matter were to undergo a change.

---

112 CAA Versailles, 22 septembre 2016, n° 14VE01080.

6.3.4. *Freedom to Choose the Appropriate Governance*

Article 13 of the draft model law,[113] entitled 'Appointment and membership of the governing board', could be a source of inspiration for improving charitable foundations.

The principle of independence described above[114] is one of the main obstacles to the development of shareholder foundations in France. In application of this principle, the founders will have to 'contribute' an initial endowment of a very large amount at the time of creation, but they will not be able to directly control 'their' foundation. In the context of a prospective study carried out in 2017 by the law firm Fidal,[115] proposal numbers 2 and 5 aim, in a relatively radical way, to reduce the scope of the principle of independence imposed on foundations which excessively limits the role of founders in governance.

6.4. CONTROL

6.4.1. *Control via Information*

Article 13 of the draft model law[116] is entitled 'Right to information'. The article allows the competent authority to make inquiries and request information if it has reason to believe that the enterprise foundation is not acting in accordance with its by-laws or the law. Transparency is one of the best ways of controlling a shareholder foundation, as the draft model law rightly proposes.

An obstacle in French case law stems from the right to privacy. According to the *Conseil d'État*, the documents relating in particular to the internal operation and financial situation of a legal person under private law, in this case a *fondation d'entreprise* (a corporate foundation), fall within its private life and the administration that holds them cannot therefore communicate them to third parties.[117] Although certain texts expressly authorise the communication of certain documents relating to private life – such as the articles of association of a foundation[118] or its accounts but only if it has received public subsidies[119] – there is no obligation to disclose them. There is therefore no general obligation

[113] A. Sanders, S. Thomsen and M. Ørberg, above n. 107.

[114] No. 3.1; no. 3.2; no. 3.3.

[115] Fidal Avocats, 'Étude Fidal: "Mécénat & Fondations en France: un nouveau souffle"' (5 October 2017) *Fidal*: https://www.fidal.com/actualites/etude-fidal-mecenat-fondations-en-france-un-nouveau-souffle.

[116] A. Sanders, S. Thomsen and M. Ørberg, above n. 107.

[117] CE, 7 octobre 2022, n° 44826, BRDA 24/22, inf. 3.

[118] Decree no. 91-1005 of 30 September 1991.

[119] Law no. 2000-321 of 12 April 2000 on the rights of citizens in their relations with administrations, Article 10.

of transparency on shareholder foundations, and consequently no right to information for the authorities.

6.4.2. Competent Authorities

According to Article 21 of the draft model law,[120] entitled 'Competent authorities':

> This model law suggests that the legislator implements a public competent authority or court which must have the right legal competences and business understanding to be able to evaluate the situations of enterprise foundations fully. The authority may primarily be an administrative agency.

In France, it is the judge who sanctions any malfunctions, but an authority would be welcome. This would provide greater legal certainty.

Such an authority dedicated to shareholder foundations could be inspired by *l'Autorité de la Concurrence* (the French competition authority), which is an independent French administrative authority that oversees the competitive functioning of the French economy. In addition to instilling confidence in shareholder foundations, such an authority would provide guidance on best practices.

6.5. LES BONNES PRATIQUES

6.5.1. Transparency and Communications

As proposed in the draft model law,[121] it would be a good idea for shareholder foundations to communicate systematically with the public, in particular via a dedicated website.[122] The trend is certainly towards transparency, as demonstrated by the recent publication of the Decree of 5 July 2024[123] on the dematerialisation and simplification of procedures applicable to philanthropic organisations, which came into force on 8 July 2024. In particular, this text changes the regulatory framework applicable to endowment funds. Stakeholders have, indeed, high expectations in terms of financial communication. With a view to harmonising the content of the activity reports of philanthropic organisations, the report must now contain an account of the organisation's activities – covering

---

120 A. Sanders, S. Thomsen and M. Ørberg, above n. 107.

121 A. Sanders, S. Thomsen and M. Ørberg, above n. 107, p. 107.

122 Ibid.: 'It is recommended that such large EFs have a home page with basic information including summary annual reports, the names of its governing board members and an and overview of its ownership (%) in companies in which the EF has a controlling interest'.

123 Decree no. 2024-720 of 5 July 2024 dematerialising and simplifying procedures applicable to philanthropic organisations, *JO* of 7 July 2024, n° 704.

both its internal operations and its relations with third parties – and a detailed description of the public interest initiatives financed by the organisation and the amounts involved, the name, registered office address, email address, telephone numbers and nature of the legal entities benefiting from the organisation's funding and the amounts of redistributions paid out as part of its general interest missions. The Decree increases the information held by the authorities on foundations and endowment funds. Consequently, as recommended in the draft model law, it would be useful for this information to be made more widely available to the general public.

6.5.2. The Duty of Care

According to the draft model law:[124]

> to secure the integrity of enterprise foundation model, it is crucial that members of the governance board take the purpose of the foundation to heart and use it rather than their own personal preferences as a guiding star in the exercise of their duties. Therefore, the best practice code recommends that the enterprise foundation governing board must ensure that the enterprise foundation remains true to the foundation purpose meaning that the purpose should be reflected in all enterprise foundation activities.[125]

And a liability action is also available to penalise any serious breach:

> Board members who breach their duties and thereby cause a loss, are liable to the enterprise foundation. They shall not be liable for losses if they have acted carefully and in good faith in a decision not prescribed by law based on appropriate information (business judgement rule).[126]

Would it be interesting to create a specific liability action for shareholder foundations in France based on the draft model law?

In France, there is the notion of '*intérêt social*' specific to corporate law, which could be transposed here for shareholder foundations. In corporate law, when the company's own interest – the '*intérêt social*' – is infringed, directors can be held liable on two legal grounds: abuse of minority and abuse of majority. The second paragraph of Article 1833 of the French Civil Code states: 'The company is managed in its corporate interests'. If a transaction decided by the managing partner or authorised by *les associés majoritaires* (the majority adminstrators) is contrary to the company's interests and harms the minority adminstrators to the

124 A. Sanders, S. Thomsen and M. Ørberg, above n. 107.
125 Ibid., p. 109.
126 Ibid., p. 51.

benefit of the majority adminstrators, it may be annulled on the grounds of abuse of majority voting rights. Similarly, if, *les associés minoritaires* (associates holding a blocking minority) refuse, in an untimely manner and in contradiction with the company's interests, a transaction that is essential for the company, on which its very survival depends, the abuse of minority rights may be characterised.

It is imperative to establish an action of this nature, analogous to the framework of corporate law. This will establish a framework for the practice, which is highly desirable because, akin to corporations, shareholder foundations wield significant economic influence. The magnitude of the financial stakes involved justifies this approach.

6.6. THE CREATION OF A COMMON LAW FOR SHAREHOLDER FOUNDATIONS

What could be '*le droit commun, les principes communs*' (the common law, the common principles) to shareholder foundations? In order to make them more attractive, such a common law adapted to the specific features of shareholder foundations would provide greater legal certainty and inspire greater confidence among investors. Major principles common to all shareholder foundations could be created, such as transparency, sustainable governance and integrity.

Political decision-makers can promote the creation of corporate foundations by increasing legal certainty regarding their establishment and operation. A separate law dedicated to corporate foundations could help in this respect.

SPANISH ENTERPRISE FOUNDATIONS

Alberto EMPARANZA SOBEJANO and Andrea MEIJOMIL GONZALEZ*

ABSTRACT

This chapter aims to give an overview of the law and practice of Spanish enterprise foundations and the current challenges in Spain. It will try to embed the special

---

* This work is part of the research outcomes conducted by the Research Group of the Basque University System (IT 1765-22), funded by the Department of Education, Universities, and Research of the Basque Government, of which the undersigned are members, serving as principal investigator and researcher, respectively.

form of enterprise foundations into the framework of Spanish foundation law and will then focus on the specific topics and challenges Spanish enterprise foundations face, such as: the governance of the foundation, the duties of the directors ('*patronos*') and the liability arising from their breach. Likewise, the chapter examines the figure of the Protectorate as an external supervisory body and the issues stemming from the plurality of registries.

1. INTRODUCTION

Foundations are entities that, in addition to having a long tradition in Spain, hold increasing economic importance in the management of matters deemed to be of general interest. Various circumstances have contributed to the current relevance of foundations, both as legal entities and as organisational forms.[1]

The first aspect confirming the relevance of foundations is of a general nature, preceding their potential legislative regulation, and concerns the position of these legal entities within the framework of the economic reality of the Spanish market. In this regard, it has been noted for years that foundations, in terms of their function, operate as market agents in the same way as commercial companies, public entities owning economic enterprises, cooperative societies or individual entrepreneurs. The differences with these actors are evident, but foundations demonstrate their uniqueness as legal entities through the necessary pursuit of a purpose of general interest.[2]

The variety of activities undertaken and the resources allocated to them have grown significantly in Spain in recent years, shaping a sector of activity that demands better identification of the characteristics defining the various types of entities operating under the legal framework of foundations.[3]

1 The El Corte Ingles Foundation and the MAPFRE Foundation are some of the entities that have demonstrated the uniqueness of the enterprise foundation as a subject in the economy, which has led many Spanish companies to choose to establish enterprise foundations.

2 J.M. Embid Irujo, 'Fundación, Empresa, Patronato' in A. Emparanza Sobejano (ed), *Nuevas orientaciones en la organización y estructuración jurídica de las fundaciones*, Marcial Pons, Madrid 2014, p. 19.

3 A. Emparanza Sobejano, 'La transparencia en la gestión del patronato de las fundaciones con actividad empresarial' in A. Emparanza Sobejano (ed), above n. 2, p. 49, notes that foundations as patrimonies created for the achievement of a purpose are undoubtedly undergoing a process of change. While traditionally configured as separate patrimonies devoted to a special purpose, the need to fulfil their objectives is compelling foundations to connect with the realities of the market, participating actively and continuously in commercial transactions, regardless of whether or not the foundation carries out economic activities.

2. THE REGULATION OF ENTERPRISE FOUNDATIONS IN SPAIN

2.1. PRELIMINARY REMARKS

A preliminary issue to analyse before addressing regulation would be to determine the framework in which the figure should be situated in Spain. At present, enterprise foundations are considered within the strict framework of foundation law, although they could also be situated within commercial law. In other words, it would be possible to incorporate the regime of enterprise foundations into the basic regulation of commercial law, namely in the Commercial Code, which, despite its name and the preservation of the concept of the merchant, is the primary framework for conceptually and systematically addressing all organisational and legal configurations that can be adopted by a company or entrepreneur.[4]

2.2. THE REGULATION OF ENTERPRISE FOUNDATIONS

Having addressed this preliminary issue, we will now discuss the regulation of enterprise foundations in Spain. Enterprise foundations are key players in Spain but lack specific regulation. As previously noted, enterprise foundations are considered within the framework of foundation law. Therefore, enterprise foundations share a basic legal framework with other Spanish foundations. Consequently, to analyse the concept of enterprise foundations, one must examine the legal regime applicable to foundations.

Article 34 of the Spanish Constitution enshrines the right to establish foundations as a second-tier fundamental right for foundations pursuing purposes of general interest. Thus, the right to establish foundations binds all public authorities, but a formal law is required to develop its essential content for it to be invoked judicially.[5] The fact that the distribution of powers in the Constitution does not explicitly mention foundation-related regulations has sparked a debate regarding the allocation of legislative powers in this area. The Constitutional Court has resolved this debate by accepting the existence of concurrent powers, allowing the state to maintain jurisdiction over foundations operating beyond the regional level and to establish a greater or lesser scope

4 J.M. Embid Irujo, above n. 2, p. 23.

5 For an in-depth examination of the right to establish foundations as a constitutional right, see A. Serra Rodriguez, 'El derecho de fundación' in J.M. Beneyto Pérez (ed), *Tratado de Fundaciones*, Bosch, Barcelona 2007, pp. 69–134.

for the rules applicable to foundations based on the constitutional reservation of civil or procedural legislation. However, regional jurisdiction is more broadly recognised for autonomous regions with their own civil law, while it is significantly restricted for those without it.[6] Therefore, foundation law in Spain is composed of legislation enacted by the state and regulations issued by autonomous communities with legislative authority in this area. This results in a broad set of legal rules with validity limited to the corresponding territorial scope, without significant substantive differences between the regulatory models of foundations established by institutions with legislative authority.[7] Given the impossibility of detailing each regulation, reference will be made to the preferred framework of Law 50/2002 of 26 December 2002 on Foundations (hereinafter referred to as the Foundations Law).

The current Foundations Law, under state jurisdiction, provides a generic limitation of the figure in Article 2. It defines foundations as legal entities based on assets oriented towards a purpose of general interest established by their founder. Despite extensive regulation regarding foundations in general, enterprise foundations lack specific regulation, so the aforementioned rules must be observed.

3. THE CONDUCT OF ECONOMIC ACTIVITIES PERFORMED BY FOUNDATIONS AND CORPORATE SOCIAL RESPONSIBILITY

As previously mentioned, the assets contributed by the founder are tied to achieving the foundational purposes for which the foundation was established, and these must be outlined in the statutes. In Spain, these purposes are mandatorily linked to the satisfaction of general interests, meaning that profit-making can never be the objective or foundational purpose. That said, it is possible for a foundation to hold ownership of a business activity. When delineating the concept of an enterprise foundation, it is necessary to consider all the essential elements of a legal foundation within the context of business activity.[8]

---

6 C. Albiñana Cilveti, 'Concepto y evolución normativa de las fundaciones. La fundación empresa' in I.S. Galán and S. Martínez Garrido (eds), *Buen Gobierno de las fundaciones*, La Ley, Madrid 2015, pp. 19–22.

7 The regulation of foundations that primarily carry out their functions within the territories of each autonomous community falls under their respective statutes of autonomy, while the state's jurisdiction is limited to regulating the basic conditions that ensure the equality of all Spaniards in exercising the right to establish foundations. Naturally, the choice between a state or regional foundation depends on the specific characteristics of the public-private collaboration project to be addressed in each case.

8 One of the questions that arises regarding the issue of profit-making is the possibility of establishing a family foundation with the sole purpose of distributing or preserving

The general interests tied to the foundational purposes do not prevent a foundation from engaging in business activities, nor from owning a legal entity conducting business activity. Foundations are therefore legally permitted to carry out economic activities in the market.[9] These activities qualify as business activities if conducted habitually and according to economic principles, meaning with the aim of achieving maximum economic performance, regardless of the final destination of the profits obtained. Thus, the prohibition against profit-making as a purpose for foundations does not preclude them from engaging in business activities.

In this context, it is acknowledged that foundations can own a business either because they have created it or because they have acquired its ownership, either gratuitously or for consideration. In any case, economic activity can serve as a tool for generating resources and new funds to be allocated to the fulfilment of the purposes for which the foundation was created.

The current legislation leaves no room for doubt regarding the possibility of foundations engaging in such activities.[10] Accordingly, foundations may either own business entities through which business activities are conducted and resources are obtained to meet the foundational purposes, or they may directly

---

the family estate. In this context, in Spain, the law specifies that the founder cannot use the foundation's assets and income primarily for their own benefit or for the benefit of a family group. Foundations are non-profit legal entities, meaning they cannot distribute the profits they generate to the founder, their family members or the directors. In other words, a foundation established solely to support a family would not be permissible in Spain. However, a foundation, such as many family foundations that contribute assets and funds for a general interest purpose and with a broader range of beneficiaries, is indeed possible. In Spain, family foundations are allowed and can offer advantages over mechanisms such as trust substitutions or guardianship, provided their purpose is not exclusively to guarantee support for specific individuals when their parents can no longer care for them. They must leave open the possibility of assisting other individuals with similar needs who are not part of the founding families. Finally, this does not mean that family members of the founder are prohibited from being beneficiaries of the foundation established by the founder, as there is no incompatibility between being a family member and a beneficiary. Nor is it prohibited for the founder to reserve some form of preference for themselves or their family members as beneficiaries of the foundation. What the law seeks to prevent is the establishment of a foundation whose primary purpose is to protect the interests of the members of a family, lineage, or descent when belonging to that family is the sole criterion for determining the beneficiaries. In conclusion, it is permissible to establish foundations whose primary purpose is to allocate their services or activities to founders, directors, their spouses and so on, as well as to legal entities that do not pursue general interest purposes, provided their exclusive or main aim is the conservation and restoration of assets that are part of Spain's historical heritage or the performance of social assistance or sports activities exempt from VAT. All provisions are understood without prejudice to the foundation's ability to participate in the shareholding of other types of entities.

9 J.M. Embid Irujo, 'Empresa y Fundación en el ordenamiento jurídico español (la fundación empresaria)' (2010) 1 *Anuario de Derecho de Fundaciones* 15, 19.

10 For an extensive study, E. Leiñena Mendizabal, 'Financiación y gestión de la actividad económica y empresarial de las fundaciones afinidades y singularidades respecto a las sociedades de capital' (2014) 35 *Revista Aranzadi de Derecho Patrimonial* 49.

organise the means of production and human resources to produce or distribute goods and services, without compromising the essence of the foundation.[11]

The Foundations Law classifies the economic activities a foundation may perform based on the destination of the potential profits obtained. It distinguishes between 'own activities' and 'commercial activities' (Article 24.1 of the Foundations Law). Own activities are those carried out by the foundation to fulfil its purposes of general interest, while commercial activities encompass all other activities undertaken to generate additional income to meet its foundational purposes.

The regulation explicitly states – although it is not strictly necessary – that if foundations engage in economic activities, whether or not they receive compensation for them, they must also comply with the regulatory norms of competition law as legal entities operating in the market. This fact is significant not only regarding the behaviour foundations may exhibit in the market but also concerning the conduct of public administrations and the granting of public aid. Furthermore, whether the foundation engages in own or commercial activities, it will be directly conducting economic activities in the market.

Foundations may also engage in economic activities indirectly, i.e. through their participation in other companies or entities. In this case, the foundation's objective is simply to generate additional income through temporary or long-term investments. Thus, the governing board may dynamically manage the foundation's assets, obtaining returns and profits therefrom.[12]

4. THE GOVERNANCE OF ENTERPRISE FOUNDATIONS

4.1. PRELIMINARY REMARKS

The particularities of foundation governance compared to that of capital companies stem from the different structures and objectives of foundations, which retain distinct characteristics setting them apart from other organisations.[13] In any case,

[11] On this point also see A. Emparanza Sobejano, above n. 3, p. 50.

[12] For further details, see C. Albiñana Cilveti, above n. 6, p. 34, who highlights that when the foundation's participation represents the majority of the capital of the commercial company, or when the foundation is the sole shareholder of the enterprise entity, this is deemed an indirect or mediated exercise of business activity. Strictly speaking, however, the status of entrepreneur is not attributable to the foundation, even if it is the majority or sole holder of the commercial company's capital.

[13] C. Alonso Ledesma, 'Particularidades del buen gobierno de las fundaciones frente al gobierno corporativo de la sociedades' in I.S. Galán and S. Martínez Garrido (eds), above n. 6, p. 117, points out that the nature of foundations, tied to achieving objectives of general interest, allows them to align with functions typical of public institutions. Additionally, they may carry out economic activities in the market, similar to those conducted by commercial entities.

the absence of an associative personal substrate is what characterises foundations and decisively influences their internal legal structure. This lack of an associative base justifies the absence of an assembly or body in which members can express their will, endowed with the capacity to oversee or control the governing board's management, as is the case with the general meeting or shareholders' assembly in capital companies.[14] As a result, all corporate governance rules referencing the general meeting as a supervisory body, or the rights of shareholders and their involvement in the company's operations, are non-existent in foundations.

Nevertheless, foundations, like all legal entities, require bodies to express their will and exercise their powers. Thus, the Foundations Law refers only to the governing board as the governing and representative body of the foundation.[15] Many authors highlight the possibility of other bodies being created by the founder's will or by the governing board itself through amendments to the statutes. However, the creation of such bodies would never entail supervisory, oversight, revocation or substitution powers over the governing board or its members.[16] Article 14 of the Foundations Law allows for organic plurality without significant restrictions, leaving the determination of additional bodies and their specific powers to the autonomy of will.

It seems logical that a complex organisational structure would only make sense in singular foundations, whether due to their significant assets or the specificity of their tasks, as is the case with enterprise foundations. In any event, the breadth and ambition of their purposes may render the governing board insufficient as the sole governing body for their proper fulfilment. Although the law does not set any limits on the possibility of creating additional bodies to the governing board, it seems reasonable to avoid an excessive number, as this could obscure the clear delineation of their respective powers, complicating the formation of the foundation's will and its execution vis-à-vis third parties. Thus, maintaining organisational hierarchy, there would be no objection to the creation of other

---

14 A. Emparanza Sobejano, 'El gobierno de las entidades público privadas: las reglas de gobierno como mecanismo de transparencia y control' in J.M. Embid Irujo and A. Emparanza Sobejano (eds), *El gobierno y la gestión de las entidades no lucrativas público-privadas*, Marcial Pons, Madrid 2012, p. 166.

15 Article 14 of the Foundations Law stipulates that 'Every foundation must have … a governing and representative body'.

16 Both the Foundations Law and the Foundations Regulation (Real Decreto 1337/2005, de 11 de noviembre, por el que se aprueba el Reglamento de fundaciones de competencia estatal. Royal Decree 1337/2005 of 11 November, approving the Regulations on Foundations within the Competence of the State) acknowledge the possibility of other bodies existing, with doctrine emphasising the convenience of establishing suitable delegated committees for the development of foundations or configuring other consultative or executive committees. See E.F. Pérez Carrillo, 'La gestión del patronato de las fundaciones y la responsabilidad social corporativa' in A. Emparanza Sobejano (ed), above n. 2, p. 92.

bodies over which the governing board would exercise supervisory and oversight functions.[17]

4.2. THE ROLE OF THE FOUNDER

The existence of an independent governing body, the governing board and the presence of a charitable interest or social purpose in the aim pursued through its creation establish three essential foundational elements of the concept of a foundation: the will of the founders, the endowment of assets and the purpose related to the common good. Despite this, the key element is the purpose of the individual who drives the creation of a new foundational entity. The founder is the person who endows the foundation with assets and determines its purpose. However, the prominence of the founders, initiators of the endeavour and determinants of the general aim pursued, diminishes with the birth of the new legal entity, at which point the assets assume this prominence with autonomy.[18]

This implies that once the foundational act has been executed, as a set of voluntary actions giving rise to the constitution of a new legal entity under the law, the founder's role takes a back seat. The judgement of the Supreme Court (Administrative Chamber, Fourth Section) dated 22 November 2005 defines the foundational act as a legal act of a transactional and *inter vivos* nature.[19] However, it subsequently establishes a series of restrictions that eliminate such legal autonomy by determining that, once granted, it becomes irrevocable as such because 'the foundation, once established, constitutes a legal transaction that supersedes the will of the founder'.

Once the foundation is constituted, there is no doubt about the prominence it acquires with assets separate from its founder. However, it is necessary to refer to the founder's relevance in the possible transformations of the foundation, ranging from a simple modification to its dissolution.

The authority to make statutory amendments rests with the governing board which may agree to modify the foundation's statutes whenever it is deemed appropriate in the interest of the foundation. Moreover, any modification or new drafting of the statutes agreed upon by the governing board must be communicated to the Protectorate, which may only oppose it on legal grounds. Nonetheless, despite granting authority to the governing board, the current

---

17 C. Alonso Ledesma, above n. 13, p. 120, positively supports this possibility, noting that it would effectively contribute to improving corporate governance, particularly in those foundations where, due to their size, the nature of their activities, or the importance of the assets they manage, such arrangements would be necessary.

18 R. Duran Rivacoba, 'La voluntad del fundador' in L.M. Cazorla Prieto (ed), *Fundaciones: Problemas actuales y reforma legal*, Aranzadi, Pamplona 2011, p. 265.

19 All laws relating to foundations recognise the possibility of establishing the original transaction through *mortis causa* acts too.

foundation law clearly establishes the primacy of the founder's will by stipulating in Article 29.1 that 'the governing board may agree to amend the foundation's statutes whenever it is deemed appropriate in the interest of the foundation, unless the founder has prohibited it'.[20] Such is the importance of the founder's will that Article 29.2 of the foundation law states that:

> When the circumstances under which the foundation was constituted have changed to the extent that it cannot operate satisfactorily under its statutes, the governing board must agree to their modification, unless the founder has provided for the foundation's dissolution in such cases.

Regarding the dissolution of the foundation, the current regulations on foundations assign the authority to declare a foundation dissolved to the Protectorate (whether state or regional), which exercises this authority either on its own initiative in some cases or at the request of the foundation's governing board in others, when one of the causes for dissolution provided for in the law or established by the founder occurs. The Foundations Law envisions different forms of dissolution depending on the cause, but fundamentally requires a decision by the governing board ratified by the Protectorate. If no such agreement exists or it is not ratified, the dissolution of the foundation will require a judicial ruling, which may be initiated by the Protectorate or the governing board depending on the circumstances.[21]

As can be seen, the founder does not have the authority to decide the dissolution of the foundation they chose to establish. However, in this regard, it is worth mentioning the possibility that the dissolution of the foundation may arise from the causes expressed by the founder in the statutes, as per Article 31(e). It is expressly provided that foundations may be dissolved for the causes set forth in the foundational charter or the statutes, that is, for the reasons established by the founder.[22]

In conclusion, once the foundation is constituted, the founder becomes entirely detached from it, being able only to join the governing body as one

20 R. Duran Rivacoba, above n. 18, p. 301, states this is an appropriate and indispensable exception, as if the founder is allowed to introduce causes for dissolution, they should all the more be able to prevent alterations to the foundation's design.

21 The regional regulations adopt similar provisions, albeit less precise. All of them foresee the involvement of the Protectorate in the dissolution process, either by authorising the actions undertaken by the governing board concerning the dissolution, intervening in or promoting the dissolution process.

22 In this regard, critical, M.T. Carrancho Herrero, 'La extinción de las fundaciones' (1996) 8 *Derecho Privado y Constitucion* 15, points out that it does not seem appropriate to leave the determination of the causes for the dissolution of the foundation to the sole discretion of the founder. This is because a foundation, despite being a private entity, justifies its existence through the pursuit of the general interest, which implies that matters intrinsically linked to the essential nature of the institution cannot be left to individual will.

member among others, but without any kind of privilege. The overarching interest that the foundation serves excludes any possibility of unjustified dissolution of the foundation.

4.3. THE GOVERNING BOARD AS THE GOVERNING AND REPRESENTATIVE BODY (*PATRONATO*)

The law recognises the governing board[23] as the sole governing and representative body of the foundation:

> responsible for fulfilling the foundational purposes by diligently managing the assets and rights comprising the foundation's patrimony, ensuring their performance and utility.[24]

Thus, the governing board monopolises the governance of the entity, without accountability to any body other than the Protectorate.

The governing board is the necessary and supreme governing and representative body of foundations. Regarding its structure, the law establishes a minimum organisational framework by requiring the presence of a president and a secretary (who may be external), determining that the board must consist of at least three members, whether natural or legal persons, and that decisions are made by majority vote, enforcing the collegiality of the body. However, the law does not clearly regulate the functioning of the governing board, leaving this matter largely to the autonomy of will, which may adopt many governance recommendations provided for capital companies.[25]

The governing board is responsible for governing and representing the legal entity, directing its actions towards achieving the purposes established in the statutes. In terms of ordinary management, this involves overseeing the proper administration of the foundational patrimony and annual budget, staying

---

23 The governing body is called 'Patronato' in Spain.

24 J.M. Embid Irujo, 'Introducción general al curso. La fundación como modelo para la colaboración público-privada' in J.M. Embid Irujo and A. Emparanza Sobejano (eds), above n. 14, p. 55, notes that the term 'governance' has raised questions regarding its scope, as the governing board does not occupy the same institutional position as the administrative body of a capital company but rather holds a superior position. Nonetheless, it is also entrusted with the competence of managing the foundation's assets and rights, which constitutes its managerial function.

25 Traditionally configured as a separate estate allocated to a special purpose, the need to fulfil their objectives has compelled foundations to connect with market realities by participating actively and continuously in transactions, regardless of whether the foundation conducts economic activities. The fact that a foundation often acts as another market operator – providing services, hiring employees, carrying out economically assessable tasks, etc. – explains why the foundational norms of classic economic operators' organisational functioning must increasingly be considered in this domain.

informed, appointing and supervising executives, etc. Concerning extraordinary circumstances, it has the authority to agree on statutory amendments, propose merger agreements, etc. Governance of the foundation is thus a complex activity involving guiding and directing the foundation's life, adapting policies to circumstances and generally limiting itself to overseeing and monitoring the management of executives, employees and collaborators of the foundation.[26]

4.3.1. *The Members of the Governing Board*

Due to the evolution of the configuration of foundations, it is evident that the founder's intent is losing the decisive role it once held, giving way to the governing board (*patronato*), which, in a sense, embodies the founder's will by being obligated to ensure the achievement of the foundation's purposes.

The management of the governing board corresponds to its members (in Spanish law, '*patronos*'). The law states that members of the board may be natural persons who have full capacity to act and are not disqualified from holding public office, or legal entities that designate the individual or individuals who will represent them (Article 15.2 of the Foundations Law).[27] Without delving into the extent of functional independence that the governing board should possess with respect to the founder's will in performing its duties, it is undeniable that this body is essential for achieving the proposed foundational purposes.

Unlike the detailed regulation in capital companies, the pre-appointment conditions and qualifications for the governing board in foundations are entirely left to the autonomy of the founder's will. Therefore, it will be the founder's intent, as set out in the statutes, that determines the number and individuals comprising the board, as well as the term of office. It is common for a director's mandate to be lifelong, contrary to the provisions for capital companies, where terms are limited but renewable.[28]

---

26 E.F. Pérez Carrillo, above n. 16, p. 92.

27 The Foundations Law does not establish qualification requirements for members of the governing board, although such requirements are present in the regulations of special or sectoral foundations, such as the Law 26/2013 of 27 December, on Savings Banks and Banking Foundations). These requirements stipulate that directors must possess specific knowledge and experience relevant to their duties. Furthermore, these requirements are recommended in some codes of good governance for foundations, such as the 'Ethical Code and Good Governance of Foundations: Principles, Values, and Good Practices' (2001), which states in point 3.2.2 that directors should be 'sufficiently prepared to set objectives, secure necessary resources, monitor both, and convey a vision for the future'.

28 The fact that the position is temporary and renewable facilitates the oversight of the work performed during the term. In contrast, on lifelong appointments of directors, as noted by A.B. Perdices Huetos, 'Hacia unas reglas de gobierno corporativo del sector no lucrativo' (2008) 17 *Revista jurídica de la Universidad autónoma de Madrid* 141, 166; 'while they may confer stability and an appearance of seriousness to the entity, can also perpetuate undesirable practices or routines, making their removal particularly complicated'.

One distinguishing feature of governance in foundations is the gratuitous nature of the governing board member's role. Article 15.4 of the Foundations Law clearly establishes the unpaid nature of the board position, without prejudice to their right to reimbursement for duly justified expenses incurred in the exercise of their function.[29] The unpaid nature of the role stems from the altruistic purpose motivating those who join a non-profit organisation.[30]

However, the current Foundations Law allows for the possibility of remuneration, unless the founder has expressly prohibited it, for directors who provide services to the foundation beyond those inherent to their role as board members, subject to prior authorisation from the Protectorate (Article 15.4, para. 2 of the Foundations Law). This remuneration differs from the right of directors to reimbursement for duly justified expenses incurred as a direct consequence of performing their duties.[31]

4.3.2. Duties of the Governing Board

The governing board's members are subject to obligations stipulated in the Foundations Law, its regulations, and special laws, consisting of positive actions (to do or give) and negative obligations (to abstain), as well as obligations of means, where compliance with a standard of conduct is legally required.

The Foundations Law, in Article 17, merely states in general terms that the directors' management must be diligent and loyal, which implies that directors must act in the best interests of the foundation, prioritising its interests over their own.[32]

The director's work must be carried out with diligence, demonstrating professionalism in their actions, and their conduct must consistently prioritise the foundation's interests over personal interests. These two duties – diligence and loyalty – are inherent to the role of director and should be distinguished, as they serve different purposes. The duty of diligence requires directors to dedicate a certain amount of time and effort to their responsibilities, as well as exhibit a

---

29 The gratuitous nature of the position is also a necessary condition for the foundation to obtain tax benefits, as the Fiscal Regime of Non-Profit Entities Act (Law 49/2002 of 23 December 2002) stipulates in Article 35 that the position of director must be unpaid for the law's benefits to apply.

30 For an in-depth analysis of the governing board's remuneration, see *in extenso*, A. Martínez Balmaseda, 'La retribución de los patronos de las fundaciones' in A. Emparanza Sobejano (ed), above n. 2, pp. 111–133. And, A. Emparanza Sobejano, 'La retribución de los patronos' in I.S. Galán and S. Martínez Garrido (eds), above n. 6, pp. 303–325.

31 To prevent abuses, such as excessive payments, mechanisms have been established, including the provision in Law 49/2002 that limits reimbursements to directors for duly justified expenses to the thresholds set by personal income tax regulations for tax-exempt allowances.

32 C. Alonso Ledesma, above n. 13, p. 130, highlights that the lack of detailed typification of directors' duties makes it more difficult to enforce compliance and, above all, accountability for breaches.

certain level of expertise in managing or supervising the foundation. The duty of loyalty, on the other hand, requires directors to prioritise the foundation's interests over their own, ensuring that the achievement of the foundation's goals is not compromised.

Despite these general duties, the Foundations Law does not provide for additional obligations stemming from the duty of loyalty, such as the duty of confidentiality, prohibition of competition or the obligation to avoid conflicts of interest. The only reference is found in Article 28, which mentions self-dealing, alongside the possibility of remunerating directors for services provided beyond their role, representing potential conflicts of interest. These scenarios, though not specifically regulated by mandatory provisions, may lead to disloyal conduct. Such actions, even if not expressly penalised, should be deemed sanctionable, not so much because they may cause financial harm to the foundation but because they suggest the director is more concerned with personal gain than with advancing the foundation's objectives.[33]

Regarding the duty of diligence, although the law requires directors to act diligently, it does not specify the standard of conduct expected of them. This raises questions about whether the required diligence corresponds to the traditional 'good family father' standard or the standard of an 'orderly entrepreneur', given the nature of the role and assigned functions. In any case, one might assume that the duty of diligence for those involved in governance and organisation implies dedicating a certain amount of time and effort, as well as possessing technical qualifications akin to those of a professional manager.[34]

4.3.3. *The Governing Board's Liability*

The Foundations Law refers to the members of the governing board's liability in Article 17, stating that directors must perform their duties with the diligence of a loyal representative and are jointly and severally liable to the foundation for damages caused by actions that are contrary to the law or the statutes, or those carried out without the level of diligence required for their position.

If a director finds themselves in any of the aforementioned circumstances or situations and fails to notify the governing board or Protectorate, the foundation, upon becoming aware of the situation, may take different measures depending

33 A. Emparanza Sobejano, above n. 3, p. 65.

34 C. Alonso Ledesma, above n. 13, p. 133, emphasises that directors' dedication and effort are not always consistent, as many directors are unaware of their managerial responsibilities and believe they fulfil their mission merely by lending their public image to the foundation or fundraising for the cause. In any case, the author notes that it would be advisable to adequately outline the duty of diligence to enhance directors' managerial awareness and professionalism in fulfilling their functions, thereby exonerating those who comply with legally established duties, as is the case with administrators of capital companies.

on the scale of the transaction conducted, its actual execution and the resulting financial effects on the foundation.[35]

In such cases, the foundation may exercise *ex post* control over the director who has failed to fulfil their duty of loyalty. Three potential courses of action may be taken in cases of breach by the director.

4.3.3.1. Action to Nullify Governing Board Resolutions

Firstly, the foundation may pursue nullification actions against resolutions passed by the governing board. Article 35.2 of the Foundations Law grants the Protectorate the right to challenge actions and resolutions of the governing board that contravene legal or statutory provisions governing the foundation. Such actions must be filed before the court of first instance in the foundation's domicile. Despite this limitation, many authors have recognised that the founder or even the governing board itself may exercise this nullification action. In this context, the key element for recognising standing is the claimant's legitimate interest. Thus, it is undisputed that the governing board holds the greatest interest in annulling any action contrary to the foundation's interests.[36]

4.3.3.2. Dismissal and Liability of Non-Compliant Members of the Governing Board

The second option is the dismissal and liability of the non-compliant director. Article 18.2(d) of the Foundations Law provides for the possibility of a director's removal in cases where they have not performed their duties with the required diligence, subject to a judicial resolution. However, this mechanism is inadequately developed and leaves certain aspects unresolved. While the possibility of dismissal through a court ruling is expressly foreseen, procedural difficulties arise. The initial action likely involves holding the director accountable for disloyal conduct, which does not automatically result in their dismissal.[37]

---

35 A. Emparanza Sobejano, above n. 3, p. 66.

36 Ibid., p. 67, reminds that alongside annulment actions, general civil actions remain available to nullify operations conducted in breach of a director's duty of loyalty. Nullification can also be pursued if it is demonstrated that the director's disloyal conduct led to the invalidity of the board decision being challenged.

37 For further analysis, see *in extenso*, I. Peñalosa Esteban and T. Sanjurjo, 'Órgano de gobierno y relación con los poderes públicos' in R. de Lorenzo García, J.L. Piñar Mañas, T. Sanjurjo, J.R. Barrera Hernández and L. Díez-Picazo (eds), *Tratado de fundaciones*, Aranzadi, Navarre 2010, pp. 237.

4.3.3.3. Restitution of Unjust Enrichment

In cases where it is proven that the director has acted disloyally, claims should aim not only to repair the damage caused but also to recover any personal gain resulting from the breach of their duty of loyalty. In this way, the director would return to the foundation any losses caused and reassign to it any personal benefits derived from their disloyal actions.

4.4. THE GOVERNING BOARD AND GOOD CORPORATE GOVERNANCE

The self-regulation of companies when designing control mechanisms for corporate management through codes of good corporate governance has demonstrated the vast potential that self-regulation offers as an explicit manifestation of the autonomy of the will.[38] Since enterprise foundations also face the challenge of establishing mechanisms to control management, this regulatory technique can be applied to such entities.

It has been observed that the principles and recommendations of corporate governance developed for commercial companies are extendable to all entities subject to private law, regardless of their specific nature and whether they are profit-making or non-profit. However, it is essential to consider the unique features arising from both the legal organisational model and the particularities of these entities compared to profit-making organisations.[39]

Foundations are entities where the governing board monopolises the management of the entity, with accountability owed solely to the protectorate. Thus, the very scope of foundations constitutes an ideal framework for implementing codes of conduct that improve the directors' management to make it more transparent and efficient. The governing board of an enterprise foundation, as the foundation's governing and representative body, needs to adapt its organisation and functioning to current demands. In this regard, the experiences offered by corporate governance in companies provide a highly useful reference.

---

38 A. Emparanza Sobejano, above n. 14, p. 166. This model brings beneficial effects by promoting greater transparency, which becomes a cornerstone of organisational functioning and management oversight. Moreover, it fosters greater stakeholder involvement in management.

39 A. Alonso Ureba and A. Roncero Sanchez, 'Relevancia del buen gobierno para las fundaciones y asociaciones de utilidad pública' in I.S. Galán and S. Martínez Garrido (eds), above n. 6, p. 97.

5. THE PROTECTORATE

The Protectorate of Foundations in Spain is an administrative body responsible for overseeing and ensuring the proper functioning of foundations. Its role is to guarantee that foundations fulfil their stated purposes of public interest and manage their resources in a transparent and efficient manner

The institution of the Protectorate was born out of the need to safeguard the public interest. Since then, the Protectorate has assumed the role not only of ensuring adherence to the founders' will but also of overseeing the entity to guarantee the fulfilment of the public interest purpose for which it was established.[40]

The current Foundations Law, continuing the approach of the previous 1994 Foundations Law, mentions in its preamble (section III) that:

> the functions of the Protectorate are reformulated, enhancing its role of supporting and advising the foundations under its jurisdiction, especially those in the process of being established.[41]

The fact that the foundational purposes are of public interest, along with the very structure of a foundation, entails the creation of a legal entity that must comply with the intent outlined in the founding act with the aim of perpetuity, with an asset base that the founder ceases to own. This means that public authorities must act as guarantors of compliance with the founder's intent. The purposes, objectives and assets allocated to the public interest are, therefore, subject to controls. These are divided into prior controls, ensuring compliance with legal requirements for their establishment, and subsequent controls regarding their operation. The latter focuses on ensuring the fulfilment of the foundation's purpose, i.e. that the assets are used in line with the founder's intent. This control is generally exercised by public authorities, including both the administration and the judiciary, sometimes combined with internal control by a private body within the same entity.

Balancing minimal administrative intervention in private entities with the necessary supervision of a sector that is social but also economic and operates in the market is not an easy objective to achieve. Accordingly, three forms of control are identified: judicial control; control exercised by the specific public authority

---

40 M.A. Cabra de Luna, 'La regulación y funcionamiento de las fundaciones. Las fundaciones de titularidad pública. Especial referencia a las fundaciones publicas sanitarias' (2000) 3(8) *Revista Española de Control Externo* 29, notes that the Protectorate was established as a guardian of the founder's intent, serving as a *ministerium legis*, seeking to prevent circumvention of the general prohibition on the creation of new foundations.

41 Autonomous communities' statutes of autonomy have assumed competencies over foundations that primarily operate within their territories. Consequently, some autonomous communities have enacted their own foundation laws and established corresponding protectorates.

designated for this supervisory role; and internal control exercised by a body within the foundation itself. Thus, alongside the governing board (*patronato*), there may exist within the same entity an independent private oversight body. Spanish legislation has opted for control exercised by a specific public authority designated for supervision. Therefore, the public body responsible for this control is the Protectorate. In enterprise foundations, the supervisory role traditionally assigned to the general assembly in commercial companies is externally exercised by the Protectorate, without any other body tasked with ensuring that the directors' management aligns with the founder's intent and the foundation's statutes.[42]

As previously mentioned, the situation in Spain is a result of the political and legal structure of a composite and multi-legislative state, which has led to a current legal framework for foundations comprising a national law, a development regulation and regional legislation. Therefore, the authorities overseeing foundations are governed by a variety of regional laws. This discussion will refer only to the single Protectorate for foundations under state jurisdiction. This body aims to ensure the proper exercise of the right to establish foundations and the legality of their establishment and operation, providing support, encouragement and advice services.

Since its implementation, all functions of the Protectorate for foundations under state jurisdiction, with the sole exception of banking foundations, have been concentrated within the Ministry of Education, Culture and Sport.[43]

As for its functions, unlike in other countries, the Protectorate performs prior supervision, focusing on the legality of the founding act and its process, which is approved by an administrative body without discretionary power and subsequently registered. Post-supervision control generally concerns legal operation, compliance with foundational purposes, and the activities carried out. This includes ensuring the beneficiaries' right to see the public interest fulfilled, the preservation of assets and tax oversight.[44] It is clear that the Protectorate is justified by the need to ensure respect for the founder's intent and the achievement of the public interest pursued by the foundation. Thus, administrative intervention is necessary to guarantee that the foundation's purpose and the founder's will are properly fulfilled.[45]

---

42 A. Emparanza Sobejano, above n. 14, p. 166.

43 For banking foundations, see A. Emparanza Sobejano (ed), *Comentarios a la ley de cajas de ahorros y fundaciones bancarias*, Aranzadi, Navarre 2015.

44 On the specific functions of the Protectorate, see J. Canal Muñoz and M. Muñoz Sánchez-Capuchino, 'El Protectorado de las Fundaciones' (2015) 1 *Anuario de Derecho de Fundaciones* 41, 66.

45 M.A. Cabra de Luna, above n. 40, 23, states that the Protectorate's role should focus more on advisory (facilitating function) and promotional (publicity and fostering function) activities rather than on auditing and control, which should be minimal and centred on fundamental

Although in all the countries within our environment there exists an authority responsible for safeguarding the public interest, the degree of intensity of such intervention varies depending on the different models they have adopted. We can conclude that the role of the Protectorate in Spain is justified by the need to ensure that the founder's will is respected and that the foundation's pursuit of the public interest is fulfilled. Administrative intervention is necessary to guarantee that both the foundation's objectives and the founder's intentions are properly carried out. In any case, the level of intervention by the Protectorate in matters concerning foundations raises numerous questions, as alternative forms of oversight could be envisaged. For instance, this could take the form of internal control within the foundation itself, or external oversight through the registry, or judicial supervision.

6. PUBLIC REGISTRY OF FOUNDATIONS AND THE COMMERCIAL REGISTRY

As noted earlier, one of the characteristics of the legal framework for enterprise foundations is its regulatory fragmentation. Foundations are governed by a national law as well as regional laws. This fragmentation also extends to the registration of entities, resulting in a state-level registry for foundations and a series of regional registries configured in diverse ways.[46]

The current framework provides for the existence of a foundation's registry under the Ministry of Justice, where acts related to foundations that operate nationwide or primarily in more than one autonomous community are registered. Such foundations are considered to fall under state jurisdiction. The registry is overseen by the Directorate General of Registries and Notaries, whose head serves as its director, and it has a unique status for the entire national territory.[47]

---

aspects (legality assurance, fulfilment of public interest purposes, accountability, and provisional exercise of board functions in the absence of directors).

46 R. La Casa, 'La publicidad registral de las fundaciones y el registro mercantil' in A. Emparanza Sobejano (ed), above n. 2, p. 203, notes that the key issue is not merely the numerical existence of multiple foundation registries but rather their subjection to a variety of regulatory frameworks of very different nature and content. For more on regional registries, see R. La Casa, 'La publicidad registral de las fundaciones y el registro mercantil' (2014) 292 *Revista de Derecho Mercantil* 121.

47 R. La Casa, above n. 46, p. 205, notes that the legal framework governing the registration of foundations is very concise (Articles 36 and 37 of the Foundations Law). However, the issue of the effectiveness attributed to the register deserves particular attention, as it is fundamental to defining its functionality. In this regard, the public nature of foundation registries is established, accompanied by the legal presumption of awareness and content of the entries. Thus, it appears to enshrine the enforceability of registered information against third parties, substantially aligning with one of the defining characteristics of legal security registries.

On the other hand, it should be noted that the publicity of foundations is legally organised outside the commercial registry. However, considering that enterprise foundations may be regarded as traders, it seems inconsistent to exclude them from the means of registry publicity intended for such entities. It is striking that even foundations qualifying as traders, due to their regular conduct of business activities in their own name, are barred from access to the commercial registry. This is due to the principle of *numerus clausus* for registrable entities. Thus, the lack of explicit legal authorisation prevents the registration of such foundations, despite their status as traders.

The consequence of this limitation is that the commercial registry does not accommodate all entities deserving the classification of traders.[48]

7. CONCLUSIONS

Enterprise foundations in Spain play a crucial role in promoting the country's social, cultural, and economic development. These entities, linked to private companies, serve as instruments to channel corporate social responsibility, fostering sustainable projects that benefit the community. Their impact is evident in key areas such as education, research, social inclusion and environmental conservation. However, they face significant challenges, including vague regulations that hinder uniform operations and administrative registration issues that impede transparency and oversight. Despite these limitations, their structure enables effective collaboration between the private sector and civil society, driving innovative and far-reaching initiatives. In the context of growing demand for corporate commitment, foundations are consolidating their position as strategic actors in addressing contemporary social challenges in Spain.

---

[48] In this regard, the possibility of dual registration – in both the foundation registry and the commercial registry – is raised. However, R. La Casa, above n. 46, p. 240, notes that if one considers the potential registration of foundations in the commercial registry as an addition to the mandatory registration in the foundation registry, it becomes readily apparent that such a situation could potentially lead to serious dysfunctions, significantly compromising transactional security, particularly in cases of discrepancies between the entries recorded in the two registries.

ENTERPRISE FOUNDATIONS IN PORTUGAL

Carolina CUNHA and Maria Inês OLIVEIRA MARTINS*

* The authors would like to express their gratitude to Rafael Mourão for the dedicated fieldwork of surveying an extensive sample of private foundation charters.

ABSTRACT

This chapter examines the legal framework of enterprise foundations in Portugal. Although not expressly recognised in law, enterprise foundations operate within the regime of private foundations, which must pursue a purpose of social interest. The analysis covers establishment requirements, governance structures, internal and external supervision, and dissolution rules, highlighting the scarcity of specific regulation and the discretion left to founders. The chapter also discusses supervisory gaps and tax implications. Drawing on field research of foundation charters, it shows that enterprise foundations indeed seem to emerge as vehicles for succession planning or socially oriented business ownership.

1. INTRODUCTION

Under Portuguese law, a foundation is a non-profit legal person, without owners, members, or shareholders, and with sufficient assets irrevocably allocated to the pursuit of a social interest purpose. For many years, at the centre of foundation law was a specific section of the 1966 Portuguese Civil Code (PCC). Its leading role was somewhat challenged since the 2012 Framework Law on Foundations (FLF) came into force, providing a more detailed regulation.[1]

Foundation law encompasses other relevant statutes, such as the 2019 Foundations Registration Act (FRA), the 2013 Ordinance on Minimum Endowment (OME) and the 2021 Framework Law on Public Utility Status (FLPUS).[2]

---

1 Even prompting several reforms in the PCC section on foundations (Articles 157–166 and 185–194), both in 2012, when the FLF was adopted, and in 2015, when the FLF underwent some modifications. The FLF was approved by Law no. 24/2012 of 9 July 2012 and modified by Law no. 150/2015 of 10 September 2015, then by Law no. 36/2021 of 14 June 2021 and Law no. 67/2021 of 25 August 2021.

2 FLF: Law no. 24/2012 of 9 July 2012; FRA: Decree-Law no. 157/2019 of 22 October 2019; OME: Ordinance no. 75/2013 of 18 February 2013; FLPUS: Law no. 36/2021 of 14 June 2021.

From the available data, it is not easy to accurately report the number of foundations in Portugal, but a sound estimate places that number at around 800.[3]

There are currently two main types of foundations: private foundations and public foundations. The typology may be misleading, as it is based solely on the private or public nature of the founders – or rather, on the private or public origin of the initial endowment, assessed by the majority of assets it includes – and does not take purpose into consideration.[4] This means that a foundation pursuing a social interest purpose (as all Portuguese foundations are required to do), if established by a private person with private capitals, will be qualified as private, despite what, in some jurisdictions, might be considered the 'public' nature of its purpose. What in those same jurisdictions might be considered a 'private' purpose (e.g. the wellbeing of the founder's family) is simply not allowed under Portuguese law. Portuguese private foundations and public foundations are separately regulated by the FLF; each one is addressed by a specific section but even in the general provisions some distinctions between them are made.

Within Portuguese private foundations, aside from general foundations, there are three narrower subtypes subject to particular rules: social solidarity foundations (Article 39 FLF), development cooperation foundations (Article 42 FLF) and foundations for the establishment of private higher education institutions (Article 45 FLF).

A private foundation can be granted public utility status or be set up as a private institution of social solidarity, which comes with several tax benefits and other advantages, as well as with some additional regulation.[5] These foundations are subject to considerable limitations and are not suitable for the pursuit of economic activities in competitive markets. We shall thus not delve into their regime, only alluding to it by way of contrast with the general norms on foundations.

---

3 See Raquel Campos Franco (ed), *O impacto social das fundações portuguesas*, Católica Porto Business School/Centro Português de Fundações, Porto 2021, pp. 35–36.

4 Private foundations are set up by one or more persons governed by private law, jointly or not with public legal persons, provided that the latter, alone or jointly, do not have a dominant influence over the foundation. Public foundations can be either 'of private law' (set up by one or more public legal persons, jointly or not with persons governed by private law, provided that the former, alone or jointly, have a dominant influence over the foundation) or 'of public law' (set up exclusively by public legal persons (Article 4(1) FLF). Dominant influence exists whenever there is either the exclusive or predominant endowing of the assets that make up the initial capital of the foundation, or the right to appoint or dismiss the majority of the members of the foundation's governing board (Article 4(2) FLF).

5 Respectively Statute of Private Institutions of Social Solidarity, enacted by Decree-Law no. 119/83 of 25 February 1983 and FLPUS.

Private institutions of social solidarity supplement the role of the state in the realisation of the citizen's social rights and normally work in cooperation with public entities. They may only engage in profit-oriented activities as a means of financing their charitable social solidarity ones (Article 1(B)(2) Statute of Private Institutions of Social Solidarity).

As to the status of public utility, it is granted upon request to foundations that have been active for at least the last three years in any of a broad range of areas (for instance, health, education, housing, science, culture, agri-food, entrepreneurship and innovation ...), cooperate with public entities in this realm and comply with requirements of transparency, capability and accounting standards (Article 4(1)–(3), Article 8(1) FLPUS). It is also automatically granted to private institutions of social solidarity (Article 28(1)(b) FLPUS).

Notably, the status of public utility can only be granted if the applicant legal entity does not exclusively or primarily engage in the production and sale of goods or services for an active and competitive market in any economic sector in such a way that the granting of said status would prevent, distort or significantly restrict competition, in whole or in part, in the corresponding relevant market (Article 8(4) FLPUS). As far as we could ascertain in the field research, the status of public utility was very rarely attributed to foundations offering any goods or services in a competitive market, even as a side activity.

2. ENTERPRISE FOUNDATIONS AND PURPOSE

Portuguese law does not acknowledge the existence of enterprise foundations. Although there is an academic debate over their admission, a significant number of authors deems enterprise foundations compatible with the current legal framework.[6] Moreover, as revealed by founders' declarations and charters deposited in the public register,[7] practice seems to tolerate enterprise foundations to some extent – mainly, insofar as the social interest purpose is not overshadowed by business activity.

---

6 See J. Sousa Ribeiro, 'Fundações: uma espécie em vias de extensão?' in *Comemorações dos 35 anos do Código Civil e dos 25 anos da Reforma de 1977*, vol. II, Coimbra Editora, Coimbra 2006, pp. 253 et seq.; D. Soares Farinho, 'Empresa e fundações: uma união mais forte?' (2012) IV(4) *Revista de Direito das Sociedades* 805, 811 et seq. With an unfavourable position regarding the admissibility of enterprise foundations, see P. Olavo Cunha, "As "fundações-empresa" – liberdade paradoxal ou paradoxo da liberdade (de instituição)", in *Direito das Fundações em Debate – Perspetivas de Reforma*, D. Costa Gonçalves/R. Soares Pereira (ed.), Princípia, Cascais, 2020, 169, 172 et seq.

7 Accessible at: https://publicacoes.mj.pt/Pesquisa.aspx.

2.1. THE LEGAL FRAMEWORK

In the current regulatory framework, enterprise foundations qualify as private foundations in the very specific Portuguese sense that they are set by private founders with private capitals (see above, section 1). It is nevertheless mandatory for all Portuguese foundations – either private or public – to pursue a purpose of social interest.[8] The definition is quite broad: a purpose that benefits one or more categories of people other than the founder, his/her relatives and family members or people or entities linked to the founder by friendship or business relationships. From the list of legal examples of social interest purposes, we can conclude the concept is similar to the idea of public benefit purpose required by the European Foundation Proposal Regulation.[9]

Family enterprise foundations are not allowed, insofar as all family foundations are prohibited: a foundation will be denied recognition if its purpose benefits the founder, his/her family or a restricted universe of beneficiaries related to them.[10]

Pure enterprise foundations, i.e. those pursuing exclusively business purposes, do not comply with the social interest requirement because they are not for the benefit of others. Thus, a foundation cannot be set up for the sole purpose of running a business or of holding shares in a company.[11]

However, a foundation can run a business either to pursue its specific purpose of social interest or as a means to obtain revenues to pursue such purpose. Within this framework, it is admissible for a foundation either to directly run a business, as its owner (operating enterprise foundation), or to indirectly run a business, by having controlling influence over a business company, i.e. owning more than 50% of the share capital and/or more than 50% of the voting rights (holding enterprise foundation).[12]

The balance between pursuing the social interest purpose and (directly or indirectly) running a business should not lean too much on the side of the latter, otherwise the Foundation Authority can enforce dissolution on the grounds that the activities carried out by the foundation reveal that the real purpose

8 Article 185(1) PCC, Article 3(1) FLF.

9 There is a clear similarity between Article 3(2) FLF and Article 5(2) of the Proposal for a Council Regulation on the Statute for a European Foundation (FE), COM(2012)35 final. Social interest should not be confused with strict public interest, as it only implies a certain usefulness for the community – see E.R. Vilar, 'Fundações – Legitimidade, responsabilidade e (auto-)regulação' in *Nos 20 anos do Código das Sociedades Comerciais*, vol. II, Coimbra Editora, Coimbra 2007, p. 538. Thus, purposes of social interest are not restricted to those of a purely charitable nature and often encompass carrying out economic activities in a business-like manner – see J. Sousa Ribeiro, above n. 6, p. 256.

10 Article 188(3)(a) PCC, Article 3(2) FLF. See E.R. Vilar, above n. 9, p. 539.

11 M.N. Serens, 'Corporate-sponsored foundations: altruísmo ou (ainda) economicidade?', *III Congresso Direito das Sociedades em Revista*, Almedina, Coimbra 2014, p. 585; J. Sousa Ribeiro, above n. 6, p. 254.

12 J. Sousa Ribeiro, above n. 6, pp. 253–258; D. Soares Farinho, above n. 6, 818–823.

does not match the purpose set in the founding act.[13] The tipping point of this required balance is at the core of the academic dispute regarding the admission of enterprise foundations.[14]

2.2. INSIGHTS FROM PRACTICE

Against this moderately flexible legal background, practice discloses the existence of some enterprise foundations. By going through numerous charters deposited in the public register, several conclusions can be drawn.

First and foremost, regardless of the foundation's specific purpose, a significant number of charters include clauses explicitly allowing the foundation to hold shares in companies, or even to create companies, provided it is useful either for pursuing its purpose or for maximising asset management. This reveals that indirectly owning a business is widely seen as acceptable, whether it aligns with the foundation's purpose (thus pursuing it) or merely constitutes a sensible investment.

In some other instances, the foundation's purpose encompasses what we can label as economic activities. They frequently cluster around a main purpose of unquestionable social interest, typically listed in the FLF as such[15] – e.g. health, wellbeing and medical care; support of children, youth or elderly; education and training; addressing people's housing problems; etc. – and in several cases these economic activities align with the foundation's purpose (e.g. running a medical clinic, a daycare centre, a retirement home, a school, etc.). What the charters seldom make clear is how these economic activities shall be pursued – i.e. from a business point of view, through a for-profit company or a directly owned for-profit enterprise, or from a charitable point of view, without adequate compensation from the users.

Some light can be shed by a common charter provision stating the foundation income may derive from all activities carried out in pursuit of its purpose, as

13 Article 192(2)(b) PCC, Article 35(2)(b) FLF.

14 With authors arguing that operating a business cannot constitute the foundation's main purpose, even if the resulting income is used to pursue a social interest purpose (M.N. Serens, above n. 11, pp. 585–587), while others reckon that foundations are defined by their social interest purpose and therefore all activities that contribute in an appropriate way to achieving such purpose are justified (J. Sousa Ribeiro, above n. 6, pp. 253–258). The former seems to consider that as long as running and preserving a specific business is paramount in the foundation structure (as can be inferred from the presence of an ownership clause – see below section 3.2.2), the existence and the effective pursuit of social interest purposes is not enough, because in such case 'the company would not be serving the foundation, but the foundation would be serving the company'. One can argue that it is not at all clear that this conclusion flows from the legal framework. Surely enough the social interest purpose must be actively pursued – and not merely proclaimed – but nothing seems to prevent simultaneously honouring the founder's will to preserve the business, as argued by D. Soares Farinho, above n. 6, 819.

15 Article 3(2) FLF lists more than 25 examples of purposes that qualify as 'of social interest'.

well as from services rendered to external parties. This suggests the possibility of a true enterprise foundation, running a for-profit business structure, even if some room is left for a nuanced approach (e.g. by distinguishing between users according to their economic status or vulnerability).[16] When the economic activity and purpose do not align – i.e. when the former is purely seen as a means to provide income to pursue the latter – the for-profit nature of the business owned by the foundation becomes much clearer.[17]

Although our field research was limited to charters deposited in the public register and therefore can only provide a narrow insight on the way enterprise foundations operate, it seems that in some cases they are possibly being used as an instrument of planned business succession – namely when company shares make for a significant part of the initial endowment. In one case, the founder was the chairperson of the board of a holding company whose shares provided for more than two-thirds of the initial endowment value, although the foundation could not be qualified as an enterprise foundation based on its shareholder status alone, since it owns a mere 6% of the shares in the company. In another instance, however, the founder made an initial endowment of all the shares in a company that runs two medical clinics and appointed himself as the foundation's lifelong president and chairperson of the board. It should be noted that the foundation purpose explicitly included 'the provision of medical services in an inpatient health facility and specialised outpatient clinical medical practice'.

In other instances, foundations seem to be chosen as the adequate ownership structure for socially oriented businesses. That was the case with a foundation the sole purpose of which was acquiring and restoring traditional houses in villages in rural areas to put them on the market at moderate rents, thus fighting the desertification of the countryside and improving housing supply.

Overall, what may be lacking in the Portuguese landscape is a sharper sociological awareness of the role of enterprise foundations, as well as dispelling lingering traditional hesitations about their compatibility with the legal framework. As steward ownership structures start to draw attention both from entrepreneurs and from academia, enterprise foundations are likely to gain some visibility.[18]

---

16 For instance, determining the medical services provided will be paid for in order to sustain the foundation's activity, although they may be free of charge depending on the financial situation of the users as ascertained by a questionnaire; or determining that the private school owned by the foundation will award scholarships to outstanding students who are economically disadvantaged.

17 For example, a foundation pursuing charitable, philanthropic, cultural and educational purposes is the sole shareholder of two for-profit limited liability companies running two four-star hotels.

18 The main problem being the extremely high minimum capital requirement – see below section 3.1.1.

3. ESTABLISHMENT, MODIFICATIONS AND DISSOLUTION – A BRIEF OVERVIEW FROM AN ENTERPRISE FOUNDATION'S PERSPECTIVE

3.1. ESTABLISHMENT

3.1.1. Initial Endowment Requirements

Besides the pursuit of a social interest purpose, a foundation must be set up with a sufficient amount of capital.[19] If the assets assigned are deemed insufficient or inadequate, the foundation will be denied legal recognition.[20]

The minimum value of the initial endowment (or rather the amount 'presumed sufficient' for such endowment) has been set rather high, at €250,000.[21] In addition, the assets that make up the initial endowment of a foundation must 'ideally' include a cash portion of at least 30% of the total and, in any case, of not less than €100,000.[22]

Those values are significantly high in the Portuguese context (where a limited liability company requires, in the stricter scenario, €50,000 to be set up) and are bound to prevent the choice of this legal form by some potential founders. Moreover, they remain equally high in comparison with the amount required by the European Foundation Proposal (€25,000)[23] or by jurisdictions in much stronger economies.[24]

By setting this threshold, the Portuguese lawmaker has avowedly disregarded the recommendation made by the Advisory Council for Foundations (see below, section 5.2), suggesting that the value of the initial endowment should be aligned with the amounts under discussion regarding the European Foundation Proposal. The justification behind the setting of a higher amount was 'the desirable sustainability of foundations … without systematic recourse to public support'[25] – a

19 Article 3(1) FLF.

20 Namely if they are burdened with charges that compromise the fulfilment of the foundation purposes or if they do not generate sufficient income to guarantee the fulfilment of such purpose – Article 188(3)(b) PCC.

21 Article 22(3) FLF, Articles 2 and 3 OME.

22 Sufficient endowment is presumed if the foundation's assets value meets the minimum capital requirement (Article 22(3) FLF), but the ultimate assessment should take into consideration the correlation between capital and purpose, so it is not impossible (although rare) that complying with such requirement proves not to be enough – or, conversely, that an initial lower capital may be deemed sufficient.

23 Article 7(2) of the Proposal, above n. 9.

24 The Austrian private foundation has a minimum capital requirement of €70,000 (S. Kalss, 'The Austrian foundation' in this volume, p.[x]; in Denmark €40,000 is sufficient (R.K. Feldthusen, 'Denmark: Enterprise Foundations' in this volume, p.[x].

25 Together with a circumstantial argument – at the time Portugal was under financial and economic rescue by the International Monetary Fund (IMF), the Council of Europe

reasoning which seems to derive from a particular model of public financing that has little to do with the structure of a private enterprise foundation.[26]

Another observation made by the Advisory Council for Foundations that was entirely disregarded warned that the initial endowment does not necessarily have the same meaning to all foundations, considering some may receive the required financial resources in regular contributions over time.[27] The Advisory Council mentioned the example of foundations set by companies, but the same reasoning should apply to foundations that own companies or businesses.

Against this background, establishing an enterprise foundation may be financially challenging for startups or smaller businesses, but as long as the enterprise or the company shares are worth (at least) €150,000 and the founder can add €100,000 in cash, the minimum capital requirements are met. Thus, enterprise foundations remain a valid option as a succession planning tool for mature businesses.

3.1.2. Founder's Declaration and Charter: Legal Recognition

The setting up of a foundation is a twofold process, requiring:

- the founder's declaration (establishment act), either through a unilateral act documented in a public deed or through a will; and
- the legal recognition by the Foundation Authority.

The founder declaration and charter provisions are usually two separate documents,[28] but some clauses can be placed in either one of them.[29] Portuguese law allows for the lack or the incompleteness of charter provisions, which can be drawn up or completed either by the Foundation Authority or by the executor of the will, always taking into account the real or presumed intentions of the founder.[30]

Development Bank (CEB) and the European Commission (EC) and had undertaken specific commitments (see the OME recitals).

26 See E.R. Vilar, above n. 9, p. 539. This assumption that foundations somehow rely on public financing also stems from the narrow concept that foundations mostly operate in areas where the state is unable to provide a suitable answer to societal needs.

27 A view commonly accepted by Portuguese scholars – see J. Sousa Ribeiro, 'As fundações no Código Civil: regime actual e projecto de reforma' (2001) 1–2 *Lusíada Revista de Ciência e Cultura* 59, 62; M.N. Serens, above n. 11, pp. 603–604; A. Ferrer Correia and A. de Sá, 'Algumas notas sobre fundações' (1989) XV *Revista de Direito e Economia* 331, 334.

28 As confirmed by Article 22(2)(b) and (2)(j) FLF.

29 Such as the location of the administrative headquarters, the terms of the foundation organisation and operation, the terms of its transformation or extinction, the destination of its assets upon liquidation – Article 186(2) PCC, Article 18(2) FLF. Nevertheless, the foundation purpose and the foundation initial assets should always be specified in the founder's declaration – Article 186(1) PCC, Article 18(1) FLF.

30 Article 187 PCC, Article 19(2) FLF.

There is a model charter available under the simplified procedure for recognising private foundations,[31] which is also intended as a reference for potential founders even in cases where the simplified procedure does not apply. Legal recognition means the foundation becomes a legal person and acquires the assets and entitlements assigned to it by the founder's declaration.[32]

Private foundations are recognised on an individual basis by an administrative decision made by the Foundation Authority.[33] The procedure is initiated online by submitting a list of documents, legal certificates and binding declarations and the final decision must be taken within 90 days.[34] There is a fast-track procedure, available under certain conditions, with fewer (but not much fewer) documents required and a faster outcome – the decision must be issued within 30 days.[35] Since one of the requirements of this simplified procedure is that the foundation's initial endowment should consist solely of cash, its usefulness for establishing enterprise foundations – where the initial endowment tends to include either company shares or an enterprise – is quite limited.

3.1.3. Irrevocability

When the foundation is established by a living founder, the transfer of property becomes irrevocable as soon as recognition is requested (or begins *ex officio*).[36] If the foundation is set up by will, the founder's heirs cannot revoke it unless compulsory succession rules are infringed.[37] This contingency should be taken into consideration when enterprise foundations are elected as succession planning tools for family businesses.

However, should recognition be refused on grounds of insufficient capital, the establishment of a foundation by a living founder will have no effect, thus releasing the assets.[38] If the founder is no longer alive, the assets shall be transferred to an association or foundation with similar purpose to be designated by the Foundation Authority, unless the founder has stipulated otherwise.

---

31 The model charter was approved by Order no. 11648-A/2016, issued by the Foundation Authority, allowing for the simplified procedure referred in Article 22(6) FLF to be implemented.

32 Article 188(2) PCC, Articles 6(1) and 20(2) FLF.

33 Article 158(2) PCC, Article 6(2) FLF.

34 Article 22 FLF.

35 Article 22(6) FLF.

36 Article 185(2) PCC, Article 17(2) FLF.

37 Article 185(3) PCC, Article 17(3) FLF.

38 Article 188(5) PCC.

3.2. MODIFICATIONS

3.2.1. Charter Amendments

Regular charter amendments may at any time be proposed by the foundation's governing board, after which they must be approved by the Foundation Authority. All amendments need to conform to a strict boundary: they can neither represent an essential change to the defined purpose nor can they contradict the founder's will (as expressed at the time the foundation was set up).[39] However, it is not completely impossible to change the foundation's purpose, even if it may prove rather difficult.[40]

First and foremost, no change of purpose can take place if the charter forbids it. When this is not the case, a different purpose may be assigned to the foundation, but only when the original purpose is facing some specific hardship.[41] The Foundation Authority then has the power to ascribe a different purpose to the foundation, upon hearing both the founder (if alive) and the board of directors.[42] In any case, the new purpose must be as close as possible to the original one.

It is interesting to note that if the original purpose is not abandoned, it can be broadened in much more flexible terms. Although both the founder (if alive) and the board still must be heard, the single material prerequisite to expand a foundation's purpose is that it promotes the social maximisation of the available resources.

3.2.2. Ownership Clauses

In the context of enterprise foundations, an ownership clause typically makes it difficult to sell the foundation's business or the shares in the company, because permission from the foundation authority would be required. The question has not been discussed in Portuguese literature, as far as we know, but there seems to be no obstacle to the foundation charter including an ownership clause – e.g. a provision stating that the business or company shares should not be sold.

---

39 Article 189 PCC, Article 31 FLF.

40 Article 190 PCC, Article 32 FLF.

41 To be more precise, when when the original purpose has been entirely fulfilled, has become impossible or is of no further social interest, as well as when the foundation's assets become insufficient to pursue it.

42 If the founder is no longer alive, it does not seem impossible to take into consideration some expression of his/her original will – e.g. the indication of a subsidiary purpose in case the main one is fulfilled or has become impossible – provided it can be found in the establishment act or in the charter.

The respect legally granted to the founder's will as stated in the charter[43] seems to allow for such a clause. In fact, the only 'negative' requirement to which the charter provisions are subject (other than 'positive' requirements related to internal organisation and some key aspects of running the foundation)[44] is general compliance with the law.[45]

If the foundation charter includes an ownership clause, it would prove quite difficult to change or supress it. As we have seen, charter amendments can neither represent essential change to the purpose nor contradict the founder's will.[46] Therefore, if the founder's will has been clearly stated through the ownership clause, suppressing it (or even modifying it) will not be allowed. Furthermore, if the ownership clause has the extra layer of being encompassed by purpose (e.g. a foundation dedicated to promoting health that owns a medical clinic), suppressing it (or even modifying it) can be seen as compromising the foundation's purpose, thus providing additional grounds for rejecting the proposed amendment.

Even in the absence of an explicit ownership clause, there is still some possibility to object to the sale of company shares or of the business itself. The law does not contain a special provision for general private foundations, but the provision set for both private foundations with public utility status and public foundations provides a useful benchmark.[47] It states that the disposal of the foundation's assets endowed by the founder, identified in the foundation charter and deemed to be of special significance for the purposes of the foundation, shall require permission from the Foundation Authority, otherwise it will be null and void. Permission can be refused if the sale would jeopardise the pursuit of the foundation's purposes in a way that would be difficult to revert. Such assets could be company shares or a business itself.

Of course, such a provision is not directly applicable to general private foundations. But its core idea can be quite useful in handling the same predicament in private foundations. It can be argued that foundation directors have the duty not to sell either company shares or the business itself if such assets are identified in the charter and are deemed to be of special significance for the purposes of the foundation. One can even go a step further and ask whether the foundation, as a legal person, has the required capacity to make such a sale. As a rule, the capacity of legal persons covers all the rights and obligations necessary or convenient for the pursuit of their purposes.[48] Since the aforementioned assets are of special significance to the pursuit of the foundation's purpose, their sale

---

[43] To the point where even if the charter provisions do not exist or are incomplete, the Foundation Authority shall draft them or complete them 'as far as possible' taking into account 'the actual or presumed will of the founder' (Article 187(3) PCC, Article 19(3) FLF).

[44] Article 186(2) PCC, Article 18(2) FLF.

[45] Article 188(3)(c) PCC, Article 23(1)(d) FLF.

[46] See section 3.2.1 above.

[47] Article 11 FLF.

[48] Article 160(1) PCC.

would not be necessary or convenient, thus falling outside of the foundation's legal capacity, making it null and void.[49]

3.2.3. Mergers

The 2012 foundation law reform explicitly acknowledged the possibility of foundation mergers, provided it would not contradict the will of the respective founders.[50] The final decision is entrusted to the Foundation Authority, under the proposal of the management bodies and upon hearing both the founders (if alive) and the directors. The merger of foundations can also be determined as an alternative to extending the foundation's purpose in case of hardship situations,[51] namely when the foundation's assets become insufficient to pursue its purpose. In any case, all the foundations involved in the merger should pursue similar purposes. There is no further regulation on the specific details of foundation merger, but rules on companies' mergers can provide sufficient legal support.[52]

3.3. DISSOLUTION

3.3.1. Grounds for Dissolution

Foundations can be dissolved on specific grounds and through several procedures.[53] Foundations can be semi-automatically dissolved upon the occurrence of a list of causes which shall be notified by the management body to the Foundation Authority, who then formally declares the foundation dissolved. The list comprises the lapse of time, if the foundation has been set up temporarily; the occurrence of any cause specified in the foundation charter; and the closure of insolvency proceedings when the continuity of the foundation is not permitted by the insolvency court.

Foundations can also be dissolved by an autonomous decision from the Foundation Authority, after hearing the Advisory Council for Foundations, when the purpose has been exhausted or has become impossible; when the activities carried out show that the real purpose does not align with the purpose set out by the founder; or when no relevant activity has been conducted during the previous three years. The law grants the Foundation Authority the powers

---

49 Because that is the consequence for breach of legal capacity, in principle and according to Article 294 PCC.

50 Article 190-A PCC, Article 33 FLF.

51 Listed in Article 190 PCC and Article 32(2) FLF – see above, n. 45.

52 Namely Article 97 of the Commercial Companies Code (CCC), Decree-Law no. 262/86 of 2 September 1986, which regulates both mergers resulting in the formation of a new legal person and mergers by absorption.

53 Articles 192–193 PCC, Articles 35–36 FLF.

to order investigations or audits to ascertain the facts. In some extreme cases – when purpose is systematically pursued by illicit or immoral means or when the foundation existence becomes contrary to public order – foundations can be dissolved by court decision, in an action brought by the Public Prosecutor's office or by the Foundation Authority.

3.3.2. Liquidation

The dissolution of the foundation sets in motion the process of liquidating its assets.[54] The Foundation Authority will be in charge and shall adopt the measures it deems convenient. If there is an express provision by the founder on the destination of the remaining assets (i.e. those that remain after creditors are paid in full) in the event of dissolution, it shall be complied with. Otherwise, remaining assets are handed over to a non-profit association or to a foundation with similar purposes, designated by the foundation board or by the Foundation Authority. As a last resort, if none of the above is possible, the assets revert to the State.

4. GOVERNANCE AND INTERNAL SUPERVISION

4.1. GENERAL REMARKS: SCARCITY OF THE EXISTING RULES

The fact that, unlike a shareholder or an associate, the founder as such remains external to the foundation's activity and performs no supervisory role in its structure, is known to enhance problems of incentives regarding the behaviour of managing bodies.[55] The rules on foundational governance are expected to compensate for such shortcomings and the FLF did bring some innovative rules to this realm – e.g. the rules detailing the organ structure and composition, those requiring the adoption of codes of conduct and several new disclosure requirements (Articles 7, 9 and 26 to 27 FLF). Nonetheless, the existing rules on governance remain very scarce.

This has the upside of giving considerable room to the founder's private autonomy, allowing for the adaptation of the governance structure to the size and scope of the foundation's activity. The FLF indeed puts a great emphasis

54 Articles 166 and 194 PCC, Articles 12 and 37 FLF. Also Article 184 PCC (the powers of the board shall be limited to carrying out purely conservative acts and those necessary either for the liquidation of the assets or for finalising pending business).

55 For mentions of this well-known problem in Portuguese scholarship, see e.g. D. Soares Farinho, 'Alguns problemas de governo fundacional de uma perspectiva normativo-orgânica' in *O governo das organizações: A vocação universal do corporate governance*, Almedina, Coimbra 2011, pp. 629–630; A. Figueiredo, 'A designação de administradores nas fundações de empresa' in *A designação de administradores*, Almedina, Coimbra 2015, p. 336.

on *self-regulation*, requiring foundations to adopt and publish codes of conduct where they self-regulate good practices, particularly regarding the participation of the beneficiaries of their activities in the life of the foundation, the transparency of their accounts, conflicts of interest, incompatibilities (Article 7(1) FLF).

On the downside, the paucity of the regime creates the risk of poorly designed governance rules and leaves room for doubt on points not addressed by the charter – moreover considering that the body of case law regarding foundational governance is very scarce.

These problems may be alleviated by the availability of model charters catering to foundations of some complexity. There is indeed a model charter prepared and made available by the Portuguese Centre of Foundations (PCF), a private association that gathers some of the more influential foundations in the country.[56] It may, however, not fit the exact needs of the founders in the case.

4.2. FOUNDATION BODIES: MAIN FEATURES

The FLF sets out a two-tier system, with separated supervisory and management bodies. It provides for two bodies with management competences: a management body, responsible for managing the foundation's assets, as well as deliberating on proposals to amend the statutes, modify, and terminate the foundation; and a governing or executive body, with functions of day-to-day management (Article 26(1)(a) and (b) FLF). Unless the charter provides differently, the management body has the competence to represent the foundation in and out of court (Article 28(1) FLF). These two bodies may be merged into a single management body, where part of the members have functions of day-to-day management (Article 27(2) FLF).

The Foundation Authority has the power to decide on key matters of particular importance to the life of the foundation – namely, those of modification of the statutes, change of purpose (termed 'transformation') or merger of the foundation, reduction or modification of the foundation's obligations or extinction. Its decisions generally require a proposal from the management body, except for changes of purpose or mergers, where consultation with the management body is sufficient (Articles 31 to 34 FLF, replicated in Articles 189 to 191 PCC). In cases of change of purpose, merger or obligation changes, the founder must also be consulted if alive (Articles 32 to 34 FLF).

Either separated or encompassing the executive body, the management body is composed of an odd number of members, one of whom is the president

56 See the Portuguese Centre of Foundations ('*Centro Português de Fundações*') website at: https://cpf.org.pt. For the model charters, see 'Modelo de Estatutos': https://cpf.org.pt/fundacoes/como-criar-uma-fundacao/modelo-de-estatutos/.

(Article 27(2) FLF and Article 164(1) PCC). The supervisory body is responsible for overseeing the management and accounts of the foundation. It may consist of a sole auditor or of a board composed of an odd number of members, one of whom is the president (Articles 26(1)(b) and 27(3) FLF and Article 164(2) PCC). Foundations thus have two or three mandatory bodies, depending on whether the managing bodies are separated or merged. As revealed by our survey of current charters, separation prevails.

As was already the case before the FLF, the charter may supplement this structure with optional bodies. The law makes express reference to the possibility of providing for a council of founders or trustees, with the mission of ensuring compliance with the foundation's statutes and respect for the will of the founder or founders (Article 26(2) FLF). Additionally, the founder has considerable leeway not only in choosing the foundation's bodies, but also in specifying their competences. He/she should however avoid that such competences overlap (Article 27(1) FLF) and should arguably respect the attribution of competences as expressly designed by the law – e.g. regarding the competence of the administrative body to propose modifications to the charter.[57]

This flexibility is very frequently used in practice to establish bodies composed of founders or a combination of founders and other individuals – typically members of the founders' families. These councils of founders or trustees are assigned with a variety of competences. The cases where they are given a purely advisory role tend to be those where either the founders are members of the management bodies or the founder is a legal entity, apparently not attached to a specific family. It is considerably more frequent that such bodies are granted critical powers such as selecting members of managing bodies or vetoing certain transactions. This is in line with the model charter made available by the PCF, which provides for a council of founders and gives it ample powers.

4.3. APPOINTMENT AND TERM OF OFFICE

Under the FLF, the initial members of the foundation's bodies are appointed by the founder, as the request for recognition must include the names of the persons who are or will be part of the foundation's governing bodies (Article 22(2)(l) FLF). There are no rules as to how subsequent appointments should be made. The terms of office are set by the charter, subject to the limitation that they cannot be lifelong, except for positions expressly created by the founder or founders with that nature in the act of establishment (Article 26(3) FLF).

57 Articles 26(1)(a) and 31 FLF and Article 189 PCC. For the latter view, A. Ferrer Correia and A. de Sá, above n. 27, 338–343, who defended that the charter cannot attribute to a different organ – namely, a council of founders – the competence to propose such a modification.

In practice, founders typically appoint themselves in the charter as members of the managing bodies, with mandates that are lifelong or terminate upon incapacity or reaching an advanced age. Family members are often also appointed in the charter under similar conditions. Charters typically also grant founders the power to appoint the governing members, whether in their capacity as founders, as members or presidents of the management body or as members of the council of founders or trustees. In other cases, future governing members are elected by co-option of the existing members. Governing members who are not directly appointed in the charter generally have limited terms of office.

4.4. THE PRESENCE AND POWERS OF FOUNDERS IN PRACTICE: COMMANDING THE FOUNDATION FROM WITHIN?

The traditional description portrays the founder as an outsider, whose influence upon the foundation crystalises in the charter, and who does not remain an active force within the entity.[58] The FLF does consider the present will of the founder in some extreme cases (change of purpose or merger of the foundation, reduction or modification of the foundation's obligations), but does not grant him/her decision-making authority over any matters. In practice, however, founders tend to exert a much more active influence on the foundation.[59] In most of the cases surveyed, foundations are instituted in the lifetime of the founders and founders play an important role in their management, either by holding the majority in the management body or by having the power to appoint its members.

All the foundation's bodies, regardless of whether they have founders as their members, are equally bound by the charter. The competence to modify it belongs exclusively to the Foundation Authority, under proposal of the management body. This may create an incentive to lay out charters that are not very detailed and which may, if necessary, be later complemented by regulations issued by the management. However, if founders with control over the foundation's bodies influence the managers to act in disregard of the charter, it is doubtful that this will have any consequence. Internal controls are unlikely to be triggered in this case and external controls are uncertain in their functioning and designed for more egregious cases.

---

58 M.A. Domingues de Andrade, *Teoria geral da relação jurídica*, vol. I, Casa do Castelo, Coimbra 1944, pp. 61–62; C.A. da Mota Pinto, A. Pinto Monteiro and P. Mota Pinto, *Teoria Geral do Direito Civil*, 4th ed., Coimbra Editora, Coimbra 2005, p. 270. Both are quoted for instance in the judgement of the Lisbon Court of Appeal of 11.12.2019, case no. 18887/18.9T8LSB.L1-7. The Legal Opinion no. 19/2023 issued by the Public Prosecutor's Office, p. 30, makes similar remarks.

59 The cases where founders remain present in the life of the foundation have been discussed in scholarship, which highlights the boundaries to their intervention – see J. Sousa Ribeiro, above n. 27, 69–70; A. Ferrer Correia and A. de Sá, above n. 27, 338–343.

4.5. RIGHTS AND DUTIES OF THE GOVERNING MEMBERS

There are no statutory rules on the rights of the governing members. In particular, there are no rules in regard of their remuneration apart from limitations that apply to private foundations with public utility status and public foundations.[60] The charters surveyed frequently set out that governing members are entitled to remuneration, or at least that they may be granted such right. In most cases, the authority to determine remuneration lies with the council of founders or trustees; this is in line with the model charter of the PCF (Article 11(1)(k)). In a relevant number of cases, such authority is assigned to the management body.

The obligations and liability of the governing members towards the foundations are defined in the charter. In the absence of charter provisions, the rules of mandate shall apply with the necessary adaptations (Article 29(1) FLF, with the same wording as Article 164 PCC).

Most of the charters surveyed lack detailed provisions on the conducts required from the governing members. A few charters adopt the provisions of the PCF model charter concerning the dismissal of governing body members. In addition to referring generally to breaches of duty, these provisions specify obligations such as safeguarding the foundation's reputation and refraining from uncivil behaviour towards other governing body members and from public conduct that contradicts the foundation's principles and values (Article 24 of the model charter).

Some of the charters include rules on conflicts of interest, generally prohibiting (direct or indirect) transactions between the foundation and members of the management body that result in personal benefit for the latter. Less commonly, charters also prohibit members of the management body from voting (either in their own capacity or as representatives) on decisions in which they or certain relatives have a direct interest. The respective provision of the PCF model charter (Article 16), which encompasses both aspects, is sometimes adopted for those purposes. One of the rare rulings on matters concerning foundations held that provisions barring members of a management body from voting when they have a personal interest in the decision do not apply in cases where those members are deciding on their own appointment to non-remunerated governing positions.[61]

The codes of conduct required by the FLF could naturally serve as a source of detailed obligations for the members of governing bodies. However, among the very few foundations surveyed that complied with the requirement to maintain

60 In these cases, personnel expenses must not exceed 15% of the annual income of foundations whose primary activity consists predominantly of granting benefits or financial support to the community, and 75% of the annual income of foundations whose primary activity consists predominantly of providing services to the community (Article 10(1) FLF).

61 Lisbon Court of Appeal, 11.03.2021, case no. 1991/19.3T8TVD.L1-6.

a dedicated website (Article 9(1) FLF), only a small number made their code of conduct publicly available. Moreover, the codes of conduct that were available generally contained broad and open-ended provisions, with only one foundation with public utility status including detailed rules on the conduct of its governing bodies.

Given the lack of detailed charter provisions regarding the duties of conduct for governing bodies, the statutory rules that supplement these provisions take on greater importance. The rules on mandate give a decisive role to the principal, who has the power to give instructions to the agent, to scrutinise and approve his/her performance or terminate the relationship (Articles 1161, 1162, 1163 PCC). There is no exact parallel to this role in foundations. The scope of the mandate is foremost defined by the will of the founder, as stated in the charter and act of institution. The governing members should thus carry out their activities in accordance with those acts and to the law. Moreover, the rules on agency do not provide guidance as to how management or overseeing tasks should be undertaken. The gaps left by the rules on foundations and on mandate may be filled in by resorting by way of analogy to the rules on commercial companies. Although this approach has not been endorsed by the scarce case law on foundations, it is favoured by scholarship.[62]

The norms on commercial companies bind the members of administration and supervision bodies to general duties of care and of loyalty (Article 64 of the Commercial Companies Code (CCC)), which have been broadly discussed by scholarship and case law. Duties of care comprise an array of specific conducts and can be summarised as duties to devote the time, effort and knowledge required by the nature of the member's functions and the circumstances. Duties of loyalty are duties to exclusively consider the interests of the company and seek to fulfil them, therefore refraining from promoting the own benefit of the member or the interests of third parties.[63] Some authors further autonomise a duty of legality, conceived as a duty to assure the compliance with the laws applicable to the company.[64] Under the general standard of performance, as

62 A. Menezes Cordeiro, 'Artigo 164.° (Obrigações e responsabilidade dos titulares dos órgãos da pessoa coletiva)' in A. Menezes Cordeiro (ed), *Código Civil Comentado: I – Parte geral*, Almedina, Coimbra 2020, pp. 467–68; J. Ferreira Gomes, '§7. Administração das fundações' in D. Costa Gonçalves and R. Soares Pereira (eds), *Direito das Fundações em Debate: Perspetivas de Reforma*, Principia, Cascais 2020, p. 156; also H. Sousa Antunes, 'Fundações: a aplicação analógica de normas sobre a convocação judicial de assembleia geral' (2007) 19 *Cadernos de Direito Privado* 58, 71. It has been refused for instance by the Guimarães Court of Appeal in the judgement under commentary in the latter article, H. Sousa Antunes, 58–63.

63 J.M. Coutinho de Abreu, *Responsabilidade Civil dos Administradores de Sociedades*, 2nd ed., Almedina, Coimbra 2010, respectively pp. 18 and 25, in regard of members of the managing bodies.

64 M.A. Carneiro da Frada, 'O dever de legalidade, Um novo (e não escrito?) dever fundamental dos administradores?' in M.A. Carneiro da Frada (ed), *Forjar o Direito*, Almedina, Coimbra 2015, pp. 399 et seq.

it applies to agents, the governing members are required to fulfil their duties with the care and skill that may be reasonably required from persons with their qualifications or members of their profession.[65]

The application by way of analogy of the norm on liability of managers or supervisors of commercial companies (Article 72 CCC) clarifies that fault is presumed in case of infringement of legal or contractual duties of the governing members – a solution that would already derive from the general rule on liability in contract (Article 72 CCC and Article 799(1) PCC).[66] The norm further entails a version of the business judgement rule, granting governing members a defence based on proof that they acted in an informed manner, free of any personal interest and according to business rationality criteria. This defence only applies in realms where the members of bodies have discretionary competences, as may be the case of the management of the foundation's assets, subject to the terms of the charter.

There are special rules for liability arising from resolutions adopted by foundation bodies with several members. Governing members cannot abstain from exercising their voting rights in resolutions passed at meetings they attend. They are liable for any damages resulting from such resolutions, unless they have recorded their dissent in the minutes (Article 29(2) FLF, with the same wording as Article 164 PCC). Some authors construe this as entailing that a member who is absent from the meeting where a resolution was adopted is exempted from any liability arising from it, whereas others consider that an absent member may be held liable even if he/she records her dissenting position in the minutes.[67]

There are no administrative sanctions for governing members who breach their duties, although such measures might arguably be necessary to address the overall underdeterrence of the system.[68]

4.6. INTERNAL SUPERVISION AND ITS LIMITS

The enforcement of liability falls upon the members of the organ who did not incur in it, as well as upon the other organs of the foundation. The management

65 M. Helena Brito and M. Lurdes Vargas, 'Art 1161.º – Obrigações do mandatário' in A. Prata (ed), *Código Civil Anotado: Volume I (Artigos 1.º a 1250.º)*, Almedina, Coimbra, 2019, p. 1490; J. Ferreira Gomes, above n. 62, pp. 160, 162.

66 The liability of members of bodies towards the company is generally deemed to be of contractual nature. J. Coutinho de Abreu and M. Elisabete Ramos, 'CSC Art. 72.º, Responsabilidade de membros da administração para com a sociedade' in J. Coutinho de Abreu (ed.), *Código das Sociedades Comerciais em Comentário*, vol. I, Almedina, Coimbra 2017, p. 900.

67 For the first view, P. Olavo Cunha, 'Artigo 164.º, Obrigações e responsabilidade dos titulares dos órgãos da pessoa colectiva' in L. Carvalho Fernandes and J. Brandão Proença (eds.), *Comentário ao Código Civil. Parte Geral*, Universidade Católica Portuguesa, Lisbon 2014, p. 360; for the second, extending his views on company law to the realm of foundations, J. Ferreira Gomes, above n.62, pp. 165–66.

68 J. Ferreira Gomes, above n. 62, p. 148.

body is particularly well placed to supervise the activity of the executive body, when separated, and the overseeing of the foundation's management is one of the competences of the supervisory organ (Article 26(1)(b) FLF). As seen above, it is also frequent that the charter instates special bodies – typically, councils of founders or trustees – and endows them with further overseeing powers.

The internal supervision mechanisms may prove effective when those endowed with powers to dismiss or bring the individual parties to liability are engaged in the foundation. However, enforcement measures will hardly be taken when all the governing members are involved in the same wrongful practices – e.g. managing the foundation to their own advantage. Even when that is not the case, law-abiding members may refrain from pursuing liability for fear of reputational harm to the foundation.[69]

5. EXTERNAL SUPERVISION

Portuguese private foundations are subject to external and public supervision, provided by a network of entities: the Foundation Authority (the 'competent authority for recognition'), the Advisory Council for Foundations and, in some extreme situations, the public prosecutor and the courts. The existence of a National Public Register of Foundations can also provide some degree of external oversight of foundations' structure and main features.

5.1. FOUNDATION AUTHORITY

The law makes numerous references to the 'competent authority for recognition', entrusting it with all the relevant powers regarding foundations from their creation to their extinction. Oddly enough, what we refer to as the Foundation Authority is not truly a special entity or an independent agency. In fact, one must piece together several legal provisions to even find out which entity is actually in charge of foundations' legal oversight.

The recognition of private foundations is the responsibility of the Prime Minister, with the option to delegate the necessary powers (Article 20(1) FLF). Should the Prime Minister exercise this option, the delegation shall cover all the competences legally attributed to the entity competent for recognition (Article 20(5) FLF). But it is not clear who could be the recipient of such delegation. Some light is incidentally shed by a provision on model charters (Article 22(8) FLF), which shall be approved by 'the member of the government

69 J. Ferreira Gomes, above n. 62, p. 148.

responsible for recognising foundations'. Following this legal thread, the 'Foundation Authority' would be the member of government to which the Prime Minister delegates all the powers related to foundations' supervision.

Currently, however, the recipient is not even a formal member of government, but a subdivision of the government called Secretariat-General of the Presidency of the Council of Ministers (SGPCM).[70] This is also the entity charged with – among other things[71] – initiating the processes of granting, renewing, or terminating the status of public utility to all eligible legal persons (including foundations) and this role seems to be paramount, somehow overshadowing its competences as a foundation authority.

It should be noted that such status quo can give rise to some concerns about political interference, as well as to a possible lack of consistency regarding foundations oversight, because it is not entrusted to single independent entity. When foundation law was reformed, in the legislative process that led to the approval of the FLF in 2012, the creation of a public independent authority (named the National Commission for Foundations) was deemed paramount by the drafters of the project.[72] Separation from the government would be assured both in its composition and in its *modus operandi*. Unfortunately, that part of the project was never passed into law. The Portuguese Foundation Authority is thus a non-dedicated body, which may not be properly staffed for matters of foundation law and exercises its competences discretionarily. These combined features do not offer reassurance on the quality or even predictability of its activity and do not allow for scrutiny. Moreover, its enforcement powers are, at the same time, limited and overreaching, targeting the foundation itself and not the liability of its governing members. Although the Foundation Authority has, as mentioned above, the power to dissolve or request the judicial dissolution of the foundation, it lacks the power to enforce the liability of governing members or to remove them, leaving it without adequate means to address wrongful individual conduct in an otherwise functional foundation.

---

70 'The Secretariat-General of the Presidency of the Council of Ministers (SGPCM) is a central service under the remit of the Presidency of the Council of Ministers with administrative autonomy and which falls under the Prime Minister directly, or a member of Government appointed by them' (see: https://www.sg.pcm.gov.pt/en/).

71 Whose 'mission is to ensure and coordinate the legal, informative, and administrative support given to the Presidency of the Council of Ministers (PCM), ensuring inspections and audits via appraising the legal and regular nature of the acts by the PCM's services and bodies, or those under the tutelage of the members of Government integrated in the PCM, as well as assessing its management and outcomes through the technical, performance, and financial audit control' (see: https://www.sg.pcm.gov.pt/en/).

72 See R. Alarcão, "Fundações: que reforma?" (2002) 292(51) *Scientia Iuridica – Revista de Direito Comparado Português e Brasileiro* 507, 512–513; J. Sousa Ribeiro, above n. 27, 80–81.

5.2. ADVISORY COUNCIL FOR FOUNDATIONS

The Advisory Council for Foundations (Article 13 FLF) also originates within the framework of the Presidency of the Council of Ministers; nevertheless, it shows a more stable and autonomous structure than the Foundation Authority. The five members, appointed for a five-year non-renewable term, are independent in the performance of their duties and cannot be removed.[73]

The Advisory Council is legally entrusted with issuing opinions on administrative acts relating to foundations and on the results of audits on foundations. At the request of the Foundation Authority, it can issue opinions on any matter relating to foundations. The Advisory Council can also, by its own initiative, take a stand on any matter relating to foundations that falls within the competence of the Foundation Authority.

Although it serves mostly as a consultative body, the Advisory Council has the powers to issue statements that bolster inspections, or even to scrutinise the Foundation Authority's actions. Such powers are exercised on a discretionary basis. Historically, the Advisory Council has taken important stands on some regulatory issues – namely, on the subject of foundations' establishment, advising for lower minimum capital requirements and against the maintenance of a formal act of recognition by the Foundation Authority.[74]

5.3. PUBLIC PROSECUTOR AND COURTS

The courts may be called upon to dissolve the foundation or to enforce the liability or remove governing members and have exclusive competence to dissolve the foundation on the grounds of unlawful activity (Article 35(3) FLF). The power to request the judicial dissolution of a foundation rests with the Foundation Authority and the public prosecutor.

Like the Foundation Authority, the public prosecutor lacks the competence to enforce the liability or remove governing members. Such competence generally lies with governing bodies of the foundation, under the terms of the charter. This severely constrains the effectiveness of the remedy that is key to align the activity of the foundation with the applicable statutes and provisions.

---

73 They shall be three personalities of acknowledged merits, recommended by associations representing foundations and appointed by the Prime Minister, one of whom shall preside; a representative of the Ministry of Finance and a representative of the Ministry of Labour, Solidarity and Social Security, appointed by the corresponding ministers. Given the political contours of the Foundation Authority (see above, section 5.1), it can be seen as a positive note that in the Advisory Council the governmental appointees are in the minority.

74 See Opinion no. 1/2012 issued on 23 November 2012, and Opinion no. 1/2016 issued on 5 May 2016.

The exception to these general rules regards foundations set up as *private institutions of social solidarity*, which are under the enhanced supervision of the services of the Ministry responsible for the area of social security. Besides overseeing and auditing the activities of these foundations, these services may request the judicial removal of the foundation's managers (Article 34 et seq. Statute of Private Institutions of Social Solidarity).

5.4. NATIONAL PUBLIC REGISTER OF FOUNDATIONS

A National Public Register of Foundations was created in 2019, by the Foundations Registration Act (FRA). It consists of a single database, available for public consultation.[75] There is an extensive list of acts subject to mandatory publication, including the founder's declaration, the foundation's charter and any amendments made to it, important events such as mergers and dissolution, as well as the appointment and removal of members of the foundation's board and supervisory body.[76] Ongoing judicial procedures and judicial decisions affecting the foundation must also be registered.[77] The National Public Register has proven to be a very useful tool for gaining some insight into the reality of Portuguese foundations, as most of the relevant information is kept in an online database with open access.[78]

5.5. DERIVATIVE ACTION OF BENEFICIARIES?

Granting the beneficiaries of the foundation's activity the right to enforce liability against governing members could mitigate the risks of underenforcement. As the FLF did not provide for this matter, these rights could be derived by analogy from provisions of the CCC that grant shareholders the right to bring derivative actions. Although scholarship has pleaded for this construction,[79] some of the few rulings on foundation law have rejected the application of commercial company norms to foundations by analogy, which suggests that the courts may be reluctant to follow this path.[80]

---

75 Article 8(4) FLF.

76 Article 2 FRA.

77 Article 4 FRA.

78 Available at: https://publicacoes.mj.pt/Pesquisa.aspx.

79 H. Sousa Antunes, above n. 62, 71, and J. Ferreira Gomes, above n. 62, p. 148.

80 Guimarães Court of Appeal, 11.07.2005, case no. 1312/05 and Supreme Court of Justice 09.02.2017, case no. 5425/07.8TBALM.L1.S1, both rejecting the application by analogy of norms on the summoning of shareholders' meetings.

6. TAXATION

There are no special rules on taxation of foundations as such: they are subject to the general rules on taxation of legal persons. As they fall under the rules for entities that do not primarily engage in commercial, industrial, or agricultural activities, they are not taxed for their profit. They are rather taxed for their total income, corresponding to the algebraic sum of the income from various categories considered for personal income tax purposes (Articles 3(1)(b) and 2(1)(a) of the Income Tax on Legal Entities Code (ITLEC)).[81]

Tax privilege is a special status that applies to two kinds of foundations mentioned above: *private institutions of social solidarity* and foundations that have been granted the *status of public utility*.

Private institutions of social security are automatically exempt from income tax on legal entities (Article 10(1)(b) ITLEC). Foundations with the status of public utility which operate predominantly or exclusively in certain sectors (e.g. culture, science, agro-bio) may be exempted by decision of the Finance Ministry when they comply with requirements regarding the independence of their bodies and application of their income in their public utility activity (Article 10(1)(c), (2) and (3) ITLEC). Both those types of foundations are automatically exempted from stamp duty, municipal tax on real estate transactions and municipal tax on real estate in regard of buildings used for their statutory purposes.[82] They are also exempted from several administrative fees – notably, court fees (Article 11(1) FLPUS). However, as mentioned, these types of foundations are ill-suited for running businesses in competitive markets.

---

81 L. Marques dos Santos, '§9. O regime fiscal das fundações em Portugal: Enquadramento e mecenato' *in* D. Costa Gonçalves and R. Soares Pereira (eds), *Direito das Fundações em Debate: Perspetivas de Reforma*, Principia, Cascais 2020, pp. 186 et seq. Decree-Law no. 442-A/88, of 30 de November 1988.

82 Article 6(c) and (d) Stamp Duty Code, Article 6(d) and (e) Municipal Tax on Real Estate Transactions Code, Article 44(1)(e) and (f) Tax Benefits Statute.

ENTERPRISE FOUNDATIONS IN IRELAND

Needles in Haystacks or Hiding in Plain Sight?

Oonagh B. Breen*

ABSTRACT

The term 'enterprise foundations' is not commonly used or understood in Ireland. That does not mean, however, that the concept does not exist. Based on interviews with Irish non-profits and charities, this chapter explores the legal space for enterprise foundations and examines the reticence of some executives to call out the business element of their operations for fear of undermining their charitable

* The author expresses thanks to those organisations who participated in this research both on and off the record.

status where this is in play. The case studies featured display some to most of the characteristics of enterprise foundations, indicating the need for such an entity if the political and legal climate can be shaped to support it.

1. INTRODUCTION

As a common law jurisdiction, Ireland's legal system does not recognise the civil law concept of 'foundation' in Irish law. Where the word 'foundation' occurs, it is used as a descriptive label implying a non-profit or charitable entity, but that entity is always underpinned by a common law legal structure – most often a company limited by guarantee (CLG) or a charitable trust. These may act as functional equivalents to the civil law foundation but there are important differences between them and the foundation. A CLG differs from a company limited by shares as a CLG has no shares or shareholders. Instead, its members act as guarantors. This means that each member undertakes to contribute a predetermined amount (usually a small sum, such as €1) if the company becomes insolvent and needs to be wound up. The CLG thus takes a corporate form, like the foundation, but it has the requirement of members, a concept alien to the foundation. Trusts, like foundations, provide stewardship of a trust corpus (whether comprising real or personal property) but the trust is not normally a body corporate, and the trustees may be natural persons who will hold legal title to the property without the protection of separate legal personality or limited liability.

Thomsen notes both the rarity of enterprise foundations globally and the difficulty of finding out information about them even when they do exist.[1] This difficulty is multiplied exponentially when one is searching in a common law jurisdiction for a concept which is not in common usage. The purpose of this chapter is therefore twofold: first to identify whether enterprise foundations are hiding in plain sight in Ireland. To this end, this chapter begins by identifying the features inherent in the civil law definition of enterprise foundations advanced by Sanders[2] and considering Irish functional equivalents which may meet some of or all these criteria. It then examines the existing Irish charity, corporate and tax law frameworks and their conduciveness to accommodating a prospective philanthropist who desires to establish or maintain an enterprise foundation. Finally, given the many similarities that exist between Ireland and England, both being common law jurisdictions, the chapter draws on the published guidance of the Charity Commission of England and Wales (CCEW) for charities owning

---

1 S. Thomsen, 'The Case for Enterprise Foundations' (4 December 2023) *ELI Project on European Enterprise Foundations*.

2 A. Sanders, 'Defining Enterprise Foundations' (4 December 2023) *ELI Project on European Enterprise Foundations*.

non-charities. To begin, it is necessary to explain briefly the Irish charity law framework and its approach to charities owning commercial enterprises or holding shares therein.

2. LEGAL FRAMEWORK

At last estimate, there were approximately 34,000 non-profit entities in Ireland.[3] Of these non-profits, approximately 11,000 organisations enjoyed registered charitable status.[4] Charitable status is a legal status granted by the Charities Regulatory Authority (CRA) to non-profit entities meeting the charity test set out in the Charities Act 2009. Certain advantages flow from having charitable status, including eligibility for consideration for charitable tax exemption from the Office of the Revenue Commissioners and greater public trust and confidence and implicitly greater public support resulting from the increased statutory regulation and oversight.

The granting of charitable status does, however, impose certain limitations on the activities of charities in political and economic spheres. In the latter instance, these restrictions flow mainly from a tax law perspective although a charity law perspective also requires some consideration. Charity law will be concerned to ensure that those individuals who control a charity (known as 'charity trustees' regardless of the legal form of their charity) act within the powers of their governing instruments regarding any engagement in economic activities. The common law and statutory law focus is on protecting charitable funds from exposure to liability or ultimate loss or erosion by direct or indirect distribution of profit to those controlling the charity. In applications for charity registration, the CRA checks that any trading activities carried out by the applicant fall into one of four broad categories:

(a) trades that are exercised in the course of the actual carrying out of a primary purpose of the organisation;
(b) trades carried out by the beneficiaries of the organisation;
(c) ancillary trading by the organisation (suitable for small-scale trading such as a café in an art gallery); or
(d) ancillary trading activity in furtherance of an organisation's primary purpose by a subsidiary. The subsidiary itself is not a charity and is fully taxable on profits, but under section 848A of the Taxes Consolidation Act 1997 it can donate its profits to an eligible charity.

3 Benefacts, 'Nonprofit Sector Analysis 2021' at: https://benefactslegacy.ie/reports/.

4 Charities Regulatory Authority (CRA), 'Charities Register' (December 2024) at: https://www.charitiesregulator.ie/en/information-for-the-public/search-the-register-of-charities.

In all cases, the CRA will require evidence that the profit of the trade is applied solely for the charitable purpose of the body.[5]

As modern charities need sustainable revenue streams beyond state grants or public donations, it is not unusual to find registered charities with subsidiary companies the income of which supports the parent charity. Examples include Dublin City University (DCU), a registered third-level education charity which owns (both directly and indirectly) and manages several companies that provide services to students, staff and members of the public (ranging from a commercial theatre space through to campus accommodation) and which also contribute financially to the University.[6] On other occasions, the economic activity is directly integrated into the parent charity itself without the use of separate subsidiary structures, as would appear to be the case for both Oxfam Ireland and Rehab Ireland, two registered charities which fundraise for their charitable purposes through their charity shop enterprises, which in Oxfam Ireland's case accounted for 46 shops across Ireland in 2023 and provided a net income of €794,000 to the charity.[7]

For a charity to hold shares in a trading or holding company, its governing document must provide the necessary investment powers. Examples of Irish enterprise foundations are hard to find. Although charitable CLGs must file annual reports and financial statements with the Companies Registration Office – and these annual filings are shared with the CRA – the quality of financial reporting is low due to the absence of charity financial reporting regulations, making interrogation of revenue streams difficult to ascertain. On the charitable trust side, while the CRA receives annual financial reports from these charities, it currently does not publish them so there is a dearth of information available on their income sources. A new Charities Amendment Act 2024, once fully commenced, will introduce new accounting reporting standards for all charities and enable better interrogation of accounts in time. However, if a charity takes the form of a private charitable trust, which is defined by the Charities Act 2009 as 'a charitable trust that is not funded by donations from the public', the trust is exempted from public disclosure of its annual report and financial statements, a situation that the Charities Amendment Act 2024 does not change. Private charitable trusts are attractive if endowing a charitable foundation with private money and are often favoured where family wealth will fund a charity.

In September 2016, the CRA undertook a review of its public Register of Charities to establish the number of registered Irish charities holding shares on trust in special purpose vehicles (SPVs) and to determine whether they fell within

---

5 CRA, 'Memorandum of Understanding between the Office of the Revenue Commissioners and The Charities Regulatory Authority' (2016) Schedule A.

6 See 'Campus Companies', *Dublin City University*: https://www.dcu.ie/ocoo/dcu-commercial-group-campus-companies (accessed 14 August 2024).

7 Oxfam, 'Annual Report 2022/23', p. 89.

the remit of the Charities Act 2009 (the Act).[8] Before examining the rationale for the CRA's sectoral review, it is worth noting two findings from the review which provide an insight into charity law's perspective of possible enterprise foundation structures. The CRA expressly recognised that registered charities can make investments and hold shares to achieve a return so that they can further their charity's aims. However, it held that the holding of shares, per se, should not be the motivation and reason for a charity's existence.[9] It also noted that any investments by charity trustees should be within their legal powers.

SPVs are typically structured under the ownership of a charitable trust to keep them off the balance sheet of the banks, hedge funds and private equity firms that use them. They are normally structured as an orphan company with the objective of providing bankruptcy remoteness and facilitating tax avoidance. To achieve this aim, the shares of the SPV are held on trust by an independent share trustee. When the share trustee is a charitable organisation, it will declare that it holds any benefit it receives from the share capital for the benefit of charitable purposes. In 2016, it was estimated that SPVs and related structures known as financial vehicle corporations held €750 billion of assets in Ireland, including distressed debt, greenhouse gas credits and catastrophe bonds.[10] Their use is standard practice in the financial services sector and is permitted by the Taxes Consolidation Act 1997 (section 110).

The CRA investigation arose following concerns raised by senior Department of Finance officials about the use of registered charities to help keep these 'tax neutral' vehicles off the balance sheets of companies to which they were linked. It should be noted that the CRA found no difference in the tax treatment of section 110 companies when the shares were held by a registered charity because the tax treatment of the SPV was specifically provided for by the relevant legislation. According to the regulator, the 'charitable status of its shareholders does not give rise to any tax benefit to the company from the use of such corporate structures'.[11]

In its inquiry, while acknowledging the difficulties of establishing the actual number of registered charities holding shares in section 110 companies, the CRA did identify four such charities. Of the four identified, one fell within the exemption provisions of section 8 of the Charities Act 2009 (i.e. holding assets in companies whose business solely consisted of leasing plant and machinery and making donations in respect of all dividends received on those shares within the previous 12 months to the review to benefit its charitable purpose).

8 Charities Regulator, 'Review of registered charities holding shares in section 110 companies on trust' (April 2017) at: https://www.charitiesregulator.ie/media/1542/review-of-registered-charities-holding-shares-in-section-110-companies.pdf.

9 Ibid. at para. 5.10.

10 J. Brennan, 'Charities Regulator examining groups over investment vehicles' (25 July 2016) *Irish Times*.

11 See Charities Regulator, above n. 8, at para. 3.5.

The unidentified charity was thus eligible for deregistration from the Charities Register although it remains on the Office of the Revenue Commissioners' list of bodies who currently hold charitable tax exemption. In the case of the other three entities, they argued that their holding of shareholdings in multiple section 110 companies was an ancillary activity to their charitable purpose. The volume of shareholding caused the CRA concern and the three entities in question decided to restructure their holdings as trust service providers due to the 'external policy uncertainties in this area, such that they were unclear as to the future status of the charities'.[12] This resulted in the Office of the Revenue Commissioners' withdrawal of the charitable tax exemptions previously extended to these charities and, consequently, the CRA's deregistration of the entities from the Register of Charities.

What appears clear from the CRA Review was that while the regulator recognised that registered charities could make investments and hold shares in order to achieve a return, the purpose of that return must be to further a charity's aims. The holding of shares, per se, could not be the raison d'être for the charity's existence, as was the implication in respect of the three charities that restructured as a result of the CRA investigation.

Apart from this thematic review, the CRA has been relatively silent on a pronouncements and published guidance front when it comes to relationships between charities and non-charities. This contrasts with the position taken by the Charity Commission for England and Wales (CCEW), which has issued a series of guidance documents addressing the legal underpinnings of the relationships between charities and 'non-charities',[13] the legal remit for charities to hold financial investments and exercise investment powers[14] and the tax consequences for a charity of having a trading arm.[15]

3. THE FEATURES OF THE ENTERPRISE FOUNDATION

The term 'enterprise foundation' or the related US concept of 'steward ownership'[16] is not used in Ireland. Introducing either of these terms into a conversation

---

12 See Charities Regulator, above n. 8, at para. 5.6.

13 CCEW, 'Charities and investment matters: Legal underpinning' (updated 1 August 2023) https://www.gov.uk/government/publications/charities-and-investment-matters-a-guide-for-trustees-cc14/charities-and-investment-matters-legal-underpinning.

14 CCEW, 'Guidance for charities with a connection to a non-charity' (29 March 2019) https://www.gov.uk/guidance/guidance-for-charities-with-a-connection-to-a-non-charity.

15 CCEW, 'Trustees trading and tax: how charities may lawfully trade' (24 February 2016) https://www.gov.uk/government/publications/trustees-trading-and-tax-how-charities-may-lawfully-trade-cc35/trustees-trading-and-tax-how-charities-may-lawfully-trade.

16 Discussion of the concept of stewardship and steward ownership in the United States dates back to the work of J. Davis, F. Schoorman, and L. Donaldson in the late 1990s (see, J. Davis, F. Schoorman and L. Donaldson, 'Towards a Stewardship Theory of Management' (1997)

necessitates an explanation of the concept at hand and a justifying rationale for its value. Once explained there is, however, a general curiosity amongst stakeholders and an interest to learn more. In attempting to identify possible Irish functional equivalents, one must first isolate the characteristic features of the enterprise foundation and then tease out whether or why these features are/are not present in the Irish models considered.

Drawing on the work of Sanders,[17] the following elements were selected for examination from an Irish perspective.

- *Chronology*: normally, the business precedes the foundation's existence with the latter created by a decision of the founder or founder's family when the wealth of the business is well-established.
- *The controlling share*: the foundation may hold majority voting rights in the company *or* have a veto or golden share right that is determinative on core issues relating to the company (direction or purpose related).
- *Purpose*: the company's dividends enable the foundation to achieve public benefit or charitable purposes, but charitable status (although often present) is not a requirement of this model.
- *Governance*: there are often common directors between the company and the foundation, but the governance arrangements ensure that no shareholders with control rights receive dividends from the entity. Governance rules often also enable the foundation a large say in the appointment of the company's board, thereby ensuring a strong mission alignment between for-profit and non-profit.
- *Structural Complexity*: In some models, economic and voting rights are split between two holding foundations that sit above the operating company.

These features were each considered in the Irish case studies undertaken in support of this research. In nearly all cases, the feature of chronology was met and in some, so too was the feature of governance. In one instance, the controlling share criterion was satisfied, while in another share dividends from the related business indirectly supported the charitable mission. In all other cases, business resources and profits were used to support the foundation and to enable achievement of a charitable or public purpose. As the case studies will reveal, an issue informing the absence of a controlling or indeed any shareholding stake by the charity was often the relative age of both the business and the associated foundation. In

22(1) *Academy of Management Review* 20). See further M. Hayek, W.A. Williams Jr, S. Taneja and R. Salem, 'Effective Succession of Social Entrepreneurs: A Stewardship-based Model' (2015) 20(2) *Journal of Applied Management and Entrepreneurship* 93; S.N. Gary, 'The Oregon Stewardship Trust: A New Type of Purpose Trust that Enables Steward-Ownership of a Business' (2020) 88 *U. Cin. L. Rev.* 707.

17 See A. Sanders, above n. 2.

several instances, the founder of the commercial activity was still running the business directly and sitting on the board of the charitable foundation, making the funding and direct control of the latter a seamless operation. As discussed with stakeholders, it is only with the imminent retirement of these self-made entrepreneurs in the coming years that the issue of succession planning will come to the fore. It is when the business founder relinquishes ultimate control (whether by transfer of the business upon sale or to a new generation of the founder's family) that decisions on how to ensure the ongoing viability of the associated charitable foundations will become pressing.

4. CASE STUDIES OF POTENTIAL IRISH ENTERPRISE FOUNDATIONS

The case studies in this section examine some existing non-profit corporate arrangements in Ireland that meet, at least in part, the characteristics of the enterprise foundation. Four organisations are considered: *The Irish Times*, a non-profit, non-charitable corporate trust; University College Dublin (UCD), a registered charity established by statutory charter; and the Small Foundation and the Lifes2Good Foundation, both registered charities established as CLGs. Consideration was also made of an unnamed private charitable trust which is supported by an entrepreneur's business profits. In each instance, background is provided for the enterprise in question and its associated charitable or non-profit entity. Consideration is then given to the way it meets or does not meet the enterprise foundation features identified in section 3 above.

4.1. THE IRISH TIMES

4.1.1. Background

The Irish Times is a national daily Irish newspaper, which is available in broadsheet and online versions. First published in 1859, it is a newspaper of record. It became a public company in 1906 with the then owners, the Arnott Family, retaining a majority shareholding in the company; a position that continued right up to the 1960s. In 1962, Major Thomas McDowell joined The Irish Times Ltd as vice-chairperson (chief executive) and the following year he also became managing director. Appointed chairperson in 1973, he became a governor and founder-chairperson of The Irish Times Trust in 1974. The formation of the trust had strong echoes of the UK *Guardian* newspaper's Scott Trust.[18] The objective in

---

[18] See: https://www.theguardian.com/about/history (last accessed 01 October 2025).

each case was to provide a secure framework for the continued publication of robustly independent journalism, driven by strong commitments to democratic ideals, social justice and high editorial standards.[19] These objectives are reflected in the terms of the trust's constitution which was incorporated as a CLG in 1974 and updated in 2016.

4.1.2. *Corporate Structure*

In terms of its corporate governance structure, The Irish Times Trust CLG comprises a maximum of 11 governors, who are appointed on the basis that they are 'representative broadly of the community throughout the whole of Ireland'.[20] The Trust is incorporated under company law and is regulated by a Memorandum and Articles of Association (or Constitution). Despite its broad primary objectives of advancing education, relieving poverty and furthering the advancement of medical, surgical and veterinary science,[21] it is not a charity and does not have charitable status. Any trust income must be applied solely towards the Trust's objectives and no profits can flow to the corporate trustee members.[22] In practice, profits are used to strengthen the newspaper, directly and/or indirectly.

The trust has a wholly owned subsidiary in the form of the Irish Times Holdings Unlimited Company, established in 1974. This investment holding company provided a mechanism to pass value to the original shareholders in The Irish Times Trust at the time of the Trust's creation, and while the company is still registered, it is not active today.[23] A more important subsidiary of the trust is the Irish Times Designated Activity Company (or DAC). Irish Times DAC is the corporate entity which houses the newspaper printing and publication business of the group. According to its financial statements for 2022, the Irish Times Trust CLG owns 100% of the preference shares of the DAC and owns, indirectly, 100% of its non-voting ordinary shares. The primary role of the Trust is to appoint the board of the DAC.[24] Membership of the DAC board currently comprises a non-executive chairperson, three executives from the news publisher and six non-executive directors, three of whom are nominated from the Trust's membership.

---

19 See Irish Times Trust CLG Constitution, Article 2(d)(ii)(B) and (C), dated 10 April 1974 and amended 7 October 2016.

20 Ibid., Article 32.

21 Ibid., Article 2(a), (b) and (c).

22 Ibid., Article 3.

23 The shares in the *Irish Times* were transferred on the eve of the introduction of capital gains tax in Ireland, leading to claims that the directors were cashing out of the company (to the tune of £325,000 each) to avoid the tax. The buy-out of the directors and the formation of the trust left the *Irish Times* with a large debt in the difficult economic period of 1974. See further, 'Obituary: Major Thomas McDowell' (12 September 2009) *Irish Times*.

24 Irish Times Trust CLG Constitution, Article 54.

Figure 1. Corporate structure of The Irish Times

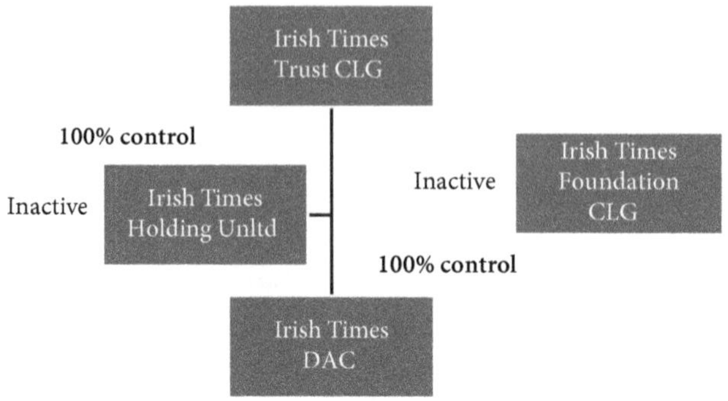

Explaining the functions and the interactions of the Trust and the DAC, the *The Irish Times* puts the matter in the following way:

> Both the Trust and the Board [of the DAC] share the responsibility of ensuring the editorial independence and financial viability of The Irish Times, but they do not interfere with the ordinary activities or decisions (commercial or editorial) of each other. They are differentiated mainly by functions of ownership and operation.[25]

In the event of any serious disagreement within the Board of the DAC, the DAC Constitution provides that the three directors nominated by the Trust may be deemed to have 50% of all votes plus one. This provision can only come into operation based on legal advice that certifies the matter to constitute a 'question of significant policy' under the Constitution.[26]

Independent of The Irish Times Trust structure is the Irish Times Foundation CLG, established in 1974. The purpose of the Foundation is that in the event of the liquidation of The Irish Times Trust, the final proceeds would be given for charitable purposes via this foundation. At present, the Foundation is not actively trading (as it is not required) and it is not currently registered as a charity due to this inactivity. It sits for all intents and purposes as a shelf company awaiting its contingent purpose.[27]

Turning to the features identified in section 3 above, Table 1 below sets out the extent to which The Irish Times Trust model satisfies the civilian concept of enterprise foundation.

---

25 'The Irish Times Trust' (updated 2025) *Irish Times*: https://www.irishtimes.com/about-us/the-irish-times-trust/.

26 Irish Times Trust DAC Constitution, Article 10.2.

27 Author interview with Irish Times CLG and Irish Times DAC Company Secretary, Colm Dunne (4 April 2024).

Table 1. The Irish Times Trust CLG

Characteristic	Presence	Comment
Chronology	Yes	Irish Times business precedes Trust establishment.
Controlling Share	Yes	Irish Times Trust owns 100% of preference shares in Irish Times DAC and holds a veto share with Trust nominees in cases of significant policy difference on the DAC Board.
Purpose	Yes	There is complete mission alignment between the Trust and the DAC to provide a secure framework for independent journalism. Any profits of the DAC must be reinvested to strengthen the newspaper directly or indirectly. The Trust has additional primary objectives relating to advancing education, relieving poverty and furthering the advancement of medical, surgical and veterinary science.
Governance	Yes	Trust is self-perpetuating and must be representative of the people of Ireland. Trust elects the Board of Irish Times DAC and nominates three of its Board to the DAC Board. Managerial distance otherwise exists.
Structural Complexity	Yes	Trust holds veto vote on the DAC Board, but the dividends do not flow to the Trust but to the operation of the DAC. If ever the Irish Times ceases to operate or is sold, the proceeds flow back to the Trust, which is required to transfer them to the Irish Times Foundation for charitable purposes.

The Irish Times Trust is thus the best and longest established Irish example of an Irish enterprise foundation. Acting as the corporate trustee of the Irish Times DAC, the legal form chosen shields the governors from the personal liability that would otherwise flow from their trusteeship. Given that the date of its incorporation precedes the introduction of the CRA by some 40 years and the fact that The Irish Times Trust had never sought charitable tax exemption from the Office of the Revenue Commissioners, it was not added to the Charities Register as a 'deemed charity' upon the Register's establishment in 2014.[28] The wording of its trust deed, however, could give rise to an obligation for the trustees to self-register with the CRA as its stated purposes are charitable. Given that the Trust does not currently give effect to the primary charitable purposes outlined in its trust instrument, this could create charity law compliance issues. The inclusion of these unactioned charitable purposes is to provide the release mechanism for the assets of the *Irish Times* newspaper should it ever cease to be operated by the Trust, ensuring that the governors could direct the proceeds to the similar purposes of the Irish Times Foundation, which too is currently unregistered as

[28] Charities Act 2009, section 40.

a charity but is essentially an inactive shelf company and is certified as being in good status with the Companies Registration Office.[29]

4.2. UNIVERSITY COLLEGE DUBLIN

Established by founding charter under the Irish Universities Act 1908, UCD is a body corporate, now governed by the Universities Act 1997. It is a registered charity and is Ireland's largest university providing third-level education to over 38,000 students. It has ten wholly owned subsidiaries, which manage UCD's property portfolio, campus leisure activities, innovation companies, global activities and campuses, its heritage properties and its professional courses.[30] In 2023, the surplus generated by these subsidiary companies for UCD amounted to €291,000, down from €3.6 million in 2022.[31] Of these subsidiaries, one (UCD Nova DAC) is a registered charity in its own right. Two are CLGs (Newman House Literary Centre and UCD English Language Academy) with the remainder being companies limited by shares. Unlike the *Irish Times*, the commercial entities in UCD's case do not precede the establishment of the University which benefits from the surpluses created. It follows that the motivation for the creation of the group structure in UCD's case is different.

As noted in the introduction to this chapter (section 1 above), direct commercial engagement by a charity in revenue-generating but non-charitable purpose activities can raise tax and charity law compliance issues even when those funds are ultimately used to support the charity. Employing a wholly owned subsidiary (or ten, as in UCD's case) to conduct the activity allows a charity to engage in risk transference of liabilities. Thus, in UCD's case, the use of separate companies to run its cultural and leisure activities gives the charity greater freedom to increase/decrease staffing levels (as happened during the Covid-19 pandemic). From a tax perspective, using a private subsidiary for its capital expansion projects enables UCD to avail of VAT advantages not available to charities. Use of a subsidiary also means that contractors can be hired at market rates and no pension liabilities accrue (which would not be possible under the public pay sector guidelines binding the University). From an accounting perspective, it also makes it easier for the University to monitor the cost effectiveness of these hived off operations and avoid cross-subsidisation.

---

29 The Irish Times Foundation CLG registered its B1C Annual Return General with the Companies Registration Office (CRO) on 11 January 2024 and it maintains its CRO Certificate of Good Standing (CGS), proving that it is incorporated and authorised to undertake business in Ireland and has been in existence since incorporation.

30 University College Dublin: National University of Ireland, 'Annual report and consolidated financial statements: Year ended 30 September 2023', p. 48.

31 Ibid., p. 41.

Turning to the characteristics of an enterprise foundation, Table 2 below considers the extent to which the UCD model satisfies these conditions:

Table 2. University College Dublin

Characteristic	Presence	Comment
Chronology	No	The existence of UCD, the University and charity, preceded the establishment of its commercial subsidiaries.
Controlling Share	Yes	In the case of the ten subsidiaries considered, UCD has either 100% direct control or 100% indirect control, often being the sole member and shareholder.
Purpose	Yes	There is complete alignment of objectives between the University and its wholly owned subsidiaries, all of which are set up to advance UCD's purpose under the Universities Act 1997.
Governance	Yes	In four of its subsidiaries, UCD employees comprise the entire board of directors. In those with an external board or independent chair, the charity has a majority of UCD *ex officio* members on the board.
Structural Complexity	Yes	This is harder to determine given the commonality of directors but the alignment of purposes and the isolation of liability within subsidiaries means that only net surpluses flow back to UCD. The Irish University Association's Code of Governance for Corporate Subsidiaries applies to each entity and is overseen by a common company secretary.

If it is accepted that an enterprise foundation can exist in circumstances where the recipient charity pre-dates the establishment of the commercial arm, then it is possible to view UCD (and indeed the corporate group structures of other Irish university institutions, such as DCU)[32] as being functionally equivalent. The majority control, coupled with the strong mission alignment of both parent and subsidiary is coupled with the transfer of risk to the subsidiaries and in return, the transfer of profits to the parent institution to fund its educational and related activities.

4.3. THE LIFES2GOOD FOUNDATION

A third example takes the form of a charitable CLG which is supported by the commercial profits of a for-profit business. The Lifes2Good Foundation (L2G) was established in 2017 by James and Maria Murphy, the founders of L2G, a

32 See 'Campus Companies', above n. 6.

successful investment partner in the health and beauty sector bringing emerging businesses to scale. The sale of the Viviscal brand to US conglomerate Church & Dwight for €150 million allowed the company to expand its business interests to include an international property and equity portfolio, while also supporting a standalone charitable foundation to fund preventative and remedial work for women and children in situations of vulnerability in Ireland and two developing countries and to carry out environmental projects. Between 2017 and 2023, the foundation contributed more than €6.6 million to charitable endeavours in the west of Ireland and in Afghanistan.[33]

The L2G corporate structure comprises L2G Group Holdings, a private company limited by shares, incorporated in 2006, through which the business activities of L2G occur, and Irish Response Ltd (founded in 1997). Related companies within the Group include the investment arm, the Mount Amber Group (comprising several strategic investment and finance unlimited companies). The group companies along with the standalone foundation share common directors.

The L2G Foundation is fully funded by the L2G Group and does not receive public funding or grants. The mechanism of funding is interesting in that in its first years of existence and up until 2021, the Foundation received annual unsecured, repayable, interest free loans from the Mount Amber Group, which it repaid in full in February 2021. In its financial statement for the year ended 2022, the Foundation confirmed that it had written confirmation from Mount Amber Investments Unlimited that it would provide the Foundation with the funds necessary to enable it to discharge its obligations for a minimum period of 12 months from the date of approval of the 2022 financial statements. Another interesting feature of the Foundation is that it employs no staff directly. Instead, foundation management happens internally within the L2G Group with services being costed out in terms of employees, accounting and finance function and charged back to the Foundation at cost. Business efficacy and economies of scale drive this approach, enabling the Foundation to receive excellent support at a rate that it could not secure itself in the private market or if it employed its own staff directly. There are, however, clear lines of separation between the company and the Foundation. The Foundation has its own bank account and grants are made from this account. The auditor of the Foundation is independent of the L2G Group and the costs of services are recognised in the Foundation's accounts each year.

So, to what extent does the L2G Foundation meet the enterprise foundation characteristics?

---

33 Author interview with CFO of Lifes2Good Foundation (7 June 2024). See also: https://lifes2goodfoundation.ie/our-work/ (last accessed 10 November 2025).

Table 3. The Lifes2Good Foundation

Characteristic	Presence	Comment
Chronology	Yes	L2G Business existed before the L2G Foundation, which was created following health and beauty business success.
Controlling Share	No	At present L2G Foundation owns no shares in L2G Group entities. The family business empire is still run by its co-founders who are strong influences within the foundation. Succession planning is however on the horizon when new models of sustainability for the Foundation will be considered.
Purpose	No	In terms of alignment of objects, the charitable foundation was established to enable its founders use their business wealth to support vulnerable women and children and subsequently switched focus to tackle environmental issues. As there is no shareholder control or veto share, the current funding arrangement is legally precarious.
Governance	Yes	There are common directors shared between the business arms and the Foundation. The Foundation has no direct staff but is supported by Irish Response Ltd on a business efficiency basis.
Structural Complexity	No	Tax driven structure. Long-term repayable loans by the Group in early years to the Foundation were repaid in full upon receipt of a bigger Group donation when the Foundation qualified for 'eligible charitable status' with the Office of the Revenue Commissioners. This status now enables the Group to make tax efficient corporate donations to the Foundation which can be directly deducted as trading expenses. Transfer of shares and division of economic/voting rights may be considered in the future when founders retire, subject to prevailing tax law.

The strength of the L2G Foundation, as with many similar charitable foundations in Ireland, lies in the fact that the founders of the business enterprise still run the business and play significant roles in the Foundation. This state of affairs provides ongoing assurance to the Foundation that funding will flow, either by way of tax efficient corporate donations, tax efficient repayable loans or through written guarantees from the founder to the charity to underwrite costs incurred in a financial year, allowing the Foundation to exist as a going concern. The challenge that will arise in the future is when the founder retires or ceases to play an influential role in the commercial arm. In the context of succession planning and ensuring the ongoing viability of the charitable foundation, the enterprise foundation model may therefore provide a useful model for consideration.

4.4. THE SMALL FOUNDATION

One charitable foundation that has begun to think through those issues is the Small Foundation. Established in 2007 as a CLG for charitable purposes with CHY tax exemption, the Small Foundation's focus is to alleviate extreme poverty in sub-Saharan Africa. It seeks to identify and support highly leveraged interventions that improve the business ecosystem for on-farm and off-farm micro, small and medium enterprises (MSMEs) by expanding access to knowledge, finance, technology, skilled human resources and markets. It aims to support initiatives that have systems change potential and in its 17 years of existence, it has spent €40 million on philanthropic endeavours to this end.[34]

Funding for the Small Foundation flows from the business acumen and success of Tim Brosnan, founder of Gandon Investment, and an early investor in an online brokerage firm, CyBerCorp, bought out by Charles Schwab in the 1990s. Brosnan began his individual philanthropic interest in Africa at this time but also cofounded Abbey Capital, an alternative investment management company specialising in managed future funds. Abbey Capital Ltd is a subsidiary of Cavendish Capital Ltd and share dividends from both companies flow to Brosnan, amongst others. Dividends and donations from these enterprises are received in a tax efficient manner by the foundation. During his time as chair of the Foundation and subsequently as a non-executive director, Brosnan provided a formal undertaking that he would personally ensure that the Foundation would have sufficient funds to honour any financial commitments made by it.[35] The guarantee expired in 2021 when he retired as a director. Funding was also previously provided by way of €2 million revolving standby facility between Brosnan and the foundation under which unsecured short-term bridging advances could be drawn down by it as needed. This facility expired in 2023.[36] Since then, a formal strategic renewable funding agreement worth €25 million over five years has been established between Cavendish Capital and the Small Foundation.

In thinking ahead to the future funding of the Small Foundation, there is a strong family connection to the Foundation with the founder's son, Conor, now serving as its chair and CEO. Succession planning is underway with the goal that the value of Brosnan's Cavendish Capital Holdings would continue to be used for charitable purposes including the support of the Small Foundation. So, again in an indirect way, we see emerging in Ireland elements of the enterprise foundation concept. Brosnan's Cavendish shareholding is not a majority one and these shares will not be held directly by the Small Foundation in the future but the value of that holding in terms of dividends will contribute greatly to the long-term sustainability of the Small Foundation.

---

34 Author interview with Chair of the Small Foundation (2 May 2024).

35 Small Foundation, 'Annual Report 2022', p. 9.

36 Ibid.

Table 4. The Small Foundation

Characteristic	Presence	Comment
Chronology	Yes	Both Gandon Investment and Abbey Capital existed before the Small Foundation, with funds from the sale of CyBerCorp used to establish the foundation.
Controlling Share	No	The Small Foundation is not a direct shareholder in the businesses, but it does benefit indirectly from share dividends and this will continue indefinitely.
Purpose	No	In terms of alignment of objects, the charitable foundation was established to enable its founders use their business wealth and knowledge to leverage local development funding in Africa. The continuation of this mission post the founder's lifetime is being actively considered.
Governance	Yes	There are common directors shared between the business arms and the foundation.
Structural Complexity	No	Tax driven structure. Donations by the companies or the founder are all tax efficient. If greater incentives existed to donate shares directly, this would be considered in future.

5. ISSUES TO CONSIDER IN THE CREATION OF AN ENABLING ENVIRONMENT FOR ENTERPRISE FOUNDATIONS IN IRELAND

Drawing on the case studies above, there is evidence of strong links between business and philanthropy in Ireland. Institutional philanthropy is still in its infancy in Ireland, and it would thus be premature to claim an Irish culture of enterprise foundations. Nevertheless, one can identify certain enterprise foundation characteristics embedded in existing legal structures. Innovative ad hoc legal workarounds are also emerging to facilitate effective funding arrangements for entrepreneurs establishing their own foundations. In light of Ireland's prevailing philanthropic-friendly climate,[37] this chapter has sought to provide a more informed context in which to understand the space for enterprise foundations. This section seeks to identify four issues that would benefit from considered – as opposed to ad hoc – solutions and proposes some related reforms that would facilitate the enhancement of the legal environment for Irish enterprise foundations.

[37] Note the Irish Government's new 'National Policy on Philanthropy 2024–2028' (December 2023): https://assets.gov.ie/280970/9db88719-c3b3-49ba-ab4b-0a0683d32021.pdf (last accessed 1 January 2025).

5.1. TAXATION RULE REFORMS

In discussion with philanthropic stakeholders during this research, several funding practices came to light which were driven by tax considerations. To seek 'eligible charity' status, charities must first meet several Office of the Revenue Commissioners requirements and exist for a period of two years as a tax-exempt charity. Eligible charities can reclaim the tax that individual taxpayers pay on their donations while corporate donors are permitted to treat their donations as deductible trading expenses. Such claims and deductions are not possible under tax law in the first two years of the charity's operation. To avoid tax, several of the businesses made interest-free repayable loans to their foundations and funded the repayment of the loan through a bigger corporate donation to the foundation once the latter received its eligible charity status. In recognition of this workaround, this chapter recommends that the Office of the Revenue Commissioners rules regarding the two-year requirement for eligible charity status recognition be reviewed so that philanthropic gifts made during those two years should be retroactively recognised for tax purposes after the charity meets the two-year requirement.[38] To further the growth of philanthropy the resulting tax refund should go to the charity rather than to the corporate donor.

A second proposed tax reform relates to the Office of the Revenue Commissioners' accumulation rules. Up until 2025, the Office of the Revenue Commissioners practice required charities to obtain prior approval from the Office of the Revenue Commissioners if they intended to accumulate funds for more than two years. Any application had to include the reasons for accumulation. The Office of the Revenue Commissioners tended to allow accumulation, for example, if it related to a capital project for which the funds were being earmarked. Philanthropic activity, however, often needs to build reserves to a certain scale before it can undertake the longer-term systemic projects for which it was established. Since those reserves may arise by way of an incremental funding stream rather than by an initial endowment, these philanthropic institutions had no guarantee of the Office of the Revenue Commissioners' accumulation approval or reassurance regarding its duration. Taking account of this reality and supported by this research, the Fiscal Incentives Subgroup of the Implementation and Monitoring Group for the National Policy on Philanthropy recommended the development of new Office of the Revenue Commissioners guidelines on philanthropic fund accumulation practices so that the Office of the Revenue Commissioners could make informed and enabling

38 This recommendation was adopted by the Implementation and Monitoring Group for the National Policy on Philanthropy and formed part of its budget submission in October 2024. The recommendation found legislative form in The Finance Act 2024. Section 16 of that Act goes one step further than the recommendation sought by completely removing the two-year requirement for eligibility for all registered charities.

decisions regarding the exercise of its approval in line with the spirit of the National Policy on Philanthropy. In response to this Budget submission, s17 of the Finance Act 2024 amended tax law to extend the period for the accumulation of charitable 'income' to five years.[39] It is hoped that this legislative change will provide the Office of the Revenue Commissioners with leeway to also consider appropriate timelines for the incremental accumulation of philanthropic funds not attributable to income.[40]

The case studies show that often the initial funding for the charitable foundations sprang from a liquidity event in the business activity – sale of product or a business producing a windfall. Where some of that windfall is donated to a philanthropic cause, the donor (whether an individual or company) does not qualify for tax relief from capital gains tax (CGT) (which is charged at 33% on capital gains made on the disposal of assets), leaving only the net amount after tax available for donation. The Implementation and Monitoring Group for the National Policy on Philanthropy has recommended that tax law be changed to allow for relief against CGT (or corporation tax on chargeable gains) where the person/company making the gain donates at least €1 million of this to a qualifying philanthropic organisation. A reform of this nature (which would cover disposal of shares) would greatly assist in the establishment of enterprise foundation functional equivalents in Ireland.

One existing perceived drawback to gifting shares to a charitable foundation is the belief that dividend withholding tax would apply to the charity and that, unlike a for-profit shareholder, the charity would not be able to reclaim this tax. However, a review of the Office of the Revenue Commissioners guidance on dividend withholding tax (DWT) would seem to indicate that charities as 'excluded persons' are considered exempt from DWT[41] and as such would be eligible to reclaim a refund of this tax.[42] While the requirement of reclaiming the tax was still seen as an additional burden not present when a corporate donation is made, stakeholders agreed that in the period when the founder had retired from the supporting business (so that corporate donations might not be possible on the same scale or at all), the possibility of gifting shares could be reconsidered in light of this explanation of the DWT rules.

---

39 The Finance Act, section 17: https://www.irishstatutebook.ie/eli/2024/act/43/section/17/enacted/en/html#sec17 (last accessed 3 October 2025).

40 It is notable that the revised guidance now refers to registered charities seeking prior approval for the accumulation of "funds" for more than five years – see https://www.revenue.ie/en/companies-and-charities/charities-and-sports-bodies/charitable-tax-exemption/conditions-retaining-charitable-tax-exemption.aspx (last accessed 3 October 2025).

41 See 'Dividend Withholding Tax (DWT)' (18 January 2024) *Revenue*: https://www.revenue.ie/en/companies-and-charities/dividend-withholding-tax/index.aspx (last accessed 10 November 2025).

42 Ibid.

5.2. CHARITY LAW LEGAL STRUCTURE RULES

A second issue that merits further consideration is the most appropriate legal structure to facilitate the shareholding for charitable benefit. Two key questions are: where does shareholder control lie and under what conditions can it be exercised; and second, can the share benefits (i.e. dividends) be directed other than to the shareholder in a tax efficient manner?

At its most basic, an entrepreneur could gift a business shareholding directly to a charity. The charity trustees would thus become the legal owners of the shares and if it was a majority shareholding certain responsibilities regarding oversight of the business may flow from this gift.[43] Depending on the legal structure of the charity and the terms and conditions attached to the gift of shares, this may or may not be a suitable mechanism of transfer. It is a common feature of continental enterprise foundations that the control of the foundation may be overseen by related family members. The Charities Amendment Act 2024, when commenced, will require a charity to have a minimum of three charity trustees who are natural persons and a majority of these may not be a connected relative of another trustee. In the case of the charity having a single corporate trustee, the corporate trustee must have at least three directors who are natural persons, the majority of whom are unrelated. The requirements of section 54A will not be welcomed by family founders who wish family members to have a dominant board influence, but this approach is in line with the proposed European Enterprise Foundation model law, which sets board independence as the default position.

Another option, as demonstrated by the *Irish Times* corporate structure, is to use a non-profit CLG to hold the shares and exercise the controlling power within the operating enterprise with the ability to transfer surpluses under the terms of its constitution to a charitable foundation (thereby separating voting rights and dividend rights). In the UK, use of a holding company structure for share ownership with power of distribution to the charity is common. The Wellcome Trust (WT), an English charitable testamentary trust established in 1936, originally held a 100% shareholding in pharmaceutical company, The Wellcome Foundation Ltd (WFL). In 1986, with the consent of the Charity Commission for England and Wales, WT formed a new holding company, The Wellcome Trust Ltd (TWTL), a non-charitable CLG and trust corporation, acting as sole trustee of WT, which replaced WT's individual trustees who became members and directors of TWTL. TWTL sold 20% of its shareholding in 1986, maintaining majority control in WFL until 1992, when further asset diversification reduced its holding to 39.5% before selling its remaining interests to Glaxo in 1995, ending its 59-year ownership of WFL.

---

43 *Re Lucking's Will Trust* [1968] 1 WLR 866.

A further useful American example of separation of shareholder control rights from dividend rights is found in the 2022 restructuring of BCorp clothing company, Patagonia. The company founders transferred their share ownership to two entities, the Patagonia Purpose Trust (PPT) and the Holdfast Collective (a non-profit 501(c)(4) organisation). The Holdfast Collective now owns 98% of the equity in the Patagonia business and all the non-voting stock. This gives Holdfast a right to dividends but no control over the Patagonia enterprise. The PPT owns 2% of the company's equity and all the voting stock. Voting stock has both economic value and decision-making authority. This splitting of control and dividend rights means that the Holdfast Collective can devote its investment income to saving the planet while the founding family (who sit on the PPT advisory committee) can continue to ensure that the business is run in line with their vision and values. Exploring similar structures in Ireland will be important in the future.

5.3. CHARITY LAW GUIDANCE

As interest in establishing enterprise foundations grows, the CRA will need to develop guidance on relationships between charities and non-charities and provide clearer investment guidance on the legal implications for charities holding a majority or controlling share in a business. To date, this matter has not been addressed by the Irish courts nor by the published guidance of the CRA outside the CRA's acknowledgement that charities can hold shares to achieve their charitable end purpose.[44] As noted earlier, the charity's governing instrument will need to authorise share investment and provide charity trustees with sufficient powers to manage such investments.

It is useful to look to the Charity Commission of England and Wales (CCEW) guidance in this respect on issues relating to both the legal underpinning of investments by charities (2023) and guidance for charities with connections to non-charities (2019). The 2023 guidance differentiates between the obligations of a charity that holds shares simply as financial investment and one that holds a controlling interest in a company. Addressing the former, the CCEW counsels that charity trustees must exercise appropriate investment criteria over time.[45] In the latter instance (and specifically referencing a gift of controlling shares by a business donor) the CCEW advises, '[w]here a gift of shares results in the charity owning a majority shareholding the responsibilities of the trustees are to manage that in the interests of the charity'.[46] Citing *Re Lucking's Will Trusts*,[47] the CCEW

44 See above n. 8 and accompanying text.
45 CCEW, above n. 13, at p.21.
46 Ibid.
47 *Re Lucking's Will Trusts* [1968] 1 WLR 866.

highlights the need for charity representation on the company's board so that '[charity] trustees holding a controlling interest ought to ensure so far as they can that they have such information as to the progress of the company's affairs as directors would have'.[48] The flow of information must be more than shareholders would be entitled to where majority control is held.[49] Where a donor imposes a condition that shares may not be sold without the consent of the donor/their family or a third party, the CCEW views this veto power as a fiduciary one, which must be exercised in the interests of the charity's purposes rather than the donor's interests. In instances where charity trustees consider they need to diversify but the donor refuses consent, the CCEW advises trustees to apply to the Commission to vary the governing document of the charity.[50]

The CCEW's 2019 guidance for charities with connections to non-charities[51] represents a very broad range of charity relationships but its scope certainly includes the enterprise foundation concept, a view further supported by the CCEW's provision of a checklist for charities 'mainly set up and funded by non-charities'.[52] The guidance, which consolidates rather than changes the existing law, sets out six principles which the CCEW expects charities to apply in the management of their non-charity relationships. These relate to recognising the risks that may arise from this connection; ensuring the connection does not result in any non-incidental private benefit to the non-charity; operating independently; identifying and addressing any conflicts of interest that may affect any trustees who are appointed by the non-charity; assessing the risks and benefits of a shared identity with a non-charity; and finally, acting to protect the charity in any shared working or resource agreements to ensure that they are in the charity's best interest. What is clear from both guidance documents is that there is an enabling space in England and Wales for enterprise foundations to exist within the charity regulatory framework.

5.4. PHILANTHROPIC SUCCESSION PLANNING

Many of the issues discussed in sections 5.1 to 5.3 above came to light following interviews with Irish philanthropic institutions. A common feature of Irish

48 Citing Cross J. in *Re Lucking's Will Trusts* [1968] 1 WLR 866, 874.

49 Ibid., Cross J. warning 'if [charity trustees holding the majority shares] allow the company to be run by the minority shareholder and receive no more information than shareholders are entitled to, they do so at their risk, if things go wrong'.

50 See above n. 13.

51 See CCEW, above n. 14.

52 See CCEW, 'Checklist 2: Charities set up and mainly funded by the non-charity': https://assets.publishing.service.gov.uk/media/5c9be6fae5274a527b865b61/Checklist_2_Charities_set_up_and_mainly_funded_by_the_non-charity_final_odt.odt (last accessed 10 November 2025).

foundations whose business enterprise preceded the foundation is their relative youth, with the majority established in the past 15 years. In most, the founder is still at the helm of the business arm and heavily involved in the foundation. Tax efficient corporate solutions to transfer funds from the business to the charity are thus the modus operandi of choice. The future sustainability of such funding models, however, does not fully prepare for the day when the founder is no longer involved in both the commercial and philanthropic activities.

The issue of succession planning, when raised with stakeholders, provoked interesting conversations about the precarious nature of funding based largely on a founder's personal goodwill. The Small Foundation's experience on the retirement of its founder prompted it to be proactive in both formalising its strategic funding agreements and beginning discussions for a succession plan regarding the ultimate direction of the founder's share dividends, which are currently earmarked for the Foundation.

In those other foundations, where these issues are not yet prescient but the question of succession planning is looming, there was strong interest in exploring the legal environment for gifting shares or at least shareholder value to the foundation in the future. The pros, cons, terms and conditions of gifting either share rights or share dividends to a foundation merits greater consideration from a corporate, charity and tax law perspective. Having a clear knowledge base on these issues would enable professional advisers to assist new philanthropists to best structure their philanthropic endeavours. It would also focus the mind of the National Policy on Philanthropy Implementation and Monitoring Group to identify statutory barriers to philanthropy which could be legally reformed in the interests of growing the sector.[53]

6. CONCLUSION

In conclusion, the business case and the philanthropic case exists for the formalisation of the enterprise foundation concept in Ireland. The previous absence of a strong institutional basis for domestic philanthropy coupled with the approaching retirement of a generation of Ireland's most successful entrepreneurs provides two essential ingredients for policy change – a problem and a solution.[54] The third key ingredient required for a policy window to open – an external catalyst – comes in the form of a welcome double act, namely, a draft model law for enterprise foundations, courtesy of the European Law Institute's European Enterprise Foundation Project[55] and the Irish government's

53 'National Policy on Philanthropy 2024–2028', above n. 37.

54 J. Kingdon, *Agendas, Alternatives, and Public Policies*, 2nd ed., Pearson, London 2010.

55 See: https://www.europeanlawinstitute.eu/projects-publications/current-projects/current-projects/eli-enterprise-foundations-in-europe/ (last accessed 10 November 2025).

current implementation phase of its 'National Policy on Philanthropy 2024–2028'.[56] Objective 3 of the policy aims specifically to stimulate and incentivise philanthropy, providing a welcoming environment for new ideas from Ireland's European neighbours that can be adapted to Ireland's common law legal system. It may be that if the forces align, in the Kingdonian sense,[57] the enterprise foundation may cease to be a needle in a haystack or forced to hide in plain sight but may hopefully become a common functional tool for future Irish entrepreneurs who wish to do good while doing well.

56 'National Policy on Philanthropy 2024–2028', above n. 37.
57 J. Kingdon, above n. 54.

ARE ENTERPRISE FOUNDATIONS POSSIBLE IN THE UNITED STATES?

Ofer ELDAR*

ABSTRACT

This chapter discusses the ability of entrepreneurs to form enterprise foundations in the US and the hurdles for forming them. The US regime for tax-exempt private foundations is very restrictive and does not practically allow them to have substantial ownership of for-profit firms. As a result, there is a perception that enterprise foundations are not feasible in the US. However, enterprise foundations, broadly defined as nonprofits that control industrial firms, need not involve ownership by a private foundation (as it is defined in the US Tax Code) and could also refer to other types of nonprofits. Such enterprise foundations are unlikely to benefit from key tax exemptions (such as tax-deductible donations or income tax exemptions), unless the for-profit itself serves a charitable purpose. This chapter evaluates recent developments to liberalize the law of enterprise foundations, such as the 'Newman's Own' exception and the perpetual purpose trust.

---

* UC Berkeley (ofer.eldar@berkeley.edu). I thank Henry Hansmann, Peter Molk, Anne Sanders, Steen Thomsen and participants at the Enterprise Foundations workshop for valuable comments. Brendan Smith also provided excellent research assistance.

1. INTRODUCTION

While enterprise foundations are common in some European countries, they have historically been extremely rare in the US. Enterprise foundations are nonprofit entities, including corporations or trusts, that lack owners and exercise control over an industrial company.[1] Until recently, the only known example of an enterprise foundation has been the Hershey Company, a chocolate manufacturer, which is controlled by the Hershey Trust, a charitable trust that operates a school for orphans.[2] But nonprofit control has gained more prominence with the emergence of OpenAI, a leading AI firm controlled by a nonprofit organization with the mission of ensuring that artificial general intelligence (AGI) benefits all of humanity.[3]

The question of whether enterprise foundations are feasible in the US is particularly timely. As I and others show, the number of founder-controlled companies going public has recently risen dramatically. Between 2017 and 2019, almost 20% of initial public offerings were dual-class firms that allocated control to the firm founders.[4] One of the motivations for adopting a dual-class structure is to enable founders to pursue their vision uninhibited by the pressure of sophisticated investors.[5] In fact, some of these firms, such as Lemonade and Allbirds, are benefit corporations that purport to pursue a public benefit which is not limited to seeking profits.[6]

Founders may wish to ensure that the business firm they control will continue to pursue their legacy or vision after their death. Enterprise foundations – if legally feasible – may provide a mechanism for accomplishing 'immortality' for founders' visions.[7] Without employing an entity to control the corporation, it is largely impossible to ensure that the firm is committed in perpetuity to pursuing

---

1 See S. Thomsen, 'Foundation Ownership around the World' in A. Sanders and S. Thomsen (eds), *Enterprise Foundation Law in a Comparative Perspective*, Intersentia, Cambridge 2023.

2 See J. Klick and R.H. Sitkoff, 'Agency Costs, Charitable Trusts, and Corporate Control: Evidence from Hershey's Kiss-off' (2008) 108 Columbia Law Review 749.

3 F.H. Pederson, 'Ownership at OpenAI: From the Perspective of Enterprise Foundation Governance' (15 April 2024).

4 D. Aggarwal, O. Eldar, Y. Hochberg and L. Litov, 'The Rise of Dual-Class Stock IPOs' (2022) 144(1) Journal of Financial Economics 122, 124.

5 Z. Goshen and A. Hamdami, 'Corporate Control and Idiosyncratic Vision' (2016) 125 Yale Law Journal 560, 588–591.

6 For analysis of benefit corporations, see O. Eldar, 'Designing Business Forms to Pursue Social Goals' (2020) 106(4) Virginia Law Review 937, 964–968; M.B. Dorff, J. Hicks and S.D. Solomon, 'The Future or Fancy? An Empirical Study of Public Benefit Corporations' (2021) 11 Harvard Business Law Review 113.

7 However, it should be noted that it is unclear whether private foundations actually do a good job of fulfilling their founders' visions; see B. Galle, 'The Quick (Spending) and the Dead: The Agency Costs of Forever Philanthropy' (2021) 74(3) Vanderbilt Law Review 757 (showing empirical evidence suggesting that managers of private foundations depart significantly from the preferences of the organization's major donors after their deaths).

the founder's vision or a defined public benefit.[8] In fact, in at least one notable case, Delaware courts have invalidated an antitakeover device that the firm's founders adopted partly as an attempt to protect the mission of the firm in perpetuity.[9]

The general perception is that the formation of enterprise foundations in the US is prohibited by tax penalties.[10] The primary restriction is the tax on excess business holdings by private foundations, which are essentially nonprofits that are controlled by their main donors. The main exception to this tax permits private foundations to invest in for-profits that further the foundation's purpose through program-related investments. A simple example would be investing in a bank that makes loans to low-income individuals. Thus, for all practical purposes, the tax on excess business holdings prevents private foundations from holding a controlling stake in industrial for-profits.

However, enterprise foundations in the broader sense need not involve ownership by a private foundation and could also be owned by other types of nonprofits. The restrictions on other tax-exempt nonprofits that do not qualify as private foundations are much less severe. For example, the Mozilla Corporation, a for-profit firm that operates the Firefox web browser, is owned by the Mozilla Foundation (which, confusingly, is not a private foundation), a tax-exempt nonprofit devoted to improving and protecting the internet. The exempt nonprofit may need to pay taxes known as unrelated business income tax (UBIT) on any income from the for-profit business if unrelated to its purpose,[11] but it may in principle continue to operate and control it.

---

8 On the use of control mechanisms to commit an organization to a social purpose, see O. Eldar, 'The Role of Social Enterprise and Hybrid Organizations' (2017) Columbia Business Law Review 92, 154–157.

9 eBay Domestic Holdings, Inc. v. Newmark, 16 A.3d 1, 34 (Del. Ch. 2010) ('Jim and Craig contend that they identified a threat to craigslist and its corporate policies that will materialize after they both die and their craigslist shares are distributed to their heirs. At that point, they say, "eBay's acquisition of control [via the anticipated acquisition of Jim or Craig's shares from some combination of their heirs] would fundamentally alter craigslist's values, culture and business model, including departing from [craigslist's] public-service mission in favor of increased monetization of craigslist."', ibid., 32).

10 H. Hansmann and S. Thomsen, 'The Governance of Foundation-Owned Firms' (2021) 13(1) Journal of Legal Analysis 172, 174.

11 UBIT is defined as 'the gross income derived by any organization from any unrelated trade or business ... regularly carried on by it', less certain deductions and modifications (26 U.S. Code (Internal Revenue Code/I.R.C.), §512). The major modifications – including income from dividends, interest, annuities, royalties, rents, sale of non-inventory property – largely serve to exclude most passive income from being UBIT (ibid, §512(b)). As defined in section 513, an unrelated trade or business is one 'the conduct of which is not substantially related ... to the exercise or performance' by the organization of its exempt purpose or another section 501(c)(3) purpose, with certain carveouts (I.R.C., §513). 'Trade or business' includes 'any activity which is carried on for the production of income from the sale of goods or the performance of services' (ibid, §513(c)). Whether a trade or business is 'regularly carried on' hinges on the 'frequency and continuity with which the activities productive of the income are conducted and the manner in which they are pursued' (Treas. Reg., §1.513-1(c)(1)). In general, activities conducted year-round will be considered regularly conducted, as will

Moreover, if the nonprofit is not tax-exempt, there seem to be very few restrictions on its control of a business firm. The only potential limitations on control are embedded in states' corporate laws. Although these do not appear to be burdensome and are rarely enforced,[12] there is little evidence that entrepreneurs use non-tax-exempt nonprofits to control industrial corporations, particularly those that are publicly listed.

While the regulatory system for forming enterprise foundations appears not to have resulted in many such organizations, two recent developments could potentially spur the growth of enterprise foundations in the US. The first one is the adoption of another exception to the tax on excess business holding, which permits private foundations to hold 100% of the voting rights of an industrial corporation without incurring the tax, subject to certain requirements relating to the foundation's independence from its founders and donors.[13] It is unclear how many private foundations have taken advantage of this exception, except that it was passed specifically to assist Newman's Own Foundation, a private foundation that received a contribution of 100% of Paul Newman's food and beverage firm.

The second development relates to changes in trust laws under certain US states' laws that permit the creation of a perpetual purpose trust. Historically, it was largely impossible to set up a perpetual purpose trust, particularly if the purpose was not charitable. However, some states, such as Delaware, have recently enabled entrepreneurs to set up perpetual purpose trusts, and such trusts may control industrial business corporations.[14] To date, control by perpetual purpose trusts has primarily been used as a substitute to employee stock option plans which are subject to hefty regulation and to ensure that controlled business corporations distribute a sizable share of their profits to the employees. But this structure could potentially be used by founders to create public firms that are controlled by a trust whose purpose is to promote the founder's values. In fact, very recently, the founder of Patagonia, a manufacturer of environmentally friendly clothing, transferred control to a perpetual purpose trust.[15]

It remains to be seen whether recent developments in US law will spur further evolution of enterprise foundations. Patagonia's structure may offer a promising

---

activities conducted seasonally when seasonal operation is the norm for the field. Whether a trade or business is 'substantially related' depends on the causal relationship between the conduct of the business and the achievement of the organization's exempt purposes, other than through the production of income (Treas. Reg., §1.513-1(d)).

12 P. Molk and D.D. Sokol, 'The Challenges of Nonprofit Governance' (2021) 62 Boston College Law Review 1497, 1522–1525.

13 See below, nn. 63–65.

14 S.N. Gary, 'The Oregon Stewardship Trust: A New Type of Purpose Trust that Enables Steward-Ownership of a Business' (2020) 88 University of Cincinnati Law Review 707, 711–712.

15 All voting power was allocated to a perpetual trust, and the nonvoting stock that carries 98% of the economic interest was transferred to a non-exempt nonprofit; see Y. Chouinard, 'Earth is now our only shareholder' (14 September 2022) *Patagonia*: https://www.patagonia.com/ownership/ (accessed 18 September 2023).

model for addressing two significant legal challenges that have historically hindered such initiatives. First, by employing a non-charitable purpose trust to control the business entity, founders or their heirs can circumvent the restrictions imposed on private foundations. Second, by utilizing a dual-class share structure, all control of the business can be vested in the trust, while the cash flows are allocated to a charitable, tax-exempt nonprofit. This arrangement ensures that the income generated by the for-profit entity qualifies as passive income, thereby avoiding potential taxation under UBIT.[16]

This chapter describes in detail the law that regulates the formation of enterprise foundations under US law. The basic takeaway is that contrary to the perception that legal institutions prohibit enterprise foundations, it is possible now to create enterprise foundations in the US. The "catch" is that if founders are interested in the tax exemptions afforded to tax-exempt nonprofits, these requirements are very restrictive.

In this chapter, I do not take a normative stance on whether the requirements under US law should be relaxed to allow private foundations to control business firms more freely while benefiting from tax exemptions, as is the case in some European jurisdictions. This question depends on the relative risks of nonprofit and for-profit mission drift and the capacity of regulatory and tax authorities to monitor these risks effectively.[17]

2. PRIVATE FOUNDATIONS

To understand the restrictions on private foundations' control, it is first necessary to understand what a private foundation is. A private foundation under US law is defined by the Tax Code and is not simply any nonprofit entity that does not have owners. The definition itself is somewhat complex. The starting point is that a private foundation is a section 501(c)(3) tax-exempt organization, and thus it is organized for a tax-exempt purpose (charitable, religious, educational, scientific or literary). It is further subject to the prohibition on inurement, which means

---

16 See below nn. 92–93.

17 See O. Eldar and M. Ørberg, 'The Anatomy of Nonprofit Control of Business Enterprise' (forthcoming, 2026) *Yale Journal on Regulation*. Eldar and Ørberg distinguish between two models of nonprofit control: the income-generating for-profit, where a nonprofit controls a business to fund its charitable activities, and the socially-oriented for-profit, where the business itself advances a social mission. They argue that the key regulatory challenge lies in addressing 'mission drift' – nonprofits neglecting their charitable goals in the former model, and for-profits straying from social purposes in the latter. The authors propose that optimal legal regimes should distinguish between these models, impose distribution duties on income-generating for-profits, introduce regulatory oversight and enforcement for socially-oriented for-profits, and more generally focus on safeguarding nonprofit independence from outside investors rather than founders or donors.

that none of the organization's earnings may inure to any private shareholder or individual.[18]

Every tax-exempt organization is a private foundation unless it falls into one of the excluded categories under section 509(a) of the Tax Code.[19] Importantly, the Code excludes organizations that are not controlled directly or indirectly by a disqualified person[20] and do not receive more than a third of their funding from such a person.[21] A disqualified person is defined to include a substantial contributor to the organization, or an entity in which such a contributor has more than 35% beneficial interest.[22] Accordingly, the result of this convoluted definition is that a tax-exempt nonprofit that is highly dependent on a private entrepreneur that contributes a substantial amount of his or her wealth to the organization is classified as a private foundation.

2.1. EXCESS BUSINESS HOLDINGS

The private foundation faces substantial restrictions on owning and controlling operating companies. The most significant one is the excise tax imposed by section 4943.[23] The base for the section 4943 tax is the 'excess business holdings' of any private foundation in a 'business enterprise'. 'Business enterprise' is defined by exclusion in the statute: it does not include: (1) a business that is a 'functionally related business'; or (2) a trade or business for which at least 95% of its gross income is derived from passive sources.[24]

A functionally related business is one which is not an unrelated trade or business[25] or which is part of an aggregate of activities related to the exempt purpose of the organization.[26] Conversely, if the business in question is an unrelated trade or business, this exception will not apply, and it will be treated by default as a business enterprise unless the passive income exception applies.[27]

---

18 I.R.C., §501(c)(3) (defining tax-exempt charitable entities as those in which 'no part of the net earnings ... inures to the benefit of any private shareholder or individual').

19 The first category includes certain specified types of organizations, such as hospitals, churches and universities. I.R.C., §509(a)(1); I.R.C., §170(b)(1)(A).

20 I.R.C., §509(a)(3).

21 I.R.C., §509(a)(2).

22 I.R.C., §4946.

23 For the purposes of section 4943, 'private foundation' includes certain deemed private foundations: notably, donor-advised funds and certain supporting organizations. See I.R.C., §4943(e)–(f).

24 Ibid., §4943(d)(3); see also Treas. Reg., §53.4943-10 (noting that a trade or business need not result in a profit to be a business enterprise).

25 Defined in I.R.C., §513 as a trade or business which is not substantially related to the exercise or performance of the organization's purpose.

26 Ibid., §4942(j)(4).

27 Treas. Reg., §53.4943-10(a)(1) ('"[B]usiness enterprise" includes the active conduct of a trade or business, including ... an unrelated trade or business under section 513').

Passive sources for purposes of the second exception mostly track the passive income exclusions from unrelated business taxable income in section 512, most notably dividends, interest, annuities, royalties, rents from real property and incidental personal property and gains or losses from disposition of property besides inventory.[28]

If a trade or business qualifies as a business enterprise, excess business holdings are calculated as the private foundation's excess interest in the enterprise over its 'permitted holdings'.[29] Permitted holdings are generally calculated as an aggregate of the interest held by the private foundation and 'disqualified persons'.[30] Disqualified persons include, broadly speaking, substantial contributors or insiders of the foundation who were able to exercise 'substantial influence over the affairs of the organization' at any time during the preceding five years, as well as certain family members and controlled entities.[31]

How permitted holdings are calculated depends on the entity form of the enterprise. For corporations, permitted holdings are generally 20% of the voting stock minus the percentage of voting stock owned by disqualified persons.[32] Two exceptions apply: first, where a third person has 'effective control of enterprise' (essentially, real control over management of the enterprise[33]), the threshold is 35%;[34] and, second, a 2% de minimis rule applies under which a foundation will not be treated as having excess holdings if it owns less than 2% of voting stock and 2% of the total share value of the corporation.[35] Additionally, as long as disqualified persons do not together own more than 20% or 35% (depending on the applicable threshold) of voting stock, all nonvoting stock held by the private foundation will be permitted holdings.[36]

---

28 I.R.C., §4943(d)(3) (citing I.R.C., §512(b)(1)–(3), (5)). For example, operating a donated apartment complex that generates more than 95% of gross income from rents could be an unrelated trade or business, but it would fall within the passive sources exception and would not be a section 4943 business enterprise (I.R.S. P.L.R. 201422027 (30 May 2014)). Notably, revenue from services besides rents in that remaining 5% (such as revenue from coin-operated laundry machines) could still be subject to UBIT, section 4943 notwithstanding.

29 I.R.C., §4943(c)(1).

30 Ibid.

31 Ibid., §4943(f)(4).

32 Ibid., §4943(c)(2).

33 Treas. Reg., §53.4943-3(b)(3)(ii).

34 I.R.C., §4943(c)(2)(B).

35 Ibid., §4943(c)(2)(C). When different classes of voting stock exist, the percentage of voting stock owned is determined by reference to the relative power of each class to vote for directors, disregarding treasury stock and authorized but unissued stock (Treas. Reg., §53.4943-3(b)(1)(ii)). The example from the regulations: a private foundation holding 20% of a stock class entitled to elect three directors and no stock from the class entitled to elect five directors is treated as holding 7.5% of voting stock (20% of the class having 37.5% of the voting power) (ibid).

36 I.R.C., §4943(c)(2)(A). For unincorporated businesses, the tests are analogous. For partnerships, the corporate tests apply with the substitution of 'profits interest' for 'voting stock' and 'capital interest' for 'nonvoting stock' (ibid., §4943(c)(3)(A)).

The initial excise tax is 10% of the value of excess holdings in an applicable business enterprise.[37] The tax is imposed on the last day of the private foundation's taxable year, but its calculation uses the excess holdings amount from the day in the foundation's taxable year on which excess holdings in that enterprise were at their greatest (by value).[38] Additionally, if excess holdings are still maintained at the end of the 'taxable period', a penalty tax of 200% of excess holding value is applied.[39] The taxable period begins on the first day on which there are excess holdings and ends on the earlier of two dates: the date of mailing of a notice of deficiency or the date on which the initial 10% tax is assessed.[40] Various grace periods may apply to permit the foundation to dispose of excess holdings before the tax comes into effect in circumstances where the foundation did not know or had no reason to know that it acquired excess business holdings.[41]

The general effect of this substantial tax penalty is that private foundations cannot, for all practical purposes, have a controlling ownership stake in a business firm. As discussed above, evaluating the policy rationale for this outcome is beyond the scope of this chapter. But it is worth noting that when adopted in 1969 through the Tax Reform Act, there was robust debate regarding its desirability.

The center of the debate was a 1965 Treasury report which found that around 14% of private foundations had ownership of at least 10% of an outstanding class of stock of a corporation.[42] The report expressed concerns about the involvement of private foundations in active commercial businesses on several grounds. The managers of foundations, often their main donors, were arguably managing the business firm in a way that compromised the interests of the foundations, for example, by refusing to distribute dividends.[43] Controlling the business firm arguably also enabled the foundations' insiders to cause the business firm to enter into self-dealing transactions with these insiders and their affiliates.[44] Investment of tax-exempt funds by foundations in active commercial ventures put taxable businesses at a competitive disadvantage.[45]

---

37 Ibid., §4943(a)(1). This was raised from an earlier rate of 5% by the Pension Protection Act of 2006, and some regulations have not been updated yet to match the new, higher rate (Treas. Reg., §53.4943-2(a)(1)(i)).

38 Treas. Reg., §53.4943-2(a)(2).

39 I.R.C., §4943(b).

40 Ibid., §4943(d)(2). 'Assessment' is used here as the term of art referring to statutorily required recording of tax liability (Treas. Reg., §301.6203-1 (method of assessment)).

41 Treas. Reg., §53.4943.

42 Senate Comm. on Fin., 89th Cong., Treasury Department Report on Private Foundations 31 (1965).

43 Ibid., 39.

44 Ibid., 15–16.

45 Ibid., 31.

On the other hand, others argued that restrictions on foundation control of business firms would be harsh and undiscriminating.[46] They argued that most foundations ran business firms without any tax abuse or abusive acquisitions, and that the tax advantages offered to private foundations were limited.[47] Moreover, the restrictions would harm small community-oriented foundations capitalized by a substantial ownership interest in a local business, and thus would be detrimental to foundations' ability to serve communities' needs.[48] Nonetheless, opponents of foundations' control of business firms prevailed, and the tax on excess business holding was adopted.

2.2. PROGRAM-RELATED INVESTMENTS

The main exception, until recently, to the tax on excess business holding has been investments that qualify as program-related investments (PRIs). A PRI is defined as a foundation investment, the primary purpose of which is to accomplish religious, charitable, scientific, literary and/or or educational purposes, and no significant purpose of which is the production of income or the appreciation of property.[49] An investment qualifies if it significantly furthers the accomplishment of the private foundation's exempt activities, and if the investment would not otherwise have been made.[50] While any investment may qualify as a PRI, so can an investment that provides the foundation with control over a business corporation. Accordingly, there are generally no limitations on private foundations if they invest in businesses that serve an exempt purpose.

The advantages of PRIs go beyond the exemption from the tax on excess business holdings. The income from PRIs is itself tax-exempt because the income flows from a related business and thus is not subject to UBIT, which is discussed is more detail below. Moreover, PRIs qualify towards foundations' mandatory distribution requirements, despite the fact they can yield some income. Foundations must annually satisfy statutorily imposed minimums for expenditure made in furtherance of their charitable purposes which generally equal at least 5% of their assets.[51] Undistributed income is subject to a 30% tax.[52] Amounts invested as PRIs thus help foundations avoid this tax penalty.

---

46 Senate Comm. on Fin., 91st Cong., Tax Reform Act of 1969, H.R. 13270: Part A – Testimony to be Received Tuesday, 7 October 1969 107 (Comm. Print 1969) (statement of James Irvine Foundation).

47 Ibid., 119–21.

48 Ibid., 116–117.

49 I.R.C., §4944(c); 26 Code of Federal Regulations (C.F.R.), §53.4944-3(a)(1).

50 26 C.F.R., §53.4944-3(a)(2); 'Program-related investments' (2024) IRS: https://www.irs.gov/charities-non-profits/private-foundations/program-related-investments.

51 I.R.C., §4942(e)(1).

52 Ibid., §4942(a).

Despite the advantages associated with PRIs, few foundations make them in practice.[53] The reason is that investments that purport to qualify as PRIs create substantial legal risks for foundations. If a specific investment fails to qualify as a PRI, it may result in failure to meet the foundation's minimum distribution requirements, leading to substantial tax payments.[54] Moreover, because such investments tend to carry high risk and lower return, they could be viewed as jeopardizing the foundation's financial ability to carry out its exempt purpose[55] and, as jeopardizing investments, they would be subject to a 10% tax.[56] In extreme cases, the investment may result in the foundation losing its tax-exempt status if the investment violates the prohibition on private inurement by creating a private benefit for the shareholders of the business firm that received the investment.

The ultimate responsibility of verifying that an investment qualifies as a PRI rests with the foundation itself. Private foundations must exercise 'expenditure responsibility' by monitoring the firm that received the investment to ensure that the funds are used for their intended purposes, obtaining reports on how the funds are spent, and making detailed reports to the Internal Revenue Service (IRS).[57] The PRI rules and several private letter rulings by the IRS mitigate the uncertainty of verifying and monitoring PRIs by providing specific examples of qualifying investments. These refer mainly to businesses that transact with disadvantaged individuals or businesses, in circumstances where conventional sources of funds are unwilling to provide funds at reasonable rates. Examples include a business that employs a substantial number of low-income persons or an investment firm organized for investing in businesses in low-income communities.[58] Nonetheless, there remains substantial legal uncertainty for foundations when making PRIs because there may be reasonable disagreements as to whether different businesses would further the purpose of the foundation, and whether these businesses can obtain capital at reasonable terms from other sources. Accordingly, it is not surprising that most foundations are reluctant to assume this responsibility.[59]

In summary, PRIs provide an exception that permits private foundations to invest in and control business firms, but this exception is relatively narrow because it is confined to businesses that serve a foundation's tax-exempt purposes. Moreover, due to the legal uncertainty associated with making PRIs, relatively few foundations make use of them.

---

53 O. Eldar, above n. 6, 959.

54 Ibid., 960.

55 Treas. Reg., §53.4944-1(a)(2)(ii).

56 I.R.C., §4944(a)(1).

57 I.R.C., §4945(d)(4); Treas. Reg., §53.4945-5(a)(2); Treas. Reg., §53.4945-4(a)(2).

58 O. Eldar, above n. 6, 961.

59 Ibid., 960.

2.3. THE 'NEWMAN'S OWN' EXCEPTION

In 2018, the Tax Code was amended under the Philanthropic Enterprise Act of 2017 to allow for another exception to the tax on excess business holdings.[60] Interestingly, the law was passed specifically to assist Newman's Own Foundation, a private foundation that received a contribution of 100% of Paul Newman's for-profit food company, called Newman's Own, that paid all its profits to charity. The foundation faced the risk of paying the tax on excess business holdings because its holdings exceeded the permitted threshold of 20% of the voting rights in the for-profit good company. Paul Newman himself apparently lobbied for the legislation.

The exception at section 4943(g) mirrors the situation faced by Newman's Own Foundation. The provision exempts from the excise tax all holdings in a business enterprise that meets three tests: (a) 'ownership', (b) 'all profits to charity', and (c) 'independent operation'.

The 'ownership' test has two requirements: the private foundation must have held 100% of voting stock in the business enterprise during the taxable year; and all its ownership interests must have been acquired by means other than purchase.[61]

The 'all profits to charity' test requires that the business enterprise distribute its net operating income (calculated as gross minus deductions, tax and a working capital allowance) to the parent foundation within 120 days of the close of its taxable year.[62]

The 'independent operation' test requires three markers of independence: first, no substantial contributor[63] to the private foundation or family member of the same may be involved in the business;[64] second, at least a majority of the board of directors of the foundation must be persons who are not directors or officers of the business enterprise or family members of substantial contributors; and, third, there must be no loans outstanding from the business enterprise to substantial contributors, their family members or the private foundation itself.[65]

---

60 Pub. L. No. 115-123, §41110, 132 Stat. 64 (2018); I.R.C., §4943. The exception does not apply to certain deemed private foundations that are otherwise subject to the excise tax. I.R.C., §4943(g)(5) (donor-advised funds; certain supporting organizations; certain charitable and split-interest trusts).

61 Ibid., §4943(g)(2).

62 Ibid., §4943(g)(3).

63 Defined at I.R.C., §4958(c)(3)(C). Generally speaking, a donor donating more than $5,000 and more than 2% of the organization's total contributions in a year would count as a substantial contributor.

64 Specifically, they may not be a 'director, officer, trustee, manager, employee, or contractor of the business enterprise (or an individual having powers or responsibilities similar to any of the foregoing)', ibid., §4943(g)(4)(A).

65 Ibid., §4943(g)(4).

Taken as a whole, these requirements are designed to address the concerns that underlie the policy rationale for the tax on excess business holdings, discussed above. As the foundation is the sole owner of the business firm, there is no risk that tax-exempt funds will be used to benefit other shareholders. There is also no risk that profits from the business will be locked in the for-profit entity and will be unavailable to the foundation. Moreover, the main donors are not permitted to control both the foundation and the business firm, and thus there is little risk they would be able to utilize both to their personal advantage.

Finally, the income from the for-profit is generally taxable as UBIT if it is unrelated to the purpose of the foundation. For example, the income from selling food products is clearly unrelated to the charitable purpose of Newman's Own Foundation and thus is taxable at the normal corporate tax rate.

Overall, the 'Newman's Own' exception is relatively narrow in scope, but it does provide foundations an opportunity to generate income from business activity. In particular, the exception may be used by philanthropists who wish to bequeath their ownership stake in business firms to private foundations, and for foundations to operate such firms to generate more income and increase their funds.

3. TAX-EXEMPT ORGANIZATIONS THAT DO NOT QUALIFY AS PRIVATE FOUNDATIONS

It is important to remember that the heavy restrictions on controlling a for-profit business firm apply only to private foundations. These restrictions do not apply to nonprofits that do not qualify as private foundations. The IRS issues a section 509(a) ruling with respect to every tax-exempt organization in order to determine whether the organization is a private foundation, or alternatively, a public charity. If the organization is a public charity, it is not subject to the tax on excess business holding.

Public charities include certain types of specified organizations, such as hospitals and churches, and educational organizations, such as schools and universities.[66] A more general category that appears to have been overlooked in the earlier literature is an organization that normally receives a substantial part of its support from a governmental unit or from the general public described in section 170(b)(1)(A)(vi) of the Tax Code. The 'substantial part of its support' requirement is generally met if the organization receives at least 33.33% of its support from the government and the general public.[67] The Mozilla Foundation

66 I.R.C., §509(a)(1); I.R.C., §170(b)(1)(A).

67 Treas. Reg., §1.170A-9(f)(ii)(2). Alternatively, the IRS may conduct a multifactor analysis based on 'facts and circumstances', but including whether at least 10% of the support of the organization is sourced from the public. Ibid., §1.170A-9(f)(ii)(3)–(3)(i).

and Open AI, discussed above in section 1, are examples of such organizations. Thus, the tax on excess business holdings does not apply to its ownership of the Mozilla Corporation.

Paradoxically, the historical prototype of a US public charity that controls a business firm, the Hershey Trust, is not representative of general practice, but is viewed as a unique anomaly. The trust owns a controlling stake through a dual-class structure in the Hershey Chocolate Company. The trust that received its assets, including the ownership stake in the chocolate company from Milton Hershey in 1918, would be treated as a private foundation. But because the trust's role is to support a school for orphaned children, it qualifies as a 'supporting organization' to an educational organization under section 509(a)(3) – an exception that Congress apparently created specifically for the Hershey Trust.[68]

Nonetheless, this ownership structure by public charities is subject to some, albeit milder, restrictions.[69] The most direct one is UBIT.[70] This tax amounts to the normal corporate tax rate imposed on trade or business which is not regularly carried on and is not substantially related to the exempt purposes of the organization.[71] The Hershey Chocolate Company's business is clearly unrelated to the purpose of the Hershey Trust. The Mozilla Corporation does, in some years, generate business income from licenses and various services it sells, and this income may be unrelated to the purposes of the nonprofit parent, and to that extent that income is taxable.[72] More drastically, if the unrelated business activity is too substantial, the organization will be deemed not to be operating exclusively for exempt purposes and will not qualify for tax-exempt status.[73] Thus, operating a business firm is risky for nonprofits even if they are willing to pay tax on the income generated by the business.

---

68 E. Brody, 'Whose Public? Parochialism and Paternalism in State Charity Law Enforcement' (2004) 79 Indiana Law Journal 937, 987–988.

69 I.R.C., §4944(c).

70 Ibid, §511. The investment in the for-profit would also be subject to a 10% tax if it is so risky so as to jeopardize the ability of foundation to carry out its exempt purpose. I.R.C., §4944.

71 Above n. 11. Note that UBIT also applies in the case of private foundations, whether or not there is excess business holding.

72 The 2019 filing of the Mozilla Foundation states: 'The foundation qualifies as a public benefit charitable organization exempt from income taxes on related income under section 501(c)(3) of the internal revenue code and applicable sections of the California revenue and taxation code. The foundation provides for tax, if any, on unrelated business income. In accordance with the accounting standard on accounting for uncertainty in income taxes, no portion of an uncertain tax position will be recognized if the position has less than a 50 percent likelihood of being sustained upon audit by the relevant taxing authority. Also, interest expense, if any, is recognized on the full amount of deferred benefits for uncertain tax positions.' (Mozilla Foundation, I.R.S Form 990: Supplemental Financial Statements, DLN. 93493321080390 (2019)).

73 See Treas. Reg., §1.501(c)(3)–1(c).

There are likewise examples where the for-profit business qualifies as a related business, and therefore the income from the business that flows to the foundation is exempt from income tax. An example is the Greyston Foundation, a nonprofit that is devoted to enhancing employment opportunities in low-income communities by promoting open hiring practices.[74] The foundation is not a private foundation, again because it receives a substantial part of its support from the general public under section 170(b)(1)(A)(vi).[75] The Greyston Foundation owns 100% of the Greyston Bakery, a commercial bakery that is committed to employing people in low-income communities that suffer from systemic unemployment. In this case, the operations of the for-profit subsidiary are likely related to the tax-exempt purposes of the parent nonprofit, and thus they are not typically classified as UBIT.

4. NON-EXEMPT PURPOSE-ORIENTED ORGANIZATIONS

In assessing whether enterprise foundations are possible in the US, it is important to emphasize that it seems entirely possible for organizations that are not tax-exempt to have a controlling stake in for-profit firms.

Taking nonprofit corporations first, just like business corporations, they can usually be formed for 'any lawful activity'.[76] It is generally possible to create a nonprofit whose purpose is to promote some nonpecuniary purpose that is related to the vision of some entrepreneur, and for that nonprofit to have voting control of the business corporation which was owned by that entrepreneur. A recent example is the transfer of all stocks of Tripp Lite, an electrical device manufacturing company, to a nonprofit formed under section 501(c)(4) to promote conservative political causes.[77]

Of course, the management of the nonprofit will be subject to the standard fiduciary duties of loyalty and care, and since the nonprofit corporation was created under the laws of a US state, the state attorney general will monitor whether managers act beyond their powers or engage in self-dealing transactions.[78] Accordingly, it may be difficult for entrepreneurs to maintain control over the nonprofit after the transfer of their ownership interest. However, state monitoring

---

74 O. Eldar, above n. 8, 114.

75 See above n. 67 for an explanation of the 'substantial support' test.

76 Revised Model Nonprofit Corporation Act 1987, §3.01.

77 K.P. Vogel and S. Goldmacher, 'An Unusual $1.6 Billion Donation Bolsters Conservatives' (22 August 2022) *New York Times*: https://www.nytimes.com/2022/08/22/us/politics/republican-dark-money.html.

78 P. Molk and D.D. Sokol, above n. 12, 1509.

of nonprofits is generally very loose, and it is rare for state attorneys general to expend substantial resources in policing the management of nonprofits.[79]

Instead of using the nonprofit form, it may also be possible to create a limited liability company ((LLC), which would be outside the ambit of state attorneys general and not subject to mandatory fiduciary duties under states' corporate laws. The LLC is an entity form that allows entrepreneurs to design all its internal governance arrangements through the LLC agreement.[80] The LLC agreement could lay out a constraint on distributing any profits to individuals, such that the LLC has no owners. The LLC could further be governed by a self-appointing board of directors that is entrusted with pursuing the purpose of the LLC, which again will be defined in the LLC agreement. The LLC, which would effectively serve as a nonprofit, could be allocated the controlling stake in a business firm and continue to run it in perpetuity.

The 'perpetual purpose trust' or 'stewardship trust' is a novel form of ownership that was recently introduced in the US,[81] and may be used to create enterprise foundations. At common law, a non-charitable purpose trust would generally fail due to the lack of ascertainable beneficiaries.[82] The Uniform Trust Code (UTC) modified the common law rule in section 409 to allow for trusts created for a specific non-charitable purpose or a valid, non-charitable purpose selected by the trustee.[83] Although this change allowed creation of purpose trusts, a durational limit remained, prohibiting perpetual trusts.[84] Additionally, section 409 UTC gave courts the power to reduce the corpus of a purpose trust to the extent the total is 'not required for the intended use'.[85] These limitations diminished the business incentives to place a perpetual entity

---

79 Ibid., 1522–1525. In fact, state attorneys general are more likely to intervene in transactions when it is politically expedient to do so – see J. Klick and R.H. Sitkoff, above n. 2, 755–756 (the Pennsylvania Attorney General intervened and obtained a preliminary injunction of the Milton Hershey School Trust's (Trust) sale of its Hershey Company stake, on the grounds that the sale would harm the local Pennsylvania economy and community).

80 Recently, Facebook's founder, Mark Zuckerberg, chose to organize his charitable activities in an LLC instead of a private foundation, partly to avoid some of the tax complexities and restrictions that foundations entail. See D.B. Reiser, 'Disruptive Philanthropy: Chan-Zuckerberg, the Limited Liability Company, and the Millionaire Next Door' (2018) 70 Florida Law Review 921, 931–948.

81 See Z. Schlag, D. Razo and C. Canon, 'Exiting to Employees through Employee Ownership Trusts' (2021) *Common Trust Partners LLC and Purpose Network US*; L. Tyson, S. Thomsen, R. Strand, E. Pelissier and E. Gurfein Borge, 'Perpetual Purpose Trust and Organically Grown Company: Rethinking Corporate Ownership for the Future' (2021) *Berkeley Haas Case Series*.

82 S.N. Gary, above n. 14, 713–716 (citing E.C. Halback Jr., *Restatement of the Law Third, Trusts*, American Law Institute, 2007, §47).

83 Ibid., 717–719 (citing Uniform Trust Code, §409 (amended 2010)).

84 Absent additional change, non-charitable purpose trusts remain subject to the duration fixed in the statute – either the default 21 years of the rule against perpetuities or an extended term adopted by the state. Ibid., 720.

85 Ibid. (citing Uniform Trust Code, §409(3) (amended 2010)).

under the control of a purpose trust. However, certain states, notably including Delaware, omitted these restrictions from their trust statutes, permitting perpetual, non-charitable purpose trusts without threat of court-ordered asset reduction.[86]

The perpetual trust has been increasingly used to create a form of employee-owned business by designating employees as the trust's beneficiaries. It is often seen as an alternative to employee stock-ownership plans (ESOPs), which are heavily regulated and highly inflexible.[87] Although the employees do not own the company directly, they may thereby be able to share in its profits.[88] The trust will also typically specify the conditions under which a sale might happen in order to ensure the protection of the purpose of the trust.[89] Although the trust may hold all the voting stock of the company, the company may retain the ability to raise capital by issuing nonvoting preferred stock.[90] The trust thus ensures that the firm will remain employee-owned throughout its lifetime.

The management of the trust is highly flexible in identifying the key stakeholders that control the business firm and determining the governing structure of the operating company. Typically, the parent trust is managed by a committee. The committee is elected by stakeholders, such as employees and community representatives. The committee's role is then to ensure that the trust upholds its purpose, and it oversees the board of the operating company.[91] The exact scope of decision-making of the committee or the board as well as the power of employees or other stakeholders in decision-making and elections are set by the trust agreement.

Overall, despite the fact that it is growing in popularity in the context of employee-owned firms, it remains a relatively rare ownership model. Very recently, the founder of Patagonia, a clothing company, announced that his family transferred the ownership of the firm by creating a dual-class structure under which a perpetual purpose trust will have the voting power in the firm and a non-exempt nonprofit organized to protect nature and the environment under

---

86 Ibid., 721.

87 ESOPs are retirement products and thus their benefits are mainly paid to participants near or at retirement age. In contrast, the trust structure allows employees to share in the company's profits throughout the life of the firm. Holding the company's shares through a trust avoids the valuation issues that arise with the circulation of shares in an ESOP under the Employee Retirement Income Security Act of 1974 (ERISA). A perpetual trust may avoid the lack of diversification inherent in an ESOP by instead applying profits as an employer contribution to a traditional 401(k) plan for the company's employees. See Z. Schlag, D. Razo and C. Canon, above n. 81, pp. 23–24.

88 Ibid., p. 23.

89 Ibid., p. 24.

90 S.N. Gary, above n. 14, 729.

91 See Z. Schlag, D. Razo and C. Canon, above n. 81, pp. 40–41.

section 501(c)(4) will be entitled to 98% of the economic profits.[92] Importantly, the founder's family will keep its influence over the company through the trust's governance structure. This structure has the advantage of avoiding UBIT, as the tax-exempt nonprofit, which holds nearly all of the cash flow rights in the business, receives only passive income. Meanwhile, the trust, which retains voting control, actively manages the business.

It remains to be seen whether Patagonia and Tripp Lite remain unique examples of a founders willing to part with their wealth, and whether more founders will form enterprise foundations. A major challenge for creating such structures is that at least in the US, the demand for them is often motivated by tax considerations.[93] A disadvantage of non-exempt entities is that any gifts or transfers to the organization would not typically be tax-deductible, including transfer of stocks in the relevant business firm.[94] However, lifetime gifts to section 501(c)(4) nonprofits are exempt from estate and gift taxes.[95] This exemption may have facilitated the transformation of Patagonia and Tripp Lite into enterprise foundations, and in the case of Patagonia, the founder's family manages to maintain its influence by allocating voting control to the trust. Further research is necessary to evaluate which tax exemptions may be critical for entrepreneurs to induce them to form enterprise foundations.

5. CONCLUSION

There is a perception that enterprise foundations are not possible in the US. In this chapter, I have shown that it is actually feasible to form them, yet they are rarely created. The reason appears to be that subject to a few exceptions, there are no tax benefits to forming enterprise foundations in the US. This suggests that at

---

92 One reason for not seeking a tax-exempt status for the nonprofit firm is to allow it to undertake political and lobbying activities, which are not permitted for tax-exempt nonprofits under section 501(c)(3); see D. Gelles, 'The climate philanthropists' (16 September 2022) *New York Times*: https://www.nytimes.com/2022/09/16/climate/yvon-chouinard-patagonia-philanthropy.html.

93 This is generally consistent with the evidence on perpetual trusts. See M.M. Schanzenbach and R.H. Sitkoff, 'Perpetuities or Taxes? Explaining the Rise of the Perpetual Trust' (2006) 27 Cardozo Law Review 2465 (demonstrating that the demand for perpetual trusts was driven by exemptions from estate tax).

94 I.R.C., §§2501, 2001. See D.B. Reiser, above n. 80, 952–956; L. Tyson, S. Thomsen, R. Strand, E. Pelissier and E. Gurfein Borge, above n. 81, p. 5.

95 I.R.C., §§2501(a)(6). See A.R. Sorkin et al., 'Philanthropy, the Billionaires' Way' (16 September 2022) *New York Times*: https://www.nytimes.com/2022/09/16/business/dealbook/philanthropy-patagonia-billionaires-way-taxes.html.

least in the US, without tax benefits, it is generally unlikely that business planners would opt to employ nonprofits to control business firms.

However, some recent innovations may potentially lead over time to the greater popularity of enterprise foundations in the US. It is possible that more private foundations will utilize the 'Newman's Own' exception to own and control business firms. The challenge is that the conditions for satisfying the exception, such as the requirement that the foundation should own 100% of the business firm, are quite restrictive.

Likewise, the emergence of the perpetual purpose trust may provide an efficient legal tool for creating enterprise foundations, without subjecting entrepreneurs to the complexities and vagueness of the Tax Code (though without important tax benefits, such as tax-deductible donations or exemption from income tax). These trusts are increasingly used to form employee-owned firms, and there are some recent examples of trusts created to control for-profit firms that purport to have a purpose that is broader than merely profit-maximization. Control by a trust that has no investor-owners may be used to ensure that such firms will not sacrifice their missions in order to make more profits.[96]

96 O. ELDAR, above n. 8, 154–157. In contrast, legal forms, such as the benefit corporation, do not provide a credible commitment device that ensures that firms pursue social missions effectively; see O. ELDAR, above n. 6, 964–968.

ENTERPRISE FOUNDATIONS IN EUROPEAN LAW

An exploration of judgments of three European courts pertaining to freedom of establishment and fundamental freedoms for enterprise foundations and their initiators

Wino J.M. van Veen

ABSTRACT

This purpose of this chapter is to explore whether there are principles or norms ensuing from EU/EEA-law and the European Convention on Human Rights, that apply to the establishment, governance and supervision of enterprise foundations. The main findings are that it seems to follow from case law of the CJEU and of the EFTA-court, that enterprise foundations are eligible to market freedoms such as the freedom of establishment if certain conditions are met. Moreover, the case law of the European Court of Human Rights holds not only that foundations as such are eligible to the fundamental rights afforded by the Convention, but also that forming foundations falls within the scope of freedom of association. These findings have ramifications for the law and administrative practice relating to (enterprise) foundations.

1. INTRODUCTION

Comparative research shows considerable, sometimes fundamental differences in the laws on foundations in Europe.[1] These differences relate to political history and characteristics and legal culture of the different states.[2] Differences include, for example, the nature of the regulation, which may have a substantial public law component in one country and in other countries be predominantly of a civil law nature. Similarly, supervision over foundations may be charged to a body of the executive branch of government, whereas in other countries supervision is charged to an independent administrative authority, or the magistrature being the public prosecutor and the courts. Such differences in themselves may affect the latitude foundations enjoy in a specific country and how foundations have developed.

Also, in some countries, foundations can only be set up for a public benefit purpose, whereas in other countries such restriction is absent.[3] Moreover, the concept of a foundation differs in countries with a civil law tradition and a common law tradition. In civil law countries the foundation typically is a specific legal form with legal personality and without members or the equivalent thereof, such as shareholders. To complicate matters a bit further, certain jurisdictions

---

1 See *inter alia*, A. Schlüter, V. Then and P. Walkenhorst (eds), *Foundations in Europe: Society, Management and Law*, Charity Aid Foundation/Directory of Social Change/ Bertelsmann Foundation, London 2000; A. Richter and T. Wachter, *Handbuch des internationalen Stiftungsrechts*, Helbing Lichtenhahn Verlag, Basel 2007; T.J. van der Ploeg, W.J.M. van Veen and C.R.M. Versteegh (eds), *Civil Society in Europe: Minimum Norms and Optimum Conditions of its Regulation*, Cambridge University Press, Cambridge 2017, pp. 75 et seq.; A. Sanders and S. Thomsen (eds), *Enterprise Foundation Law in a Comparative Perspective*, Intersentia, Cambridge 2023.
For a regularly updated overview of country reports on foundation law in Europe, see: https://philea.eu/how-we-can-help/policy-and-advocacy/analysing-the-legal-environment-for-philanthropy-in-europe.

2 See *inter alia*, A. Richter, 'German and American Law of Charity in the Early 19th Century' in R. Helmholz and R. Zimmermann (eds), *Itinera Fiduciae, Trust and Treuhand in Historical Perspective*, Duncker & Humblot, Berlin 1998; T.J. van der Ploeg, 'A Comparative Legal Analysis of Foundations' in H.K. Anheier and S. Toepler (eds), *Private Funds, Public Purpose: Philanthropic Foundations in International Perspective*, Kluwer Academic/Plenum Publishers, New York 1999; W.J.M. van Veen, 'Public benefit law from a comparative perspective' in F.W. Hondius and P. Bater, *The Tax Treatment of NGOs: Legal, Ethical and Fiscal Frameworks for Promoting NGOs and their Activities*, Kluwer Law International, The Hague/London/New York 2004.

3 Also, within one jurisdiction, public benefit may have a different content in tax law and in foundation law. See W.J.M. van Veen, above n. 2, also published in German: 'Gemeinnützigkeitsrecht aus vergleichender Sicht' in H.K. Anheier and V. Then (eds), *Zwischen Eigennutz und Gemeinwohl: Neue Formen und Wege der Gemeinnützigkeit*, Verlag Bertelsmann Stiftung, Güthersloh, 2004, pp. 203–222.

have two or more different legal entities that meet the basic characteristics of a foundation that are available for certain applications.[4] In countries with a common law tradition the foundation is as such not known as a specific form of legal entity. In these countries, other legal forms are available that are functionally equivalent to the foundation.[5] In short, in Europe the laws on foundations have a distinctive '*couleur locale*'. It goes without saying, this entails challenges when designing a model law for (enterprise) foundations that is widely acceptable.

Comparative research is a logical and adequate method for a better understanding of the enterprise foundation and finding common grounds for the evaluation of its regulation. In addition to that, it may be useful to explore whether there are principles or norms ensuing from European institutions that apply to the establishment, governance and supervision of enterprise foundations. This chapter departs from that thought. At the core of this chapter are two, arguably the main, sources of European law. The first concerns the common market, with at its core the Treaty on the Functioning of the European Union (TFEU)[6] and the Agreement on the European Economic Area (EEA Agreement).[7] The second concerns the classical fundamental rights, laid down in the European Convention on Human Rights (hereafter, the Convention or ECHR).[8] These treaties provide for a court with the authority to issue judgments that are binding on all their Member States. The Court of Justice of the European Union (CJEU) is the competent court in regard to the TFEU and the EEA concerning EU Member States (see Article 2(2)), the European Free Trade Agreement (EFTA) Court in regard to the EEA concerning EFTA states and the European Court of Human Rights (ECtHR) in regard to the Convention.[9] The case law of these courts

4 For example, in France the law distinguishes and regulates the following forms of foundations: (i) *fondations reconnues d'utilité publique*; (ii) *fondations d'entreprise*; (iii) *fondations de recherche*; (iv) *fondations partenariales*; (v) *fondations universitaires*; (vi) *fondations de cooperation scientifique*; (vii) *fondations hospitalières*; and (viii) *fonds de dotation*. And there is also a regulation for foundations without legal personality: the *fondations abritées* or *sous égide*.

5 For instance the trust, company limited by guarantee, and in England and Wales, the Charitable Incorporated Organisation (CIO), which can be organised as a membership or non-membership organisation. See M. Synge, 'Civil society in England and Wales' in T.J. van der Ploeg, W.J.M. van Veen and C.R.M. Versteegh (eds), above n. 1, pp. 363–364. In addition, even though the trust has no legal personality, the trustees of a charitable trust can be incorporated. See the Charities Act 2011, Part 12. And there is also the phenomenon of the 'corporation sole' which is not known in civil law countries but has many applications in common law countries. See L.M. Salamon, *The International Guide to Nonprofit Law*, John Wiley & Sons, New York 1997, p. 312.

6 Treaty on the Functioning of the European Union [2012] OJ C326/47.

7 Agreement on the European Economic Area [1994] OJ L1/3. The EU counts 27 Member States, the EEA counts 30 Member States, including the 27 EU Member States.

8 All 46 members of the Council of Europe have ratified the Convention.

9 To this I add that the CJEU also is the competent court in regard to the Charter of Fundamental Rights of the European Union. Where appropriate, I shall refer to judgments in regard to the Charter as well.

provides authoritative interpretations of the rights afforded by the treaties and the admissibility of restrictions on such rights.

The basic questions to explore in this chapter are, first, whether the establishing of foundations, and enterprise foundations in particular, falls within the scope of the rights afforded by either one of these treaties. The second question is whether enterprise foundations are eligible to such rights and what that means for their functioning and regulation.

The enterprise foundation is defined in the context of this project as a foundation that holds a controlling interest in a business.[10] This definition covers two manifestations of the enterprise foundation: the foundation that runs a business itself, defined as 'operating foundation'; and the foundation that exercises control over a subsidiary company or a group of companies by means of shares and/or shareholders' agreements, defined as 'holding foundation'.[11] I shall use these same definitions. In addition, the introductory chapter observed that enterprise foundations can have a public benefit or social purpose or can be created to serve the interest of a specific family. A combination of these two objects is possible as well. Where relevant, the distinction between foundations with a public benefit purpose and a private purpose shall be taken into account. For the sake of clarity, the term 'public benefit' shall be used to indicate objects that are of a philanthropical, idealistic, social or other altruistic nature.

For reasons set out elsewhere in this book, the definition of enterprise foundation also includes functional equivalents of the civil law foundation, such as trusts or companies and structures composed of a combination of such entities. Including all possible functional equivalents of the civil law foundation concept would render this exploration practically unfeasible. In this chapter, therefore, I will focus on the foundation as a legal form as it is commonly understood in civil law systems. Since the European treaties have their own definitions that are autonomous from the definitions in national legislation of their Member States, the findings in this chapter are likely to apply to other legal forms as well. As we shall see in the next section, case law pertaining to trusts and companies in regard to freedom of establishment and other market freedoms is partly underlying the analysis pertaining to the position of foundations in relation to that right.

To this I add that there are other interesting documents with a 'European signature' as well, such as Recommendation CM/Rec(2007)14,[12] proposals by

---

10 See the introductory chapter of this volume.

11 Enterprise foundations in some countries can also take the shape of a parent foundation, managing subsidiary foundations possibly in combination with companies. Including this as a separate manifestation of the enterprise foundation next to the holding foundation is not conducive for the purpose of this chapter.

12 Recommendation CM/Rec(2007)14 of the Council of Europe Committee of Ministers to member states on the legal status of non-governmental organisations in Europe.

international experts for a European foundation statute published in 2006[13] and the Proposal for a Council Regulation on the Statute for a European Foundation (FE).[14] I will make reference to these documents in connection with findings from the exploration of the treaties and the case law of the relevant court.

2. ENTERPRISE FOUNDATIONS AND EU/EEA LAW

2.1. SCOPING AND RELEVANCE IN REGARD TO ENTERPRISE FOUNDATIONS

The TFEU provides four market freedoms and rules on competition law. The market freedoms comprise free movement of persons (Articles 45 et seq. TFEU), freedom of establishment (Articles 49 et seq. TFEU), freedom to provide services (Articles 56 et seq. TFEU) and the free movement of capital (Article 63 TFEU). All four market freedoms may be relevant in some way for foundations that are taking part in economic life.[15] In regard to the creation, migration and restructuring of enterprise foundations, however, the freedom of establishment is the single most important. I will therefore focus on freedom of establishment.

Freedom of establishment obliges Member States to allow nationals of another Member State to set up undertakings, in particular companies or firms within the meaning of Article 54 TFEU, under the conditions that apply for such Member State's own nationals. A measure restricting freedom of establishment may in certain circumstances be justified but only for imperative reasons in the public interest and on the condition that such a restrictive measure is appropriate for ensuring the attainment of the objectives pursued and does not go beyond what is necessary to attain them.[16] Pursuant to Article 54 TFEU, freedom of

---

13 K.J. Hopt, W. Rainer Walz, T. von Hippel and V. Then (eds), *The European Foundation: A New Legal Approach*, Verlag Bertelsmann Stiftung, Gütersloh 2006.

14 Proposal for a Council Regulation on the Statute for a European Foundation (FE) (2012) COM(2012) 35 final, Document 52012PC0035. Further interesting reading includes Council Regulation (EU) 2019/127 of 16 January 2019 establishing the European Foundation for the improvement of living and working conditions (Eurofound) [2019] OJ L30/74.

15 See for free movement of capital *inter alia*: (i) cross border donations and bequest and scope of free movement of capital, Joined Cases C-578/10 to C-580/10, *Staatssecretaris van Financiën v. L.A.C. van Putten*, ECLI:EU:C:2012:246 and Case C-485/14, *Commission v. France*, ECLI:EU:C:2015:506; (ii) tax treatment of foundations and donors, Case C-386/04, *Centro di Musicologia Walter Stauffer v. Finanzamt München für Körperschaften*, ECLI:EU:C:2006:568 and Case C-318/07, *Hein Persche v. Finanzamt Lüdenscheid*, ECLI:EU:C:2009:33; and (iii) transparency measures regarding foreign funding, Case C-78/18, *European Commission v. Hungary*, ECLI:EU:C:2020:476.

16 See *inter alia*, Case C-411/03, *SEVIC Systems AG*, ECLI:EU:C:2005:762, paras. 28 and 29; Case C-378/10, *VALE Építési kft*, ECLI:EU:C:2012:440, para. 39.

establishment is not only conferred to natural persons who are nationals of the Member States, but also to:

> Companies or firms formed in accordance with the law of a Member State and having their registered office, central administration or principal place of business within the Union …[17]

Freedom of establishment, like all market freedoms, is relevant in a cross-border context. In regard to establishing 'companies and firms' within the meaning of Article 54 TFEU, freedom of establishment obliges the Member States to treat nationals of other Member States the same as their own nationals. 'Companies and firms', governed by the laws of a Member State and having their registered office, central administration or principal place of business within the Union, are considered to be nationals in this context as well.

To mention some key implications of freedom of establishment following from case law of the CJEU, Article 49 taken with Article 54 TFEU obliges Member States to recognise the legal capacity of a company formed and existing under the laws of another Member State.[18] Moreover, the right to establishment prohibits Member States to impose certain elements of its domestic company law on a company governed by the laws of another Member State.[19] This is also the case if that company was originally formed under the laws of that Member State but has converted into a company governed by the laws of another Member State, while carrying on its main activities in the Member State of origin.[20]

Furthermore, it follows from the case law of the CJEU that a Member State must allow nationals of other Member States and, therefore, companies governed by the laws of another Member State to use the same means of formation of a company within the jurisdiction of a Member State that are available to its nationals, including its domestic companies. An example of this is found in the *Sevic* judgment in which the CJEU held that the freedom of establishment obliges a Member State to allow a cross-border merger when it would allow the merger if the merging entities were governed by its own laws.[21]

---

17 This applies to freedom to provide services as well. See Article 62 TFEU.

18 Case C-208/00, *Überseering BV v. Nordic Construction Company Baumanagement GmbH*, ECLI:EU:C:2002:632.

19 Case C-167/01, *Kamer van Koophandel en Fabrieken voor Amsterdam v. Inspire Art Ltd*, ECLI:EU:C:2003:512. The Court added: 'The reasons for which the company was formed in that other Member State, and the fact that it carries on its activities exclusively or almost exclusively in the Member State of establishment, do not deprive it of the right to invoke the freedom of establishment guaranteed by the Treaty, save where the existence of an abuse is established on a case-by-case basis'.

20 Case C-276/22, *Edil Work 2 Srl and S.T. Srl v. STE Sàrl*, ECLI:EU:C:2024:348.

21 Case C-411/03, *SEVIC Systems AG*, ECLI:EU:C:2005:762. From a German perspective it concerned an inbound merger by acquisition. From the perspective of EU law, particularly Article 54 TFEU, a cross-border merger by acquisition or cross-border conversion is regarded

This principle of non-discrimination also surfaces in the case law concerning cross-border conversions: the process in which a company governed by the laws of one Member State transforms into a company form governed by the laws of another Member State. The CJEU ruled in the *Cartesio* judgment that a provision of national law that would require the winding up or liquidation of a company, in preventing a company from converting itself into a company governed by the law of the other Member State, is prohibited under the freedom of establishment unless it serves overriding requirements in the public interest.[22] This judgment, therefore, addresses the obligations emanating from freedom of establishment of the Member State under which the company resides. The message in *Cartesio* on this point ultimately is that the provisions concerning freedom of establishment 'also prohibit the Member State of origin from hindering the establishment in another Member State of one of its nationals or of a company incorporated under its legislation'.[23]

The *Cartesio* judgment is complemented by the *VALE* judgment, the latter addressing the obligations of the envisaged Member State of immigration. In this judgment, the Court essentially ruled that if legislation of a Member State enables its domestic companies to convert in another legal form, the freedom of establishment obliges such Member State to accept that also companies governed by the laws of another Member State can convert into a legal form governed by the laws of the host Member State.[24] To conclude this overview, the European Court held in the *Polbud* judgment that Article 49 TFEU does not require the company that wishes to convert to have or to pursue actual economic activities in the host Member State.[25]

In essence it follows from the case law of the CJEU that the freedom of establishment entails *inter alia* that a Member State cannot categorically deny companies governed by the laws of a Member State the use of manners of corporate restructuring that it provides for its domestic companies. This is a manifestation of the principle of non-discrimination.

To this I add that each Member State remains autonomous in regard to the rules governing the incorporation and functioning of companies governed by its laws. Consequently, the freedom of establishment does not oblige Member States to accept manners of formation of companies that are not provided for in its own laws.[26] Consequently, a cross-border conversion into a specific form of company

as 'forming' a company in the host Member State. See W.J.M. van Veen, 'Opgericht' naar het recht van een lidstaat' in F. Ibili, M.E. Koppenol-Laforce and M. Zilinsky (eds), *IPR in de spiegel van Paul Vlas*, Kluwer, Deventer 2012, pp. 229 et seq.

22 Case C-210/06, *Cartesio Oktató és Szolgáltató bt*, ECLI:EU:C:2008:723.

23 Explicitly earlier, Case 81/87, *Daily Mail and General Trust*, ECLI:EU:C:1988:456, para. 16; Case C-264/96, *Imperial Chemical Industries plc*, ECLI:EU:C:1998:370, para. 21.

24 Case C-378/1, *VALE Építési kft*, ECLI:EU:C:2012:440.

25 Case C-106/16, *Polbud – Wykonawstwo sp. z o.o.*, ECLI:EU:C:2017:804.

26 See para. 112 of *Cartesio*, above n. 22, as further explained in paras. 29–31 of *VALE*, above n. 24.

governed by another Member State only falls within the scope of freedom of establishment if the envisaged form of company can be formed by way of conversion pursuant to the laws of the recipient Member State. The same *mutatis mutandis* applies to other cross-border restructuring operations such as a cross-border merger and cross-border demerger. The freedom of establishment requires the recipient Member State to observe the principle of non-discrimination vis-à-vis companies governed by the laws of another Member State.[27] It does not oblige recipient Member States to accept the formation of a company governed by its laws in a manner that is foreign to it.

Whether a Member State of origin is obliged to allow an outbound restructuring that it does not afford to its own legal persons is still under debate.[28] Can, for example, a Member State take the position that an outbound conversion of a foundation governed by its laws – assuming that it is eligible to invoke freedom of establishment – is prohibited, if the laws of that Member State prohibit the conversion of a foundation altogether? So far, this specific question has not been dealt with this explicitly.[29] In this regard, one can say that this matter is undecided. On the other hand, the judgments express that also the Member State of origin must allow outbound migrations as a corollary of freedom of establishment. As set out above, Member States may impose restrictions on freedom of establishment, but only for imperative reasons in the public interest, on the condition that the restricting measure is suitable for attainment of the objectives pursued and does not go beyond what is necessary to attain them. Although in the underlying cases it was the host country that opposed the migration, these considerations apply to the Member State of origin too, given that they must respect the freedom of establishment of their own nationals and companies as well.

Excluding the foundation converting into another legal form, such as an association or company, is understandable and arguably justified order to protect the designation of its assets in conformity with the will of the founder(s). This said, the same level of protection might be afforded by the laws of another Member State. Assuming that freedom of establishment can be invoked by a foundation, the question arises whether an absolute prohibition of outbound migrations is proportionate. Following this line

---

27 The freedom of establishment also obliges the host Member State to observe the principles of equivalence and effectiveness. See paras 42–63 of *VALE*, above n. 24.

28 See for example F. Möslein and A. Sanders, 'Corporate Asset Locks: A Comparative and European Perspective' (2023) 1 *French Journal of Legal Policy* 51, 68 et seq., and F. Möslein and A. Sanders, 'Vermögensbindung und Europäisches Gesellschaftsrecht' (2022) 77(19) *JuristenZeitung* 923, 926 et seq. with further references. See for Dutch literature W.J.M. van Veen, 'Grensoverschrijdende omzetting, -fusie en -splitsing: theorie en praktijk' in W.J.M. van Veen (ed), *Grensoverschrijdende omzetting, -fusie en splitsing: Vrijheid van vestiging, vennootschapsrecht en fiscaalrecht*, ZIFO-series Part 10, Kluwer, Deventer 2013 (open access), pp. 27 et seq., with further references.

29 Although in the case underlying the *VALE* judgment, above n. 24, the company wishing to convert had already ceased to exist as a legal person pursuant to its law of origin (Italian law) and could no longer convert pursuant to Italian law. This matter is, however, of a different nature than a prohibition for a certain type of legal person to convert altogether.

of thinking, it seems that an outbound migration might have to be accepted as a corollary of freedom of establishment, provided that an equal level of protection of the will of the founder is achieved under the laws of the host Member State. The same applies, in my opinion, in regard to restrictions on outbound migrations of companies that are subject to an asset lock.[30] If and to the extent that enterprise foundations qualify as the equivalent of a company in the sense of Article 54 TFEU, the case law of the CJEU discussed above also applies to enterprise foundations. In this respect it is to be established whether enterprise foundations fall within the category of 'other legal persons' that are 'profit-making', all within the meaning of Article 54 TFEU. We shall go into that in section 2.3.

2.2. FREEDOM OF ESTABLISHMENT – DIRECT EFFECT IN EU AND EEA LAW

The aim of the EEA Agreement is to create a common market between the EU Member States and the so-called EFTA states (currently Iceland, Norway and Liechtenstein). It provides for the same four market freedoms that are worded substantially identically to their counterparts in the TFEU. Freedom of establishment for companies follows from Article 31 taken with Article 34 of the EEA Agreement. This section deals with the question whether freedom of establishment has the same implications for EFTA states and for EU Member States.

For reasons that are out of the scope of this chapter, the EEA is set up in a two-pillar system consisting of EU institutions in parallel with EFTA institutions. This applies to the courts as well. The CJEU has jurisdiction in matters involving EU Member States' obligations ensuing from the EEA Agreement, whereas the EFTA Court has jurisdiction in such matters involving EFTA states. Interestingly, there is no hierarchy between EU and EFTA institutions, including the two courts.[31] Clearly, in order to achieve its aim it is necessary that the judgments of the two courts are homogeneous.[32]

30 For example, companies that are formed by means of conversion of a foundation pursuant to Dutch law. Their articles of incorporation must show that the foundation's property, as it was on the moment of conversion, and the fruits (benefits) thereof may only with authorisation of the court be used in another way than as required prior to the conversion. See Article 2:18(6) Dutch Civil Code. For a thorough piece on the compatibility of the asset lock with EU law, see the articles by F. Möslein and A. Sanders, above n. 27.

31 The EFTA Court is pursuant to Article 6 EEA Agreement, only bound by judgments of the CJEU pertaining to provisions of (*inter alia*) the TFEU that are substantially identical to the provisions in the EEA Agreement, given prior to the date of signing of the EEA Agreement, which took place on 2 May 1992.

32 See the preamble to the EEA Agreement: 'WHEREAS, in full deference to the independence of the courts, the objective of the Contracting Parties is to arrive at, and maintain, a uniform interpretation and application of this Agreement and those provisions of Community legislation which are substantially reproduced in this Agreement and to arrive at an equal treatment of individuals and economic operators as regards the four freedoms and the conditions of competition'.

For that reason, certain mechanisms have been built in the EEA Agreement.[33] Also, the EFTA Court has affirmed conform interpretation as a principle of EEA law in a number of cases.[34] One can assume, therefore, that the market freedoms, including freedom of establishment, materially result in the same obligations for the EFTA states and for the EU Member States.

This said, there is one issue deserving further attention. This concerns the very nature of these treaties. With respect to the EU treaties, the CJEU ruled that they supersede national law and practices where these interfere with the right to effectively enjoy the fundamental rights and freedoms provided for by the treaties.[35] In line with this judgment, the *Sevic* judgment holds that the absence of harmonisation rules cannot be made a precondition for invoking freedom of establishment.[36] Member States should allow, for example, corporate restructurings that are possible in a national context to be executed in a cross-border context within the EU, even if they are categorically prohibited by their national laws. Such prohibitions in national law are set aside by the obligations ensuing from the TFEU, without having to change the law.[37] The practical importance of this characteristic is demonstrated by the cases mentioned above in section 2.1.

This principle of primacy of Community law over national law is not so evident under the EEA Agreement. Protocol 35 to the EEA Agreement and its preamble express that the contracting parties are not required to transfer legislative powers to any institution of the EEA and that the objectives of the EEA consequently will have to be achieved through national procedures. In case of conflicts between implemented EEA rules and other statutory provisions, Protocol 35 holds that 'the EFTA States undertake to introduce, if necessary, a statutory provision to the effect that EEA rules prevail in these cases'. This lead the CJEU to opine that the EEA Agreement is (to be) established on the basis of a classic international treaty which, essentially, merely creates rights and obligations as between the parties and provides for no transfer of sovereign rights to the intergovernmental institutions which it sets up. And furthermore, it appears from Protocol 35 to the EEA Agreement that the principles of direct effect and primacy do not apply to EEA law.[38]

---

[33] See P. Spleitler, 'Judicial Homogeneity as a Fundamental Principle of the EEA' in C. Baudenbacher (ed), *The Fundamental Principles of EEA Law: EEA-ities*, Springer International Publishers, Cham 2017, pp. 19 et seq.

[34] See for example, Case E-1/94, *Restamark* [1994] OJ C398/18, para. 80; Case E-1/01 *Hörður Einarsson v. The Icelandic State* [2002] OJ C115/13, para. 54; and Case E-2/10 *Þór Kolbeinsson v. The Icelandic State* [2011] OJ C141/11.

[35] Case 6-64, *Flaminio Costa v. E.N.E.L.*, ECLI:EU:C:1964:66.

[36] Case C-411/03, *SEVIC Systems AG*, ECLI:EU:C:2005:762, para. 26.

[37] The absence of laws permitting such restructurings, however, in practice can complicate their implementation. More on this: A. Fici, W.J.M. van Veen and B. Van Baelen, *Study supporting an impact assessment on cross-border activities of associations*, Publications Office of the European Union, Luxembourg 2023.

[38] Opinion 1/91 of the Court, 14 December 1991, ECLI:EU:C:1991:490, in particular para. 27.

This view is, however, criticised in literature.[39] It goes beyond the ambitions of this chapter to dive into the intricacies and details of this debate. Instead, I will try and set out the practical relevance of the main part of the EEA Agreement, more specifically the market freedoms included in the EEA Agreement, based on the case law of the CJEU and EFTA Court. To start with the CJEU, it follows from its case law that agreements entered into by the EU on the basis of Article 216 TFEU have the status of EU law in the Member States' legal order.[40] Consequently, it is widely accepted that such agreements, including the EEA Agreement, are capable of sorting direct effect in the legal order of the EU Member States,[41] that is, if they are unconditional and sufficiently precise.

In regard to the EFTA states, it should be noted that Protocol 35 does not stand in the way of direct legal effect of EEA law as a result of the laws of a Member State.[42] In regard to Liechtenstein, once a treaty is ratified, it becomes part of national law from the time of its entry into force for Liechtenstein.[43] As a result hereof, the main part of the EEA Agreement has become part of Liechtenstein law. In regard to Norway and Iceland, the EFTA Court ruled in a number of cases that Protocol 35 of the EEA Agreement does not stand in the way of direct effect. The Court interprets this protocol thus, that a precondition for direct effect is that the provisions of EEA law have been made part of the national law by means of implementation in national law of the EFTA states. Once it is implemented, it follows from Article 3 of the EEA Agreement that provisions of EEA law produce direct effect, provided that the provision is unconditional and sufficiently precise.[44] Assuming that the main part

---

39 See (also for further references) *inter alia* W. van Gerven, 'The genesis of EEA law and the principle of primacy and direct effect' in J. Stuyck and A. Looijenstijn-Clearie (eds), *The European Economic Area EC-EFTA*, Kluwer Law and Taxation Publishers, Deventer 1994, pp. 33 et seq.; C. Baudenbacher, 'Reciprocity' in C. Baudenbacher (ed), above n. 33, pp. 35 et seq.; M.K.F. Dystland, F.B. Finstad and I. Sørebø, 'Article 7: Binding effect and implementation of EU legal acts' in F. Arnesen, H.H. Fredriksen, H.P. Graver, O. Mestad and C. Vedder (eds), *Agreement on the European Area: A Commentary*, Nomos, Baden-Baden 2018, pp. 248 et seq.

40 See Case 181-73, *Haegeman v. Belgium*, ECLI:EU:C:1974:41, paras. 4 and 5; Case 104/81, *Hauptzollamt Mainz v. C.A. Kupferberg & Cie KG a.A.*, ECLI:EU:C:1982:362, paras. 3 and 7. Reciprocity is not a condition of direct effect within the EU. See Case 87-75, *Conceria Daniele Bresciani v. Amministrazione Italiana delle Finanze*, ECLI:EU:C:1976:18, para. 23.

41 See C. Baudenbacher, above n. 39, p. 42; M.K.F. Dystland, F.B. Finstad and I. Sørebø, above n. 39, p. 261 (no. 38), with further references.

42 See the Joint Declaration to the EEA Agreement Protocol 35: 'It is the understanding of the Contracting Parties that Protocol 35 does not restrict the effects of those existing internal rules which provide for direct effect and primacy of international agreements'.

43 Moreover, if the provisions are sufficiently precise, they are capable of producing direct effect. See 'Liechtenstein Country Report: First Report Pursuant to Article 40 of the International Covenant on Civil and Political Rights of 16 December 1966' (10 June 2003), p. 12.

44 See for example, Case E-1/94, *Restamark* [1994] OJ C398/18, para. 7; Case E-1/01, *Hörður Einarsson v. The Icelandic State* [2002] OJ C115/13, para. 55; and Case E-11/22, *RS v. Steuerverwaltung des Fürstentums Liechtenstein* [2023] OJ C2023/365, paras. 40 et seq., 50 and 58.

of the EEA Agreement is implemented in the national law of Norway and Iceland, in keeping with their obligations ensuing from Article 3 of the EEA Agreement and Protocol 35,[45] provisions such as Article 31 and Article 34 of the EEA Agreement have direct effect in the legal order of the EFTA states. Both the CJEU and the EFTA Court have found, after all, that the prohibition of discrimination between national subjects and subjects of other Member States is sufficiently precise to produce direct effect.[46]

Consequently, one can conclude that freedom of establishment has the same implications in the EU Member States and EFTA states.

2.3. THE ENTERPRISE FOUNDATION AND THE CONCEPT OF A 'COMPANY' AND 'PROFIT-MAKING' IN ARTICLE 54 TFEU/ ARTICLE 34 OF THE EEA AGREEMENT

Enterprise foundations come in different manifestations. There are operating foundations and there are holding foundations. Enterprise foundations can have public benefit objectives and devote their income to philanthropical, idealistic or other altruistic purposes. There are also enterprise foundations that distribute income among members of a specific family and there are enterprise foundations the purpose of which is primarily to promote the continuity and independence of the company. To establish the relevance of freedom of establishment for enterprise foundations, it must first be established whether enterprise foundations can qualify as a 'company or firm' within the meaning of Article 54 TFEU and if so, if this goes for each of the manifestations above.

2.3.1. The Concept of 'Profit-Making' and Operating Enterprise Foundations

The concept of 'company' in connection with the freedom of establishment is rather broad. Article 54 TFEU, second paragraph reads:

> 'Companies or firms' means companies or firms constituted under civil or commercial law, including cooperative societies, and other legal persons governed by public or private law, save for those which are non-profit-making.

45 See Case E-1/01, *Hörður Einarsson v. The Icelandic State* [2002] OJ C115/13, para. 51. This is ultimately for the national courts to determine. See *Hörður Einarsson v. The Icelandic State*, paras. 48 and 51.

46 For instance, see in regard to freedom of establishment specifically already: Case 6-64, *Flaminio Costa v. E.N.E.L.*, ECLI:EU:C:1964:66. See further *inter alia* Case 104/81, *Hauptzollamt Mainz v. C.A. Kupferberg & Cie KG a.A.*, ECLI:EU:C:1982:362, paras. 3 and 7; Case E-11/22, *RS v. Steuerverwaltung des Fürstentums Liechtenstein* [2023] OJ C2023/365, para. 41, concerning direct effect of the EEA Agreement, Article 28.

It follows from this provision that the concept of 'company' is considerably wider than what is commonly understood to be a company. Basically, it includes any legal entity, be it governed by public law or private law. Since the foundation is a legal person, the key question to determine whether it qualifies as a company that is eligible to freedom of establishment, is whether it can be considered to be 'profit-making' within the meaning of Article 54 TFEU. To be more precise, the key question is whether one should infer from its legal form that a foundation is non-profit-making and, consequently, as such are excluded from the scope *ratione personae* of the freedom of establishment.[47]

The concept of 'profit-making', again, is an autonomous concept of Community law. There are a few judgments that shed light on how to interpret this concept. A key judgment in this context, in my opinion, is the CJEU judgment in *Commission of the European Communities v. Kingdom of Belgium*.[48] This case concerned laws on non-profit-making associations which contained certain mandatory nationality requirements for members and directors in order to be eligible for obtaining legal personality.[49] The issue in this case was whether this provision was in conflict with the freedom of establishment. If the answer is affirmative, the implication is that entities that are not allowed to distribute profits can qualify as a 'company' within the meaning of Article 54 TFEU.

The Court ruled in this judgment that the provisions referred to indeed conflicted with the freedom of establishment. It substantiated its ruling by referring to the reasoning of the Commission in its application. The reasoning of the Commission in its application is therefore important in this context. The Commission had argued that the concept of profit-making is an autonomous concept of Community law which should not be taken literally. It argued that it follows from the case law of the CJEU that also entities that pursue an informative, cultural, sportive, philanthropical, scientific, pedagogical (etc.) purpose and that do not pursue the maximalisation of profits can invoke freedom of establishment.

47 This position seems to be taken in de opinion of the Legal Service of the Council of the European Union (CLS) of 7 January 2025 (https://data.consilium.europa.eu/doc/document/ST-5125-2025-INIT/en/pdf). This CLS position relies heavily on CLS' interpretation of para. 25 of the *Sodemar Judgment* of 17 June 1997 (ECLI:EU:C:1997:301), which however in my opinion is not conclusive on this matter. To this I add that Case C-172/98, *Commission of the European Communities v. Kingdom of Belgium*, ECLI:EU:C:1999:335 – which is of a more recent date than *Sodemar* - is not at all mentioned in by CLS in this opinion, whereas, in my opinion this judgment is key in this matter, as will be set out below. See for a detailed, critical analisis of CLSs' opinion, T. Wöffen, *Response to the Opinion of the Council's Legal Service (CLS-Opinion) on the Legal Bases of Articles 50 and 114 TFEU of the proposed ECBA-Directive*, which can be found at https://civilsocietyeurope.eu/.

48 Case C-172/98, *Commission of the European Communities v. Kingdom of Belgium*, ECLI:EU:C:1999:335.

49 In particular: the Law of 25 October 1919 conferring legal personality on international associations which pursue philanthropic, religious, scientific, artistic or pedagogical objectives and the Law of 27 June 1921 conferring legal personality on non-profit-making associations. See Opinion of A-G Cosmas, 28 January 1999, Case C-172/98, *Commission of the European Communities v. Kingdom of Belgium* [1999] ECR I-03999.

What is required is that they pursue to take part in economic life by offering goods or services for a consideration.[50]

It follows from this judgment that a key criterion that defines an entity as 'profit-making' and therefore as 'another legal person' eligible to invoke freedom of establishment, is that the entity takes part in economic life. It also follows from *Commission of the European Communities v. Kingdom of Belgium* that entities with a public benefit purpose are not as such excluded from the freedom of establishment. The fact that a legal entity is prohibited to distribute profits is not relevant in this context either, nor is the aim to maximise profits through its activities. To this I add that I presume the activities must relate to the realisation of their objects. Economic activities that are purely marginal and ancillary probably will not suffice to qualify as 'genuine' economic activity.[51]

Consequently, based on this judgment, one can conclude that operating foundations qualify as a 'another legal person' that is 'profit-making' within the meaning of Article 54 TFEU, regardless their objects being of public benefit or not.[52] Operating foundations, therefore, are eligible to invoke freedom of establishment.[53]

2.3.2. *The Concept of 'Profit-Making' and Holding Foundations*

Holding foundations do not run a business themselves but hold a controlling interest in a company that is (directly or indirectly) carrying on business activities. Therefore, their qualification as 'profit-making' in the sense of Article 54 TFEU does not follow immediately from *Commission of the European Communities v. Kingdom of Belgium*. The question whether this manifestation of

---

50 The Commission referred to several CJEU judgments to underpin its reasoning including among others Case 36-74, *Walrave*, ECLI:EU:C:1974:140; Case 13-76, *Dona*, ECLI:EU:C:1976:115; and Case 196/87, *Udo Steymann v. Staatssecretaris van Justitie*, ECLI:EU:C:1988:475. In addition, the Commission referred to its 1984 'Television without frontiers: Green Paper on the Establishment of the Common Market for Broadcasting, especially by Satellite and Cable' (1984) COM (84) 300 final, pp. 205 et seq.

51 Compare Case 53/81, *D.M. Levin v. Staatssecretaris van Justitie*, ECLI:EU:C:1982:105, para. 17; Case 196/87, *Udo Steymann v. Staatssecretaris van Justitie*, ECLI:EU:C:1988:475, para. 13; Case C-176/96, *Jyri Lehtonen and Castors Canada Dry Namur-Braine ASBL v. Fédération royale belge des sociétés de basket-ball ASBL (FRBSB)*, ECLI:EU:C:2000:201, para. 44.

52 The CJEU in fact ruled in other areas of EU law that foundations with a public benefit purpose can conduct genuine economic acitivities. See Case C-222/04, *Ministero dell'Economia e delle Finanze v. Cassa di Risparmio di Firenze SpA, Fondazione Cassa di Risparmio di San Miniato and Cassa di Risparmio di San Miniato SpA*, ECLI:EU:C:2006:8, paras. 122, 123.

53 In the same vein and including other forms of non-profit organisations, *inter alia* A. Fici, W.J.M. van Veen and B. Van Baelen, above n. 37, p. 31; C.R.M. Versteegh in T.J. van der Ploeg, W.J.M. van Veen and C.R.M. Versteegh (eds), above n. 1, p. 47; F. Möslein and A. Sanders, above n. 28, 925. See also S. Lombardo, 'Some Reflections on Freedom of Establishment of Non-profit Entities in the European Union' (2013) 14(2) *European Business Organization Law Review* 225, who also stresses the importance of *Commission of the European Communities v. Kingdom of Belgium*, ECLI:EU:C:1999:335 in this matter.

the enterprise foundation can qualify as profit-making in the sense of Article 54 TFEU, consequently, needs to be examined separately.

In connection to this point, two judgments in particular are of interest. The cases underlying these judgments involved trusts to which shares in family-held companies were transferred. These judgments are relevant in relation to the eligibility of the holding foundation to invoke freedom of establishment because the trusts at handheld shares in companies and did not carry on business activities themselves. The trusts in these cases, therefore, in this respect are functionally similar to a holding foundation. The cases involved are the EFTA Court judgment in *Fred. Olsen and Others and Petter Olsen and Others*[54] and the CJEU judgment in *Trustees of the P Panayi Accumulation & Maintenance Settlements.*[55]

The case underlying *Olsen* involved a discretionary, irrevocable and perpetual trust, governed by the laws of Liechtenstein. The trust was set up in order to hold the interests of the Norwegian Olsen family in certain companies. The trust held the shares in a Dutch company which was the parent company of a group structure comprising a substantial number of limited liability companies. Because the judgment mentioned that the trust held 'the' shares in the parent company, I take it that the trust held all shares, i.e. a controlling shareholding, in that company. The trust was registered in Liechtenstein as an asset management trust. The key question in this case was whether the trust at hand could invoke freedom of establishment (Article 31 of the EEA Agreement/Article 49 TFEU), and by implication, qualify as a company within the meaning of Article 34 of the EEA Agreement, which is the counterpart of Article 54 TFEU.

In this judgment the EFTA Court held that to be eligible for freedom of establishment, the person or entity concerned must conduct a 'real and genuine economic activity' in a Member State. The Court held that an essential feature of real and genuine business activities that constitute establishment is that a person or an entity carries on a business, such as by offering services, which are effected for consideration, for an indefinite period through a fixed establishment. It is not required that the economic activities take effect in the EEA state of establishment. It suffices that they take effect in the EEA.

Subsequently, the EFTA Court held that:

> Whether the entity in question conducts a real and genuine economic activity cannot be answered in the abstract. It depends on the actual terms of the entity's statutes, such as, in the case at hand, the trust's deed, and the actual activities of that entity

54 Joined Cases E-3/13 and E-20/13, *Fred. Olsen and Others and Petter Olsen and Others v. The Norwegian State, represented by the Central Tax Office for Large Enterprises and the Directorate of Taxes* [2015] OJ C68/5.

55 Case C-646/15, *Trustees of the P Panayi Accumulation & Maintenance Settlements v. Commissioners for Her Majesty's Revenue and Customs*, ECLI:EU:C:2017:682.

> and its management. If a specific assessment reveals, for example, that the trust is involved in the management of a group's companies or other activities for a group, such as managing a pool of resources, and its actual incorporation reflected its actual activities, it has to be regarded as a real and genuine economic activity, which constitutes establishment.

One could argue that holding a controlling shareholding in a company is sufficient for eligibility for freedom of establishment. Pursuant to Article 54 TFEU/Article 34 of the EEA Agreement, such shareholding, i.e. holding a subsidiary, after all is a form of exercising freedom of establishment.[56] As a consequence one could argue that holding a subsidiary is a means of taking part in economic life in the Member State of establishment of the subsidiary. It appears from the considerations quoted above, however, that the EFTA Court holds the view that the mere holding of a controlling shareholding is not sufficient to conclude that the entity holding the shares is conducting a real and genuine economic activity.[57] Following this line of reasoning, for an entity that is 'a legal person' in the sense of Article 54 TFEU/Article 34 of the EEA Agreement that only qualifies as a company within the meaning of that provision if it is 'profit-making', the mere holding of a controlling shareholding is not sufficient to consider it as such to be eligible to invoke freedom of establishment. In the consideration quoted above, the Court sets out what it deems necessary to find that such an entity is economically active. This requires that the entity is involved in: (i) the management of the company or companies in which it holds the shares; or (ii) other activities for the group or as the case might be, in my opinion, the company in which the entity concerned holds the shares.

Interestingly, the first additional criterion resonates with the interpretation of 'economic activity' of the CJEU and the EFTA Court in other areas of EU law, such as tax law and competition law. In, for instance, *Ministero dell'Economia e delle Finanze*, which concerned the tax treatment of Italian banking foundations (holding foundations by our definition) in the context of competition law the CJEU stated that:

> In that regard, it must be pointed out that the mere fact of holding shares, even controlling shareholdings, is insufficient to characterise as economic an activity of the entity holding those shares, when it gives rise only to the exercise of the rights attached to the status of shareholder or member, as well as, if appropriate, the receipt of dividends, which are merely the fruits of the ownership of an asset.[58]

---

56 See Case C-251/98, *C. Baars v. Inspecteur der Belastingen Particulieren/Ondernemingen Gorinchem*, ECLI:EU:C:2000:205, para. 22.

57 See also N. Appermont, 'Adrift between Scylla and Charybdis? The trust caught between a civil law rock and a fiscal hard place' (2016) 22(10) *Trusts & Trustees* 1134, 1147.

58 Case C-222/04, *Ministero dell'Economia e delle Finanze v. Cassa di Risparmio di Firenze SpA, Fondazione Cassa di Risparmio di San Miniato and Cassa di Risparmio di San Miniato SpA*, ECLI:EU:C:2006:8, para. 111. In the same vein: Case C-155/94, *Wellcome Trust Ltd v.*

And also:

> ... an entity which, owning controlling shareholdings in a company, actually exercises that control by involving itself directly or indirectly in the management thereof must be regarded as taking part in the economic activity carried on by the controlled undertaking.[59]

The second additional criterion the EFTA Court brought up in para.99 of *Olsen*, quoted above, is the involvement of the entity holding a controlling shareholding 'in other activities' of such (group of) companies. Such activities apparently can also be regarded as genuine economic activities of that entity. The Court mentions managing a pool of resources (providing for instance financing)[60] as an example, but these services could arguably also consist of administrative, accounting, information technology, know-how and general management services or insurance coverage.[61]

To conclude, the Court made a connection between the terms of the entity's statutes and its actual activities, more specifically that its actual incorporation reflects its actual activities. In these considerations I read that the activities of the entity must be in conformity with its objects and, by implication, are not to be regarded 'as purely marginal and ancillary'.[62]

In *Trustees of the P Panayi Accumulation & Maintenance Settlements*, the CJEU seems less concerned with providing guidance for determining whether 'another legal person' can qualify as 'profit-making' in the sense of Article 54 TFEU. The case underlying this judgment involved four trusts ('the Panayi trusts') governed by UK law, which were created by a Cypriot national for the benefit of his children and other family members. He transferred to those trusts 40% of the shares of Cambos Enterprises Limited, the holding company of the

Commissioners of Customs and Excise, ECLI:EU:C:1996:243, paras. 32–34, regarding the interpretation of 'economic activity' in the Sixth Council Directive 77/388/EEC of 17 May 1977 on the harmonization of the laws of the Member States relating to turnover taxes – Common system of value added tax: uniform basis of assessment [1977] OJ L145/1.

59 Case C-222/04, *Ministero dell'Economia e delle Finanze v. Cassa di Risparmio di Firenze SpA, Fondazione Cassa di Risparmio di San Miniato and Cassa di Risparmio di San Miniato SpA*, ECLI:EU:C:2006:8, para. 112.

60 Which could, but not necessarily, qualify as economic activity for VAT purposes. See Case C-306/94, *Régie dauphinoise – Cabinet A. Forest SARL v. Ministre du Budget*, ECLI:EU:C:1996:290 and Case C-142/99, *Floridienne SA and Berginvest SA v. Belgium*, ECLI:EU:C:2000:623.

61 Considered to be economic activity in the context of competition law by the EFTA Court, Joined Cases E-4/10, E-6/10 and E-7/10, *Principality of Liechtenstein, Reassur Aktiengesellschaft, Swisscom RE Aktiengesellschaft,vs. EFTA Surveillance Authority* [2011] OJ C294/7, para. 54.

62 Compare Case 53/81, *D.M. Levin v. Staatssecretaris van Justitie*, ECLI:EU:C:1982:105, para. 17; Case 196/87, *Udo Steymann v. Staatssecretaris van Justitie*, ECLI:EU:C:1988:475, para. 13; Case C-176/96, *Jyri Lehtonen and Castors Canada Dry Namur-Braine ASBL v. Fédération royale belge des sociétés de basket-ball ASBL (FRBSB)*, ECLI:EU:C:2000:201, para. 44.

businesses established by him. In relation to the matter of eligibility of the trusts to invoke freedom of establishment the Court reiterated its case law, holding that freedom of establishment is one of the fundamental provisions of EU law and that, consequently, exceptions to that freedom must be interpreted strictly.[63] These considerations are set in the key of eligibility of the trusts at hand to freedom of establishment. With respect to the matter whether the trusts at hand qualified as 'profit-making', the CJEU considered:

> [33] As regards whether the trusts at issue in the main proceedings are profit-making, suffice it to state that it is clear from the documents submitted to the Court that those trusts have no charitable or social purpose and that they were created in order that the beneficiaries might enjoy the profits generated from the assets of those trusts.
>
> [34] It follows that an entity such as a trust which, under national law, possesses rights and obligations that enable it to act in its own right, and which actually carries on an economic activity, may rely on freedom of establishment.

In the considerations above, the CJEU seems to take a different approach than the EFTA Court did in *Olsen*. The CJEU ruled that an entity can be deemed to be profit-making if it is created to manage shares in order to distribute the proceeds to certain beneficiaries, while the trusts in this case did not hold a controlling interest in the companies concerned. Moreover, an active involvement in the management of the companies concerned was not mentioned as a prerequisite to qualify as profit-making in the sense of Article 54 TFEU. Seemingly, it sufficed that the trusts had no charitable or social purpose and were created to distribute profits from its assets to its beneficiaries.

Interestingly, the Court must have been aware of *Olsen* and apparently did not consider it opportune to repeat or reflect on the considerations of the EFTA Court pertaining to the profit-making criterion of Article 54 TFEU/Article 34 of the EEA Agreement. It is true that the cases were different, the main difference being that in *Olsen* the trust held all shares in the company whereas in *Trustees of the P Panayi Accumulation & Maintenance Settlements* the trusts did not hold a majority shareholding. However, in neither case did the trusts have a charitable or social purpose. Therefore, the question arises what, if any, is the message of the CJEU in this matter?

Assuming that it is no coincidence or slip of the pen that the CJEU did not refer to *Olsen*, it seems that the CJEU takes a considerably broader interpretation of the concept of profit-making than the EFTA Court, at least with regard to entities such as trusts and foundations that do not have a public benefit purpose. If such trusts or foundations are created in order that profits generated from their

---

63 See Case C-646/15, *Trustees of the P Panayi Accumulation & Maintenance Settlements v. Commissioners for Her Majesty's Revenue and Customs*, ECLI:EU:C:2017:682, paras. 26–27.

assets are distributed to beneficiaries, such entities are considered to be profit-making. Reflecting on the relevance of this judgment for holding foundations, it seems to follow from this judgment that if such foundations are created in order that certain beneficiaries, for example the members of a family, might enjoy the revenues generated by the shares, the CJEU will consider them profit-making in the sense of Article 54 TFEU.

With regard to holding foundations with public benefit objects, however, the analysis is different since the Court explicitly limited its finding to trusts that have no charitable or social purpose. Since there is, in my view, no relevant difference between the trust and foundation on this particular matter, it would seem logical that foundations with a charitable or social purpose can be expected to be treated no differently than trusts in this regard. I submit that it does not follow from the considerations of the Court that a charitable or social purpose of an enterprise foundation would block its eligibility to freedom of establishment altogether. It is also unlikely that that is implied by the Court. That would, after all, be irreconcilable with *Commission of the European Communities v. Kingdom of Belgium*. Moreover, it follows from *Ministero dell'Economia e delle Finanze* that holding foundations with public benefit objects can be economically active.[64] The same follows by implication from *Wellcome Trust* in regard to charitable trusts. In the latter case, the trust was found not to be economically active, however, that was not on account of its purpose but on account of the fact that it was explicitly forbidden to be involved in the management of the company in which it held the shares.[65] The fact that these cases pertained to competition law and VAT law respectively is, in my opinion, not relevant in this matter. If anything, the criteria for 'economic activity' in these fields of EU law are more specific than for freedom of establishment.[66]

My understanding of *Trustees of the P Panayi Accumulation & Maintenance Settlements*, therefore, is that the CJEU seems to be prepared to accept that holding foundations that do not have a public benefit purpose and that are created to manage shares in order that beneficiaries may benefit from the profits, are considered to be profit-making in the context of freedom of establishment, without the need for other activities from which it appears that it actually carries on an economic activity.[67] In this respect, such entities are treated the

64 Case C-222/04, *Ministero dell'Economia e delle Finanze v. Cassa di Risparmio di Firenze SpA, Fondazione Cassa di Risparmio di San Miniato and Cassa di Risparmio di San Miniato SpA*, ECLI:EU:C:2006:8, paras. 10 and 112–124.

65 Case C-155/94, *Wellcome Trust Ltd v. Commissioners of Customs and Excise*, ECLI:EU:C:1996:243, para. 35. Same, N. Appermont, above n. 56, 1156.

66 See also Opinion of A-G Kokott, 21 December 2016, Case C-646/15, *Trustees of the P Panayi Accumulation & Maintenance Settlements v. Commissioners for Her Majesty's Revenue and Customs*, ECLI:EU:C:2016:1000, para. 39.

67 The CLS seems to read in this judgment that it suggests that if legal person's purpose is to further charitable or social purposes rather than to pursue profits for its members or

same as companies with a share capital or limited by guarantee. I submit that this conclusion might be premature, given that the reasoning of the CJEU is somewhat apodictic.

With respect to holding foundations with a public benefit purpose, the logical interpretation of the CJEU's case law is that additional conditions apply in order that they can be regarded as 'profit-making'. Assuming that the CJEU will respect the principle of conform interpretation between itself and the EFTA Court and considering its interpretation of 'economic activity' in other areas of EU law, as was set out above, holding foundations with a public benefit purpose are considered to be economically active, i.e. profit-making, provided that the criteria in *Olsen* are met. That is, if they are (directly or indirectly) involved in the management of the company (or group) in which they hold shares, or, at the present state of case law, if they are involved in other activities for such companies or groups, all on the condition that the controlled entities are economically active within the EEA. This position is robust, in my opinion, given that it is in line with the interpretation of 'economic activity' in the case law of the CJEU and the EFTA Court in other areas of EU/EEA law.

In regard to the first criterion, the remaining question is whether the active use of shareholders' rights suffices to consider the foundation economically active in the context of freedom of establishment. As we have seen, the mere use of shareholders' rights was not considered an economic activity in the context of competition law and tax law.[68] In my opinion, this means that the involvement with the management needs to go beyond controlling the management *ex post* in order to be considered economic activity. It remains to be seen whether the Courts will be more lenient on this point in this regard to freedom of establishment.

3. ENTERPRISE FOUNDATIONS AND THE EUROPEAN CONVENTION ON HUMAN RIGHTS

3.1. RELEVANCE IN REGARD TO ENTERPRISE FOUNDATIONS

The European Convention on Human Rights, hereafter the 'Convention' or ECHR, guarantees classical fundamental rights and freedoms to any natural

beneficiaries, it is not considered to be profit-making. See para. 32 of its opinion referred to in footnote 47. In my opinion, this does not follow logically from this judgement. Moreover, this reading is not in line with *inter alia Commission of the European Communities v. Kingdom of Belgium, ECLI:EU:C:1999:335*, which judgment seems not to considered by the CLS.

68 See quote above from C-222/04, *Ministero dell'Economia e delle Finanze v. Cassa di Risparmio di Firenze SpA, Fondazione Cassa di Risparmio di San Miniato and Cassa di Risparmio di San Miniato SpA*, ECLI:EU:C:2006:8, para. 111, and Case C-155/94, *Wellcome Trust Ltd v. Commissioners of Customs and Excise*, ECLI:EU:C:1996:243, paras. 32–34.

person, non-governmental organisation or group of individuals. See Article 34 ECHR. It follows from this provision that the relevance of the Convention in regard to the regulation of (enterprise) foundations potentially has two aspects. The first concerns the right to form and to participate in an enterprise foundation. The main question here is whether incorporating and participating in a foundation falls within the scope of a fundamental right afforded by the Convention. Is establishing and joining a foundation – as a co-founder, director, supervisory director or another capacity – a fundamental right under the ECHR? The second aspect regards the protection of foundations themselves against infringements on their fundamental rights and freedoms. The main question here is what, if any, are the implications of the Convention on the law and administrative practices pertaining to the governance and supervision of (enterprise) foundations?[69]

Before addressing these questions, it should be noted that a restriction on a fundamental right or freedom afforded by the Convention is not per se inadmissible. These rights and freedoms are not absolute. Member States may impose restrictions on them, provided that they meet certain criteria. The first of these criteria is that the restriction must be prescribed by law. This requires that the restriction is of a general nature,[70] sufficiently clear[71] and made publicly known,[72] in order that citizens are able to determine their behaviour. Furthermore, safeguards against misuse, such as appeal with an independent court, must be incorporated in the regulation holding the restriction.[73] The second criterion is that the restriction must be justified on account of a limited

[69] For the sake of clarity, I submit that all Member States provide for a foundation or an equivalent legal form. The question whether Member States are obliged to provide for a foundation-type legal entity as a corollary of a fundamental right afforded by the Convention, therefore, does not need to be addressed.

[70] *Sunday Times v. The United Kingdom*, ECtHR no. 6538/74, 26 April 1979, para. 47; *Silver and others v. The United Kingdom*, ECtHR no. 5947/72, 6205/73, 7052/75, 7061/75, 7107/75, 7113/75, 7136/75, 25 March 1983, para. 86; *Malone v. The United Kingdom*, ECtHR no. 8691/79, 2 August 1984, para. 66; *Kruslin v. France*, ECtHR no. 11801/85, 24 April 1990, para. 27.

[71] *Groppera Radio AG and others v. Switzerland*, ECtHR no. 10890/84, 28 March 1990, para. 68; *Autronic AG v. Switzerland*, ECtHR no. 12726/87, 22 May 1990, para. 57; *Sunday Times v. The United Kingdom*, ECtHR no. 6538/74, 26 April 1979, para. 49; *Silver and others v. The United Kingdom*, ECtHR no. 5947/72, 6205/73, 7052/75, 7061/75, 7107/75, 7113/75, 7136/75, 25 March 1983, para. 88; *Malone v. The United Kingdom*, ECtHR no. 8691/79, 2 August 1984, para. 67.

[72] This does not necessarily imply that the rule must be published through the official journal. Depending on the circumstances, availability on order can be sufficient: *Groppera Radio AG and others v. Switzerland*, ECtHR no. 10890/84, 28 March 1990, para. 68 and *Autronic AG v. Switzerland*, ECtHR no. 12726/87, 22 May 1990, para. 57.

[73] *Silver and others v. The United Kingdom*, ECtHR no. 5947/72, 6205/73, 7052/75, 7061/75, 7107/75, 7113/75, 7136/75, 25 March 1983, para. 90; *Malone v. The United Kingdom*, ECtHR no. 8691/79, 2 August 1984, para. 67.

number of grounds.[74] Third, a restriction must be necessary in a democratic society, in order to be admissible. It follows from several cases that a democratic society is characterised by pluralism, tolerance and open mindedness.[75] It is not required that a restriction is indispensable for it to be deemed necessary in a democratic society and it is, on the other hand, not enough that it is reasonable or useful.[76] Decisive is the nature of the restriction in relation to its purpose. The principle of proportionality is one of the factors to be taken into account when assessing whether a measure of interference is 'necessary'.[77] A restriction that is too general of character or unsuitable to achieve its purpose, for example, is considered not to be necessary in a democratic society.[78] The ECtHR has elaborated the various elements in numerous judgments, for which I refer to the textbooks on the Convention and the Court's website.

Moreover, for the purpose of this chapter, one should note that the Member States have a certain margin of appreciation with regard to imposing such restrictions. This margin of appreciation depends on the right or freedom involved,[79] but also on the specific circumstances in that Member State. Given the country-specific evaluation, it is possible that a specific restriction is justified in one Member State but not in another.

The aim of this section is not to try and give an overview of restrictions that are justified or not. Given the country-specific evaluation that this would require, such exercise would be practically unfeasible. Instead, the focus will be on the question whether certain elements that can be found in foundation laws constitute a restriction of some fundamental right or freedom. If this would

---

74 Depending on the right involved, such grounds include the interest of national security, territorial integrity of public safety, to prevent disorder and criminal acts, the protection of public health or good morals, the good name or rights or freedoms of others, to prevent the disclosure of information received in confidence and to guarantee the authority and impartiality of the courts.

75 See *Handyside v. The United Kingdom*, ECtHR no. 5493/72, 7 December 1976, para. 49; *Müller and others v. Switzerland*, ECtHR no. 10737/84, 24 May 1988, para. 33; *Young, James and Webster v. The United Kingdom*, ECtHR no. 7601/76, 7806/77, 13 August 1981, para. 63; *Kjeldsen, Busk Madsen, Pedersen v. Denmark*, ECtHR no. 5095/71, 5920/72, 5926/72, 7 December 1976, para. 50, in which the Court states that pluralism in education is essential for the preservation of a democratic society.

76 See, e.g. *Handyside v. The United Kingdom*, ECtHR no. 5493/72, 7 December 1976, para. 48. Also *Sunday Times v. The United Kingdom*, ECtHR no. 6538/74, 26 April 1979, para. 59; *Silver and others v. The United Kingdom*, ECtHR no. 5947/72, 6205/73, 7052/75, 7061/75, 7107/75, 7113/75, 7136/75, 25 March 1983, para. 97; *Barthold v. Federal Republic of Germany*, ECtHR no. 8734/79, 25 March 1985, para. 55.

77 *Rassemblement Jurassien & Unite Jurassienne v. Switzerland*, ECommHR no. 8191/78, 10 October 1979, p. 121.

78 *Sigurdurjónsson v. Iceland*, ECtHR no. 16130/90, 30 June 1993, para. 41.

79 With respect to the freedom of association for example, the ECtHR holds that 'the exceptions set out in Article 11 are to be construed strictly; only convincing and compelling reasons can justify restrictions on freedom of association': *Case of Sidiropoulos and others v. Greece*, ECrtHR no. 26695/95, 29 May 1997, paras. 38 and 40.

result in reflecting on any restrictions and the question whether such restriction is justified, the aim of this chapter shall be achieved.

3.2. THE INCORPORATION OF A FOUNDATION – A FUNDAMENTAL RIGHT?

The Convention confers certain freedoms that are connected to establishing a foundation, such as freedom of expression and freedom of association. The ECtHR has expressed in *Refah Partisi* that these rights are connected in the sense that the protection of the freedom of expression (Article 10 ECHR) is one of the objectives of the freedom of association (Article 11 ECHR).[80] Furthermore, the Court made it clear in *Bowman* that the right to dispose of money for the purpose of imparting information and ideas is a component of Article 10 ECHR.[81] It follows therefore from these judgments that one of the objects of the freedom of association is also to protect the right to designate funds or other means for the purpose of imparting information and ideas. Enter the foundation.

Not many constitutions explicitly recognise the right to establish a foundation.[82] Neither the wording of the Convention nor the *travaux préparatoires*[83] suggest that the freedom of expression or the freedom of association confer the right to establish a legal person. The Court has found, however, in a number of judgments that such a right does indeed follow from Article 11 ECHR. The freedom of association entails that 'citizens should be able to form a legal entity in order to act collectively in a field of mutual interest'. The Court qualified this as one of the most important aspects of freedom of association.[84] Underlying these judgments is the obligation of the Member States to ensure that persons within their jurisdiction can effectively enjoy the fundamental rights and freedoms. The line of reasoning of the Court is that freedom of association and, in relation to that, freedom of expression can only be enjoyed fully if an entity that exists separately from its membership can be established.[85]

80 See for example, *Refah Partisi (The Welfare Party) and Others v. Turkey*, ECtHR no. 41340/98, 41342/98, 41343/98 and 41344/98, 31 July 2001, para. 88 and *Gorzelik and others v. Poland*, ECtHR no. 44158/98, 17 February 2004, para. 91.

81 *Bowman v. the United Kingdom*, ECtHR no. 24839/94, 19 February 1998.

82 See J. García-Andrade, 'Establishment, amendment and liquidation of foundations' in A. Schlüter, V. Then and P. Walkenhorst (eds), above n. 1, pp. 629–631, although it may be restricted to public benefit purposes.

83 European Court of Human Rights, 'Travaux Préparatoires to the Convention' available at: https://www.echr.coe.int/documents/d/echr/library_travprep_table_eng.

84 See *Sidiropoulus and others v. Greece*, ECtHR no. 26695/95, 10 July 1998, para. 40; *Gorzelik and others v. Poland*, ECtHR no. 44158/98, para. 88.

85 The same applies to the freedom of religion (Article 9 ECHR). See *Religionsgemeinschaft der Zeugen Jehovas and others v. Austria*, ECtHR no. 40825/98, 31 July 2008.

In line with the Court's finding that the concept of association is an autonomous concept of the Convention,[86] the Court has ruled that forming a foundation is also a component of the freedom of association. This is apparent from the following consideration:

> 39. Quant à la nécessité de cette mesure dans une société démocratique, la Cour rappelle que la possibilité pour les citoyens de créer une personne morale, dotée d'un patrimoine à son service dans le cas d'une fondation, afin d'agir collectivement dans un domaine d'intérêt commun constitue un des aspects les plus importants du droit à la liberté d'association énoncé à l'article 11 de la Convention …[87]

In the unofficial German translation on the Courts' website (an English translation apparently is not available) this consideration reads:

> (39) Hinsichtlich der Notwendigkeit dieser Maßnahme in einer demokratischen Gesellschaft erinnert der GH daran, dass die Möglichkeit der Bürger zur Gründung einer juristischen Person, der im Fall einer Stiftung Vermögen zur Verfügung steht, um damit im Rahmen eines gemeinsamen Ziels gemeinschaftlich wirken zu können, einen der wichtigsten Aspekte des von Art. 11 EMRK gewährleisteten Rechtes auf Vereinigungsfreiheit darstellt.

It follows from this judgment that the right to establish a foundation is indeed a fundamental right ensuing from Article 11 ECHR. Interestingly, in the context of freedom of association, ex Article 12 of the Charter of Fundamental Rights of the European Union,[88] the CJEU too expressed that the concept of 'association' includes foundations.[89] Apparently the ECtHR and CJEU are on the same page on this point. Although this may be counter-intuitive from a civil law perspective, foundations too are to be regarded as associations in the context of freedom of association.

In the same vein, the scope of Article 11 ECHR extents to endowing and joining a foundation's organisation. One can join a foundation's organisation, for example, as a member of its board or its supervisory board or in another capacity catered for by the law or the foundation's articles. By doing so, one can be said to have voluntarily joined for a common purpose. The fact the founder(s) has(/have) determined that purpose as such does not detract from that. In this respect it is not that peculiar that the Court considers the foundation as an association within the meaning of Article 11 ECHR. Moreover, from the

---

86 See *A. Cēsnieks v. Latvia*, ECtHR no. 56400/00, 12 December 2002, in which the Court accepted that freedom of association pertains to taking part in companies with a share capital as well.

87 *Fondation MİHR c. Turquie*, ECtHR no. 10814/07, 7 May 2019.

88 Charter of Fundamental Rights of the European Union [2012] OJ C326/2.

89 Case C-78/18, *European Commission v. Hungary* ECLI:EU:C:2020:476, paras. 115 et seq.

perspective of the fundamental rights involved, the availability of the foundation as a legal form arguably certainly is relevant, because of its distinct characteristics that sets it apart from typical membership-based organisations such as the association.[90] The judgments in *Refah Partisi*, *Bowman* and *Fondation MİHR* in my opinion clearly and robustly underpin that incorporating, endowing and joining a foundation are fundamental rights afforded by the Convention, more particularly the Court's interpretation of Article 11 ECHR and Article 10 ECHR.[91]

3.3. IMPLICATIONS CONCERNING ESTABLISHING (ENTERPRISE) FOUNDATIONS

The observation that Article 11 ECHR includes establishing foundations implies *inter alia* that requirements and administrative practices pertaining to the establishment of foundations must be assessed in the light of Article 11 ECHR. If establishing a foundation involves a procedure that is too cumbersome – for example, because it is too costly or takes too long – this may infringe on freedom of association. This is also the case if the law does not provide for an appeal with an independent court if approval by a public authority for incorporating a foundation is required but denied. Moreover, procedures involving the approval of a public authority based on vague or unpublished criteria or even the discretion of that authority – a concession system – probably constitute an unacceptable infringement on the freedom to establish a foundation.[92]

Other requirements for the incorporation of foundations that require further attention, especially in relation to enterprise foundations, are requirements regarding their endowment and their purpose. To start with the endowment of foundations, in some countries no minimum amounts apply, whereas in other countries there is no absolute minimum endowment but an open norm that the endowment must be sufficient to realise the foundation's objects. It is also not uncommon that a country's law or administrative practice prescribe a fixed minimum endowment for the incorporation of a foundation. In some cases, these

90 For example, the protection of the will of the founder (objects, governance, etc.) and the absence of parties that are entitled to profits or surplus after liquidation. I submit that if the same results can be achieved by means of an association or other form of legal entity, arguably there is no disproportionate restriction of freedom of expression or association. Member States are autonomous in structuring their legal order and system of legal forms, provided that they observe their obligations ensuing from the Convention.

91 Compare W.J.M. van Veen in T.J. van der Ploeg, W.J.M. van Veen and C.R.M. Versteegh (eds), above n. 1, pp. 25–27, who argued that these rights flow from Article 10 ECHR taken with Article 1 of the First Protocol ECHR and Article 11 ECHR.

92 See for a description of the characteristics of a proper approval/registration procedure, Recommendation CM/Rec(2007)14, above n. 12, and T.J. van der Ploeg, W.J.M. van Veen and C.R.M. Versteegh (eds), above n. 1, pp. 96 et seq.

amounts are quite significant.[93] Clearly, requiring a high minimum endowment restricts the freedom of association, i.e. the freedom to establish a foundation.

In order to be allowed, such requirements must be necessary in a democratic society in order to protect public interests mentioned in Article 11 ECHR or the rights of others. One could argue that minimum endowment requirements serve to promote that only viable foundations are established. However, a foundation could potentially also raise funds after its incorporation or depending on its objects and *modus operandi*, be effective in achieving its purpose with little financial means. Also, the Court has ruled that mere sensible or useful restrictions do not suffice to justify infringements on freedom of association.[94] Instead, one could argue that suppressing the formation of smaller foundations is detrimental to pluriformity, whereas pluriformity, according to the Court, is one of the key characteristics of a healthy democratic society.[95] I doubt therefore that suppressing the formation of smaller foundations and foundations established to raise funds in the course of their existence, will easily be considered as necessary in a democratic society.

The other issue noted above regards restrictions on the objects a foundation can pursue. In some countries, no restrictions apply other than that the objects and activities must be lawful and that the foundation may not make any distributions, except donations for idealistic or charitable purposes. It is not uncommon, however, that foundations can be established only for a public benefit purpose and that engaging in political activities is restricted.[96] Given that establishing a foundation is a fundamental right afforded by Article 11 ECHR and that this provision also serves to promote freedom of expression, a restriction to objects and activities that are of public benefit is a restriction of that right.

This does not mean that such restriction is per se inadmissible. It means that the restriction has to be tested against the criteria set out above. Much will depend on how broad or how strict permissible objects are demarcated and how much discretion is afforded to the authority designated to approve the

---

93 In France for example, the minimum endowment for establishing a '*fondation reconnues d'utilité publique*' is €1 million. See the sources referred to above in n. 1, also for the endowment requirements in more jurisdictions.

94 See e.g. *Handyside v. The United Kingdom*, ECtHR no. 5493/72, 7 December 1976, para. 48. Also *Sunday Times v. The United Kingdom*, ECtHR no. 6538/74, 26 April 1979, para. 59; *Silver and others v. The United Kingdom*, ECtHR no. 5947/72, 6205/73, 7052/75, 7061/75, 7107/75, 7113/75, 7136/75, 25 March 1983, para. 97; *Barthold v. Federal Republic of Germany*, ECtHR no. 8734/79, 25 March 1985, para. 55.

95 See *Handyside v. The United Kingdom*, ECtHR no. 5493/72, 7 December 1976, para. 49; *Müller and others v. Switzerland*, ECtHR no. 10737/84, 24 May 1988, para. 33; *Young, James and Webster v. The United Kingdom*, ECtHR no. 7601/76, 7806/77, 13 August 1981, para. 63; *Kjeldsen, Busk Madsen, Pedersen v. Denmark*, ECtHR no. 5095/71, 5920/72, 5926/72, 7 December 1976, para. 50. The same: Case C-78/18, *European Commission v. Hungary*, ECLI:EU:C:2020:476, para. 112.

96 See the sources referred to above in n. 1.

establishment of the foundation. Also, the availability of another legal form with essentially the same features as the foundation could be a relevant aspect. This being said, I consider that a discretionary power to determine if the foundation is of public benefit will most likely not be acceptable, because the criteria by which an application is to be evaluated are not (sufficiently) clear and precise. The same goes for a restriction that the foundation's objects must be in line with public policy. The latter restriction also stands in the way of promoting pluralism and therefore is likely to be regarded as not conducive to a healthy democratic society, in the view held by the Court of such society.

Apart from these examples, that are reminiscent of a concession system, one would expect that the margin of appreciation of Member States to restrict the objects for which foundations can be created is limited, given the connection between freedom of association and freedom of expression that the Court affirmed. To my knowledge, the Court has not yet had the opportunity to rule on the question whether restricting the use of a foundation for certain (public benefit) objects is a justified restriction or not and, if so, under what circumstances and conditions.

Another question is whether engaging in economic activities falls within the scope of Article 11 ECHR. This is a relevant issue because in regard to foundations there is much diversity on this point in Europe.[97] Arguably, it follows from the observation that establishing a foundation is a fundamental right afforded by Article 11 ECHR that the right of foundations to engage in economic activities in accordance with their objects falls within the scope of Article 11 ECHR. Classic examples are hospitals, educational institutions, elderly homes, etc. that provide services for a consideration. These examples involve purposes and activities that are generally accepted as being of public benefit. Given that public benefit foundations are generally accepted, it is to be expected that foundations are allowed to be economically active in pursuit of their objects. As a corollary of their obligation to actively promote that fundamental freedoms afforded by the Convention can be enjoyed effectively, the Member States are obliged to ensure that these entities can pursue their aims and objectives.

A perhaps more challenging question is whether Article 11 ECHR can also be invoked in relation to other business activities that are not widely accepted as being of public benefit, for instance construction, packaging or brewing beer. In my opinion, there are indeed arguments that underpin this view. For a start, the Court held in *Cēsnieks* that commercial 'associations' are not excluded from the concept of association in Article 11 ECHR.[98] In the underlying case Cēsnieks claimed a violation of (negative) freedom of association because he was allotted

97 See the sources referred to above in n. 1.

98 *A. Cēsnieks v. Latvia*, ECtHR no. 56400/00, 12 December 2002. The consideration is not numbered and reads: 'toutefois, l'applicabilité des garanties de l'article 11 à des "associations" commerciales n'a jamais été expressément écartée'.

shares in a company as a result of a conversion of a cooperative society into a public limited liability company. It follows from this judgment that commercial 'associations' like cooperative societies as well as, apparently, companies are regarded by the Court as 'associations' within the meaning of Article 11 ECHR. The claim that the negative freedom of association was violated, after all, held that the applicant had become a shareholder against his will. By implication, the purpose to engage in business activities is not excluded from the scope of Article 11 ECHR.[99] Since the Court has accepted that establishing a foundation falls within the scope of Article 11 ECHR, the logical implication seems to be that the default position is that a prohibition on creating foundations for business activities (that are not of public benefit) is a restriction on freedom of association.

To this one can add that the foundation has certain unique characteristics that could make it the single most suitable legal form for the objects that the initiators may wish to pursue. If, for instance, the initiator(s) would aspire to create an enterprise that is and will remain to be run in accordance with certain principles or standards, the foundation is better suited to accomplish that goal than a regular company or other membership-based legal form.[100] Arguably, the freedom to make such a choice may also fall within the scope of freedom of expression, for example, when such principles are of an idealistic nature. Also, from this perspective one can argue that depriving citizens of that choice interferes with the effective enjoyment of freedom of expression and freedom of association.

I submit that one can argue that Member States are autonomous in regard to structuring their legal order and as a corollary, its system of forms of legal persons with different characteristics, that are tailored to certain social needs. Consequently, they must be afforded a margin of appreciation in this respect. This is a valid argument. However, this does not alter the fact that a Member State in doing so could impose restrictions on freedom of association. The key question is whether, taking their margin of appreciation into account, such restrictions are justified or not. To my knowledge, the Court has not yet had the opportunity to rule on the question whether excluding foundations from being established for business activities can be a justified restriction and, if so, under what circumstances and conditions.

The discussion above relates to an operating foundation. There may be good reasons to choose a structure in which the enterprise is run by a company in which the foundation holds shares. In the case of a holding foundation as defined for this chapter, the foundation holds a controlling interest in that company. From

---

99 Also, commercial activities may be protected under Article 10 ECHR. See *Autronic AG v. Switzerland*, ECtHR no. 12726/87, 22 May 1990, para. 47.

100 *Inter alia* because amendment of the articles can be excluded and there is no one entitled to profits generated by the enterprise that might seek to push for maximalisation of profits over other interests, such as members or shareholders.

a human rights perspective, the analysis pertaining to a holding foundation is not fundamentally different than with regard to an operating foundation.

This being said, the holding foundation, from a comparative perspective, is less controversial than the operating foundation.[101] This is so because the foundation is broadly accepted as a legal form for designation of assets to pursue a certain purpose. Fundamental freedoms might come into the picture in case the laws would prohibit a foundation to be involved in the management of its subsidiaries or to exercise its voting rights. This could hinder the foundation and therefore its initiator(s) from pursuing certain objectives, for example, ensuring compliance with certain principles or standards when conducting the business. In this regard, I note that the right of a shareholder to exercise voting rights and to influence the company fall within the scope of Article 1 of the First Protocol to the Convention.[102] Prohibiting a foundation to exercise such rights, consequently, is an infringement of its entitlement to peaceful enjoyment of its possessions.

To conclude, it follows from the above that, departing from the normative framework of the Convention, establishing an enterprise foundation is a fundamental right afforded by the Convention. Consequently, the default position is that the foundation as a legal form should be available for both running an enterprise as well as holding shares in a company and to influence that company. Furthermore, given the Member States' obligation to actively promote that their nationals can effectively enjoy the fundamental rights ensuing from the Convention, the default position is that Member States should facilitate the establishing of enterprise foundations. Any restrictions on these rights must be evaluated against the testing criteria set out in section 3.1 above.

3.4. FUNDAMENTAL RIGHTS FOR ENTERPRISE FOUNDATIONS

It follows from Article 34 ECHR that foundations can invoke the fundamental rights afforded by the Convention to the extent that they are suitable to apply to legal persons. This includes, for example, the right to a fair trial (Article 6 ECHR), the right to respect for private life, home and correspondence (Article 8 ECHR),[103] the freedom of expression (Article 10 ECHR), the freedom of assembly and association (Article 11 ECHR), the right to an effective remedy

[101] Although in some countries (Hungary, Slovenia) the holding foundation is forbidden. See N. Bitterová and H. Surmatz, 'Comparative Highlights of Foundation Laws: The Operating Environment for Foundations in Europe' (2021), p. 31, available on Philea's website.

[102] *Marini v. Albania*, ECtHR no. 3738/02, 18 December 2007; *S-S., I. AB and B.T. against Sweden*, ECtHR, 11 December 1986.

[103] See *Société Colas Est and Others v. France*, ECtHR no. 37971/97, 16 April 2002, para. 41, in which the Court ruled that 'in certain circumstances the rights guaranteed by Article 8 of the Convention may be construed as including the right to respect for a company's registered office, branches or other business premises'.

(Article 13 ECHR) and the right to property (First Protocol, Article 1 ECHR). An interesting topic in the context of this chapter is what, if any, implications these fundamental rights could have for the regulation of (enterprise) foundations.

Foundations are commonly subjected to supervision by one or more public authorities, separately from supervision by tax authorities. The measures in this area are more elaborate in regard to foundations than in regard to legal entities with a membership base. The lack of a membership base means that the foundation has no inherent internal organ to oversee the functioning of the board of the foundation and to take appropriate measures in the interest of the foundation if circumstances so require. This renders the foundation vulnerable for inactivity – i.e. caused by the absence of a functional board or by objects that can no longer be attained – and for misuse by its directors to remain unnoticed because they are not internally accountable. Also, foundations may continue to exist although they are no longer viable. Supervision by a public authority can serve to address these deficiencies in the governance of foundations.

Comparative research shows that the instruments to address these deficiencies are fairly similar. This being said, there are significant differences regarding the approach to the role of the state in the supervision of foundations and the conditions under which the measures can be executed. In some jurisdictions, for example, the role of the supervisory authority is to promote effective and efficient management of foundations, i.e. legitimacy and efficiency, whereas in other jurisdictions the supervisory authority's mandate is restricted to address inactivity of foundations and cases of breach of duties by their directors, i.e. legitimacy only.[104] Another difference is that in some jurisdictions the supervisory authority may have the power to inspect the books and records, annul resolutions, replace directors or dissolve a (public benefit) foundation without prior court consent, whereas in, for example, the Netherlands only the court can take such measures.[105] In jurisdictions with a more restricted mandate for the supervisory authority, self-regulation is an important component of the supervision of foundations to address its governance deficiencies. As a matter of policy, self-regulation is also seen in certain jurisdictions as an alternative for certain functions of state supervision.[106]

---

104 A more subtle difference especially in regard to public benefit foundations is that in some jurisdictions the will of the founder is the focal point whereas in other jurisdictions public benefit considerations relatively may carry more weight. See T.J. van der Ploeg, W.J.M. van Veen and C.R.M. Versteegh (eds), above n. 1, p. 150.

105 See for an overview T.J. van der Ploeg, W.J.M. van Veen and C.R.M. Versteegh (eds), above n. 1, pp. 187–188.

106 See T.J. van der Ploeg, W.J.M. van Veen and C.R.M. Versteegh (eds), above n. 1, pp. 124 et seq.; O.B. Breen, A. Dunn and M. Sidel, *Regulatory Waves: Comparative perspectives on State Regulation and Self-Regulation Policies in the Nonprofit Sector*, Cambridge University Press, Cambridge 2017. This approach is also found in K.J. Hopt, W. Rainer Walz, T. von Hippel and V. Then (eds), above n. 13, pp. 35 and 239 et seq. See also A. Sanders, 'Enterprise Foundations in Germany' in A. Sanders and S. Thomsen (eds), above n. 1, p. 48.

This overview is far from comprehensive. It merely serves to illustrate that within Europe there are remarkably different views on the responsibility of authorities for the functioning of foundations and the degree of their independence from government. The question is to what extent the Convention provides a normative framework for the evaluation of certain elements of state supervision of foundations. For the reasons set out in section 3.1 above, it is not feasible to conclusively answer this question. The broad spectrum of measures and powers in this area, combined with the country-specific analysis of the admissibility of a restriction and the limited scope of this chapter, stand in the way of such endeavor. Instead, the aim is to paint the general picture.

As was mentioned in section 3.1 above, there is one judgment of the Court that explicitly deals with the exercising of powers by a supervisory authority. The case underlying this judgment regarded the dissolution of a foundation and the transferral of its assets to another foundation, initiated by the supervisory authority on the ground that the foundation's assets did not yield enough to undertake activities in pursuit of its objects and there was no prospect that that would change. The Court considered the following:

> 42. La Cour observe aussi que les objectifs de la fondation requérante, prévus d'une façon substantielle par ses statuts (recherche, conseil et publications dans le domaine des principales sciences naturelles ou sociales, établissement d'universités ou de facultés dans le but de réaliser ces recherches, activités économiques et commerciales, différentes aides sociales, etc.) correspondent à des objectifs d'utilité publique et d'intérêt général. Elle estime, à l'instar du Gouvernement et à la lumière du rôle assumé par des fondations en droit et en pratique turcs pour assurer la cohésion sociale, que le fait d'exiger de la fondation requérante qu'elle remplisse des critères financiers minimums provenait du besoin de préserver l'efficacité et la crédibilité du système des fondations d'utilité publique en Turquie.
>
> 43. Dans ces circonstances, la Cour considère, sans préjudice à la question du rétablissement de la fondation requérante (question encore pendante devant les juridictions nationales), que les raisons invoquées par les juridictions nationales pour constater que la fondation requérante avait été dissoute pour difficultés financières étaient « pertinentes et suffisantes », que cette mesure répondait à un besoin social impérieux, était proportionnée au buts légitimes poursuivis et, dès lors, était nécessaire dans une société démocratique.[107]

More on this: W.J.M. van Veen, 'Corporate Governance for Non-Profit Organisations; a Legal Approach' in H. Kohl, F. Kübler, C. Ott and K. Schmidt (eds), *Zwischen Markt und Staat, Gedächtnisschrift für Rainer Walz*, Carl Heymans Verlag, Cologne/Berlin/Munich 2007, pp. 755–766, and specifically in regard to fundraising: W.J.M. van Veen, 'Comparing regulation of fundraising: self-regulation or governmental regulation?' in K.J. Hopt and T. von Hippel (eds), *Comparative Corporate Governance of Non-Profit Organizations*, Cambridge University Press, Cambridge 2010, pp. 662–698.

107 See *Fondation MİHR c. Turquie*, ECtHR no. 10814/07, 7 May 2019.

It follows from these considerations that measures imposed by a supervisory authority to ensure the effectiveness and credibility of (public benefit) foundations in general can be seen as necessary in a democratic society, depending on the circumstances of the case. In this context, the Court explicitly refers to the role of public benefit foundations in the Turkish legal and social setting. However, this does not mean that the considerations are not relevant to other countries as well. On the contrary, the foundation as a legal form is known in all countries as a non-membership legal entity, the objects and functioning of which (as a rule) are determined by their founder(s). Moreover, it is widely recognised – also by the ECtHR and CJEU – that public benefit organisations, including public benefit foundations, fulfil an important role in society.[108] The foundation, thus, provides for a specific need in the legal and social order, not only in Türkiye, but in jurisdictions in general. In my opinion, the main message of *Fondation MİHR* is that from a fundamental rights' perspective it is legitimate to restrict freedom of association by means of measures aimed at addressing the deficiencies in the governance of foundations that render it vulnerable for neglect and misuse. This is legitimate because these measures are aimed at maintaining the credibility of the foundation as a legal form for its social functions. For this reason, such measures can be regarded as necessary in a democratic society provided that they are prescribed by law and sufficiently narrowly tailored.

Departing from this, certain transparency and reporting requirements and measures to enable inquiries of books and records should be permissible. Without such measures, after all, effective supervision is illusionary. However, in certain jurisdictions, the supervisory authorities have the power to access the offices of a foundation and to investigate their books or bank accounts, without a prior court order.[109] Such a generic power has been found to be an infringement on the right afforded by Article 8 ECHR in regard to companies.[110] Arguing that such a power is justified in regard to foundations, therefore, seems challenging.[111] Another example of a measure that is questionable in regard to the right to privacy is that the meetings of the organs of a (public benefit) foundations are open to the public.[112]

On a more general note, freedom of association not only includes the ability to create or dissolve an association or foundation but also covers that it must

---

108 See *inter alia* C.R.M. Versteegh, 'Civil Society and Civil Society Organisations in the Institutional and Legal Framework of the European Union' in T.J. van der Ploeg, W.J.M. van Veen and C.R.M. Versteegh (eds), above n. 1, pp. 35 et seq. with further references.

109 See T.J. van der Ploeg, W.J.M. van Veen and C.R.M. Versteegh (eds), above n. 1, p. 167.

110 See *Société Colas Est and Others v. France*, ECtHR no. 37971/97, 16 April 2002, para. 41.

111 See Recommendation CM/Rec(2007)14, above n. 12, paras. 67–69 and T.J. van der Ploeg, W.J.M. van Veen and C.R.M. Versteegh (eds), above n. 1, pp. 165–166.

112 See for example, E. Hartay, 'Legal aspects of civil society organisations and their relation with government: Hungary' in T.J. van der Ploeg, W.J.M. van Veen and C.R.M. Versteegh (eds), above n. 1, p. 435.

be able to pursue its activities and operate without unjustified interference by the state.[113] *Inter alia* measures which affect the capacity to receive financial resources,[114] and threat of penalties, in particular of dissolution,[115] are to be classified as interference in the right to freedom of association. Therefore, legislation subjecting the capacity to receive certain gifts or bequests to approval by the supervisory authority is an interference with freedom of association. One could question if such an interference, depending on its exact nature, serves a pressing social need and, if so, if it is necessary in a democratic society.[116] The same goes for a requirement that a certain number of directors must be civil servants,[117] or powers such as replacing directors, reversing board resolutions and dissolution of a foundation without court approval. Evidently, in regard to actions by the supervisory authority, the foundation should be able to challenge such action in a court of law as a corollary of Article 13 ECHR. Yet, taking such action is potentially burdensome for the foundation in terms of management time and costs, while limiting its freedom to act before the matter is decided in court. These are potentially relevant aspects in the context of the proportionality test. Such measures are, obviously, less intrusive on fundamental rights if prior court approval is required. It would be interesting to learn the Court's view on matters such as these.

4. CLOSING REMARKS

The basic question underlying this disquisition is whether the European treaties pertaining to the common market and the ECHR are relevant in relation to establishing enterprise foundations and to their regulation. The main findings are that enterprise foundations that carry on business activities are regarded as 'profit-making' in the sense of Article 54 TFEU/Article 34 of the EEA Agreement and are therefore eligible to invoke freedom of establishment (see section 2.3.1 above). For holding foundations, this has to be determined on a case-by-case basis. The CJEU might be prepared to take a more lenient view in this respect than the EFTA Court, at least in regard to holding foundations that do not have a

113 See *Moscow Branch of the Salvation Army v. Russia*, ECtHR no. 72881/01, 5 October 2006, paras. 73 and 74. Concurring, CJEU 18 June 2020, Case C-78/18, *European Commission v. Hungary*, ECLI:EU:C:2020:476, para. 113.

114 *Parti nationaliste basque – Organisation Régionale d'Iparralde v. France*, ECtHR no. 71251/01, 7 June 2007, paras. 37 and 38.

115 See *Moscow Branch of the Salvation Army v. Russia*, ECtHR no. 72881/01, 5 October 2005, para. 73.

116 See *inter alia* Recommendation CM/Rec(2007)14, above n. 12, para. 7 and T.J. van der Ploeg, W.J.M. van Veen and C.R.M. Versteegh (eds), above n. 1, pp. 165–169 with further references.

117 Which is a matter of administrative practice in France in regard to *fondations reconnues d'utilité publique*.

charitable or social purpose (see section 2.3.2 above). See, for the implications of eligibility to invoke freedom of establishment, sections 2.1 and 2.2 above.

Furthermore, it appears that establishing, funding and joining a foundation fall under the protection of freedom of association, freedom of expression and the right to property (see section 3.2 above). This may have implications for the permissibility of restrictions of the objects for which a foundation can be created, given also that protecting freedom of expression is a component of freedom of association (see section 3.3 above). It may also have implications for certain powers granted to supervisory authorities, because freedom of association also covers that foundations must be able to pursue their activities and operate without unjustified interference by the state (see section 3.4 above).

The general picture is, therefore, that European law is indeed unmistakably relevant in regard to foundation law, and therefore for foundations in general and enterprise foundations in particular.[118] As has become apparent as well, there are still issues that need to be developed further by the relevant court. Consequently, the impact of European law in this fascinating area is not fully unfolded yet.

---

118 For minimum and optimum norms based European fundamental rights and principles, T.J. van der Ploeg, W.J.M. van Veen and C.R.M. Versteegh (eds), above n. 1, Chapter 5 (pp. 256 et seq.).

ENTERPRISE FOUNDATION LAW IN A COMPARATIVE PERSPECTIVE

Concluding Observations

Anne Sanders, Steen Thomsen and Mark Ørberg

ABSTRACT

This chapter undertakes a comparative analysis of enterprise foundation law across 17 jurisdictions, focusing on the institutional design choices that shape this ownership form. Enterprise foundations raise recurring legal questions concerning admissibility, permissible purposes, founder flexibility versus irrevocability, governance safeguards, tax treatment, and disclosure obligations. The chapter shows that jurisdictions diverge sharply: Denmark stands alone with a specialised framework, while most countries rely on general foundation law or functional substitutes such as trusts or certification vehicles. These differences reflect fundamental policy trade-offs between founder autonomy, regulatory oversight, and market accountability. Enterprise foundations thus emerge as a distinctive governance structure with important implications for succession, capital markets, and corporate control.

1. INTRODUCTION

The chapters in this book demonstrate the remarkable variety in the regulation of enterprise foundations in different legal systems. This concluding chapter provides a comparative overview. We briefly address the following issues: the definition of foundations and especially enterprise foundations in different legal systems (section 2); the admissibility of enterprise foundations (section 3); different notions and practices in relation to the purpose of enterprise foundations (section 4); the flexibility founders enjoy in the creation of foundation charters and their influence on the administration of foundations (section 5); foundation governance (section 6); enterprise foundations as a tool for succession planning (section 7); tax law (section 8); and the economic significance of enterprise foundations (section 9). The concluding remarks (section 10) summarise the main findings of the chapter and offer suggestions for the legislator.

We typically rely on scales to assess and illustrate similarities and differences between different legal systems. We are, of course, aware that assessments using such scales oversimplify issues and are somewhat subjective. However, we nevertheless decided to add them in order to improve the readability and foster further comparative debate.

2. DEFINITIONS: WHAT IS AN ENTERPRISE FOUNDATION?

Defining an enterprise foundation is no trivial matter. Depending on the jurisdiction, such a definition may determine whether a given enterprise foundation is legal, how it is regulated and how it is taxed. Failure to grant official recognition to a foundation will prevent it from obtaining legal personhood, and legal liability will revert back to the founders and directors.

2.1. WHAT IS A FOUNDATION?

The European chapters in this volume show a common legal understanding of the foundation as an entity without members or shareholders, and with legal personality, which is independent from its founder and requires an (in principle) irrevocable transfer of property to pursue a purpose established by the founder

under some form of public supervision. Setting up a foundation requires some form of registration, even if the special approval formerly required is no longer technically necessary. A foundation's charter must usually be in writing and may be included in a will.

Table 1. Foundation definition elements by country

Separate legal entity (separate from founder) with separate administration	Without members or shareholders	Irrevocable transfer of property to serve a certain purpose	Supervision by public authority
Denmark	Denmark	Denmark	Denmark
Sweden	Sweden	Sweden	Sweden
Austria (private and federal foundations)	Austria (private and federal foundations)	Austria (only federal foundations)	Austria (mainly federal, i.e. public benefit foundations)
Germany	Germany	Germany	Germany
Switzerland	Switzerland	Switzerland	Switzerland
Italy	Italy	Italy	Italy
Czech Republic	Czech Republic	Czech Republic	Czech Republic (only public benefit foundations)
Portugal	Portugal	Portugal	Portugal
Netherlands	Netherlands	Netherlands	Netherlands (mainly public benefit foundations)
Liechtenstein	Liechtenstein	Belgium	Liechtenstein (mainly public benefit foundations)
Belgium	Belgium	Poland (only public benefit foundations)	Belgium (mainly public interest foundations)
Poland	Poland	Spain	Poland (mainly public benefit foundations)
Spain	Spain	France	Spain
France	France		France
Hungary	Hungary		

Source: Compiled by the authors.

A main characteristic of the foundation is that it is founded as a legal entity of its own without members or shareholders. It is administrated and represented by its directors who are meant to realise the foundation's purpose. While all the European legal systems discussed in this book agree on these fundamental principles, there are considerable differences with respect to the purpose a foundation may propose and the ensuing requirements in respect to the foundation's board of directors, especially if the board has to be independent from the founder. Such differences will be discussed below.

However, there are remarkable exceptions: while the exclusively charitable Austrian federal foundation lives up to all requirements of a foundation set up above,[1] the Austrian private foundation is a special case: the founder may not only reserve a right to change the charter of the foundation, but may also revoke the gift completely for the 'price' of a tax burden.[2] Moreover, after 100 years, the foundation may be dissolved completely if the beneficiaries decide not to continue the foundation.[3] In addition, public supervision only plays a minor role in relation to Austrian private foundations.[4] In this respect, it may well be argued that the Austrian private foundation is not a foundation in the classic sense; rather, it might be considered as an alternative to the family trust, which does not exist in most civil law countries like Austria. The legal frameworks for the Polish and Dutch private foundations also allow a founder to reserve a right to revoke the foundation.[5]

The discussion of the law of foundations in the US shows a different understanding which considers federal tax law as the major source of foundation law – a foundation is defined as an entity without owners set up for the purpose of tax exemption for charitable purposes (section 501(c)(3) of the Internal Revenue Code).[6] The material legal rules – typically state law – concerning the organisation of such entities are not the focus of the discussion. Likewise, Ireland's legal system does not recognise the civil law concept of 'foundation' in Irish law, and due in part to rather restrictive investment rules for charities, examples of Irish enterprise foundations are hard to find.[7] Therefore, this comparative overview will only briefly refer to the US and Irish examples in relation to a few issues.

However, one issue is worth mentioning: the German,[8] the Irish[9] and the US chapters[10] show that alternative legal entities outside foundation law may be used to construct foundation-like entities. In Germany, the charitable limited company – the GmbH – enjoys the same tax benefits as a charitable foundation but is easier to set up and is not under public supervision. In the US, limited

---

1 S. Kalss and T. Barth, 'The Austrian Foundation' in this volume, section 1.1.
2 Ibid., sections 1.4, 6.
3 Ibid., section 1.4.
4 Ibid., section 2.2.2.
5 K. Osajda and A.-M. Weber, 'Enterprise Foundations: A Polish perspective' in this volume, section 3.3; I.A. Koele, 'The Dutch private foundation in comparison with trusts: for the same purpose but rather different' (2016) 22(1) *Trusts & Trustees* 140, 142.
6 O. Eldar, 'Are Enterprise Foundations Possible in the United States?' in this volume, section 2.
7 O.B. Breen, 'Enterprise Foundations in Ireland: Needles in Haystacks or Hiding in Plain Sight?' chapter in this volume, section 2.
8 A. Sanders, 'Enterprise Foundations in Germany' in this volume, section 1.3.3.
9 O.B. Breen, 'Enterprise Foundations in Ireland: Needles in Haystacks or Hiding in Plain Sight?' in this volume, section 2.
10 O. Eldar, 'Are Enterprise Foundations Possible in the United States?' in this volume, sections 3 and 4.

liability companies (LLCs) and perpetual purpose trusts[11] are used for comparable reasons. In Ireland, although the use of charitable trusts or companies limited by guarantee (CLG) does not appear widespread, they are in fact used to set up non-profit entities that own business enterprises.[12]

2.2. ENTERPRISE FOUNDATIONS: LEGAL DEFINITION AND REGULATION

This comparative overview shows that enterprise foundations have a significant presence in the countries covered in this book. However, with the exception of Denmark,[13] there is no special legislation for enterprise foundations and thus no legal definitions, although some general foundations laws make reference to them. Consequently, defining a foundation as an enterprise foundation is of little legal significance in the different legal systems, but is merely of practical interest. Therefore, most chapters in this book work explicitly or implicitly with the functional definition set up by Thomsen at the beginning of this book. According to this pragmatic view, which is also the approach taken in the Danish law on enterprise foundations, an enterprise foundation is a foundation with a controlling influence in a business.[14] It does not matter whether the foundation has a charitable purpose and only happens to own a company by chance or for historical reasons. For example, the Swedish chapter describes an enterprise foundation as a grant-making foundation which conducts business or owns shares. A distinction made in a draft Swedish Foundation Act between grant-making and activity-based foundations has not become law.[15]

Probably because of this lack of legal definitions, there is also no discussion in the chapters on whether being an enterprise foundation requires that a foundation holds 100% of shares in a business or whether a majority or even controlling minority of shares is still enough. Danish enterprise foundation law speaks of 'controlling influence', which would include all foundations with a voting majority larger than 51%, but a smaller ownership stake of 20% or less might be sufficient for effective control, depending on the circumstances.[16]

However, there is a discussion in different countries as to whether a foundation may manage a business itself (a direct enterprise foundation) or may simply hold shares in it (an indirect enterprise foundation or holding foundation).

---

[11] In the UK, a perpetual purpose trust is possible for a charitable purpose.

[12] O.B. Breen, 'Enterprise Foundations in Ireland: Needles in Haystacks or Hiding in Plain Sight?' chapter in this volume, section 4.

[13] R.K. Feldthusen, 'Enterprise Foundations in Denmark' in this volume, section 6.2.

[14] S. Thomsen, 'Foundation Ownership around the World' in this volume, section 2.

[15] K. Olsson, 'Enterprise Foundations in Sweden' in this volume, section 1.

[16] R.K. Feldthusen, 'Enterprise Foundations in Denmark' in this volume, section 7.

The Austrian private foundation may only act as a holding foundation by owning shares,[17] while most other countries permit both.

The European chapters in this volume show that in relation to large enterprises, holding foundations are much more common. In Germany, the Zeiss foundation used to be the most prominent example of a direct enterprise foundation. However, it was restructured because in German legal scholarship, there is agreement that the foundation does not offer the best structure for managing a business directly.[18] Direct enterprise foundations usually employ the business in question as a way to pursue their purpose directly – e.g. a hospital is managed by a charitable foundation as a means to improve healthcare or a museum runs a museum shop and café. In contrast, holding foundations are also concerned with financial value creation. Denmark is not only the sole country that has developed a legal definition for enterprise foundations, but also provides special legislation for enterprise foundations and general (non-enterprise) foundations.[19] These specialised rules take into account the fact that for market participants, interacting with a foundation owning a business may raise the same issues as would be the case for a business with a corporate owner. The Danish rules concerning enterprise foundations therefore show many similarities with legal entities conducting business activities.[20] In other countries, such as Italy,[21] foundations must simply follow general rules for all entities conducting business.

Like Denmark, Austria offers two legal regimes for foundations,[22] however, the distinguishing factor is not whether the foundation conducts business or not but whether the foundation pursues a private or charitable purpose. While the latter is free to act commercially in pursuit of its charitable purpose, the former faces limitations with respect to the direct involvement in the business. Netherlands, Belgium, Poland, Czech Republic, and Hungary also offer two or more legal regimes for foundations and functional equivalents.

The US offers specialised tax law for foundations undertaking commercial activities. However, other countries discussed in this book offer only one legal regime for foundations. The emergence of specific third-sector rules, as is the case in Italy,[23] with its Third Sector Code, may influence this development in the future. In particular, the recent developments in Central Europe show new attitudes towards regulating enterprise foundation structures. Poland, for example, introduced new rules in 2023, with the explicit aim of facilitating the succession of family businesses that can be owned by foundations with private

---

17 S. Kalss and T. Barth, 'The Austrian Foundation' in this volume, section 4.

18 A. Sanders, 'Enterprise Foundations in Germany' in this volume, section 1.4.

19 R.K. Feldthusen, 'Enterprise Foundations in Denmark' in this volume, section 6.2.

20 Ibid., section 6.

21 T. Horvarth, *Stiftungen als Instrument der Unternehmensnachfolge*, Peter Lang, Frankfurt 2010, pp. 87–91.

22 S. Kalss and T. Barth, 'The Austrian Foundation' in this volume, sections 1.1, 1.2.

23 E. Barcellona, 'Industrial Foundations Under Italian Law' in this volume, section 6.

purposes such as family purposes.[24] In 2019, Hungary enacted a new legal structure called the 'asset management foundation', allowing for hybrid trust-structures and foundations managing businesses.[25] A reform in Czech Republic in 2014 liberalised the legal framework so that foundations and 'foundation funds' are permitted to be involved in business activities such as holding majority shares in a business to generate income for the foundation.[26] And in 2019, France changed its rules on public benefit foundations to ensure that they can own and control (but not manage) traditional business enterprises.[27]

There seems to be a tendency to develop different legal forms to allow for foundation-like structures such as trusts. Since 2014, Czech 'trust funds' – a trust-like device inspired by a Quebec accommodation of the common law trust instrument – have been possible to establish.[28] Similar legal transplants of structures usually associated with common law legal systems are seen in Liechtenstein with the 'business trust[29] and in Netherlands with the 'trust foundation'.[30] Moreover, Belgian law's acceptance of so-called certification arrangements offers legal structures where a foundation is part of a certification agreement that functionally resembles common law trust-structures, enabling private foundations to hold control of business enterprises.[31]

Many countries (e.g. Belgium,[32] Germany,[33] Italy,[34] Netherlands,[35] Sweden[36] and Switzerland) do not require that a foundation is established with a certain minimum level of capital. The only requirement is that a foundation receives enough capital to be able to pursue its purpose in a sustainable way. The situation is different in Denmark[37] and with Austrian private foundations.[38] In Denmark, at least DKK 300,000 (approximately €40,000) must be donated to form a foundation. Enterprise foundations use the same capital structure as Danish limited liability

---

24 K. Osajda and A.-M. Weber, 'Enterprise Foundations: A Polish Perspective' in this volume, section 3.
25 I. Sándor, 'Enterprise Foundations in Hungary' in this volume, section 3.
26 I. Comstocková and K. Ronovská, 'Enterprise Foundation in the Czech Republic' in this volume, sections 2.1.1 and 2.2.
27 S. Dupouy, 'Enterprise Foundations in France' in this volume, section 3.1.
28 I. Comstocková and K. Ronovská, 'Enterprise Foundation in the Czech Republic' in this volume, section 1.2.
29 F.A. Schurr and A. Butterstein, 'Enterprise Foundations in Liechtenstein' in this volume, section 7.1.
30 C. Stokkermans and M. van Uchelen-Schipper, 'Enterprise Foundations in the Netherlands' in this volume, section 3.
31 H. De Wulf, 'Enterprise Foundations in Belgium' in this volume, sections 3 and 4.1.
32 H. De Wulf, 'Enterprise Foundations in Belgium' in this volume, section 1.1.
33 A. Sanders, 'Enterprise Foundations in Germany' in this volume, section 2.3.
34 T. Horvarth, above n. 21, p. 67.
35 C. Stokkermans and M. van Uchelen-Schipper, 'Enterprise Foundations in the Netherlands' in this volume, section 2.2.
36 K. Olsson, 'Enterprise Foundations in Sweden' in this volume, section 7.
37 R.K. Feldthusen, 'Enterprise Foundations in Denmark' in this volume, section 6.2.
38 S. Kalss and T. Barth, 'The Austrian Foundation' in this volume, section 5.

companies (*anpartsselskaber*) and joint stock companies (*aktieselskaber*) with a division between base capital and free reserves. An enterprise foundation may only make distributions from its free reserves. In Austria, the initial minimum assets of the foundation are €70,000. The assets need only be actually present at the time of the establishment and registration of the foundation. Portugal,[39] Hungary[40] and Czech Republic[41] also require a minimum capital. While the question of minimum capital may not be decisive, it may be considered an interesting sign of the professionalisation of the founding process.

3. ADMISSIBILITY OF ENTERPRISE FOUNDATIONS

Table 2. Admissibility

Full endorsement	Some restrictions	Serious limitations
Denmark	Austria	USA
Sweden	Germany	
Switzerland	Italy	
Hungary	Czech Republic	
Netherlands	Portugal	
Liechtenstein	Spain	
Poland	France	
Belgium	Ireland	

Source: Compiled by the authors.

All the countries discussed in this book allow enterprise foundations to exist. However, there are differences in relation to the limitations set by the regulatory system. The situation is very clear in Denmark with specific legal rules on enterprise foundations and – in recent years – a political goal to facilitate the formation of enterprise foundations through the tax system. Danish enterprise foundations are not merely tolerated but are also understood as an important policy tool to enable the long-term ownership of businesses.

In Sweden, enterprise foundations also play an important role and are admissible after a conscious decision by the legislator in 1993.[42] However, apart from that, the Swedish handling of enterprise foundations is far less transparent than in Denmark. For example, most of the major enterprise foundations – like

39 C. Cunha and M.I. Oliveira Martins, 'Enterprise Foundations in Portugal' in this volume, section 3.2.2.
40 I. Sándor, 'Enterprise Foundations in Hungary' in this volume, section 3.3.
41 I. Comstocková and K. Ronovská, Czech Republic chapter in this volume, section 2.1.3.
42 K. Olsson, 'Enterprise Foundations in Sweden' in this volume, section 6.

the Wallenberg Foundations – are considered to be charitable foundations rather than enterprise foundations, even though they are both according to the approach taken in the chapter on Sweden.

In Switzerland, enterprise foundations are admissible without restrictions,[43] so the legal system may be put on the same level as Sweden. However, the discussion in this chapter shows that some recent tax and regulatory issues provide some obstacles to enterprise foundations. The latest developments, which might broaden the scope for family foundations, may make Switzerland even more interesting for founders.

German federal law has clearly allowed enterprise foundations since 2002.[44] Both running the business directly by a foundation as well as serving as a holding foundation are possible, even though there are very few examples of the former. The law allows a foundation to exercise fully its rights as a shareholder. However, running an enterprise may not be stated as a foundation's only purpose because of the so-called *Verbot der Selbstzweckstiftung*, which demands that a foundation may not only pursue the purpose of administering its own property without any effect on the world.[45] This point has been challenged by academic writers, but is not a great hindrance to practitioners who can add a general philanthropic purpose. Other, additional purposes can be found and stated in the foundation charter. So far, foundation authorities have been hesitant to force foundations to exercise their shareholders' rights in order to receive maximum dividends for their other (often charitable) purposes. However, the interpretation of such rules may differ among different supervisory bodies and there is no guarantee that the practice will not change in the future.

As mentioned earlier, almost all countries in this sample allow that foundations run businesses directly and indirectly as shareholders. However, the latter approach, in which a foundation owns a company running the business in question, is more common for larger business in all examined countries.[46] The former approach may be taken, for example, by a charitable foundation using a business to pursue its purpose, e.g. providing healthcare services through foundation-run hospitals. Yet, in Austria, the *Privatstiftung* may not engage in entrepreneurial activities itself, although it may hold shares in companies (often through holding companies), but is not allowed to get too involved in the day-to-day running of the organisation of its subsidiaries (*keine straffe Konzernführung*).[47] Nevertheless, the most important decisions may be taken at the foundation level. The federal foundation (*Bundesstiftung*) which needs to pursue a charitable purpose may hold shares and

43 D. Jakob, 'Swiss Enterprise Foundations' in this volume, section 2.2.1.

44 A. Sanders, 'Enterprise Foundations in Germany' in this volume, section 1.2.

45 Ibid., section 2.1.

46 For a sample of holding enterprise foundations see O. Eldar and M. Ørberg, 'The Anatomy of Nonprofit Control of Business Enterprise' (2025) *European Corporate Governance Institute*, Law Working Paper No. 820/2025, Appendix.

47 S. Kalss and T. Barth, 'The Austrian Foundation' in this volume, section 1.5.

run a business as long as the dividends are used for that charitable purpose. In Italy, setting up enterprise foundations was not possible for a long time due to established hostility towards foundations in general and an understanding that owning and leading a business was impossible for a charity-oriented entity like a foundation. However, currently, following critical scholarly work since the 1960s, it is possible to form them, even if the legal environment still cannot be described as welcoming. There are still uncertainties in the case law, especially the risk of a foundation being classified as a de facto company with its directors as personally liable de facto associates.[48]

France adopted new rules in 2019 to better facilitate enterprise foundations. However, active ownership by foundations is limited due to unfavourable tax law and statutory restrictions, requiring that the foundation manage its controlling shares without interfering in the management of the company. The example of the Pierre Fabre Foundation shows that enterprise foundations are possible under French law. Their ability to actively influence the management of the foundation-owned firm is somewhat limited, although it is not entirely clear what the prohibition entails.[49] This restriction on influence potentially removes some of the benefits of foundation control over business enterprise.[50] However, through appointments and informal contact, it appears that French enterprise foundations are still able to influence the strategy of their subsidiaries. More important, however, seem to be the deep rooted ideological and cultural aversions against enterprise foundations in France. However, given that there seems to be new interest in enterprise foundations in France, the number of enterprise foundations in France may increase in the future. In Spain and Portugal, enterprise foundations are possible, but as in France, their stated purpose must be public benefit.[51] In Italy, some of the reservations in France were of importance as well but have been largely overcome by now.

Dutch foundation law provides immense flexibility for enterprise foundations. Although active ownership by an enterprise foundation is difficult to combine with public benefit status, the so-called double foundation models – setups with e.g. a public benefit foundation holding economic rights and a golden share, and a foundation holding voting rights – show the flexible approach to foundations in the Netherlands.[52] In Belgium, the law allows for enterprise foundations, and they are typically used to maintain family control of a business. Enterprise foundations with public good purposes are possible if they use their income to their public good purpose, but they are a rarity in

[48] E. Barcellona, 'Industrial Foundations Under Italian Law' in this volume, section 3.2.

[49] S. Dupouy, 'Enterprise Foundations in France' in this volume, section 3.1.

[50] O. Eldar and M. Ørberg, above n. 46, section I.

[51] C. Cunha and M.I. Oliveira Martins, 'Enterprise Foundations in Portugal' in this volume, section 2.

[52] C. Stokkermans and M. van Uchelen-Schipper, 'Enterprise Foundations in the Netherlands' in this volume, section 2.7.

practice.[53] Like in the Netherlands, in Belgium, it is common that shares are held by a foundation in trust for the benefit for beneficiaries, the DRS-holders (Depositary Receipts for Shares). While the foundation exercises voting rights, dividends go to the DRS-holders (STAK). This is a popular way for a founder to keep influence over a business centralised while securing the financial position of family members.[54] Liechtenstein foundation law is also highly flexible, and Liechtenstein is home to large enterprise foundations such as the Interogo Foundation.[55] The Czech Republic has different types of foundation-like structures, including foundations (*nadace*) that are permitted to control business activities. In enterprise foundations that have public benefit purposes, the business activities must serve the public benefit purpose of the foundation. However, private foundation structures such as the 'foundation funds' (*nadační fond*) allow for business activities and private purposes. In those cases, the foundation is not eligible for tax benefits.[56]

Placing the US in Table 2 above is not easy because of the country's unique legal approach to foundations, which focuses on federal tax rather than the material state law structuring the foundation as a legal entity. This is understandable from the perspective of federal tax law while the organisation of corporations of different kinds are regulated by the individual states. Therefore, in the US, the term 'foundation' does not have the same legal meaning as in civil law Europe. In the US foundations are defined in federal tax law as non-profit tax-exempt organisations, which are not covered under certain exemptions. In terms of tax, it is highly unattractive for such foundations to own and control property. However, there are certain exceptions, including the 'Newman's Own' Exception in the Philanthropic Enterprise Act 2017. Moreover, LLCs and perpetual purpose trusts are now used in certain states as non-tax-exempt alternatives.[57] Ireland is also difficult to place in Table 2 due to the complexities of common law and statutory law regulating non-profits. Ireland does have non-profit charities holding controlling stakes of businesses, for example, a trust owning the newspaper *The Irish Times*, but charity law requirements impose strong restrictions on investments by charitable non-profits.[58]

---

53 H. De Wulf, 'Enterprise Foundations in Belgium' in this volume, section 7.

54 C. Stokkermans and M. van Uchelen-Schipper, 'Enterprise Foundations in the Netherlands' in this volume, section 3.1; H. De Wulf, 'Enterprise Foundations in Belgium' in this volume, section 3.2.

55 F.A. Schurr and A. Butterstein, 'Enterprise Foundations in Liechtenstein' in this volume, section 1.

56 I. Comstocková and K. Ronovská, 'Enterprise Foundations in the Czech Republic' in this volume, sections 2.1.1 and 2.2.

57 O. Eldar, 'Are Enterprise Foundations Possible in the United States' in this volume, sections 2.3 and 4.

58 O.B. Breen, 'Enterprise Foundations in Ireland: Needles in Haystacks or Hiding in Plain Sight?' in this volume, section 2.

4. PURPOSE

Foundations do not have shareholders or members. Their direction is determined by a purpose decided by the founder. The extent of the founder's freedom to determine and modify this goal is of crucial importance for the regulatory approach to enterprise foundations.

In the past, legal systems including Italy, Austria and Germany demanded that foundations pursue a charitable goal. However, today, only the Austrian federal foundation, Portugal, Spain and France still demand such a purpose. Most countries now accept all kinds of purposes as long as they are not harmful to the public. Pursuing charitable goals is generally only demanded as a prerequisite for enjoying tax benefits. Although foundation purposes in Portugal must be exclusively for public benefit, foundations are allowed to have controlling influence over businesses and to have ownership clauses in their charter – that is, a charter clause requiring the foundation to keep ownership of certain assets unless qualified circumstances are present.[59] While Italy started with the inadmissibility of enterprise foundations and a requirement that foundations must serve public utility, scholars now, after a reform in 2000, hold that foundations may now pursue any lawful purpose.[60] Germany accepted the lawful foundation that does not necessarily pursue public benefit by federal law in 2002.[61]

Table 3. Do enterprise foundations have to have a charitable purpose?

Yes	No
US (tax law)	Denmark
Austria (federal foundation)	Sweden
Portugal	Switzerland
Belgium (public interest foundations)	Austria (private foundation)
Spain	Italy
France	Germany
Ireland (charities)	Czech Republic
	Netherlands
	Liechtenstein
	Belgium
	Poland
	Hungary

Source: Compiled by the authors.

59 C. Cunha and M.I. Oliveira Martins, 'Enterprise Foundations in Portugal' in this volume, section 3.2.2.

60 E. Barcellona, 'Industrial Foundations Under Italian Law' in this volume, section 5.1.

61 A. Sanders, 'Enterprise Foundations in Germany' in this volume, section 1.2.

However, not all kinds of purposes are now acceptable. There are limitations to selfish goals. A foundation may not be set up to support the founder. Nevertheless, supporting a family may be a foundation's purpose in most countries, with some limitations. In this respect, there is, in many countries, a noticeable tension with rules against perpetuities and the longstanding rejection of the *fideicommissum*,[62] which are – for example – forbidden in the Danish Constitution.[63] *Fideicommissa* were used to preserve noble property over generations. They had no legal personality and consisted of unsaleable property bound for the purpose of preserving the name and glory of a noble family. Liberal forces all over Europe rejected them for some time claiming that they preserved noble privilege and indulgence and impaired economic development in general by withdrawing property from market forces.[64] Thus, it is understandable that foundations set up for the support of a family are viewed with suspicion in many countries.[65]

In Denmark, foundations founded after 1985 may distribute benefits to family members born after the founding of the foundation only on an equal footing with other members of the public.[66] In Sweden, unwritten foundation law requires that a foundation set up for the benefit of family members without any limitation in time requires a certain purpose on which the foundation's board can make a decision, e.g. poverty of family members or financial needs to pay for education. In Germany, family foundations may be used more freely and commentators have remarked that, in fact, the family foundation may be used for the same purposes today as *fideicommissa* in the past.[67] Limitations on the number of years such a foundation may last have been debated but have not been introduced so far.[68] In

---

62 For *fideicommissa* in Denmark, see R.K. Feldthusen, *Succession*, DJOEF Publishing, Copenhagen 2001; see for the history in Germany: J. Eckert, *Der Kampf um die Familienkommisse in Deutschland*, Peter Lang, Frankfurt 1992; B. Bayer, *Sukzession und Freiheit*, Duncker & Humblot, Berlin 1999.

63 R.K. Feldthusen, 'Enterprise Foundations in Denmark' in this volume, section 6.6.

64 E. Barcellona, 'Industrial Foundations Under Italian Law' in this volume, section 5.1; R. Eckert, above n. 62, pp. 533 et seq.

65 P. Rawert, 'Der Stiftungsbegriff und seine Merkmale' in K. Hopt and D. Reuter (eds), *Stiftungsrecht in Europa*, Carl Heymanns Verlag, Cologne 2001, pp. 118–122; H. Kronke, 'Familien- und Unternehmensträgerstiftungen' in K. Hopt and D. Reuter (eds), *Stiftungsrecht in Europa*, Carl Heymanns Verlag, Cologne 2001, pp. 159–173.

66 R.K. Feldthusen, 'Enterprise Foundations in Denmark' in this volume, section 6.6.

67 On the 'functional equivalence' with a *fideicommisum* and a family foundation that requires no further requirements for supporting family members and for a critical view, see D. Reuter in *Münchener Kommentar zum Bürgerlichen Gesetzbuch*, 6th ed., C.H. Beck, Munich 2012, §81, para. 96; A. Dutta, *Warum Erbrecht?*, Mohr Sieback, Tübigen 2014; B. Weitemeyer in *Münchener Kommentar BGB*, 9th ed., C.H. Beck, Munich 2021, §80, paras. 186–192; and R Hüttemann and P. Rawert in *J. von Staudingers Kommentar zum Bürgerlichen Gesetzbuch mit Einführungsgesetz und Nebengesetzen*, Sellier/de Gruyter, Berlin, 2017, 'Vorb. zu §§80 ff.', paras. 264 et seq.; the differences between a family foundation and *fideicommissa* and the legality of the former stresses, BverfGE 37, 328, 336 and RG 26.5.1905 – Rep. VII 508/04 RGZ 61, 28, para. 2.

68 A. Dutta in A. Richter (ed), *Stiftungsrecht Handbuch*, C.H. Beck, Munich 2019, §5, paras. 35 et seq. with further references.

this light, the possibility for the beneficiaries of an Austrian private foundation to wind up the foundation after 100 years[69] seems understandable.

Table 4. May enterprise foundations support a family as its purpose?

Yes (under certain conditions)	Yes, but subject to debate	Only under certain conditions	No
Austria (private foundation) Germany Switzerland Czech Republic (private foundations) Netherlands Liechtenstein Belgium Poland (private foundations) Hungary	Italy	Denmark Sweden	Austria (federal foundation) Czech Republic (public benefit foundations) Portugal Spain France

Source: Compiled by the authors.

This is in a way surprising if one considers a foundation as a non-profit organisation in the sense of Hansmann. Such a non-profit organisation is barred from distributing its net earnings to anyone exercising control over it. Hansmann has called this prohibition on distribution of profits the 'nondistribution constraint'.[70] However, a foundation's beneficiaries do not necessarily have control over the foundation and usually do not have a legal claim to support from the foundation.

The country chapters in this book show that many jurisdictions in the centre of Europe allow for foundations that have both charitable purposes and family purposes. Besides in Denmark, Sweden, Germany and Austria, mixed-purpose foundations are found in Liechtenstein,[71] Poland[72] and Hungary.[73] But mixed purpose foundations are rare especially in the jurisdictions geographically located in the Western part of Europe. In Switzerland[74] and the Netherlands,[75] double

69 S. Kalss and T. Barth, 'The Austrian Foundation' in this volume, section 1.4.
70 H. Hansmann, 'The Role of Nonprofit Enterprise' (1980) 89(5) *Yale Law Journal* 835.
71 F.A. Schurr and A. Butterstein, 'Enterprise Foundations in Liechtenstein' in this volume, section 1.
72 K. Osajda and A.-M. Weber, 'Enterprise Foundations: A Polish Perspective' in this volume, section 3.1.
73 I. Sándor, 'Enterprise Foundations in Hungary' in this volume, section 3.2.
74 D. Jakob, 'Swiss Enterprise Foundations' in this volume, section 2.2.5.
75 C. Stokkermans and M. van Uchelen-Schipper, 'Enterprise Foundations in the Netherlands' in this volume, section 2.7.

foundation models are used to combine family purposes with philanthropic purposes,[76] while France, Spain and Portugal prohibit foundations mixing family purposes and philanthropic purposes.[77] In Ireland and the Czech Republic, tax laws or charity laws discourage mixed purpose foundations.[78]

Since most foundation laws now accept all kinds of lawful purposes, it could be argued that pursuing a business purpose as a foundation's only purpose (for example, owning a business and ensuring its growth and development but without any additional duty to pursue the public or private good through donations or philanthropically aimed business activities) should also be acceptable. However, this issue is slightly unclear or under debate in most countries. For example, Belgian law requires the purpose of a foundation to be 'disinterested', and in Liechtenstein law a self-serving purpose is not possible, but in both countries the exact content of such requirements remain unclear.[79]

In Germany, the predominant opinion among academics and also the legislator is that such a pure business purpose would violate the so-called probation of the *Selbstzweckstiftung*.[80] It is argued that a foundation must have an outward-directed purpose and must not simply administer its property. It is claimed that merely managing a business without any additional purpose would be the same as simply administering property, for example holding a bank account. Most countries do not follow this approach clearly, but this is a topic that is still the subject of debate, even though in Germany, it poses few limitations to setting up enterprise foundations in practice. Finding an additional purpose in drafting the charter is not difficult. For example, a foundation owning a furniture business may also put in its charter that it supports architecture, even though only little is done in this area. However, some scholars claim that supervisory authorities could call upon such 'fake' purposes at any time and demand that a foundation pursues its 'real' purpose, even to the detriment of running the

---

76 See also section 7 of this chapter.

77 S. Dupouy, 'Enterprise Foundations in France' in this volume in section 3, 6.3.1; C. Cunha and M.I. Oliveira Martins, 'Enterprise Foundations in Portugal' in this volume, section 1; A. Emparanza Sobejano and A. Meijomil, 'Spanish Enterprise Foundations' in this volume, section 3.

78 O.B. Breen, 'Enterprise Foundations in Ireland: Needles in Haystacks or Hiding in Plain Sight?' in this volume, section 2; I. Comstocková and K. Ronovská, 'Enterprise Foundations in the Czech Republic' in this volume, section 4.

79 H. De Wulf, 'Enterprise Foundations in Belgium' in this volume, section 2.3; F.A. Schurr and A. Butterstein, 'Enterprise Foundations in Liechtenstein' in this volume, section 5.1.

80 A. Sanders, 'Enterprise Foundations in Germany' in this volume, section 2.1; see also P. Rawert, 'Der Stiftungsbegriff und seine Merkmale' in K. Hopt and D. Reuter, above n. 65, pp. 117–118. The discussion on pure self-purpose foundations is not always directly comparable in the different states. In the 'Feasibility Study on a European Foundation Statute: Final Report' (2009), pp. 60–61, Hopt et al. stated that: 'The German view is, in the main, that such "trade protection" foundations ("Unternehmensselbstzweckstiftungen") are not allowed, because the assets of a foundation should be subordinate to its purpose … The same view also holds sway in Austria'.

business. Moreover, from an academic perspective, it is interesting to ask why managing and developing a business should not be considered an outward-directed purpose. After all, every business interacts with society through its various stakeholders.[81] A question related to this point is whether and to what extent foundation must be under a duty to distribute benefits. In Sweden, the discussion on admitting a pure business purpose seemed more focused on the question on whether a foundation with its unchanging purpose and without shareholders may offer a suitable tool for business activities. However, this question was decided in favour of enterprise foundations.[82]

Table 5. May a foundation pursue a business purpose (i.e. owning a business) as its sole purpose?

Yes	No
Denmark (with considerable arguments to the contrary)	Austria
Sweden	Germany (with considerable arguments to the contrary)
Switzerland	Portugal
Italy	Liechtenstein
The Netherlands	Belgium
Hungary	Poland
	Spain
	France
	Ireland
	US

Source: Compiled by the authors.

5. FLEXIBILITY AND IRREVOCABILITY

As discussed above, the irrevocable donation of assets is part of the general definition of a foundation. Nevertheless, retaining some flexibility can be of crucial importance in order to adjust a foundation to a changing environment. In most countries, including Germany[83] and Sweden,[84] some parts of the foundation's charter may be changed if the founder has reserved the right for the governing body of the foundation to do so and receives the approval of the

---

81 On arguments against the permissibility of foundations with no externally aimed purpose, see M. Ørberg, 'Enterprise Foundations and Faithful Agency as Drivers of Sustainable Long-Termism in Philanthropy' (2024) 25 *European Business Organization Law* 765, section 3.5.

82 K. Olsson, 'Enterprise Foundations in Sweden' in this volume, section 6.

83 A. Sanders, Germany chapter in this volume, section 2.5.

84 K. Olsson, 'Enterprise Foundations in Sweden' in this volume, section 7.

supervisory body. In countries like Switzerland and Austria (private foundations, not federal foundations), founders may even reserve the right to change the charter themselves. In Germany, the introduction of such a right was discussed in the recent reform process. However, this step was not taken.[85]

In Italy, the Civil Code explicitly states that the settlement of a foundation can be revoked by the founder only until the foundation has obtained 'legal personality' or has de facto started to operate (Article 15). This has traditionally been interpreted as an indication that, once the foundation exists, as a matter of general principle, the founder has no special prerogatives. Furthermore, if it is held that the fundamental 'purpose' of the foundation cannot be materially changed at all, it is unclear if a founder can preserve the right to themselves or the board to change the charter. If it is at all permissible, such a change would require the consent of the supervisory authority.

However, in some countries (Austria for example), the founder may reserve the right not only to change the charter but also to revoke the foundation in general.[86] This degree of flexibility might be welcome to founders and may encourage them to establish a foundation in the first place. Yet, as mentioned earlier, it might be questioned whether the Austrian private foundation can still be called a foundation in the classical sense.

Table 6. Flexibility of the foundation's charter

Founder can preserve the right to revoke the foundation	**Founder may preserve the right to change the charter of the foundation**	**Founder may preserve the foundation's board the right to change the charter**
Austria (private foundation)	Austria (private foundation)	Denmark
Poland (private foundation)	Switzerland	Sweden
The Netherlands	The Czech Republic	Austria
Hungary	Netherlands	Germany
	Belgium	Switzerland
	Poland (private foundation)	Portugal
		Liechtenstein
		Spain
		France
		Poland (public benefit foundation)
		Ireland

Source: Compiled by the authors.

85 A. Sanders, 'Enterprise Foundations in Germany' in this volume, section 2.5.

86 S. Kalss and T. Barth, 'The Austrian Foundation' in this volume, sections 1.4 and 2.2.1.

6. GOVERNANCE/TRANSPARENCY

6.1. FOUNDATION GOVERNANCE

Foundation governance is a topic of central importance across Europe. While shareholders or members of a corporation may be expected to ensure that directors do not squander 'their' money, foundations without owners or members may be in need of special protection.[87] Traditionally, this protection is provided by supervisory authorities. These authorities are usually limited to legal supervision and do not question business decisions. Supervisory authorities generally have the right to dismiss directors and demand special audits in serious cases. In Denmark since 2014, enterprise foundations have been under the legal supervision of the Business Authority, which can, for example, request that a special audit is undertaken.[88]

It is interesting to note that in Austria, private foundations are not under the supervision of a foundation authority but are supervised to a limited extent by the Commercial Court.[89] However, Austrian private foundations have a legal duty to establish internal governance mechanisms. This movement away from public supervision towards internal governance is also noticeable in Germany. Private foundations, like family foundations, may be exempt from public supervision, as in Bavaria, or may only be subject to limited supervision. Other jurisdictions that allow private foundations to be subject to private governance mechanisms rather than public supervision are Belgium, the Netherlands, the Czech Republic, Poland and Hungary. The discussions in this volume show that public supervision is no replacement for internal governance mechanisms and transparent registration in general. How to establish such mechanisms may be considered as one of the most important topics of the law of enterprise foundations.

In many countries, such as Germany, Switzerland, Sweden and Italy, the law is silent about foundation governance. In Germany, for example, only one director is necessary. This director may be the founder or members of the founding family. There is no prerequisite to establish an additional body to supervise the director or directors and no rule demanding that its members or at least some of them should be independent from the founder. The new foundation law of 2021 did not change that but at least made it clear that additional bodies may be established.[90] In Switzerland,[91] the law is silent on

87 For a general discussion of this topic, see D. Jakob, *Schutz der Stiftung*, Mohr Siebeck, Tubingen 2006.

88 R.K. Feldthusen, 'Enterprise Foundations in Denmark' in this volume, section 7.

89 S. Kalss and T. Barth, 'The Austrian Foundation' in this volume, section 2.2.2.

90 A. Sanders, 'Enterprise Foundations in Germany' chapter in this volume, section 2.4.

91 T. Sprecher, P. Egger and G. von Schnurbein, Swiss Foundation Code, Stämpfli Verlag, Bern 2021: https://www.swissfoundations.ch/wp-content/uploads/2021/06/9783727277931.pdf.

this and lawyers consult the Swiss Foundation Code as a source of inspiration for best practice and recommendations. In Sweden, foundations may even be administered by another legal entity (attached administration), an opportunity approximately 50% (20,000 foundations) have taken.[92] Swedish foundations are under supervision by the local County Administration Board. While the founder can exempt the foundation from supervision, this is not possible for enterprise foundations, which provides at least some special regulation for enterprise foundations.

In Italy, there are governance rules in the 'Third Sector Code' (TSC) applicable to third sector foundations, but no specific governance rules are contained in the Italian Civil Code. When dealing with the foundations, the Civil Code simply states that the foundation has its 'directors' (Articles 18 and 25) and implicitly assumes that more than one director makes up a 'board of directors', but nothing more than this. Therefore, nothing in the Civil Code prevents a foundation from having the founder or their family members as directors.

Table 7. Governance regulation

High prerequisites	Some special governance rules	Low prerequisites
Austria	Sweden	Germany
Denmark	Portugal	Switzerland
France	Poland	Italy
	Spain	The Czech Republic
		The Netherlands
		Liechtenstein
		Belgium
		Ireland
		Hungary

Source: Compiled by the authors.

The situation is different in Denmark and Austria, where the law demands that at least half (Denmark)[93] or all (Austria) members of the board of directors must be independent of the founding family. In Denmark, each board of directors must at least have three members who must be natural persons. At least one-third of the board of directors must be independent of the founder of the foundation. Moreover, rules are in place to guarantee that the foundation acts independently of its subsidiaries and other companies over which the foundation

---

92 K. Olsson, 'Enterprise Foundations in Sweden' in this volume, section 7.

93 According to the Danish Law on Enterprise Foundations, section 40, the founder and founding family members cannot constitute a majority of the board without the approval of the foundations authority.

exerts influence. The majority of board members and the chair and vice-chair of the board cannot be executives of the foundation. Moreover, the management of subsidiaries or companies over which the foundation exerts significant influence may not appoint members to the board of the foundation. The chair or vice-chair of the foundation may also only be an executive of a subsidiary with the special permission of the Business Authority.[94] In 2014, Danish law went a step further: a Committee on Foundation Governance was established, the purpose of which was to issue a set of recommendations upon which enterprise foundations were obligated by law to report on a comply-or-explain basis.[95]

Austrian law provides some special rules for the governance of private foundations: its board must have a minimum of three directors who must all be natural, independent persons. According to the case law of the Austrian Supreme Court, this independence requires that directors of the foundation cannot be directors of subsidiary companies and cannot be related to the foundation's beneficiaries up to the third degree.[96] The foundation is registered, but supervision is provided by a special auditor who checks the legality of the annual financial statements.[97]

6.2. TRANSPARENCY

In foundation law, transparency concerns what information enterprise foundations should be obligated to disclose and to whom such information should be disclosed. These issues are of great importance in order to hold foundations accountable. In public corporations, holding company directors to account is an important task for shareholders. In foundations which do not have shareholders, other actors must ensure that foundations are held accountable.

Danish law is at the forefront with regard to transparency. As enterprise foundations are separate legal entities running a business or controlling an operating company, the disclosure requirements have generally been the same as for other Danish LLCs, i.e. public annual reports and registration in a central public business registry. In 2015 new legislation on enterprise foundations entered into force and with it came additional requirements in relation to disclosure and transparency. It is now a requirement that all transactions with related parties, whether at market value or not, are disclosed in the annual reports.[98] In Germany, a federal foundation register will be introduced for the first time in 2026. In terms of transparency, this is definitely a step forward; however, public annual accounts cannot be expected even then.

---

94 R.K. Feldthusen, 'Enterprise Foundations in Denmark' in this volume, section 6.5.
95 Ibid., section 8.
96 S. Kalss and T. Barth, 'The Austrian Foundation' in this volume, section 8.2.
97 Ibid., section 8.3.
98 R.K. Feldthusen, 'Enterprise Foundations in Denmark' in this volume, section 8.

7. ENTERPRISE FOUNDATIONS AS A TOOL FOR SUCCESSION PLANNING

There are indications that foundations have become more popular as vehicles to structure the succession of family businesses in some European jurisdictions such as Germany,[99] the Netherlands,[100] Liechtenstein,[101] Poland[102] and Switzerland.[103] As mentioned, new rules on family foundations were introduced in Poland with the explicit aim of facilitating the succession of family businesses, and private foundations are used to facilitate succession of family businesses in Belgium and Austria.[104] The current political motion to liberalise Swiss family foundations and the potential lift of the ban on 'family maintenance foundations' may – depending on the result – further promote enterprise foundations as a succession tool in Switzerland in the future.[105] These developments might be seen as response to the demographic development in Europe which leaves many businesses without a successor.

Whether or not enterprise foundations are attractive as tools for succession planning in Europe depends on organisational law, regulatory law and tax law. Proponents of the use of enterprise foundations in succession planning emphasise that enterprise foundations can serve as effective instruments for ensuring long-term sustainability and that they can facilitate business continuity by transitioning family-owned enterprises into foundation-owned entities. This ownership structure helps mitigate common succession challenges in family businesses, such as conflicts among heirs or the lack of a suitable successor. By transferring ownership to a foundation, the business can adhere to the founder's vision beyond the founder's lifetime.[106]

Even in the US – which traditionally has been very resistant to accept families effectively maintaining control of businesses through foundation-like legal structures – family foundation structures exist. Families can keep significant influence over a business through perpetual purpose trust ownership of voting rights, if the family is willing to transfer the dividend rights to charitable non-profits.[107] The Patagonia dual ownership model in the US illustrates an ownership structure similar to the double foundation models found in European

99 A. Sanders, 'Enterprise Foundations in Germany' in this volume, section 1.2, 1.4, 2.5.

100 C. Stokkermans and M. van Uchelen-Schipper, 'Enterprise Foundations in the Netherlands' in this volume, section 3.1.

101 F.A. Schurr and A. Butterstein, 'Enterprise Foundations in Liechtenstein' in this volume, section 3.5.

102 K. Osajda and A.-M. Weber, 'Enterprise Foundations: A Polish Perspective' in this volume, section 3.

103 D. Jakob, 'Swiss Enterprise Foundations' in this volume, section 2.2.3.

104 S. Kalss and T. Barth, 'The Austrian Foundation' in this volume, section 1.4.

105 D. Jakob, 'Swiss Enterprise Foundations' in this volume, section 4.

106 S. Thomsen, *The Danish Industrial Foundations*, DJOEF Publishing, Copenhagen 2017, pp. 34–36; D. Jakob, 'The role of foundations in family governance' (2020) 26(1) *Trusts & Trustees* 4.

107 O. Eldar, 'Are Enterprise Foundations Possible in the United States?' in this volume, section 4.

countries, for example the two foundations owning the Swiss knife manufacturer Victorinox or the owners of the German Bosch enterprise.[108] So, although many regulatory frameworks across Europe still discourage founders from establishing enterprise foundations with 'family distribution purposes', there appears to be a legal development towards more countries accepting structures with family influence over enterprise foundations and also distributions to family. For tax reasons, formation of enterprise foundations with both charitable (public good) purposes and family purposes seems to be limited in many countries, but the many countries accepting different variations of double foundation models show that legal innovation, alongside legal reforms, drives the development.

8. TAX

The tax system may influence the formation of enterprise foundation in various ways.[109] It can provide tax deductions which allow founders to make deductions in their taxable income. It can also provide tax penalties by taxing foundations with business holdings (as is the case in the US) or it can require founders to pay inheritance tax even though they donated their wealth to a foundation (as was the case in Denmark until recently). However, in most cases, foundation law has chosen a middle way in which founders neither receive tax deductions nor are required to pay inheritance or capital gains taxes when establishing an enterprise foundation. However, there may be certain tax benefits for charitable foundations.[110]

All chapters in this book stress the high importance of tax law for enterprise foundations, especially when they are used as tools for succession planning. However, placing countries in a table is particularly hard in this case, as in tax law, a number of different rules work together to create a more or less favourable environment. The common denominator seems to be that enterprise foundations are taxed at the same rate as companies running a business or holding shares in other companies in Denmark, Sweden and Germany. There does not seem to be a special foundation tax law in most countries. Setting up a foundation may

---

108 D. Jakob, 'Swiss Enterprise Foundations' in this volume, sections 2.2.1 and 2.2.3; A. Sanders, 'Enterprise Foundations in Germany' in this volume, section 1.5.3.

109 S. Thomsen and N. Kavadis, 'Enterprise Foundations: Law, Taxation, Governance, and Performance' (2022) 6(4) *Annals of Corporate Governance* 227: http://dx.doi.org/10.1561/109.00000031.

110 In some countries, enterprise foundations can essentially avoid taxation of their income from subsidiaries to the extent that the income is in fact distributed to the public good purposes stated in the foundation charter. In such cases, the income has already been taxed in the subsidiary. See M. Ørberg and L. Blichfeldt Fjord, 'Enterprise Foundations as "Non-profit Organizations" Under the EU Pillar Two Directive' (2023) 51(6–7) *Intertax* 472.

cause inheritance and gift tax. However, there are capital gains and inheritance tax exemptions for foundations with a charitable purpose in Denmark, Germany and Switzerland. In Sweden, there is no inheritance tax at all. In both Germany and Switzerland, double foundations are used to combine the tax benefits of a charitable foundation with the advantages of a family foundation.[111]

In both Denmark[112] and Austria in the past, setting up foundations was to some degree encouraged by the avoidance of capital gains, private wealth and inheritance taxes, which were historically substantial. In Austria, for example, the introduction of private foundations was supported by considerable tax benefits in relation to inheritance tax in the process of succession planning. However, later, with decreasing tax incentives, the number of private foundations dropped. Today, private foundations are often dissolved and their property is distributed to the beneficiaries. The 'price' for this is the tax burden on the donated (currently valued) assets with capital gains tax.[113]

In Denmark, where the formation of enterprise foundations was largely blocked by an onerous tax regime between 1998 and 2018, the tax due on succession to a foundation ownership has recently been lowered and foundations have been allowed to succeed in paying taxes with the goal of encouraging the founding of new foundations.[114]

Table 8. Was the tax environment more favourable before?

'Yes, it used to be better'	'Stable'	'It is improving'
Denmark (before 1998)	Germany	US
Austria	The Czech Republic	Denmark (since 2021)
Switzerland	Portugal	Poland
	The Netherlands	
	Liechtenstein	
	Belgium	
	Spain	
	France	
	Ireland	
	Hungary	

Source: Compiled by the authors.

111 D. Jakob, 'Swiss Enterprise Foundations' in this volume, section 2.2.3; A. Sanders, 'Enterprise Foundations in Germany' in this volume, section 1.5.3.

112 R.K Feldthusen, 'Enterprise Foundations in Denmark' in this volume, section 10.

113 S. Kalss and T. Barth, 'The Austrian Foundation' in this volume, section 1.3.

114 R.K. Feldthusen, 'Enterprise Foundations in Denmark' in this volume, section 10.

9. ECONOMIC SIGNIFICANCE, CHALLENGES AND OPPORTUNITIES

9.1. ECONOMIC SIGNIFICANCE

Assessing the economic significance of enterprise foundations in the legal systems discussed in this volume is not easy. According to all the data presented by Thomsen[115] and Feldthusen[116] in this book, the economic significance of enterprise foundations in Denmark is impressive. Among the countries discussed here, Denmark takes pole position in terms of the economic significance of enterprise foundations.

However, it is difficult to precisely ascertain the actual significance of enterprise foundations in other countries. Only Denmark registers enterprise foundations separately. Therefore, while in countries like Germany, Switzerland and Sweden, the significance of enterprise foundations also seems to be considerable, to some degree they may fly 'under the radar', without any precise data on their economic importance. In Austria, there are roughly 3,000 private foundations, but not all of them are enterprise foundations in the sense discussed here. So far, Germany has not even established a central foundation register, let alone one for enterprise foundations specifically.

Nevertheless, on the basis of the data presented in this book, it can be assumed that the importance of enterprise foundations is considerable.[117] With respect to listed foundation-owned companies,[118] the economic significance of enterprise foundations in the countries discussed here may be ranked as follows:

Table 9. Economic significance of enterprise foundations owning listed companies from high to low in relation to % of stock market capitalisation (2024)

Country	% of Stock Market Cap
Denmark	77.98%
Belgium	42.01%
Austria	23.03%
Sweden	21.07%
Luxembourg	12.22%
Italy	7.64%

(continued)

[115] S. Thomsen, 'Foundation Ownership around the World' in this volume, sections 5–7.

[116] R.K. Feldthusen, Denmark chapter in this volume, section 2.

[117] See also D.J. Schröder, 'Publicly Listed Foundation-Owned Firms around the World: An Overview' (2021) unpublished working paper: https://www.enterprisefoundations.dk/wp-content/uploads/2021/11/Publicly-listed-FoFs-Descriptive-Paper-02112021.pdf.

[118] S. Thomsen, 'Foundation Ownership around the World' chapter in this volume, Table 2.

Table 9 *continued*

Country	% of Stock Market Cap
Norway	7.37%
Switzerland	7.17%
Spain	6.01%
Germany	2.54%
The Netherlands	1.77%
Poland	1.11%

Source: Thomsen (2025) in this volume.

In general, the relative positions on the scale may correspond with the more or less welcoming regulatory historical approach to enterprise foundations summarised in this chapter. In particular, the extensive special regulation of enterprise foundations in Denmark and private foundations in Austria corresponds to a high significance of enterprise foundations in both countries.

However, there are two exceptions to this. First, in relation to Italy, the relative position may be surprising given the formerly hostile approach to enterprise foundations. This is no doubt due to the important role of the Italian banking foundations which the Italian government created by privatising former financial mutuals. Second, country ranking could be different if foundation ownership of privately owned companies was taken into account. Given the assumed growing importance of enterprise foundations as a tool of succession planning for small and medium-sized enterprises, it is to be expected that a considerable number of enterprise foundations are difficult to assess.

9.2. HISTORICAL BACKGROUND AND FUTURE CHALLENGES

Discussing the economic importance of enterprise foundations and how this corresponds to the regulatory approach towards them illustrates the importance of the social and historical context in different legal systems. In Denmark and Germany, historical foundations like the Carlsberg Foundation (1876) and the Zeiss Foundation (1889) are closely linked to the public perception of such foundations.[119] The Swedish discussion also shows a history of foundations, and even if the beginning of enterprise foundations is less clear, they have become influential after World War I. A closer look also often reveals fascinating

[119] R.K Feldthusen, 'Enterprise Foundations in Denmark' in this volume, section 1; A. Sanders, 'Enterprise Foundations in Germany' in this volume, section 1.2.

developments in the different countries – for example, there are the unique Swedish pension fund foundations (*löntagarfondsstiftelserna*).[120]

The most important insight that the historical perspective may offer is the fact that different policy makers and consequently legal systems have both welcomed and rejected enterprise foundations as the table below (Table 10) shows. Austrian legislators saw potential benefits in strengthening foundations with tax advantages in order to combat foreign competition, such as by Liechtenstein foundations in Austria.[121] On the other hand, the chapters on Italy[122] and the US show that some policy makers have looked and still look at enterprise foundations with suspicion.

Table 10. Regulatory approach in the past

Welcoming	Neutral	Hostile/suspicious
Denmark	Sweden	US
Austria	Switzerland	Italy
The Netherlands	Germany	The Czech Republic
Liechtenstein	Portugal	Belgium
	Spain	Poland
		France
		Hungary
		Ireland

Source: Compiled by the authors.

The discussions in the chapters in this volume illustrate that the approach to enterprise foundations in any legal system is not fixed. The experience in Denmark and Austria shows that the enthusiasm for foundation building diminishes considerably once the initial tax benefits are removed. Moreover, both the chapters on Austria and Switzerland show that an increasingly challenging regulatory environment and case law of the courts may reduce the attractiveness of a legal system for enterprise foundations. While the Austrian courts' case law makes foundation governance difficult,[123] the new case law on asset management in the Swiss Federal Supreme Courts may severely affect enterprise foundations in the future.[124]

However, the chapters also show that the regulatory environment is improving in some countries, even if slowly. The German legislator, for example,

120 K. Olsson, 'Enterprise Foundations in Sweden' in this volume, section 2.
121 S. Kalss and T. Barth, 'The Austrian Foundation' in this volume, section 1.3.
122 E. Barcellona, 'Industrial Foundations Under Italian Law' in this volume, section 2.
123 S. Kalss and T. Barth, 'The Austrian Foundation' in this volume, section 8.4.
124 D. Jakob, 'Swiss Enterprise Foundations' in this volume, section 3.4.

while improving the regulatory system under the new foundation law, especially by introducing a foundation register, has arguably missed the chance to make an even bigger step towards a more flexible foundation law.[125] In the US, the 'Newman's Own' exception[126] and state legislation on the perpetual purpose trust may lead the way. In Italy, the acceptance of enterprise foundations has changed with the TSC.[127] All this may at least be partly due to an increasing interest in the third sector, and different forms of long-term purpose-oriented businesses organisation that do not focus on shareholder value maximisation. In that respect, enterprise foundations may offer attractive opportunities in a changing world.

Table 11. Trend in legislation/case law

Legal regime is improving	Stable	Legal regime is getting more difficult
Germany	Denmark	Switzerland
Italy	Sweden	Austria
US	Liechtenstein	
The Czech Republic	Ireland	
Portugal	Spain	
The Netherlands		
Belgium		
Poland		
France		
Hungary		

Source: Compiled by the authors.

10. CONCLUSION

Enterprise foundations exist in all 17 jurisdictions covered in this book, even in common law jurisdictions such as Ireland and the US. Country-specific restrictions complicate comparisons and generalisations. However, it is remarkable that all jurisdictions actually allow foundations – or foundation-like structures – to own and, at least to some extent, control companies and to have ownership of specific companies stipulated in the foundation charter. Permissible levels of founder influence differ greatly, and foundation influence in

125 A. Sanders, 'Enterprise Foundations in Germany' in this volume, sections 4.1 and 4.3.
126 O. Eldar, 'Are Enterprise Foundations Possible in the United States?' in this volume, section 2.3.
127 E. Barcellona, 'Industrial Foundations Under Italian Law' in this volume, section 6.

business matters in its subsidiary may also, in some states, be restricted. But the overall picture is that enterprise foundations (or functionally similar structures) are possible in Europe and the US. And the development in most of the covered states seems to be similar, as legal regimes for enterprise foundations are generally improving. Nevertheless, there is considerable room for improvement of national legal regimes.

Summarising the findings of this book into one table is almost impossible, because a simple ranking oversimplifies the information and paints with much too broad a brush. On the other hand, we still tried to do so, knowing full well that every placement on the table is highly debatable. We are also aware that every such ordering includes a value judgement weighing up different aspects. Moreover, it should be noted that all countries discussed in this book embrace enterprise foundations to varying degrees. Therefore, even in countries such as Germany, France, Spain, Portugal and Italy, which have been depicted here as relatively lukewarm, enterprise foundations can be and are founded.

Denmark is regarded as the frontrunner in this respect because it is the only country with a proper legal framework specifically designed for enterprise foundations that regulates governance, transparency and also a tax environment which (again) encourages the establishment of enterprise foundations. Sweden comes second behind Denmark. Even though enterprise foundations mostly fly 'under the radar' there and are not specifically regulated (as they are in Denmark), they still enjoy great freedom of purpose, governance and are subject to favourable tax laws.

The legal environments in Liechtenstein, Poland, and Hungary all offer legal frameworks for enterprise foundations that provide a high degree of flexibility for founders. The private foundations in Poland and Liechtenstein, as well as the asset management foundation in Hungary, are examples of vehicles that can be tailored to a broad range of needs in terms of purpose and management. In this sense, all three countries have rules that are very similar to the Swedish legal framework.

Confirming the order of Austria and Switzerland in this sense is especially difficult. Both have a strong tradition in relation to enterprise foundations. In Austria, the private foundation is of considerable economic importance. Moreover, it allows great flexibility to its founders. However, it should not be forgotten that part of the attractiveness of the private foundation was built on tax benefits which have now been removed. Moreover, the case law of the Austrian Supreme Court makes governance difficult.

Switzerland is famous for having many enterprise foundations, partly because it allows great flexibility to founders with respect to purpose, governance and charter amendments. With a possibly more welcoming approach to family foundations, it might be perceived as more welcoming to founders in the future.

In Germany, foundations have become increasingly popular as vehicles for structuring the succession of family businesses. However, the legal environment – characterised by the division between federal and state foundation law – has so far left much to be desired. The German reform in 2021 was an important step, but it could have gone further by increasing flexibility, improving governance and embracing business purposes.

The Netherlands provides significant flexibility for enterprise foundations. The founder's freedom of choice is considerable. However, receiving favourable tax treatment is difficult for enterprise foundations. To obtain tax benefits, founders must use double foundation structures, combining business and philanthropic purposes.

In Belgium, although many family businesses are controlled by private foundations, tax laws appear to hinder enterprise foundations that mix public benefit purposes with business objectives. The Czech approach to enterprise foundations is similar, in that it is typically not possible to combine the flexibility of a private enterprise foundation with the tax benefits granted to foundations pursuing public benefit purposes.

Italy presents a more complex case. As described in the Italian chapter, although the legal environment for enterprise foundations has been significantly strengthened, persistent legal uncertainties continue to pose challenges in Italian foundation law.

The legal frameworks for enterprise foundations in Portugal, France and Spain remain relatively modest compared to other jurisdictions. In Portugal, there is no specific legal framework for enterprise foundations, and the existing foundation laws are generally geared toward public benefit purposes. Similarly, in Spain and France, while foundations are recognised and regulated, the legal environments do not provide tailored solutions for enterprise foundations. As a result, all three countries currently offer limited options for founders seeking to establish enterprise foundations that combine business and philanthropic purposes. But importantly, Portugal, France and Spain allow for foundation ownership of business and for 'ownership clauses' in the foundation charters.

Ireland has no specific legal framework for enterprise foundations, as described in the Irish chapter. With its current charity law, it seems unlikely that enterprise foundation structures will flourish.

The US should be seen as outside the table because the chapter in this book and this analysis has only looked at federal tax law rather than all the other elements discussed in this chapter. Still, it might be reasonably concluded that US tax law generally discourages founders from setting up foundations,[128] although recent developments involving Patagonia and OpenAI show that foundation-like structures do exist and that such entities may receive significant tax benefits.[129]

128 For a comparison of US and European law on non-profits and enterprise foundations, see O. Eldar and M. Ørberg, above n. 46.

129 See O. Eldar and M. Ørberg, above n. 46.

Table 12. Overall assessment of the legal environment for enterprise foundations

From left to right: most to least favourable																
Denmark	Sweden	Liechtenstein	Poland	Hungary	Austria	Switzerland	Germany	The Netherlands	Belgium	The Czech Republic	Italy	Portugal	Spain	France	Ireland	US

Source: Compiled by the authors.

10.1. POLICY CONSIDERATIONS

Policy makers wishing to encourage the formation of enterprise foundations in their country may use the material in this book as a tentative guide. Moreover, policy makers and others may use the European Legal Institute 2025 Report on Enterprise Foundations in Europe, including its model law, as inspiration.[130]

Policy makers that wish to facilitate the creation and governance of enterprise foundations should first and foremost ensure the legality and legitimacy of the enterprise foundation form. Enterprise foundations with a charitable purpose should be permitted. In addition, foundation law should recognise that the responsible, long-term-oriented ownership of a business company is a legitimate goal for a foundation.[131] Policy makers may or may not want to mandate additional goals like support for the descendants of the founder. Family support is a deviation from pure foundation ownership in the direction of family ownership and may be deliberately limited – for example, as a share of donations or in tax treatment of foundations established with a family purpose. However, admitting a (limited) family purpose is certain to make succession to foundation ownership more popular with founding entrepreneurs and may allow them to sustain some of the positive characteristics associated with family businesses.

Second, policy makers should ensure that the tax treatment of enterprise foundations is reasonably favourable without being overly generous. The idea would be to aim for neutrality so that founders do not establish enterprise foundations for tax reasons, but only when they believe that this is the right

130 See S. Thomsen, A. Sanders and M. Ørberg, 'European Law Institute Model Law on Enterprise Foundations' [Formal title and page numbers can be inserted when ready].

131 Even with a stated business objective, enterprise foundations may qualify for status as nonprofits under EU law, see M. Ørberg and L. Blichfeldt Fjord, above n. 110.

approach for the company. This is economically feasible since the supreme economic sacrifice required by founders – donating the bulk of their wealth to foundations – will in any case limit the number of founders who wish to follow this path. The tax system should avoid both income tax exemptions and fines on controlling business ownership but should also avoid requiring founders to pay wealth taxes (inheritance and capital gains taxes) on funds that they give away to enterprise foundations with a charitable purpose.

Third, policy makers should put in place regulation to ensure the good governance of enterprise foundations which will help ensure their efficiency and legitimacy. This includes governance rules which ensure the independence of the foundation board vis-à-vis the founding family and employees or directors of the company. A majority of the foundation board should in principle be independent. However, involving some members with a material interest in the proceeds of foundation (e.g. as beneficiaries) may provide a good balance. Moreover, a good argument can be made to allow a strong family presence on the board to preserve the character of a family business even in an enterprise foundation. Moreover, regulators should create a foundation register (for all types of foundations), to which enterprise foundations in particular should be required to submit audited annual reports. Appropriate transparency will help assuage ill-founded fears from the general public about mismanagement and shady dealings in enterprise foundations.

Fourth, the authorities should establish efficient foundation supervision which should ensure the legality of all foundations and enterprise foundations in particular. Legality supervision would require regulators to protect foundations against abuse by the founding family, foundation board members and company management. However, it should avoid micromanaging the foundation businesses which regulators are ill-equipped to do. In particular, enterprise foundations should be allowed to take risks which may sometimes lead to bankruptcy, although obvious recklessness may be regarded as contrary to the foundation purpose. We are aware that some jurisdictions – instead of regulators to protect foundations against abuse – traditionally have chosen a combination of courts and private party governance mechanisms, such as supervisory boards. But at least in enterprise foundations with tax benefits and public good distribution purposes, our policy recommendation is to have foundation regulators (be they government agencies or courts) specialised in foundation law in addition to having tax law oversight performed by tax authorities. The reason is that tax law is typically focused primarily on revenue collection, while enterprise foundation law involves hard questions on both organisational law and regulatory law. Such questions arguably fall outside the general area of expertise in most tax authorities. Moreover, having one public authority with both taxing powers and intervention powers regarding organisational law and regulatory law matters could in practice become problematic.

10.2. FUTURE RESEARCH AND CLOSING REMARKS

This second edition of the book is only one of the first steps in our understanding of enterprise foundation law. As pioneers, we are very conscious that many errors must remain and that future research will be needed to weed out mistakes and improve our knowledge of this important area. Furthermore, we have covered only some countries leaving out important foundation countries like Norway, the UK and other countries beyond Europe. Future work would do well to take their experience into consideration.[132]

Nevertheless, we are happy to present the second edition of this book to a wider audience and the experience of editing it has only increased our interest in enterprise foundations as a unique and attractive ownership form which has much to teach us about business ownership and much to contribute to the global business community. After all, long-term, purpose-driven businesses are now generally promising contributors to the economy of the future. Enterprise foundations are uniquely qualified to play a major role in this endeavour.

[132] For some information in German, see the chapters in the still-excellent K. Hopt and D. Reuter, above n. 65.

INDEX

m/pod-product-compliance
UK Ltd.
nes, MK11 3LW, UK
926
0017B/1786

9 781839 705601